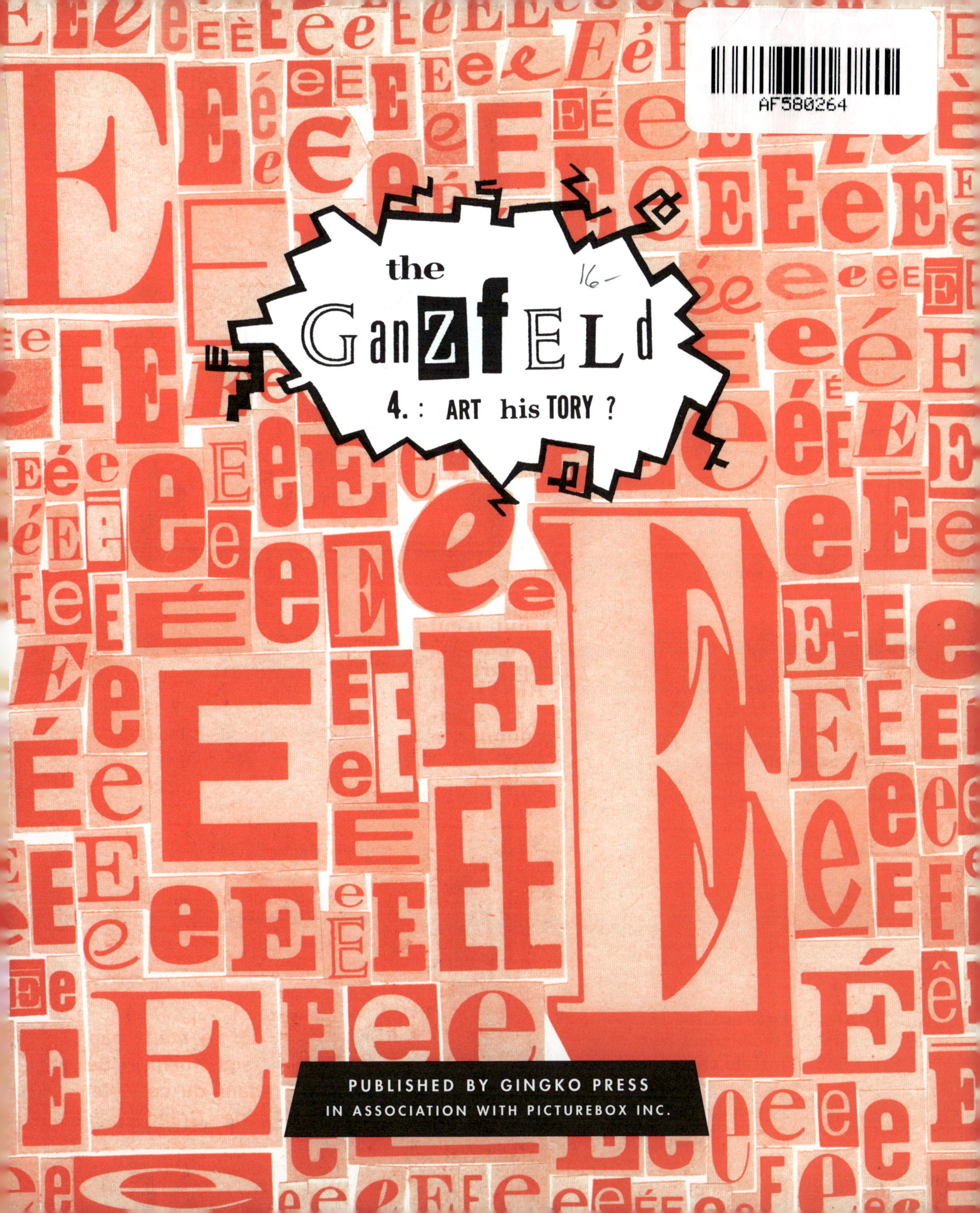

AF580264

The Ganzfeld 4

A PictureBox Book

DAN NADEL
Editor in Chief, Art Director

JESSI RYMILL
Associate Editor, Designer

RACHEL CHURNER
Grant Writer

NIKKI ZUBER
Adviser

Special thanks to:
Alexander & Bonin, Brooke Davis Anderson, Paola Antonelli, Adam Baumgold, Christine Burgin, Peggy Burns, Tom Devlin, Michael Epstein, Red Grooms, Steven Guarnaccia, Steven Heller, Maira Kalman, David Lopes and Gingko Press, Patrick Moos, the Nadel family, Mark Newgarden, Jeff Speck, Fred Tomaselli, Jeff Tweedy and Wilco, and Carl Williamson

Extra special production thanks to:
David Heatley

The Ganzfeld is produced by The Monday Morning Foundation, a 501(c)(3) not-for-profit corporation, for PictureBox Inc.

The Monday Morning Foundation wishes to thank the National Endowment for the Arts for its generous support.

First published in 2005. Printed in Hong Kong.
Package and design copyright © 2005 PictureBox Inc.
All contents copyright © 2005 their respective authors.
No part of this publication may be reproduced without permission in writing from the publisher or author.

Published by Gingko Press
in association with PictureBox Inc.

Gingko Press Inc.
5768 Paradise Drive, Suite J
Corte Madera, CA 94925
www.gingkopress.com

ISBN: 1-58423-201-3
LCCN: 2005904648

For a list of Ganzfeld special editions and related books, please visit
theganzfeld.com
and
picureboxinc.com

CONTENTS

All cover artwork (inside and out)
Julie Doucet

INTRODUCTIONS

4 Foreword: The Thing Behind the Trees
Dan Nadel

6 On Numinous Objects and Their Manufacture
Peter Blegvad

ART HISTORY

14 The Cosmic Sympathies of Athanasius Kircher
John Glassie

22 Daring Little Lady Swing like a Pendulum, Do...
Jonathon Rosen / Tom Gunning

24 A Gloucester View
Greg Cook

32 Stringing Along: Harry Smith Figures
John Cohen

42 Lippincott Inc.
Jonathan Lippincott

52 Men with Hats
Billy Epton/Dan Nadel

60 Under Hipgnosis
Oliver Broudy

74 The Anti-Art Agitprop of Jonah Kinigstein
Owen Phillips

DRAWINGS

90 Free Estimate
Gary Panter

104 The Fastest in the Business: Frank Moser
Mark Newgarden

116 Art by the Dozen
Phil Patton

120 Untitled
Alex Hanimann

126 Day to Day with John Dunn
Amid Amidi

ARTISTS ON ART

140 Unsent, Uncalled-for Letters 2 a Dead Artist
David Sandlin

160 Bureau for the Investigation of the Subliminal Image
Adam Dant

170 How to Draw Dick Tracy
Karl Wirsum

176 Paintings for Dali
Peter Saul

184 The Enigma of Marie Taglioni
Paul Etienne Lincoln

196 Gustun on These Layers of the Eath
Marc Bell

COMICS

212 Walking Distance
Frank Santoro

218 Drug Street *(also pages 248, 273, 274)*
Paper Rad

219 Galactic Putty
Leif Goldberg

224 Shigeru Sugiura
Kosei Ono

247 Ganmodoki
Shigeru Sugiura

249 The Forgotten Dream of a Melancholy Chef
Ted Stearn

258 Blond Atchen & The Bumble Boys: Including Weapons "In the Second's Layer"
C.F.

275 The Island of Silk and Ectoplasm
Matthew Thurber

280 Die Candle
Jim Drain

284 Jest Passin' Thru
Mark Newgarden

286 CONTRIBUTORS

Artwork appearing on section openers (in order of appearance): *Yazza (detail, this page); Gummez; Hadiddou; Haut Pays; Yazza (detail); Glow Falls (last page)*
Tom Burckhardt
(Courtesy Tibor de Nagy Gallery)

FICTION

THE HIGH DIVIDE

BY CHARLES D'AMBROSIO

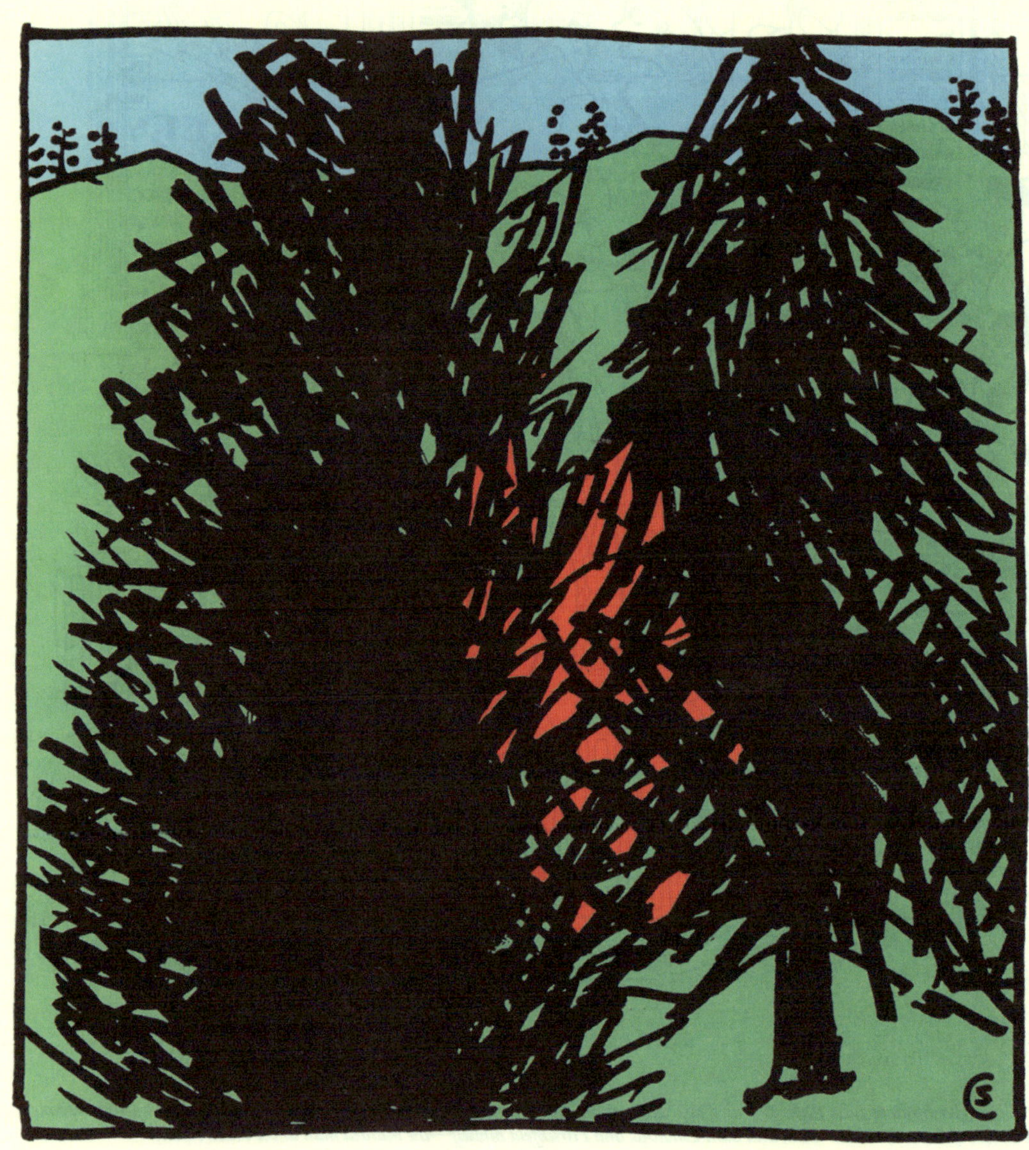

The Thing Behind the Trees

Dan Nadel

The illustration across the page is by Seymour Chwast. It appeared in a January 2003 issue of *The New Yorker.* It is one of my favorite images, and it's been tacked to my wall since I first gawked at it. In the last couple of years I've run across numerous artists who've pinned the same page to their own walls—all of them mystified by it. Meanwhile, I've never read the story it was meant to illustrate. When a drawing is as evocative as this, context just isn't necessary.

There's such rich mystery here: That red shape could be a fire, or crumpled wrapping paper—a red bush, a flag, or even a hand. And obscuring it are trees made up of simple bundles of gestures. These trees, awkwardly cropped, sit against three hills; some other quickly rendered trunks and branches dwell in the background. Nearly anything (or perhaps nothing at all) could happen in this tableau—it is a perfectly constructed enigma. This piece shows what skilled image-making can do: It can simultaneously affirm the presence of authentic mystery in the world and render you hungry to see and experience more of it. But—most pleasantly—it can also make you pull up short, suddenly aware of the possibilities for vision lying right in front of you.

The desire to open up those new vistas was the basis of *The Ganzfeld 4.* We jokingly called this "the art-history issue," and it sort of became one. (There is a section of art about artists, and plenty of writing on various facets of art history.) But—most importantly—the work within was chosen because it has the verve of real image-making—an act of will and imagination that communicates thought and feeling. Like that color behind those lines, the more you give an image, the more it gives back. We hope *The Ganzfeld 4* rewards that attention, folding you in and leaving you with a bit more than you had when you arrived. By the way, look for *The Ganzfeld 5: Japanada!* in about a year.

On Numinous Objects and Their Manufacture

PETER BLEGVAD

"The eagerness of objects
to be what we are afraid to do
cannot help but move us. Is this
willingness to be a motive in
us what we reject?"

(from INTERIOR, *Frank O'Hara)*

OBJECTS PROLIFERATE AS NEVER BEFORE, BUT THEY ARE MOSTLY DEAD HUSKS, the shells of things, wherein no daemon[1] resides. We merely own them or covet them—we are not nourished. Meanwhile, the fundamental appetite for numinous objects[2] grows ravenous. Nevermind that it remains unconscious in most citizens and unacknowledged by the authorities. Only numinous objects can make possible the communication between people and so-called dead matter, a connection that must be established if we wish to avert calamity.[3]

I am not here referring to fetishes, which are means to evoke systems of belief and are not properly ends in themselves. Nor am I referring to fantasy constructs—for example, the ship made of fingernail parings described in Norse mythology. This ship is a fine thing, but it is feebly numinous compared to a block of sodium in a meadow, its edges mollified by the tongues of cows into a lopsided loaf, like snow. And, while my more skeptical readers may scoff, it is a fact that if this salt lick is removed from the meadow and placed in a confined enclosure or—better still—sealed into a lead container, its numinous charge will be boosted manyfold.[4] It may be, as some have theorized,

KEY

FIRST MORPHOLOGICAL TABLE (CURVED)

1. Sphere, Ball, Globe, Orb
2. Crescent
3. Horn
4. Pillar, Column, Pole, Cylinder
5. Roll
6. Cylinder
7. Tube, Pipe, Hose (if flexible)
8. Hoop (a large Ring)
9. Rod, Wand, Dowel (if wood)
10. Pencil or Stick (as of chalk)
11. Straw (a thin tube)
12. Needle
13. Drum or Cylinder
14. Bell
15. Crook
16. Cane
17. Coin (a small Disk)
18. Disk
19. Grommet (a small Ring)
20. Ring, Terret
21. Circlet
22. Hole
23. Hemisphere (a solid Cup)
24. Hemisphere (a solid Bowl)
25. Elipse
26. Cone
27. Spine, Spike, Tang (a thin Cone)
28. Dot
29. Funnel
30. Arch
31. Wheel
32. Circle (bisected)
33. Oval
34. Barrel, Keg, Tun
35. Hourglass (a verticle Dumbell)
36. Belt or Band
37. Spool } w/ cross-sections
38. Reel } w/ cross-sections
39. Fan
40. Coil
41. Spring, Coil, Gyre, Helix
42. Spiral, Coil, Helix, Whorl, Gyre
43. Heart
44. Kidney
45. Bean (a small Kidney)
46. Spoon, Paddle
47. Cigar
48. Pear
49. Noose
50. Scallop, Shell
51. Puck, Quoit
52. Curl, Loop
53. Teardrop
54. Bulb
55. Egg
56. Scroll
57. Lens (cut in ½ to show convex)
58. Lens (cut in ½ to show concave)
59. Pill
60. Bullet
61. Button
62. Mushroom
63. Almond
64. Serpent
65. Saucer (with cross-section)
66. Donut or Doughnut
67. Sausage
68. Magnet, Horseshoe

SECOND MORPHOLOGICAL TABLE (STRAIGHT)

1. Brick, Box, Rectangle
2. Ladder
3. Plank, Board, Rectangle
4. Line
5. 8-pointed star
6. Pentagram
7. Seal of Solomon, Star of David
8. Envelope
9. Swastika
10. Asterix
11. Trellis
12. "L", right-angle
13. Octagon
14. Hexagon
15. Cube
16. Square
17. Diamond
18. Parallelogram
19. Frustum
20. Sheet, Page, Leaf
21. "T"
22. Prism
23. Zigzag
24. Cross
25. Saw-tooth
26. Crennelation
27. Pennant, Tri-angle
28. Obelisk
29. Arrow
30. Wedge
31. Triangle
32.
33. Ziggurat
34. Pyramid
35. Chevron, "A"-Frame
36. Coffin
37. Grid
38. Trident, Fork
39. "Y", Fork
40. Tripod
41. Staircase
42. Gallows, Gibbet
43. Presence

THIRD MORPHOLOGICAL TABLE (AMORPHOUS)

1. Cloud
2. Ditch, Trench
3. Pile
4. Puddle (with Rill or Runnel)
5. Batch
6. Mass
7. Flap
8. Mound
9. Lump
10. Papule
11. Nugget
12. Blob
13. Bolus
14. Heap
15. Loaf
16. Clod, Clump
17. Plug
18. Wad
19. Glob
20. Morsel
21. Crumb
22. Flake
23. Chip
24. Speck
25. Smear
26. Chunk
27. Slice or Flitch
28. Strip
29. Stroke
30. Strand
31. Mountain
32. Hill
33. Talus
34. Tangle
35. Block
36. Cudgel, Club
37. Swathe
38. Thong
39. Hunk
40. Streak
41. Scratch
42. Wedge or Wadge
43. Scrap
44. Swatch
45. Shard
46. Seam
47. Slab
48. Patch
49. Flocculus, Tuft
50. Crack

[MISSING - Nodule & Bump]

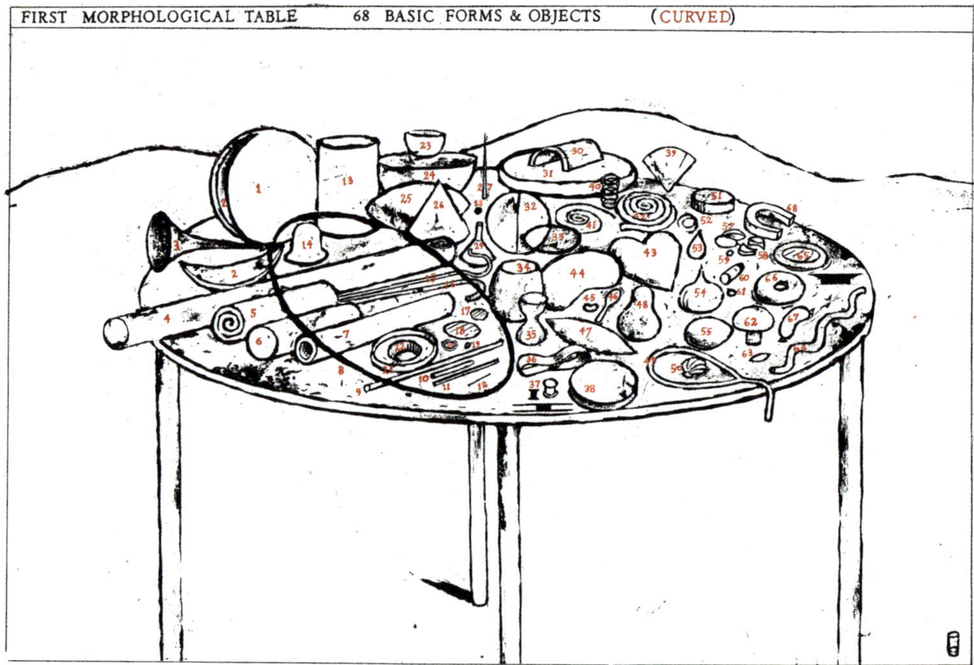

that the object au naturel or in its accumulator[5] is numinous to the degree that it functions as a mirror of the spirit—to the degree that you or I can imaginatively see something of ourselves, something for which we do not have a name or an image, made objective in it. The fact that salt can function as a mirror of anything, especially when sealed in lead, may smack of blatant hocus-pocus to skeptics—but it is in such unlikely ways that the imagination actually works.

A numinous object is charged like a capacitor. It disturbs induction and resonates ambiguously. In Surrealist parlance, it is "convulsive," meaning it has the power to drain definition from its surroundings and to become the solitary and radiant focus—the omphalos, or navel—of an entire world. An object with sufficient numinous charge can stop time.

The numinous objects existing in our environment are easily overlooked by our harassed and addled species. Education is the remedy, teaching people of all ages to resist distraction and become sensitive to the subtle radiations emanating from these items (which often masquerade as common street refuse). I imagine students returning from expeditions bright-

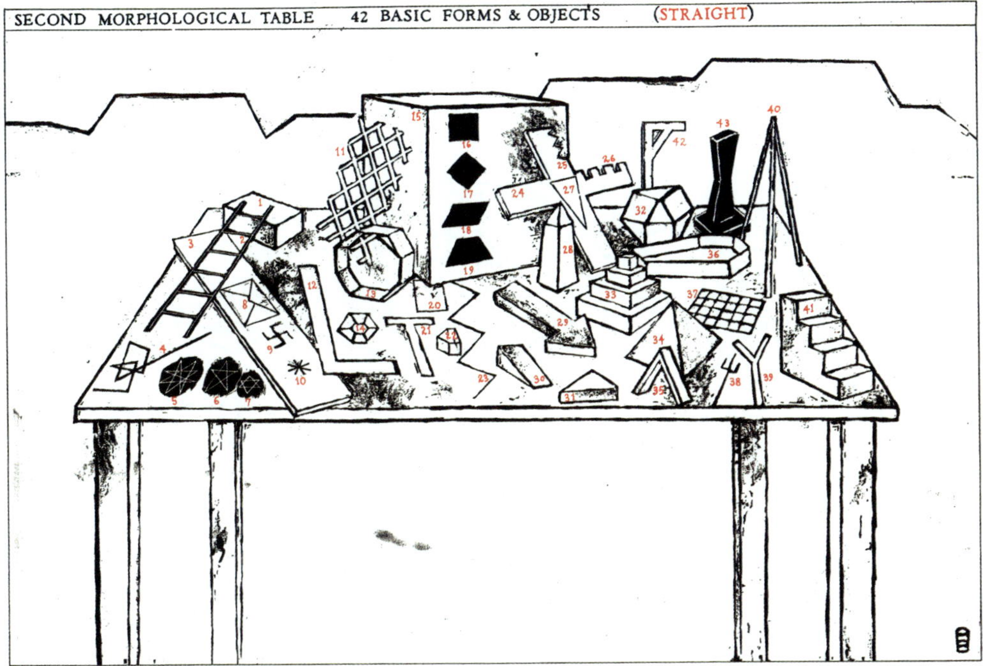

eyed and exultant with eclectic spoil—objects being tested, graded, and catalogued before being made available to the public in a chain of lending libraries.

Due to the under-abundance of numinous found objects, fresh numinous objects must be manufactured. To meet this need a new field of science is being developed here at the offices of Amateur. The Morphological Tables illustrate the first phase of this work: discovering the morphologies or forms most conducive to numinosity. We're still compiling the list of materials from which these forms may be compounded.[6] The selection is vast and the distinction is critical, in terms of numinosity, between, let's say, a ball of snow and a ball of the same size composed of soluble glass—although both balls, when viewed from a certain distance, might otherwise be twins.

How would an alchemist seeking the *lapis*, or Philosopher's Stone, picture it in his mind? (The *Tractatus aureus* describes the precious Stone as "altogether vile," but aside from that provides little aid.) Would he imagine an amorphous lump, a perfect sphere, or a brick? Would it be oily or dry? Dull or polished? Cold or warm to the touch? Would it be fused into a dense solid or porous, ventilated like a

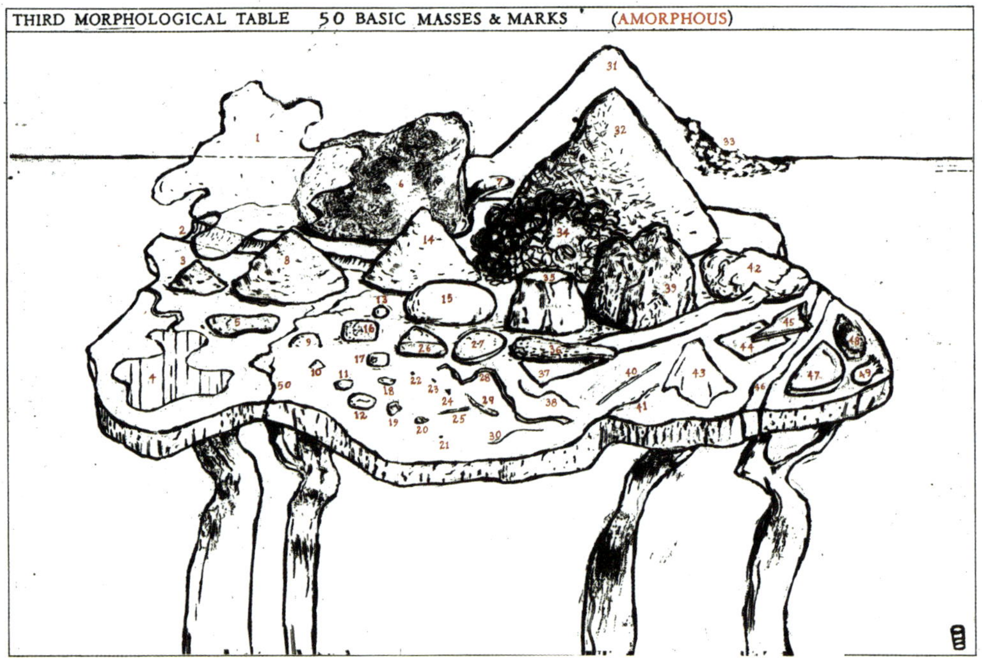

honeycomb? Such grossly materialistic speculations demean the spiritual associations the Stone evokes, no doubt, but in seeking the recipe for numinous objects we have found it useful to ask such questions....

To return to the morphologies: We have deliberately restricted the choice to basic forms and objects, at least for our first tentative experiments. If an object can be inserted in the phrase "the object is _____ -shaped" (e.g., *cigar-*, *bullet-*, *barrel-*, or *teardrop*-shaped), it will usually qualify for selection. Other objects serve as nearly archetypal signs for themselves (e.g., *gallows* or *gibbet*, *coffin*, *house*, etc.). It is a basic building-block quality that we seek. Certain forms, by their inclusion, automatically disqualify others. *Hourglass*, for instance, renders *dumbbell* redundant, because the latter is too nearly the former turned on its side.

Forms and objects are separated into three categories: those composed entirely of straight lines (*straight*); those in whose lineaments curves and circles are involved (*curved*); and those indefinite units of matter—the humble blob, chunk, chip, lump, heap, hill, etc.—that, while sometimes suggesting the quantity of matter involved, do not imply more than a very approximate form (*amorphous*). The reader will notice that some two-dimensional figures have been included on the Tables, as have a few negative shapes (*holes, cracks, crenellations*). They are there because it seems certain that an aperture or apertures could contribute to the numinosity of an object, and that a two-dimensional tattoo or illustration might do likewise.

Many forms and objects are missing but should be included. Could more letter shapes qualify? L, T, V, O, S, U, X, and Z all seem to be basic forms; perhaps the rest of the alphabet's 26 are, too. One wonders if a numinous object could not, therefore, be a word....

It may transpire that unless we find the appropriate context in which to place a finished object, it will not "convulse"; its numinosity will remain dormant. Conventional gallery design since the middle of the last century would indicate that the aesthetic qualities of art objects are best savored in antiseptic spaces under electric lamplight. But an object such as we propose to manufacture, and which we do not think of simply as "art," might require a specific site, a specific hour of the day or night, specific supporting props, specific weather conditions, and so on, before "its soul, its whatness, leaps to us from the vestment of its appearance"[7] and it becomes numinous.

---

1 Daemon—the animating spirit of a place or thing Cf. the painter Giorgio de Chirico's dictum: "One must discover the daemon in everything."

2 Numinous—invested with power or spirit

3 Guy Davenport: "...science and poetry from the Renaissance forward have been trying to discover what is alive and what isn't. In science the discovery spanned three centuries, from Gassendi to Niels Bohr, and the answer is that everything is alive." Davenport also quotes Einstein: "...every clod of earth, every feather, every speck of dust is a prodigious reservoir of entrapped energy." (from *The Geography of the Imagination*)

4 Cf. Leonora Carrington: "The explosion...had momentarily dispersed the powers that always gathered around the Cup in enclosed areas. This is a magic law and true for nearly all charged objects." (from *The Hearing Trumpet*)

5 Cf. Wilhelm Reich and his "accumulators" and "boosters" (of "orgone energy")

6 One reason the list of materials is potentially endless is that science keeps inventing new, potentially numinous matter. Dr. Cyril Drake, for example, "accidentally made a glass that dissolved in water." "Without silicon, using phosphorous, calcium and sodium oxides," the ingredients in Dr. Drake's soluble glass can be adjusted to dissolve as swiftly or as slowly as required, in "from a few minutes up to ten years."

7 James Joyce, descibing an epiphany

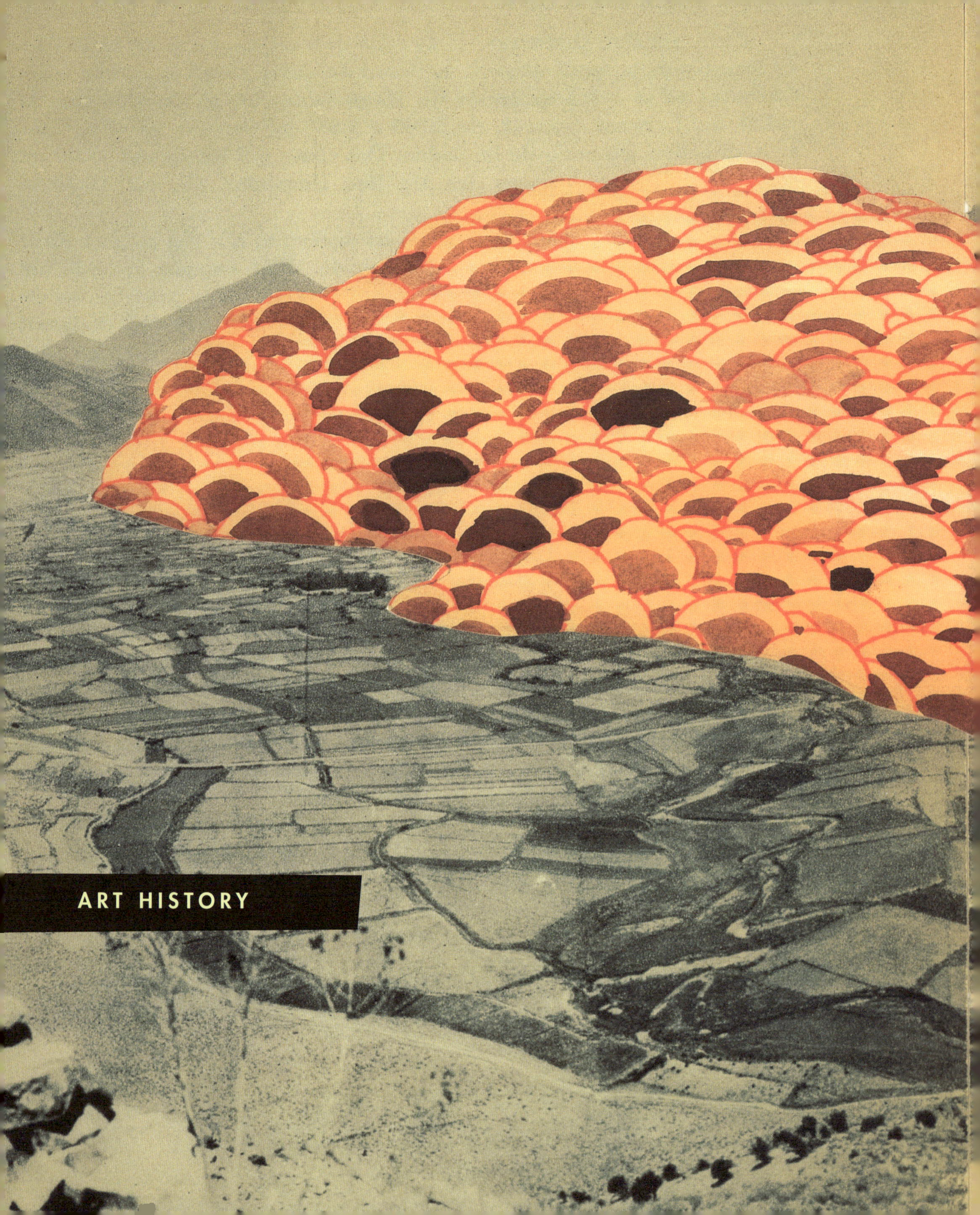

ART HISTORY

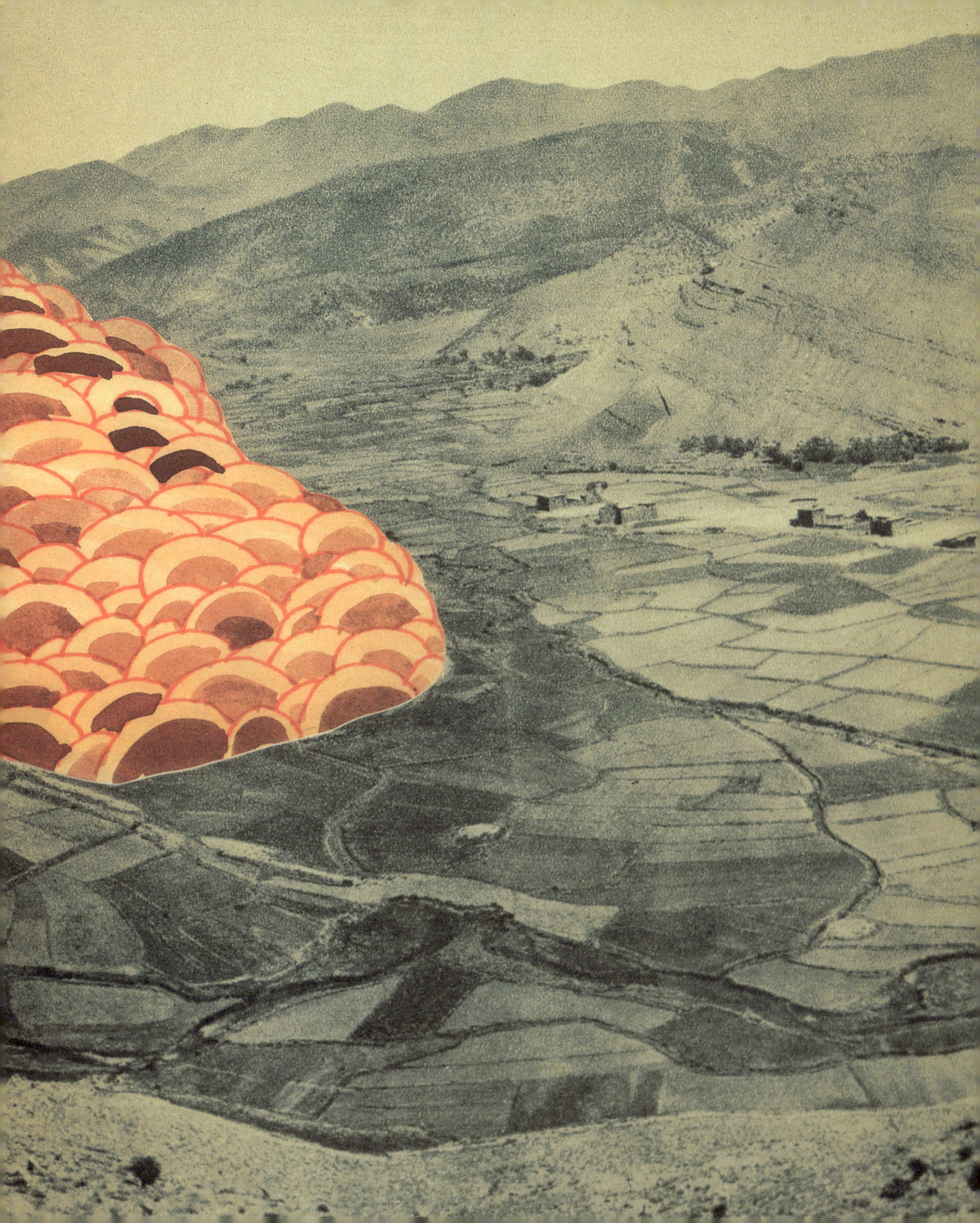

THE COSMIC SYMPATHIES

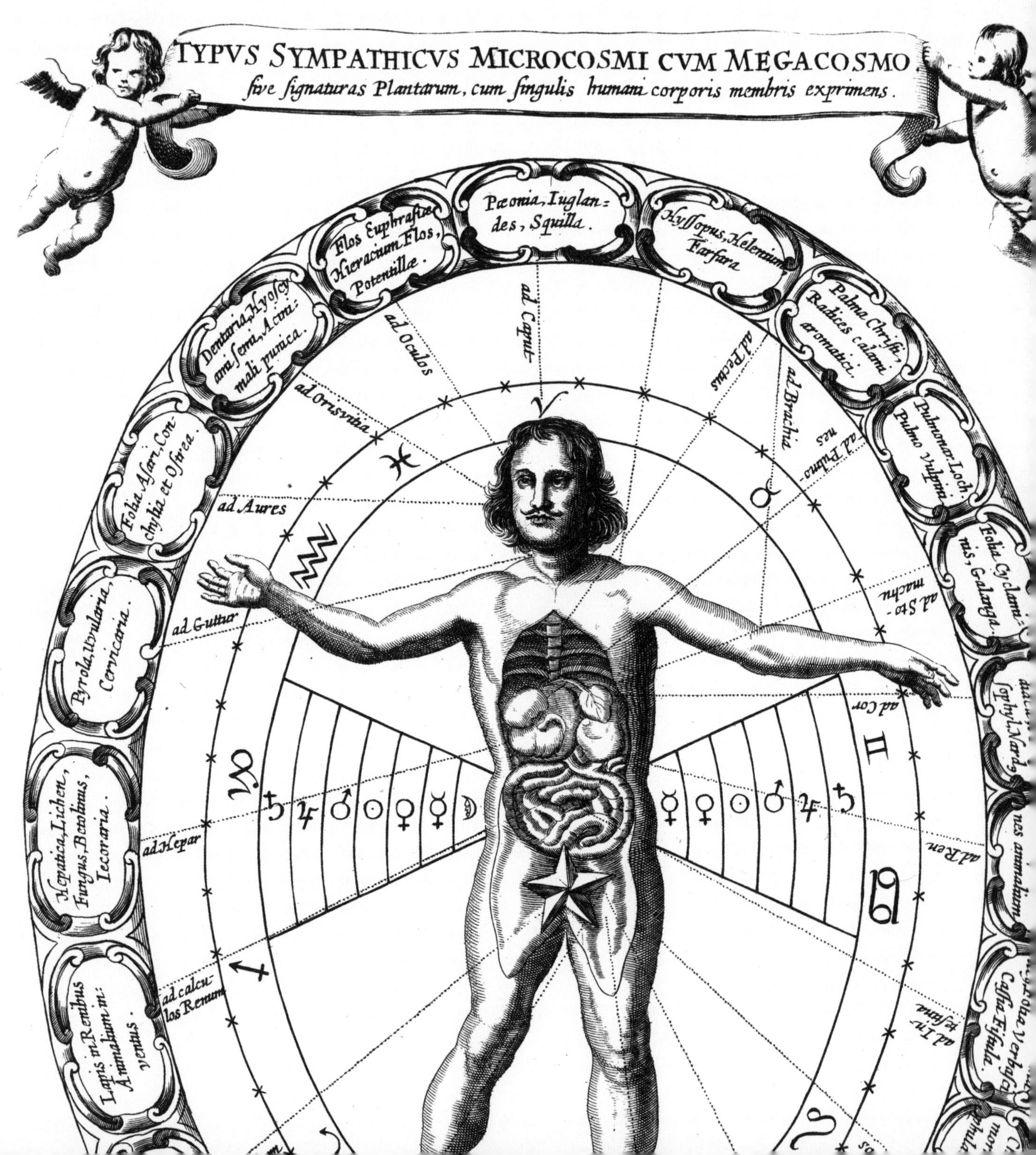

OF ATHANASIUS KIRCHER

John Glassie

"We approach now the vast and terrifying subject of Athanasius Kircher," began historian René Taylor 33 years ago. *Vast* because anything else would be an understatement for the scope of work covered by the seventeenth-century Jesuit polymath (who engaged in acoustics, optics, geology, Egyptology, mechanics, astronomy, cosmology, linguistics, biology, medicine, and mathematics—among other fields). *Terrifying* because, from the viewpoint of modern science, Kircher got so many things wrong. If his contemporary René Descartes stood for scientific skepticism, Kircher was seen to represent credulity; his holistic worldview, which featured secret webs of cosmic influence, was predicated on biblical history, in particular the story of Noah's Ark and the events surrounding the Tower of Babel. (Kircher's schematic recreations of the Ark included allotted places for both gryphons and mermaids. He exhibited tailbones of the latter at his museum at the Collegio Romano.)

But more recently, academics have begun to place Kircher in his proper context: a time, despite the presence of certain brilliant minds, before real science existed or was inevitable—a world where even Johannes Kepler was into astrology and Isaac Newton passionate about alchemy. And, rather than being terrified of Kircher, people are now becoming quite fond of him. He and his work have appeared in the fiction of Umberto Eco, have been appreciated by (the now late) Stephen Jay Gould, and have been exhibited at the Museum of Jurassic Technology by David Wilson (who was himself brought to greater attention by Lawrence Weschler's *Mr. Wilson's Cabinet of Wonder*). Kircher's admirers are rightly amazed by the breadth and depth of his investigations and inventiveness, and especially by the more than 30 multi-volume, suitcase-sized folio treatises he published. Spectacularly illustrated with engravings and woodcuts, these works served as encyclopedias of contemporary knowledge and theory as well as venues for Kircher's own research, experimentation, and—in no short supply—speculation. They are his great, lasting, and bizarre gift to the world.

Kircher was born in 1602 near Fulda, in what is now Germany. In his youth, according to his own account, he was swept under a mill wheel (unharmed), stampeded by horses (unscathed), and stricken with life-threatening gangrene (which he survived by praying to the Blessed Virgin). He then joined the Society of Jesus, studied and taught everything from Hebrew to mathematics in Cologne, Würzburg, and Avignon, and began to produce shows of fireworks on the side.

Kircher didn't restrict himself to the subject at hand in his massive works. In *Mundus subterraneus* (*The Subterranean World*), he laid out the "sympathies" between the zodiacal realm, the planetary realm, and the parts of the body, as well as diseases and their corresponding remedies.

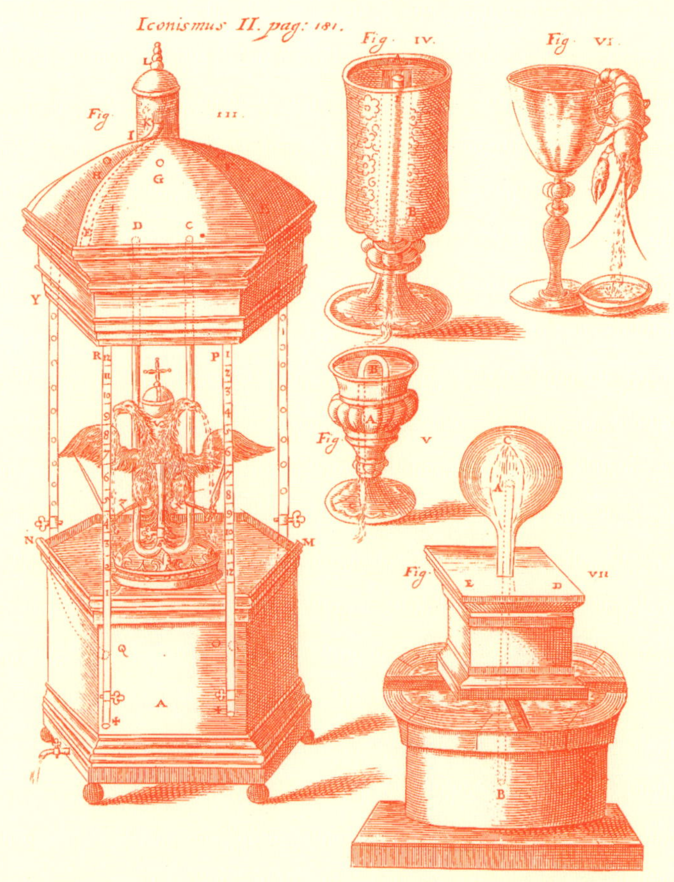

Examples of the hydraulic devices displayed in Kircher's museum include a "two-headed Imperial Eagle, vomiting water copiously from the depth of its gullets" *(left),* and a "cancer vomitor," or vomiting lobster *(top right).*

In 1633 he was called to Vienna to succeed Kepler as mathematician to the Habsburg court, and then redirected by Pope Urban VII to Rome, where he worked on almost every conceivable thing for the next 40 years. There he not only produced his immense, widely read volumes, but created one of the first public museums in history, the Museum Kircherianum. Along with antiquities, artifacts, and curiosities from around the world (amassed with the help of the Jesuit missionary system), Kircher exhibited dozens of his own inventions, including magic lanterns, magnetic clocks, perpetual-motion devices, vomiting machines, and a single "cat piano."

This was the kind of man who pursued his interest in geological matters by lowering himself down into the smoking crater of Vesuvius. He then put 25 years into his massive *Mundus subterraneus* (*The Subterranean World*), in which he described the oceans and great fires at the center of the earth. Believing that the secrets of the world's cultures and beliefs could be found in ancient Egypt, he filled six books on Egyptology and spent decades deciphering hieroglyphic texts—inaccurately, as it turns out. He examined all aspects of the nature of music and acoustics in his *Musurgia universalis* (*Universal Music-Making*), offering comparative studies of the ears of dif-

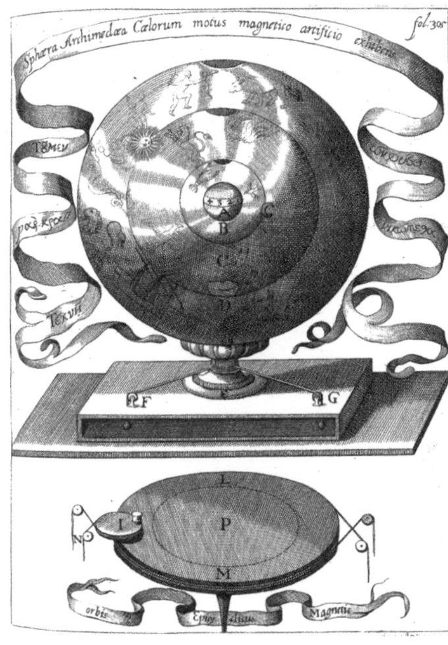

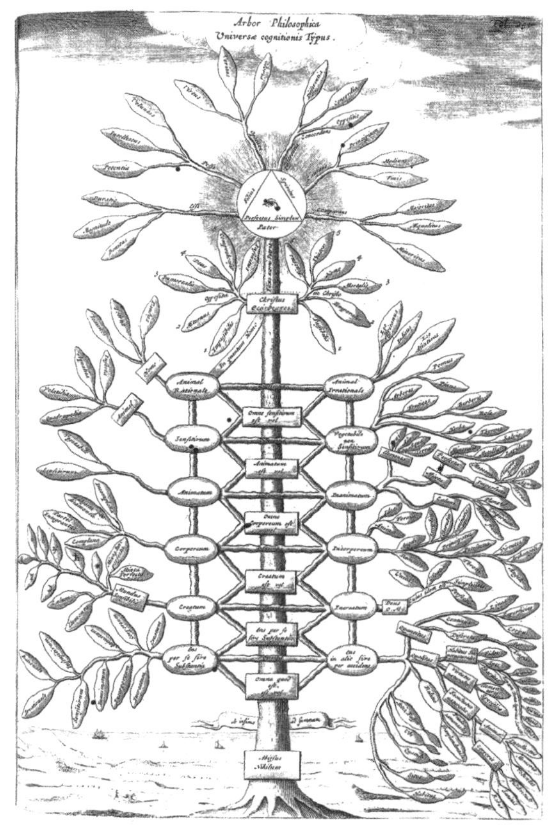

Left: Kircher exhibited dozens of his own mechanical devices in the museum at the Collegio Romano, including this sphere of Archimedes. (The motion of the planets is driven by magnets.)

Right: In *Ars magna sciendi* (*The Great Art of Knowing*) Kircher showed readers how all branches of knowledge are ordered on this diagrammatic "philosophical tree." Knowledge runs from "nothingness" at the trunk to that which emanates from the Holy Trinity at the top. Animate, corporeal beings and rational animals are on the left; their inanimate, incorporeal, and irrational counterparts are on the right.

ferent animals, describing his acoustical creations (speaking tubes, eavesdropping machines, hydraulic organs), and explaining that musical harmony was an expression of the harmonious relationships within the cosmos. And on and on.

"The master of a hundred arts," as Kircher was called, was indeed mistaken about a great deal. Magnetism, for instance, is not the operative force at work in everything from the motion of the planets to human relationships to divine love. On the other hand, microorganisms are in fact responsible for the spread of disease, as Kircher proposed after examining the blood of plague victims through a microscope. (And in the years after Galileo had been threatened with the stake and Giordano Bruno burned, it's not too surprising that a devout Jesuit would take a weak stance on Copernicus.)

Kircher lived at a time when, as least as he believed, one man could still reasonably try to gather and understand all that could be known—and then put it all together. In a sense, he was the last person to come anywhere close. The images here represent his attempt to answer questions about the nature of the universe and the underlying systems that guide it—the biggest questions of all.

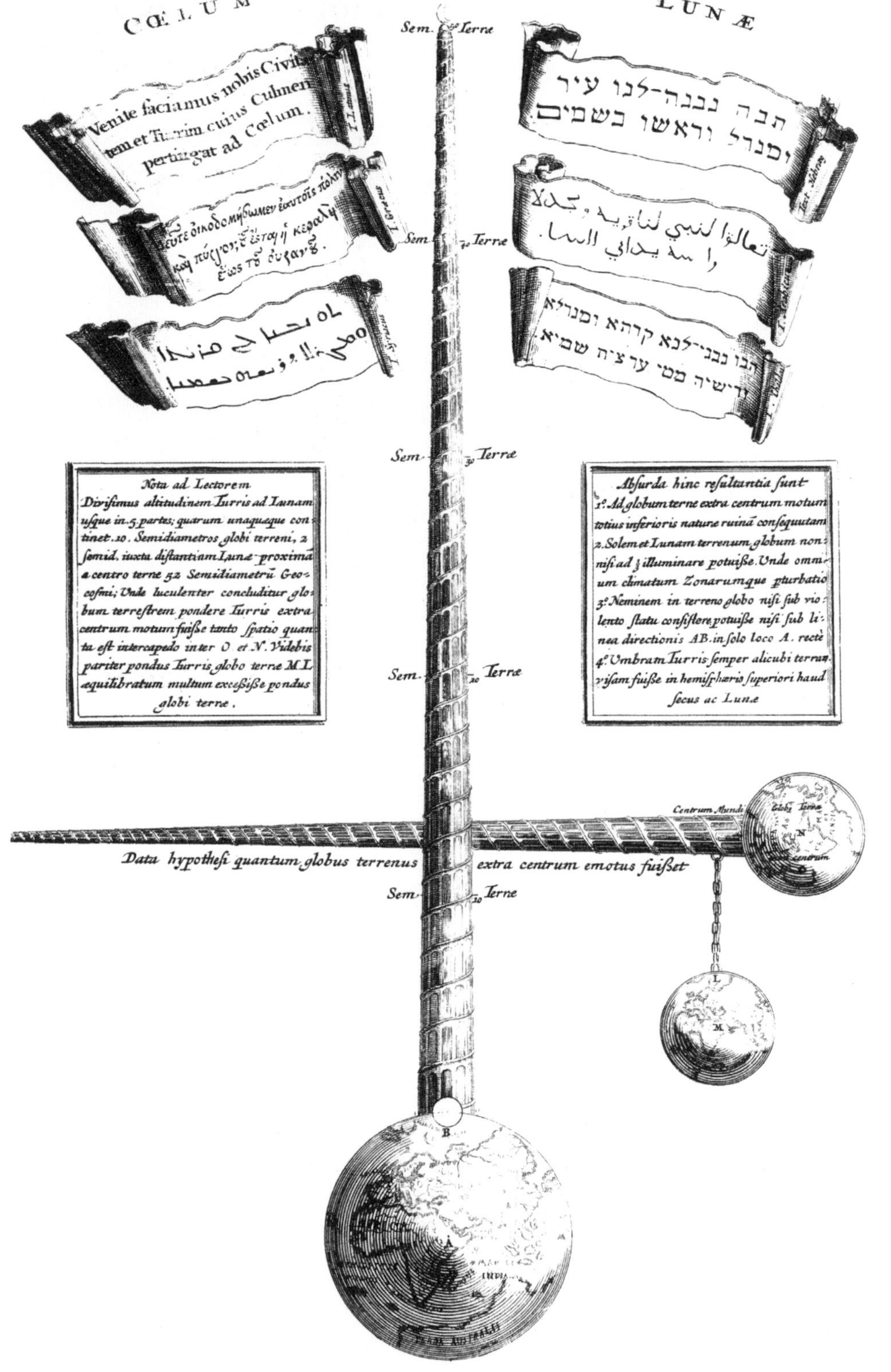
CŒLUM
LUNÆ
Venite faciamus nobis Civitatem et Turrim cuius Culmen pertingat ad Cœlum.
Sem. Terre
Nota ad Lectorem
Dirisimus altitudinem Turris ad Lunam usque in.5.partes; quarum unaquæque continet.10. Semidiametros globi terreni, 2 semid. iuxta distantiam Lunæ proximā a centro terre 52 Semidiametrū Geocosmi; Unde luculenter concluditur globum terrestrem pondere Turris extra centrum motum fuiße tanto spatio quanta est intercapedo inter O et N. Videbis pariter pondus Turris globo terræ M.L. æquilibratum multum exceßiße pondus globi terræ.
Absurda hinc resultantia sunt
1º. Ad globum terre extra centrum motum totius inferioris naturæ ruinā consequutam
2. Solem et Lunam terrenum globum non nisi ad ⅓ illuminare potuiße. Unde omnium climatum Zonarumque pturbatio
3º. Neminem in terreno globo nisi sub violento statu consistere potuiße nisi sub linea directionis AB. in solo loco A. rectè
4º. Umbram Turris semper alicubi terram visam fuiße in hemisphærio superiori haud secus ac Lunæ
Centrum Mundi
Data hypothesi quantum globus terrenus extra centrum emotus fuißet
N
L
M
B
A
INDIA

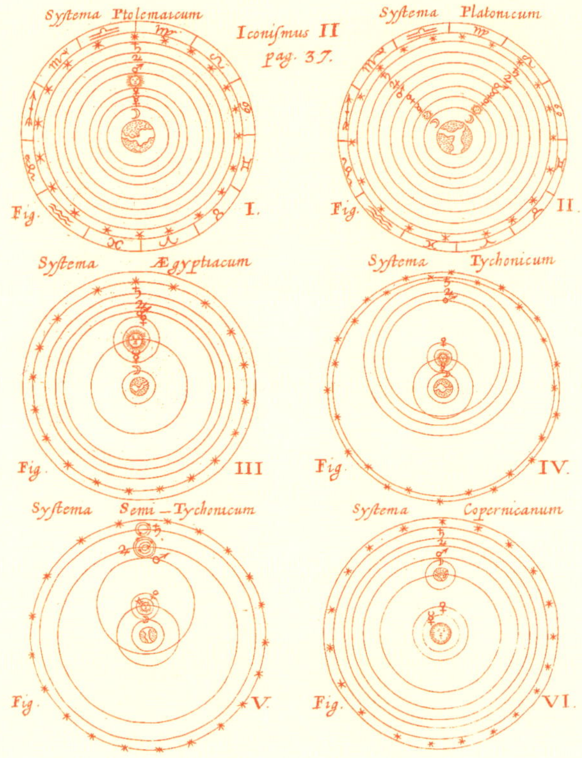

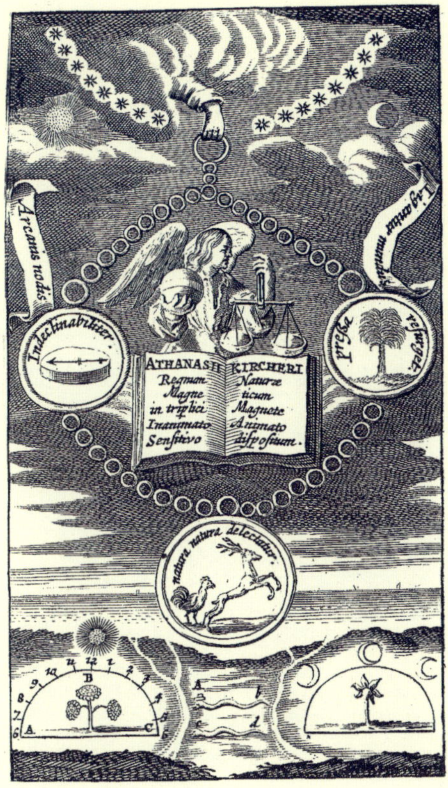

Opposite: In his book *Turris Babel* Kircher showed why the Tower of Babel could never have reached the moon. Even if such a tower could be built, he explained, its weight would pull the earth away from the center of the universe and wreak cosmic havoc.

Above, left: Perhaps because supporting a non-geocentric planetary order could get one condemned, Kircher resorted to fiction in his *Itinerarium extacticum* (*Estactic Journey*) of 1660, taking an imaginary cosmic voyage through six possibilities, including the geocentric systems of Ptolemy and Plato *(top row),* the semi-geocentric scheme of Tycho Brahe *(middle, right),* and the helio-centric system of Copernicus *(bottom, right).*

Above, right: In the frontispiece to *Magneticum naturae regnum,* God holds the chains of "magnetic" sympathy that bind and influence all beings and levels of existence—and, in particular, power the resurgence of plants. The motto reads "The world is bound by secret knots."

CLASS. VII. MATHEMATICA HIEROGLYPH. 193

ΔΩΔΕΚΑΤΟΠΟΣ

Siue XII. Manſiones Cœli,iuxta mentem Aegyptiorum, Græcorum, & Modernorum.

ΕΠΑΝΑΦΟΡΑ. MANSIO X. ΑΠΟΚΛΗΜΑ.

MANSIO XI. MANSIO IX.

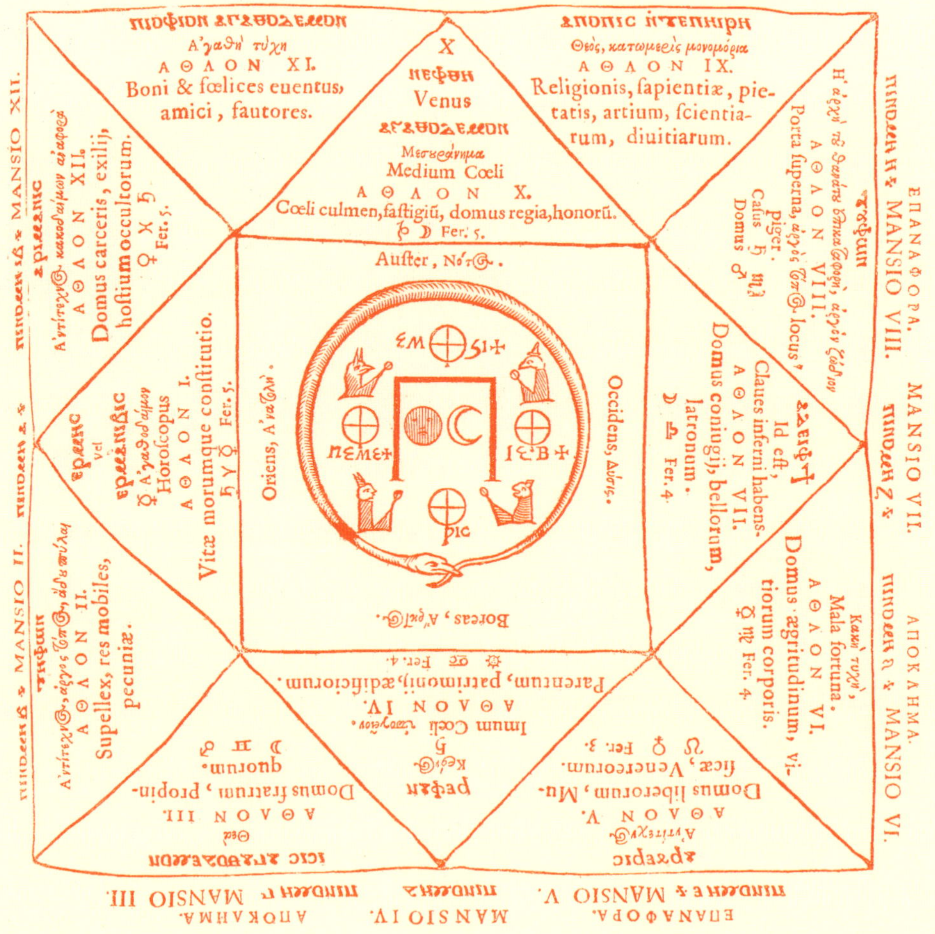

Bb Con-

Above: In this diagram of the 12 astrological houses according to the Egyptians, Greeks, and Moderns, Kircher displayed his linguistic virtuosity. He is said to have learned dozens of languages, including Hebrew, Aramaic, Coptic, Persian, Latin, Greek, Chaldean, and Armenian.

Right: The allegorical frontispiece of Giosefo Petrucci's 1677 work *Prodomo apologetico alli studi chircheriani* (*Apologetic Forerunner to Kircherian Studies*) depicts Kircher sitting on a crocodile, writing with both hands—the only way to explain his prolific output?

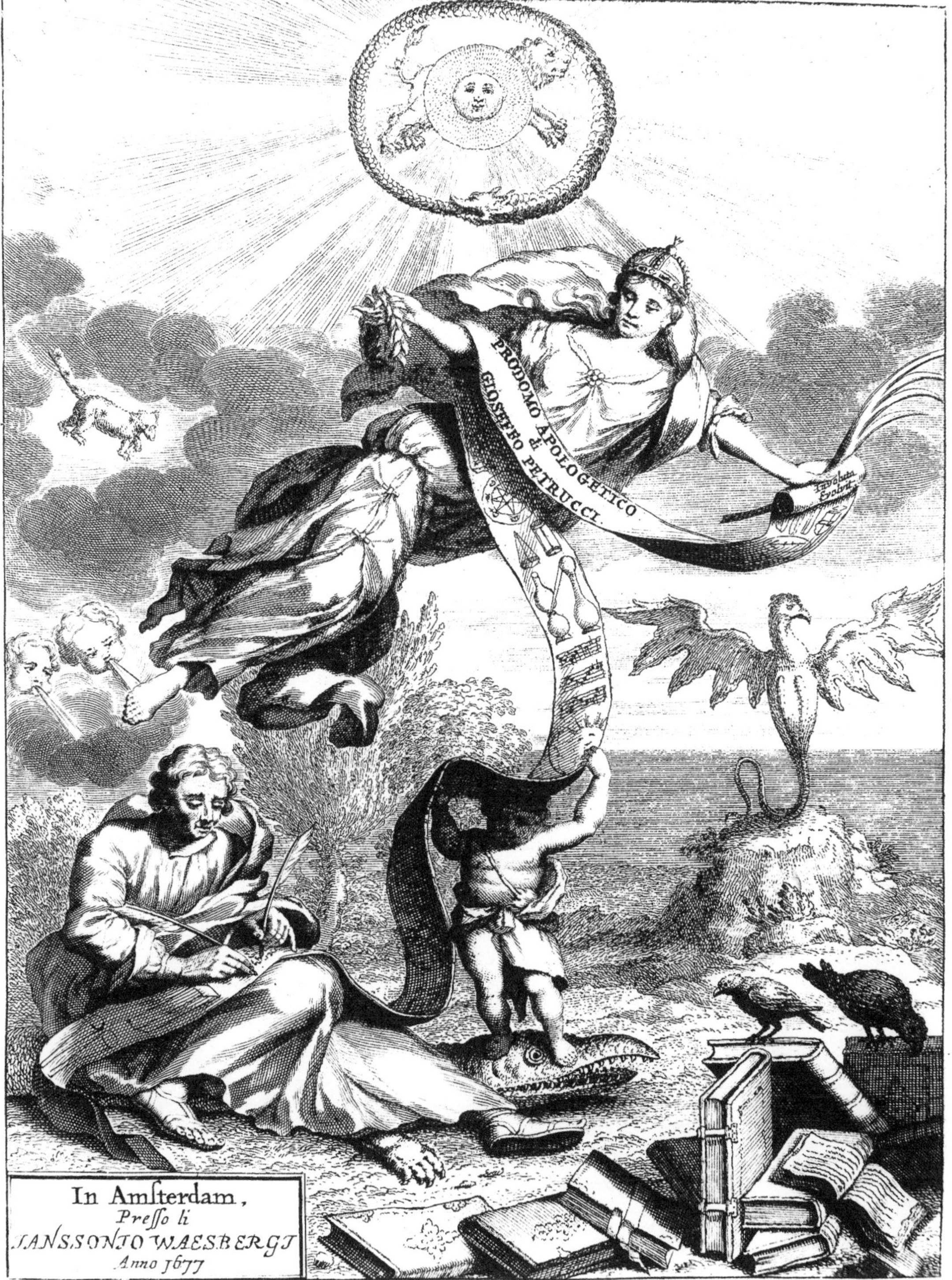
PRODOMO APOLOGETICO
di
GIOSEFO PETRUCCI
In Amſterdam,
Preſſo li
IANSSONIO WAESBERGI
Anno 1677

Daring Little Lady Swing like a Pendulum, Do

TOM GUNNING on JONATHAN ROSEN's Painting

Some months after I went to the Hall;
Was greatly surprised to see on the wall
A bill in red letters, which did my heart gall,
That she was appearing with him.
He'd taught her gymnastics and dressed her in tights,
To help him live at his ease,
And made her assume a masculine name,
And now she goes on the trapeze.

CHORUS:
She'd fly through the air with the greatest of ease,
You'd think her the man, young man on the flying trapeze.
Her movements were graceful, all girls she could please,
And that was the end of my love.

That is the final, not-so-famous verse from George Leybourne's popular song of 1868 "The Daring Young Man on a Flying Trapeze"—with an unexpected gender reversal. Women and men of the trapeze were popular attractions in the nineteenth-century urban circuses of Europe and the vaudeville theaters of America, their notoriety coming as much from their athletic death- and gravity-defying feats as from their tight-fitting costumes. (The leotard's namesake, Jules Leotard, also invented the trapeze itself.) The trapeze act's eroticism resulted from a combination of revealing costumes and the broad, skilled motion in which the leotard-clad bodies turned. The performers appeared in defiance of gravity while in reality they exploited it—to create momentum and rhythms of a nearly mechanical nature.

The motion, costume, and form of the trapeze act defined a modern freedom of the body in space. And, like Leybourne, artists took notice. James Tissot's 1885 painting *The Sporting Ladies* depicts men dressed in revealing leotards seated on trapezes glowering at ladies below, while Degas' 1879 *Miss La La at the Cirque Fernando* observes La La suspended by her teeth as she ascends to the ceiling, pictured from a low, cinematic angle. Varvara Stepanova, a Soviet Constructivist of the 1920s, applied modernist principles to clothing design; she created and donned costumes that seemed modeled on those of daring, young, trapeze-juggling ladies—but without the spangles or the sequins. "Modern clothing," Stepanova declared, "should be designed for motion, for labor, for activity." Clothing should be, in effect, a machine for wearing. And the trapeze artist is a body-become-machine, a machine for viewing—a machine that sways and moves from man to woman to woman to man, from machine to human, from clothed to naked. A wonderful modern body/machine/toy, dedicated to our lady of perpetual motion.

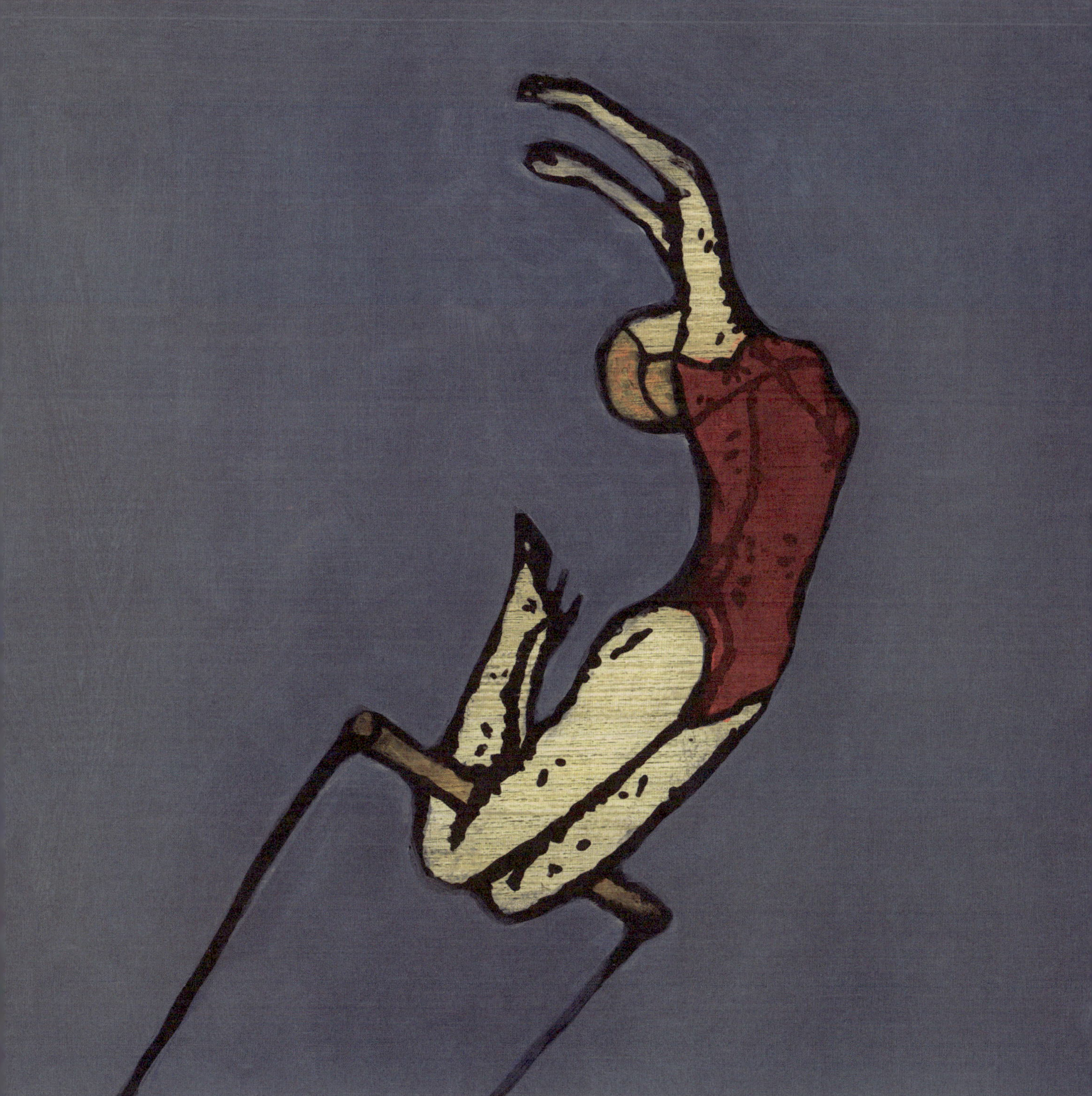

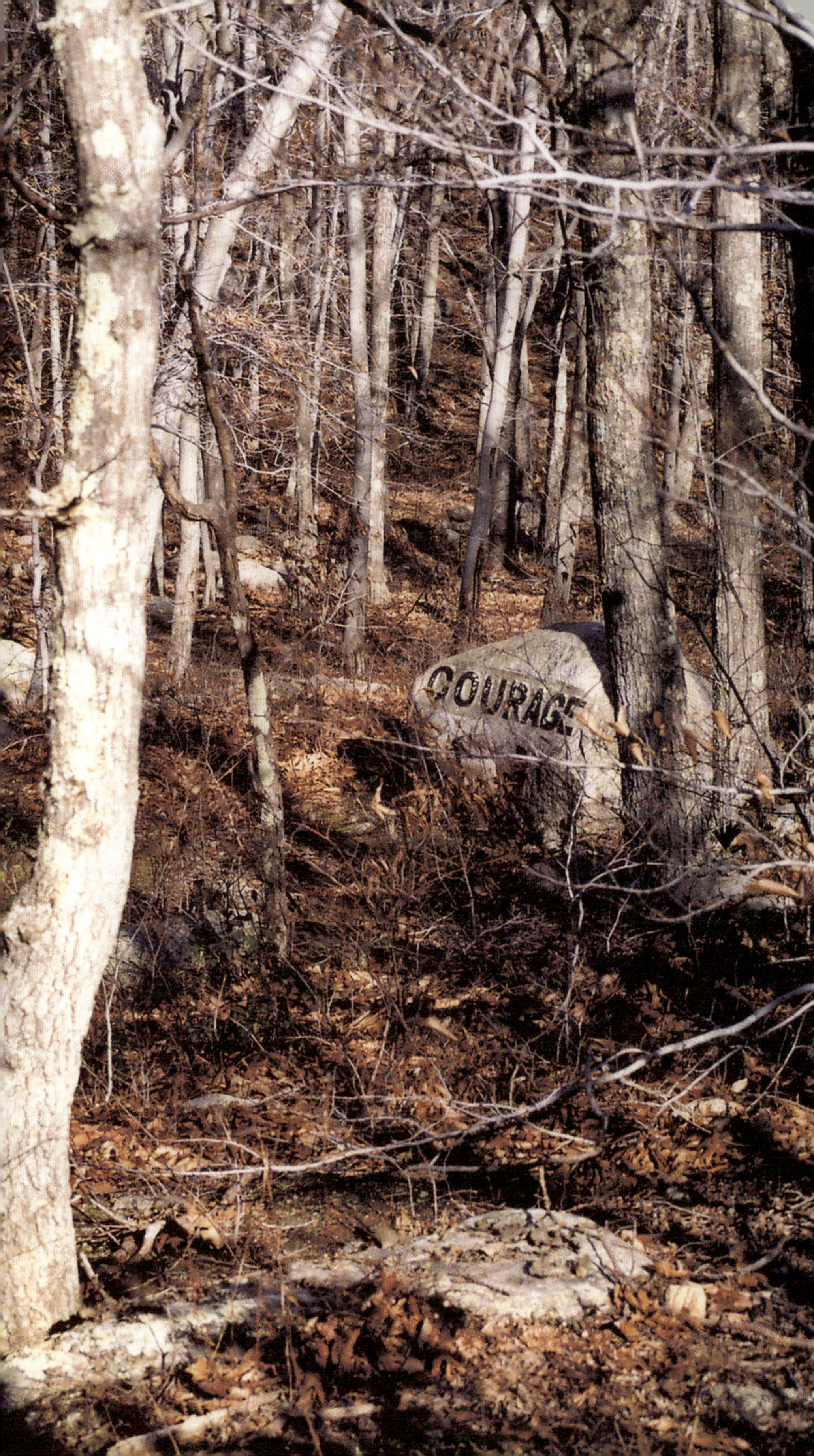

Investment counselor Roger Babson, who donated 1,100 acres of Dogtown to his native Gloucester in the first half of the twentieth century, commissioned the carving of edifying slogans into several boulders there.

In his autobiography, *Somehow a Past,* Hartley noted: "Dogtown is no longer in its original state—one of the days in the early fall [of 1931] when I went up there to make drawings—I heard the tap-tap of steel on stone—and soon found a laborer who proved to be a Scandinavian hewing out letters of some economic mottoes on the subject of labor. I asked him who had commissioned him—and he said—the owner. Hence an intervention of the worst sort it seems to me...."

A Gloucester View

Greg Cook

One. Marsden Hartley arrived in Gloucester, Massachusetts, from New York (by way of boat from Boston) in mid-July, 1931. The painter and poet had suffered a debilitating case of bronchitis over the past winter and hadn't painted in nearly a year. He was losing his hearing. He felt alienated from American culture and longed for Europe. He wondered if art was worth the trouble. Gloucester has attracted more than its fair share of artists over the years, but unlike most of them, Hartley wasn't much drawn to the city's gritty waterfront. "There is little for me to work from," he complained in a letter to his niece in August, "though I go every day to Dogtown."

Hartley was fascinated with Dogtown, an abandoned colonial village now hidden in the woods at the center of Gloucester. He wanted to stake out untraveled territory. He was attracted by its history, its severe look, and its name (which, some say, recalled the feral canines left behind by its last inhabitants). The tired, sad-eyed, hound-dog–faced man pioneered his mature style at Dogtown that summer—a roughhewn, folksy way of painting that produced pictures distinguished by heavy outlines and bold sculptural shapes.

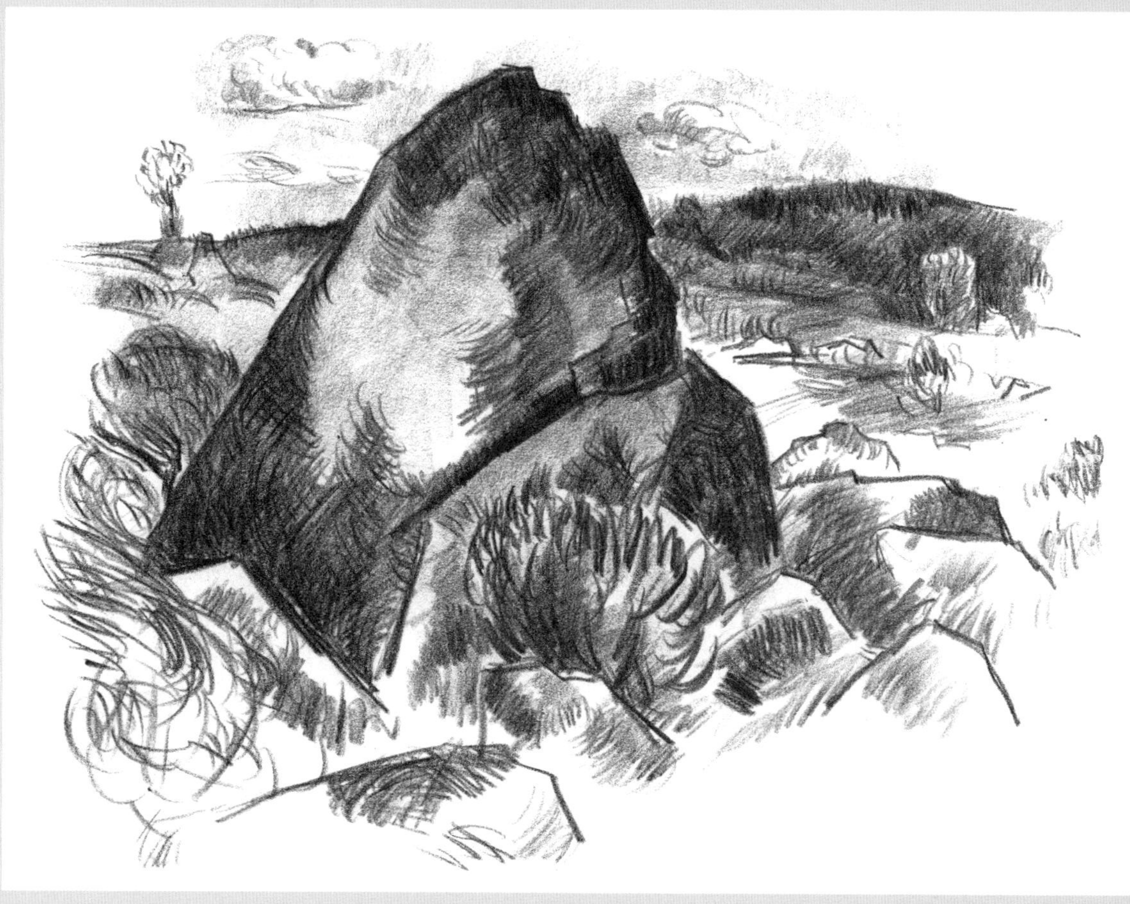

Two. Gloucester sits near the end of Cape Ann, a fist of granite an hour's drive north of Boston that punches out into the icy North Atlantic. One recent morning, I parked my car in an industrial park in Gloucester's center and hiked into the surrounding magnolias, pines, birches, and beeches of Dogtown—then down a hill, across a black amber stream, through a tangle of bittersweet decked with red berries and gold husks, over railway tracks bridging the end of the city reservoir, and up a rocky hill. A woodpecker investigated one tree trunk and then flew off. Walls of boulders, stacked three and four high, rambled through the trees and over hills, marking the property bounds of English settlers who cleared "Town Parish" or "Upper Town," as it was then known, for planting and pasture in the late 1600s. The thin soil was never well suited for farming and the village dwindled as Gloucester threw its lot in with fishing and clustered around the harbor downtown. They say the last resident of Dogtown was taken to the poor house in the 1830s, but people continued to graze their cattle, sheep, and horses there until Hartley's time. Now it's all gone to seed.

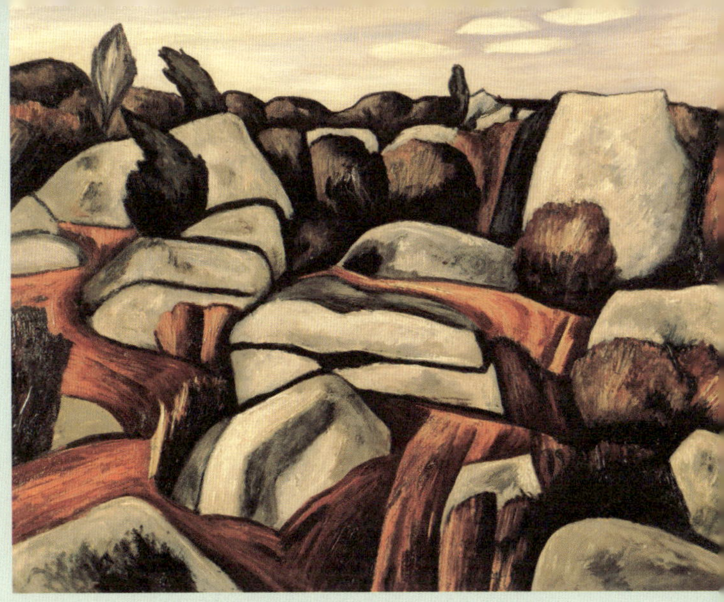

Three.

Hartley spent his mornings in Gloucester reading, writing, or at the beach. He might catch a movie downtown in the evening. But in the afternoons he hiked the five miles to Dogtown. He didn't have the strength to haul his painting materials with him, so he painted from crayon, pencil, or ink sketches, as well as from memory. I imagine the 54-year-old wheezing as he thumped up and down Dogtown's boulder-studded hills, hunting for a spot to sit alone among the scrub and stone and saturate himself in the austere, elemental landscape. He noted the blueberries, junipers, and, here and there, the odd cellar hole—the only remains from colonial houses.

He quickly found his artistic footing, but remained distracted and annoyed by the old ladies he ran into at meals in the guesthouse on the eastern side of the harbor where he boarded, and by what he described as the tawdry goings-on of the idle and the snobby who had gathered there for the summer. "Industry seems to be at a standstill—if there is any outside of cod fishing—Poor old New England so done in because of its beauty—so utterly sold out to the tourist," Hartley wrote to his dealer, the photographer Alfred Stieglitz, on August 12.

Opposite: Marsden Hartley, *Rock;* charcoal drawing, 12 × 15 inches; New Britain Museum of American Art, New Britain, Connecticut (gift of Alex W. Stanley Estate, 1954.63); photo credit: E. Irving Bloomstrann

Above: Marsden Hartley, *Rock Doxology, Dogtown,* 1931; oil on panel, 18 × 24 inches; private collection

Overleaf: Fitz Hugh Lane, *Gloucester from Rocky Neck,* 1844; Cape Ann Historical Museum, Gloucester, Massachusetts

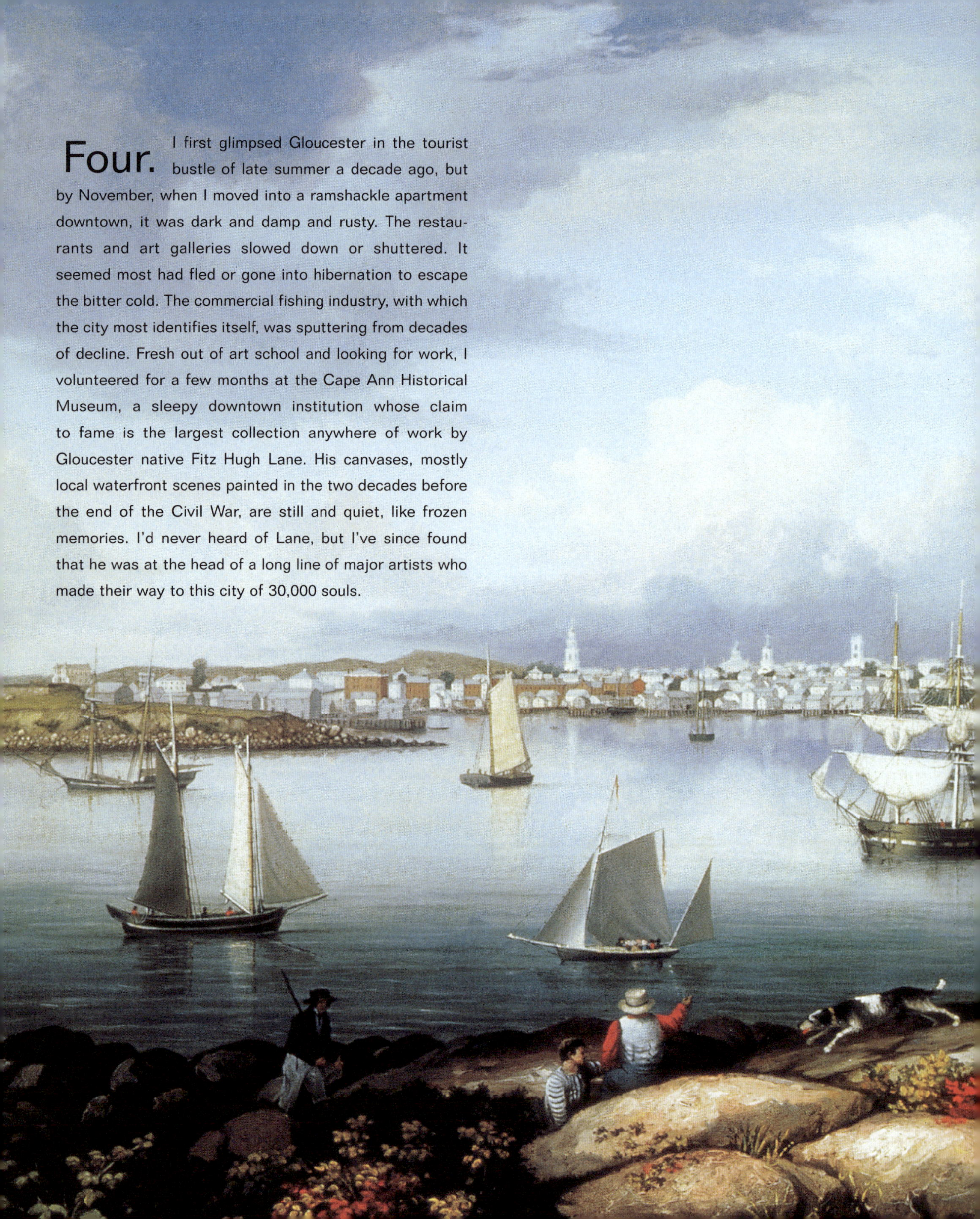

Four. I first glimpsed Gloucester in the tourist bustle of late summer a decade ago, but by November, when I moved into a ramshackle apartment downtown, it was dark and damp and rusty. The restaurants and art galleries slowed down or shuttered. It seemed most had fled or gone into hibernation to escape the bitter cold. The commercial fishing industry, with which the city most identifies itself, was sputtering from decades of decline. Fresh out of art school and looking for work, I volunteered for a few months at the Cape Ann Historical Museum, a sleepy downtown institution whose claim to fame is the largest collection anywhere of work by Gloucester native Fitz Hugh Lane. His canvases, mostly local waterfront scenes painted in the two decades before the end of the Civil War, are still and quiet, like frozen memories. I'd never heard of Lane, but I've since found that he was at the head of a long line of major artists who made their way to this city of 30,000 souls.

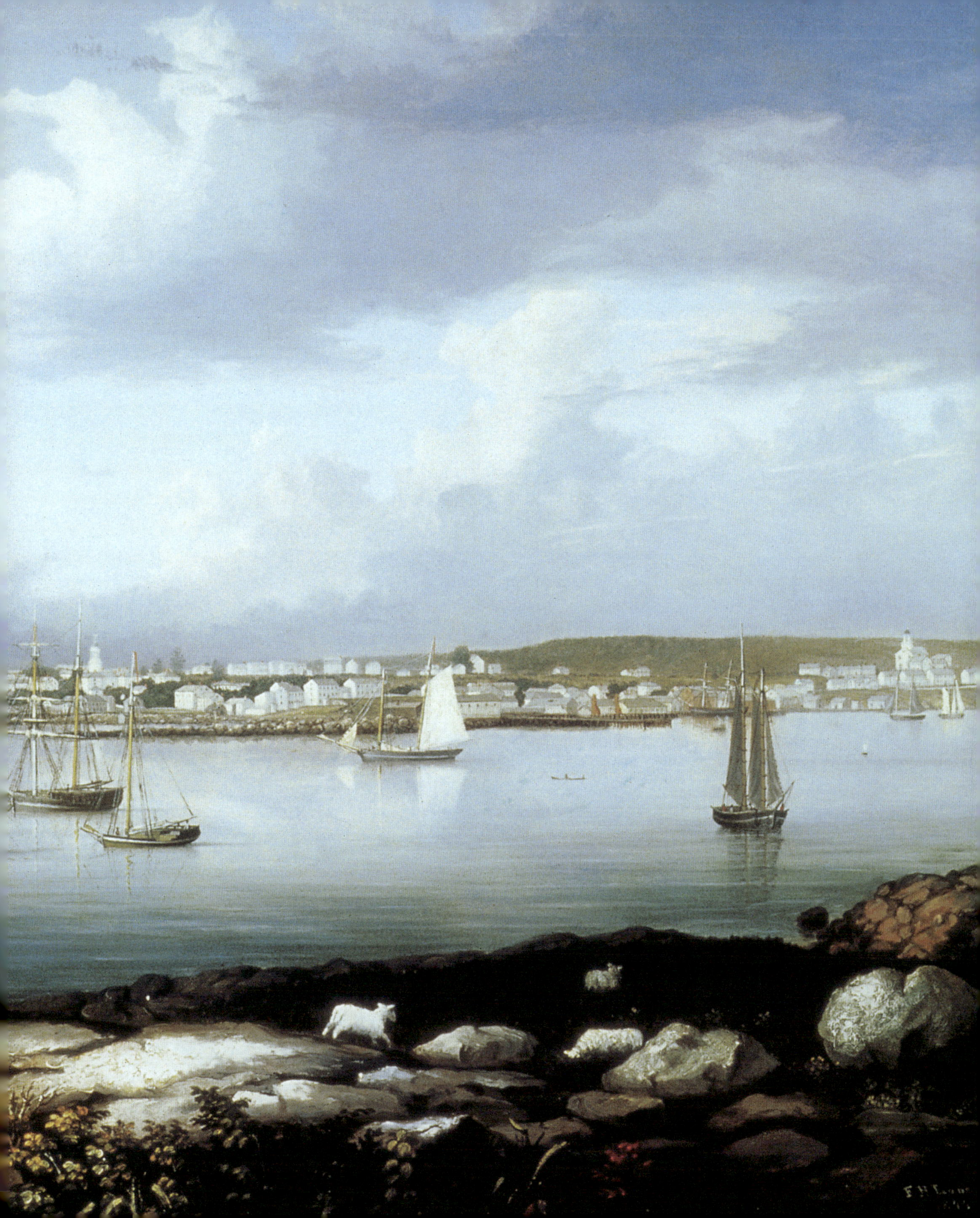

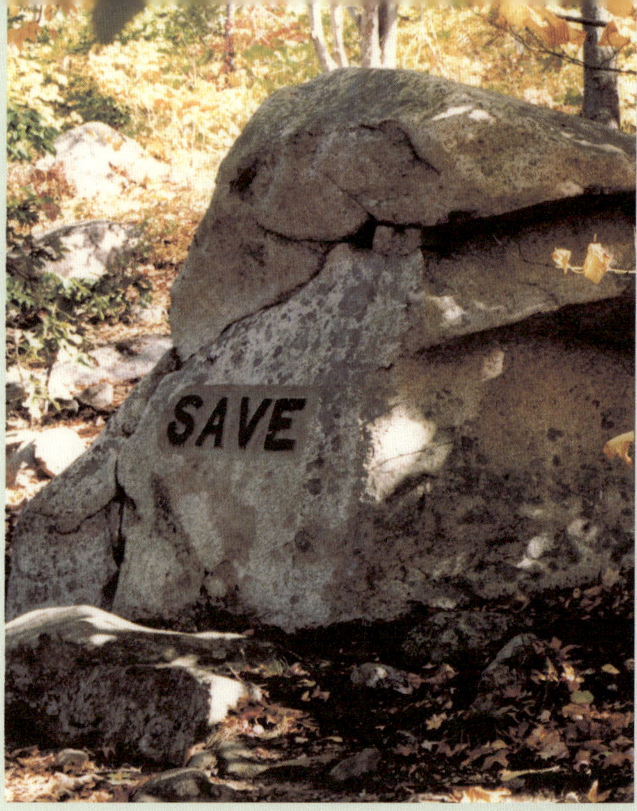

Five. Gloucester was already a tourist town by the time Winslow Homer first summered here in 1873. Visitors arrived by train, coach, or steam ship and settled into grand hotels or rented houses for the season. Homer installed himself in a room at the end of Main Street and painted sunny scenes of waifs playing around the waterfront, seeing in them hope after the devastation of the Civil War. He returned in 1880, boarding with a lighthouse keeper on an island in the harbor, to paint schooners under fiery sunset skies. Edward Hopper painted lonely Gloucester streets and alleys in 1911 and again in the 1920s. Ash Can School painter John Sloan summered here in the 1910s, convincing his friend Stuart Davis to follow. Milton Avery came in the 1940s and attracted his friends Mark Rothko, Adolph Gottlieb, and Barnett Newman. T.S. Eliot (who summered here as a child), Rudyard Kipling, Charles Olson, and Henry Wadsworth Longfellow wrote about this place.

Artists were attracted by Gloucester's crisp clear light, rugged natural beauty, and working harbor. Some turned defunct sail lofts into studios. American Impressionists found here a rocky coastline that recalled Monet's French shores, while urban realists appreciated that, despite the tourist influx, it remained a working-class city, a fishing town complete with roughneck bars and prostitutes plying the waterfront. Some fancied they could know Gloucester completely because it was a small island city, the cape peninsula severed from the mainland by the Annisquam River. And this all was conveniently located just a day's trip from New York.

After World War II, though, major artists stopped coming here. The growing interstate highway system and air travel opened up the West. And as the art world shifted from realism to abstraction, artists no longer required Gloucester's picturesque scenery. Today, visiting Cape Ann's galleries, I find a thriving art scene—but one dominated by painters churning out sentimental harbor scenes for the tourist market. Perhaps this was always the way.

Six. Hartley decided to stay in Gloucester for the fall, and his usual crankiness fled him after the tourist crowd departed. By the end of September, he wrote to a friend about his paintings: "I am wanting them to be painted sculpture and not ordinary paintings and I think they mostly are. I feel as if I am casting off a worrisome chrysalis and hope to emerge a clear and more logical and consequent being." Hartley was up in Dogtown every afternoon until sundown through late October, sketching drawings for new paintings. The leaves turned red and gold, contrasting with the greenish hew of the lichen-speckled boulders. The sun hung lower in the sky, offering a warmer light that accentuated the sculptural masses of trees and stone. His paintings distilled these components down to the essential, uncanny air of the place, which lingers in the memory along with the paths and brambles, hills and boulders of Dogtown. "And I assure you I have never seen anything so unique as the coloring is up on the Cape just now. It comes the closest to the analogy of music that I have ever seen.... I am relieved to find nature at last being thoroughly visual again—and for once she evades all the painters save me, or so I am inclined to think as I never see one up there," Hartley wrote on October 22. "...It cannot appeal to dull painters because it calls for deep contact and study and I am capable of both. And while my pictures are small—they are more intense than ever before—and I have for once immersed myself in the mysticism of nature."

Hartley left Gloucester in mid-December to spend the holidays in New York and then continued on to Mexico on a Guggenheim Fellowship. His Gloucester work sold poorly in New York the following spring, but he returned here one last time in 1934. He was distracted by financial worries and the looming war in Europe, and couldn't recapture the electricity he'd tapped here three years before. Hartley wrote on July 20, 1934: "I had lived it over in my imagination so intensely that the thing looked like nothing when I got here."

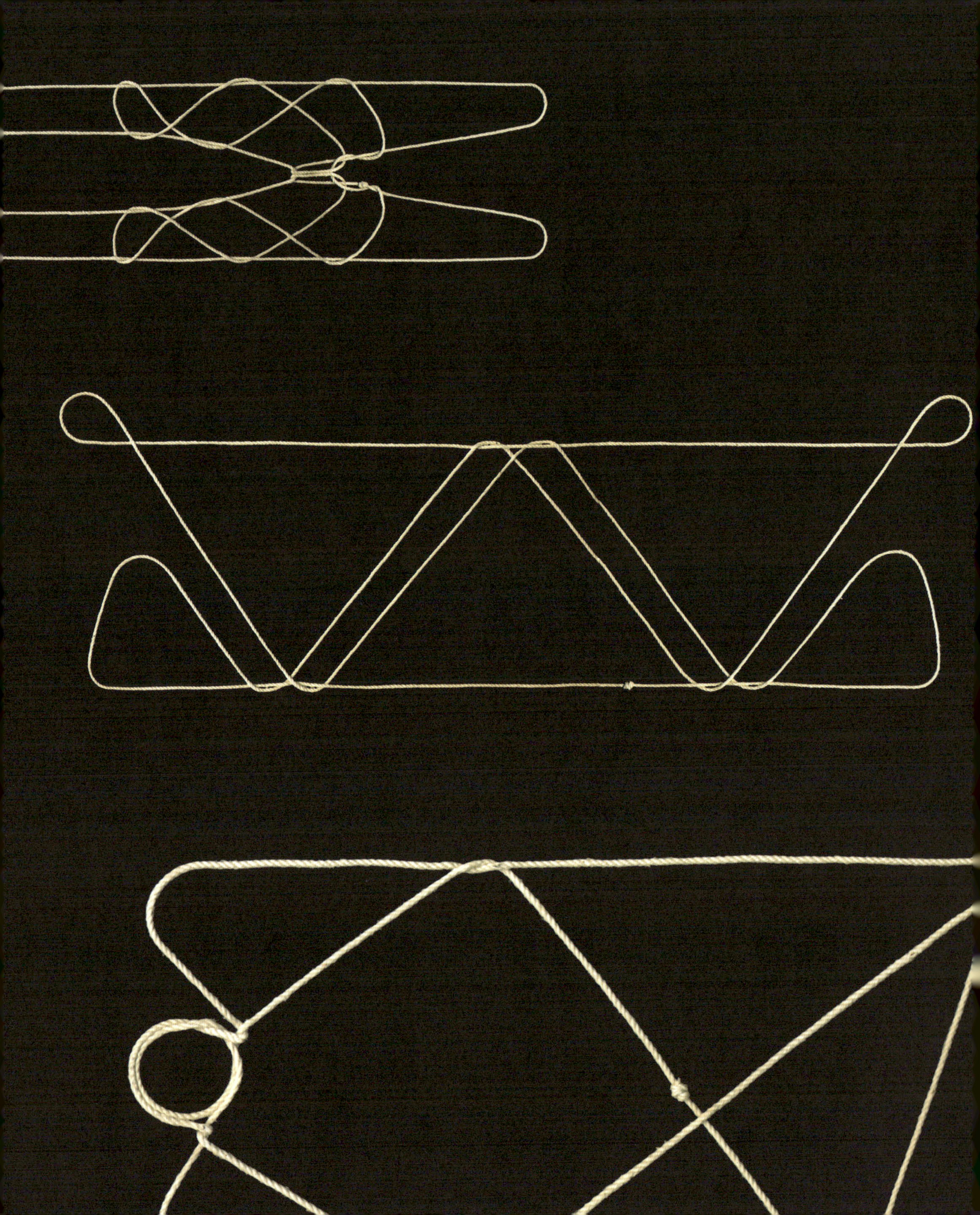

Stringing Along

Harry Smith Figures

John Cohen
1968

Despite himself, Harry Smith has emerged as the unheralded genius behind the scenes of the folk movement in America. He is also greatly respected as an avant-garde filmmaker by avant-garde filmmakers, and his works have been shown at the Museum of Modern Art.

A visit to his room is a somewhat mystifying experience, for what appears on first impression as orderly piles of books and objects is actually a storehouse for cross-disciplinary investigations of visual, anthropological, and musical phenomena. The closet is filled with women's dresses from the Florida Seminole Indians. One corner of the room, marked with a Keep Off sign, is filled with Ukrainian Easter eggs; on the bureau are stacks of mounted string figures; behind the table is a movie camera alongside portfolios of his paintings and graphic work. In another corner is a clay model of an imaginary landscape that has been recreated from a dream. On the walls hang empty frames from which the pictures have been torn. Under the desk lamp is the only living thing besides Harry: a solitary goldfish in an orange clay bowl. A nineteenth-century Pennsylvania Jacquard spread covers the bed. At other times there have been piles of beautiful quilts and other weavings from that area, as well as a collection of paper airplanes from the streets of New York. Small file cabinets of index cards are distributed between the stacks of research books. Each book becomes more exotic by its juxtaposition with the others—Mayan codices beside Eskimo anthropology studies, under a collection of Peyote ceremonial paintings, etcetera.

In the notes to the Folkways anthology, Harry included this quote: "Civilized man thinks out his difficulties—at least he thinks he does; primitive man dances out his difficulties," along with another from Aleister Crowley: "Do as thy wilt shall be the whole of the law."

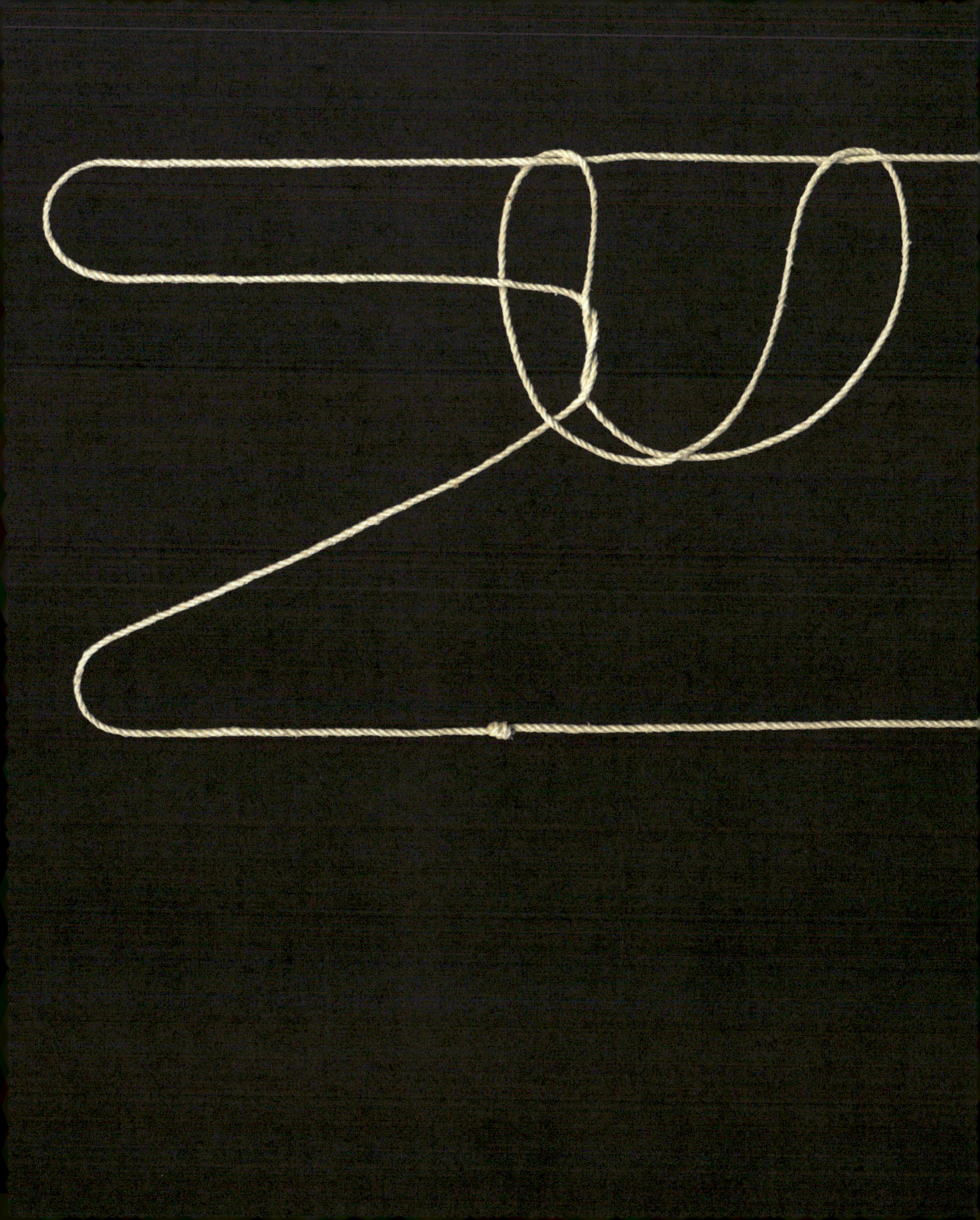

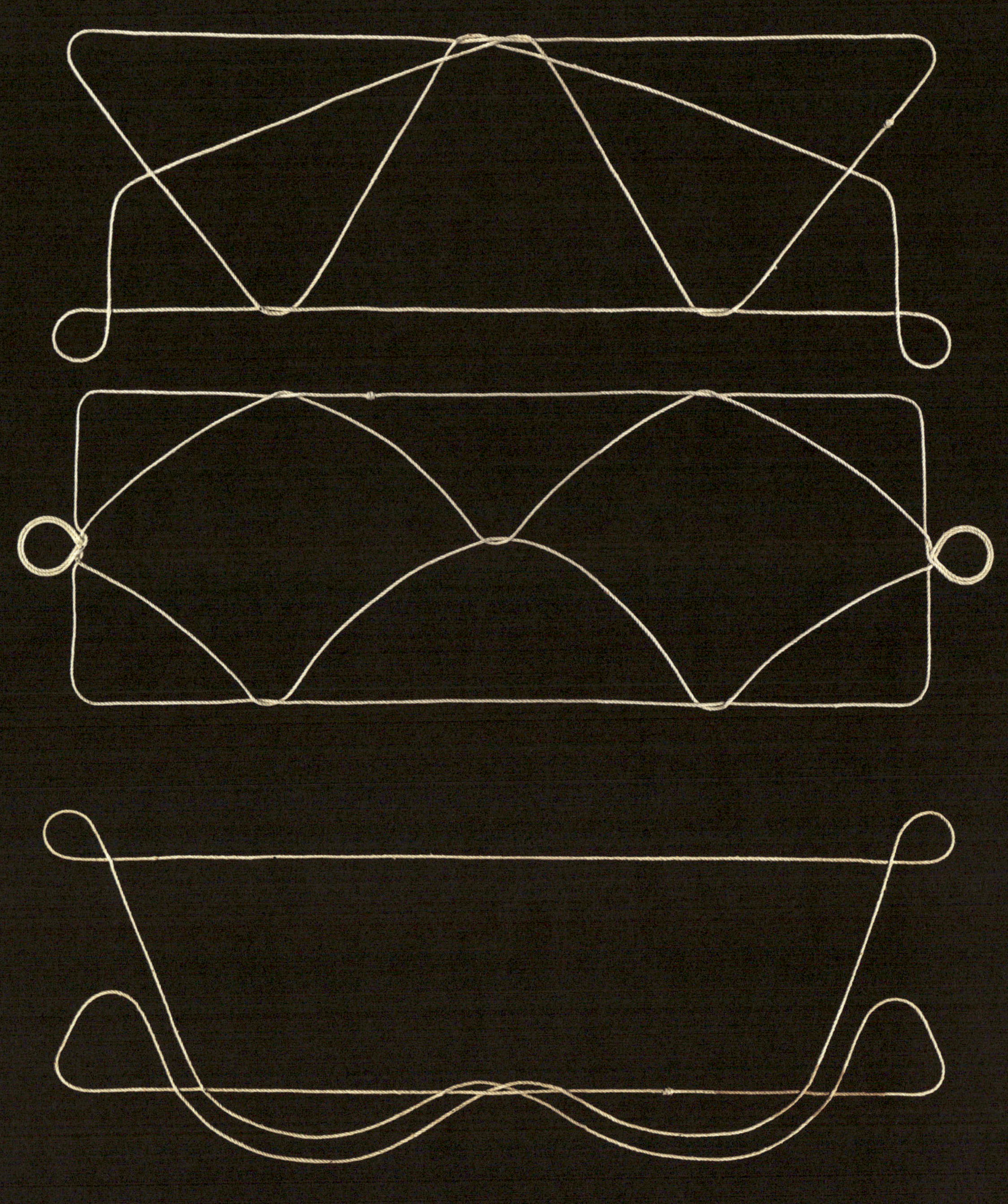

John Cohen interviews Harry Smith

"Every few years I get interested in string games, but I don't have all the apparatus for doing them."

Don't you just need a piece of string?

No, no—you need the instructions. I'm writing a book on the subject. Thousands of pages of it are written, but it has to have the references corrected, etc.

What is it that you saw in the strings?

Oh, it was some universal thing that seemed to be more widely distributed than anything else in places that didn't have so-called "civilization." It was the only thing that I could isolate offhand that was produced by all primitive societies, and by no "cultured" societies. String figures are found everywhere in the world except Europe and Asia (except for a few peripheral areas like the hills in the Philippines and Scotland). None of these places like France, Russia, Japan, China, Turkey have string figures—despite a great interest in games. It is a bit difficult to understand how the same thing is done in Patagonia as is done within the Arctic Circle or the Kalahari Desert, without leaving some evidence in Europe and Asia. I've had various theories for that. Possibly, it has to do with the parts of the brain that memorize letters (of which there usually seem to be around 30 or 50), the things you have to learn to write a language, because string figures don't occur in places where writing is done.

What do you see in a figure?

It depends on where it's from. Some places make realistic figures. The Eskimos make complicated, realistic, asymmetrical figures, whereas most Micronesian and Australian figures are geometric, and are consequently named after flowers and stars and things. The techniques developed in these places are suitable for such geometric figures, while those of the Eskimos are suitable for realistic animals, birds, and people.

I remember that some of the Eskimo strings act out little dramas—like a house falling down and a man running away.

That occurs everywhere. The reason that there is a lot of drama in the string figures I have from the Eskimos is that those were part of a carefully made collection. Anywhere that a careful collection is made (which would take a number of years to do in any place), there would always be moving figures.

The other oddity is that the string is always the same length, no matter where it is, and that only one person makes the string figures. Something similar to the string figure is the cat's cradle, which is done all over Europe and Asia. But the cat's cradle is a game, while string figures are essentially pictures of things.

String figures do have many uses in the cultures where they're created. But my interest in them is merely as something created by a lot of people who are usually grouped together as "primitive." The distribution of anything else across cultures—bows and arrows, pottery, basketry, clothing—isn't the same. As far as I know, string figures are the only universal thing other than singing. And singing might exist universally for the same reason—that a lot of experiences are lumped together as songs. But in tonal languages, as in Aruba, many things identified as songs turned out to be poetry recited at a certain pitch. And there's a Seneca tradition that is spoken, but when it's transcribed from a recording it's possible to indicate what tone each word is sounded on. Because of this possibility of transcription from tape recordings, it becomes very difficult to determine when speech ended and singing began. It is an artifact of the technical methods of handling the productions of people's vocal chords that enables us to classify certain sounds as songs. And it may be the same way with string figures—they may be derived from many different sources.

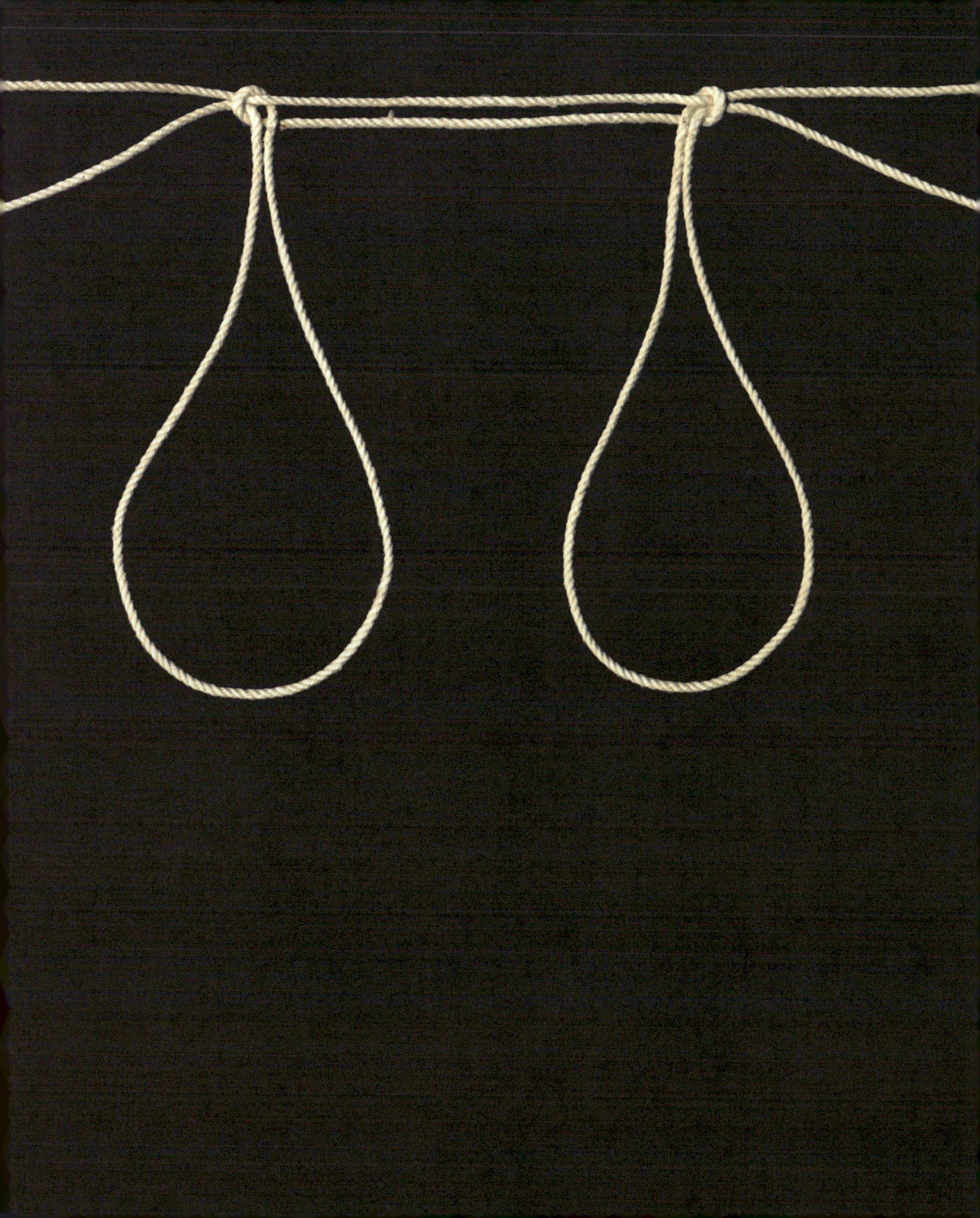

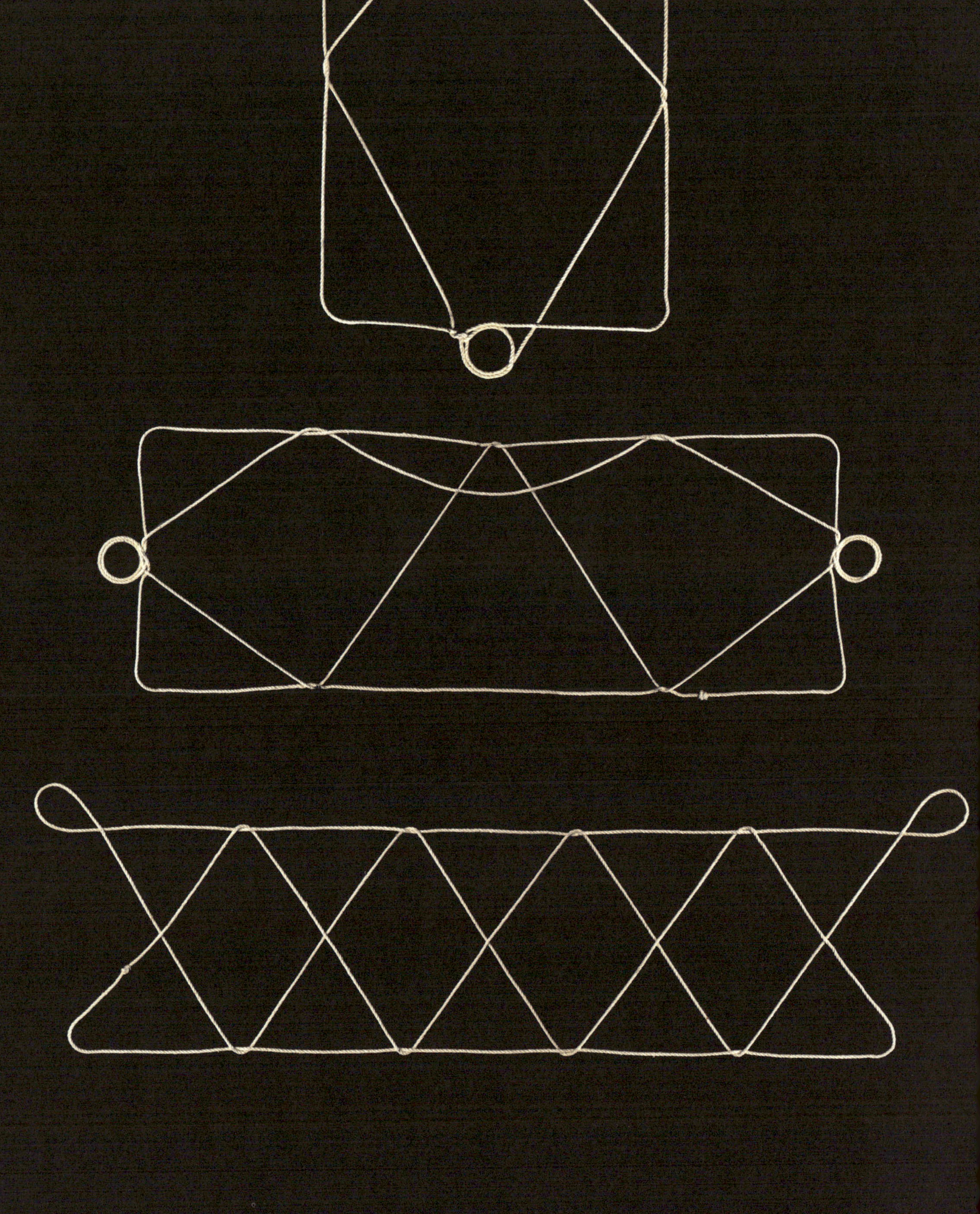

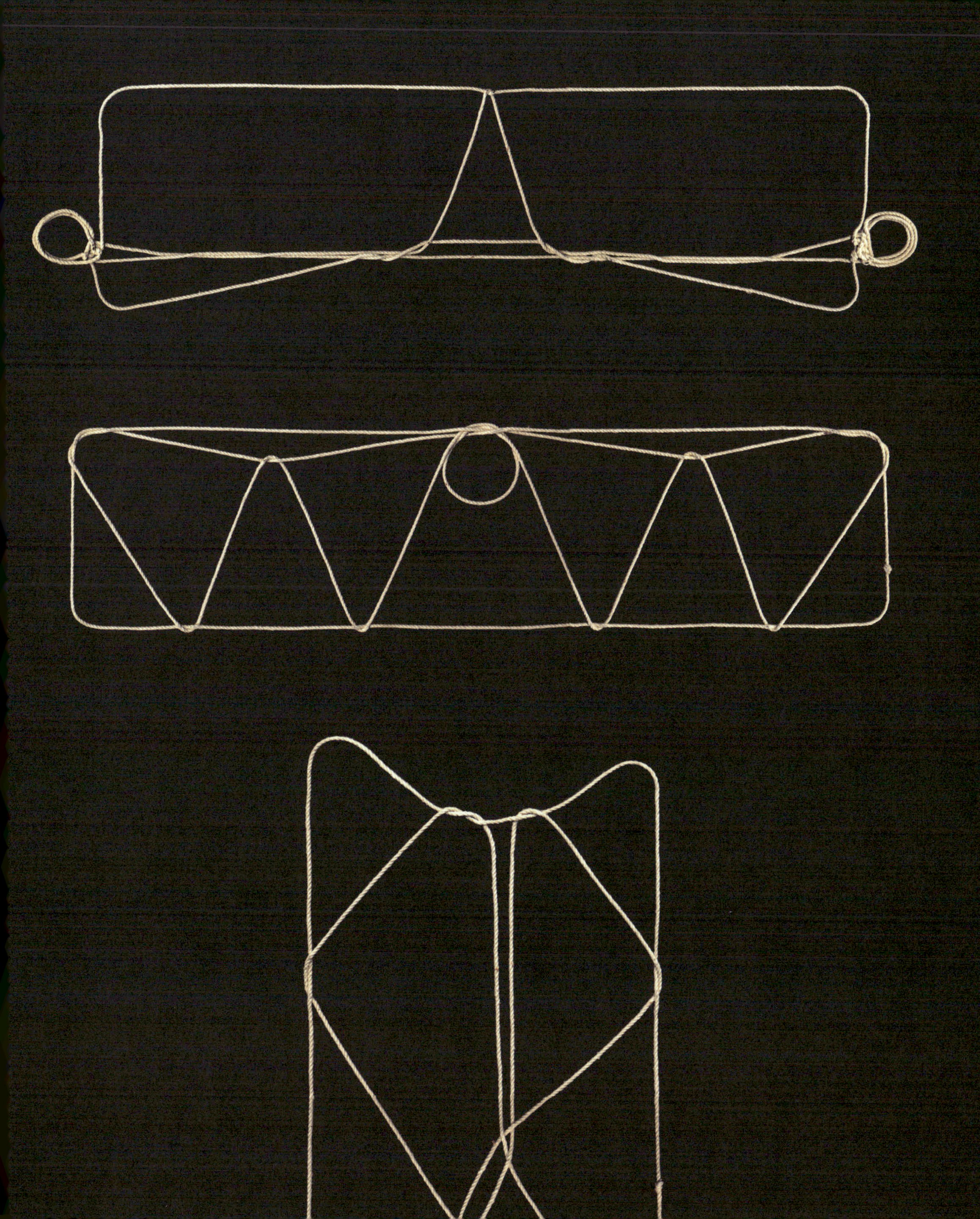

Lippincott Inc.

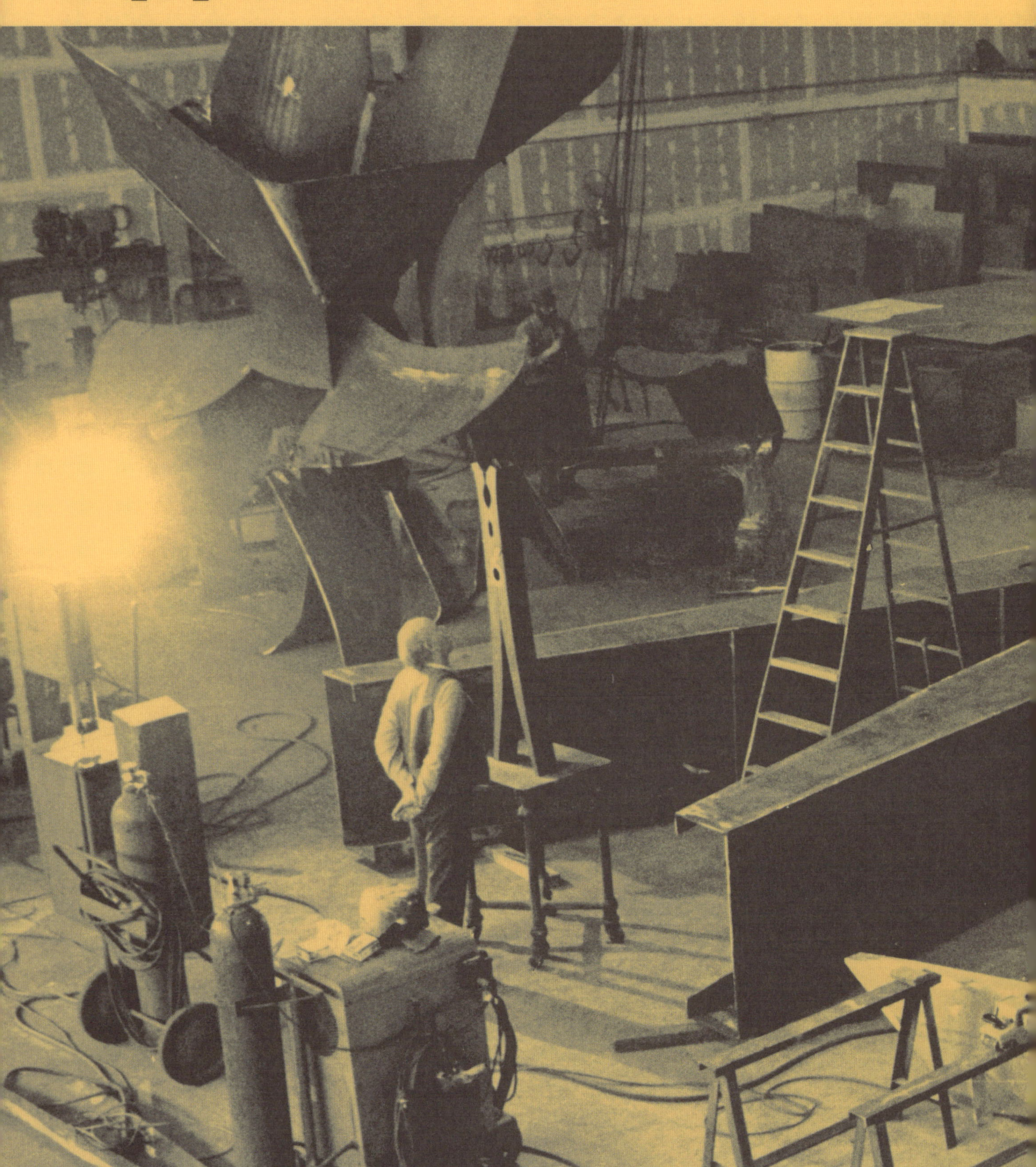

JONATHAN LIPPINCOTT

All photographs
copyright
Lippincott Inc.

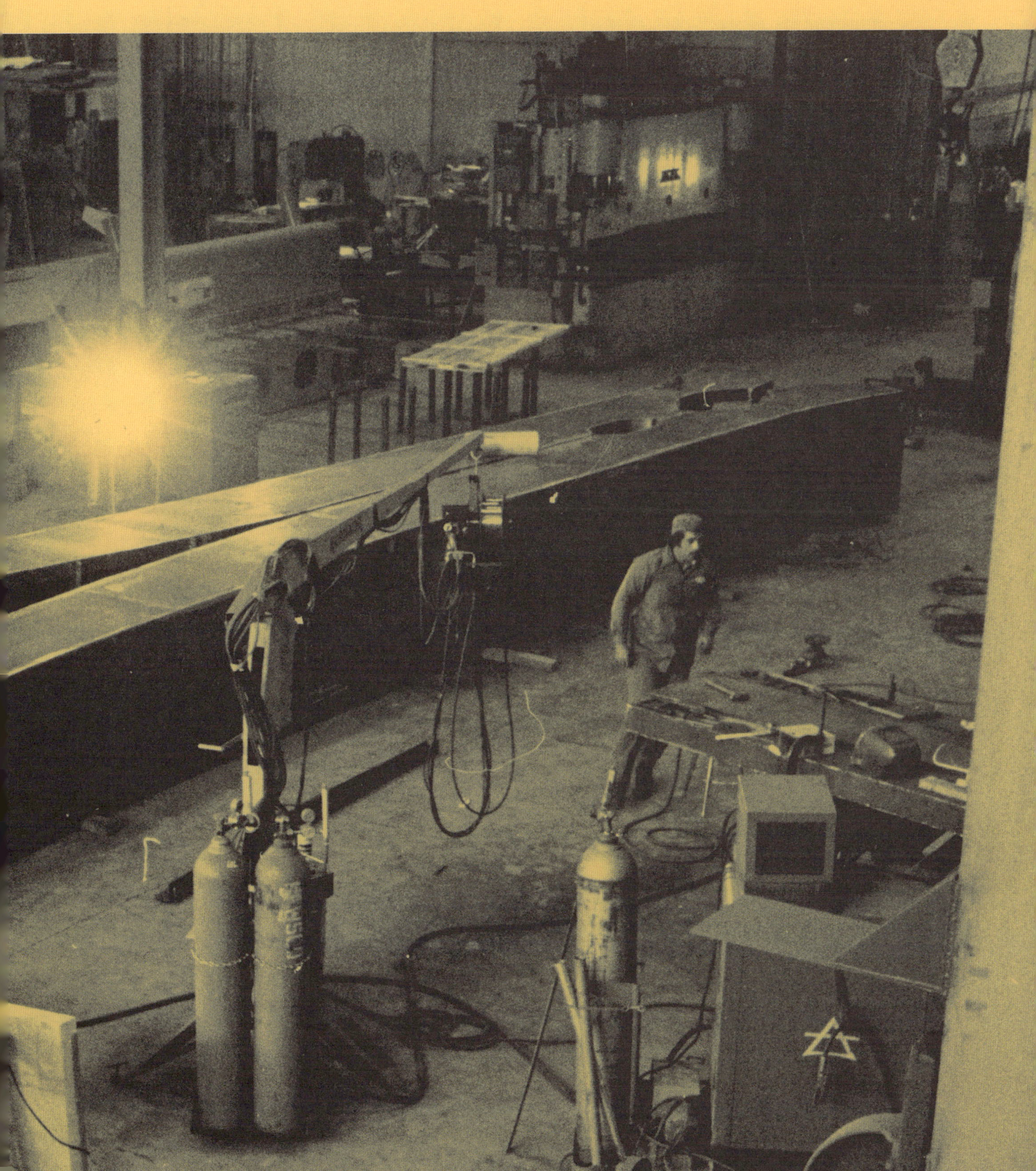

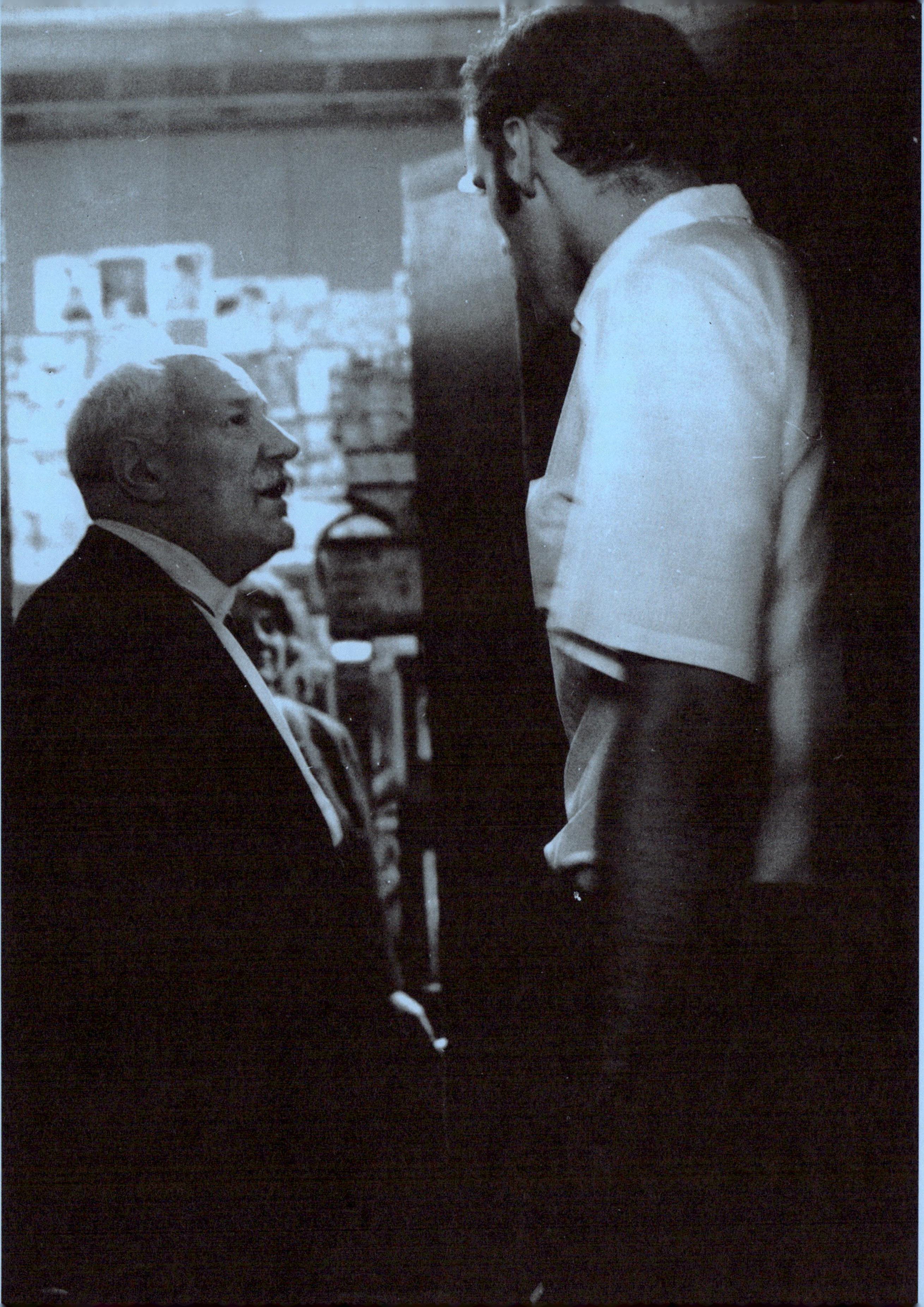

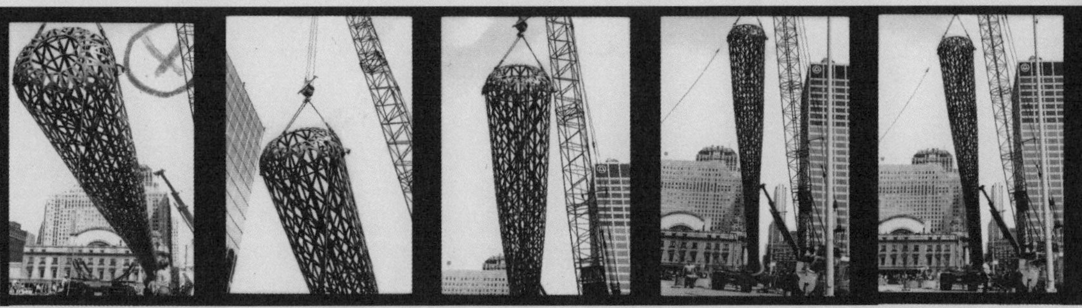

In 1977, when I was in fourth grade, my parents let my brother and me miss a day of school to go see my dad at work. My father owned and ran a metal shop called Lippincott Inc. that fabricated large-scale artwork in a town outside New Haven. When we arrived at the shop with our mother, we joined the small group of photographers and journalists gathered to watch a 100-foot–tall, 20-ton sculpture called *Batcolumn,* by the Pop artist Claes Oldenburg, be loaded onto a truck. The sculpture, made of 3"-wide steel bars welded together into a lattice creating the silhouette of a baseball bat, was on its way to permanent installation in Chicago. We had been watching it grow across the floor of the shop for several months, and in the end the sculpture was so long that the doors of the building had to be left open so it could stick out into the parking lot. I remember seeing Oldenburg standing by the truck with my dad and his crew for a photograph before the great departure. Looking around the field that day, I could see two or three of Louise Nevelson's black layered-steel collages and a brightly colored geometric piece by George Sugarman. While the departure of a 10-story baseball bat was unusual enough to warrant skipping school, making large-scale sculpture was, to me, simply what my father did at work.

My father, Donald Lippincott, started the company in 1966. Prior to the creation of Lippincott Inc. if artists wanted to create works larger than their studios or their own metalworking abilities allowed, they had to work with industrial manufacturers—usually steel fabricators or boat builders. Concerns about the unknown costs and the problems of engineering artwork discouraged many companies from taking on these projects. Lippincott Inc. was able to address these challenges and put the tools of industrial fabrication at the disposal of artists. It was the first—and for nearly a decade and a half, the only—company of its kind working exclusively with artists.

Dad and his crew embraced the artists' creative processes and expected each job to be a little different from the last. They gave artists the chance to explore the possibilities of the manufacturing process and the materials available. The shop always had a problem-solving quality to it—the problem being translating an artist's vision to a realized work of art. From the elegant silhouette of an Ellsworth Kelly sculpture to Robert Indiana's 12-foot *LOVE* to Louise Nevelson's complex assemblages, my dad and his crew worked with the artists to make their ideas large-scale realities. Their willingness to engage with the artists and to remain open to experimentation were what made the venture a success.

In the early days of the company, Dad and his business partner, Roxanne Everett, approached several artists whose work they admired and invited them to work at Lippincott Inc. They wanted to recruit a variety of artists to create a range of work showcasing the possibilities of industrial fabrication. This first group included Bernard Rosenthal, Marisol, Robert Morris, Robert Murray, Clement Meadmore, James Rosati, and Barnett Newman. Don and Roxanne always kept up the search for interesting artists, and artists also came to the company through introductions from friends or through their galleries. Lippincott Inc. later attracted artists like Forrest Myers, Donald Judd, Keith Haring, George Sugarman, and David von Schlegell.

Above: Claes Oldenburg's *Batcolumn* during installation in Chicago

Opposite: Barnett Newman and Donald Lippincott at the shop; Newman's *Zim Zum* and Annalee Newman in the background

Overleaf: Claes Oldenburg contemplating the small-scale edition of *Clothespin;* large-scale *Clothespin* under construction (Sugarman's *Yellow Ascending* to the back left)

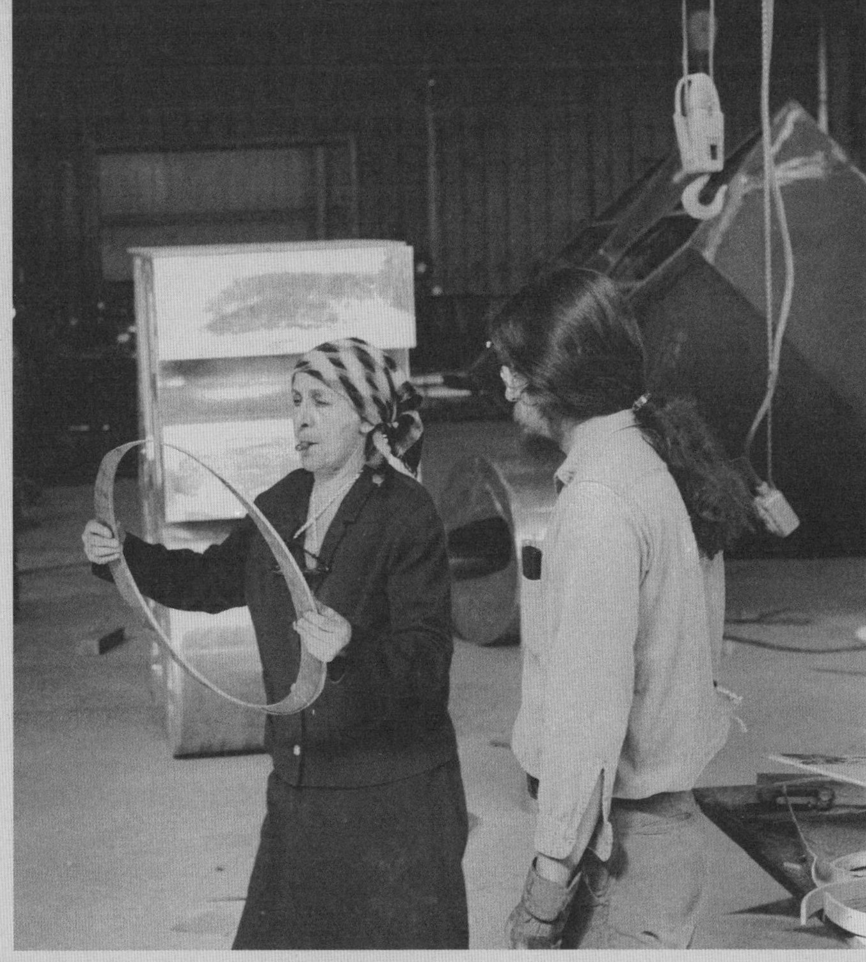

Work on a project began at the shop with discussions between Dad, the artist, an engineer, and the shop manager. Together they would resolve structural issues of building the sculpture, choose materials, and establish the final size of the piece. Usually, artists would arrive with models or drawings. For instance, Oldenburg made an early prototype of *Crusoe Umbrella* from the branches of his Christmas tree, which he stripped of needles, bent, and joined to form the shape of an umbrella. Sugarman created many of his models with the cardboard used in hat brims, which was waterproof and well suited to painting. Murray made some of his models using tin, which he could easily cut with snips and spot-weld together. The finished sculpture might echo the way the model was made—for instance, recreating the line of the model's snipped tin edges in the steel sheets of the final piece. Throughout all phases of fabrication the artist was encouraged to be at the shop, interacting with and reacting to the work as it proceeded, and guiding the look of the finished sculpture.

For the artists, the company served as an extension of their studios and of their own hands. The knowledge and skill of the crew allowed the artists to explore creative possibilities that were unavailable to them when working alone. The crew members were mostly welders and metal workers, and there were two people who focused on painting and finishing. My father kept the company small, with a staff of between 10 and 15, in order to foster a feeling of collaboration. An artist would often work with the same welders on several projects over the years, and this time together allowed them to develop a mutual creative language.

Above: Louise Nevelson directing the assembly of a sculpture, with Peter Verseeg; in the background, the partially complete *LOVE* by Robert Indiana

Opposite: Bobby Giza and Bob Stanford working on one of the sculptures in Nevelson's *Seventh Decade Garden* series

Of all the artists, Louise Nevelson engaged most actively in the fabrication process. Rather than start with a model or drawings, she would usually create directly at scale. Her metal sculptures, similar to her assemblages in wood, consisted of found elements—in this case, culled from the collection at the shop. These shapes were scraps from other artists' projects, as well as metal collected for her by my father. She would use these pieces as they were, or have them cut or bent to her specifications.

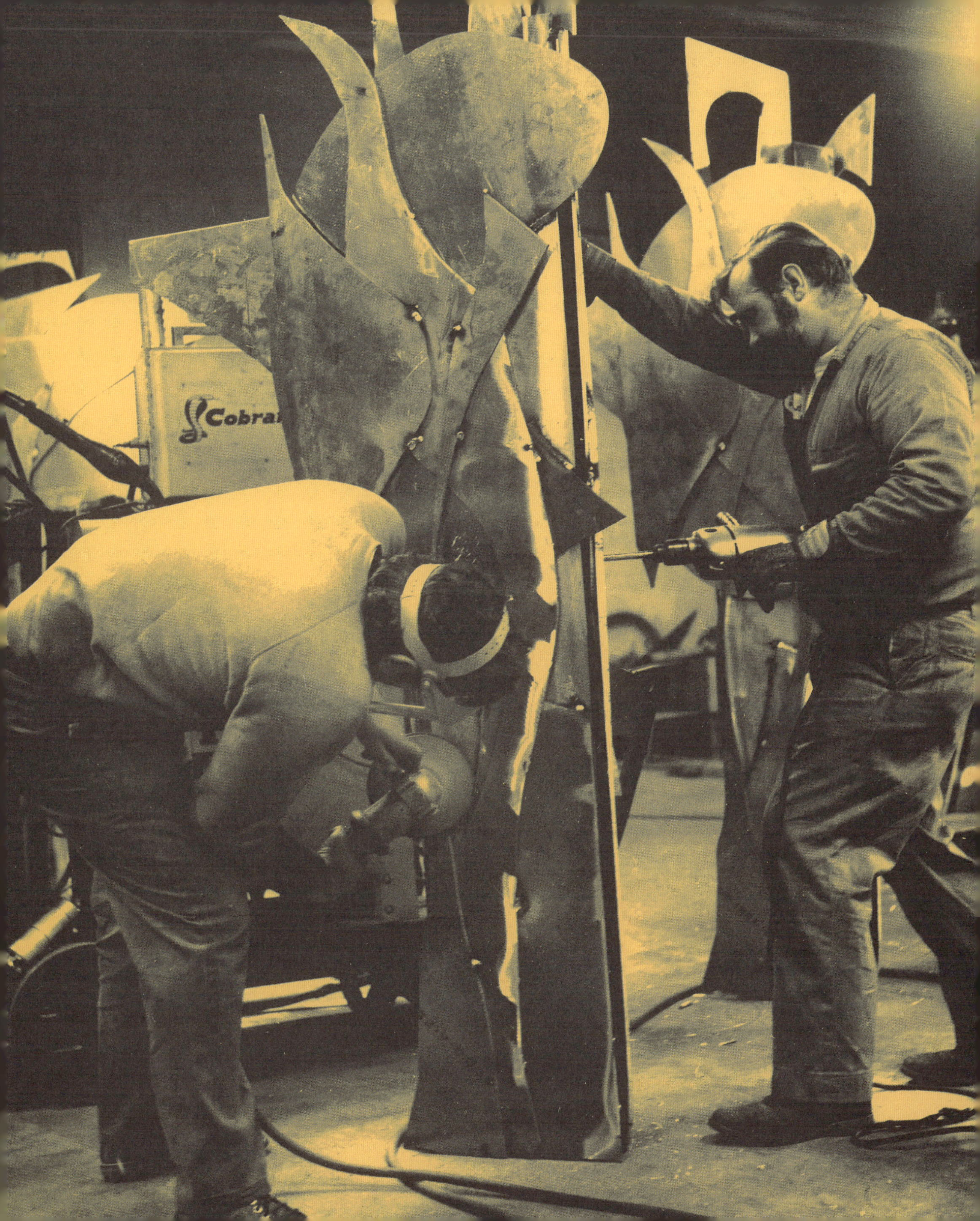
Cobra

Below: Robert Murray's *Quinnipiac* during setup for viewing in the yard

Opposite: George Sugarman and Peter Verseeg examining an element of one of Sugarman's sculptures

George Sugarman describing his experience at Lippincott Inc.: "I have felt for a long time as if it's really an extension of my studio, as if here is a group of workers who are really my assistants.... With the close personal attention they give to each sculpture, I can be sure that my aesthetic goals will be realized."

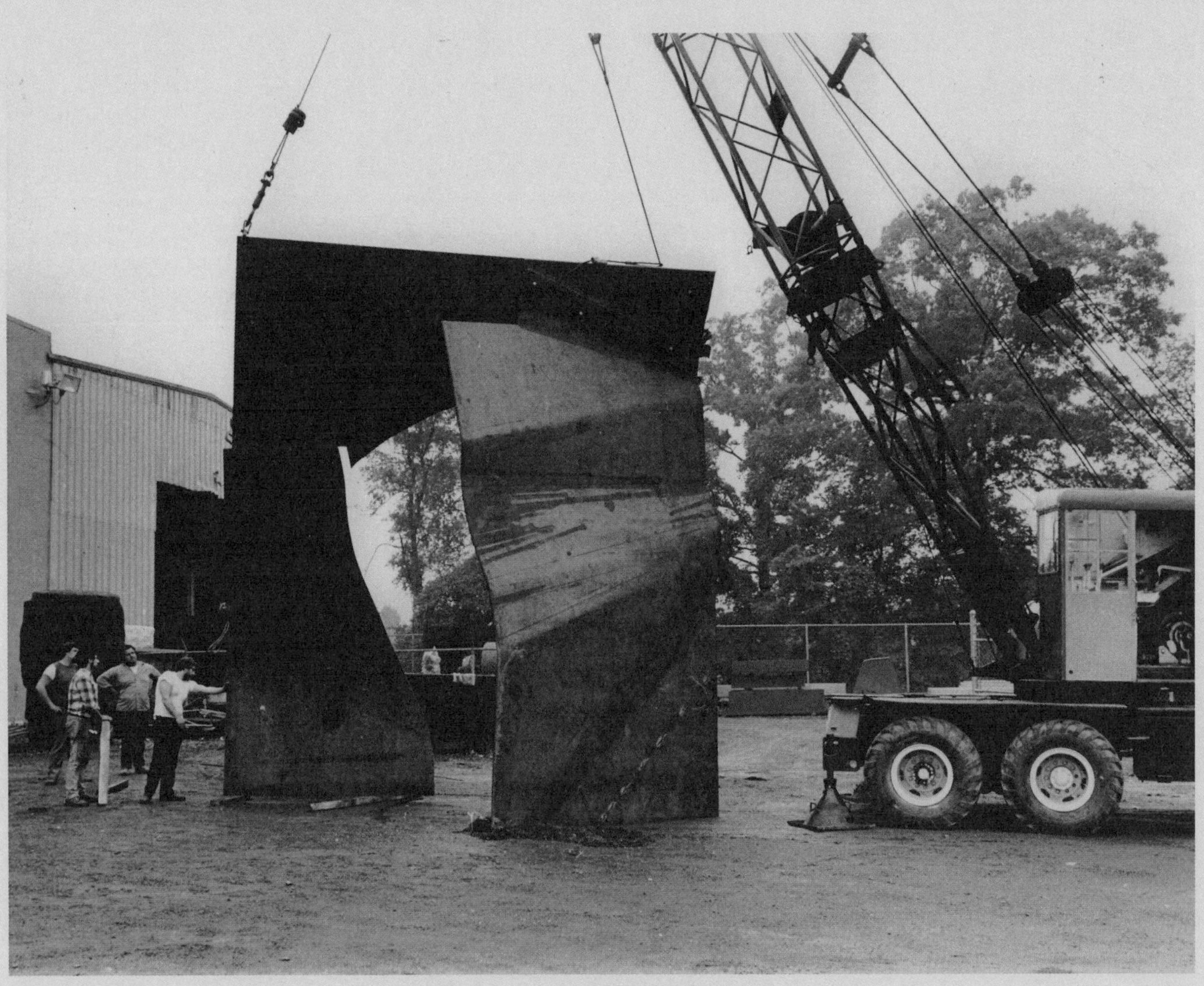

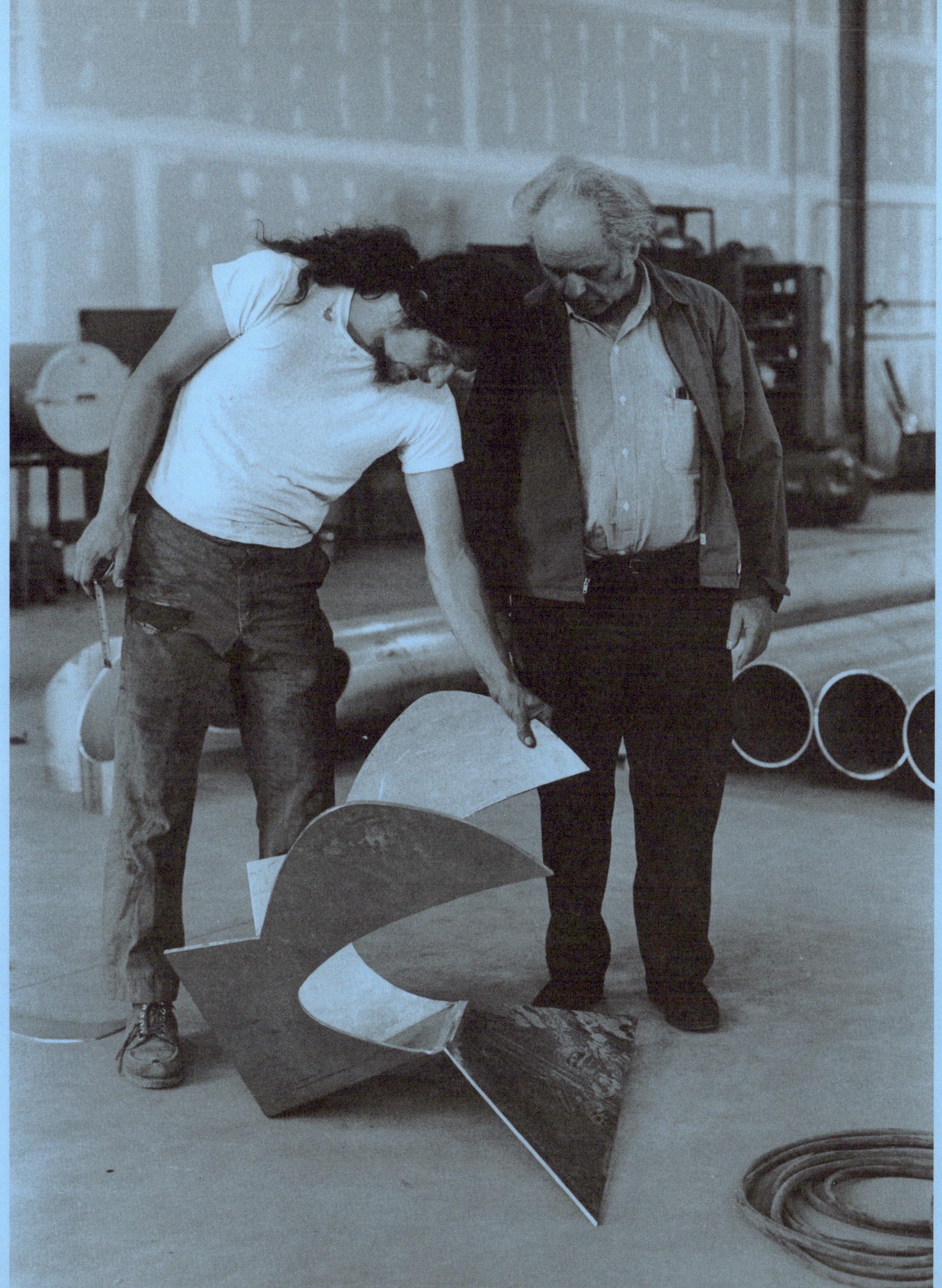

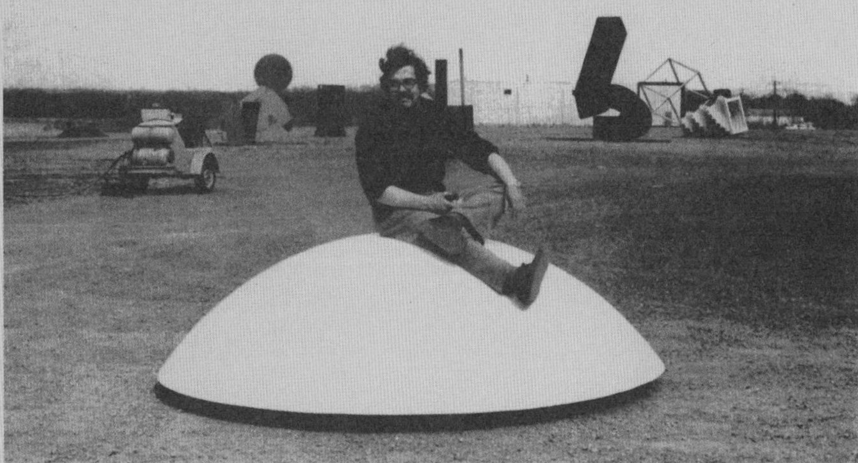

The building at Lippincott Inc. was an airplane-hangar–like 22,000 square feet, with 25-foot ceilings and two overhead cranes. The space was large enough for sculptures by several different artists to be underway at the same time. The main room was 120-feet square and used for layout, cutting, and assembly of the elements of a sculpture. Finishing work was done in the paint room adjoining the main workroom. Sandblasting was done outside in back of the shop, where the Cor-ten sculptures were put out in the field to weather. The five-acre field in front of the building also provided a viewing space for completed work.

This field was the destination of many school trips over the years, from nursery school to college. It was a great place to see (and, occasionally, to climb) recent work. Of course, my schoolmates and friends were not the only audience for all this artwork; plenty of adults came to look and explore as well. In the same way that most industrial fabricators were leery of manufacturing pieces of art, architects and developers, as well as private collectors, were hesitant to commission large-scale work based on drawings and models alone. They needed to experience finished work. My dad and the artists offered prospective buyers a chance to see works realized at full scale and to develop a greater understanding of the impact and importance of the work.

The conclusion of a project at Lippincott Inc. was the installation of the sculpture at its permanent site. The construction plan always anticipated the final installation and the need for the work to travel. In public spaces, installations often became performances as well, with people stopping to watch the unloading and assembly of the artwork. I remember going to New York with my dad to install a Calder mobile that the company had restored and painted. The piece was on loan and being shown in Central Park near the Plaza Hotel. After the mobile arms were set atop the base and the lifting straps removed, the gathered crowd burst into applause as the piece began to move. As the crowd dispersed, we gathered up the moving blankets, tools, and tape, climbed back in the truck, and headed home.

Above: Robert Breer atop one of his kinetic sculptures in the field; in the background *(from left to right)* are sculptures by Oldenburg; Nevelson; Murray; Meadmore; Myers; and Sugarman

Opposite: Installing Barnett Newman's *Broken Obelisk* at a show of outdoor sculpture in Detroit; watching are Annalee Newman *(left)*, Barnett Newman *(third from left)*, and Don Lippincott *(far right)*

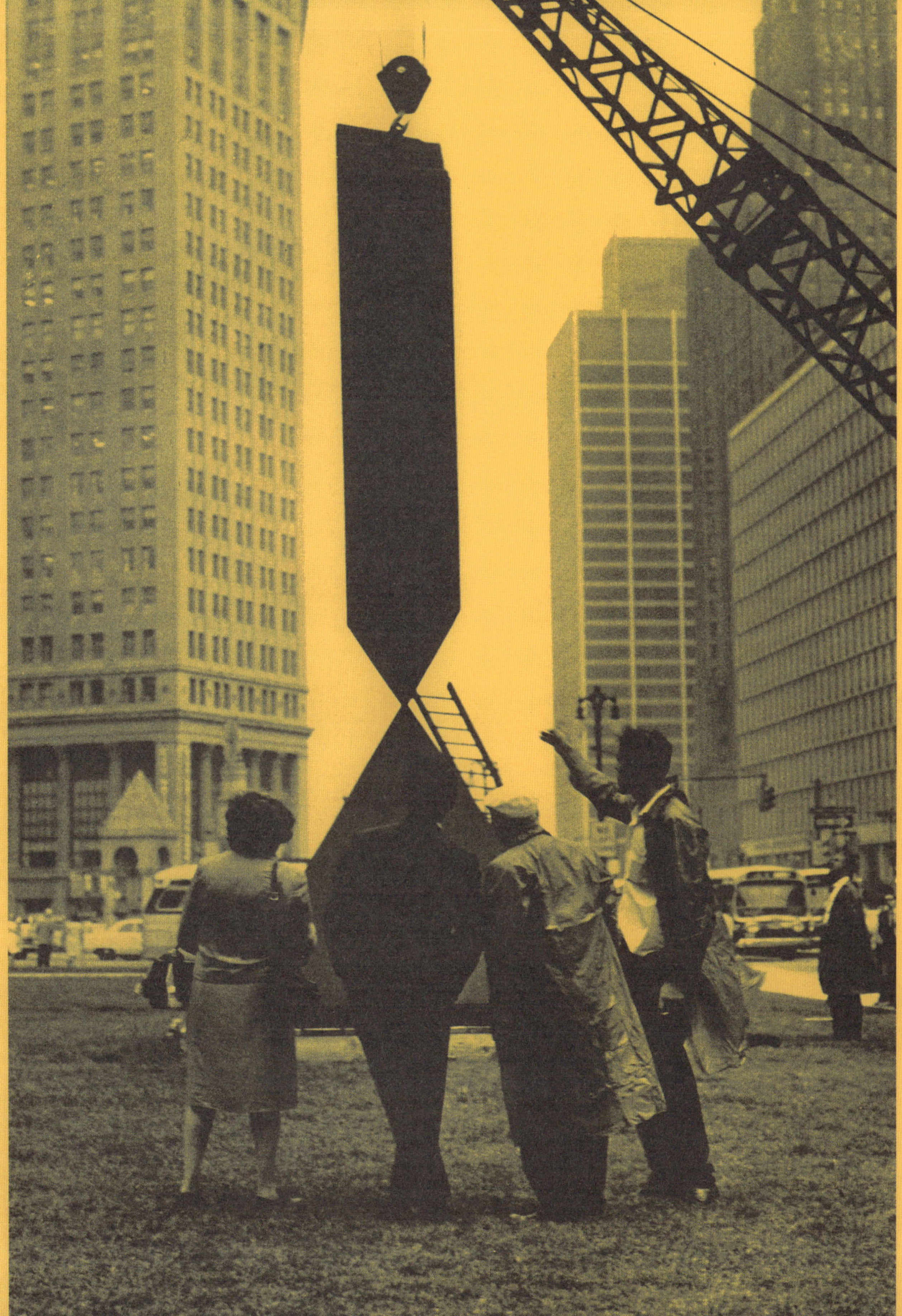

MEN WITH HATS

Billy Epton

"I think that there's no style, as such. I think there's a style of thought, maybe."

Billy Epton begins his own story: "A brief biography of an object maker. There are no prizes, honors, or grants—just my trophies."

Fitting pride and modesty for a man born in Oklahoma in 1936. A true son of the Midwest, Epton was schooled in painting at the University of Oklahoma and in art history at Washington University in St. Louis. He went on to teach art history at the University of Missouri–St. Louis, and then (from 1975 to 2000) sculpture at the Maryland Institute College of Art. Upon retirement he moved to New York City, where he and his wife, Carolyn Brady, spent a few years in the late '60s. All the while, Epton has been making art. He is a poet of the everyday, taking innocuous objects and literally recasting them as objects of wonder, surprise, and delight. He thrives on verbal and visual puns; works like *Dead Lead Soldiers* are simultaneously hilarious, tragic, and beautiful. The density of meaning in his work results from both the length of their gestation within him and the sense that he's packing in as much meaning—from the title to the shape to the very weight of each sculpture—as possible. Now back in New York, he lives among his "trophies," displayed in immaculate glass cases—each sculpture signifying a thought or moment in his life precious enough to warrant a space behind the panes. DN

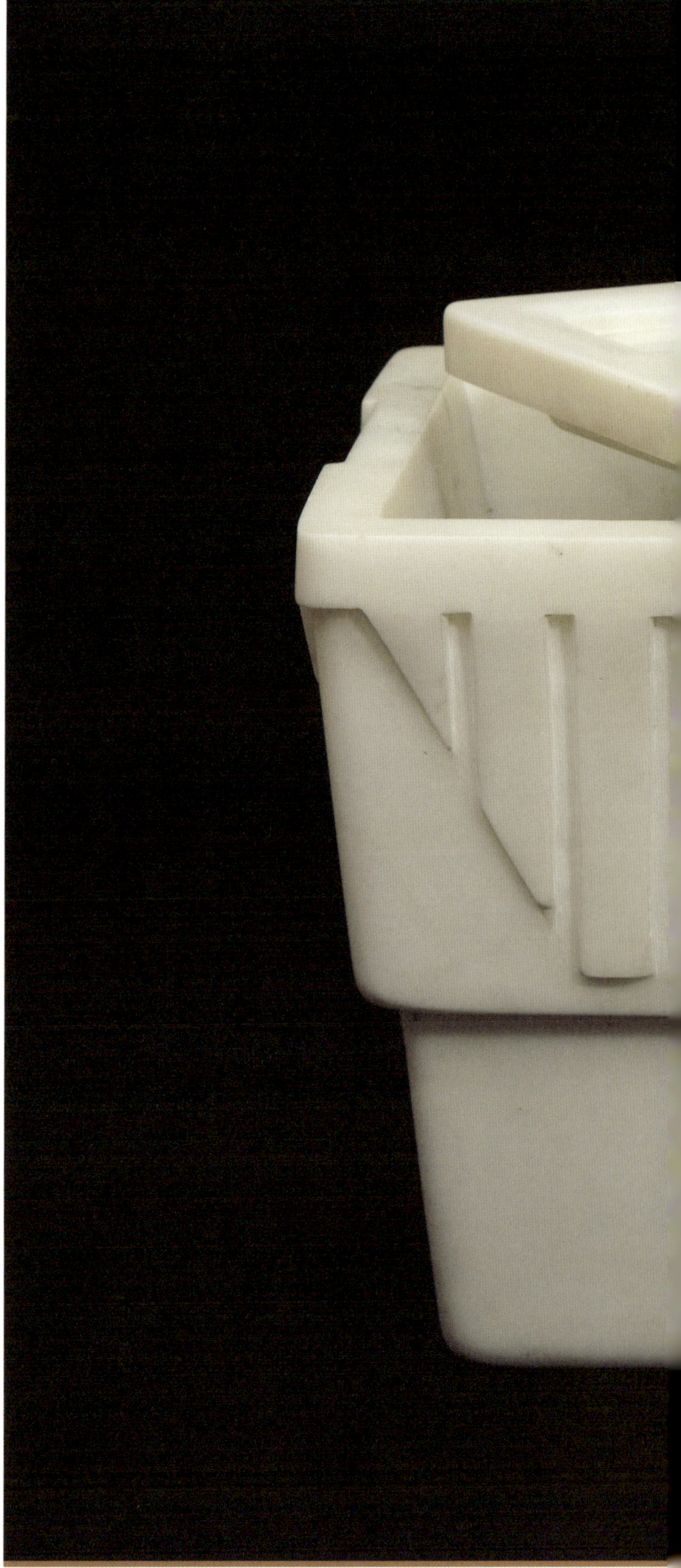

SIX-PAC COOLER

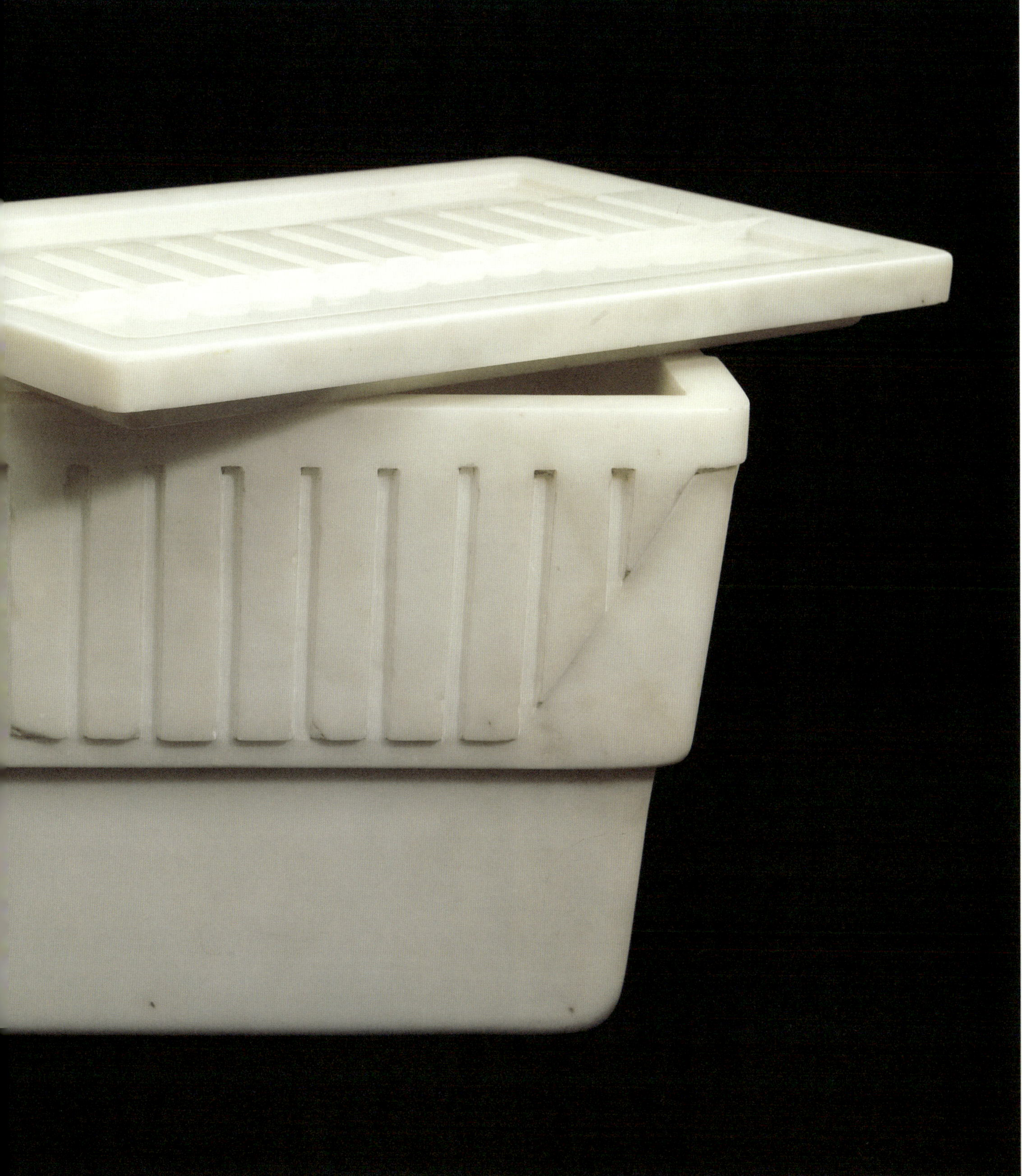

Six-Pac Cooler
1980, 1982
White Carrara marble
17.25 × 12 × 12.75 inches

A marble copy of a Life Forms polystyrene beer cooler.

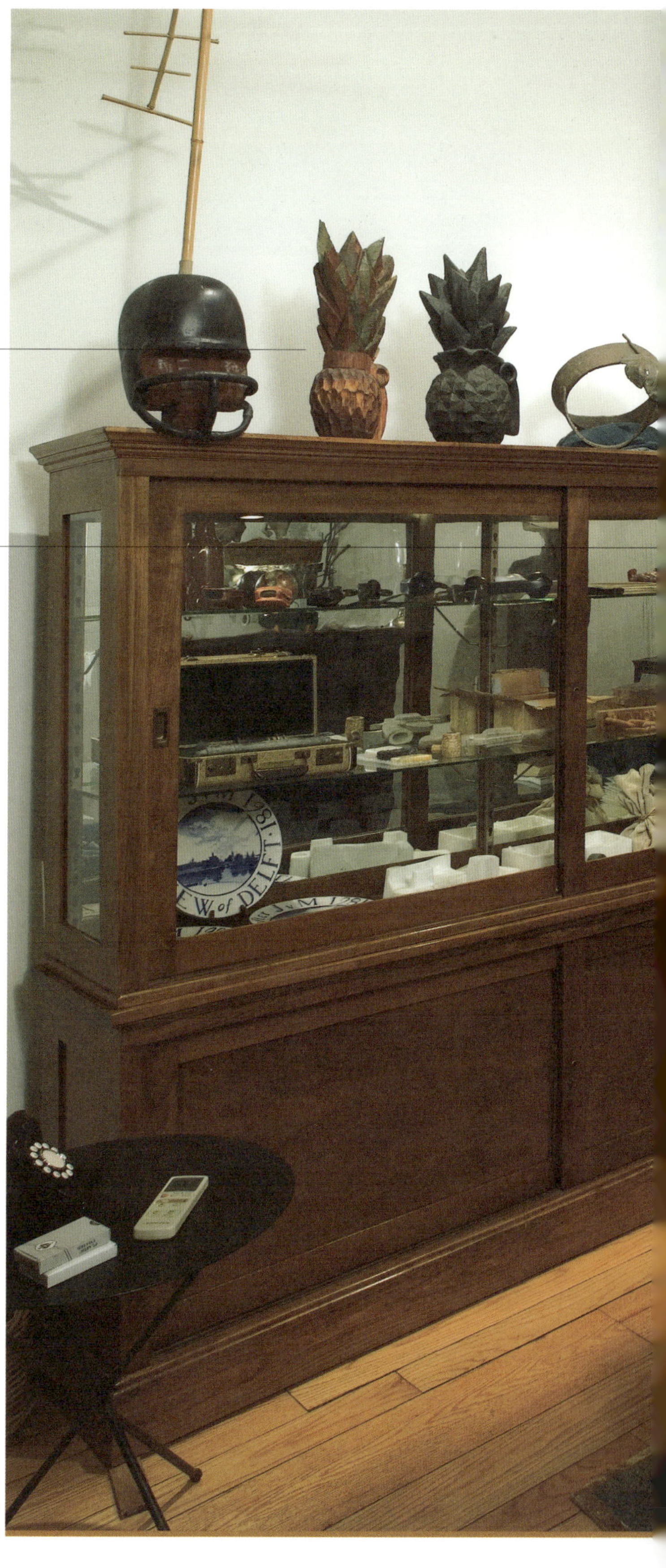

Pineapple Bomb
1990
Mulberry, hand-painted with oil (left), soapstone (right)
8 × 17 inches

The pineapple was a symbol of welcome in early America, and also a G.I.'s term for a hand grenade.

Flag
1967
String with vegetable dye
36 × 24 inches

I was just thinking about doing Warhol and Johns one better (and maybe Claes Oldenburg), and it was a Pop-Art thought. Johns's flag had only 48 stars, so mine does, too. I was trained in the abstract world, so I thought *Flag* was a way of dealing with the subject matter.

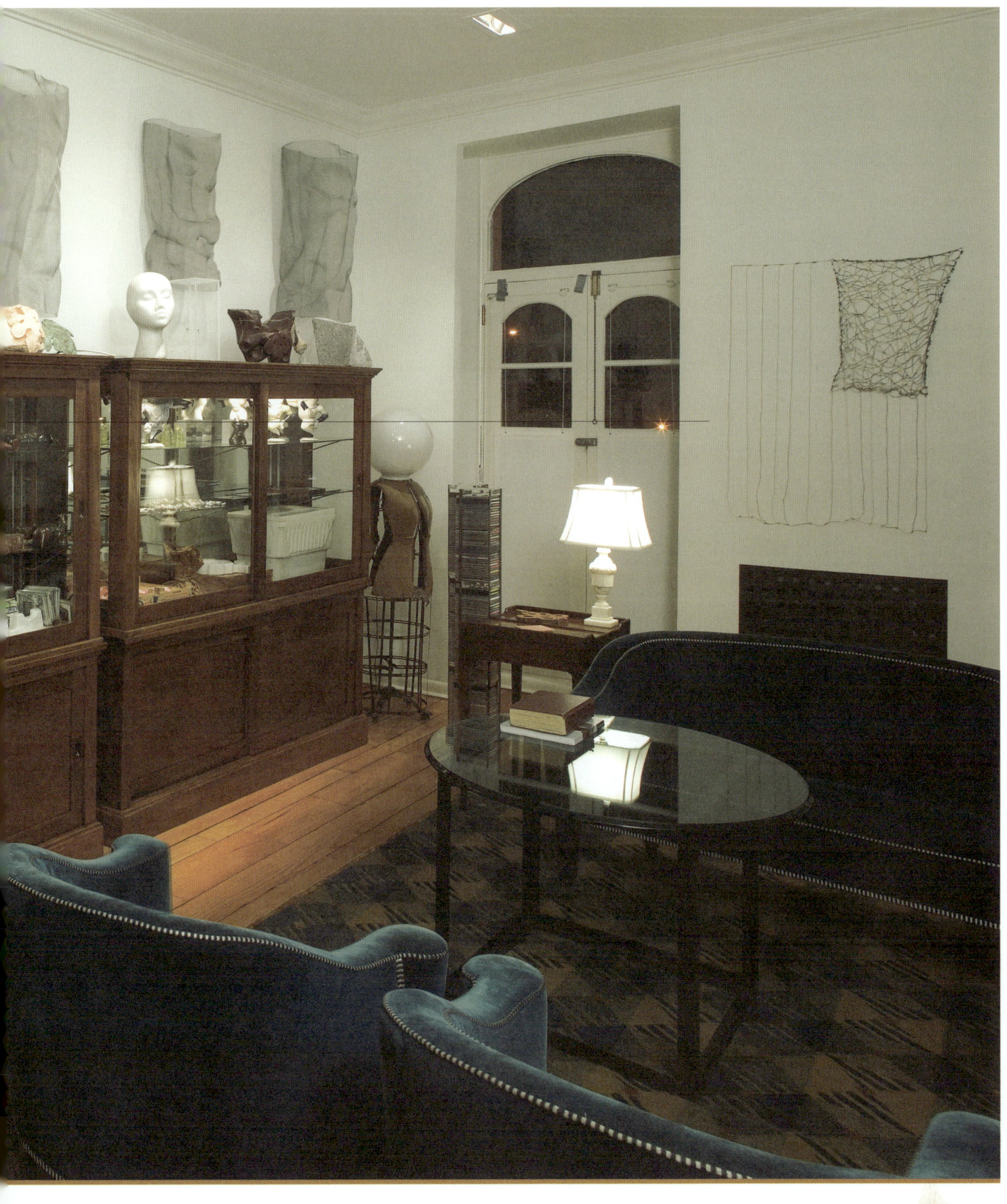

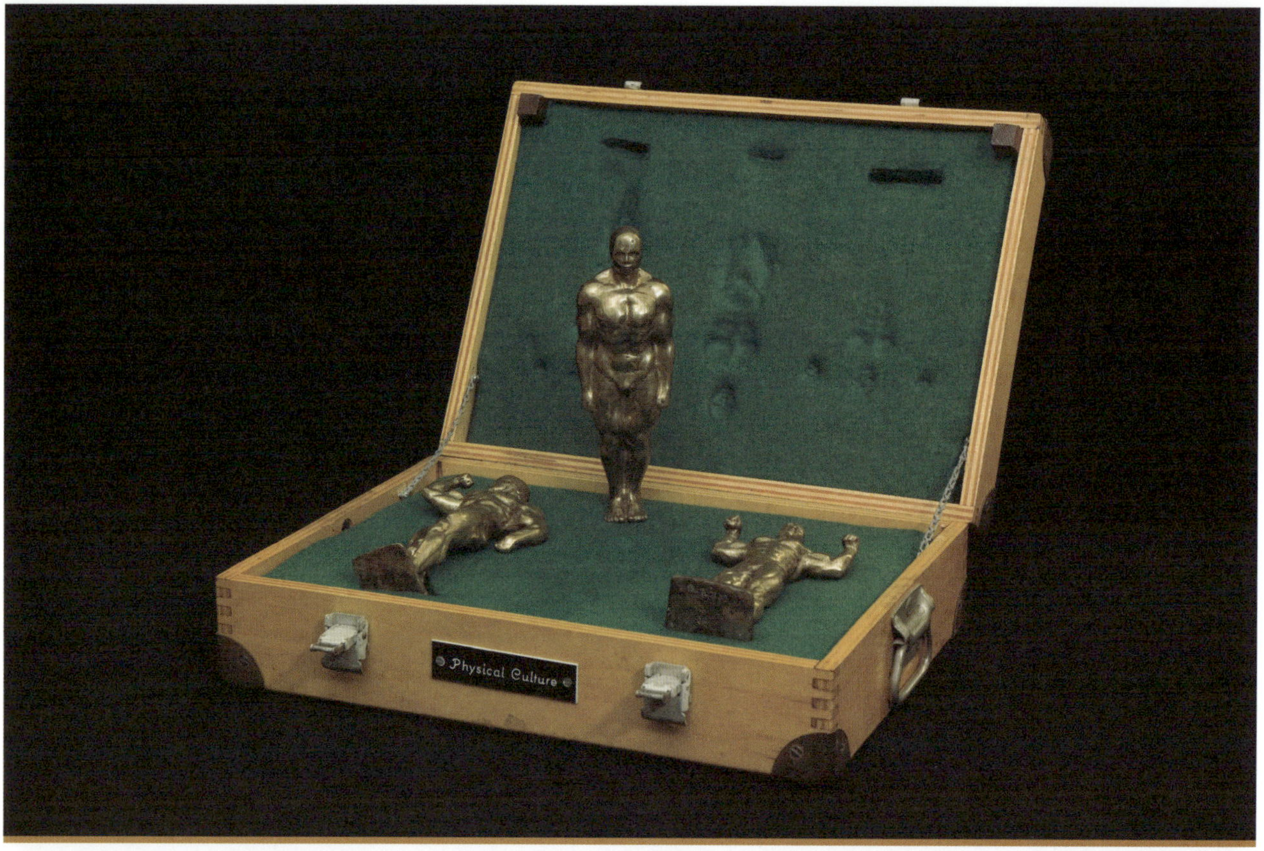

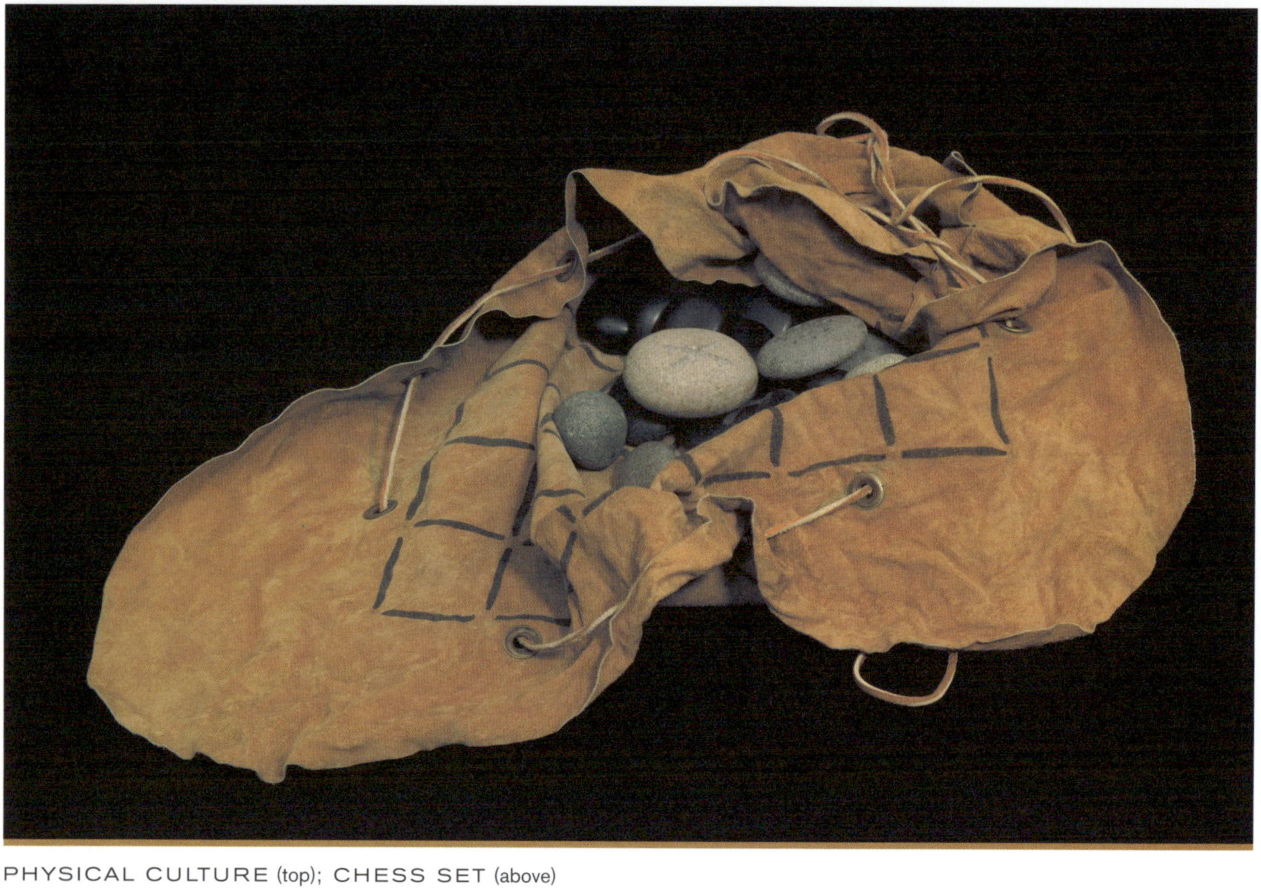

PHYSICAL CULTURE (top); CHESS SET (above)

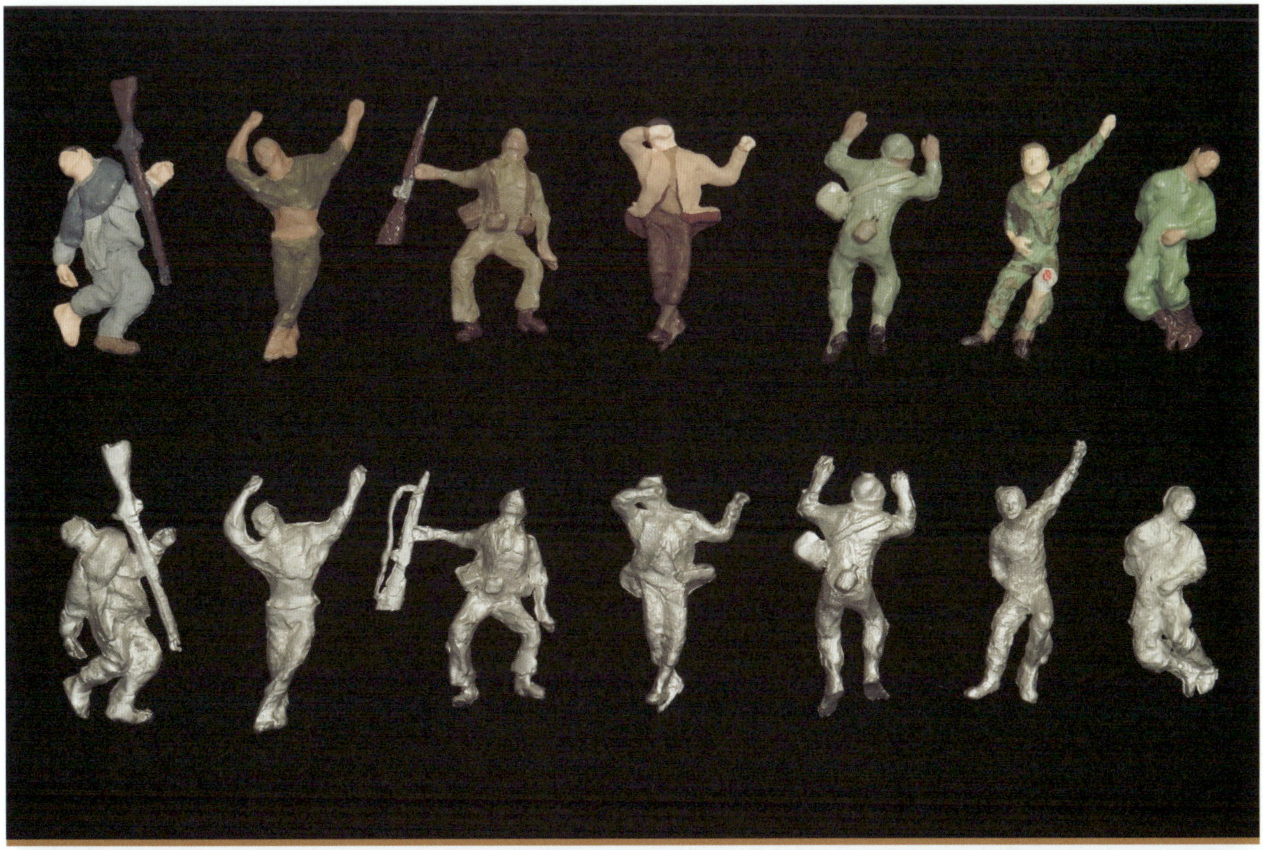

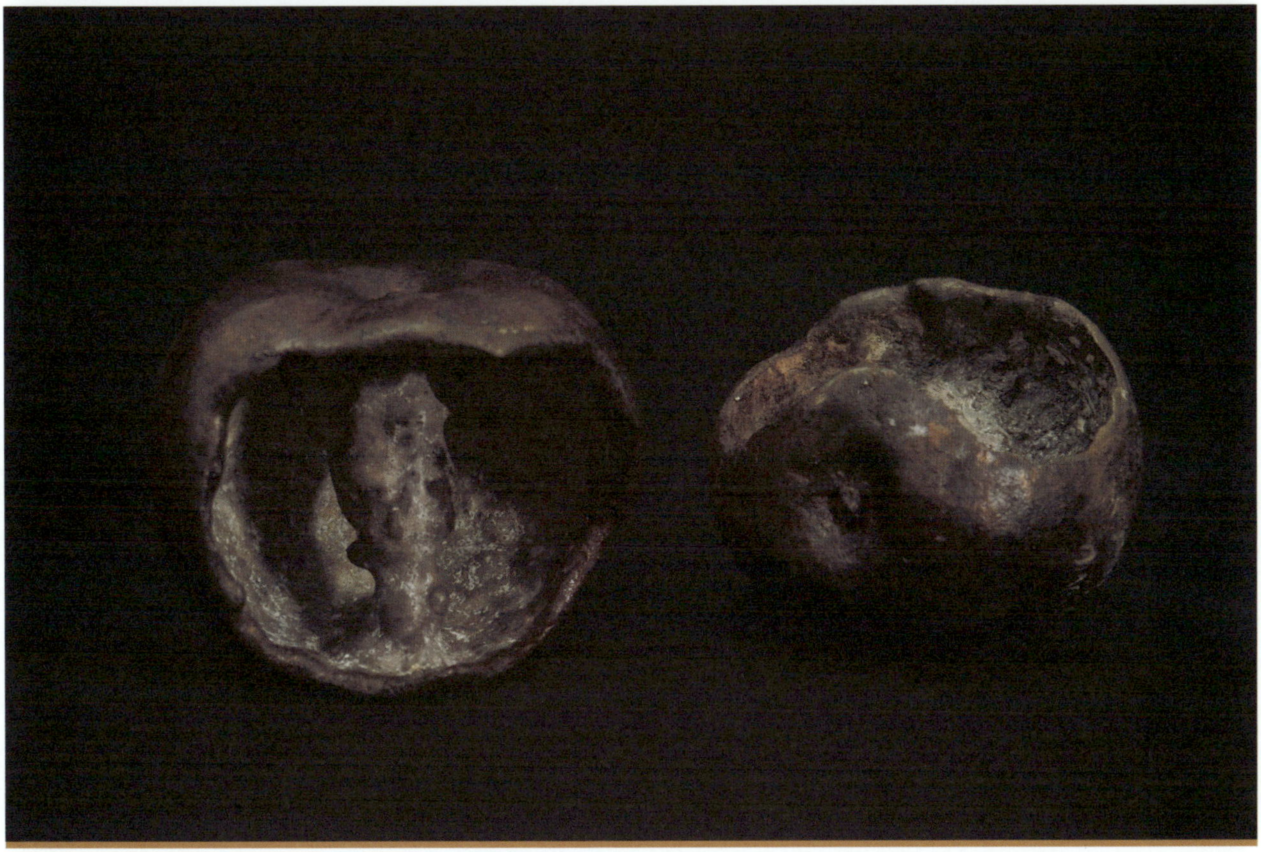

DEAD LEAD SOLDIERS (top); APPLE CORES (above)

Physical Culture
1976
Found wooden ammunition box with green-felt fitted lining; three bronze casts
12.25 × 16.75 × 5 inches

These statues were meant to be like trophies. One is the light-weight champion Ed Gorney, and the heavyweight is Arnold Schwarzenegger; the other is the Oscar.

I remember buying a muscle magazine, which I couldn't stand to look at. Of course, here in New York City, everybody looks in the mirrors at every subway stop. Because I was from the Bible Belt, I didn't dare look at myself in the mirror. So, for that reason, the Schwarzenegger was a hard one.

Chess Set
1960
Hand-painted black grid on irregular chamois skin with brass eyelets and leather drawstring; chess pieces made from found stones including basalt from Brimstone Island and granite from Vinalhaven Island; all stones have sandblasted engravings
17 × 17 inches

The chess set was one of the first things I made, and several copies of it were actually sold by Multiples Gallery for a hundred dollars the first time I lived in New York. And Marcel Duchamp bought one of the sets, so I thought I'd made it then. But, of course, nothing happened. I just missed meeting him, but I saw him on the street: a grumpy guy with a cigar in the corner of his mouth.

Apple Cores
1981–87
Wax cast in bronze
3 inches tall

I would walk home from the Maryland Institute for lunch, and buy an apple from Safeway, and I would take a bite out of it and I would say, "Geez, that's terrible." And, of course, it was Golden Delicious from Washington State, so I just threw it aside. And when I came back, I would see that the ravens or somebody who was hungry had gotten to it and eaten everything out of it except for the core. So I picked up the cores and took them home where I was casting wax, and I just dipped them in wax and then did a burn-out, and then cast them in bronze.

We had a saying in the Midwest when I was a kid: "Apple core, Baltimore, who's your friend?" Then you'd throw your apple core at your friend and try to hit him.

Dead Lead Soldiers
1986
Zinc and lead
3.5 inches tall
Eight figures constitute a set

They comprise: Christian Poveda, Robert Capa, Timothy O'Sullivan, Dimitri Baltermants, Larry Burrows, Matthew Brady, George Strock, and anonymous.

They are lead soldiers, like Churchill used to play with when he was a kid. One set is painted because I assumed that the paint would keep kids from licking their fingers after they'd played with them, so that they wouldn't get lead poisoning. They were all based on photographs of dead soldiers from different eras. In most cases, I tried to research the uniforms as thoroughly as I could.

Father
1985
Carved from a single Osage orange tree
17 inches diameter × 70 in. tall

My father had a good eye, was very honest, and never told a story that he hadn't lived. He also never told a joke, but he was a great storyteller. He was like this statue: he always had his jacket and his coat on, and he always had his hand out to shake hands. I hardly wore a hat until I got old enough to imitate him, and bald enough, and then I realized that it was necessary to wear a hat to keep warm and to keep the rain off.

In his left hand could be anything. It could be his briefcase, or it could be an umbrella—anything. It was just a hole that I bored through there. A hat was a signal for what you did. Nobody wears a hat now, and you can't tell where they're coming from. I sometimes consider myself a traveling salesman....

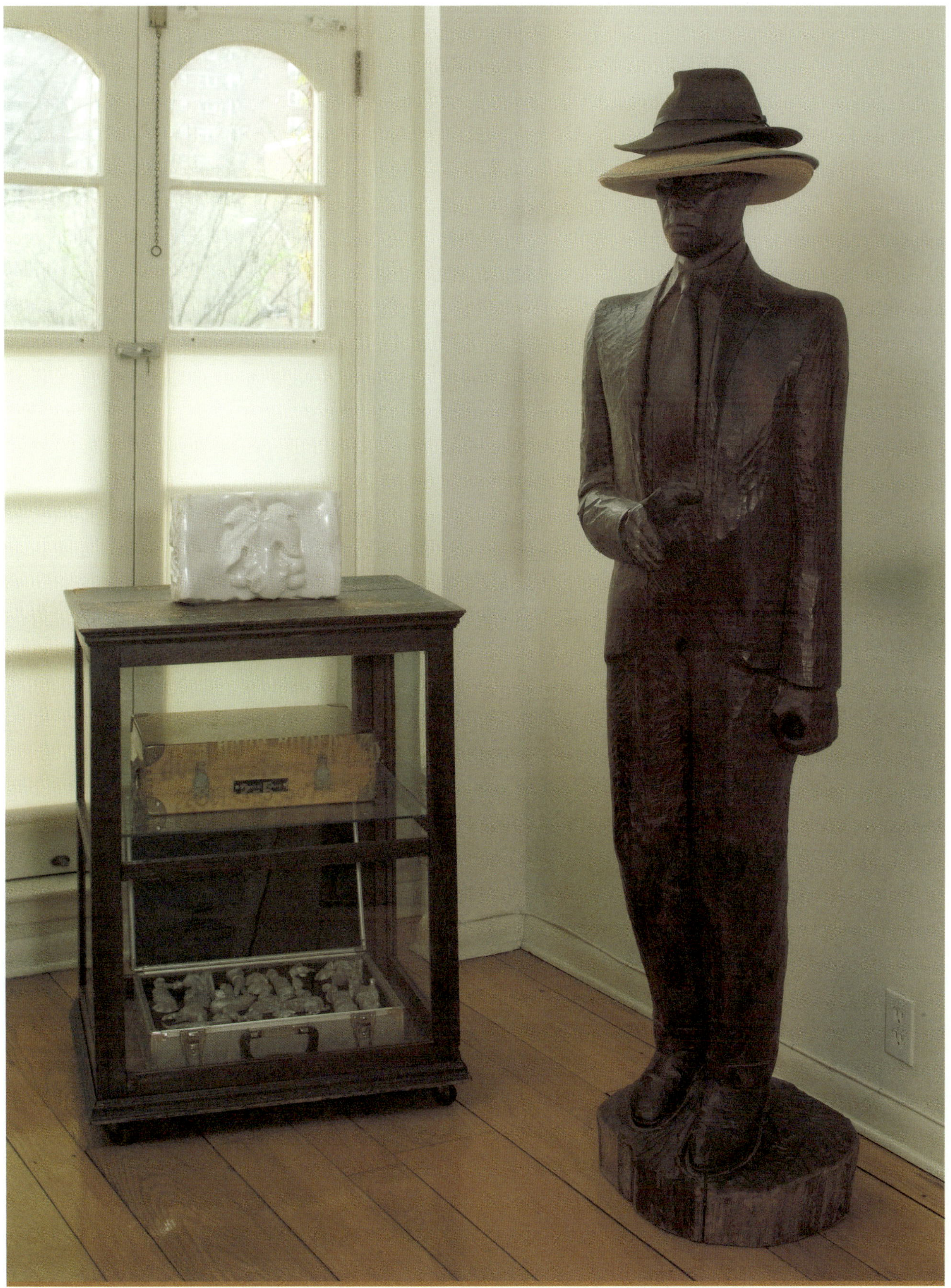

FATHER

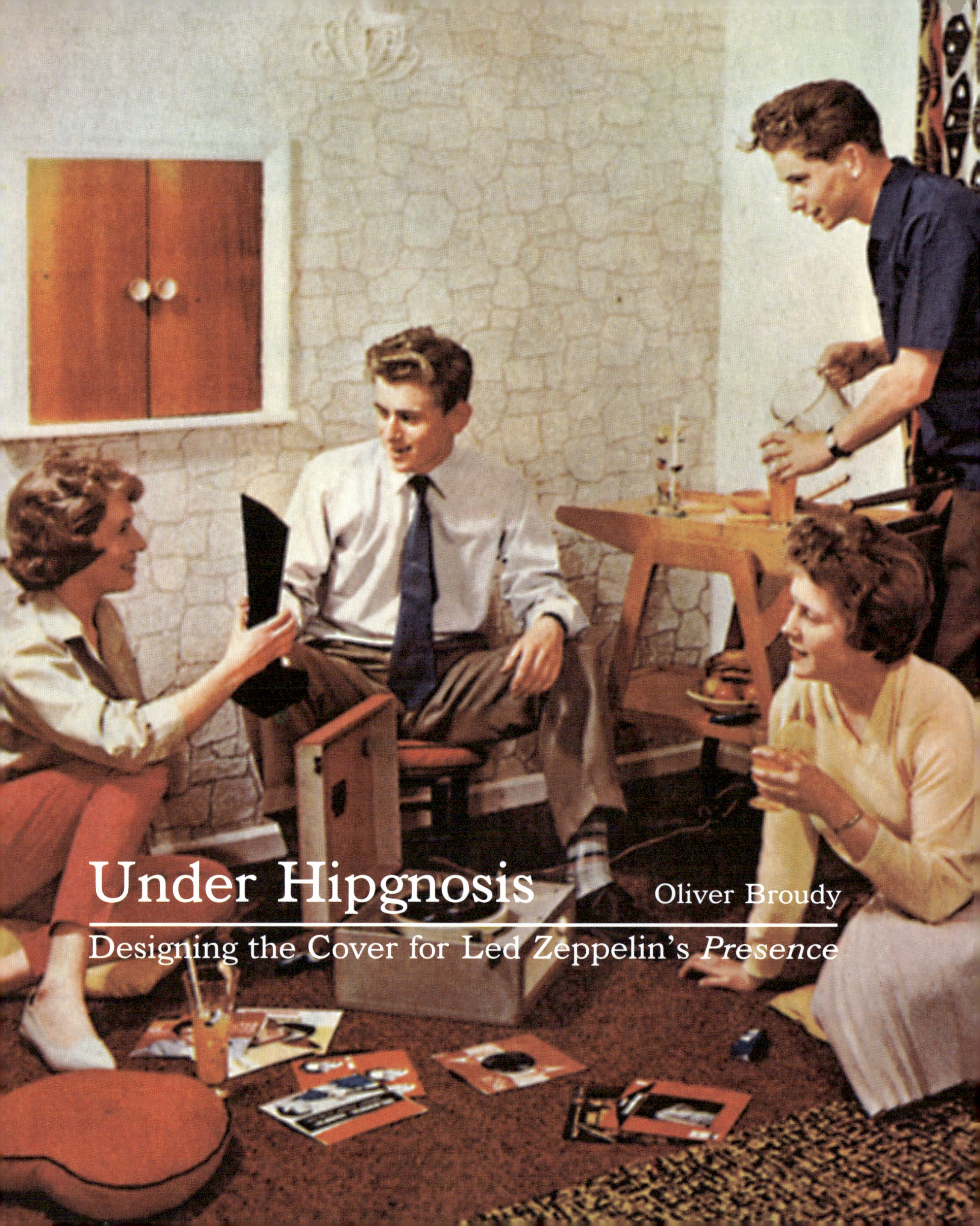

Under Hipgnosis

Oliver Broudy

Designing the Cover for Led Zeppelin's *Presence*

"It's true what they say—all album cover designers really want to be pop stars."
—Aubrey Powell

"Who the hell needs to understand everything anyway?"
—Robert Plant

In 1976, the English music magazine *Sounds* held a competition to see who could come up with the most convincing explanation for the mysterious object on the cover of the new Led Zeppelin album, *Presence*. The cover depicts a stereotypical nuclear family—dorky dad, glammy mom, two grabby kids—seated around a small table with a white tablecloth. The object sits in the middle of the table, like some hideously weird and blackened saltshaker. It appears slightly smaller than a box of aluminum foil stood on end, except for a tilted top and a pinched indentation at the waist—or else these are merely visual distortions resulting from a slight helical twist. The true proportions are difficult to discern because the matte black surface of the object hides its lines.

The context seems to offer clues: the boatyard behind them; the fact that—except for the little boy—they all have their hands on the table, ready to make a move, as if the object were some sort of game involving reflexes; but perhaps most importantly the expressions. The children are facing away but the parents' expressions are fully visible, and one imagines that it was their ambiguous smiles that the readers of *Sounds* were interpreting as much as the shape of the object itself. The object is less a part of the image than a hole in it; it casts no shadow, it has no texture, and perhaps even no depth. Upright on its small pedestal, it floats on the image, held in place mainly by the family's single-minded attention.

Sounds received thousands of submissions. The object, said one reader, was "a window which we can either look at or through thus creating a totally illusory image floating in a material world. Its implacable depths are the fast-flowing rivers of the tunnel of life at the end of which the searchers' souls will be joined as one." Another entry identified the object as "a Telepathic Wave Receiver and Transmitter (TWRT). In the year 2108, the specific static factor of telepathic linkage was finally defined. It was electronically synthesized, made infinitely turnable and incorporated in the TWRT. Some TWRTs were projected into the mid-twentieth century as an experiment in four-dimensional communication." Another reader suggested, more modestly: "Its precise function is still obscure, but scientists have noted that it induces trance-like automatism in its faithful adherents."

The cover was the product of a London-based design group called Hipgnosis. Hipgnosis was founded in 1968 by Storm Thorgerson and Aubrey Powell, and in the years that followed they designed covers for everyone from Peter Gabriel to Black Sabbath. In 1976, at the time of the release of *Presence*, Hipgnosis was at its peak, in high demand by successful bands, and—in this pre–music-video era—enjoying a proven track record of ingenious answers to the question *What does music look like?*

Illustrated covers had been around since 1939, when a young advertising director at Columbia Records, Alex Steinweiss, recognized the then untenanted twelve inch's potential as a miniature billboard. Steinweiss was pretty much on the same page as his counterparts in parallel industries, which were undergoing a minor revolution thanks to advances in color-printing technology.

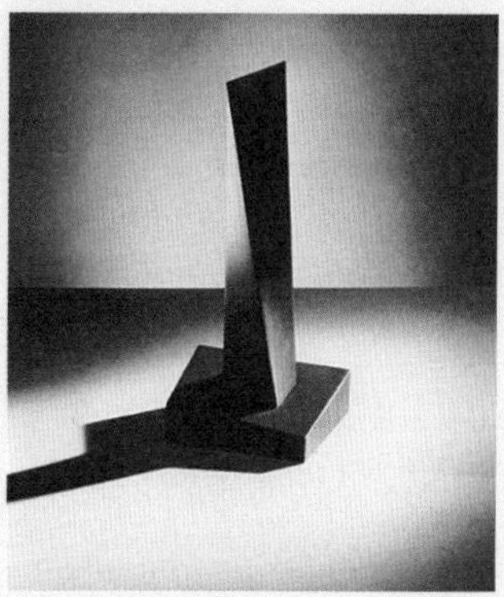

Soon everyone was concealing products in packaging that showed pictures of the products, which practically doubled the pleasure of consuming them. You could now own the advertisement for the product as well as the product itself. Of course the music could not be pictured, per se, but the band was illustratable—either in the stylized lines of artists such as Jim Flora, or, more commonly, with a photograph of the band grinning, mugging, or blowing on horns.

The relatively short history of album covers (short compared to, say, painting) is largely a history of the form's vacillation between competing impulses, the commercial and the artistic: born of one, it was 30 years before changing circumstances in popular culture and in the music industry itself would give rise to the other, a countermove to that made by Steinweiss in 1939. In 1967 the Beatles released *Sgt. Pepper's Lonely Hearts Club Band.* Peter Blake designed the cover. Blake's cover, which pictured the band gabardined in spiffy satin amidst a psychedelic collage of celebrity heads, broke all the rules—or almost all; the band was still on the cover, but the literalism was gone—the sense of the cover as an attempt to convey a literal picture of what was inside. As highly successful bands like the Beatles gained leverage with record companies and were increasingly able to choose their own designers, the designers, like cats in a new room, began to explore more fully the artistic possibilities unique to the album cover, thus marking its emergence as a form unto itself.

As a form, the album cover was ideally sized for the individual listener, who could study the cover as the music played. The covers helped to personalize the musical experience at a time when music was becoming more personal, and the personal was becoming more powerful. A new era was dawning, for various sociological and pharmacological reasons. It was the summer of 1967—the summer of love, and so on and so forth. "Everybody was wearing flowery shirts and velvet trousers and pink high-heeled boots and earrings and chains and everybody had very long hair and we were all very hip and groovy," says Powell.

Hipgnosis's entrée to the scene came with the cover for Pink Floyd's first album, *Saucer Full of Secrets,* one year after the release of *Sgt. Pepper's.* Thorgerson and Powell were in their early twenties, fresh out of art school, impoverished but hopeful. "He was a better designer," Powell says of Thorgerson, "and I was a better photographer and businessman, so I primarily did the photography and business side of it and he primarily came up with ideas." Peter Christopherson joined them later as a full partner in 1974, and throughout this time they relied frequently on freelancers—like Richard Manning, who handled their airbrush needs, and the illustrator George Hardie, who brought a mechanical expertise for lines, lettering, and logos.

It is difficult to assess Hipgnosis's influence today since the medium in which they worked basically ceased to exist sometime in the early '80s, but in the years when they were active, from 1968 to 1981, they broke boundaries in album cover design, experimenting with a range of techniques—from collage to airbrush to photographic manipulation—to exert a new sort of control over the image. They were not designers so much as image-makers. "Fundamentally what we do is to dream up pictures that we have to go out and shoot," Thorgerson wrote in 1978 in his book about Hipgnosis, *Walk Away René.* They drew heavily on the surrealists—especially Man Ray, Marcel Duchamp, and Magritte

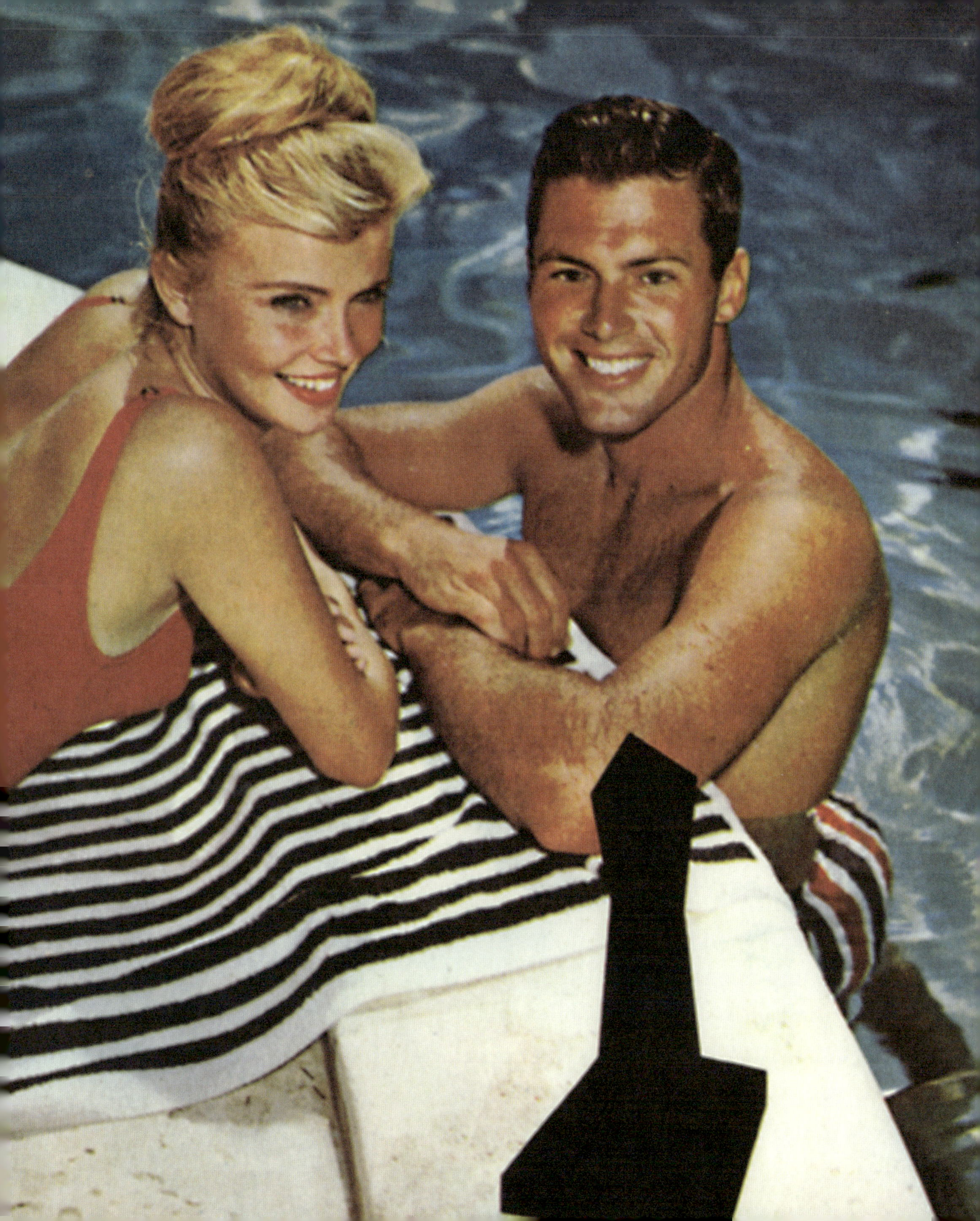

(the René of Thorgerson's title)—whose work integrated image and concept with a conciseness that perfectly suited the album cover's limited real estate. Surrealism provided a precedent for how to make images that were highly economical and at the same time visionary: the two men shaking hands on the cover of Floyd's *Wish You Were Here,* for instance, one of whom is on fire; or the trail of red balls stretching away into the distance of a Dali desert on the cover of *Elegy* by The Nice. Although they were not, like Steinweiss's covers, the product of commercial thinking, the Hipgnosis covers nevertheless proved highly successful. It was as if, as the French writer Lucien Lucelle observed a few decades before, surrealist imagery provided the shock necessary to "give birth to the acquisitive desire."

Like the pop songs they contained, the covers were brief, shiny, and—their creators hoped—catchy as well. Both Thorgerson and Powell studied film in art school, and—as with Cindy Sherman 10 years later—the film influence brought a narrative sense to their work, one which found expression in photographic vignettes that behaved a lot like pop hooks. On one cover, a man with frightened eyes peeks through Venetian blinds (*What is he afraid of?*). On another, a man looks up at what appears to be a UFO while a woman stands in the foreground holding a camera (*Is that a real UFO, or did the man just toss a Frisbee?*).

The *Presence* cover exemplified the Hipgnosis approach, incorporating elements of surrealism and narrative photography while at the same time speaking directly to what made the client unique. It was 1976, and Zeppelin was still huge. A year earlier, during their last American tour, they sold out 120,000 tickets for six shows in New York in 36 hours. In Long Island, fans overran a Ticketron outlet and had to be dispersed with fire hoses. Three years earlier, an audience of 56,800 at a Zeppelin concert in Tampa, Florida, broke an attendance record previously held by the Beatles for their legendary concert at Shea Stadium in 1965. In the spring of 1975 Zeppelin became the first band in history to have six albums on the Billboard charts at the same time, with *Physical Graffiti* at number one. In April 1976, Charles Shaar Murray, reviewing *Presence* for *New Musical Express,* wrote, "Zeppelin are rock and roll's greatest ground-to-ground tactical nuclear missile.... If the Russkies start any hoohah, we'll just beam this mutha at Moscow...."

There was an ambition to Zeppelin's music that exceeded all that had gone before. They didn't just adapt the blues, they untethered it from literal storylines—bad women, bad weather, bad booze—and took it into outer space. In the absence of these grounding narratives there no longer existed an easy explanation for the music's gripping power. What did it mean? To the average Zeppelin fan sitting by the stereo, lost in the depths of the music like a sonar operator in a submarine with headphones pressed tight, it might mean anything. Perhaps the answer lay in Robert Plant's

---

George Hardie on searching picture archives for *Presence* imagery:

I went to lots of picture libraries and I did the initial dummy for the front cover: a family sitting eating crab at Fisherman's Wharf in San Francisco. We literally painted out the tablecloth and put the black object in the middle. And then when the idea was accepted we got in touch with *National Geographic* and they wouldn't let us use the photograph. So the boat show had a fake village in the middle of London, a show that sells yachts, and so the background was shot there, and Po styled the photograph and got all those models in to try and look as though it was from some kind of non-specific period.

The back cover was shot at my wife's school, Westminster City School in London, in a real classroom. (Again styled by Po.) And the little girl in the foreground is one of the naked figures on the *Houses of the Holy* cover, from years before. And the sum on the blackboard gives you Hipgnosis's number, or something like that. This is all nonsense. And I think it was my idea to have a kid's drawing of the black object on the cover, hanging up in the classroom.

And then I went to hundreds of picture libraries—which was really good fun because in those days there were hundreds of dusty boxes of big transparencies—and with a kind of mental list of things like "young love" and "science" and "family" and "entertainment" and so on I chose the pictures for the inside sleeve, which are genuinely old pictures, with no real change—except, you know, bits being retouched to put the black object in.

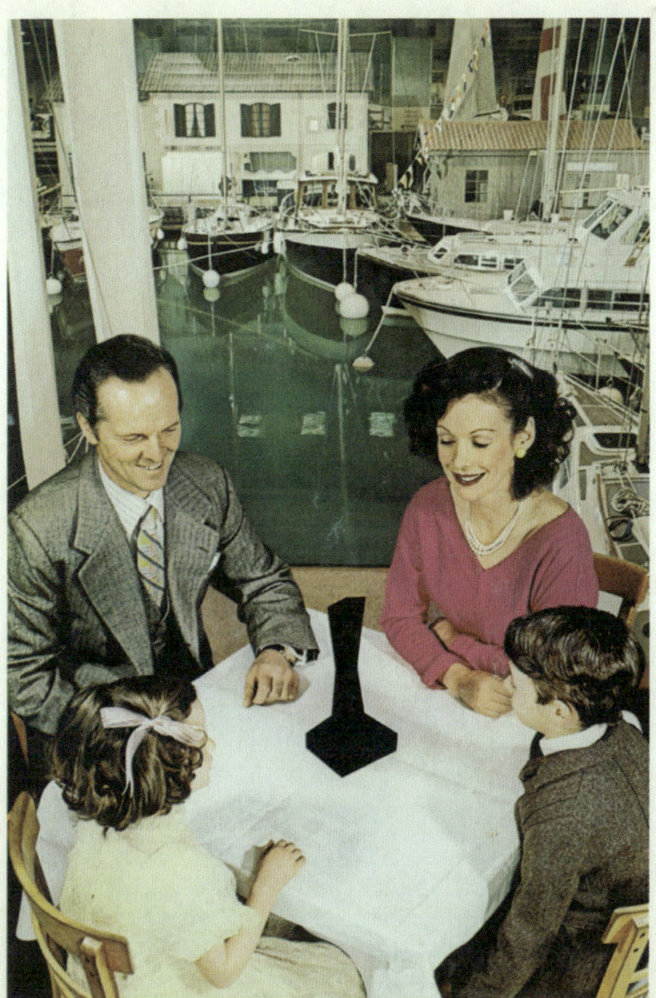
LED ZEPPELIN
PRESENCE

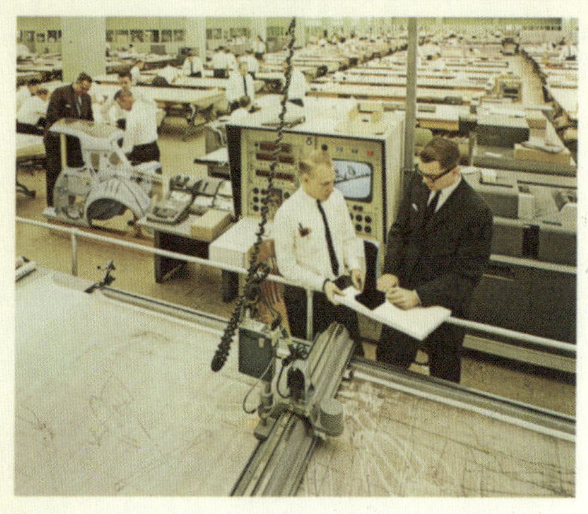
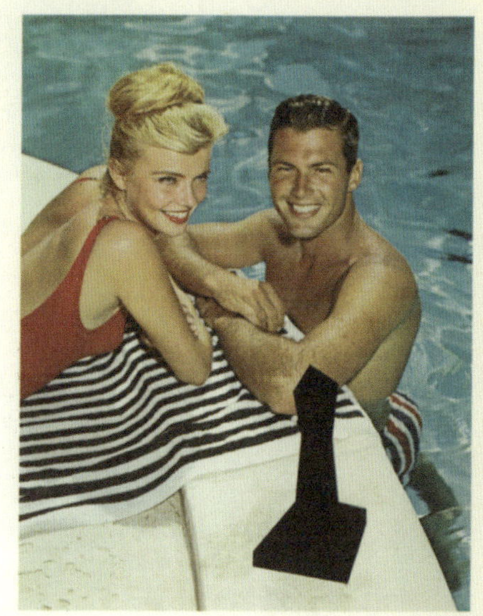
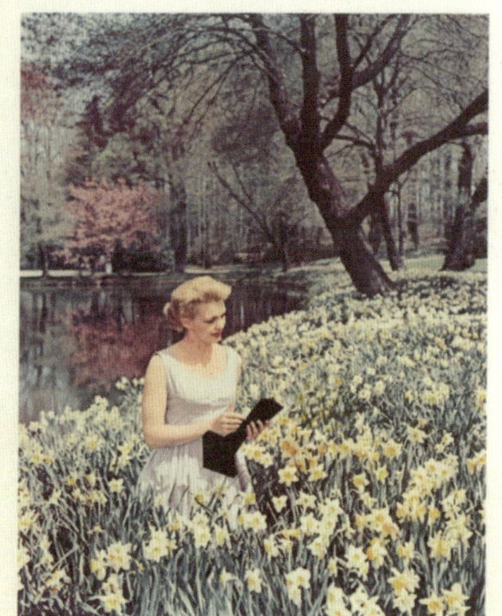
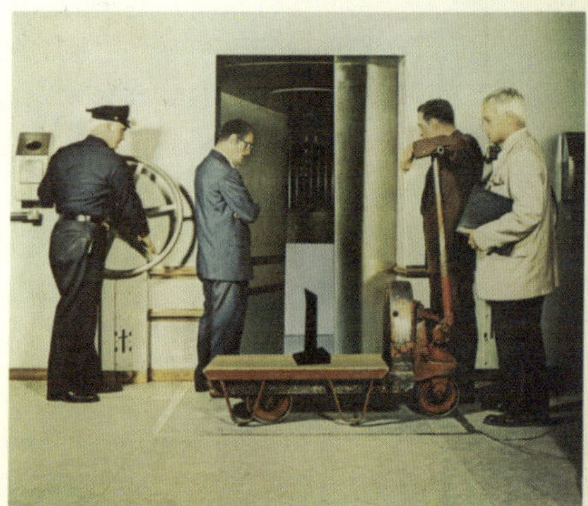

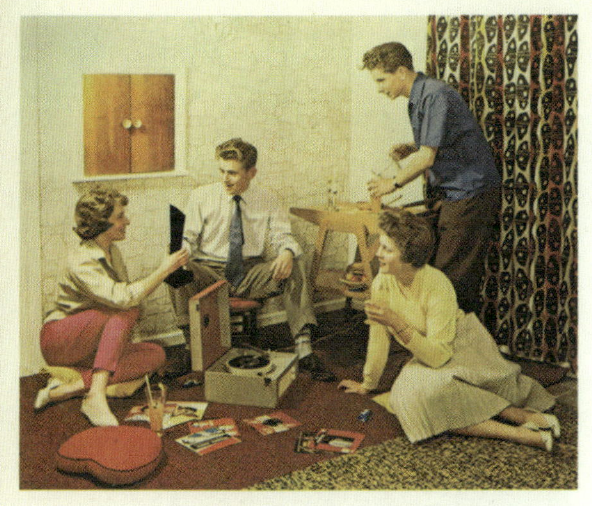
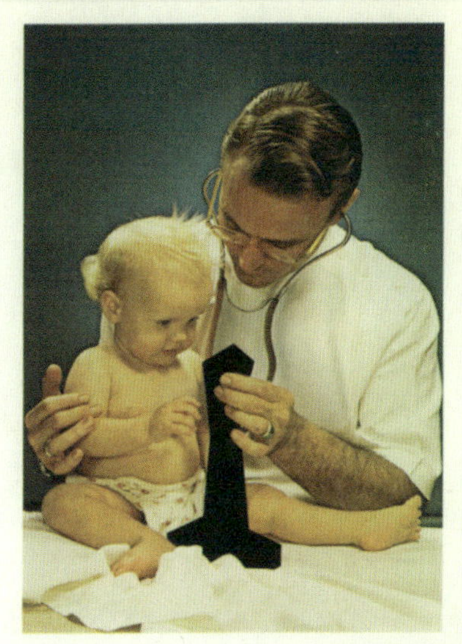
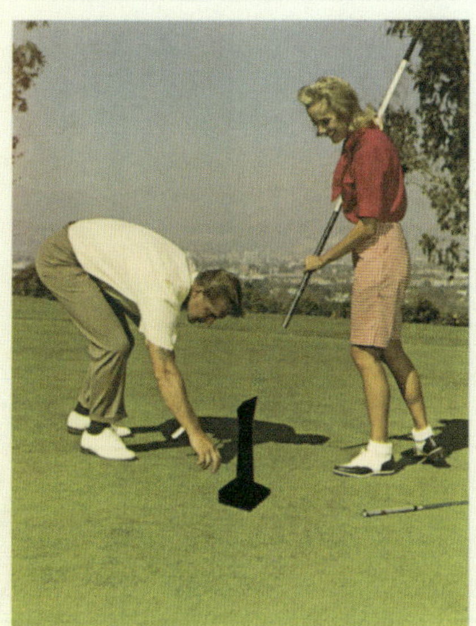
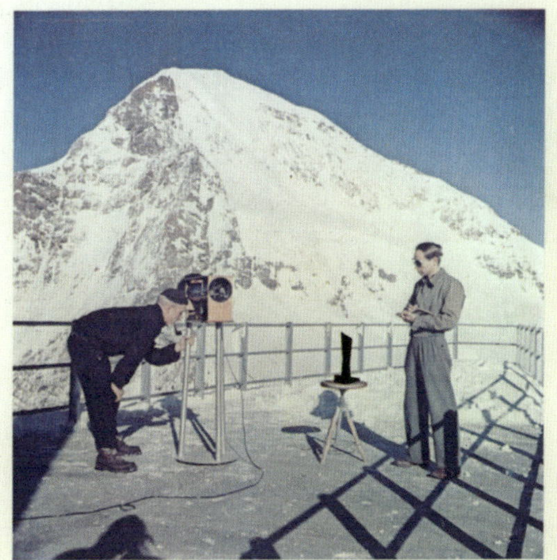

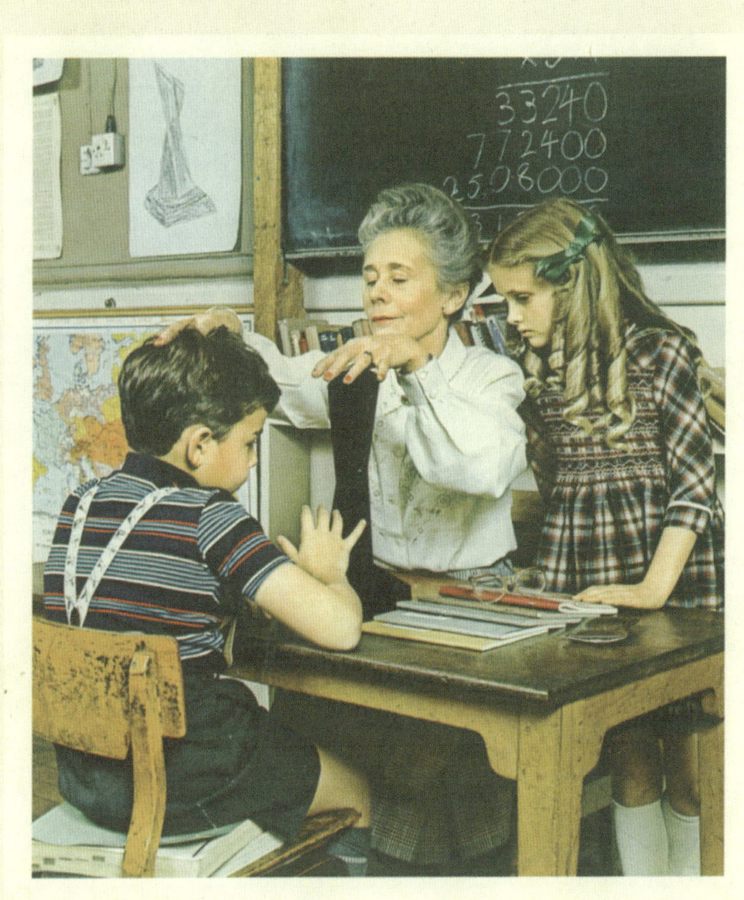
33240
772400
2508000

Celtic mysticism, or in the black magic of Aleister Crowley, with whom Jimmy Page was known to have an unhealthy preoccupation. Or perhaps there was no explanation, and the appeal of the music is that it allowed fans to provide their own.

Or else the mystery was of a more musical nature. Like no other band before them, Zeppelin managed to tap the energy latent within the four-man structure on which so much rock and roll was based. Each instrument spoke with such a uniquely emphatic voice, pulling out so strongly against all the others—Bonham's pummeling drums, the wiry metal ride of Page's guitar, Plant's witchy vocals, Jones's steady bass—that the music crested along on a wave of sheer amazement that, despite all of these disparate forces, the band somehow managed not to explode. That it actually might was part of what made the music so exciting, particularly to Zeppelin's fan base, which consisted overwhelmingly of havoc-hungry teenagers.

Ever since *Sgt. Pepper's,* fans had been accustomed to reading into covers for secret meanings. The strategy of the *Presence* cover was to answer the mystery of Zeppelin's powerful allure by suggesting another mystery in its place. What was the object? Was it, in fact, a Telepathic Wave Receiver and Transmitter? Or else some sinister, hypnagogic totem designed to bring about the downfall of Christian civilization? In a sense, the pursuit of one mystery is the pursuit of the other. For Zeppelin, the mystery was not the question but the whole point. Mystery was their style, just as straightforwardness had been the style of traditional blues. Thorgerson explains in Walk Away René:

> We'd been interested in holes, or frame breaks—any device that might temporarily throw a picture "out" or suspend disbelief for a moment and cause a picture to appear fractionally as though it were indeed three dimensional, that it stretched away from the viewer. It was felt appropriate that the disturbing presence in the anachronistic picture should be a "hole," a blackness, a nondimensional thing (no depth cues), although it could have a shape—a hole can have a shape. Then someone suggested that the obsessional object that everyone needs is not just a self-obsession but, in fact, inflicts itself upon people from outside. It is a power source which people cannot do without. It is true that objects of obsession are also things that people cannot do without, but the change of emphasis was to consider the object as deliberately sent from another time or insidiously employed by some secret society to subjugate people.

As evocative of Zeppelin as this is, one wonders how much the Hipgnosis designers were actually thinking about the band when they first came up with the idea. "Sometimes the music isn't made when you made the cover," George Hardie says. He continues:

> I did an analysis of this book, *The 100 Best Album Covers.* The book says a lot about how designers worked with the bands, but I did an analysis and there are very, very few covers that are straight responses to the music. Quite often the cover is a response to one song on the album, which then got dropped, or even to the title of the song, rather than the music. So if you read through that book there are two or three percent where people said, 'I've sat down and listened to the music and that gave me the idea.' It's a kind of strangely parallel thing, but the results sometimes are ridiculously appropriate.

Hardie also seems to recall that the *Presence* cover was initially designed for a band called 10CC, who passed on it. It was common to keep designs around after they had been rejected, and then re-pitch them to other bands as the opportunity arose. There were some images that got pitched over and over again but were never used, like the three bloody ducks stapled to the wall above a mantelpiece—much loved by the designers, but perhaps a little too gross for anyone else. This ability to recycle images was new, a result of the switch

---

Storm Thorgerson on placing the object everywhere

The object was essential to all parts of society, whether it be lovers by a pool or workers in a factory, whether it be leisure or serious scientific investigation. You see, they were still trying to discover what the object was, what it was made of, and where it came from. It was important, also, to introduce it to young infants to help them grow properly, and in education to teach them that, of all things in life, the "presence"— the nameless, unknown, and undefined black object—was of paramount significance.

---

from a literal to a non-literal design approach. In the past, for instance, an album-cover design for Elvis featuring a picture of Elvis could not exactly be re-pitched to the Four Tops.

As images became recyclable, a new sort of marketplace was born, a marketplace of imagery where bands and images could be mixed and matched. In the end, the covers were often related to the music only to the extent that the same people who made the music also signed off on the design. Powell describes the moment: "I was in my hotel room and had all the ideas around the room and the black object in the middle and [Jimmy Page] walked in and he said 'That's it.' Just like that. There wasn't any question about any of the others, there wasn't any question of any thought that something else might be appropriate. He just looked at the black object and said, 'That's it.'" Why? Who knows? To understand that you'd have to know what goes on inside Jimmy Page's mind. And if you knew that, then you'd know why Zeppelin was so powerful in the first place. At this point, though, one might understandably begin to tire of all the hocus pocus, and develop a craving for the refreshing bluntness of punk rock. Consider Sex Pistols manager Malcolm McClaren's explanation for the first Pistols cover, *Never Mind the Bullocks*: "The colors were meant to make it look like a packet of washing powder—no better, no worse, just disposable rubbish." In the same spirit, it is tempting to simply accept, as someone had put it, that the mysterious object on the *Presence* cover was Aleister Crowley's dildo, and leave it at that.

Powell's explanation is not quite so terse, but it is perhaps more believable than Thorgerson's, which sounds like it was cooked up after the fact:

> Twice a week we met until about four in the morning, and this one night we were talking about cats, about how people love cats, and like to stroke cats, and how cats are often used for therapy. So we were talking about how interesting it would be if everyone had a cat, because it would make them feel better. So imagine how fantastic it would be if you had a party and every single person was holding a black cat. And then we thought, *No, that's too silly for Led Zeppelin.* So we thought something black would be interesting, but what could it be? And then it was like, *Well, what are we trying to say, here: something that would charge you up, give you the same feeling as touching a cat, give you the same sense of well being.* Well, a battery. But you can't just have a battery, you know, in the middle of a room—everybody with a battery. So then we came round to an object, like the object in [Stanley Kubrick's] *2001,* we don't know what that was, but something that was, you know, mysterious, and yet somehow everybody needed it, and when they had it they felt good, and you always had one with you to sort of recharge your battery, or relate to, or send messages on, or whatever.

Given the customary reliance of any creative collaboration on accident, serendipity, and (frequently) pure nonsense, one might well ask whether the explanations of the designers should carry any more weight than those suggested by the readers of *Sounds*. George Hardie's entry is as follows:

> There was a phrase going around at that time which went "Nostalgia isn't what it used to be." So we started talking about nostalgia and remembering things, and there's a nice story that architects talk about which is the point at which the fireplace stopped being the center of the room and the television started being the center of the room. I don't know if you have a fireplace in your house, but it's a big problem if you have two centers to the room. Very difficult to arrange everything. But so when television was invented your family would be oriented around a television instead of a fireplace, and we were trying to invent something similar, something that was at once nostalgic but which no one knew quite where it came from. So we thought of inventing an object that wasn't a fireplace and wasn't a television, but which was really important to everyone. And that's where it came from, I think.

Hardie's version, setting aside its historical accuracy for the moment, raises interestingly trippy questions about nostalgia and the bearing one generation has on the next. The story can be told as an evolution of attention, shifting over time from one sort of object to another. In each case the object is different, but it always remains that which we gather around, define ourselves by, or even enslave ourselves to. Led Zeppelin supplanted the Beatles, and later, the Sex Pistols supplanted Led Zeppelin (which is putting it kindly), just as, the suggestion is, TV replaced the fireplace. Of course there was no way of knowing, in 1976, that the personal computer would someday supersede the TV, but one gathers that the *Presence* object was intended to symbolize whatever this ultimate replacement might be. "I have to say it's not a film I've ever seen right through," Hardie says, referring to *2001.*

Aubrey Powell on digital look in the pre-digital age

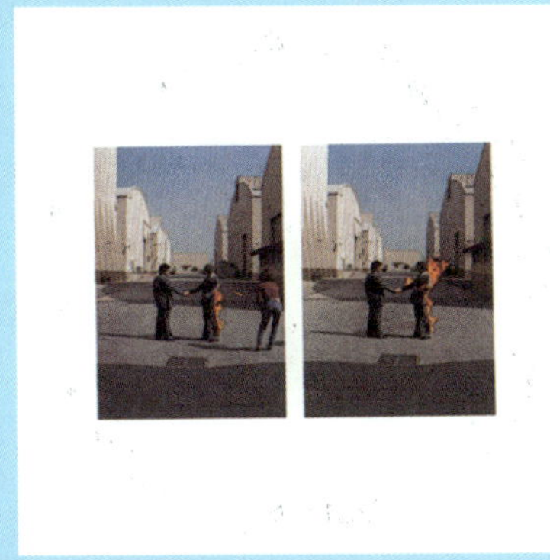

Pink Floyd
Wish You Were Here
(Hipgnosis)

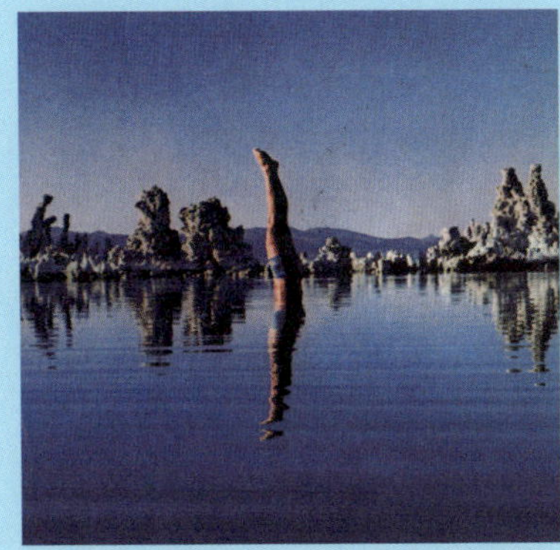

Pink Floyd
Wish You Were Here (back cover)
(Hipgnosis)

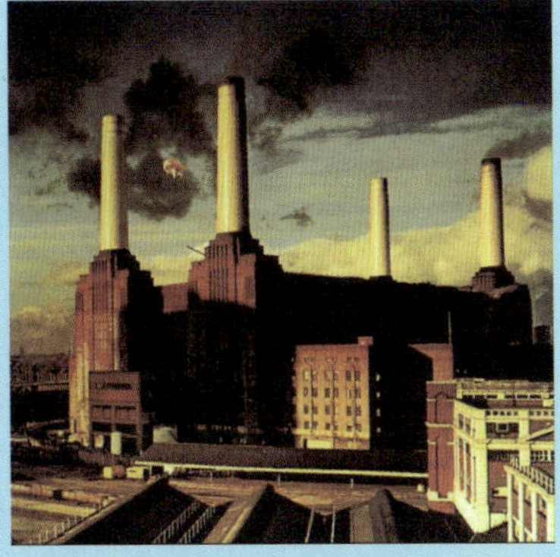

Pink Floyd
Animals
(Hipgnosis)

Basically, in those days, there were two ways of doing things: We either cut things out and stuck them together and then re-photographed them and then had them retouched so that you couldn't see the joins; or we used to shoot things for real. I mean, if you look at, let's say, *Wish You Were Here* by Pink Floyd, the man on fire in the front picture is really on fire. We got two stuntmen and we set fire to one of them. In Hollywood.

And the guy on the back of the cover who is diving into a still lake, Mono Lake in California—I had a special chair brought for a stuntman who could hold his breath for two and a half minutes. It was a kind of yoga chair and we sank it into the mud and then he did a handstand as slowly as he could so the ripples would be as little as possible and stood there for a minute and a half underwater, holding his breath. And we took the photograph.

I mean, these were not cheated pictures. But so many people said, "How did you do that!? You must have stripped that in!" But it wasn't so.

The one picture that we did cheat on was the pig over the power station on *Animals* by Pink Floyd. Because the pig flew away. It was a huge 40-foot by 60-foot pig floating over the power station, but the rope broke, and it sailed away. And we got the most fantastic shot of the power station and the clouds and wonderful light and everything, so we stripped it in. I've got it hanging on my wall downstairs.

George Hardie on illustrating an idea

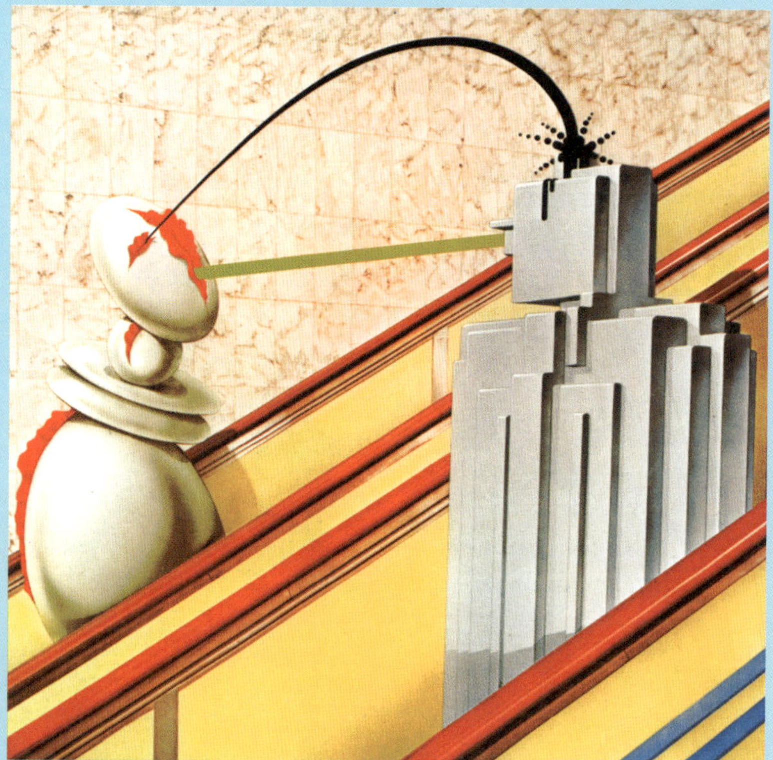

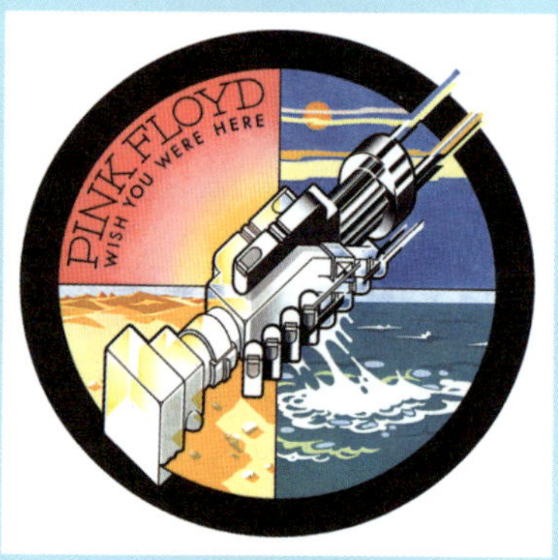

Pink Floyd
Wish You Were Here (sticker)
(Hardie/Hipgnosis)

Black Sabbath
Technical Ecstasy
(Hardie/Hipgnosis)

They wanted to call it *Technical Ecstasy* and Storm said, "That's about two robots falling in love." And then I went in and invented the two robots—I've still got the rough drawings somewhere—and then we looked at it and we decided that it would be a lot more poignant if they were falling in love in a situation where they couldn't get together, like up and down on an escalator. So I redrew all that.

And then I did really accurate drawings of the robots with pencil shading, and they were done by an airbrush artist, this guy Richard Manning, and the escalator is bits of photograph, bits of airbrushing. So it's a real good combination job, with lots of input from everyone.

"But it was in the air, this looming central issue. I don't see how we could have not noticed that. No one said, 'Let's do a cover with a mini-computer on it.' It didn't arrive from there, but that's maybe why it looked like it did."

If there is a problem with the *Presence* cover, it's the object itself—or, more exactly, the pedestal on which it stands. The object aspires to a kind of sinister ubiquity, a pan-dimensionality that is literally expressed by the photographs in the sleeve design, each of which depicts the object in a different context: in the arms of a young woman amidst a field of daffodils; standing on a trolley in the door of a bank vault; on the lip of a swimming pool beside a flirtatious young couple; between a doctor and an infant (replacing, in the original picture, a test tube); and so on. It is the object for all occasions, for all times and places. Like a rock star, it aspires to dominate any context in which it might appear—and yet at the same time remain independent of that context. The pedestal, however, constitutes a tacit concession to context, and has the effect of instantly according the object a specific scale and bearing—something about the size of a bowling trophy comes to mind, the sort of thing you might be awarded by your fellow band mates for having performed a particularly naughty deed, like seducing a 14-year-old (Page), or dicing a Tokyo hotel room with a samurai sword (Bonham). Certainly, there's something sinister about the object, but it's also kind of... well, cute. In its miniature attempt at massiveness it bears a closer resemblance to the midget Stonehenge prop in *Spinal Tap* than to the obelisk in *2001*; the obelisk in *2001* had no pedestal (presumably because there are no kitchen tables in outer space).

Hipgnosis continued to work with Zeppelin, contributing design elements for both *In Through the Out Door* and *Coda*. But their business was winding down. Pop stars weren't interested in Escher or Magritte or any of the usual hippie fixations anymore. Punk had arrived, and no one wanted to be associated with the guys who did the covers for Zeppelin and Floyd. In the words of Paul Simonon, the Clash bassist (the one smashing his instrument on the famous *London Calling* cover), "Led Zeppelin? I don't need to hear the music. All I have to do is look at one of their album covers and I feel like throwing up."

In 1976 Zeppelin was beginning to wind down as well. They were still strong, but they would not be as strong again. In March of that year, *Melody Maker* reported that Foghat had beaten Zeppelin's attendance record at the Pittsburgh Civic Center. In July, *New Musical Express* reported that Jimmy Carter liked to listen to Led Zeppelin. By the fall of 1980, John Bonham was dead, and the band split up. And a few years later, heralded by the famous commercial directed by Ridley Scott, a new kind of computer was released, faster than any that had come before, and ideal for personal use. As it turned out, it was not black like the *Presence* object, but beige.

Aubrey Powell on the evolution of attention: Exit Olivia Newton John, enter the Sex Pistols

I lived in the same building as Malcolm McClaren [the Sex Pistols manager] and the Sex Pistols. Hipgnosis's studio was right in front of a courtyard and in the courtyard were the Sex Pistols—we watched them rehearse every day. We were all very polite to each other. Oh yeah, really nice. "Hi, how ya doin', John," and so on. And then they started dressing more garishly—and this was before they had even released a single.

And then one day, I was photographing—I think it was—Olivia Newton John. Do you remember her? And I could hear all this spitting going on from out the back window in the courtyard, and I thought "Oh fucking hell, who's that? Man, this is really interrupting my session." And I went out there and leaning out the window were Syd and Johnny Rotten—well, John Lydon—gobbing into the courtyard below. And I said, "What the fuck are you doing!? Y'know I'm doing a photo session upstairs!" And they said, "We're fucking practicing our stage show, man." Y'know. And we were definitely by then the old men of rock and roll. And within six months the whole thing had changed and they moved out of there with Malcolm McClaren and were gone. But it was very interesting seeing the transition from four very polite boys who used to hold the door open for each other.

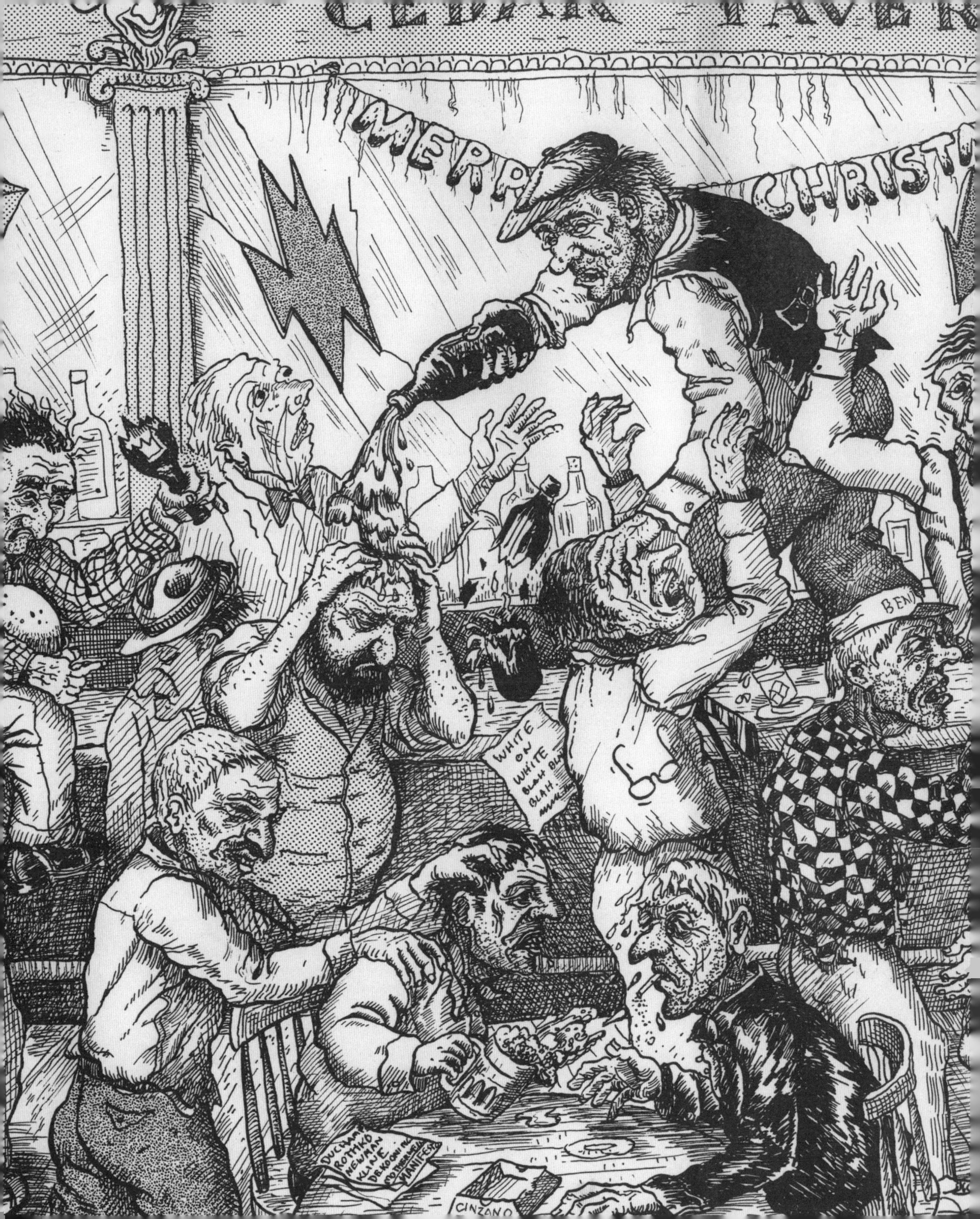
MERR
CHRIST
BEN
WHITE ON WHITE BLAH BLAH BLAH.
DUCHAMP
ROTHKO
NEWMAN
KLINE
DE KOONING
MANIFESTO
CINZANO

The Blasphemer of Flatbush; or, On Beer Cans, Stuffed Goats, and Blank Canvases: Fraud! Incest! Collusion! The Anti-Art Agitprop of Jonah Kinigstein

Owen Phillips

On the plywood surrounding a construction site across the street from Fanelli's in SoHo was a rain-ravaged poster titled *The 10th St. Intellectuals Hammering Out Their Manifestos.* In the scratchy drawing, drunken Abstract Expressionists sling chairs and beer mugs at each other in a Cedar Tavern brawl. A sign on the bar mirror reads "Heavy pondering to the back." Farther down Prince Street, among the concert posters, highbrow graffiti, and the odd lost-dog sign, was a poster depicting gallery owners Leo Castelli, Ivan Karp, and Mary Boone and art critic Clement Greenberg as the Horsemen of the Apocalypse. Boone, in a spear-tipped brassiere, holds up a Julian Schnabel painting, which spews its broken china shards over a crowd of scraggly, hardworking artists wielding obsolete brushes and palettes. The horses' blinders cover their eyes as they trample Old Master art books.

It was 1992. The construction site across the street would eventually become the super-sleek Mercer Hotel. Downtown art still mattered enough that year for the Guggenheim to open a SoHo branch. A block west there was still a post office.

The posters bore a large red stamp that read "The Scarlet Pimpernel," but in the corner was a tiny signature: Jonah Kinigstein. I tracked him down at his Victorian house in Flatbush. Stocky and sporting a goatee, he was 66 but had lately been spending his nights wheatpasting his photocopied pen-and-ink drawings on SoHo walls. All 40 posters in the series show the museums, the major galleries, and the art critics as allegorical figures fondling each other and cooperating in a massive swindle: selling pure, unadulterated garbage to John Q. Public. They are cartoons, but they are also savage attacks on the art industry—as likely to make you cringe as laugh.

Kinigstein showed me around his cluttered attic studio, pointing out his own oil paintings among art books, a taxidermied blowfish, a variety of animal skulls, and a broken crucifix. "The posters are attacks on an avant-garde that has become the Academy it is rebelling against," he said. He pushed back his hair and adjusted his thick glasses. We had been talking for a few minutes and he was already getting angry. "Yeah, I single out Castelli. He's a snake-oil salesman. Sure, he's a genius, but he's a *marketing* genius." As he began to rant, he started to bounce and wave his arms. He said things like "Hucksters!" and "Hoodwinked!" He lurched across the room and grabbed a book, something called *Art Now!*, which was next to *Hoax* and *Fake!* Flipping through the pages, he said, "This guy here, he's a joke.... This one, forget it.... Nothing.... Nothing.... There's nothing here!" Kinigstein pointed at a painting by Josef Albers, one of the pioneers of Modernism. It was a lime square within a tangerine square. "Albers is shit," he said in disgust. "I have more respect for Norman Rockwell than Willem de Kooning. I am a sinner to them. It's a sin what I do. It's blasphemy. It's anathema. I am anathema. I call them 'The Academy of the Avant-Garde.' Fraud! Incest! Collusion!"

Now he was furious. "They pretend to make a total break with the past," he said. "The biggest insult in the world is to hear that your work looks like someone else's. Yeah, I'm influenced. I'm proud of my influences. Listen, if you walk away from a Caravaggio at the Met and you don't take something away, if it doesn't touch you, then what kind of person are you?"

Kinigstein began pulling examples of his drawings, piling them quickly on a dirty gray couch. He

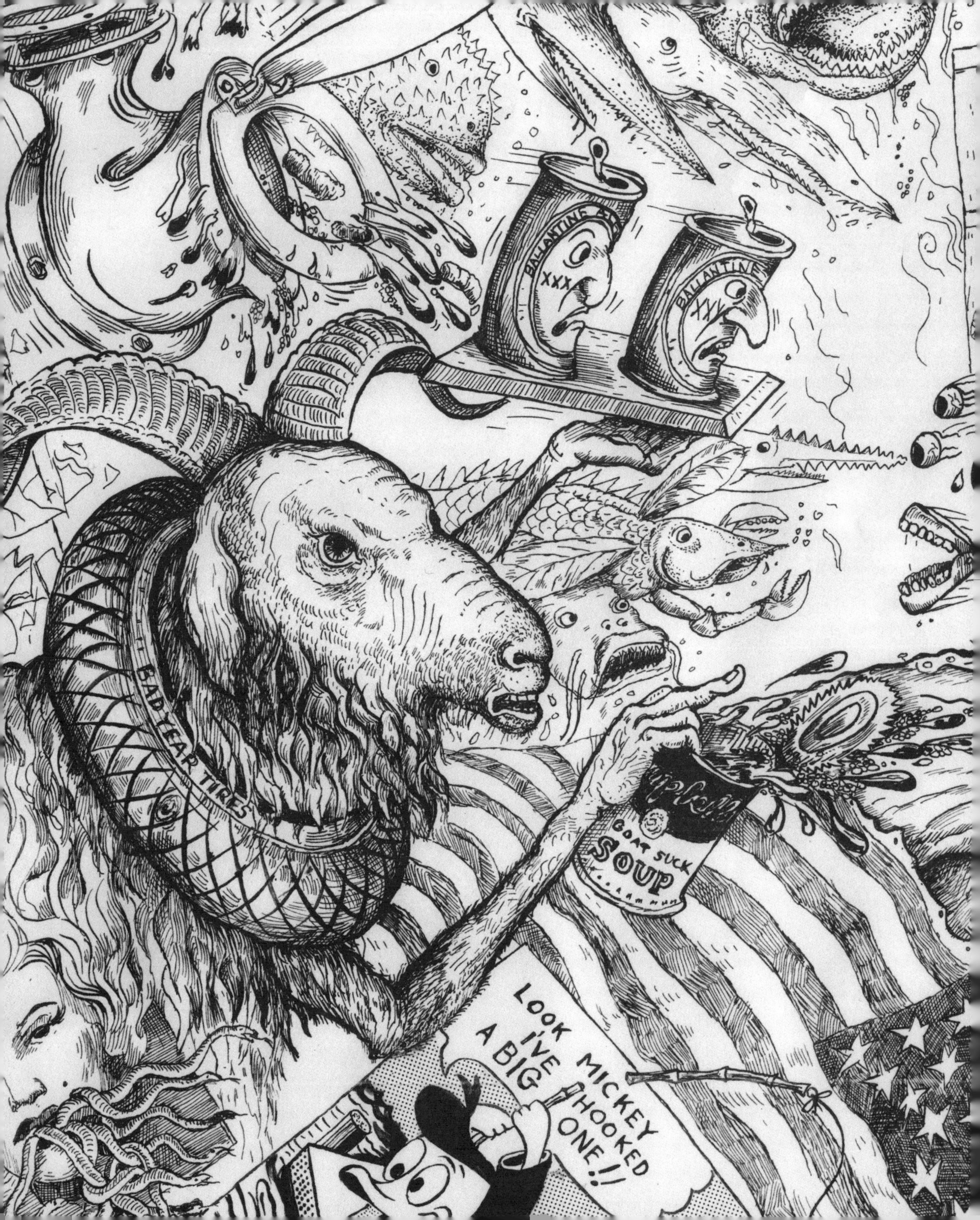
BALLANTINE
XXX
BALLANTINE
XXX
BAD YEAR TIRES
GOAT SUCK
SOUP
LOOK MICKEY
I'VE HOOKED
A BIG ONE!!

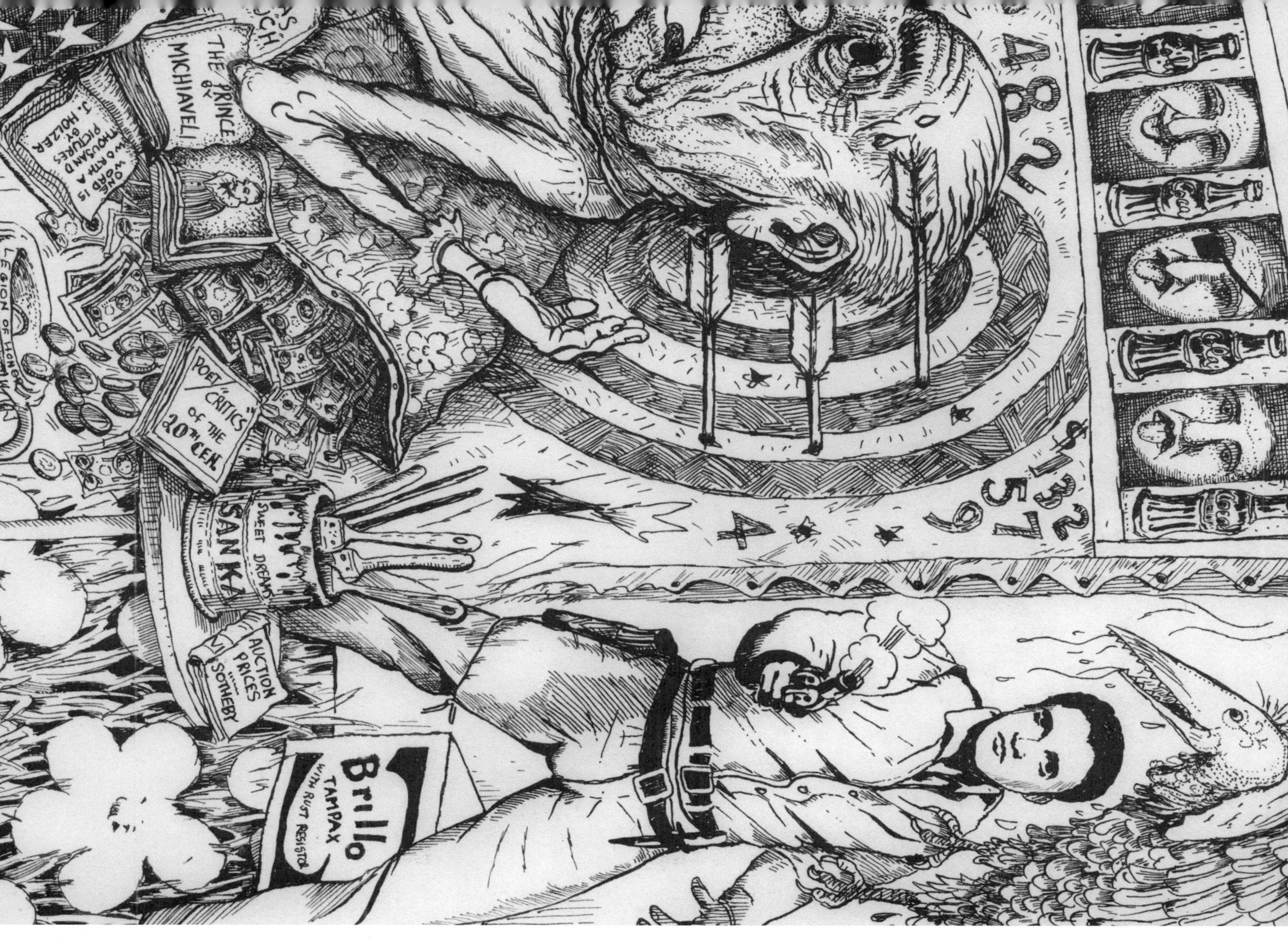

The Dream and Lies of L. Castelli *(detail)*

uses all kinds of art-historical sources. There is *The Last Supper* with Clement Greenberg at the center of a table full of Abstract Expressionists asking, "Why is this night different from any other night?" There is a sendup of Géricault's *Raft of the Medusa* on which the dying and naked "last real artists left" cling to easels and fend off SoHo gallery sharks. In Kinigstein's *The Roots of Evil Bring Forth Rotten Fruit*, Castelli and his ex-wife Ileana Sonnabend stand in for Durer's *Adam and Eve,* and a version of Rauschenberg's *Monogram*, the angora goat with a tire around its middle, replaces the phlegmatic ox.

Kinigstein claimed to know what he was talking about. "I've been there," he said. "The Cedar Tavern? I saw Pollock puke at the Cedar Tavern. I know what these artists are doing and I've done it all myself." He started yanking canvases from stacks of hundreds, flinging them in my direction. He showed me his early *St. Jerome*, the figure of the desert hermit obscured by Expressionist brushstrokes. "Sure, it's there, a lot of *Sturm und Drang*. But that fades fast—just the record of the artist's muscle. You've got to go beyond that, incorporate it into something more. And anyway, it's been done before. John Singer Sargent, of all people, did more with the quick expressive brushstroke than all of them."

Next it was the critics: "The Critics! They're poets. They're giving their own Rorschach inkblot-test results. They're good poets, sure; they tell us what they see in pretty ways. But don't tell me what I see in that cloud!"

Kinigstein's conspiracy theory rivals that of the most dogged Grassy Knoll enthusiast. "Everyone is so damn afraid of doing the same thing they did to van Gogh that they buy everything that comes along. It's the Tyranny of the New. How fresh is it? How fresh do you want it?" In his drawings, commandments are listed on stone tablets or dribbling out of the mouths of gallery owners in saints' robes and halos: "Make it so outrageous there are no values to judge it"; "Less is more, ergo, least is best"; "Thou shalt not make anything recognizable."

Kinigstein started doing the cartoons around 1990 and just sent them to friends. "To be honest," he says, "the reaction wasn't that great. But I started putting them on the streets because I wanted more people to get the message, and I thought someone might see them and want to show them or publish them so even more people would see them. But I was wrong. I sent them to a few places and no one wanted to touch them." He told me an editor at *Art in America* turned down a reporter's story on him, calling it scatological (piles of poop on pedestals often sum up Kinigstein's view of contemporary art in his posters, as do disembodied genitalia and massive orgies of art insiders). "In the very next issue they ran photos of what's-his-name's *Piss Christ*, an aquarium full of urine with a crucifix in it," he said. "Everybody's got their vested interests. The magazines need their advertisers, and anybody already involved has too much at stake to question what they're doing now. They've invested their cash in the whole myth."

Kinigstein put up his posters about once a week for a year. They didn't last long, and both his fans and enemies were to blame. He used to do his own forensic work and could tell if they'd been cut down carefully, as souvenirs, or if they'd been torn down in anger. "There are loads of people who see it the way I do," he said. "They come up to me on the street when I'm putting them up. They say, 'Thanks. I didn't know it was okay to feel this way.'" (Most of us only vent our suspicions every two years, in honor of the Whitney Biennial.)

When adopting a pseudonym, Kinigstein chose The Scarlet Pimpernel over Don Quixote—though he claimed to know he was tilting at windmills—because the hero of Baroness Orczy's novel was successful. Kinigstein, belying the unmistakable cloud of bitterness hanging over his crusade, had some early success as a painter. He was born in Coney Island in 1927 and raised in the Bronx. He learned to paint at Cooper Union and went on to win a Fulbright to study in Rome in 1951; by 1956 he was in MoMA's Young Americans show. He got shows right away but never sold much. "I worked in the Brooklyn Navy Yards as a loftsman. This was very early. We'd lay the metal ship plates right down on these giant blueprints. Later I did some research and development for Seagram's. They don't do it so much any more, but they'd have these moving displays in bars, pushing their whisky—little mechanical things where people's heads would move, something to look at. Later I was a chromist, ghosting lithographs by hand for other painters."

Over the years his paintings made it into the permanent collections of many museums, including MoMA, the Whitney, and the Albright. The subjects of his oil paintings are anything but conservative; they're likely to depict full-bodied women in garters riding bishops like horses, tattooed fortunetellers, and maniacal clowns, all crammed into menacing

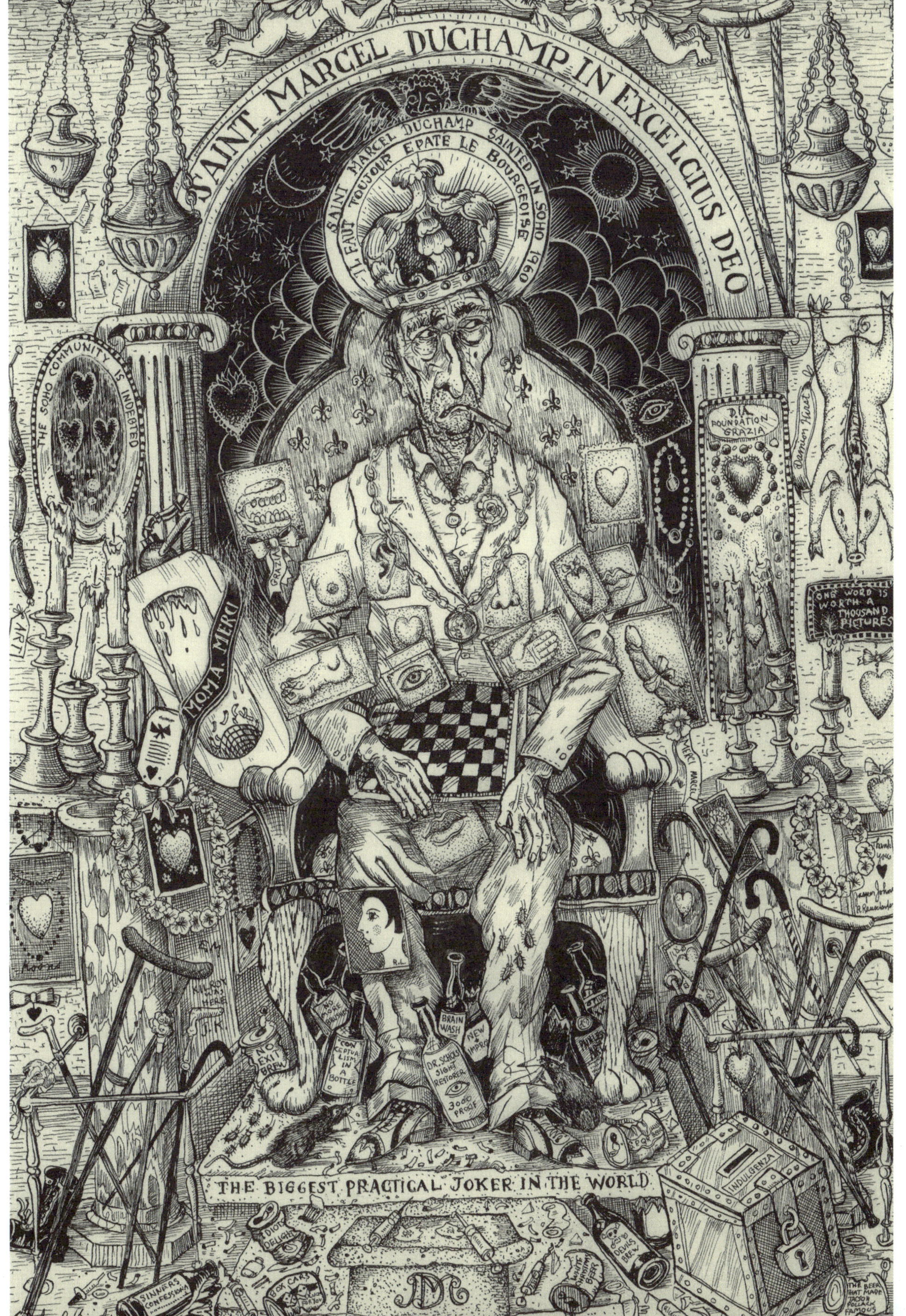

Saint Marcel Duchamp in Excelcius Deo; or, The Biggest Practical Joker in the World *(detail)*

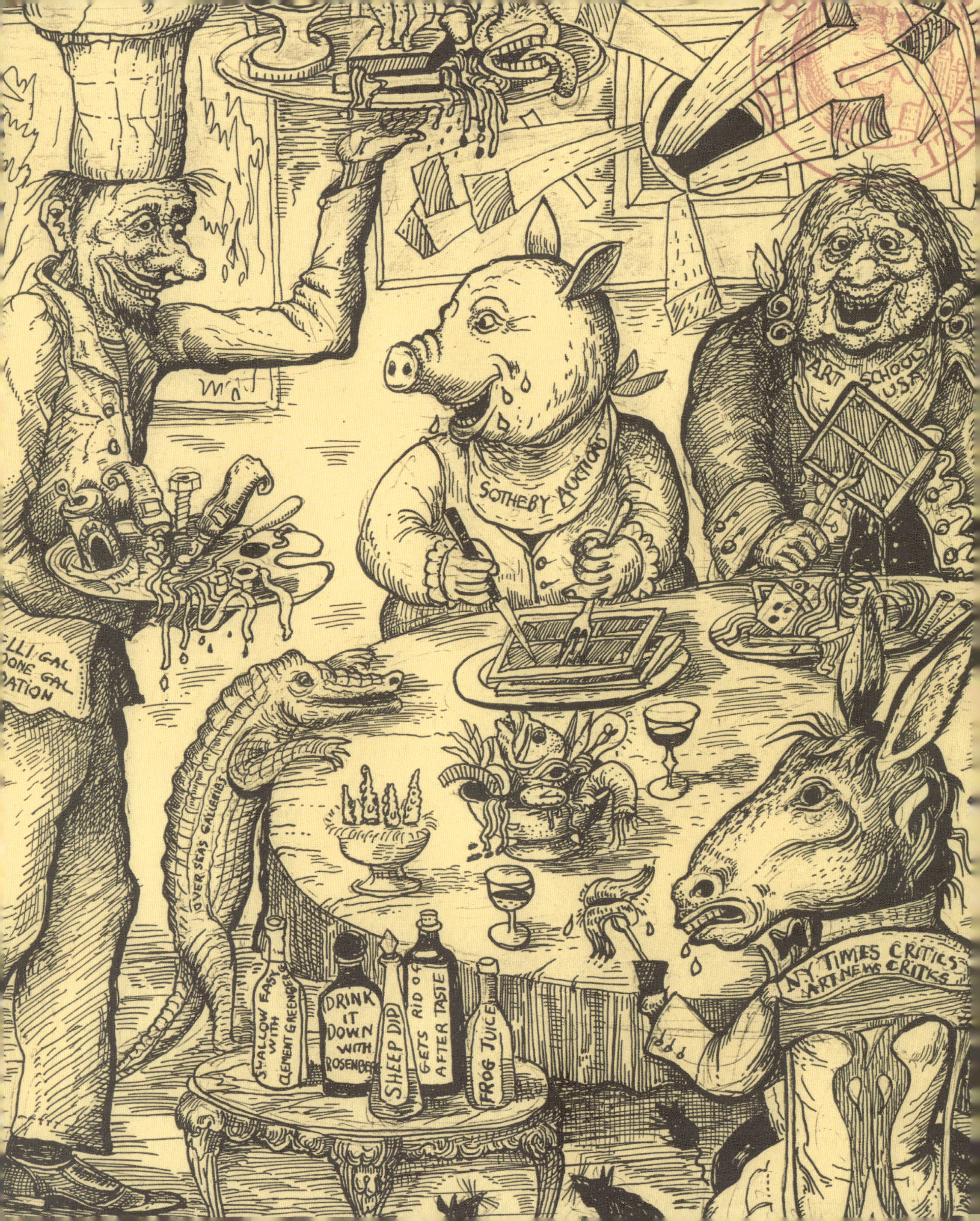
SOTHEBY AUCTIONS
ART SCHOOLS U.S.A.
OVER SEAS GALLERIES
N.Y. TIMES CRITICS
ART NEWS CRITICS
SWALLOW EASY WITH CLEMENT GREENBERG
DRINK IT DOWN WITH ROSENBERG
SHEEP DIP
GETS RID OF AFTER TASTE
FROG JUICE

sideshow scenes. There's a little George Grosz in the creeping, sagging flesh and jaded eyes of his characters, and some Georges Rouault in the weight of the paint and the depth of the shadows.

He showed me his favorite posters. In *The Adoration of the Magi*, three representatives of the gallery world come bearing gifts of mounted private parts and feces to MoMA, an obese whore with a Picasso tattoo and torn stockings. The headline reads "Ask not what you can do for us—Ask only how you would like it done to you." He showed me *The Tower of Babel*. He said, "This critic with the Pinocchio nose and donkey ears says, 'Personal volumetric illusionistic Stolichnayism persists!' And here's Castelli, he's got cash flowing out of his pockets, saying, 'Spontaneous plastic argh gleek MacDonaldism!'" Throughout the drawings, critics talk gibberish, dealers and curators are blind, and holy relics of art—like Jasper Johns's Ballantine Ale cans, Malevich's *White on White*, and Duchamp's urinal—mix with trash and vermin.

In Kinigstein's attic, 12 years later, there are now so many paintings on wooden panels that we have to shove them aside to get from room to room. Kinigstein at 78 is a little gaunter than I remembered but just as animated. He still has the goatee and thick glasses, and he's wearing a lumberjack shirt under a canvas work vest. When he gets wound up he looks like he could still kick your ass. "Things have absolutely gotten worse," he begins. "This Matthew Barney...." He doesn't seem to know even where to begin about Matthew Barney. "At that time I didn't think things could get much worse. But now it's really all just shortcuts to fame." There's no solace for him in the demise of SoHo as the center of serious art in New York, or in the fact that Leo Castelli is dead.

He shows a more recent drawing: *The Old Wave Shocked and Abhorred by the New Avant-Garde*, subtitled *What Goes Around Comes Around*, in which his usual targets—Duchamp, Warhol, Castelli, Kline, De Kooning, and Pollock—stare aghast at an eviscerated pig, covered in worms and set on a butcher-block table, meant to represent Damien Hirst's work (there's a shark flopped over on another table for good measure). Maybe the old avant-garde looks a little better to Kinigstein now. De Kooning in this picture is at least holding a dripping house-paint brush, and Castelli is so upset that his false teeth have popped out. Even Warhol has the sense to try to flee.

He doesn't post on walls anymore, and any other audience he had has dwindled. "I've lost more friends than I've made doing the cartoons. One friend called me and said, 'Stop sending them to me!' I stopped. A few friends turned from figurative art into abstraction and I stopped sending drawings to them, too. I didn't wait for them to tell me."

For the first time, recently, he's done a full-size oil painting of one of his agitprop cartoons, *The Anatomy Lesson of Professor Tulp Recycled; or, The Quacks Operate on 20th Century Art*. The six-foot–wide canvas shows a devastated character called Figurative Art, with his split-open skull upon a cinderblock, being completely disemboweled by educators, critics, and curators. As a painting it's promising. He's not naming names, so the attacks seem less like personal vendettas, and perhaps leave more room for thought. It's set to hang at the National Academy of Design soon.

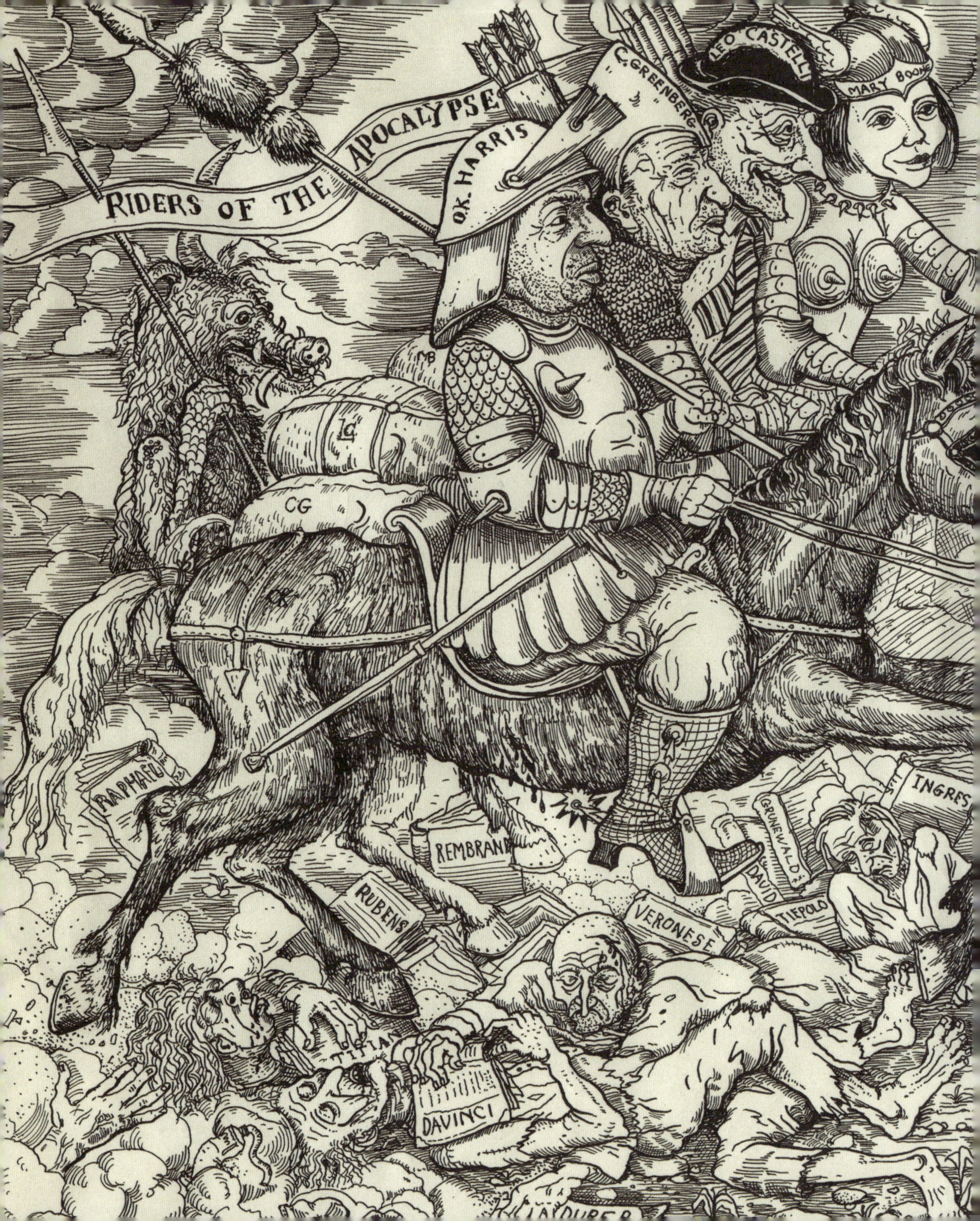
RIDERS OF THE APOCALYPSE
O.K. HARRIS
C. GREENBERG
LEO CASTELLI
MARY BOONE
MB
LC
CG
RAPHAEL
REMBRAND
RUBENS
VERONESE
TIEPOLO
DAVID
GRUNEWALD
INGRES
TITIAN
DAVINCI

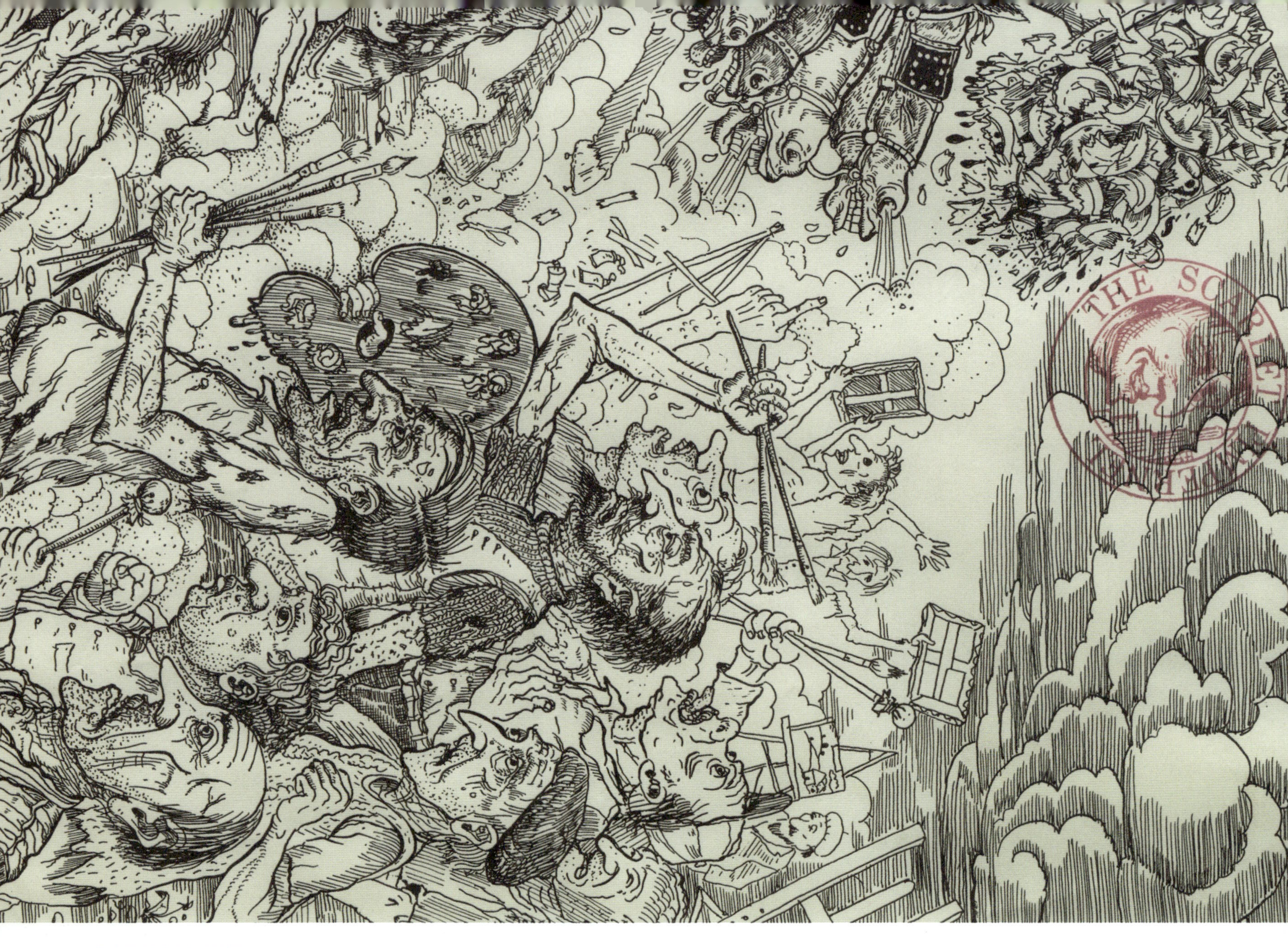

Riders of the Apocalypse

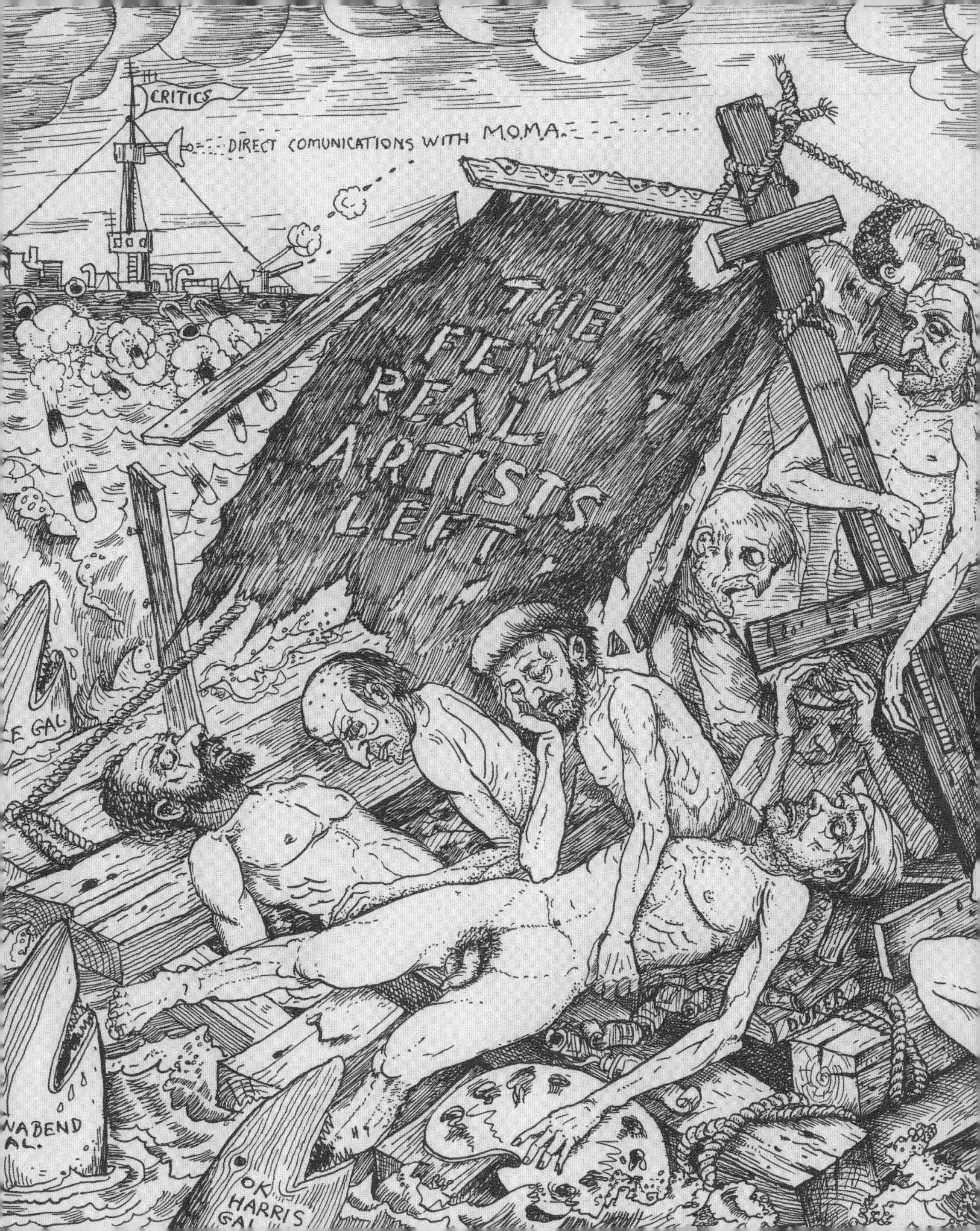
CRITICS
DIRECT COMUNICATIONS WITH M.O.M.A.
THE FEW REAL ARTISTS LEFT
E GAL
NABEND
AL.
OK
HARRIS
GAL
DURER

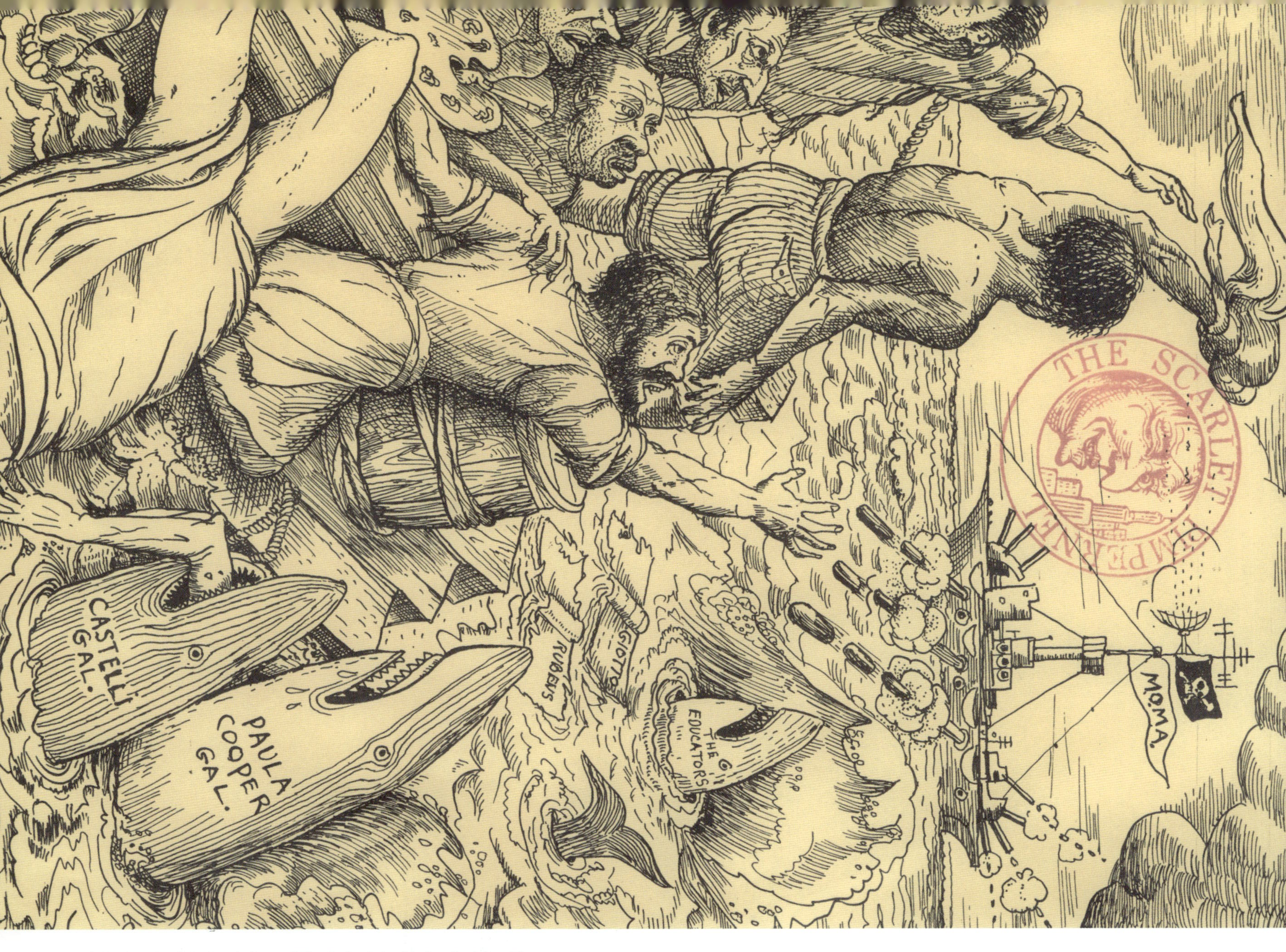

The Few Real Artists Left; or, "The Raft of the Medusa" of Our Time

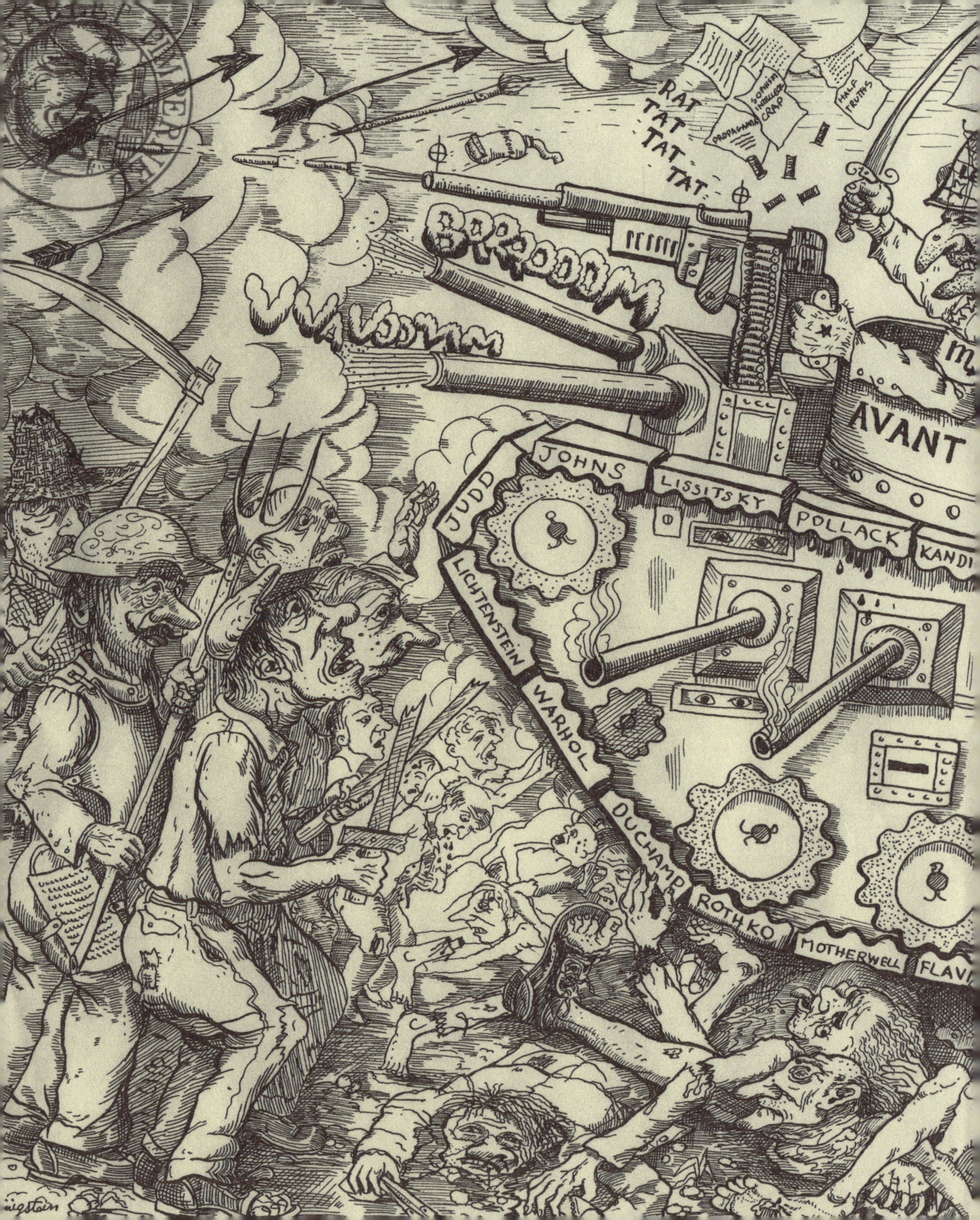
RAT
TAT
TAT
TAT
PROPAGANDA
CRAP
HALF TRUTHS
AVANT
JOHNS
JUDD
LISSITSKY
POLLACK
LICHTENSTEIN
WARHOL
DUCHAMP
ROTHKO
MOTHERWELL

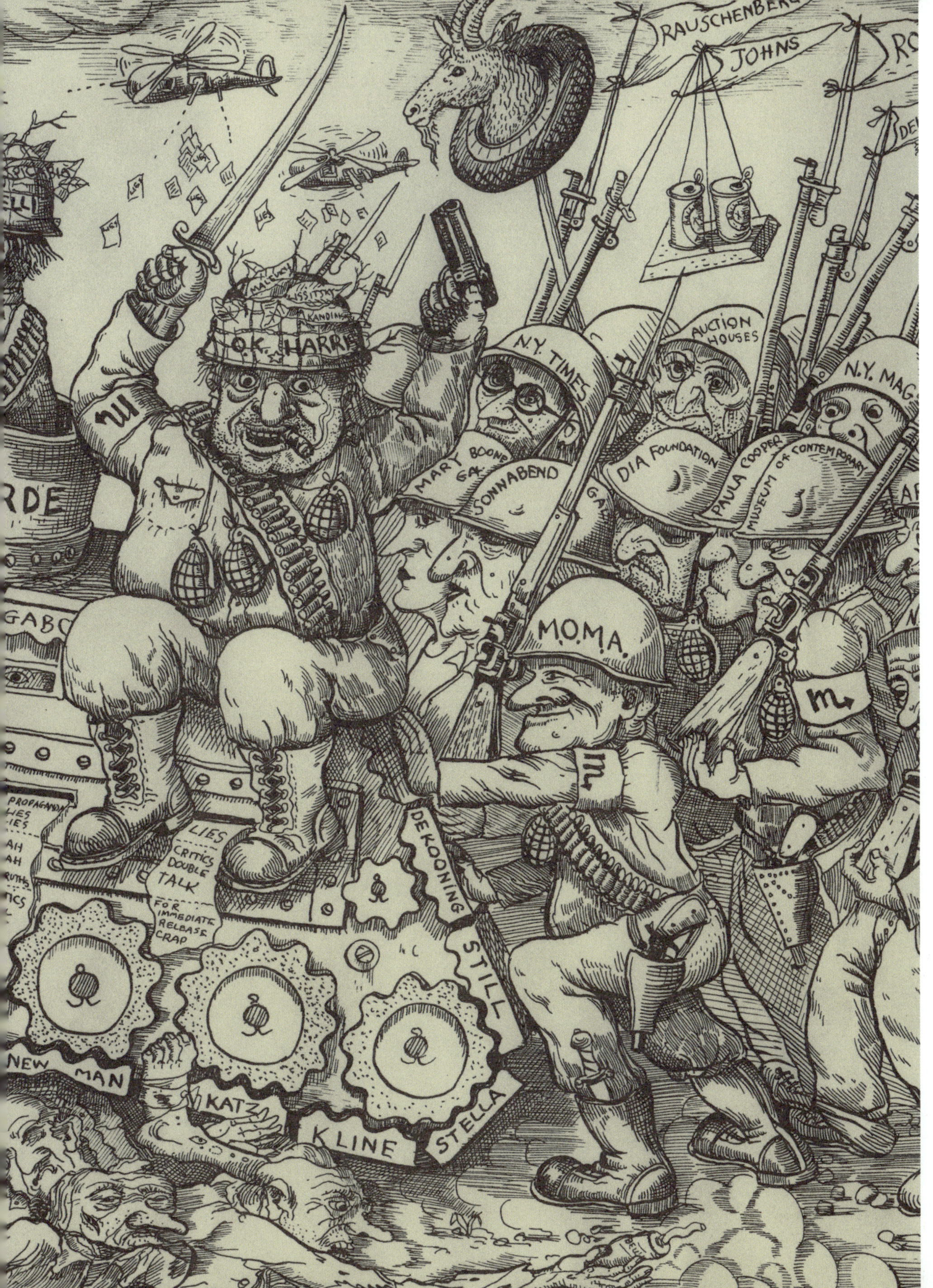

The Overwhelming Number of Soldiers and Equipment of the "Avant Garde" Crushing the Loyalist Rebellion

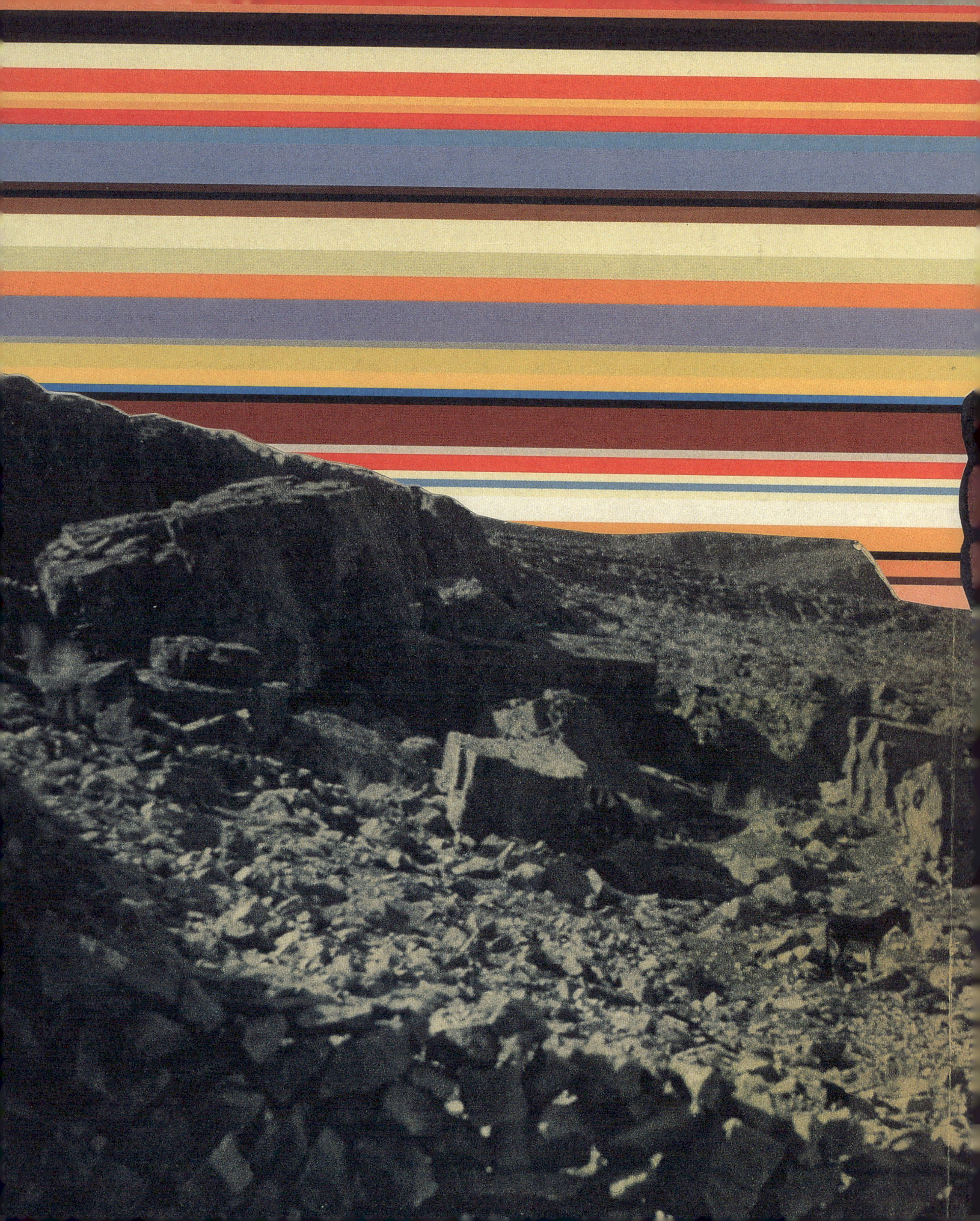

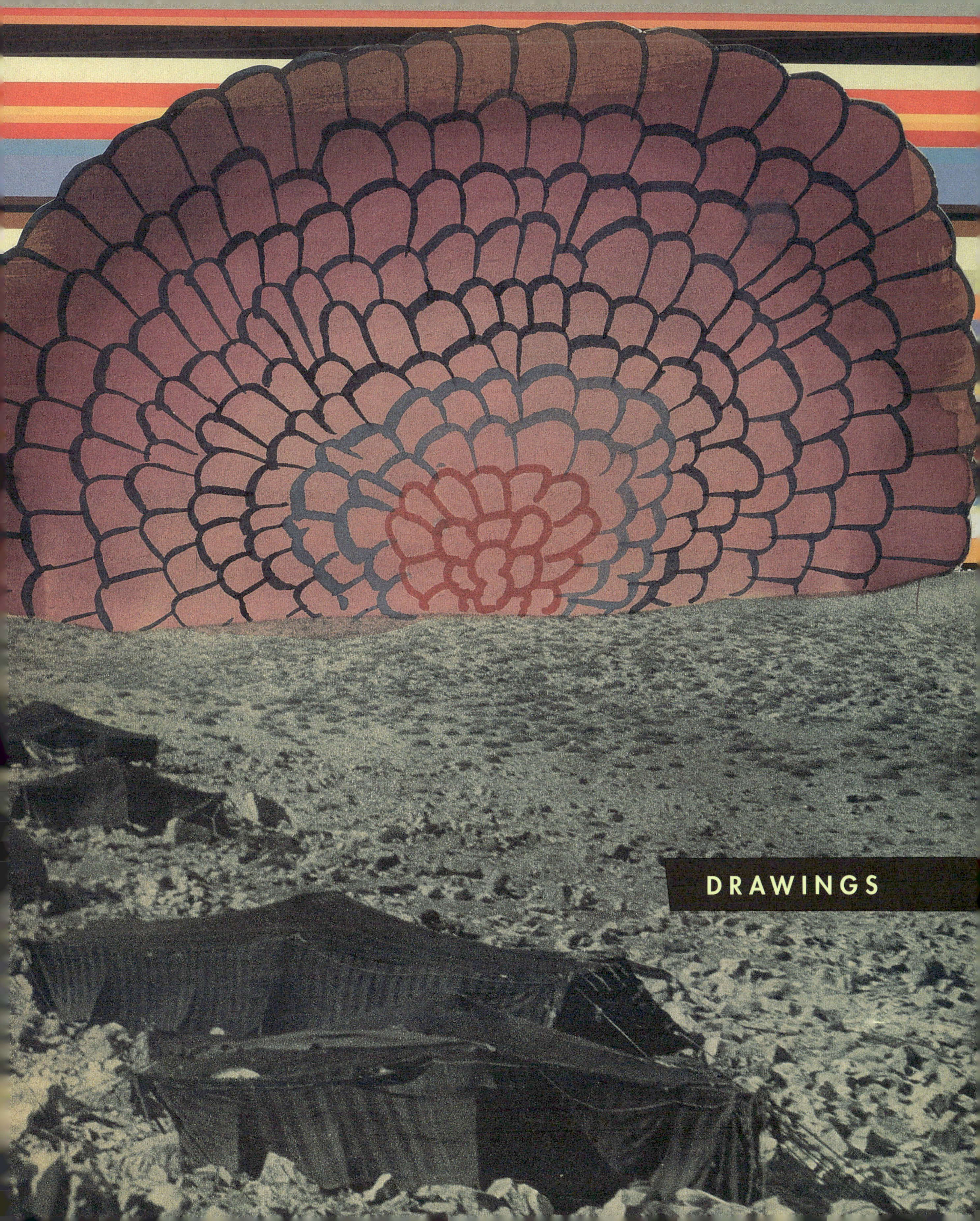

DRAWINGS

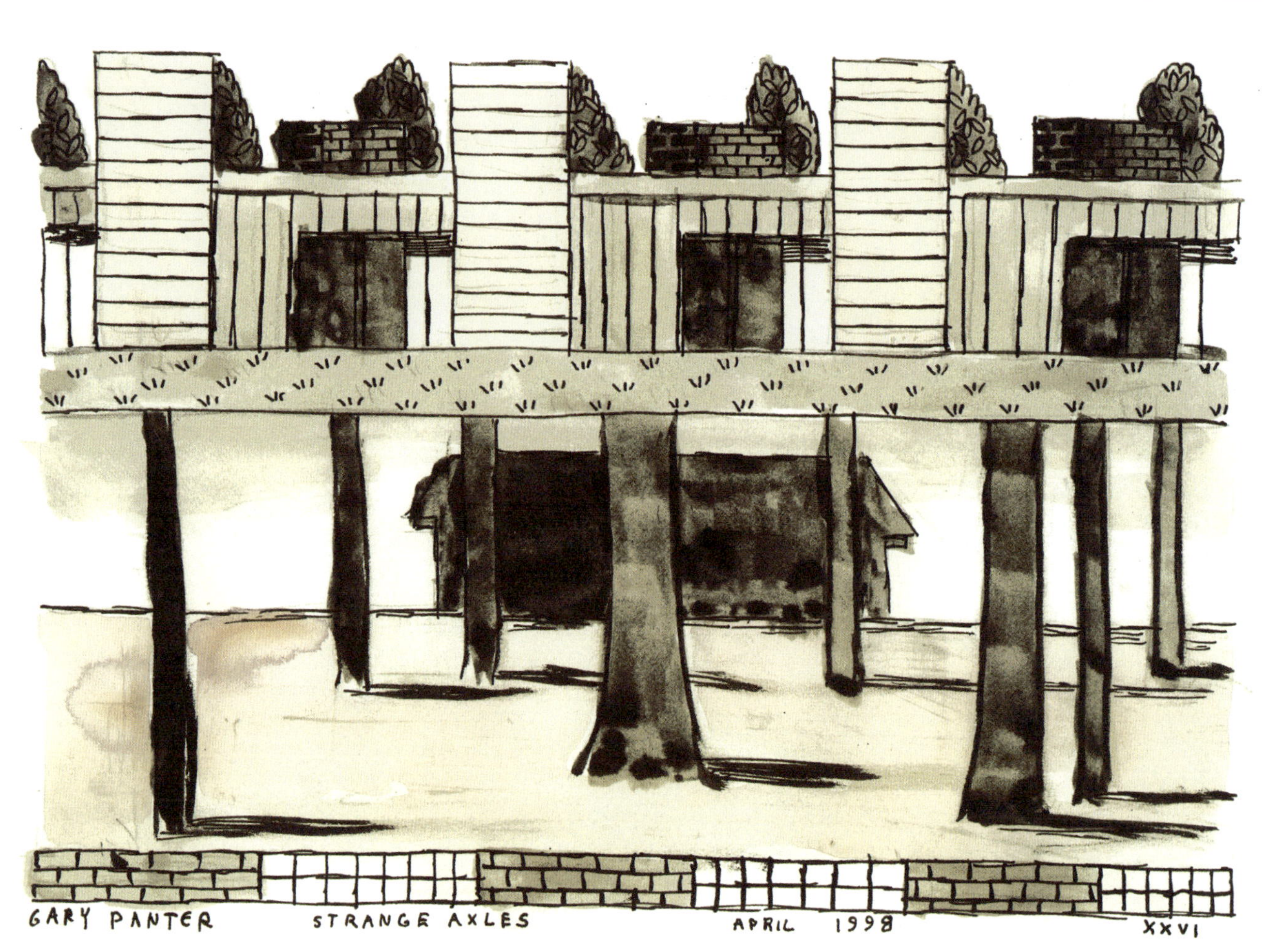
GARY PANTER
STRANGE AXLES
APRIL 1998
XXVI

FREE ESTIMATE

GARY PANTER FREE ESTIMATE BKLN NY TITLE PAGE SEPT 1998

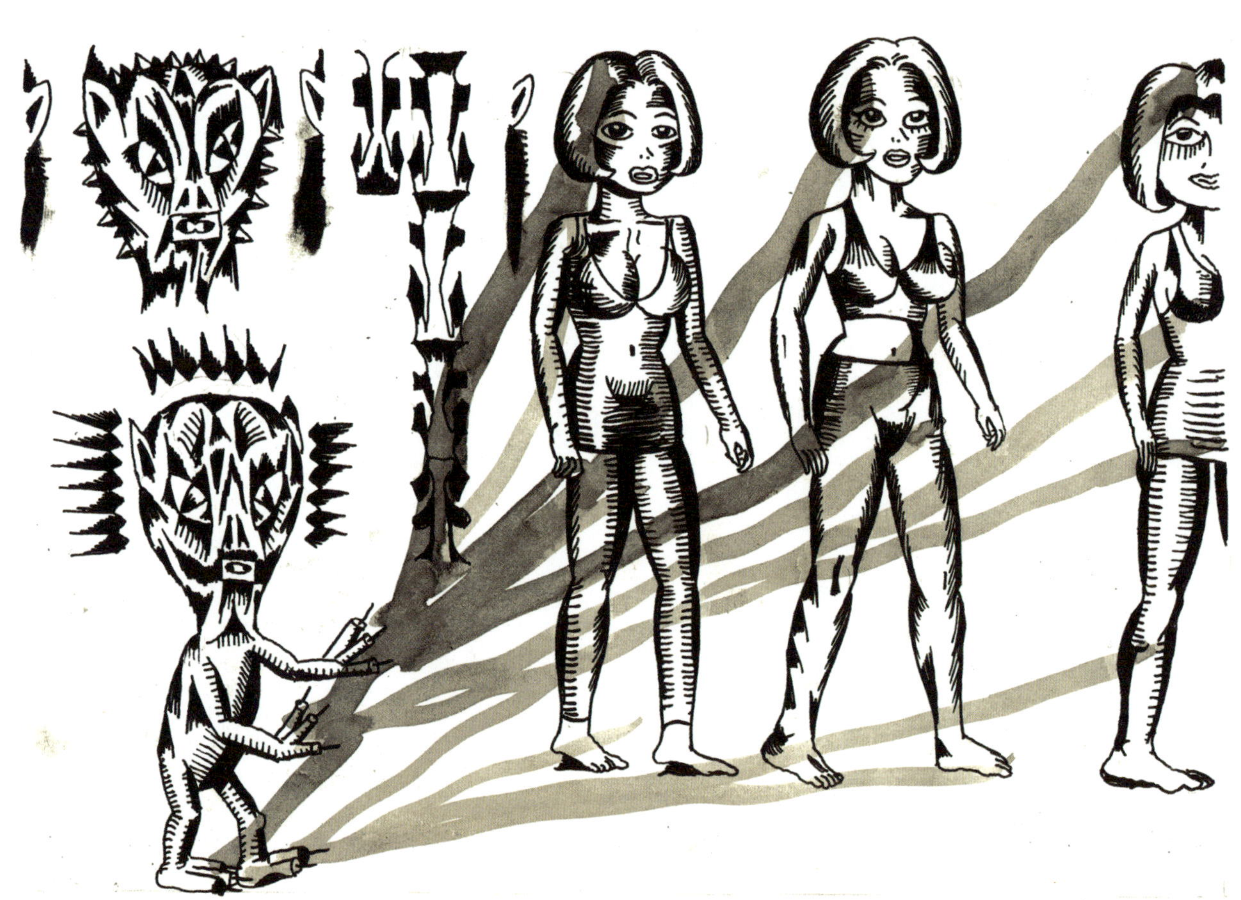
GARY PANTER
BLISTEX BALM
BROOKLYN
4 · 12 · 1998 EASTER
XXIV

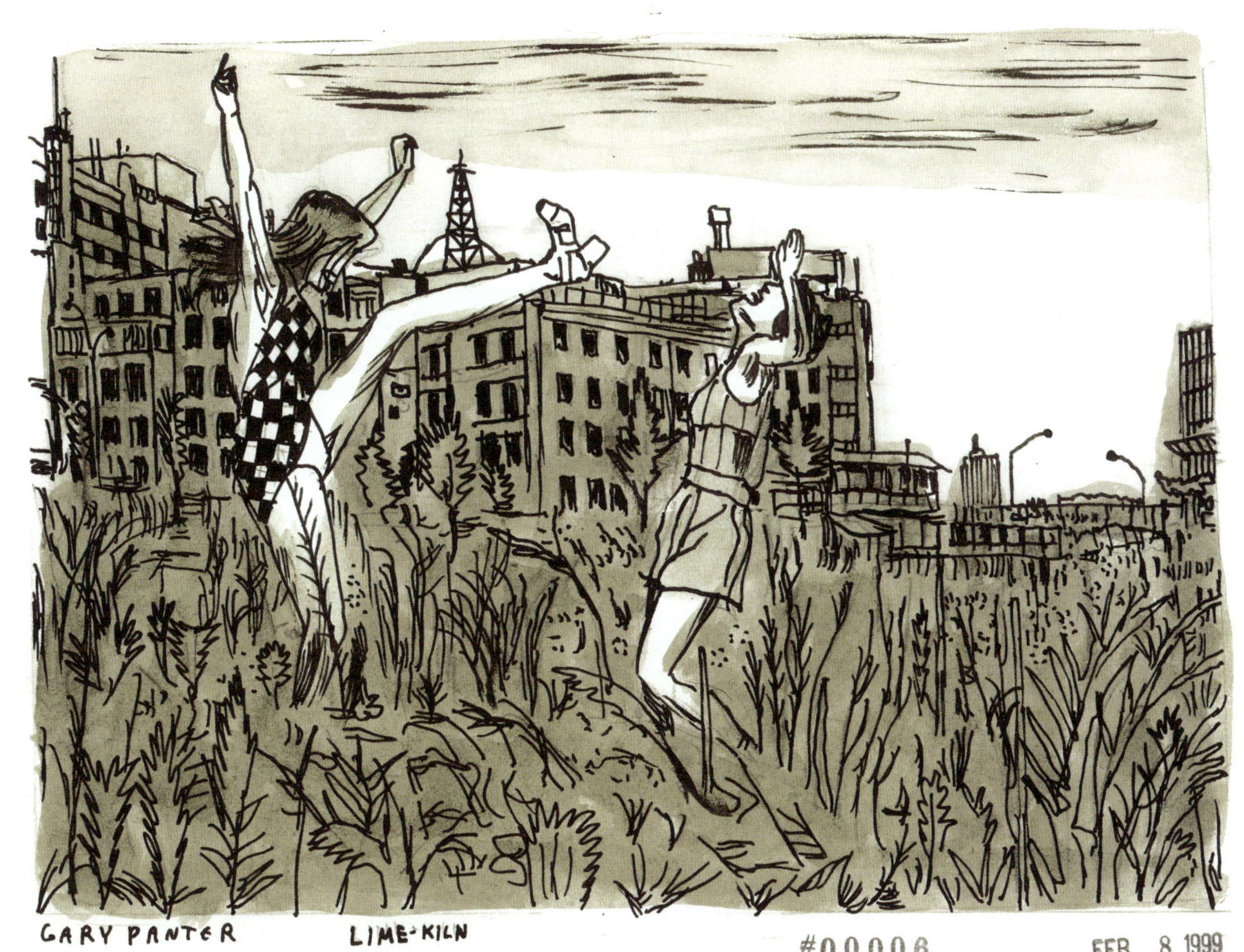
GARY PANTER
LIME-KILN
#00006
FEB 8 1999

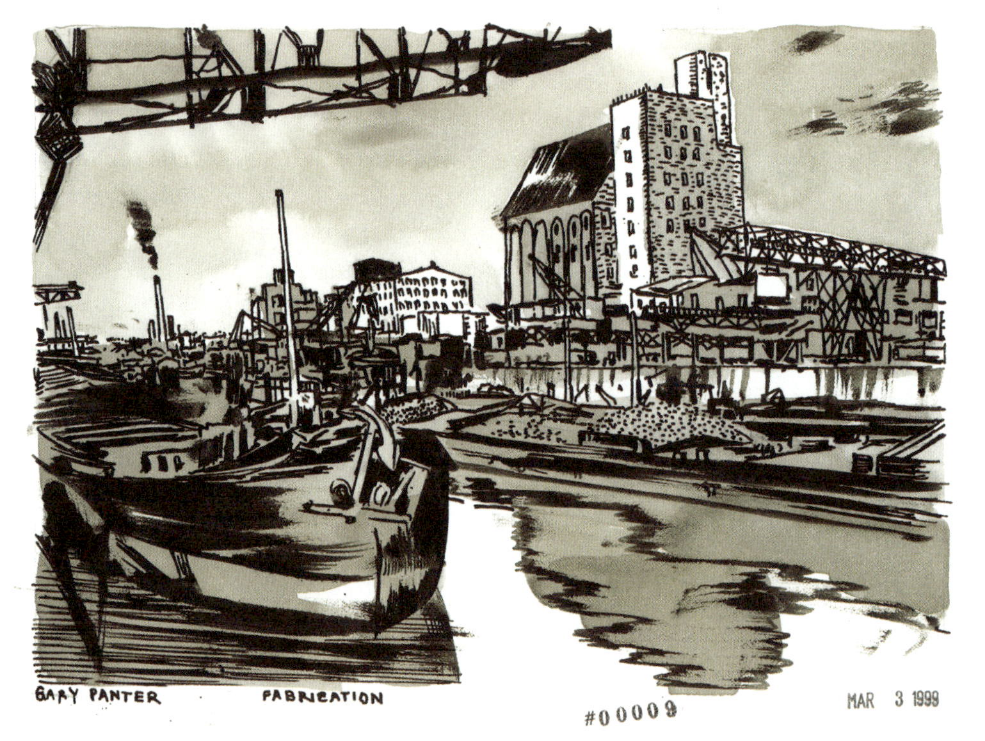
GARY PANTER
FABRICATION
#00009
MAR 3 1999

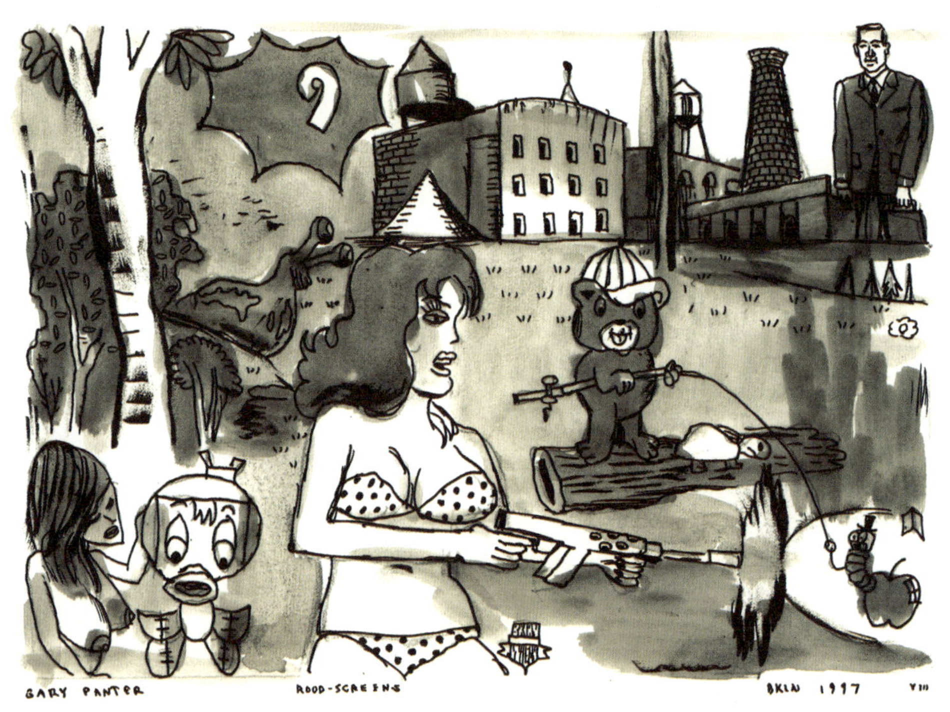
9
GARY PANTER
ROOD-SCREENS
BKLN 1997

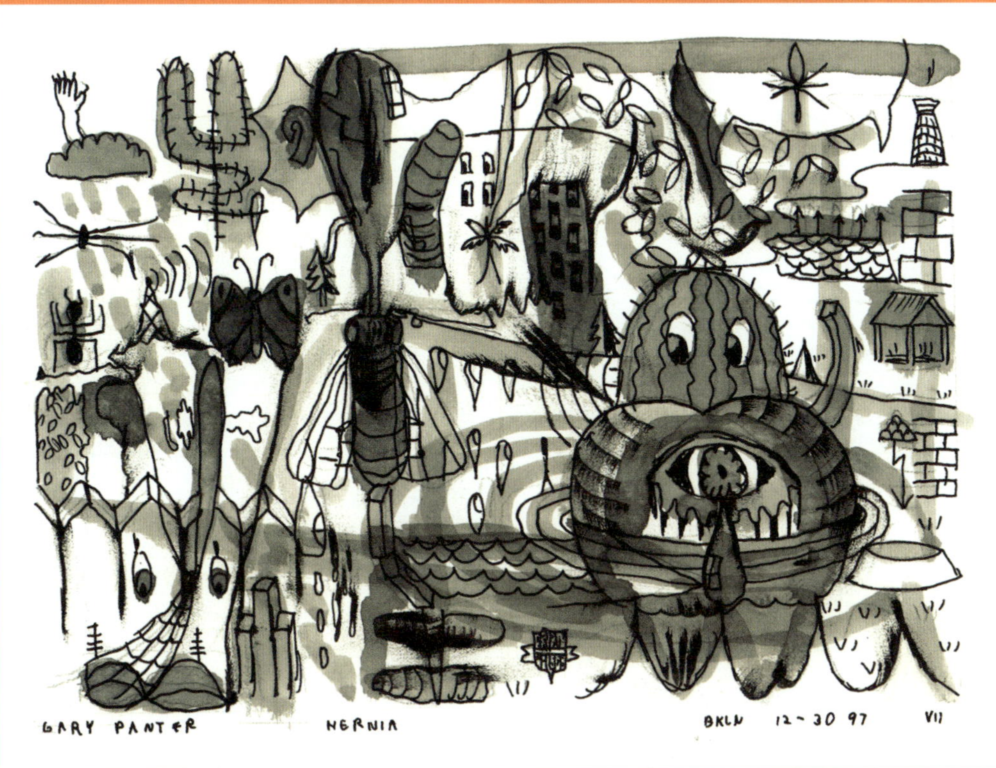
GARY PANTER
HERNIA
BKLN 12-30 97
VII

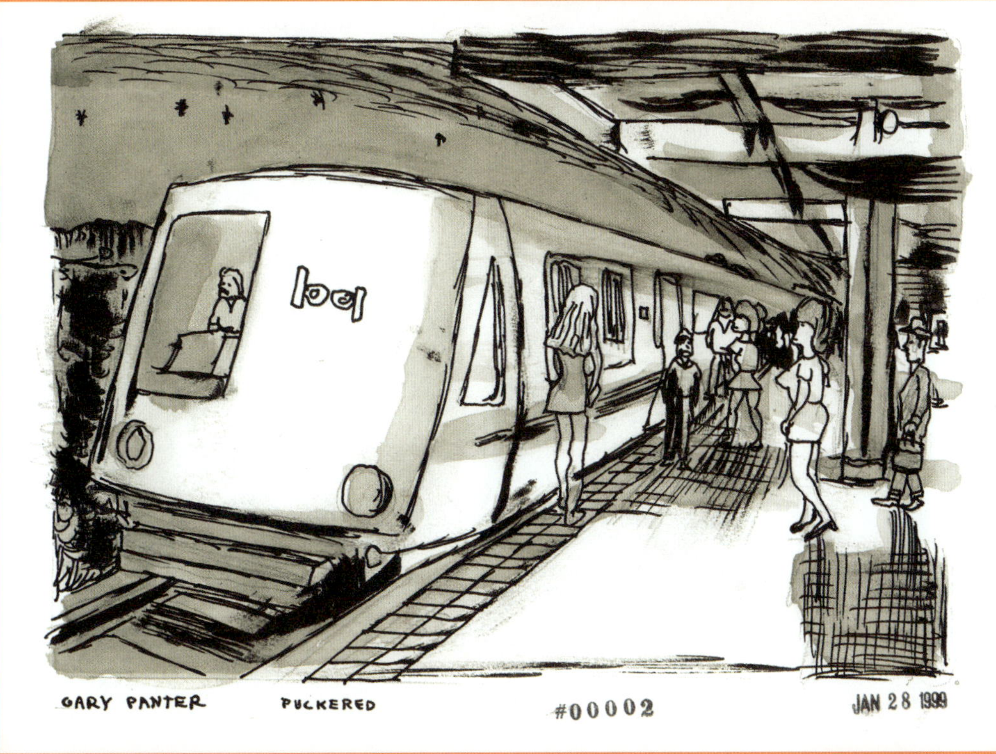
GARY PANTER
PUCKERED
#00002
JAN 28 1999

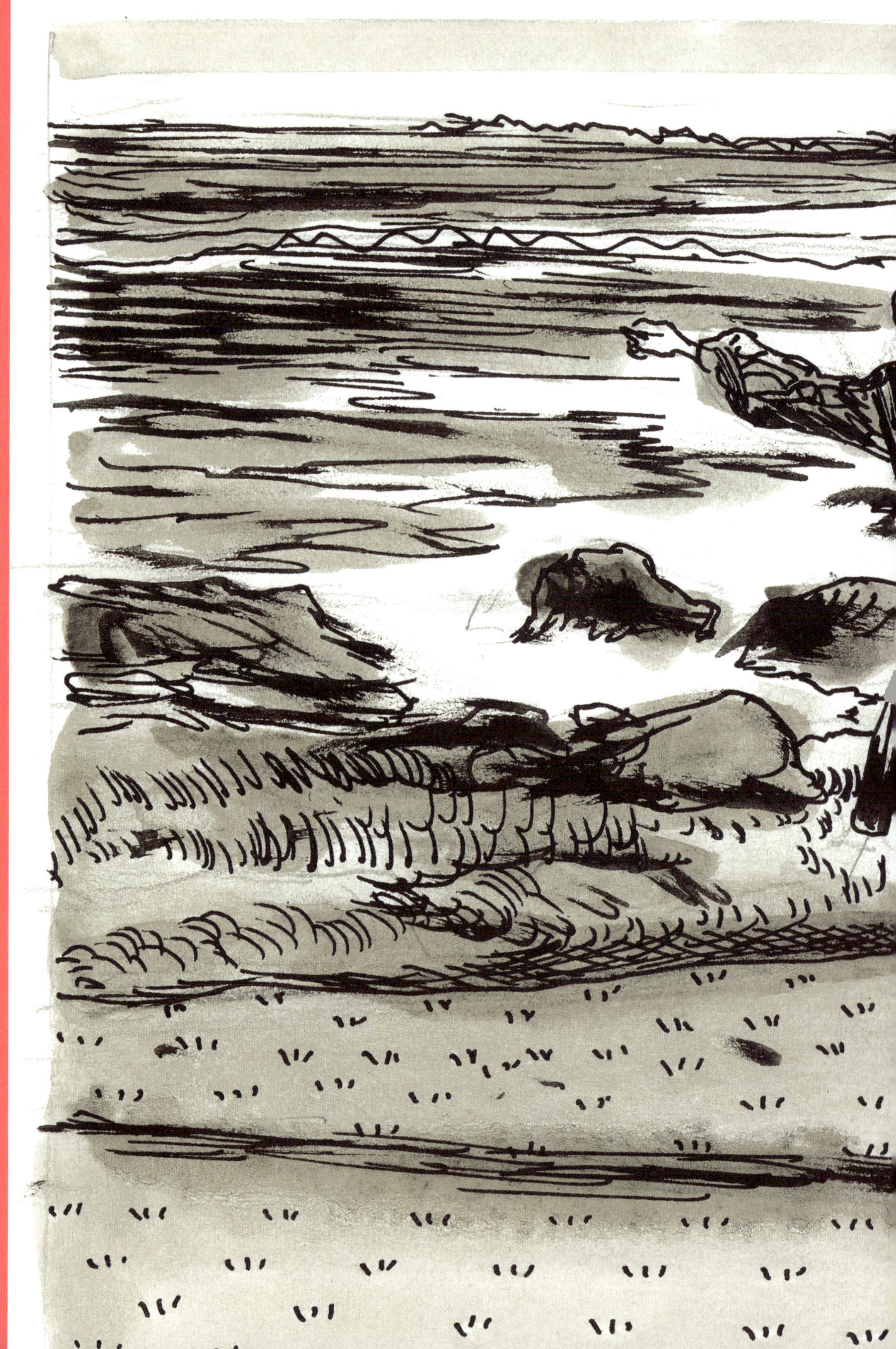

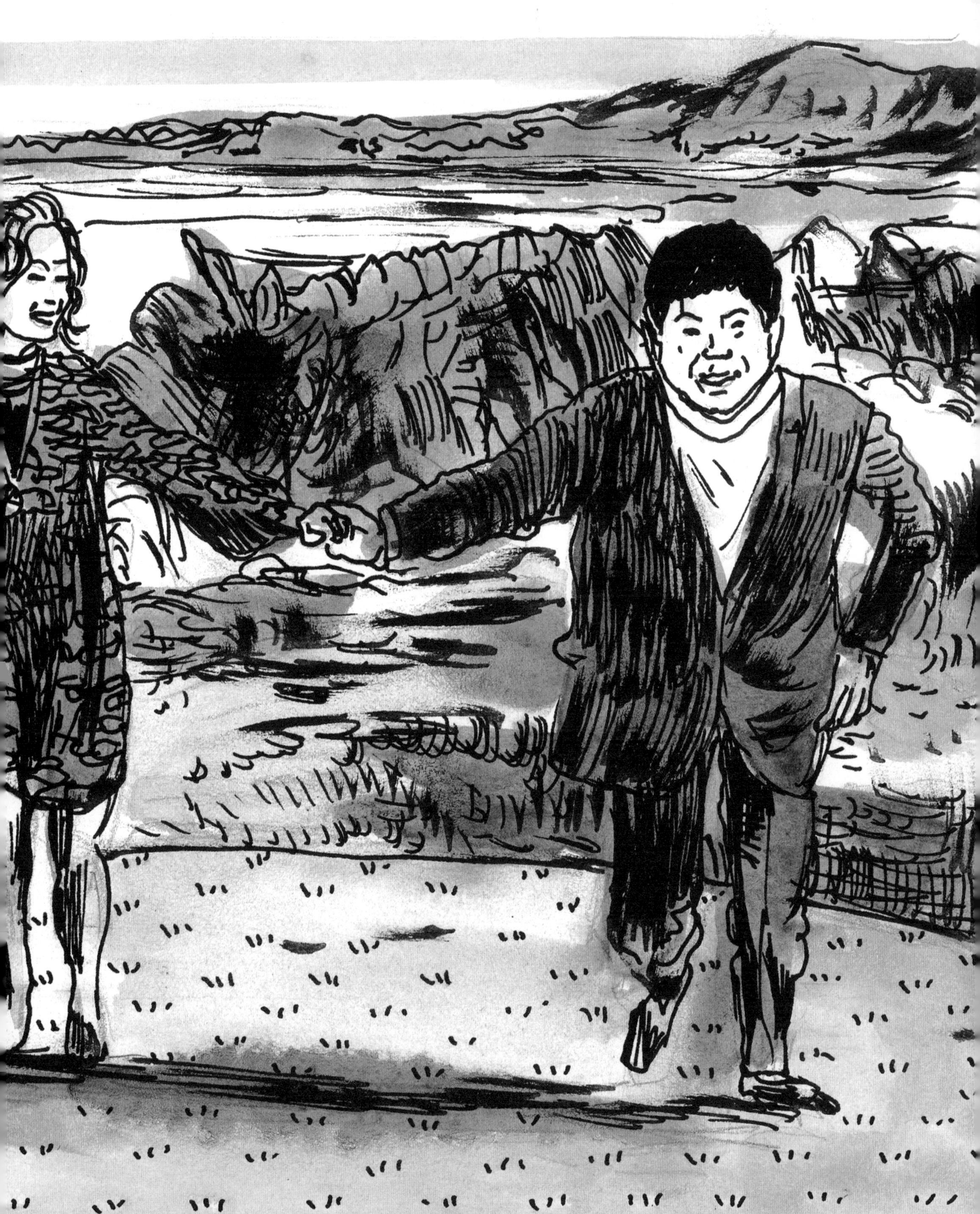

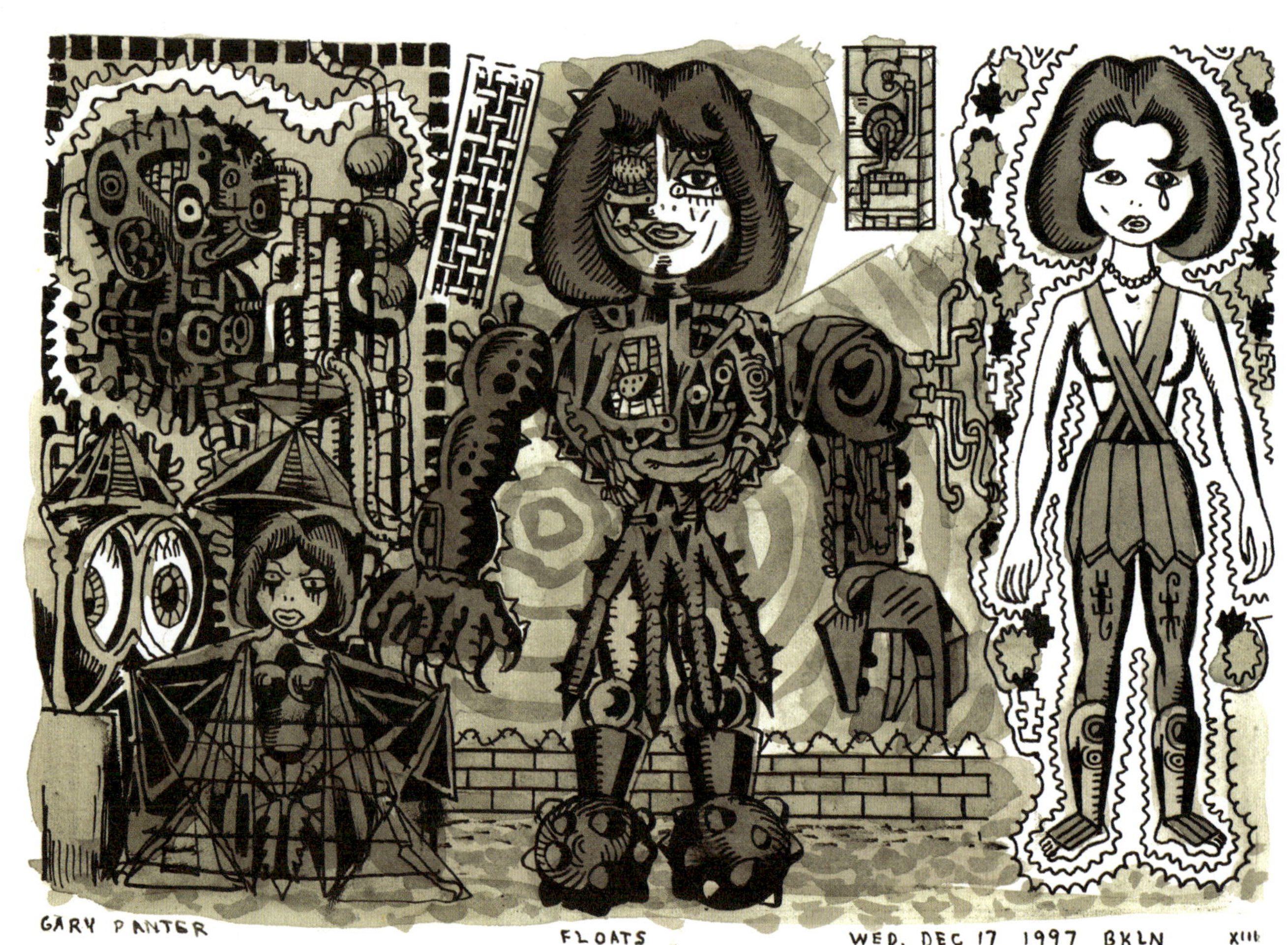
GARY PANTER
FLOATS
WED. DEC 17 1997 BKLN

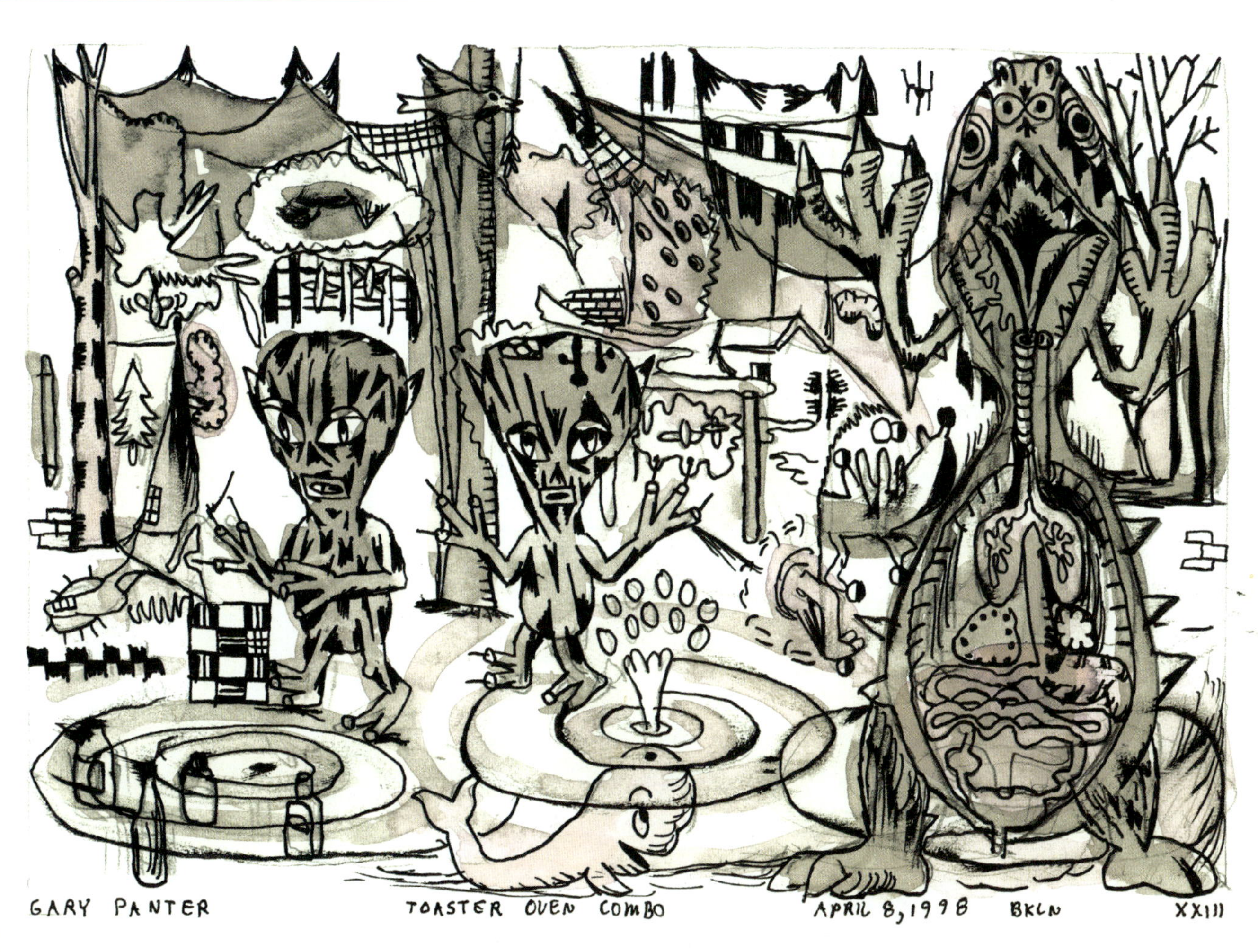
GARY PANTER
TOASTER OVEN COMBO
APRIL 8, 1998 BKLN
XXIII

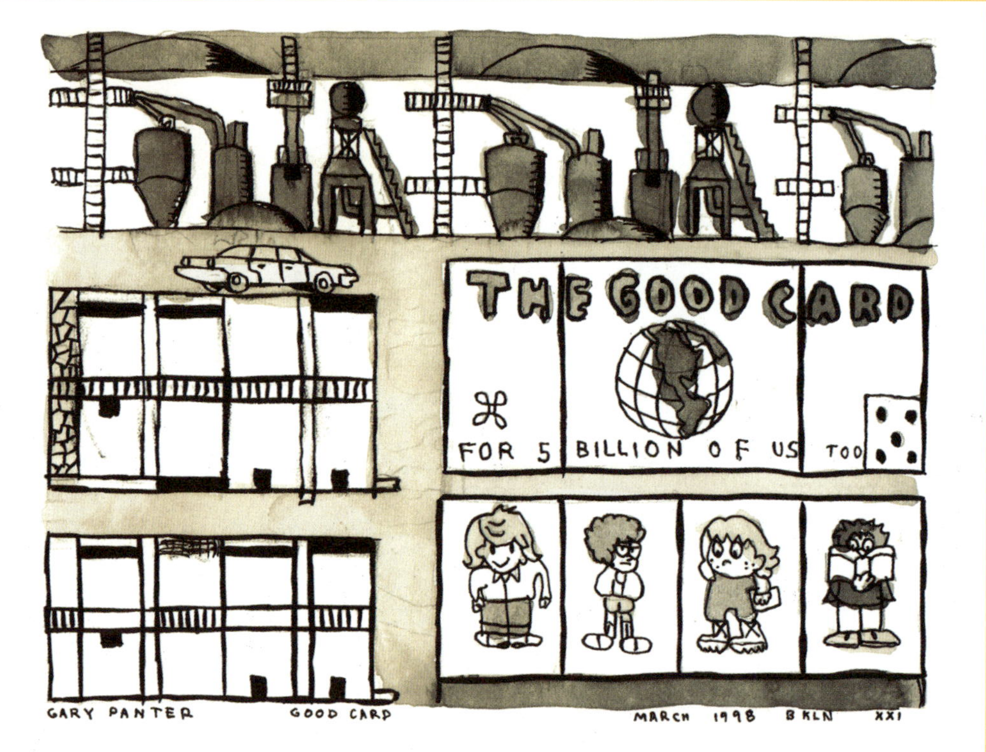
THE GOOD CARD
FOR 5 BILLION OF US TOO
GARY PANTER
GOOD CARD
MARCH 1998 BKLN XXI

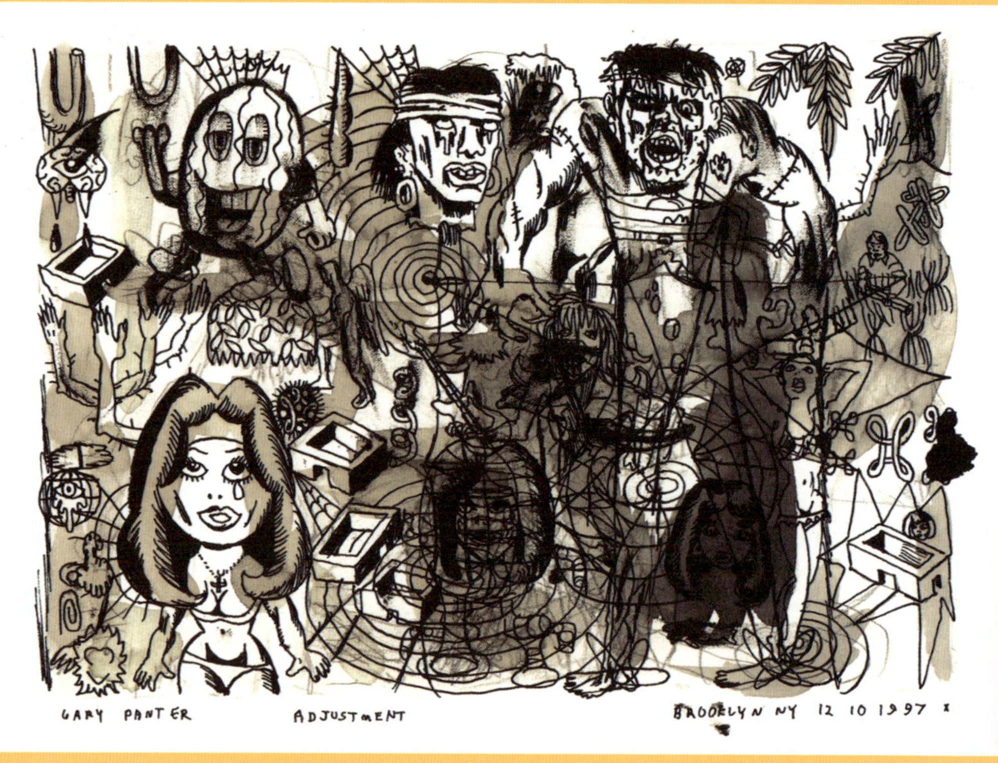
GARY PANTER
ADJUSTMENT
BROOKLYN NY 12 10 1997 X

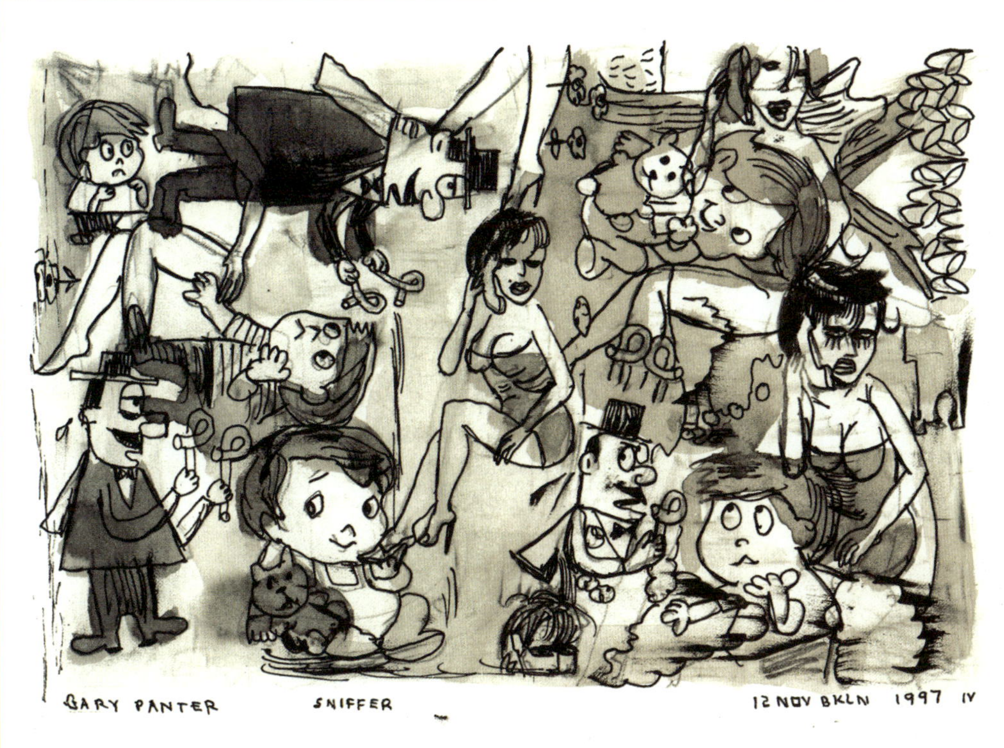
GARY PANTER
SNIFFER
12 NOV BKLN 1997 IV

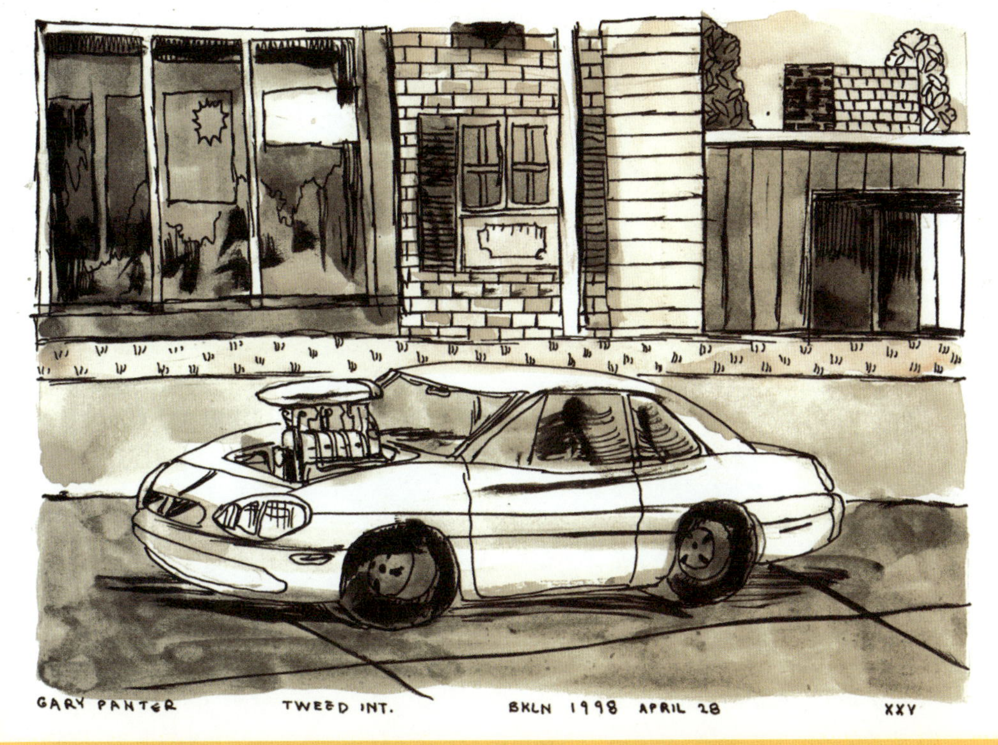
GARY PANTER
TWEED INT.
BKLN 1998 APRIL 28
XXV

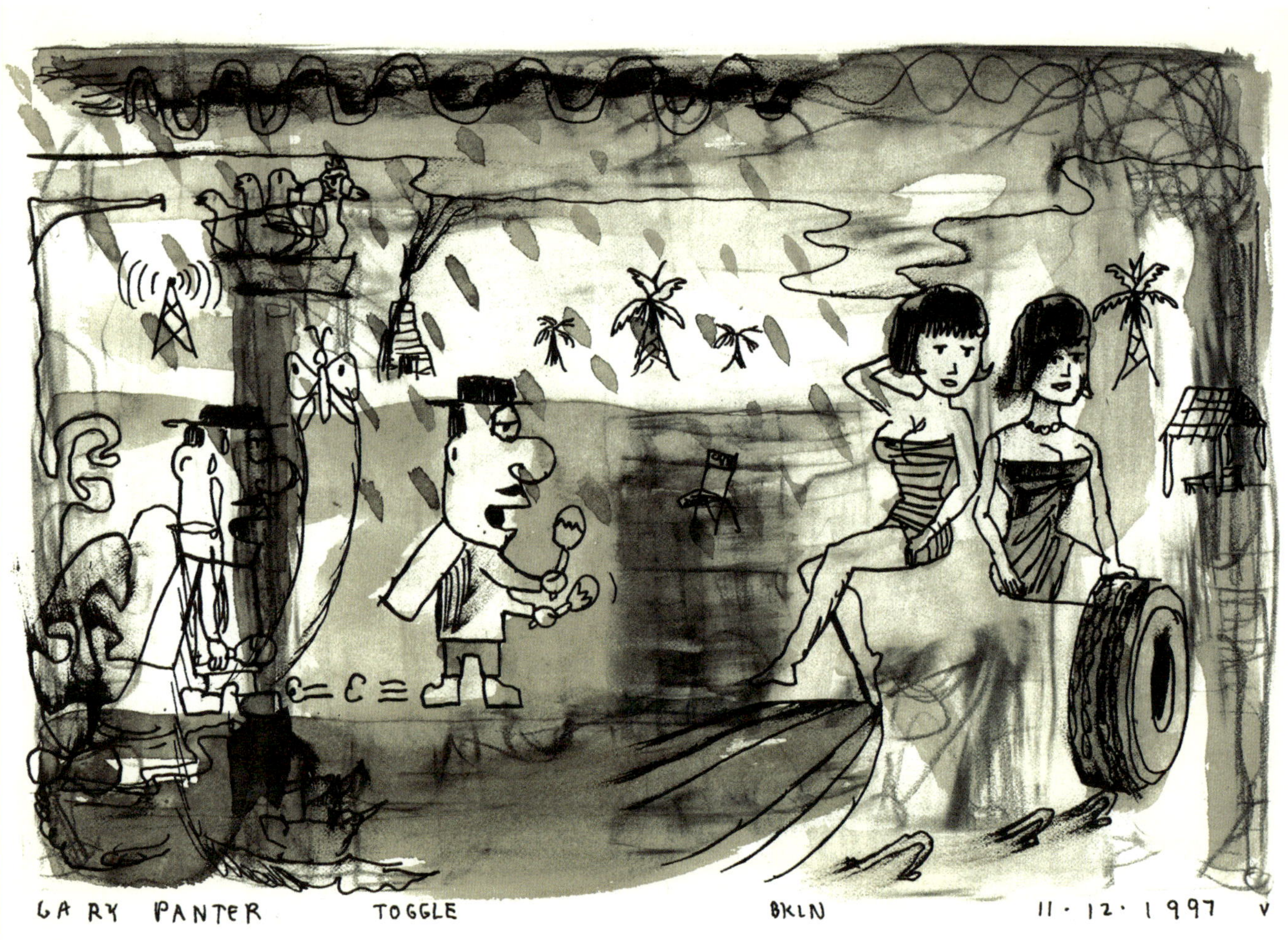

GARY PANTER
TOGGLE
BKLN
11 · 12 · 1997
V

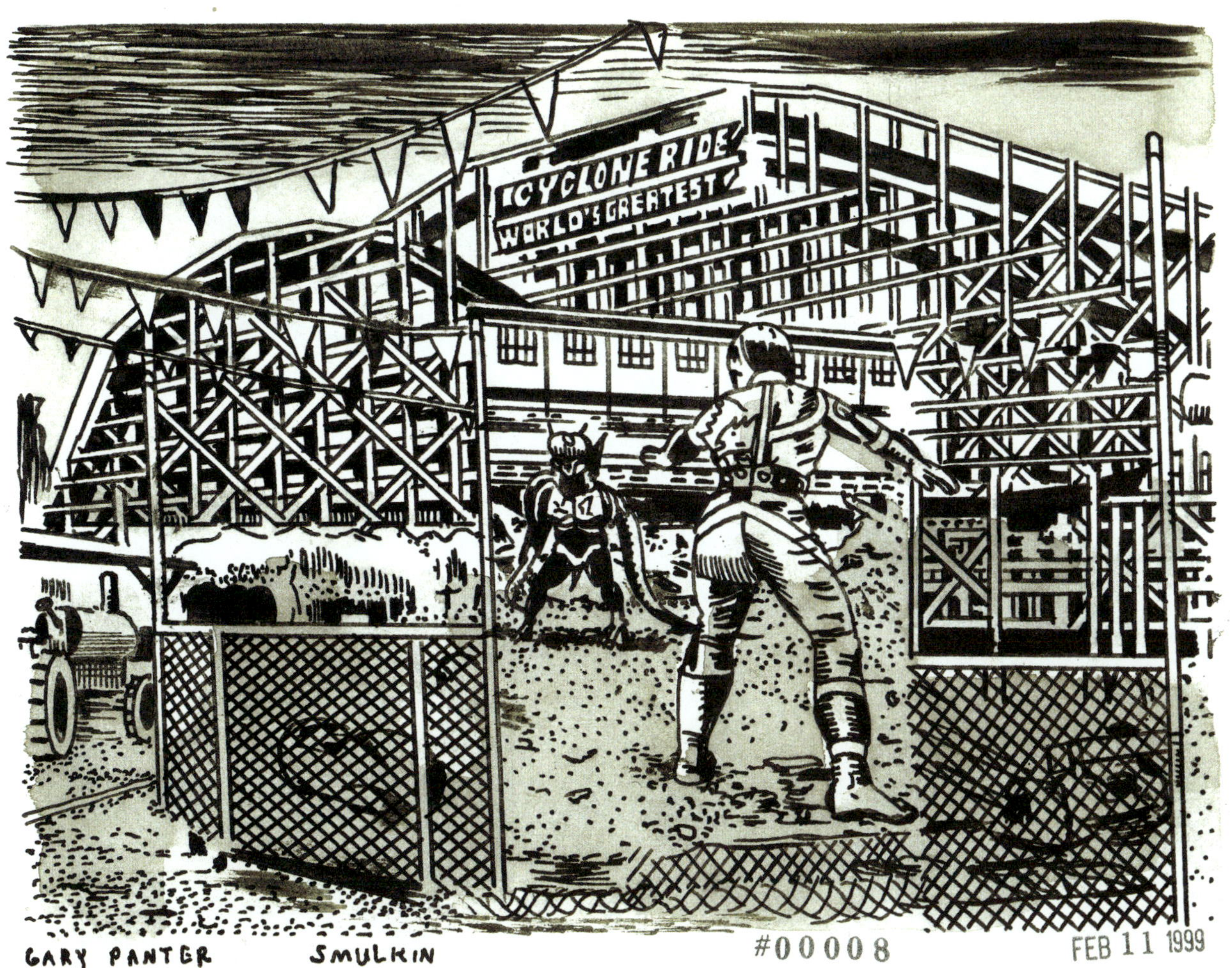
CYCLONE RIDE
WORLD'S GREATEST
GARY PANTER
SMULKIN
#00008
FEB 11 1999

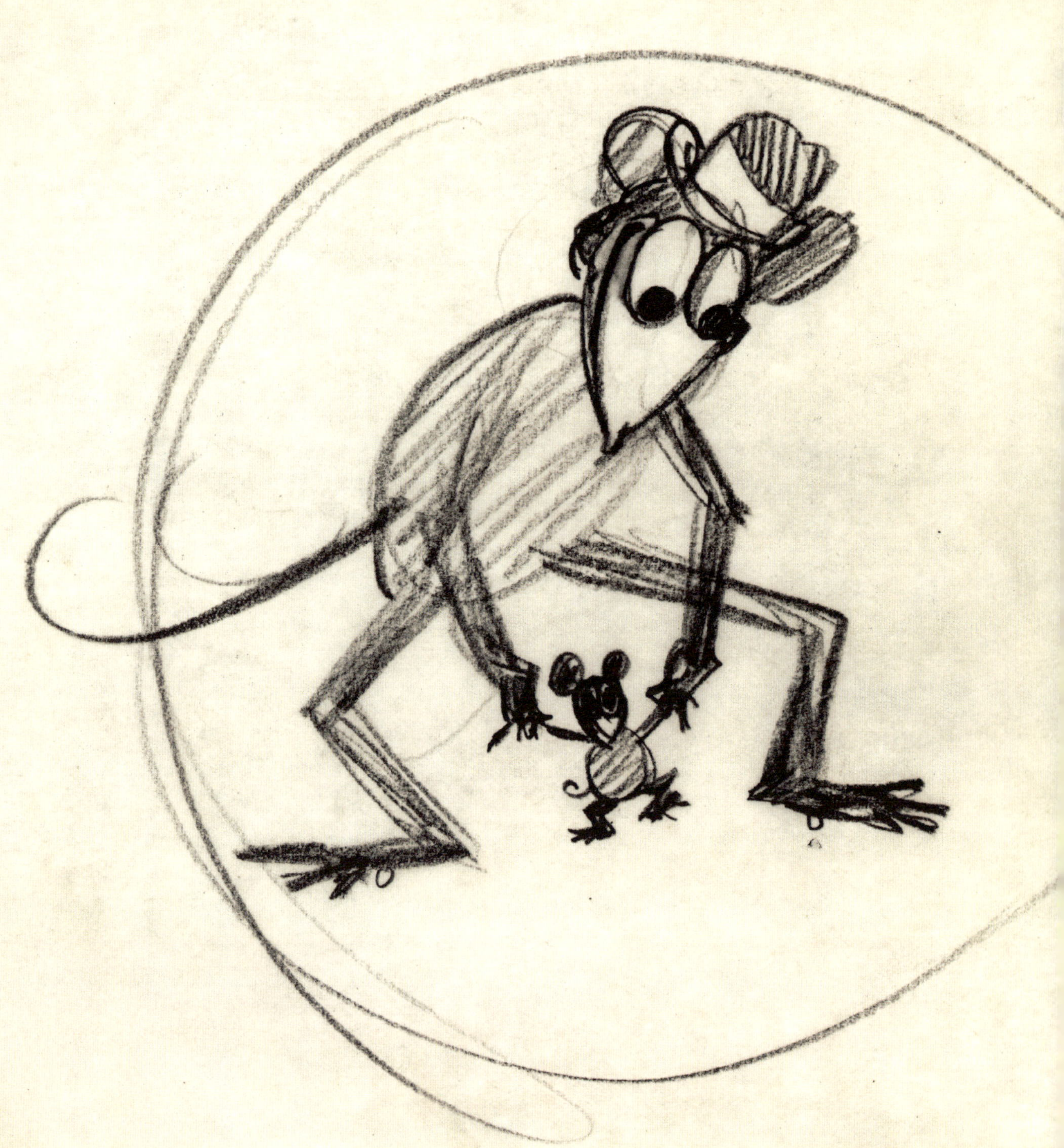

the fastest

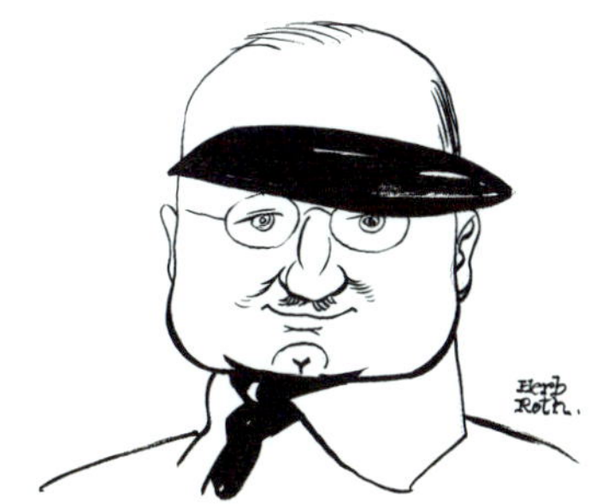

in the business

Mark Newgarden

One morning in 1925, a former newspaper cartoonist named Moser punched a clock, sat hunched at a desk in a dimly lit Manhattan office, and proceeded to produce pictures like these—of cats and mice and dogs and bugs and hills and trees and dinosaurs and derbies. Then maybe more mice. Then maybe lunch. Then maybe a quick something from a flask. Then back to it. He was by then a 10-year veteran of cartoon animation who bore the burden of his employer, Aesop's Fables Pictures, Inc., which had contracted with the theater chain that owned it to release a new animated short every single week that year.

The titles included: *A Transatlantic Flight, Bigger And Better Jails, Fisherman's Luck, Clean Up Week, In Dutch, Jungle Bike Riders, The Pie Man At The Zoo, The Housing Shortage, S.O.S., The Adventures Of Adenoid, Permanent Waves, Deep Stuff, House Cleaning, Darkest Africa, A Fast Worker, Echoes From The Alps, Hot Times In Iceland, The Runt, The End Of The World, The Runaway Balloon, Wine Women And Song, When Men Were Men, Bugville Field Day, Office Help, Over The Plate, A Yarn About Yarn, Bubbles, Soap, For The Love Of A Gal, Window Washers, Barnyard Follies, The Ugly Duckling, Hungry Hounds, Nuts And Squirrels, The Lion And The Monkey, The Hero Wins, Air Cooled, Closer Than A Brother, Wild Cats Of Paris, The Honor System, The Great Open Spaces, More Mice Than Brains, A Day's Outing, The Bonehead Age, The Haunted House, The English Channel Swim,* and *Noah Had His Troubles.*

Frank Moser (1886–1964) was once known as "the fastest in the business," which meant he was also the best. That's the part I like. However, at the same time—according to the histories—there were at least three other animators who were considered, with some validity, to be "the fastest in the business." In New York City and points west, scattered darkened burrows could be found, thick with pencilmen furiously delineating the wiggle of a fish's nose or the teetering of a farmer's heel, reducing already abstract figures into increasingly simpler, faster glyphs like there was no tomorrow. These pencilmen retreated nightly to speakeasies and garrets, vowing to return and beat those results the very next day. Though stationed separately, members of the industry were drawing the same pictures spontaneously—circle, stick, squiggle, lump—endlessly and devotedly crafting the cats and mice and dogs of dreamland. Just like salmon know where to spawn and squirrels know which way is up—like doorknobs, they all worked about the same way. If a few moth-wing–thin pages blew off Frank Moser's desk, went out the window, flapped across town and onto, say, the desk of Bill Nolan (another of "the fastest in the business"), I'd like to think that neither of those men would mind much or hardly even notice. They would both be too busy acting as cartooning machines.

Aesop's Film Fables cartoons (1921–1933) were often cited as "the guys to beat" by Walt Disney and other ambitious

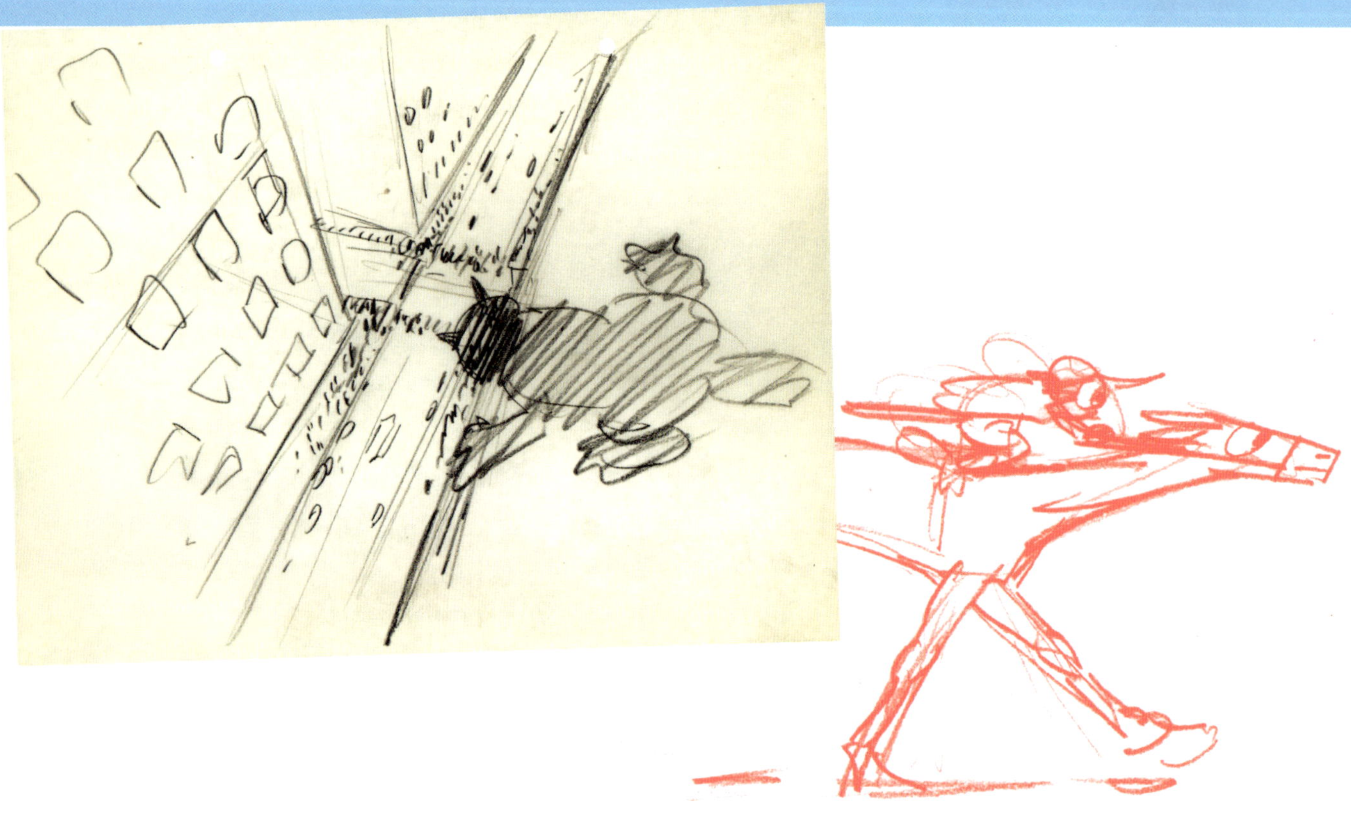

Johnnies-come-lately. But it's a little hard to see why. The films were sausage-cut off a rigid assembly line and executed under such enormous deadline pressure and poverty of attention that the results were absurdly disconnected gestures strung along slim situational threads and enacted by cycling multitudes of inky spastic beasts, and not really a whole lot else, for six minutes, more or less—depending on the speed of the theater projectionist's crank. As an animator of that time and place remarked decades later, "Today [these cartoons] wouldn't mean a damn thing." But they were there, without fail, "like a milk delivery," as Moser's problematic business partner Paul Terry was fond of quipping.

As purely functional design, they were seminal and powerful and they survive in the subliminal picture files of our culture as a sort of lost house style—closer to a working picture language than perhaps anybody realized. To discern an individual hand in the lines of a cat or mouse of this period would be the work of a detective, graphologist, or psychic. Liberated from individuality and originality and self-expression—and even coherent thought—what remained for these animation artists were speed and efficiency and the sheer pleasure of performance. The real skill of "the fastest in the business" was akin to that of a long-distance athlete or a marathon dancer. And so the sweetest fruit of Moser's effort never quite translated to the screen, where even seemingly casual details are, necessarily, highly deliberate effects. That "moment caught in time" quality evinced by drawings like his vaporized on contact with the next station on the factory line.

Moser, who entered the business in its infancy by way of the Thomas Edison Studio, left Aesop's Fables Pictures, Inc., in 1929 and created his own studio with Paul Terry. Within a decade "the fastest in the business" was out of the business entirely and suing his somewhat faster partner and associates for conspiracy and fraud. By 1955, when Terry sold the business to CBS for a cool 3.5 million, Moser's animation had flooded the TV airwaves for years—without any mention of his name. So he went on to paint landscapes of the Hudson River Valley and lived to be 78.

Still, the secret beauty that "the fastest in the business" created can be savored in these fragile souvenirs, these isolated pencil sketches that quantify the hundred-millimeter dash for the tip of a mouse's tail, or the staggered graphite broad jump onto the next donkey ear or wedding ring. These drawings seem to exist as effortlessly as breathing, and ultimately, each is as valuable as a single breath. They have as much meaning as any page pulled from a hard worker's desk mid-task. They are just as concerned with the ticking clock and the bottom line, but maybe just a little more free. Take a look, drink them in, and then admit you'd like to have tried to outrun him yourself.

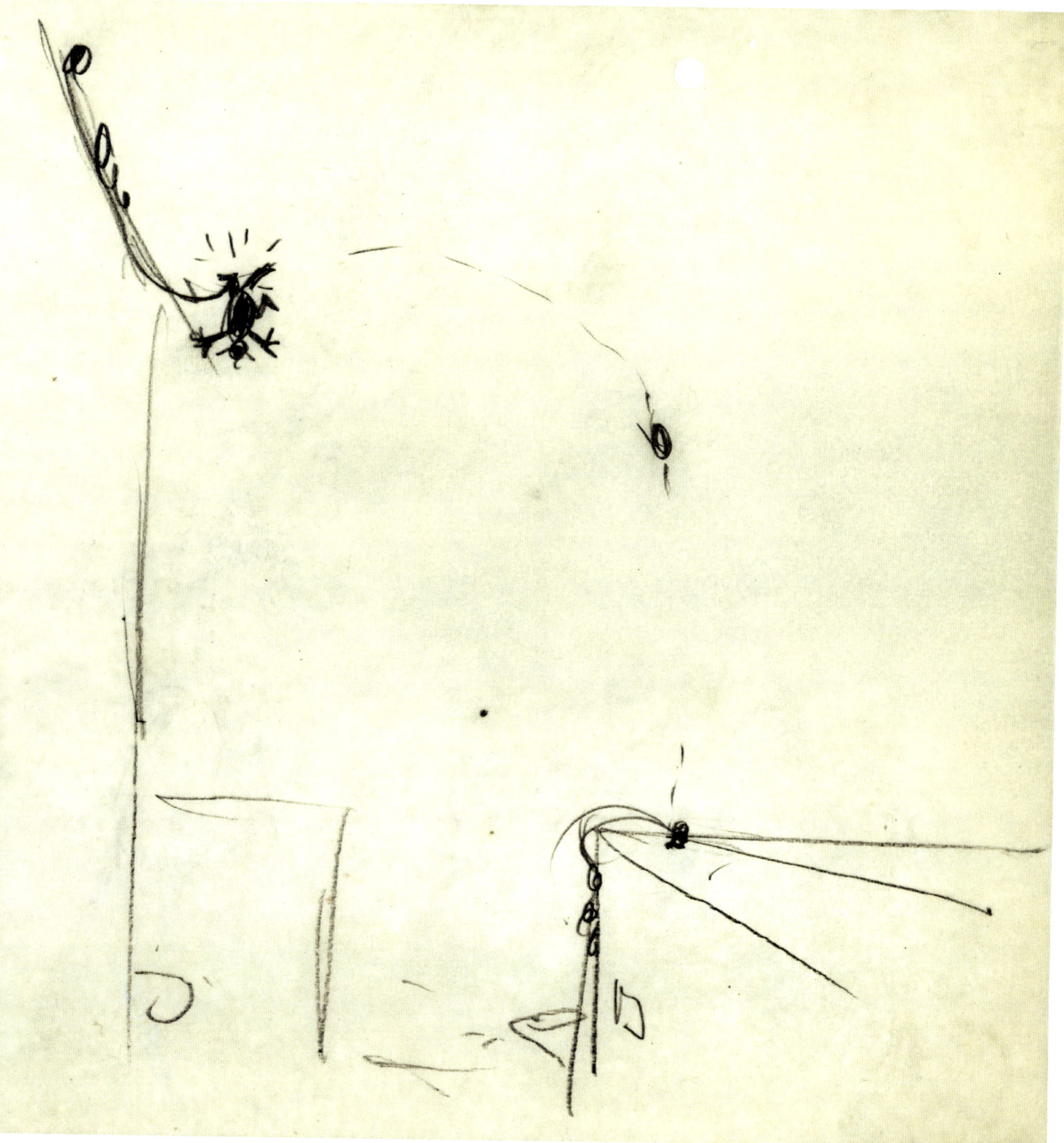

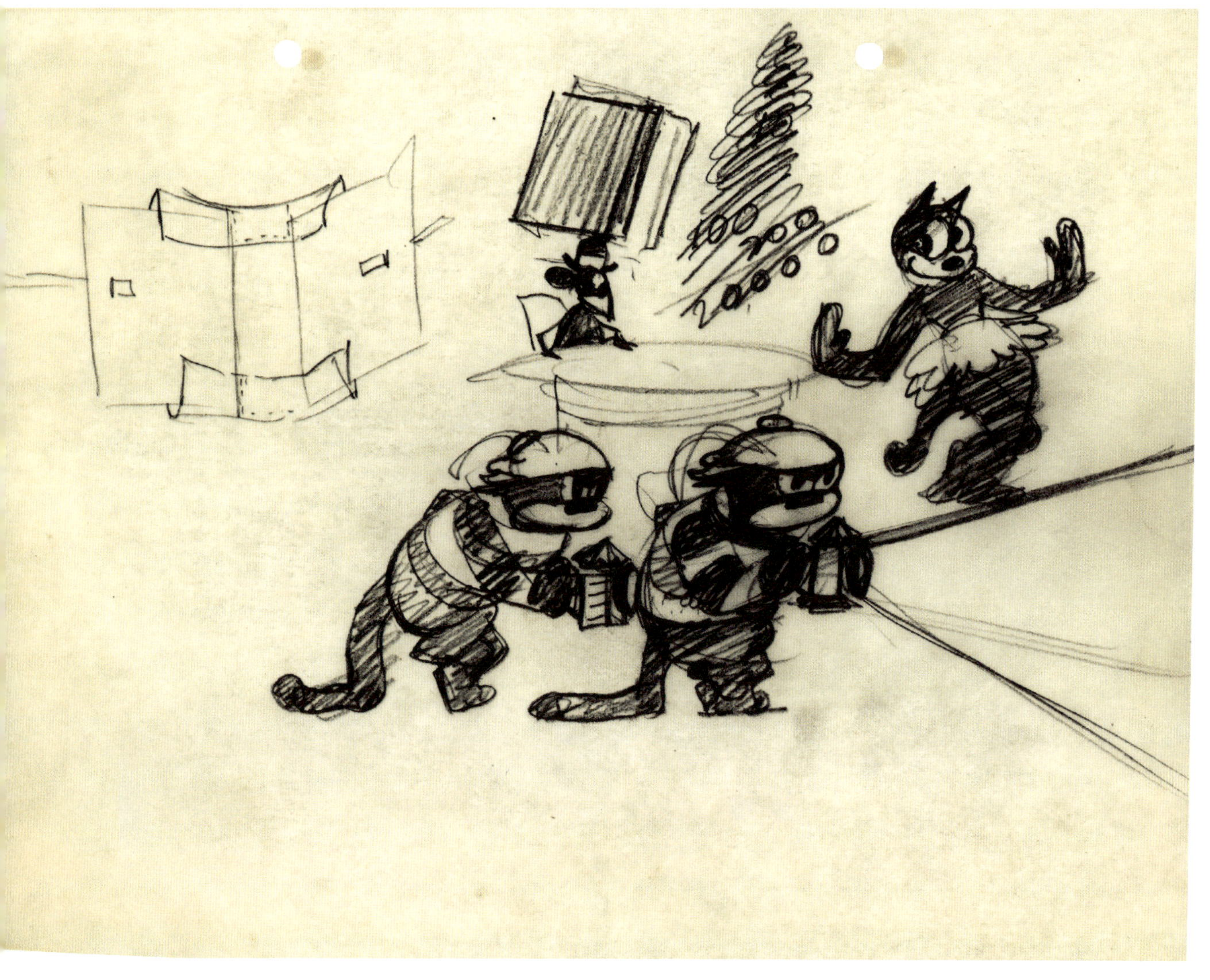

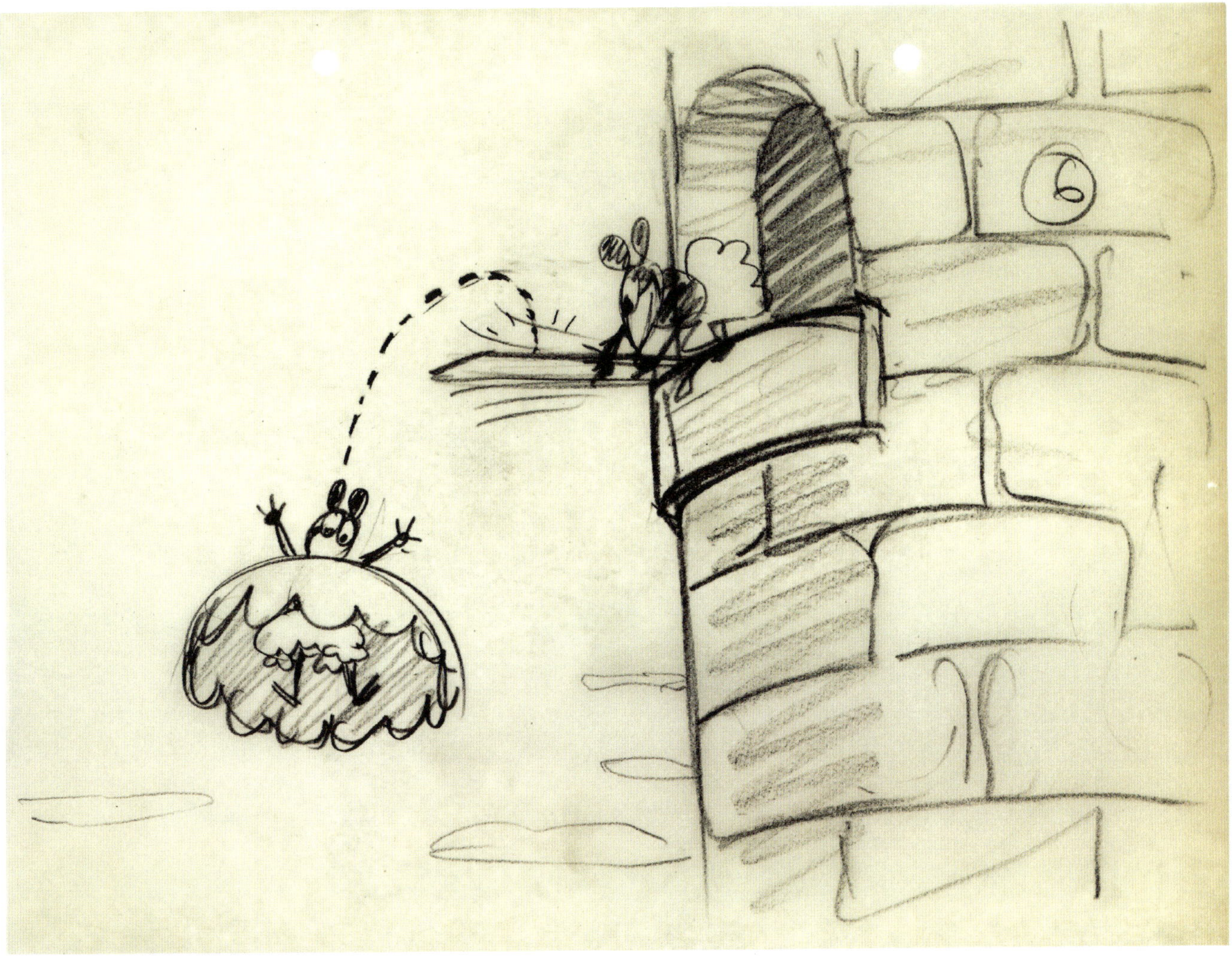

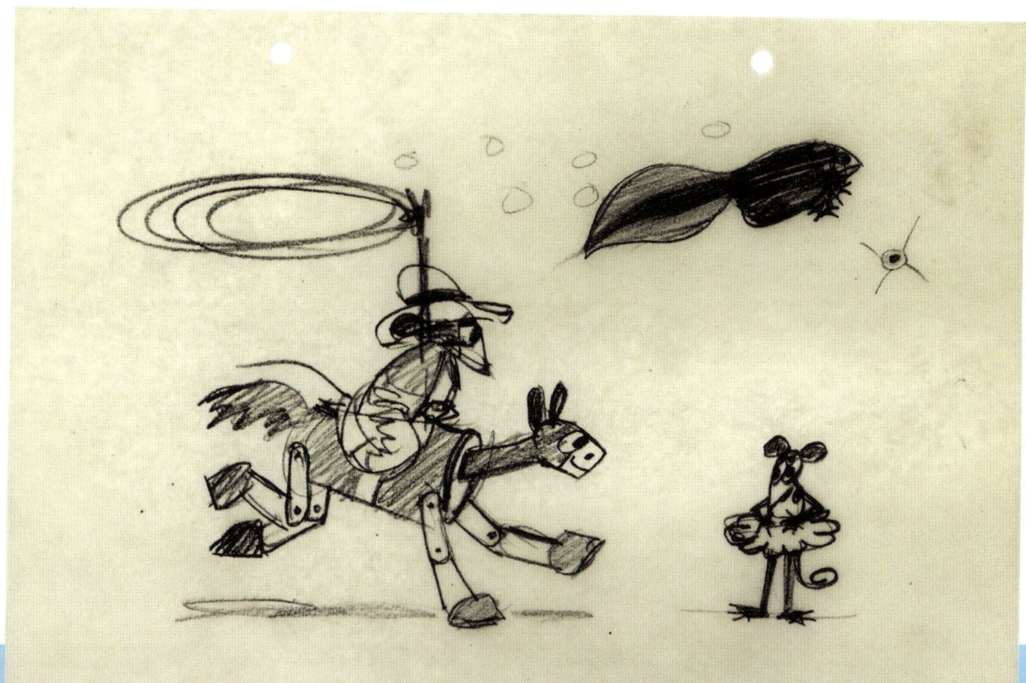

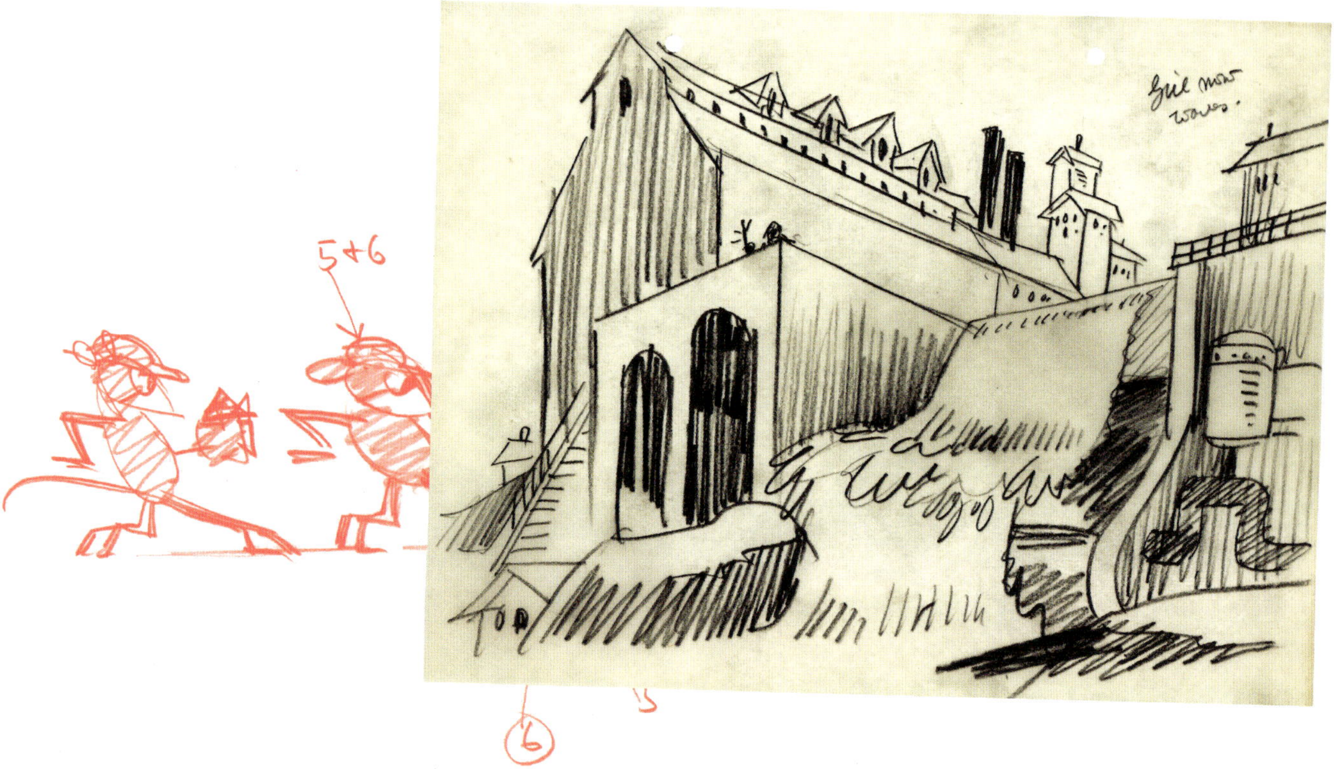

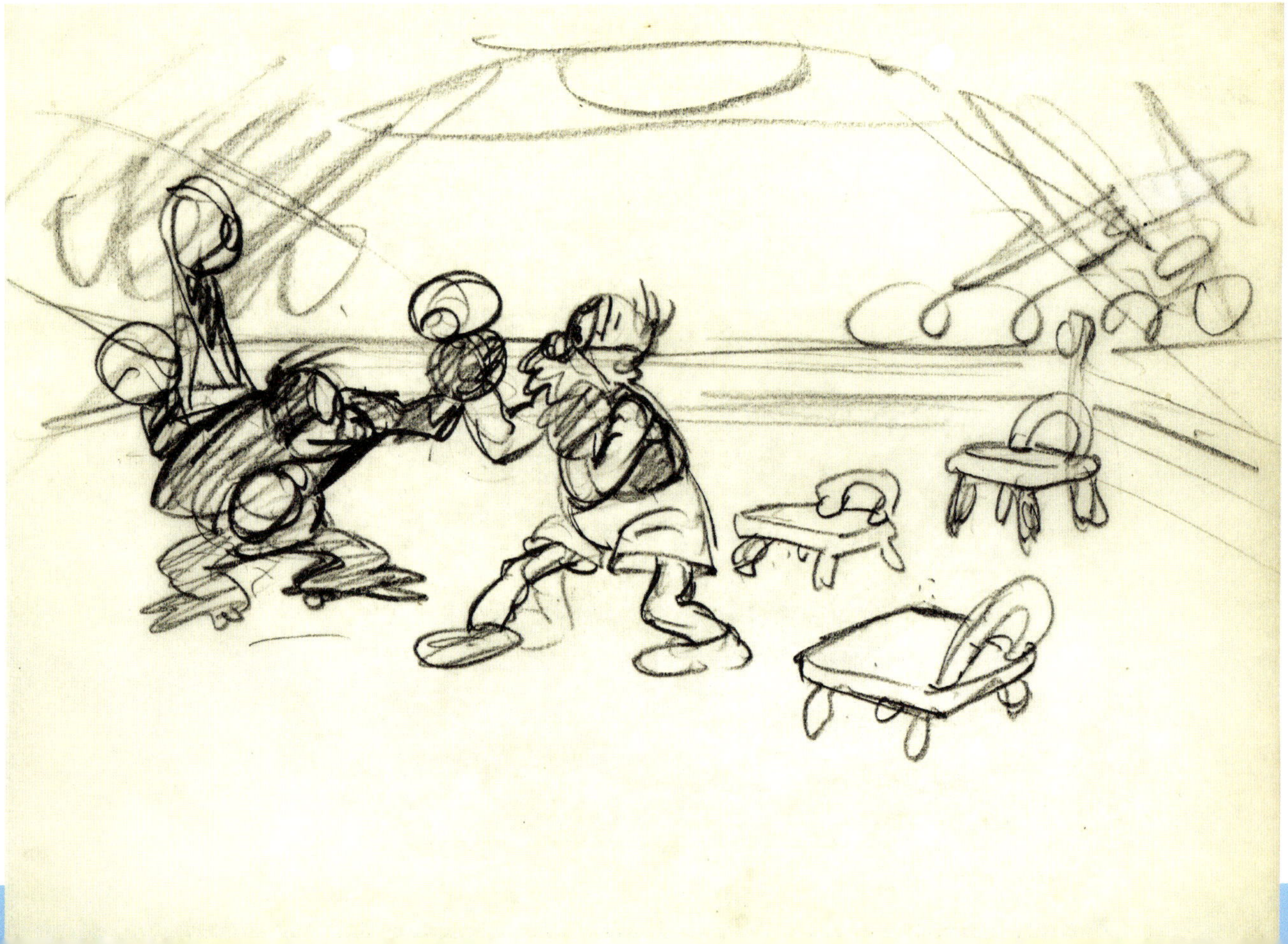

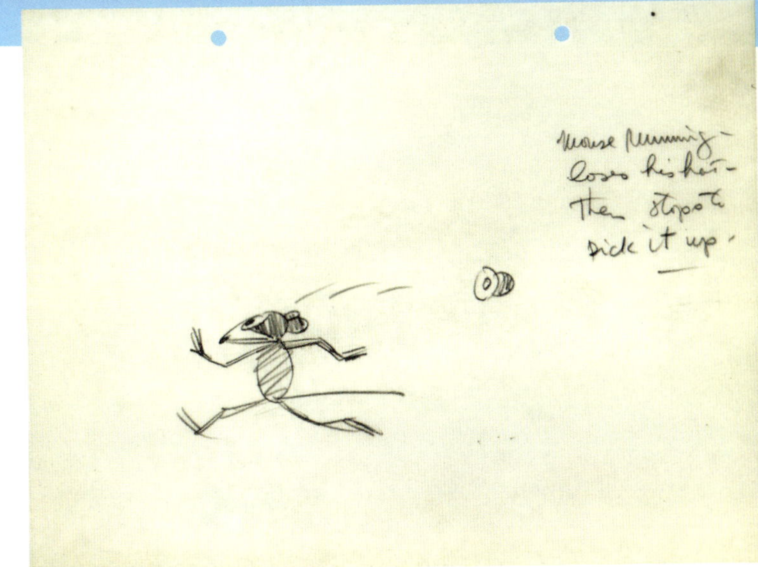

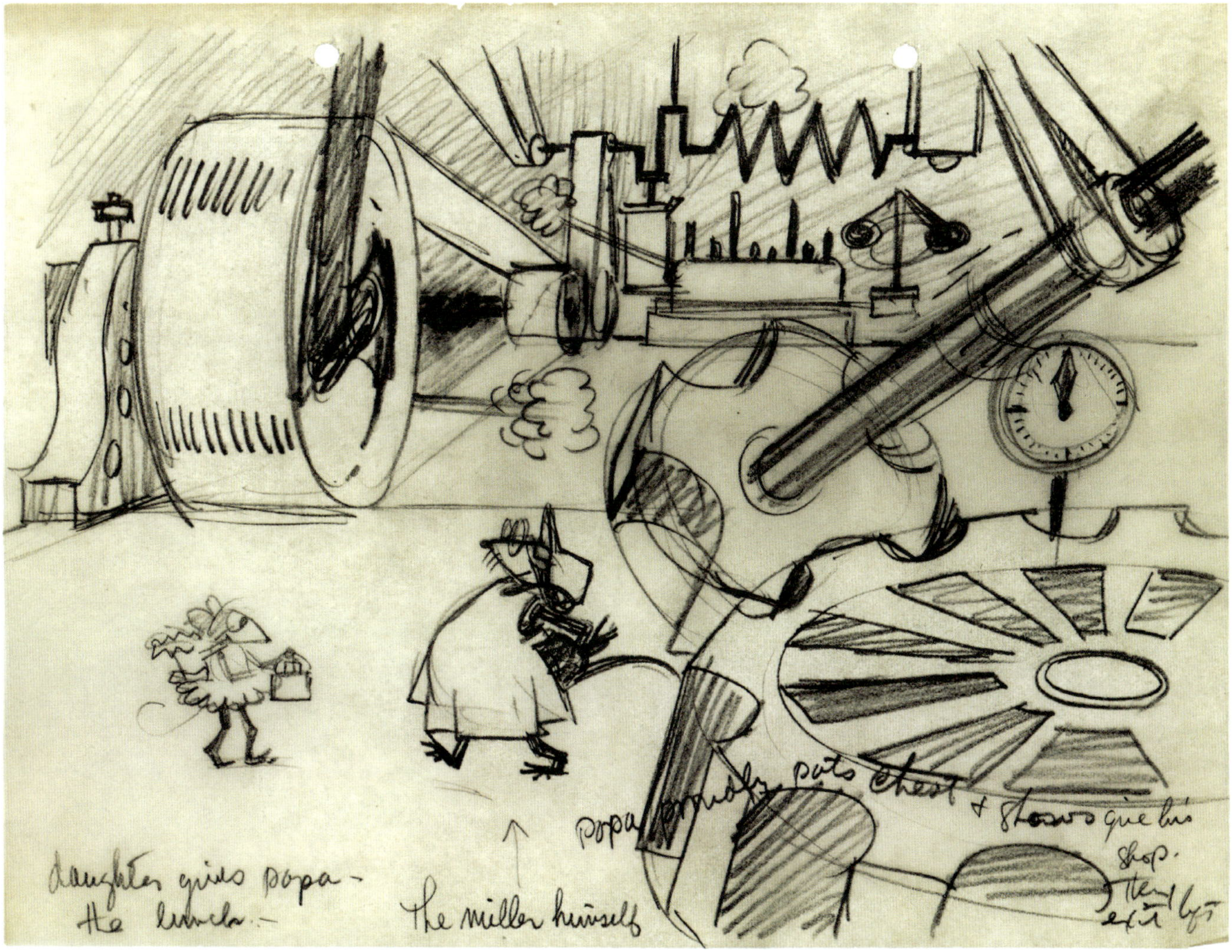

daughter gives popa -
the lunch.-

The miller himself

popa proudly pats chest + shows [illegible] his shop. Then exit [illegible]

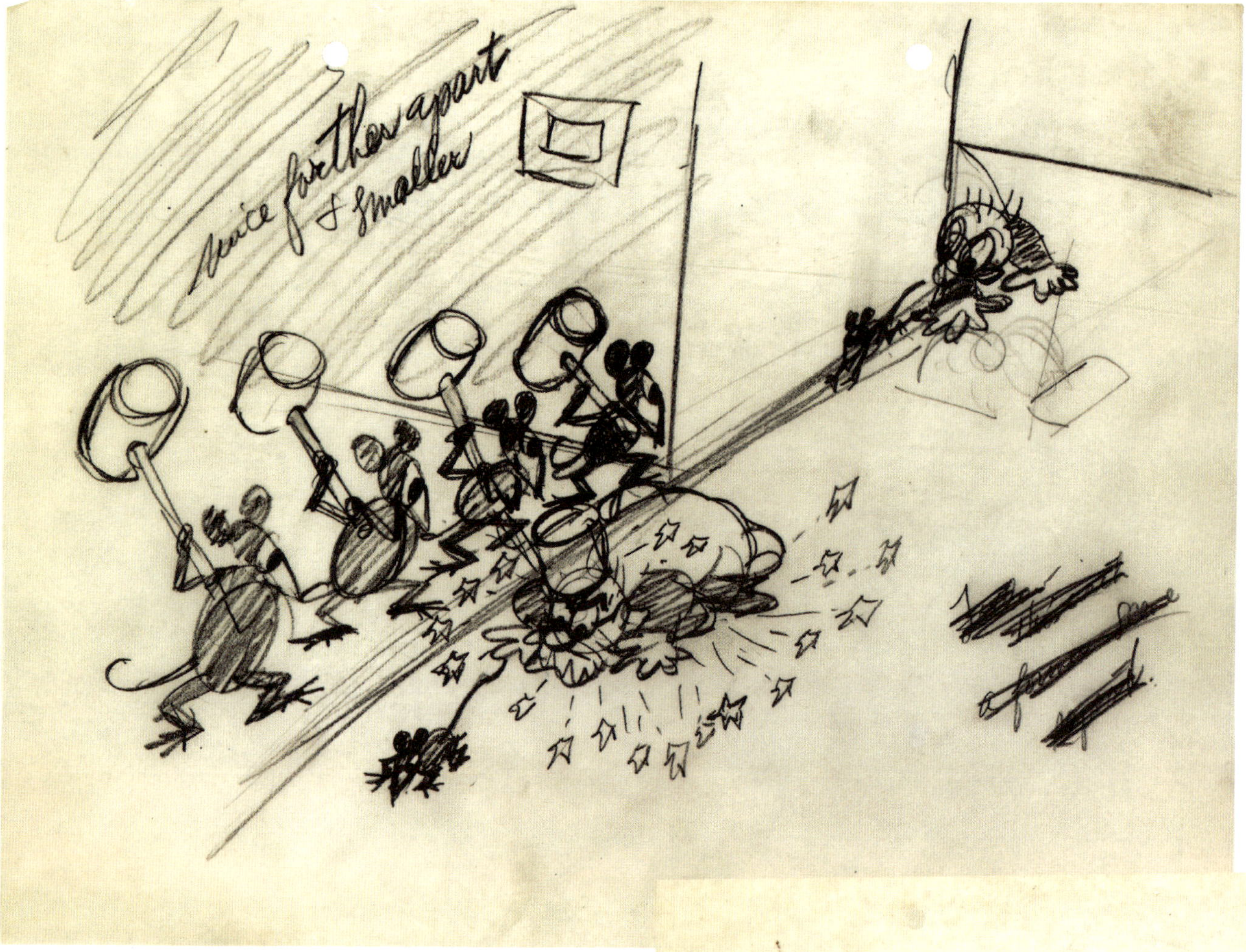

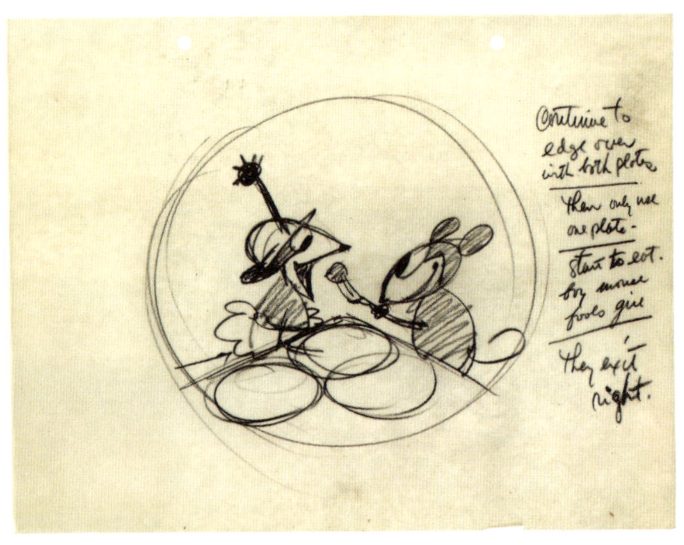
Continue to edge over with both plates
Then only use one plate -
Start to eat. Boy mouse fools girl
They exit right.

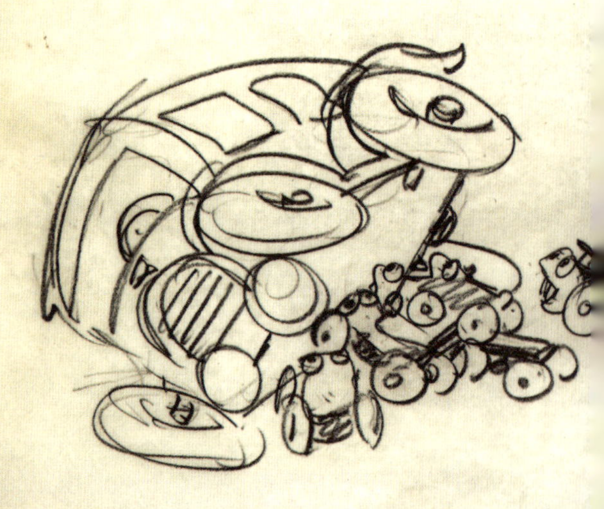

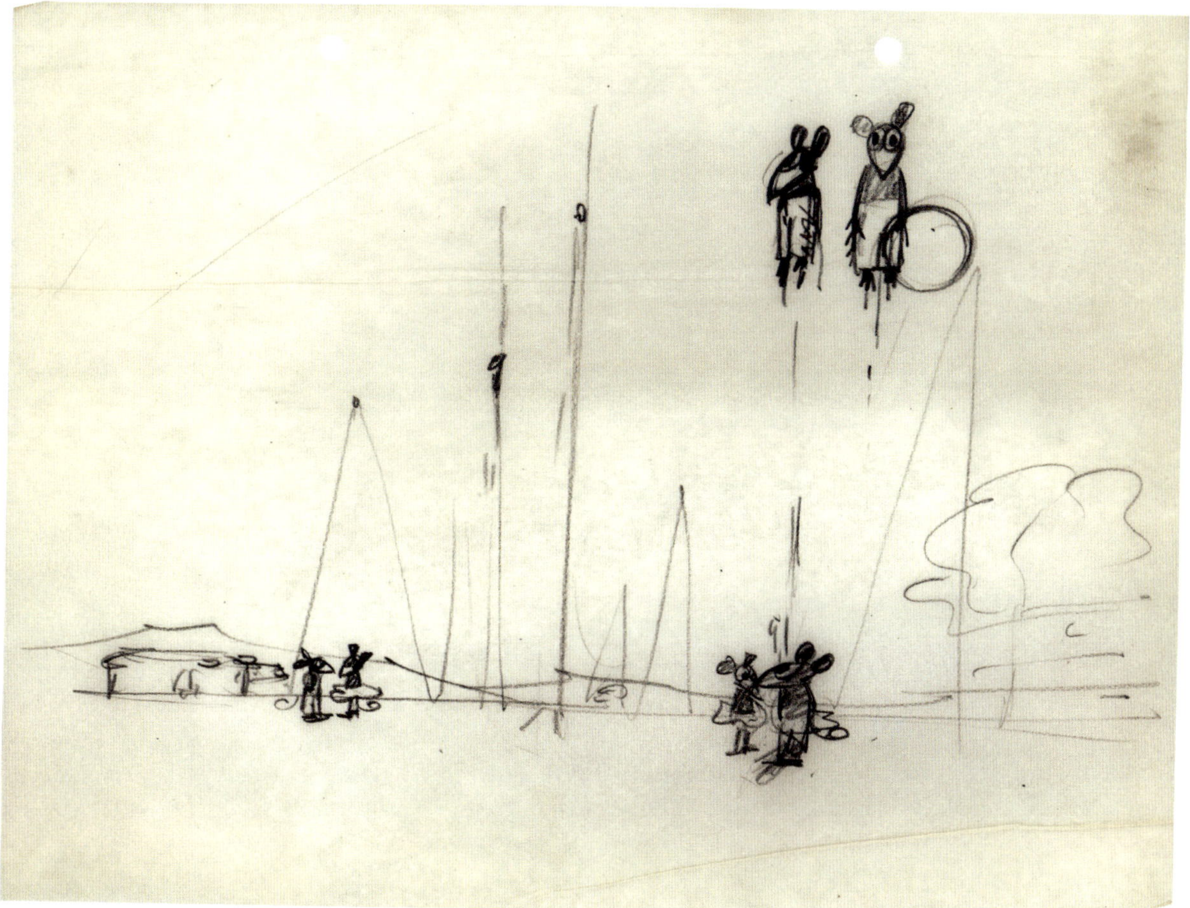

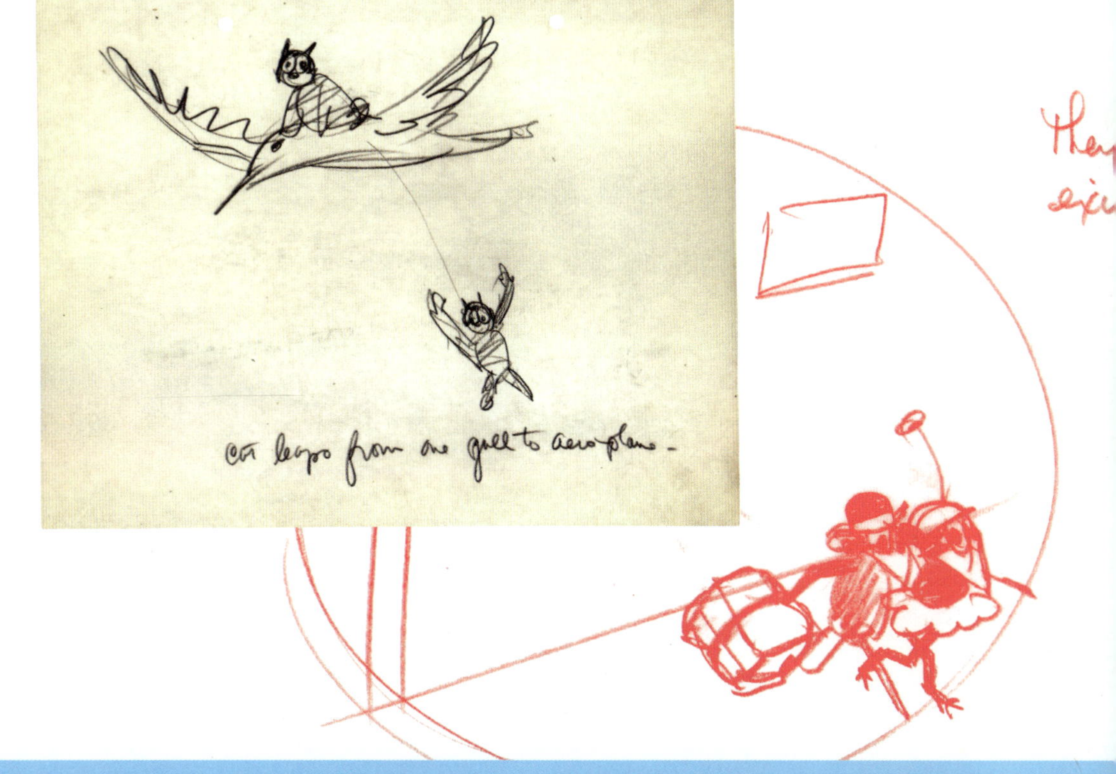
cat leaps from one gull to aeroplane -

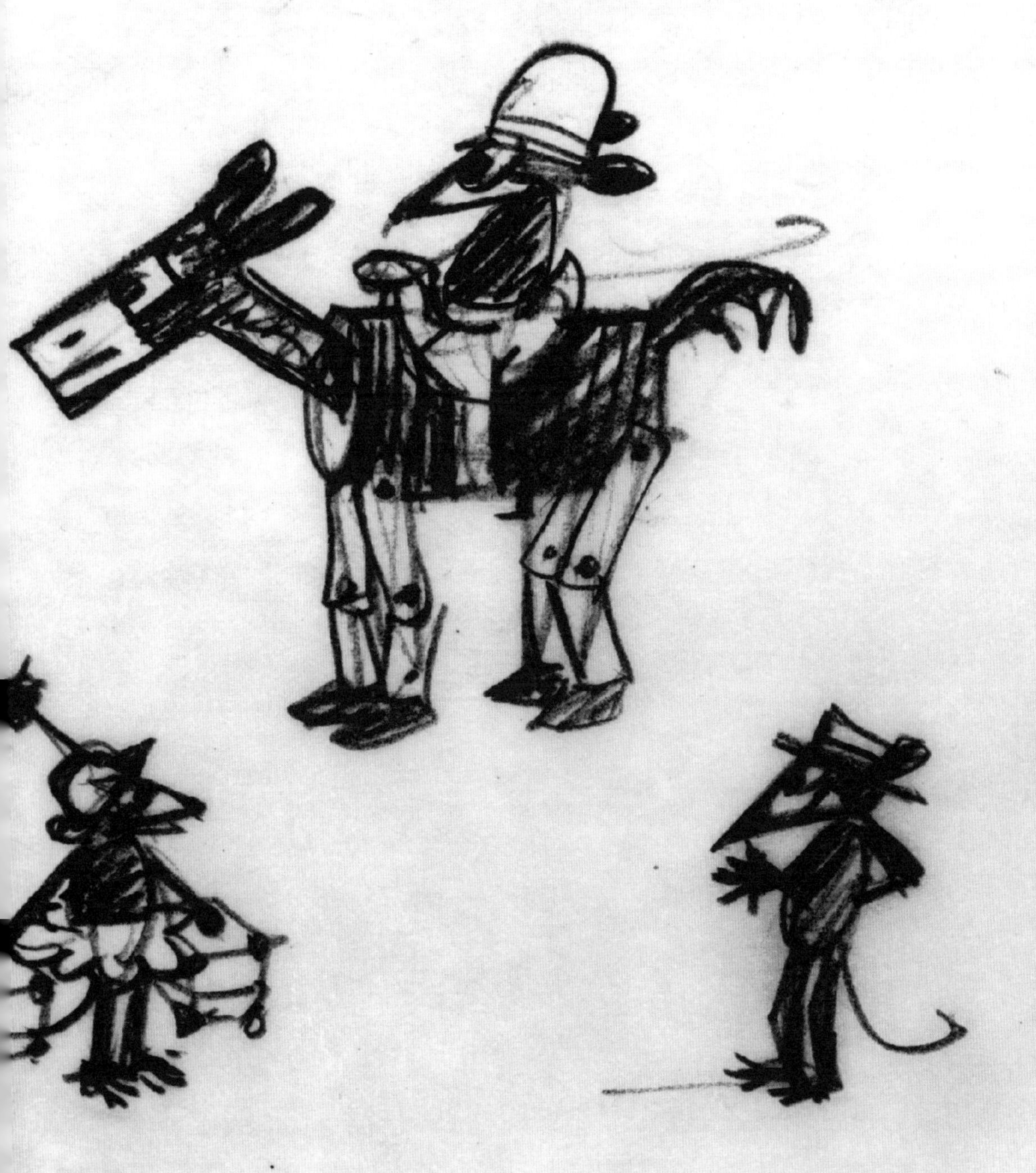

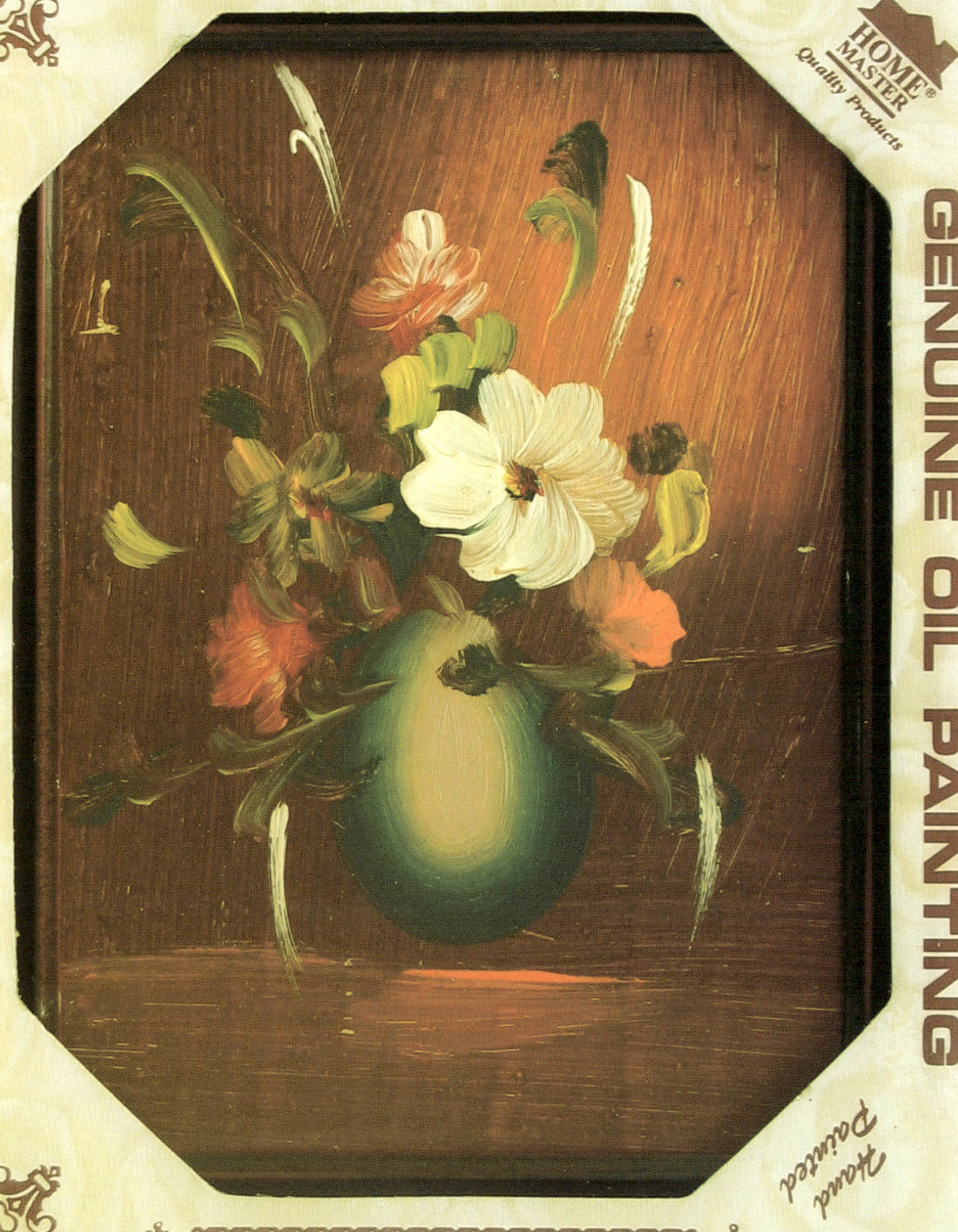
GENUINE OIL PAINTING
HOME MASTER®
Quality Products
GENUINE OIL PAINTING
Hand Painted

99-Cent Store Paintings

Phil Patton

Dollar stores or 99-cent stores—with names like Dollar Dreams, Everything 99 Cents, and Dollar Tree—are the successors to the five-and-dimes of the past—the Woolworth's, Roses, Kresges, and Kresses that were once the linchpin of American retailing. Dollar stores are fascinating. They reward browsing. You never know what you will find. They can be seen as 3-D catalogs of all the stuff people don't need yet think they do. They are studded with oddities—mother-of-pearl–finish plastic toy helicopters; pastel mod and modern salt- and peppershakers; toilet and pastry brushes; gilt-framed mirrors.

But what most caught my eye were the oil paintings. They sat in bins—small framed oil paintings, packaged in slip-in cardboard frames bearing the words "Genuine oil painting," "hand painted," "Made in China," and a barcode. I wondered: How were they made? On assembly lines? In homes? In factories? Production of shoes or toys in China, we've heard, is unsavory—with low wages and long hours. Still, looking at these paintings, it is hard not to see some pleasure in their making. There is energy in the brush strokes. They don't seem a strictly rote collective work.

Careful consideration of the total production could reveal to a connoisseur patterns of authorship. Was there an assembly line? A person applying red sitting beside one applying blue and so on? A background expert stationed beside a flower specialist? Who do we imagine painted them? One could impute a single hand, perhaps—a notional "master of the discount bin." But looking at my favorites, I saw a woman, maybe at home, in a Silas Marner–style setup—watching children while she worked. How hard was it to keep painting the same painting over and over again? Was the run limited to a few hours, a few days? Did some patterns sell better than others? Was there market feedback? Sitting there at the dull, repetitive work, did the painter make a game of trying to get each painting perfect, or instead set a record for completing it fastest? Did she or he concentrate, now on the peach, now on the grapes—a frustrating game given the pressures of time? Are these painters paid by the piece or by the hour? Some of the paintings had inspirations in recognizable masterpieces. There were Van Gogh hillsides, for instance—loosely interpreted—with varying numbers of haystacks. Had a model been held up and the painting recreated from memory?

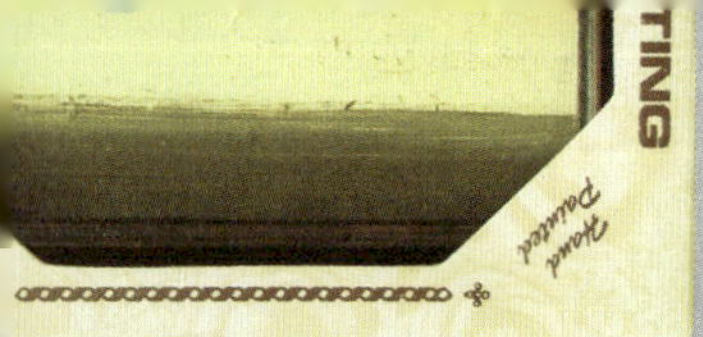
Hand Painted
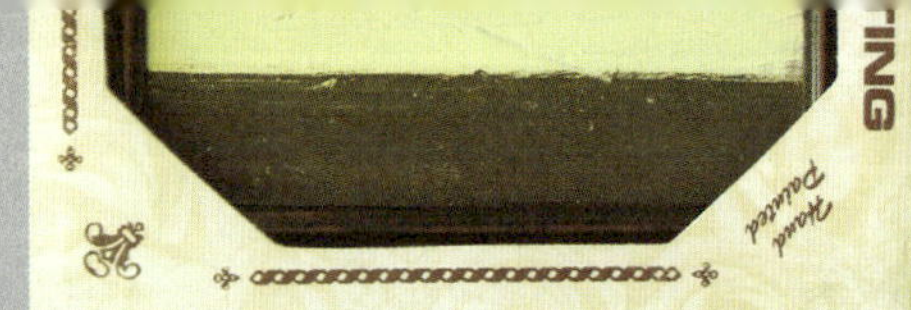
Hand Painted
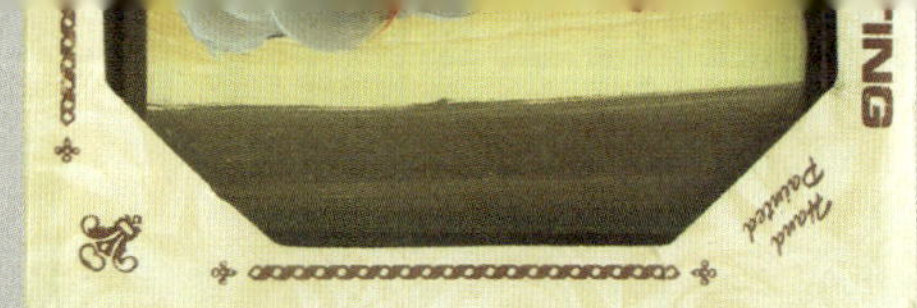
Hand Painted
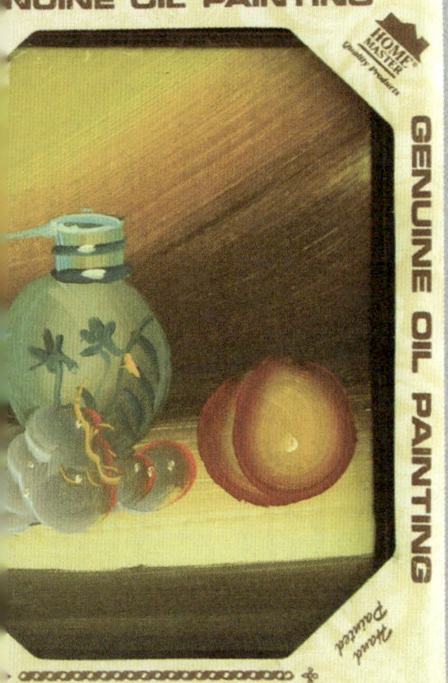
GENUINE OIL PAINTING
HOME MASTER
Quality Products
Hand Painted
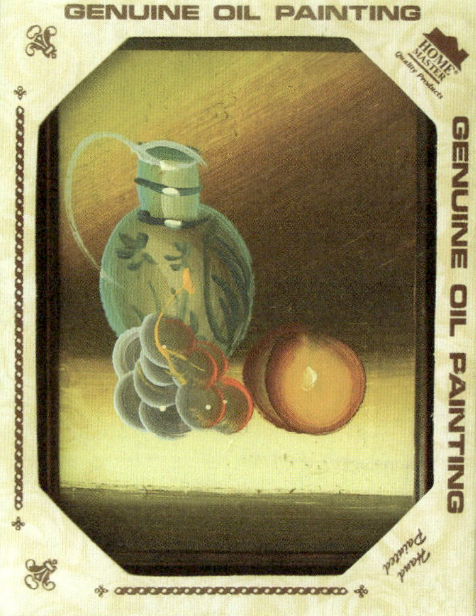
GENUINE OIL PAINTING
HOME MASTER
Quality Products
GENUINE OIL PAINTING
Hand Painted
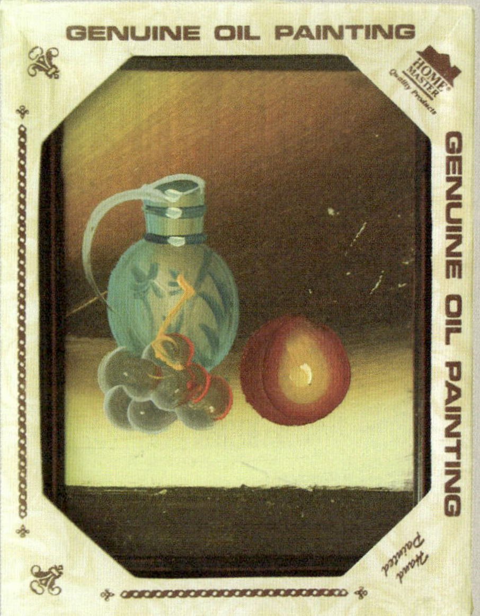
GENUINE OIL PAINTING
HOME MASTER
Quality Products
GENUINE OIL PAINTING
Hand Painted
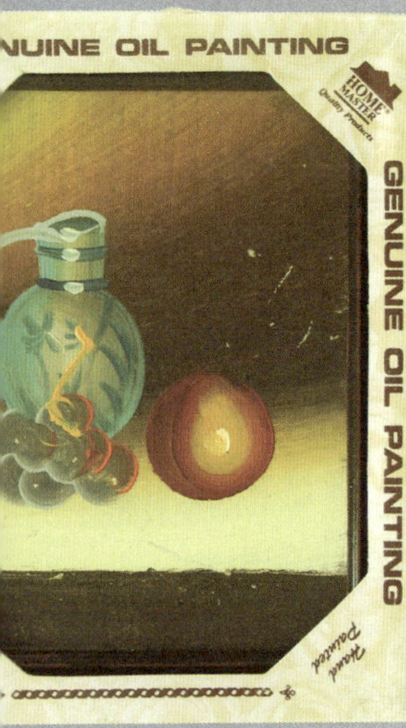
GENUINE OIL PAINTING
HOME MASTER
Quality Products
Hand Painted
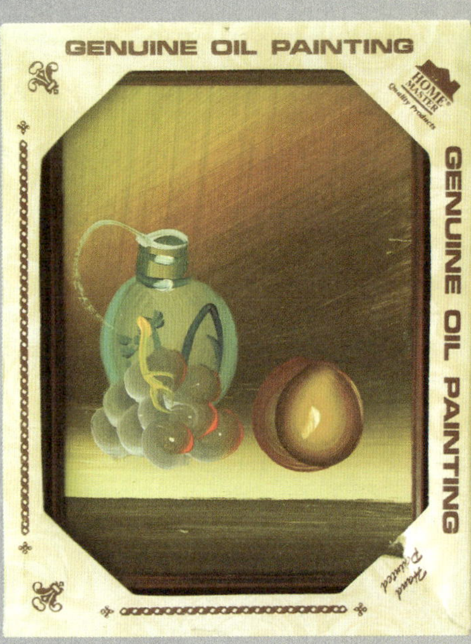
GENUINE OIL PAINTING
HOME MASTER
Quality Products
GENUINE OIL PAINTING
Hand Painted
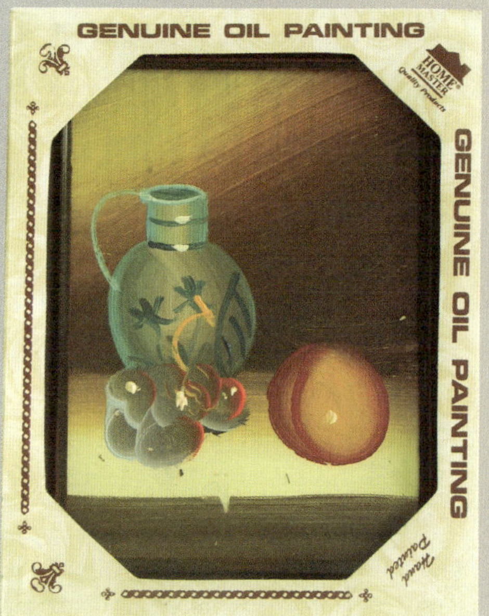
GENUINE OIL PAINTING
HOME MASTER
Quality Products
GENUINE OIL PAINTING
Hand Painted
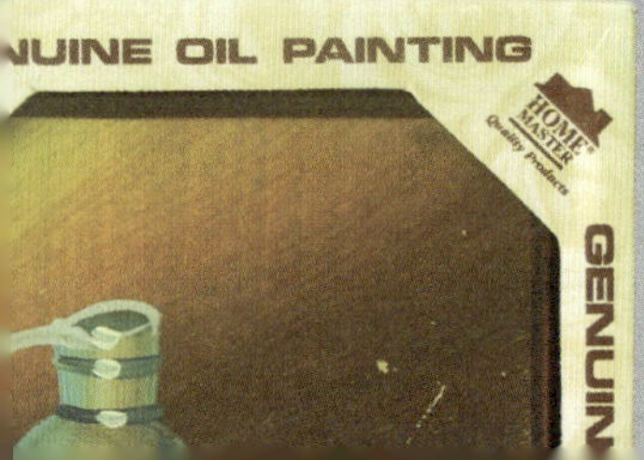
HOME MASTER
Quality Products
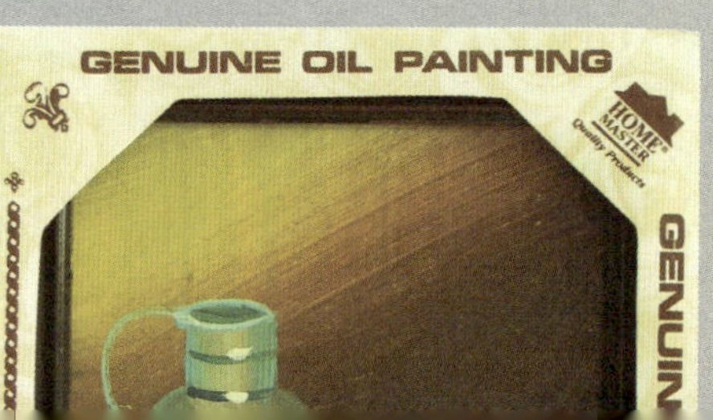
GENUINE OIL PAINTING
HOME MASTER
Quality Products
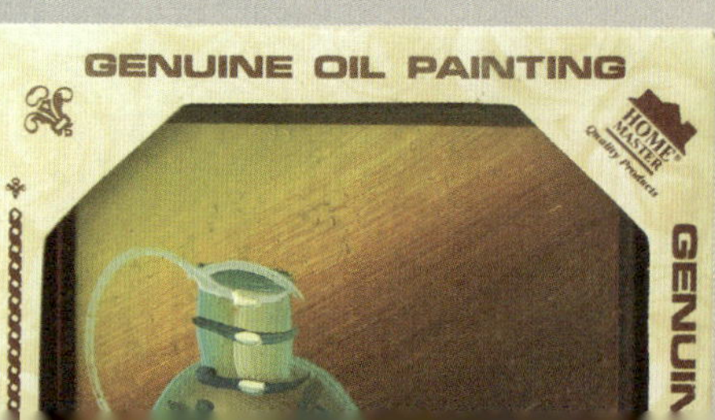
GENUINE OIL PAINTING
HOME MASTER
Quality Products

Objects made on the assembly line are supposed to be identical—each perfect in the same way. But can my imagined painter dream of creating one "perfect" painting on her assembly line? Part of the appeal of her painting is freshness—like that of untrained artist Henri Rousseau. But these dollar-store hands are not wholly untaught. Their style is naïve—shades of Rousseau or Howard Finster—mixed with gimmicks of technique, like those taught by TV oil-painting instructors—such as painting a wave by brush-blending one color into another. The painter behind these works, I imagine, might have absorbed some of the steady calm of Bob Ross—as has, perhaps, his audience. And yet how much craft do American television viewers demand when they buy art themselves? Art and mass production seem opposed, of course, but do patrons of—for example—the flourishing Thomas Kinkade empire recognize that Kinkade's assistants are the real painters? Do they accept the work of these assistants as if they were members of Rubens's atelier laying on acres of flesh for him?

The paintings often show up in the dollar store in groups of multiple variations on a single theme or scene. My favorite is a still-life series: a gray-blue jug; a peach; and a bunch of grapes—each upon an abstract surface in front of an abstract wall. They attracted not so much individually, but collectively. I would never have bought one—but I did buy many. What I loved about them were the variations. There are, of course, many art works built on the idea of the multiple—from Warhol's soup cans to Ed Ruscha's gas stations. There is also collecting, in which the variants of multiples are more important than the individual works. As a child, I collected stamps, with their series and variant systems, and later such items as coffee lids, air fresheners, and antenna balls. In such categories, the thing collected is almost pretext—the system is the key. Individual pieces might be nearly worthless—financially—and without interest—aesthetically. It is only in groups that they fascinate. At least for this collector, the play of change across type is what attracts.

In choosing from among the bins at the dollar stores I was making the same sort of choices I would if buying paintings at Castelli or Christie's. You could hang dollar-store paintings on the wall of a gallery and become, well, not just collector, but connoisseur or curator. Could you even become an artist, the paintings your materials, your readymades? The paintings aspire to the identical nature of the reproducible, but they never achieve it. The assembly line produces identical products that can be sold at identical prices; the artist produces unique products that can be sold at unique prices. The worker/painter constantly striving to produce the perfect painting is of course always failing, because there is no perfect painting. That failure is also the measure of humanity; and it may be why the dollar-store paintings appeal.

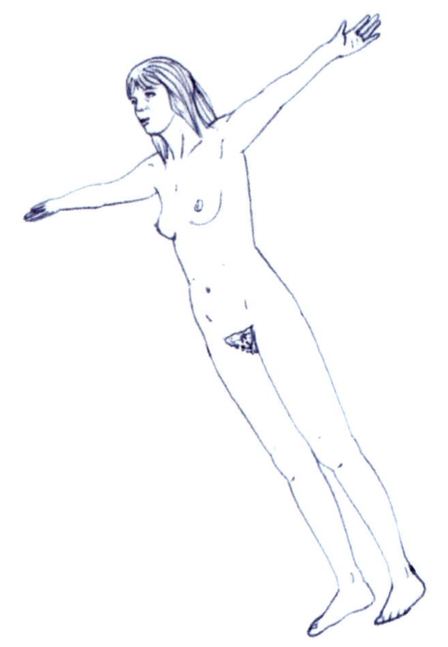
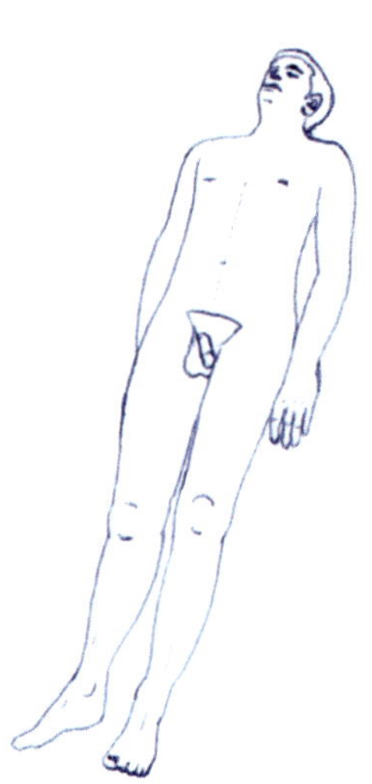
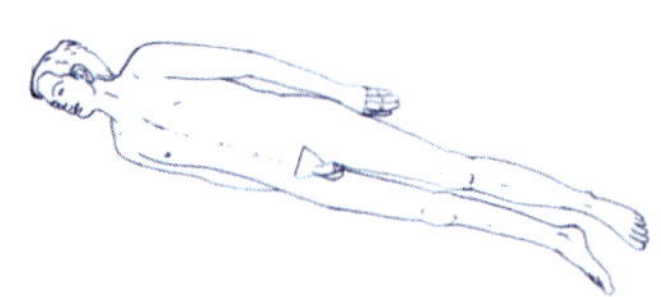
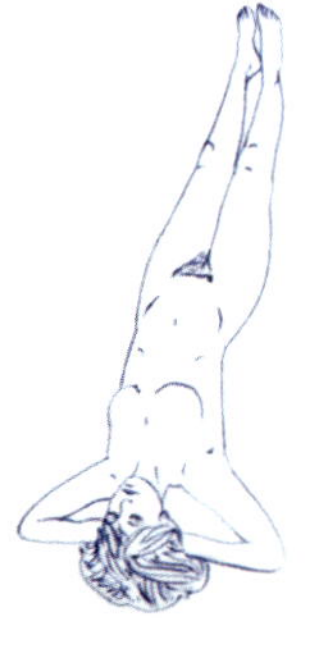

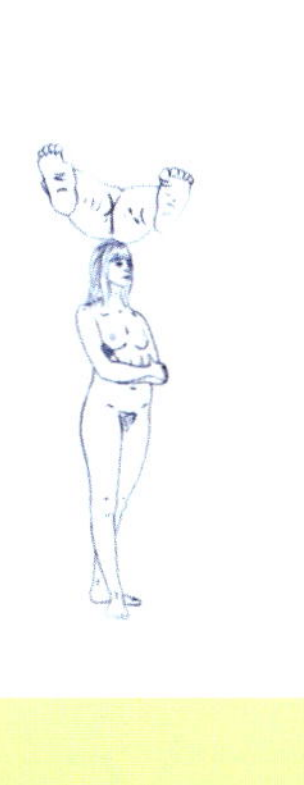
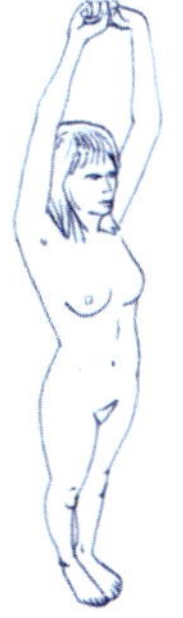
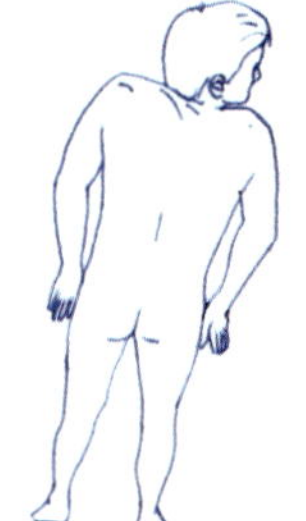
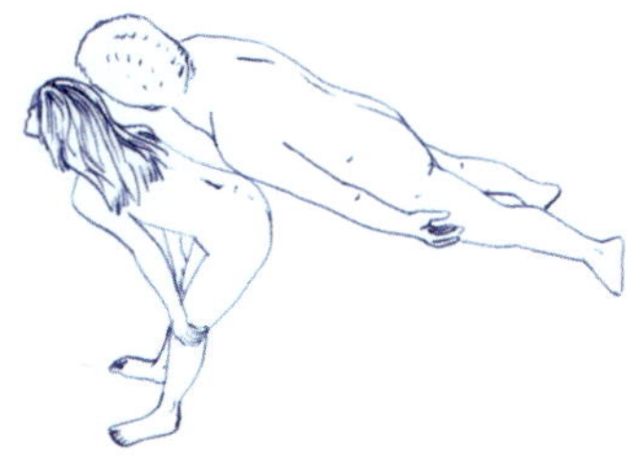

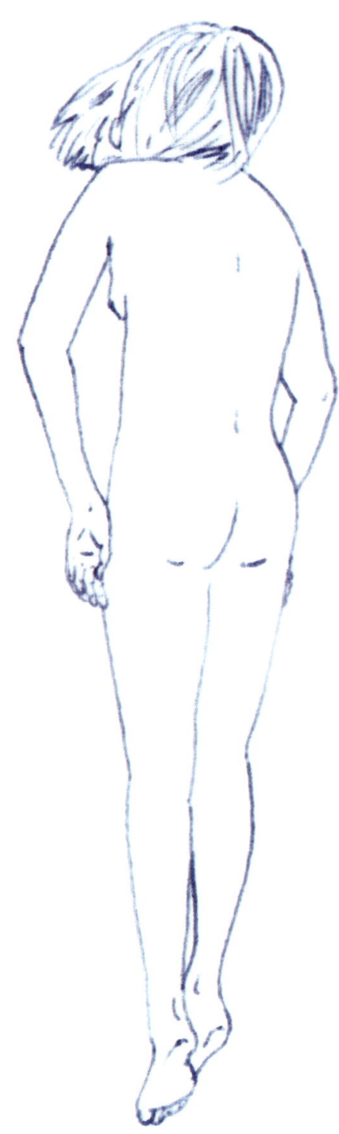

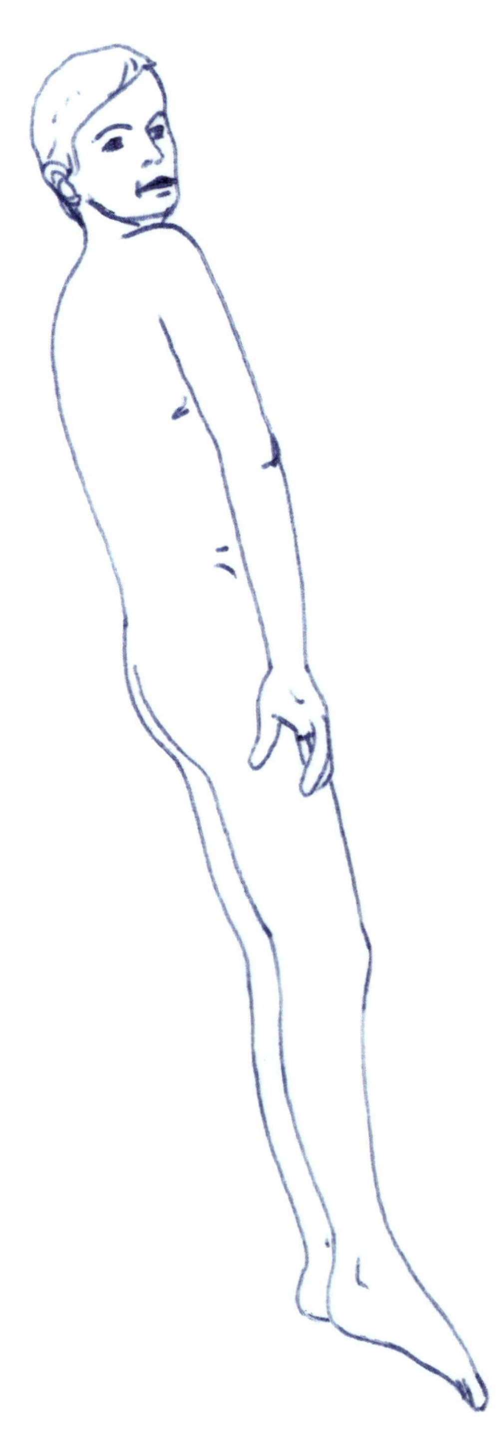

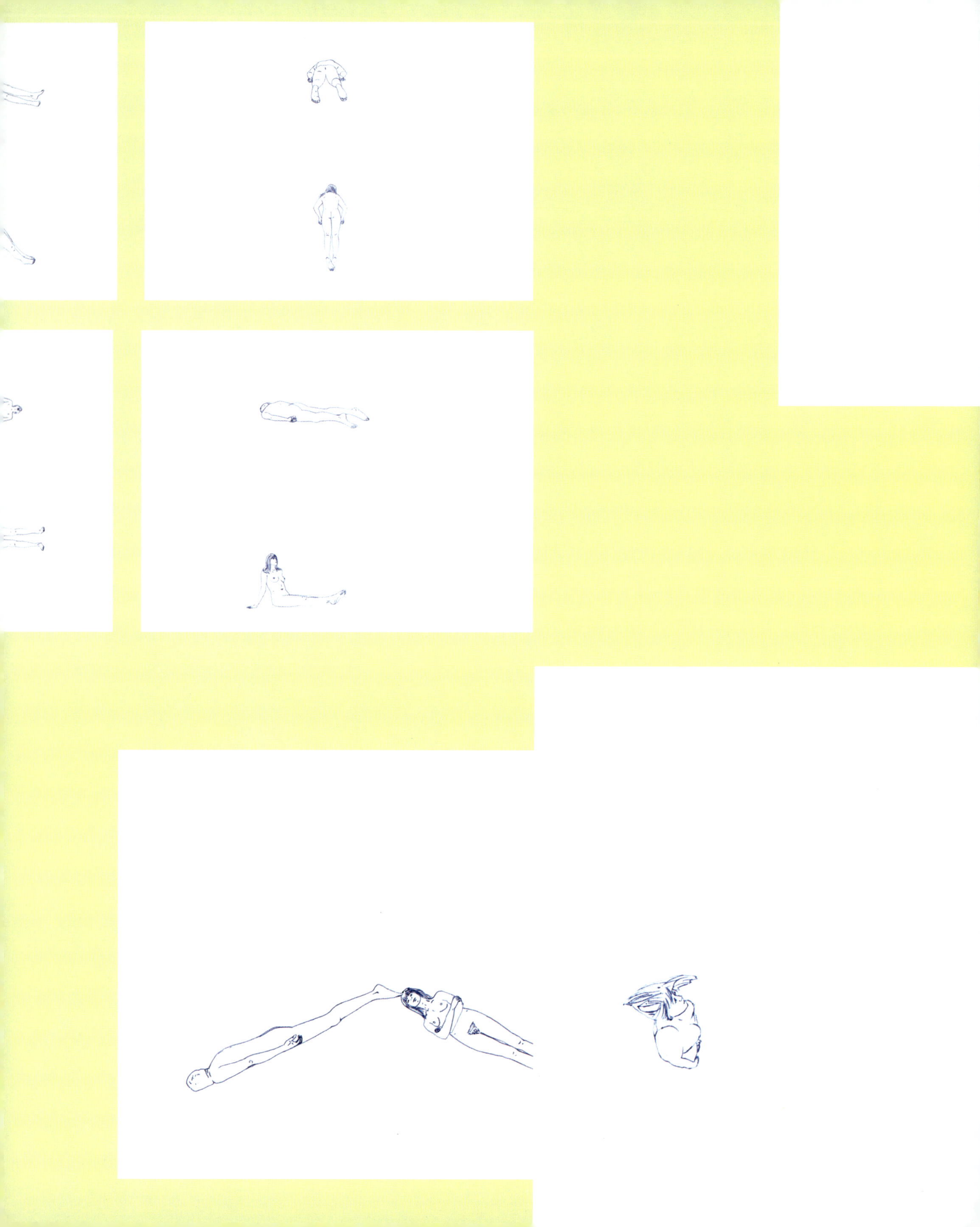

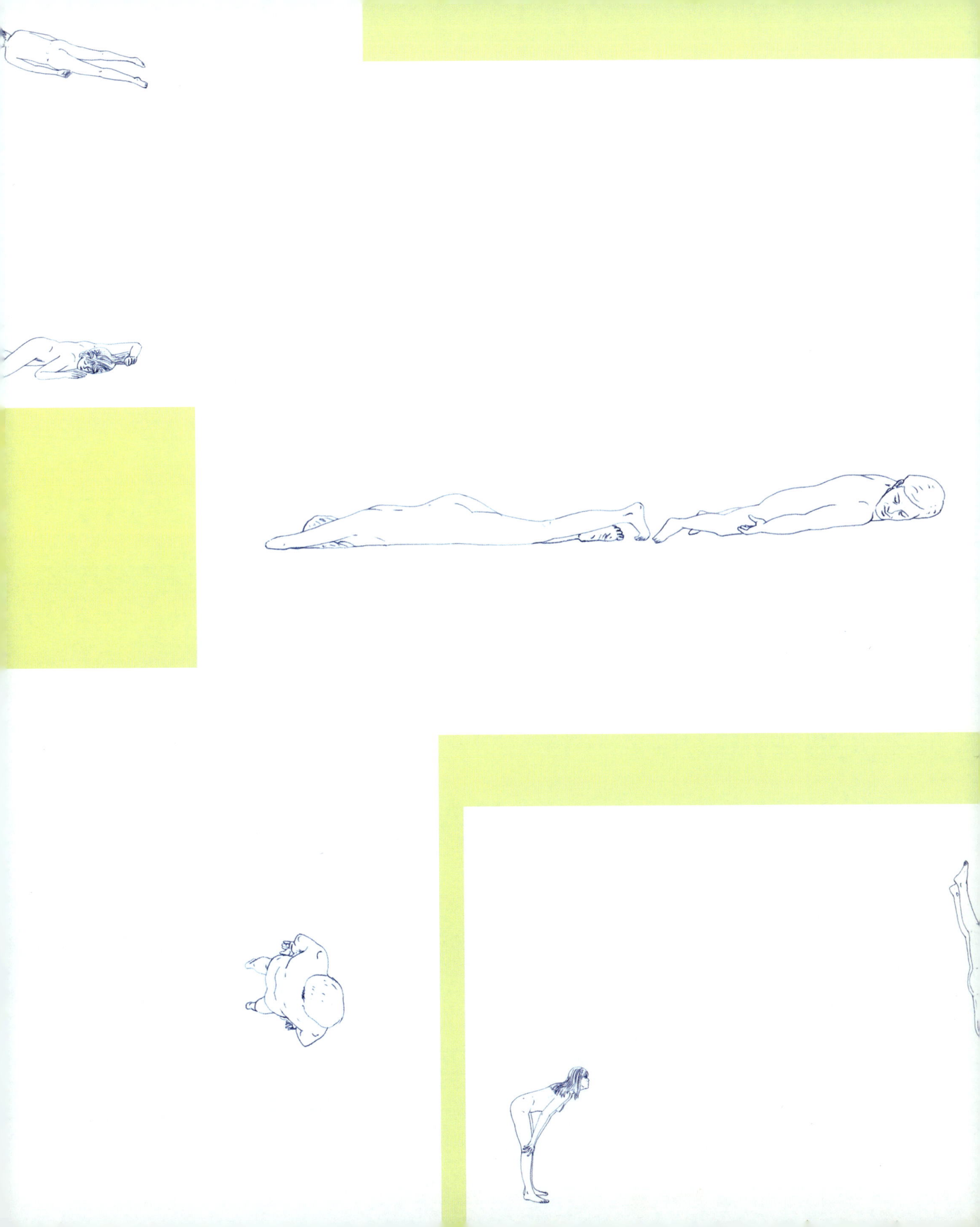

5 6 7 8 9 10 11
12 13 14 15 16 17 18
19 20 21 22 23 24 25
26 27 28 29 30 31

6 7 8 9 10 11 12
13 14 15 16 17 18 19
20 21 22 23 24 25 26
27 28

Mon

ED DURING NIGHT - HARD TO BREATHE - IN-
PRIMITINE MIST - CLEARED PASSAGES - WENT
SLEEP - (SAME THING A FEW HOURS LAT-
WOKE AT 11:00 = MARCE IN KITCHEN
MADE ME AN EGG ON TST. = READ
MARCE WATCHING MOVIE = I SHAVED - CHA-
FILLED OUT BANK SLIP = M. READY = WE
B. OF A. - (STUDIO CITY) = I CASHED CHKS +
EW $100.00 = GAVE M. $100.00 = DRV. TO
R LATE LUNCH - ($17.75) = DRV. TO VON'S
AN F.) = M. GOT GROC. = I GOT PRIMATINE
$11.62) = TO 2003 = (SHORT OF BREATH) =
T OF MIST HELPED = SHOWERED = TRICKLED
ESTA SOIL = JANIS HME 6:20 = (I GOT CHKS)
SUPS = M. + I WTCH. "THREE'S COMPANY" =
) = JANIS WATCHING MOVIE IN KITCHEN =
EEP = I WTCH. "M.A.S.H." (1) = JANIS FEEDS THE
= WTCHD. "SQUARE PEG" (NAH!) = "PVT. BEN-
"M.A.S.H." (2) = "BOB NEWHART" (SO-SO!) =
ZILCH!) = JANIS IN BED = M. TURNS IN = I GO TO
(SPRITZED MYSELF WITH PRIMATINE SPRAY) =
= (PLUS ACTIFED) = SOLITAIRE = ACED THE BULB =
E Z-TRAIN TO THE BOULEVARD OF BROK-
EAMS - Z - Z - Z =

LN. $238.23 COMP. $61.00 LS (2) $51.93 (1) $46.47

2 Tues

UP SEVERAL TIMES DURING NIGHT SPRITZING = ROSE AT
7:30 = JANIS NOISY = M. UP = I MAKE ME A CUP OF INST.
COFFEE = I BROUGHT IN THE PAPER = READING + SLURPING =
JANIS GOES TO DR'S APPT. = M.'S CO-WORKER
(SHIRLEY) CALLS - LVS. NO = M. BCK. = CALLS SHIR-
LEY = I DRESS IN ST. CLOTHES = M. + I GO AND
VOTE = (WINDY DAY) = TO VON'S MKT. FR. SW'TROLLS =
TO 2003 FR. LATE B'KFAST = TK. A NAP = AROSE AT
2:45 = (SPRITZED) = M. ON PHONE = (DOCTOR'S) REGIS-
TRATION = JIM D. HRE WITH PART FOR JANIS' CAR =
M. + I TK. TRASH CANS OUT TO CURB = JIM CALLS JAN-
IS = M. FIXING SUPPER = I WATCH "PINK PANTHER" = M.
+ JIM JOIN ME = (JANIS LATE) = BILL CALLED M. = JANIS HME
- (VOTED) = JIM WORKS ON JANIS' CAR HORN = M., JANIS +
I EAT CHICKEN, RICE + BROCCOLI FR. SUPPER = (CHOCOLATE
CAKE FOR ME) = M. + I REPAIR TO FRNT. RM. = WATCH
"THREE'S COMPANY" = WTCH. "M.A.S.H." (2) = JIM FXED
JANIS' CAR HORN - HAS SUPPER = M. + I WATCH ...
"SLEEPER" = (BOB CALLED M.) = JIM LEAVES = JAN-
IS FEEDS THE PETS = SHE RETIRES = ELECTION NEWS =
M. TO BED = I WASH - ENVELOP MYSELF IN SLEEPY -
TIMETUX = TK. MY MED. = UNWIND WITH SOLITAIRE -
BELAY THE BULB - PITTY-PAT INTO MY SNORESACK
AND PLAY TAPS ON MY BAZOO - Z - Z - Z =

3 Wed

UP 5:20 = (BREATHING DIFFICULT) = PUT WATER ON TO BOIL = GOT AN
MADE INST. COFF. = STUDIED ELECTION RESULTS = JANIS UP
CHER #2 = SHE HAD A NEW TEA = WENT
SHOWER = I HAD SW'TROLLS + COFF. = I RECLIN
AWHILE = JANIS TO WRK. = MARCE UP = MADE
AND TST. = COULDN'T EAT - (SMILEY GOT EM!) = HARD
BREATHE - (SPRITZING + ACTIFED) = M. FIN. HER B'KFAST
WENT OUT TO SIT IN SUN = M. TO WIND
CAME INDOORS = ON CAL. = REMINISCING = NAPPED AT 10:
UP AT 12:00 = WASHED / SHAVED = M. AT DOOR = WE HAVE SOUP
I SAT OUTSIDE IN SUN = MARCE TAKES THE HOSE OUT FRONT
WE SAW BIT OF "ILLEGAL" = HAD HAM, MACARONI + CHEESE
SALAD FR. LUNCH - (SUPPER, THAT IS) = GOT SOC. SEC. CHK =
DRESSED = DRVE TO AA COUNCIL = (5:44) = (6:10) GUY TEL
US THEY MOVED TO MACLAY ST. = I DRV. TO NEW ADDRES
IN AGITATED STATE OF MIND = M. GASPING FR. BREATH
HAD TO PARK SOME DISTANCE OFF AND PARK - (SWELL
I GOT THRE STOPPING TO REST NOW AND THEN) = (MUST
BEEN 6:20 AT LEAST) = I EXPLAINED TO GUY (BETWEEN GAS
AND HE LET ME IN = GUY WITH BLACK PATCH OVER HIS EY
IS CLASS DIRECTOR = SIGNED THE ATTENDANCE FORM
OUT AT NINE = DRV. TO 2003 = PARKED ACROSS ST. = M. UP
LET ME IN = SHE WAS READING ON FRNT. RM. COUCH = J
IS IN BED = (ANIMAL'S FED) = I SHOWER = DECK THE BOD
DIAPHANOUS DREAM DUDS = MARCE IN BED = SOLITAIR
I WTCH. "JOHNNY O'CLOCK" = I SNERG THE ERGS ....
RECLINE ... AND DO A LITTLE SNORING TIME - Z - Z - Z
SOC. SEC. CK $520.00

Mon

UP AT 5:00 AM AFTER SLEEPLESS NIGHT =
DRESSED = BROUGHT PAPER IN = MADE CUP
OF INST. COFFEE = READ - SLURPED = SMIL-
EY SLEPT IN ALL NIGHT = CARTOONS = JIM
UP = JANIS UP = THEY MAKE THEIR LUNCHES
= I MADE A SANDWICH = (COLD A.M.) = M. UP = J + J LVE
- M. FXES POT OF COFF. - EGGS - TST. - WE EAT = RICH-
HRE = WRKNG IN BCK = DEBBIE HRE = M. MAKES DRS
T FR. ME - DRVS ME THRE = X-RAYS - PERSCRIPTIONS =
Y BALANCE $64.00 = (NEW BAL. $65.00) = M. + I DRV
SAVE-ON = M. GOT PERSCS. REFILLED = I WAIT IN CAR =
ARD TO BREATHE) = TO 2003 - (VERY BAD ATTACK) =
A SPRITZ = SHOWERED / CHANGED = M. FXD SOUP FOR
= I MAILED H-W FORM TO DR. = READING [book] = WATCHED
ARNEY MILLER" WITH M. = M. NAPS ON FR. R. COUCH =
UP + FXES SUPPER = SOLITAIRE = TK. MED = (DEBBIE'S
CERNED CALL ABT THE STATE OF MY HEALTH) = M. SERVS
PER - MACARONI SLUMGULLION + SQUASH = WE WTCH
NTHER" = M. TO BED = SOLITAIRE - (WON AGAIN!) =
= ROUNDS UP HER SUPPER = EATS = (WE WTCH "THREE'S
= M.A.S.H. = JANIS TO HER ROOM = I TK. MY MED - WTCH
) = READING [book] = (SLEEPY) = BOILED WATER = WATCHING
ANIS IN BED) = SMILEY BARKING - JANIS BROUGHT HIM
BCK TO BED = M. UP - MADE TEA FR. HERSELF - WATCH
WITH ME = M. TO WK = I WASH - MODEL LATEST STYLE
- JOGGING SUIT = A LITTLE SOLITAIRE - A LITTLE [book] =
P MED = I PRESS THE BLACKOUT BUTTON AND BOUND
BLANKET BIJOU - Z - Z - Z =

(M'S CALL FRM HOSP... 8 YOWLERS)

9 Tues

UP 4:30 = RECURRING BAD DREAM = FIRST SOLID NIGHT'S
SLEEP I'VE HAD IN DAYS = WRT 4 A.M. = TK. HBP MED. = I
WENT OUT + BROUGHT PAPER IN = COFFEE +
NEWS = SMILEY IN ALL NIGHT = (CAN'T LET
HIM OUT WITHOUT A KEY = JANIS UP - ORD-
ERS ME TO SHUT OFF LIGHT IN KITCH + IF I HAVE
TO READ TO DO IT ON FRONT RM. = I LEFT HER WITH
MY ABSENCE + SOJOURNED TO MY ROOM + READ = I
FELL ASLEEP = AWOKE TO FIND JANIS HAD LFT AND M.
WAS HRE = M. MADE FRENCH TST. FR. B'FAST = M. TO BED =
I TK. 9-O'CLOCK MED. = READING [book] = ROLLED OVR + TK.
A NAP = WOKE AT 11:00 = THUNDER + LIGHTNING =
RAINING HARD - I LET SMILEY IN = JANIS CALLED - HER CO-
MPANY BLACKED OUT BY STORM = TOLD ME TO EXPECT
JIM OVR. TODAY = I WRAPPED UP IN BLANKET + WENT TO SLEEP =
WOKE UP - STILL RAINING HARD - READ A BIT = TOOK 1:00 MED. =
ATE L'FTOV'R ROCKHEN = (RAIN STOPPED) = COLD = READING [book] =
STOPPED RAINING - PUT SMILEY OUT = SOLITAIRE = WATCHED
"BARNEY MILLER" = M. UP = (SMILEY'S FOLLY) = 5-O'CLOCK MED =
M. + I HVE SUPPER IN FRONT RM. ON TRAYS = (I HAD CHICKEN SOUP
+ TST.) - JIM'S DAD CALLED = M. + I WTCH. "PINK PANTHER" -
POWER OUTAGE - LIT CANDLE = JIM CALLS DAD = JIM FXES HIS
LUNCH FR. TOMORROW = "HAWAII FIVE-O" = M. TO BED = JANIS
+ JIM EAT = I WTCH. "THREE'S COMPANY" (1) = JANIS CRITIC-
IZES MY SHAVING HABITS = I WTCH "M.A.S.H." = I SHAVE =
TK. 9-O'CLOCK MED. = "THREE'S CO." (2) =
JANIS HITS THE SACK = JIM RETIRES =

RAIN (THAT WAY)

10 Wed

UP 6:30 = OUT TO GET NEWSPAPER = JANIS
+ JIM UP EATING B'KFAST = I MAKE CUP OF
INST. = DRINK IT IN FRONT
ROOM WHILE PERUSING
NEWS = JIM LFT FOR COLL = I COUGHED A LO
DURING NIGHT = NO SLEEP = (READ SELECTIONS FROM
MAULDIN'S BK. "THE BRASS RING" = (WET OMINOUS DA
JANIS LFT. FR. WORK 7:50 = SMILEY OUT ALL NIGHT = I
HBP MED. = M. HME 8:45 - (WORKED O.T.) = M. GOT GROC. + T.V. GU
= M. MDE EGGS + TST. FR B'KF'ST = (SWEET ROLLS) = I HELPED
HER TAKE TRASH CANS OUT = M. TO BED = I SHWR. = CLIMB INTO
MY SNORIN' CLOTHES = ON T.V.G. = (TOOK 9:00 MED.) = SLEPT = WOKE
11:40 = SMILEY BARKING = ON T.V.G = I WARMED L'FT'IVER SLUM
GULLION FR. LUNCH - M. UP = I WTCH. BARNEY MILLER = TK
5:00 O'CLOCK MED = NEWS = M. FXING SUPPER = I DRESS
LVE = DRV. TO AA COUNCIL = SIGNED ROSTER = SUBJECT: FA
ILY RELATIONS = MEETING BROKE UP AT 9:00 = DRIVE T
CHIVERS ST., = PARKED ACROSS FROM 2003 = M. LET ME
JANIS IN BED ASLEEP = I SHOWER... INSERT THE FRAM
INTO HIGH-FASHION FLOPWEAR = M. SERVED ME A HO
DOG + COT. CHSE FR. SUSTENANCE = SHE + I WTCH THE
NEWS = ENUFF NEWS! = M. TO BED = I TO RM. = COUPLA
HANDS OF SOLITAIRE ... A PAGE OR TWO OF "BRASS RI
+ (STRIKE THE LIGHT! GROPE WAY ONTO POSTUREPE
= FLING MYSELF INTO SLEEP - Z - Z - Z =

RAIN

Mon

KIDS UP = LVE. FR. WRK. + SCHL = M.
DRVS. UP = (RICHARD HRE.) = M. LVES.
(FOR GAS FR. LAWNMOWER) = RETURNS
= I GET UP AT 8:05 = COFFEE + JELLY
S'NDWICHES = M. HAS CEREAL = (M. STOPPED
BY HOSP. TO SEE M.N. - M.N. IN SURGERY) = WE
DISCUSS THE NEWS = M. TO BED = I GO BACK TO
BED = M. UP AT 2:00 = I GOT UP = M. + I DRV. TO
SAVE-ON - I GOT LGE. PRIMATENE, CANDY = WE
DRV. TO SERRA HOSP. TO SEE M.N. = M.N. GROGGY
FRM. TESTS = OK = (HAD TEDDY BEAR) = MARCE +
I DRV. TO BEAR PIT FR. EARLY SUPPER = (GOT
TAKE-HOME DINNER FR. JANIS) = STOPPED TO
GET MILK = TO 2003 = M. TO BED = I SHOWER +
SLIP INTO SLEEPWEAR = WTCH. PINK PANTHER =
) = THREE'S COMPANY = M.A.S.H. (2) = (DROWSY) =
ME (GROUCHY) = LET SPIKE IN = JANIS PREPARES
= ENJOYS RIBS = FEEDS SMILEY + OLD OTHER =
L FR. MARCE = JANIS TO BED = WATCH... MOVIE ON T.V. -
SED TO KILL" = M. UP = I BOIL WATER FR. HER.
ARCE DRVS. TO WORK = NEWS = I CALL UP MARCE
- SKETCHING + READING = SNUFF THE BULB = HOP
SNOREBAG AND DO MY THING! - Z - Z - Z =

16 Tues

READING "CINNAMON SKIN" = FELL AS-
LEEP = HEARD JANIS UP = SMILEY IN = JAN-
IS WARMING CAR = OFF TO WORK = HEARD
M. ARR. = I SLEPT TILL 9:05 = GOT UP = (A
DULL GRAY DAY) = HAD COFF. - READ PAPER
= WATERED - (TO SHUT SMILEY UP) = TK. MEDICINE =
SCRUTINIZING CAL. = HAD 11:30 TOMATO SOUP +
RYE BREAD = TOOK A NAP = M. UP - HAS SOUP =
M. GIVES ME READER'S DIGEST = GOES TO SEE
M.N. IN HOSP. = I GOT LINC. SAV. CHK $16.45 IN
MAIL = (?) = I WTCH. BARNEY MILLER = M.
HOME WITH ARBY'S BURGERS + MILK SHAKES -
(- AND BAD NEWS ABT. M.N.) = M. CALLS LINDA
T. = PINK PANTHER = AFTER REPAST M. + I
REPAIR TO FRNT. RM - WTCH. M.A.S.H. - ALICE -
THREE'S COMPANY = JANIS HME 7:00 = EATS
RIBS + ARBY = M. SLEEPING ON FRNT. ROOM COUCH = I
SHAVE = SEE "THREE'S COMPANY" = BIT OF "LAVERNE
+ SHIRLEY" = JANIS FEEDS SMILEY - GOES TO BED = "THREE'S
COMPANY" - (2) = BILL CALLED - TALKED WITH MARCE =
NEWS = "ALL IN THE FAMILY" = I WASH = M. TO BED = I
READ "CINAMON SKIN" = SOLITAIRE = LIGHTS OUT! =
I COLLAPSE INTO MY COZY COCOON AND COVER-UP! -
Z - Z - Z =

LINC-SAV. CHK $16.45

17 Wed

AWOKE AT 3:00 AM FEELING STUFFY = USED SPRITZER - CLEA
ED AIR DUCTS = WENT TO SLEEP = AWOKE AT 4:30 - SAME
THING = READ A LITTLE OF "CINNAMON SK
WENT TO SLEEP = AWOKE (CLOCK HAD STO
AT 5:00 AM) - GOT UP - (IT WAS 9:30) = M.
ME EGGS + TST. = READ PAPER = OUT IN BCK (SUNNY
INSPECTING = BILL OVR. - TK. TRASH CANS OUT = IN
DOGHOUSE = WE HVE SOUP + SANDWICHES - BILL BROU
CANS IN = LOOKING FR. ROSES = BILL LFT. WITH FLOWE
I TK. A NAP = WOKE AT 3:25 = TK A SHOWER = WATC
"BARNEY MILLER" = (WITH MARCE) = NEWS = I DRES
= LFT. FR. A.A.C. MEETING AT 5:30 = GOT THRE EAR
SIGNED IN = TOPIC: "ALCOHOL + THE LAW" = BROKE
AT 8:45 = DRV. TO 2003 = M. LET ME IN = JANIS IN
- (SMILEY IN) = I SHOWERED - MODELED THE LATE
IN NIGHTY-NIGHT FASHIONS = HAD HOT DOGS + BEAN
M. SLEEPING ON FRNT. RM. COUCH = I SAW "QUINC
- "IN SEARCH OF - - -" (OAK ISLE TREASURE) =
MY ROOM = READING "CINNAMON SKIN" = F
ING SOLITAIRE = SNUFFED THE WICK = PILED
MY PILLOWY PADDED PALLET AND PRODUCED
PULMONARY PULSATIONS OF THE PROBOSCIS - Z
- Z =

Mon

OKE! UP AT 3:50 = STUFFED UP! = USED SPRITZER
LEAR PASSAGES = NODDED OFF TO SLEEP = RE-
AWOKE AT 5:30 = GOT NEWSPAPER = MDE.
COFF. = READ NEWS = (COOKIES + SM-
ILEY) = RETURNED TO BED = WENT
TO SLEEP AGN. = WOKE UP AT 7:45 = CHNGED =
M. UP = RICHARD + DEBBIE HRE. = I RESTED =
E EGGS + TST. = SCE MEN HRE. = SMILEY IN = H-W
TO MAIL = M. GOES TO STRE = (RESTED = I GOT UP
BREATHE) = DEBBIE LFT. = M. BCK. FRM. STRE - (I
$14.62 FR. MED. + 50% TURKEY) = SOUP FOR LUNCH =
. HER MED. = M. BCK. - (I'M CONGESTED) = GOT TWO
= SCE GUYS PCK UP + LV. = M. CALLS M.N. —
NEWS = M. + I WTCH. "BARNEY MILLER" = BREATH-
ER = M. GETTING SUPPER = M. + I HVE PORK-
GE + GR. BEANS = "PINK PANTHER" = M. GOES TO
A.S.H." (1) = JANIS HME - SMILEY IN = RELAYED
AGE TO JANIS = JANIS GETS READY FOR BED =
T + EATS = (JIM'S LONG CALL TO JANIS) = I
HREE'S COMPANY" = "M.A.S.H." (2) = JANIS FED
I PLAYED SOLITAIRE - WON! = JANIS TO BED =
FRNT. RM. - WTCH. T.V. - "M.A.S.H." (3) = "NEWHART"
M. UP - MDE. HERSELF TEA = M. OFF TO WRK = I
TAIRE = (M. FRGOT TO CALL - I CALLED HOSP.) = I
APE P.J.'S ON THE BOD = READ A BIT OF "FREE -
RIMSON" = SACK THE RADIANCE = LEAP INTO
AND DRIFT INTO THE WONDERFUL WORLD OF
IA - ? - ? - ? =

23 Tues

RAIN

UP 5:30 = READING "FREE FALL IN
CRIMSON" = MDE. COFF. + LISTENED
TO NEWS ON FRNT. RM.
T.V. = JANIS UP = GOES TO WRK. = I GOT PAP-
ER IN = READ IT = M. HME 8:30 = FXED US
EGGS + TST = M. GOES TO BED = I GO BACK
TO BED = WOKE AT 10:30 = (SMILEY BARKING) = THE
SCE GUYS ARR. = I WTCH TV = I LIE DOWN FOR AWHILE =
READ "F.F.I.C." - (FIN. IT.) = TV. = HEADACHE - TK. TWO ASPIR-
INS = SOME T.V. HITCHCOCK - (DULL) = SAT AROUND SPRITZ-
ING = ELECTRIC GUYS LVE = CARTOONS = M. UP = WE WATCHED
"BARNEY MILLER" = NEWS = M. COOKS HERSELF A HAMBURG-
ER = I HVE LESS CONGESTION (?) - FEEL QUEASY = WTCH
PINK PANTHER = M.A.S.H. - (1) = M TO BED = JANIS HOME =
SHE CALLED LINDA T. - (LONG TALK) = JANIS COOKED HAM-
BURGERS FOR US - ALSO HAD POT. SAL. + COT. CHSE = SAW
"THREE'S COMPANY" (1) = M.A.S.H. - (2) = WATCHED —
"SMILEY'S PEOPLE" FOR AWHILE = (WTH. JANIS) = JANIS
SHOWERED = THEN TIDIED UP KITCHEN = I WTCHD "THREE'S
COMPANY" - (2) = M. UP = MADE TEA = NEWS = M. GOES TO
WRK = ON NOTES = M. CALLED FRM. HOSP. - (9 HELLERS) =
I SHWRD. / SHAVED = DOLLED UP IN NAPPERIES = I
TK. MED. - COVERED PETE = LOCKED UP = SOLITAIRE =
READING = ZAPPED THE ERGS - CURLED UP IN LOWER
BERTH AND THE SUGAR-PLUM PIXIES SHANGHAIED
ME TO SHANGRI-LA! - Z - Z - Z =

24 Wed

WOKE 3:45 - (SPRITZED) = WOKE - (SPRIT
SLEPT ON + OFF TILL 7:30 = GOT UP = JA
UP - STARTS TO NAG = I MDE A CUP OF CO
TO FRNT. RM. - WTCHD T.V. NEWS = PINK PA
THER - BROUGHT PAPER IN - READ IT = JANIS
LFT FOR WRK - (SAID, "GOOD BY") = M. HM
MDE SCR. EGGS ON TST = WE HAD B'KFAST
M. TO BED = I LIE DOWN = WOKE AT 10:
NOTES = BACK TO SLEEP TILL 12:00 = T
MOVIE - "UNKNOWN WORLD" (1:30) = OU
SIDE - SUNNY - CLEAR = COOKIES + MIL
RESTED = M. UP 2:30 = WE HAD SOUP
WE WATCH "BARNEY MILLER" = NEWS =
TAKE OFF FOR AA CLASS = (5:25) = GOT
THRE EARLY = (HAD EMPHYSEMA ATTAC
AT BREAK) = COULD HARDLY BREATHE
THROUGH REST OF CLASS) = DRV. TO 20
PARKED ACROSS ST. = M. GOT ME SPRITZ
= SPRAYED = INST. RELIEF! = JIM D. THRE
JANIS, JIM + M. WATCHING "SMILEY'S PEO
I ATE FISH + CHIPS = REPAIRED TO ROOM =
OTHERS TO BED = ME TOO! - Z - Z - Z

Mon

RAIN

OMNIA = FIN. READING "GOODBYE
" = AT 5:30 BROUGHT IN PAPER =
MADE INST. COFF. = READ
NEWS = WTCHED T.V. NEWS = CARTOONS =
"THE PINK PANTHER" = M. HME 10:00 -
WKD. O.T. = COOKED US EGGS + TST. FR. B'KFAST = M.
SHWRD = WENT TO BED = I DRESSED = DRV. TO SAVE-ON
(2) SPRITZERS = TO MKT. FR. FROZEN FISH +
GE = TO 2003 = SHOWERED / SHAVED = CHANGED =
HD. T.V. = "ALL IN THE FAMILY" = M. UP 2:30 = WTCHD
RNEY MILLER" = NEWS = WE HAD CRACKERS +
ATO SOUP = M. ASLEEP ON FRNT. RM. COUCH = I FELL
EEP IN MY RM. = WOKE 5:30 = GOT CHK = [?] = SAW
NK PANTHER" = M.A.S.H. (1) = JANIS HME. = SHWRS =
KS SUPPER = "THREE'S COMPANY" = WE THREE
E SEA BASS IN LEMON BUTTER SAUCE + PEAS FR.
PER = "M.A.S.H." (2) = M. + JANIS WTCH. T.V.
TE = SORTING CHKS. = JANIS TO ROOM = MARCE
EPING ON COUCH = I WTCH "M.A.S.H." - (3) = NEWS =
S FED ANIMALS = GOES TO BED = "ALL IN THE FAM-
I LET OLD CAT OUT

30 Tues

RAIN

SOME SLEEP = WET, COLD NIGHT = UP AT
6:30 = JANIS UP - GETTING READY FR. WK.
= I GET PAPER = PUT OUT OLD
CAT = COFFEE + NEWS = JANIS LVES. FR. WK.
7:45 = I WTCH. "PINK PANTHER" - "BUGS
BUNNY" = "BEAVER" = M. UP = MKES. FRENCH TST = B'K-
FAST FR. TWO = (SMILEY OUTSIDE CHASING IMAGINARY
SQUIRRELS) = SUN OUT. = DOODLING = M. ASLEEP IN FRNT. RM =
SOLITAIRE - (I WON!) = DROPPED OFF TO SLEEP = WOKE AT 12:15 =
M.N. CALLS M. = I SLEPT AGAIN = (TILL 2:00) = M. GONE - (WENT TO
RENA H.'S FUNERAL) = I WTCH. "ALL IN THE FAMILY" = MADE TWO
SANDWICHES = M. HME - WE TOOK TRASH CANS OUT = M. MAK-
ING SOUP = WE WATCH "BARNEY MILLER" = READING T.V.
GUIDE = M. + I WTCH "THE PINK PANTHER" = "HAWAII
FIVE-O" = JANIS HME = WE EAT CHICKEN + HASH BROWNS -
"THREE'S COMPANY" = JANIS GOT PACKAGE IN THE MAIL =
JANIS FED SMILEY + OLD CAT = (I LET HER OUT) = J. TO RM. =
M. ASLEEP ON FRNT. RM. COUCH = "THREE'S COMPANY - (2) =
NEWS = "ALL IN THE FAMILY - (2)" = JANIS ASLEEP = M. GOES
TO BED = I TK. MY MED. = I SHOWER = SLIP INTO P.J.'S = I
READ A LITTLE [book] = DOODLED = DIMMED THE BRIGH

NOV. 25TH

TO MUSIC = I WTCH. FRNT. RM. T.V. - "TOO CLOSE FOR
COMFORT" = "TAXI" = M. UP - MKES TEA - SHE / I W
NEWS = M. LVES. FR. WRK. = CLEAR MOONLIT NIGHT =
T.V.G. = M. CALLS - JANIS TAKES IT = JANIS FEEDS OLD
JANIS TO BED = JIM TO BED = I PUT OLD CAT OUT = SOLITAIRE =
READING "THE GOODBYE LOOK" = SACKTIME =

3	4	5	6	7	8	9
10	11	12	13	14	15	16
17	18	19	20	21	22	23
24	25	26	27	28	29	30

ESA + PAULHRE = TERESA GIVES JIM A HAIRCUT = THEY LVE = M. HAS ROCKHENS + VEG. FOR DINNER = I HAVE EMPHYSEMA ATTACK = I SHOWER AND GET INTO JAMMIES = WE ALL WATCHING MOVIES = READING "KRAMER VS. KRAMER" = JIM GOES TO BED = JIM AND I WATCH = JIM GOES TO BED = I PLAY SOME SOLITAIRE AND READ = SCRAGG THE CANDLES = NEWS = TUMBLE INTO MY NAPSACK + SAW WOOD - Z - Z - Z -

NOV 13TH = JANIS FED BEASTIES - WENT TO BED = JANIS + I WATCH "CAHILL - US MARSHAL" = JIM TO BED = I TK. MED. = WASH UP = DRAPE THE PHYSIQUE IN SOPORIFIC GARB = INDUCE DARKNESS = GO SLUMMING IN SLUMBERLAND - Z - Z

[illegible] AT 3:00 - (COUGHING) = WOKE AG'N AT 3:30 - (DITTO) = [illegible] AT 3:40 = ROSE AG'N AT 6:00 !! = PUT WATER ON TO BOIL = GOT PAPER = MADE COFF. = READ PAPER = (BCK. TO BED) = (UP) = JANIS UP = I GOT UP AND I DRY TST. + JELLY - (LOANED JANIS \$10.00) = I DID A WASH = JANIS OFF TO WORK = M. UP - (COLD A.M.) = HUNG UP CLOTHES [illegible] TO NAP - (CONDITION) = SHOWERED + SHAVED = [illegible] = OUTSIDE SITTING IN SUN + I FALL ASLEEP IN FRNT. [illegible] NING HER NURSING SHOES = M. DRV. MY CAR TO STORE = PARKED IT IN FRNT [illegible] T.V. GUIDE = SOUP. TST. FR. LUNCH = I WATCH "BARNEY MILLER" [illegible] = M. SISTER [illegible] IN DES MOINES = SOLITAIRE = M. [illegible] HER SISTER FLO IN DES MOINES = SOLITAIRE = M [illegible] MESS CALL = SLUMGULLION = SALAD FR. SUPPER = [illegible] "M.A.S.H." = I WATCH "M.A.S.H." = JANIS FED THE FANG SET = [illegible] CAMEOS = WON (?) = JANIS SHOWERS = GETS HER [illegible] PHONE CALL FRM. JIM) = JANIS SHOWERS = GETS HER [illegible] FR. BED = SHE EATS = HIT THE HAY = I TK. M. [illegible] CALL FRM. THE HOSP. = I WATCHED "CARRIE" [illegible] = WE WATCH NEWS = M. LVES FR. WRK. = [illegible] = I WASH = PILE INTO MY LULLABYE LEVIS = [illegible] SOLITAIRE = FOOL AROUND = [illegible] = INTO MY CRUSTY CRIB - (I DON'T WAKE MYSELF UP [illegible] UP NOISES) - Z - Z - Z

4 THURS

[illegible] CALLED M. AT HOSP. = SHE FORGOT)

UP SEVERAL TIMES DURING THE NIGHT = FINALLY AROSE AT 7:00 = MADE COFF. = BROUGHT IN PAPER = READ IT = JANIS UP = [illegible] = BACK TO BED AND CRAWLED UNDER COVERS = VERY UNCOMFORTABLE UNTIL I FELL ASLEEP = MY HEAD PROPPED ON MY NIGHT STAND = JANIS IN KIT. ROOM = WOKE UP = JANIS GONE TO WRK. = MARGE FELL ASLEEP ON COUCH IN FRNT. RM. = M. COUCH = M. GOES TO BANK = I MKE TWO TST. = JELLY SANDWICHES = COFF. = M. BCK. = I TK. MED. = M. TO BED = PLAYING SOLITAIRE = BATTERIES = (I WON) = MATINE CLEARS MY BREATHING = I GOT UP 12:50 = COUCHING = AN. SALLED 10:45 = I SAT OUTSIDE WITH SMILEY IN THE SUN = (CHANGED DOG WATER) = WATCH TWO "ARCHIE BUNKERS" = OUTSIDE VIEWING = HEATED SOUP FR. OUR LUNCH = SHE TK. MED. = IN FRNT. RM. = SMILE'S BONE COLLECTION = I TK. MED. = M. FR. RM. WTH. M. = WE WTCH. "BARNEY MILLER" = M. PREPARING SUPPER = I CALLED M.N. - (SHE WAS SICK AT HOME) = WE DINED ON CREAMED CHICKEN + RICE WITH THE PINK PANTHER = M. TO BED = JIM D. HRE = JANIS ARR'D. = JANIS' ABLUTIONS / CHANGED = JIM TALKING = JANIS = JIM LVE = TK. M'S CAR = WTCH. "THREE'S COMPANY" = OFF T.V. = BIT OF AUDREY ROSE = DR. DROWSY'S DENTONS = WTCH. T.V. = M. UP = I MADE (JIFFLE) IN END OF "MIDWAY" = JANIS GOT HAIRCUT = WE WATCH NEWS = JANIS + JIM BCK. = JANIS + JANIS TOOK THEY HAD CANDLELIGHT SUPPER = M. TO WORK = JANIS CALLED M'S CALL FRM HOSP. = I TO RM. = JANIS + JIM CHATTING (ABOVE)

5 FRI

STAYED UP TIL 3:00 WATCHING A MOVIE = HORSED AROUND = SEEMED AFRAID TO GO TO SLEEP = CRAWLED IN BED AND FELL ASLEEP = [illegible] = READING BOOK = M. BROUGHT [illegible] = ATE MOST OF = JANIS + JIM PLAYED [illegible] SOME SOLITAIRE = JANIS' = HE MADE A SANDWICH = JIM UP = JIM AND HE [illegible] = I HAVE CEREAL = JANIS + JIM OUT [illegible] = STEERING WHEEL = M. TO BED = JANIS STUDYING GIFT CATALOGS = "BLOOD ALLEY" = M. OBS. = NAP = JANIS / JIM FR. A GREAT [illegible] JIM DRV. OFF = M. UP = I TK. MED. = M. FIXES ME TV DINNER = THIRD MACH = M. UP = I TK. MED. [illegible] = SHE, JANIS + JIM GO OUT FR. DINNER - (ON JANIS) = I SIFT THROUGH "THREE'S COMPANY" = I WTCH "ONE SHOE MAKES IT MURDER" - (GOOD) = JANIS + JIM HOME = JANIS READIES HERSELF FOR BED (ABOVE)

6 SAT

UNABLE (OR UNWILLING) TO SLEEP MOST OF THE NIGHT = WAS IN A PANIC = I SPENT = [illegible] = WHEN I FOUND OUT THE FORGOT HER SPRAY WAS EMPTY = MY CHEST CONGESTED = I MANAGED TO GET PAPER IN = MAKE HOT COFFEE = READ PAPER = JIM MAKES UP AND HOT COFFEE = I FR. WASH = JIM = BLOWN HIS BED = JANIS TAKES SHOWER IN FRNT. BATHROOM = JIM TAKE SHOWER IN THE BCK. BATHROOM (!) = M. BCK. WTH MEDIC = LUNCH FOR JIM = TV = FR. CHURCH = M. FIXES = I TK. MED. = JIM + JANIS = RELIEF! = I TK. DECONGESTANT = M. BCK. = [illegible] = JIM ON T.V. = BCK. TO BED = WOKE AT 11:00 = JANIS + HUSBAND IN BCK. R. = JANIS MKE COFF. = [illegible] = SOLITAIRE = A HAM OF TOLD ME = SNIFF = J + J LISTENING TO CLASSICAL MUSIC IN FRNT. RM. = [illegible] (UP!)

7 SUN

[illegible] = TIMES DUE TO BREATHING DIFFICULTY = UP FOR [illegible] A.M. = GOT PAPER IN = OLD CAT HAD STOMACH + COF. [illegible] = READ HEADLINES = JANIS UP = (I RAN OUT OF SPRITZ) = JANIS TO WORK = I (RE-CLINE) = M. UP = COOKING EGGS = [illegible] FIX OUT OF A PRESCRIPTION = I TK. MED = M. TO RIVERS HOSP. = M. DRESSING = M. TAKES INTO STORM [illegible] (NOT OPEN) = M. BCK. = WE DRV. TO SVC. STATION [illegible] (FILLED TIRES) = DRV. TO VONS = GOT MED. [illegible] STUDIO CITY B. OF A. = I DEPOSIT CHKS. = I TURN [illegible] DRV. TO PICKWICK FR. LUNCH 1:15 TO DRIVE [illegible] = M. NAPS = I SHWR. = CHANGE = TIE = GO CLOCK [illegible] READING "BRASS RING" = M. LVS. FR. NURSES [illegible] AT HOSP. = TERESA'S CALL FR. JANIS = CALL FRM. [illegible] FR. M. = CARTOONS = (DONAHUE, CAVETT, GRIFF [illegible] KIND) = WTCH "BARNEY MILLER" = NIBBLING WITH [illegible] = "NEWS" = M. DRV. M. + I TO KROFT = KITCH [illegible] LASAGNA + SALAD FR. M. [illegible] RM. = WATCHING "THREE'S COMPANY" = J. + J. GO [illegible] STROLL = "M.A.S.H." - (2) = M. + I WATCH MOVIE "BENJAMIN" = J. + J. RETURN = ATE SOUP [illegible] REPAST IN KITCH. = JANIS TO BED = JIM TOO [illegible] SAYS GOODNIGHT = M. TK. TO CLOCK - MED AT [illegible] - (WITH HER MED) = GIRD LOINS WITH [illegible] DUDS = SNUFFED THE GLEAM = BOUGHT A TICKET [illegible] REALITY TO NEVER Veterans Day NEVER LAND - Z - Z.

✱ M'S HEART CONDITION

11 THURS

WOKE UP AT 4:45 = PUT WATER ON TO BOIL = GOT PAPER = MADE COFF. = READ NEWS = HAD SWTR'S = JANIS UP = (NOTHING PLEASANT COMES OUT OF THAT FACE IN THE A.M.!) = I WATCHED T.V. = READING "THE BRASS RING" = JIM UP = HAS B'FAST WITH JANIS = BOTH ON DIETS = JIM USES JANIS CAR TO START HIS = (I'M SHAVING) = JIM LVES FR. SCHOOL = JANIS LVES FR. WORK = READING = MARGE UP = SHE COOKS EGGS + TST. FR. B'FAST = I DRESS = (OLD WEIRD HAROLD GOT A PARKING TICKET) = I DRV. TO DR. = M. TO HOSP. = DIDN'T CATCH CAB = DOG (?) = MARGE'S BAD NEWS ABT M.N. = M. LVES FR. HOSP. = I SHOWR. / CHANGE = JANIS CALL ABT. M.N. - (BILL TOLD HER) = I READING = FELL ASLEEP = I WOKE AT 1:20 = HAD LEFTOVERS FR. LUNCH = BCK. TO BOOK = SOLITAIRE = MARGE HME = M.N. UNDER STRESS = WE WATCH BARNEY MILLER = M. LVES FR. WRK. = M. TO STREAM = NAP = GOT INTO CAR = M. DRV. = WE WATCH PINK PANTHER (WITH MAGIC TOUCH OF CHEEPIE PIE!) = JIM + I AT LAUNDRY = HE = JANIS HME = SHE + JIM DO WASH = M. + I EAT CHICKEN + CORN FROM T.V. TRAYS = PRETTY RM. = WE WTCH. M.A.S.H. - (1) = J. + J. LVE FR. NIGHT ON THE TOWN = WE WATCH M.A.S.H. - (2) = ALSO OUR PHONE CALLS = (ABT. M.N.) = M. TO BED = (STILL PHONING) "BULLITT" TALKED TO BOB (UP!)

(MAILED 2ND H-W DR. BILL)

12 FRI

SPASMODIC COUGHING WOKE ME UP - (4:30) = GOT UP = TK. MED. = MADE CUP OF COFF. = NO NEWS PAPER = WOKE AGAIN AT 5:00 = STILL NONE = RETURNED TO BED = AROSE AT 9:00 = EVERYONE ASLEEP = I DRV. ONE OF [illegible] = READING SUNDAY PAPER = MAKE MOKES = M. UP = BROUGHT SWEET ROLLS = M. HAS EGG = GOES TO BED = (BROWN IN) [illegible] = PINK PANTHER CARTOONS = JANIS + JIM = GETS A 40 GUN [illegible] KITCHEN CAB = 4:10 STUFFING CAKE = WAITING FOR [illegible] JANIS SRVS. SCR. EGGS, SAUSAGES + TST. = (DELISH!) = I GO TO DR. [illegible] = JANIS = I HAD A NAP = NOT CONNECTED = GO TO PRINTER [illegible] = JANIS = COOKING = T.V. = M. HAS = THEY GO TO BANK = M. FEEDS SMILEY = M. + I SIT DOWN TO HAVE BEEF, BROCCOLI, + HASH BROWNS = M. CALLS UP M.A.S.H. = (DOWN)

14 SUN

PETER = GOT UP AT 5:00 = MADE INST. COF. = READ PAPER = FINISHED WORD STYLES = JANIS SMOKING = AN SWEATER = BANKING SMILEY'S CUP = WARM UP = TO BED = (FIN. !!) = MARCELLA UP = COOKS EGGS TST. FR. B'FAST = JANIS + M. GO = JANIS LTF 10:15 = TK. MED = M. BAKE = SHAVE = SHOWER = CLEAN UP = JIM D. CAME = [illegible] = NEWSPAPER = GIRL = BILL MAIL = BOOK CALLED = FORGOT HIS BIRTHDAY = [illegible] = THREE'S COMPANY = M. + I WTCH. "SOAP" = M. HOROWITZ = JANIS FED SMILEY + PORK = [illegible] = LEFTOVERS FR. SUPPER = (CHICKEN, CORN, MASHED POTS, + GRAVY) = M. + I GO = M. + J. GO BED = M. MARGE MED = (MEDICINE) = I WATCH T.V. = (M'S CALL - JANIS TOOK IT) = J. + J. IN KITCH. (ABOVE)

13 SAT

WAKING AROUND AT 6:15 = M. UP = [illegible] TO BED = JANIS OFF TO WRK. [illegible] I DON ROBE - MAKE CUP OF INST. = M. MKES POT OF GRAY GUNNERY FOR US = CONGREGATION OF CROWS = EGGS ON MUFFINS = CONGREGATION OF CROWS IN BCK. = MAKING SMILEY NERVOUS = I SHAVE [illegible] DRESS = OFF TO BED = DR. AT 10:00 = M. AND I DROVE ON = M. = TO THE = WE WENT TO VONS = M. GETS GROCS. = GET PRIMATEN SPRAYS AND CANDY = (T.V. GUIDE) = CHANGE CAR - (OUT OF BREATH) = I HVE SOUP = (GAVE T.V. GUIDE) = I NAP = WHILE M. GOES TO BED = M. \$70.00 = I NAP WHILE M. BRING IN COOKIES [illegible] AT 1:50 = M. BCK. = (I HELP M. BRING IN COOKIES) = ON T.V. G. = TO FIX TURN INS ON M'S CAR [illegible] TO JIM = I READ = M. + I WITH "THE PINK [illegible] CALLED = ELEANOR = CALLED = M. + WE TO BED [illegible] (JANIS WORKING O.T.) = M. + I EAT = JIM D. CONCEDES [illegible] + HASH BROWNS = SHE + JIM EAT = CROSS STREET [illegible] JANIS HME = I WTCH. "THREE'S COMPANY" = SOUP [illegible] CAROL H. = M. + I WTCH. "THREE'S COMPANY" = "TAXI" = J + J [illegible] M. + I WTCH "TOO CLOSE FOR COMFORT" = "TAXI" = J + J [illegible] M. + I WTCH "TOO CLOSE FOR COMFORT" = ROOM ⊕ = [illegible] TO BED = I BROKE UP CONFAB. IN JANIS' ROOM ⊕ = I [illegible] BED = JANIS LET SMILEY IN = GOES TO BED = NEWS = I [illegible] = BLOSSOM OUT IN SNUGGY-BUG REGALIA = SOL- [illegible] = FURTHER ADVENTURES OF T. M'GEE = DARKEN- SCENE = SETTLED DOWN ON SIESTA SLAB TO SLEEP - - Z - Z - Z =

18 THURS — RAIN

FOLKS IN THE KITCHEN = LOW VOICES = COMINS' = GOINS' = M. UP 7:00 STUFFED UP ALL NIGHT = (FREQUENT RESORTINGS TO SPRITZES) = JIM D. GONE = JANIS HERE = IN BEDROOM = M. MAKING COFFEE = I HAD A CUP = PERUSED PERIODICAL = M. SERVED EGGS ON A MUFFIN = M. - GOOD! = JANIS LFT. FR. WRK. = I TK. MED. = ON T.V. G. = G.C.E. MEN DRIVING = M. + DR. = (DOWN + AROUND) = CREWING = (RAINING) = I SHWR. / SAVE / DRESS = M. BCK. = FIRST HOSP. FR. 3:30 = BACK TO BED = M. + I TO BARTON 11:20 = PHONES M.N. = LEFT AGN. AT 11:50 = CARTOON = [illegible] = SHOOPING AGN! = LET GO = SOLITAIRE - (I WON!) = COOKIES AND MILK = "BARNEY MILLER" = ON T.V. G. = CROSSWORD PUZZLE = WAITING FOR M. = JANIS CALLED = GOING TO EAT AND SEE A SHOW WITH JIM = "BARNACLE" = COME HME LATE = I WTCH. "PINK PANTHER" = M. HME 5:35 = BROUGHT ARBY'S BEEF + MILKSHAKES = LONG CHAT = M. TO BED = I WTCH. M.A.S.H. = "ALICE" = "THREE'S EVERYTHING SMOOTH AT HIS PLACE" = DRIFTED OFF TO SLEEP COMPANY" = M.A.S.H. - (1) = WTCHD END OF "MR. MAJESTYK" = SOLITAIRE - (I WON AGAIN!) = BOILED WATER FR. M'S TEA = (I HAD = MARGE UP = NEWS = BOILED WATER FR. M'S TEA = (I HAD COFFEE) = WE WATCHED NEWS = M. OFF TO WRK = I READING "CINNAMON SKIN" = M. CALLED FRM. HOSP. - (GT. 4 CATER-WAULERS) = I SHWR. - GARB THE PHYSIQUE IN SOMINEX EN-SEMBLE = JANIS CALLED FRM. JIM'S HME AT 11:05 - (HME IN 1 HR.) = PICKING MOVIES - READING = JANIS HME (DOWN)

19 FRI — RAIN

WOKE AT 5:00 = READ "CINNAMON SKIN" TIL 5:30 - (FIN. !) = 5:35 = GOT PAPER IN = READ NEWS OUT = COFF. = BCK. TO BED = [illegible] BACK TO ROOM = NAPPED = (ON + OFF) 3:00 = UP = FED CAT = M. [illegible] = "THREE'S COMPANY" = M. + JANIS BCK. = LEFTOVERS FR. SUPPER = I SHOW SHAVE - DON P.J.'S = (STUFFY FEELING) = JANIS WTCHING A MOVIE = M. TO BED = JANIS + I WTCH. "THE MAN WHO CAME TO DINNER" = JANIS = I TK. OUR MEDS. JANIS TO BED = I PLAY SOLITAIRE = READ SOME = FREE FALL IN CRIMSON = Z. D. THE LIGHTS + DIVED INTO THE DOZING POOL = Z - Z - Z

20 SAT

ALL STUFFED UP = COULDN'T SLEEP = LIGHT ON = BED = WTCH. MOVIE "ANATOMY OF A MURDER" = GOT PAPER = READ IT WHEN LAY DOWN IN BCK. = (BREATHING) = M. UP = (?) [illegible] = BACK TO BED = SLEPT = BCK. TO BED [illegible] CAR STORES = [illegible] = STUDIO CITY = M. BCK. WITH BOB = MENCHE = M. + [illegible] COOKING PHILIPPINE DISHES = BOB + I WATCH "THE QUIET MAN" = LNCH. FR. 5 - SHRIMP DISH + PORK ON A STICK (PUMPKIN PIE) = BILL, J: YOUNG + ELISSA HRE = GAVE ME [illegible] (THEY ATE = THEY LFT. - (BILL DRVNG B. + M. HOME) = I SHOWER DON P.J.S + ROBE = BIT OF RIPLEY = "MATT HOUSTON" - (SH[illegible]) "BOB HOPE PINK PANTHER SPECIAL" = JANIS GOE TO GET GA[illegible] BCK. = SHE MAKES HERB TEA = M. TO BED = (SMILEY IN) = JAN[illegible] BED = SOLITAIRE = READ = LIGHTS KAPUT! = INTO THE SNOR[illegible] = JUST CALL ME "THE VICER OF WAKEFUL!" -

21 SUN

[illegible] 1:30 BY FIT OF COUGHING = (SPRITZED) = TO B.R. = SAME (SPRITZED AGAIN) = ON T.V. G. = BACK TO SLEEP 3:30 = WOKE UP STUFFY = 6:30 - (SPRITZED) = HEARD M. IN KITCHEN 7:00 = I GOT UP = BROUGHT IN PAPER = READ IT = M. WRASSLED TURKEY INTO THE OVEN = JANIS UP = JIM UP LATER = M. COOKED SCR. EGGS + TST. FR. B'KFAST TOGETHER WTCHING THANKSGIVING DAY PAR-[illegible] TO SHAVE = I DRESSED = M. + I WENT TO BOY'S [illegible] DRY. TO SAVE-ON - I GOT TWO LARGE SPRITZERS = BK. [illegible] = JIM LEFT TO PICK UP BOB + MENCHE = BILL, J: [illegible] + BABY HRE = ELISSA FEEDING SMILEY GRAHAM [illegible] THROUGH HOLE IN SCREEN DOOR = WAITING FR. [illegible] OF THE SHOW = CLYDE, MARGOT, NELL, LINDA + SHELLEY [illegible] UXIE ARR'S = CLYDE MIXING DRINKS FR. HE, LINDA, [illegible] = M.N. EATING KIMCHE - I TASTED IT - (HOT STUFF!) [illegible] IN FRNT. RM. WATCHING "TWILIGHT ZONE" MARATHON = [illegible] B + MENCHE HRE = BOB + CLYDE GO TO THE STRE FR. [illegible] (BUT NOT FOR ME!) AND POP = RETURN = EVERYONE SETTLED DOWN TO EAT TURKEY, GRAVY, MASHED [illegible] SWEET SPUDS, CHOPPED ZUCHINI, + PIE = HEN PRTY [illegible] BEDROOM = OTHERS WTCH. T.V. - "T.Z." - "PINK PANTH[illegible] M.A.S.H. (1)" = PARTY BREAKS UP = JANIS SQUABBLES [illegible] BOB TAKING BOOKS W'THOUT PERMISH = JANIS, JIM + [illegible] CLEAN UP KITCH. = M. TO BED = I WTCH. "THREE'S [illegible] ANY" - I SHOWR. - SIDLE Thanksgiving INTO JAMMIES = JIM ASLEEP ON FRNT. RM. COUCH = JANIS THRE. LISTENING

25 THURS

WOKE UP COUGHING VARIOUS TIMES = SPRITZED = WENT BCK. TO SLEEP AGN. = CAT YOWLING WOKE ME = I ROSE AND DAMPENED HER MUSICAL AMBITIONS = BCK. TO BED - SLEPT = AWAKENED BY DOOR BELL RINGING - I HAD INARDVERTANTLY LOCKED M. OUT = ROSE + OPENED DOOR = BACK TO BED + UP AT 8:25 = M. HAVING CEREAL = M. TO BED = JIM UP = JAN UP FEELING POORLY = RESTS ON F.R. COUCH = JIM MAKES FRNCH. TST. + BACON B'KFAST FR. HE + I = WE WTCH. PART OF "THE ALAMO" = J. + J. IN F.R. = I GO TO MY RM. = FELL ASLEEP = WOKE AT 1:30 = SHAVED = JANIS DRV. TO GET GAS REFILL = JIM. READING IN RM. = CAT YOWLING AGN. = JIM + JANIE GO FR. WALK = M. UP = I MDE. TURKEY S'DWICH = M. HAD TURKEY DINNER = J + J BCK. = THE NEW REMOTE TV. CONTROL BATTERY DOESN'T WORK = (?) = THEY LVE. TO EXCHANGE IT = M. CALLS M.N. = I WTCH "THE PINK PANTHER" J + J COME BACK = I GOT (3) CHKS = M. TO BED = JANIS SAID NEW BATTERY CHECKED OUT FINE = I FIDDLED AROUND WITH IT - IT WORKS FINE = J + J EAT SUPPER = I DO A WASH = WTCH "THREE'S COMPANY" + "MASH" = BIT J + J IN KITCH. LOUNGING = "THE NEW ODD COUPLE" = BIT OF R. HOOD = JIM LVES = JANIS WATCHES FLYNN MOVIE = I EAT (2) TURKEY SANDWICHES = M. UP = HAS TEA = JANIS TO RM. = NEWS = M. LVES FR. WRK = COLD NIGHT = ON CAL. = M'S CALL = I TK. MED = SHOWR = INTO P.J.'S = EVENTUALLY TO BED. -

COAST-FED (2 CHS) \$56.35 - \$66.86 = HOME-SAV \#66.86

26 FRI

SLEPT SPARINGLY - SPRITZED A LOT = HEARD M. DRV. UP [illegible] ROSE AT 9:00 = M. AT B'KFAST = I MDE CUP OF INST. - JOINE[illegible] AT TABLE READING NEWS = M. TO BED = JANIS UP - HER VITUP[illegible] ATION DROVE ME BCK. TO BED = SLEPT TILL 11 [illegible] DRESSED = JANIS LFT. TO GO SHOPPING [illegible] TERESA = WANDERED OUTDOORS = WENT B[illegible] BED = WOKE UP AT 2:15 = COOKIES + MILK = T.V. = M[illegible] I NAPPED = WOKE AT 6:00 = GOT CHK. ⊙ = M. HEATED FROZEN DINNERS = WTCHD "HAPPY DAYS" - "LAV. + SHIR" - "T[illegible] COMPANY" = "MTM" = M. TO BED = SOLITAIRE = TERESA'S CALL [illegible] IS ON THE WAY = JANIS HME. = SMILEY IN = JANIS' NEW WA[illegible] I WTCH T.V. = SLEPT = WOKE AT 10:00 = BOILED WATER = M. [illegible] MADE TEA = NEWS = JANIS GOT HASSLE - JANIS TO RM. = M[illegible] WRK. = JANIS TK. M'S CALL FRM. HOSP. = JANIS FED CRITTE[illegible] (FRESHLY SHAVEN) - SLID INTO SLEEPWEAR - READING "GOO[illegible] LOOK" - TUMBLED INTO BLANKETS + BLANKED OUT - Z - Z

27 SAT

COULDN'T SLEEP = GOT UP AT 2:00 + WATCHED "THE CORSICAN BROS." = BACK TO BED AT 4:00 STILL COULDN'T SLEEP = AROSE AT 5:15 DRESSED = BROUGHT PAPER IN = READ [illegible] JANIS UP = I WTCH. TV. IN FRNT. RM. = I FLOP [illegible] ON BED 8:20 = (M. LATE) = JANIS READIES HER[illegible] FR. CHURCH - LVES. 8:25 = I MK. TST., JAM + COFF. = GO TO BED AGN. = JANIS HME. AT 11:00 = M. HME. AT 11:30 = TO BED = DOG BARKING = (PHONE RANG - I'M TOO GR[illegible] TO ANSWER IT) = J. HRE. = SHE HEATED LUNCH = WE HAD SOUP + TST. = JANIS LIT Advent FIRE IN F.P. = STUDY[illegible] BIBLE = I WTCH. "WINCHESTER '73" = I [illegible] (DOWN)

28 SUN

NOV 25 — **LEE PATRICK** NOV. 28TH — **HUGH HARMON**

NOTES.

⚡ "DIRTY STORY" BY ERIC AMBLER ⊕ HOW MANY TIMES DOES BONEHEAD HAVE TO BE TOLD? = ⊙ LINC-SAV \#1 CHK \#26.00 =

NOV 14TH = SOME HOPE = J + J BACK = DINE = I WTCH. "SUPERMAN" ON FRNT. RM. = WATCH IT ON KITCH. T.V. = M. UP = I MKE. HER. TEA = SMILEY IN = M. DRV. TO WRK. = M'S CALL TO JANIS FRM. HOSP. = JANIS TO BED = FINDS NEW DRAWINGS = JIM LOOKS AT SOME OF MY CARTOONS = JIM TO BED = I SHOWR / SHAVE = CHANGED TO MATTRESS MUFTIS = SOLITAIRE = AS THE MOON SINKS SLOWLY INTO THE WEST - I SINK SLOWLY INTO SLUMBER - Z - Z - Z

NOV. 19TH WITH SURPLUS PIZZA = I HAD A SLICE = JANIS GETS READY FR. BED = SHE LETS SMILEY IN AND CUTS OUT FOR BED = I READING "C.S." = OFF MITT DER BRIGHT! - UND INTO DER BLANKETBEDDEN UND TO GESNORING - Z - Z - Z =

NOV. 28TH THINGS FR. SUPPER = WOKE M. = TURKEY STUFFING, MASHED POTS, + GRAVY = M. GOES BCK. TO BED = SOLITAIRE - JANIS TIDYING UP KITCH. = A. BUNKER = JANIS TO BED W[illegible] PARTING SHOT = I BOIL WATER FR. M'S. TEA = LISTEN TO NEWS [illegible] FRNT. RM. = (LET ANCIENT FELI[illegible] OUT) = M. UP. - WTCHES NEWS [illegible] WITH ME = M. LVES. FR. WRK. = I LISTEN TO REST OF NEWS = (CALLED M. AT HOSP. = SHOWRD = EDGED INTO JAMMIES =

RAIN

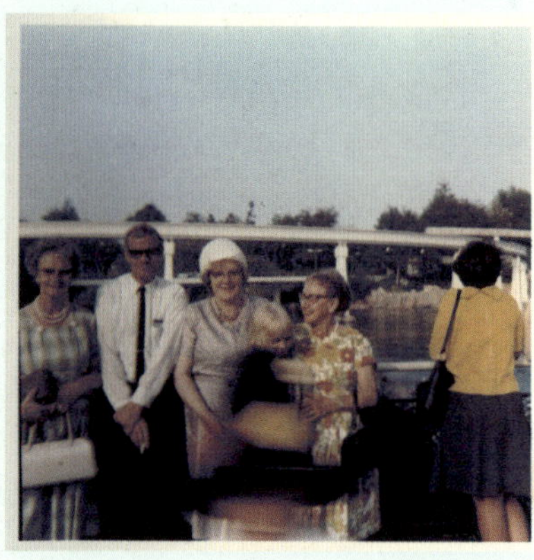

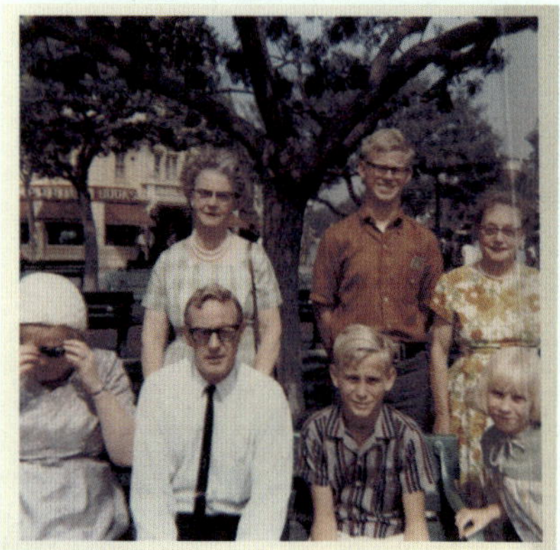

Day to Day with John Dunn

Amid Amidi

The legacy of animation designer/writer John Dunn (1920–1983) is secure—if unheralded—as the author of hundreds of animated shorts for Ward Kimball, Chuck Jones, Bob McKimson, Friz Freleng, and others. In the waning days of theatrical animation, he created some of the field's last cartoon characters—Ant and the Aardvark, Roland and Rattfink, Tijuana Toads, Blue Racer, and Hoot Kloot, to name a few. When I started researching his life, I borrowed a variety of artwork from his children: storyboards, paintings, comic strips, character designs. But the most unusual possession I received was a Ziploc bag full of Security Pacific Bank calendars that Dunn maintained for the last 18 years of his life. The first ten years' worth of calendars were of no particular note—just places for him to jot down notes about his career (weekly deadlines at the animation studio, vacation dates, meetings, and the like). With each passing year, though, the notes on his calendars grew increasingly detailed.

In 1976, when Dunn semi-retired from animation, he created in the calendars an utterly unique form of self-expression. Every square inch of the 5.75" × 6" calendar pages, both front and back, became a miniature canvas for Dunn's writings and drawings. He began to keep detailed accounts of what he ate, which television shows he watched, which books he read, as well as notes on his daily encounters with family members and animation colleagues. John's son Bill doesn't recall which sort of writing instrument his father used to write so small—that question has been a source of debate among the many artist friends who've seen the calendars—but he does remember that his father retired to his study every evening to work on the calendars, using a magnifying lens to help him fit as much as he could into his daily one-inch-square space.

Dunn's devotion to the calendars manifested itself in peculiar ways: he recorded monthly rainfall tables, dates of death of actors and animation-industry coworkers, and charts logging the number of times he'd eaten at various restaurants. A most unlikely item was noted on the back of one calendar: "From Oct. 3, 1977 to Jan. 22, 1980 the number of times I have walked back and forth on Hayvenhurst between Sherman Way and D.F.E. [DePatie-Freleng Enterprises] has been 845!!!" In the final year of his life, Dunn upgraded to a 7" × 10" engagement calendar; Security Pacific's complimentary annuals could no longer contain his copious notes on daily life.

Dunn was both an artist and a writer, so it's little surprise that his calendars are filled with nearly as many drawings as words. He worked mostly on the reverse sides of calendar pages, right over the text-heavy almanac data—the layer of words underneath adding a textural quality to his drawings on top. Dunn had been a fan of newspaper comics since childhood and his drawings reflect a strong print-cartoon sensibility, recalling artists like E.C. Segar (*Popeye*), Sidney Smith (*The Gumps*), and particularly Milt Gross. Disney animation director Ward Kimball once told me, "You would ask [Dunn] to do a page full of crazy-looking dogs and it was very hard to pick the craziest." His inventiveness was unhindered even when reduced to Lilliputian proportions.

The raw, unfiltered details of Dunn's recorded life shed a fascinating light on the man himself—his foibles and insecurities, his likes and dislikes—what made him tick. But beyond the personal aspects revealed here is the purely visceral effect of these calendars: their keeper's craftsmanship elevate them to unlikely, enchanting, beautiful works of art.

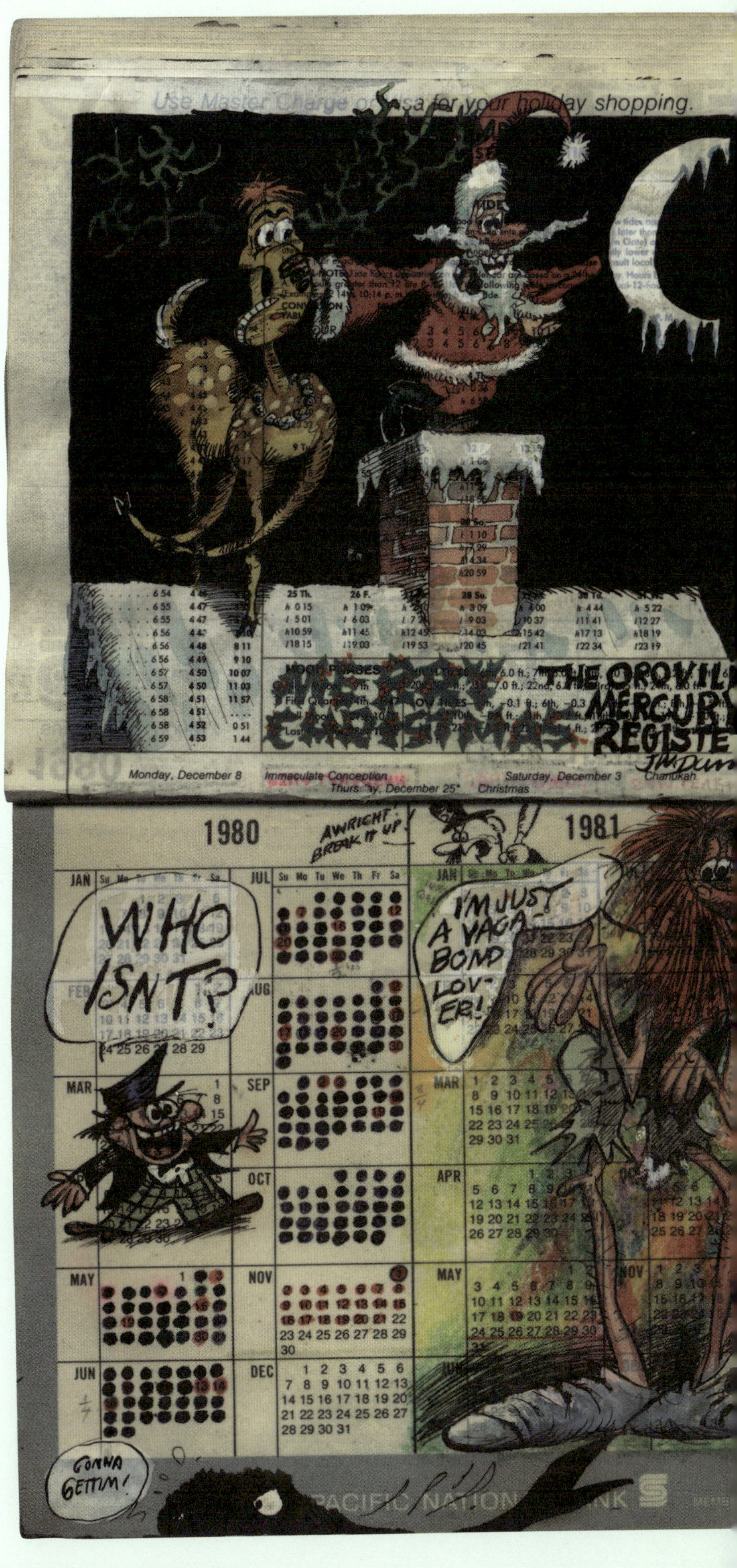

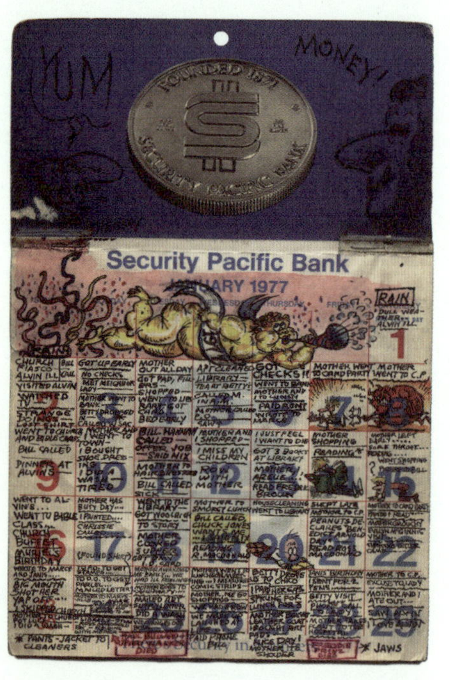
YUM
MONEY!
FOUNDED 1871
SECURITY PACIFIC BANK
Security Pacific Bank
JANUARY 1977
RAIN
JAWS

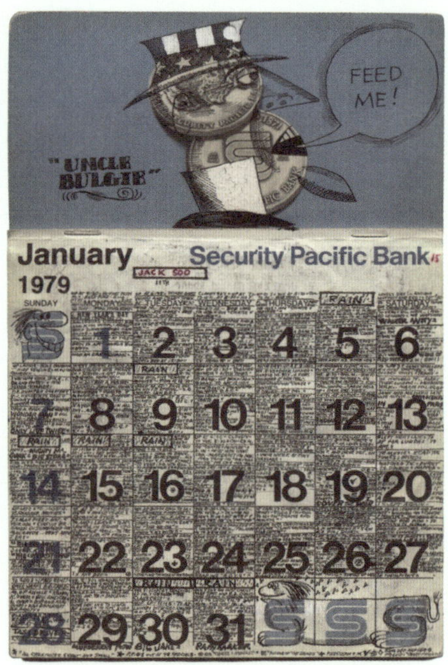
FEED ME!
"UNCLE BULGIE"
January
1979
Security Pacific Bank
JACK SOO
RAIN

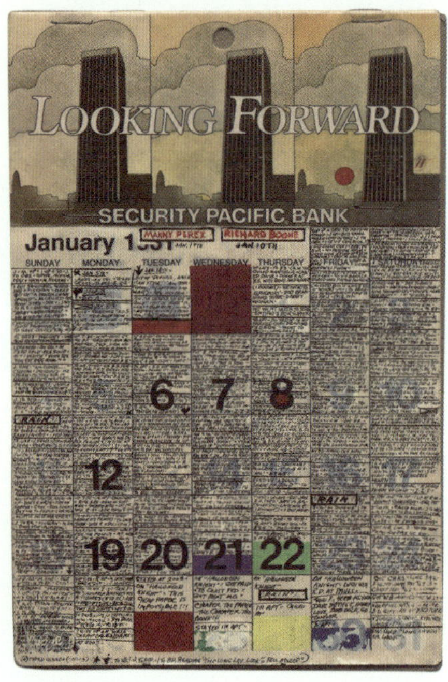
LOOKING FORWARD
SECURITY PACIFIC BANK
January
MANNY PEREZ
RICHARD BOONE
RAIN

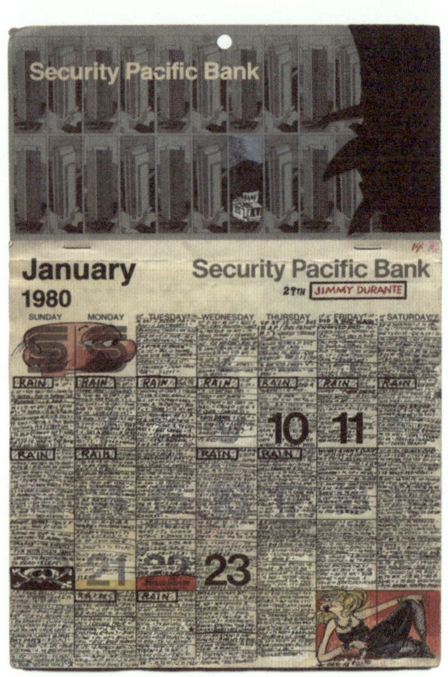
Security Pacific Bank
January
1980
Security Pacific Bank
JIMMY DURANTE
RAIN

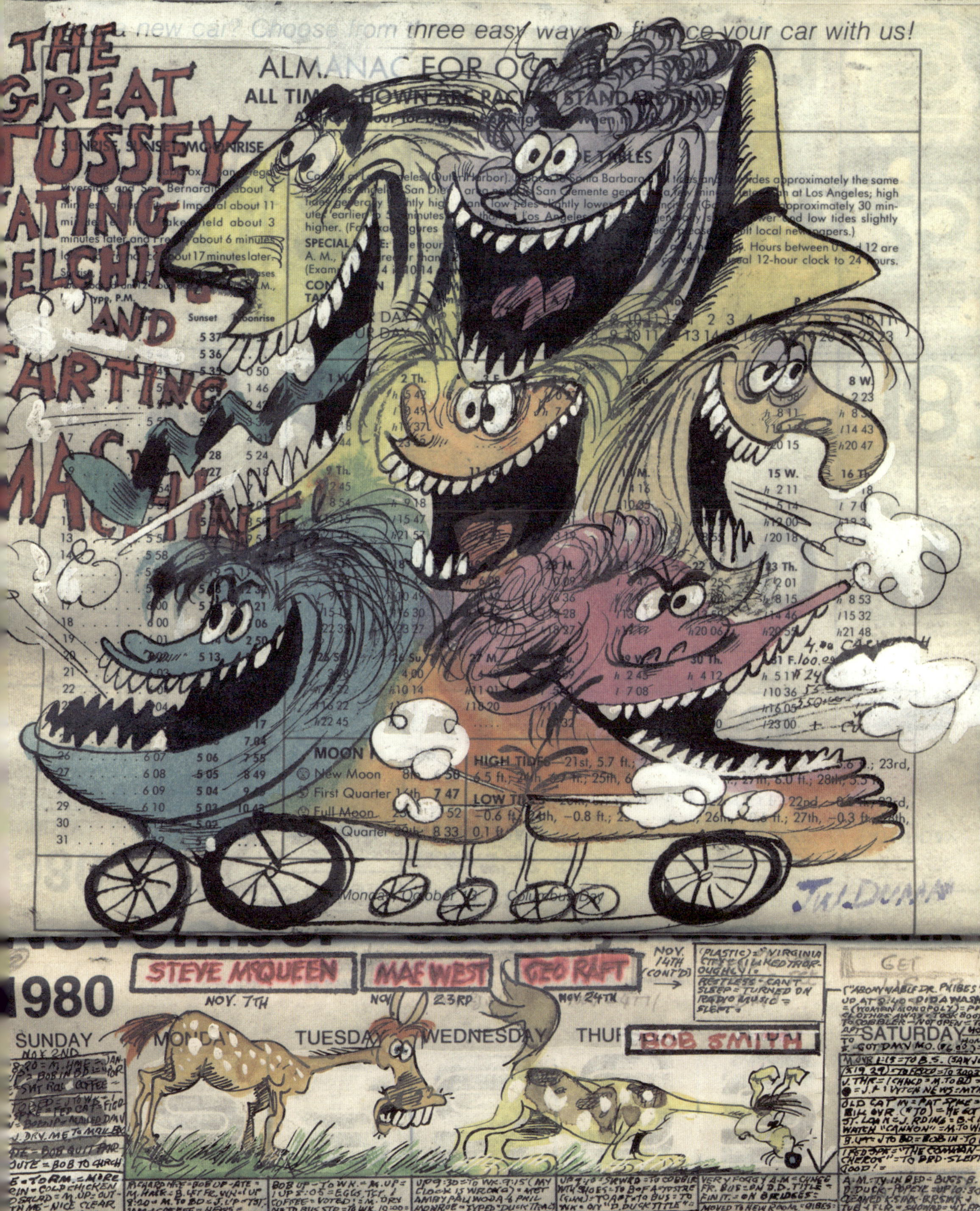
THE GREAT TUSSEY
ATING
ELCHI
AND
ARTING
MACHINE
J.W. DUMM
1980
STEVE McQUEEN
MAE WEST
GEO RAFT
BOB SMITH
NOV. 7TH
23RD
NOV 24TH
SUNDAY
TUESDAY
WEDNESDAY
SATURDAY

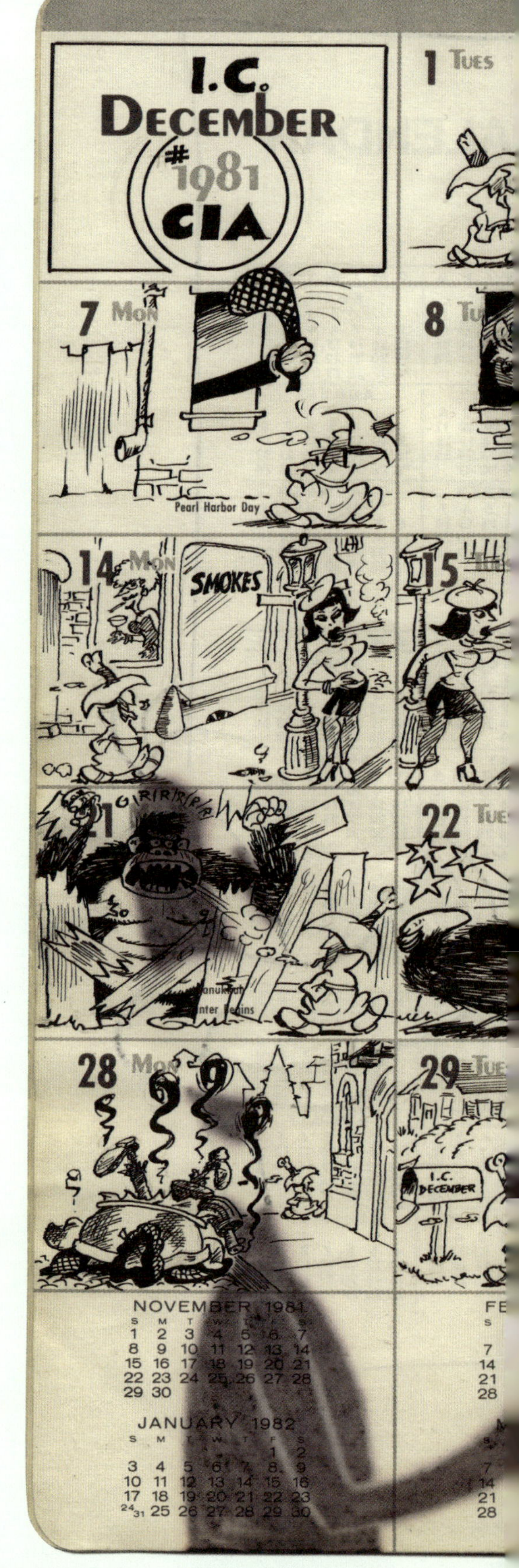
I.C.
DECEMBER
#1981
CIA
1 TUES
7 MON
Pearl Harbor Day
8
14 MON
SMOKES
15
21
22
28
29
I.C.
DECEMBER
NOVEMBER 1981
S M T W T F S
1 2 3 4 5 6 7
8 9 10 11 12 13 14
15 16 17 18 19 20 21
22 23 24 25 26 27 28
29 30
JANUARY 1982
S M T W T F S
1 2
3 4 5 6 7 8 9
10 11 12 13 14 15 16
17 18 19 20 21 22 23
24/31 25 26 27 28 29 30

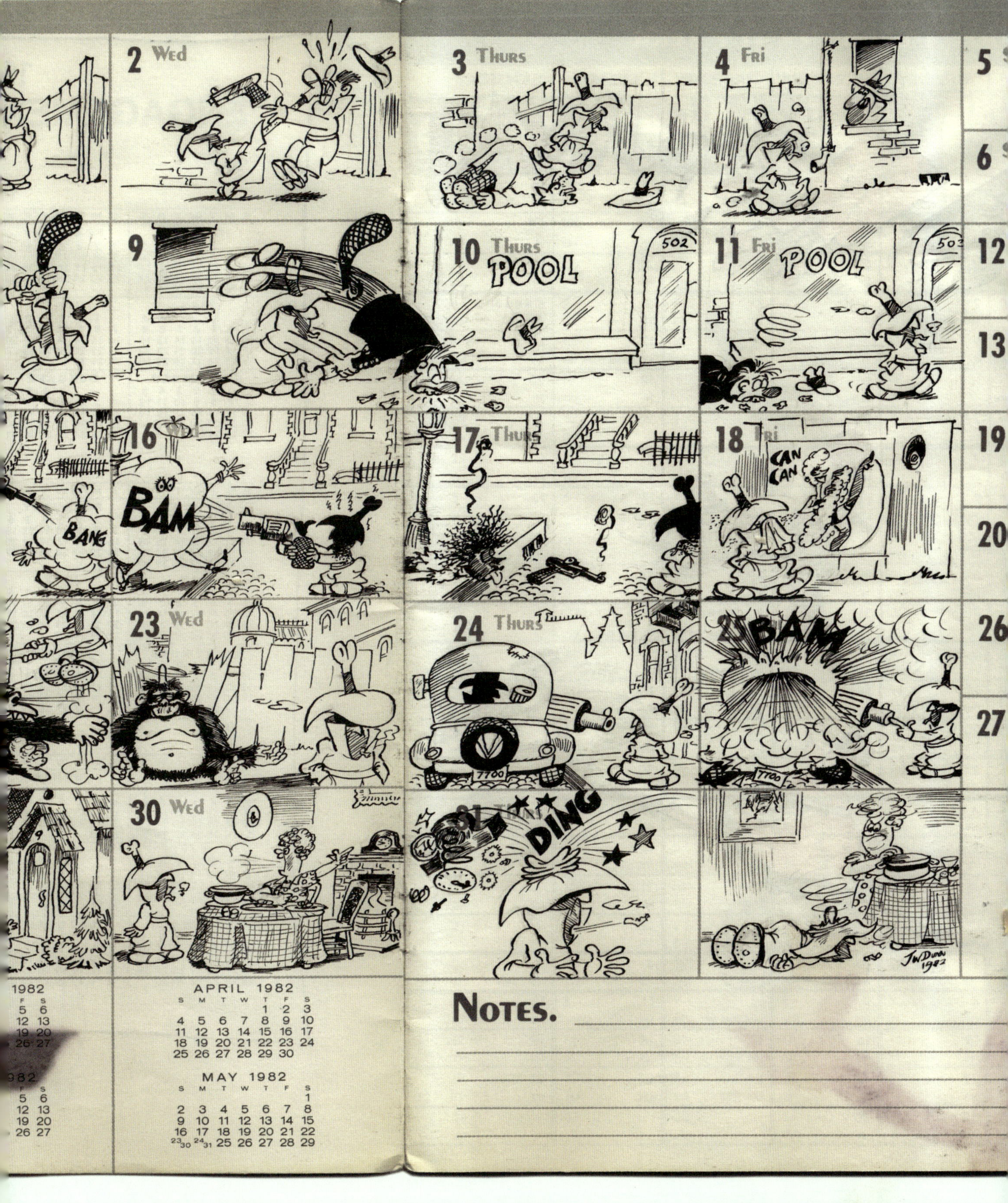

2 Wed
3 Thurs
4 Fri
5
6
9
10 Thurs
POOL
502
11 Fri
POOL
12
13
16
BAM
BANG
17 Thurs
18 Fri
CAN CAN
19
20
23 Wed
24 Thurs
7700
BAM
26
27
30 Wed
DING
JW DUNN 1982
APRIL 1982
S M T W T F S
1 2 3
4 5 6 7 8 9 10
11 12 13 14 15 16 17
18 19 20 21 22 23 24
25 26 27 28 29 30
MAY 1982
S M T W T F S
1
2 3 4 5 6 7 8
9 10 11 12 13 14 15
16 17 18 19 20 21 22
23/30 24/31 25 26 27 28 29
NOTES.

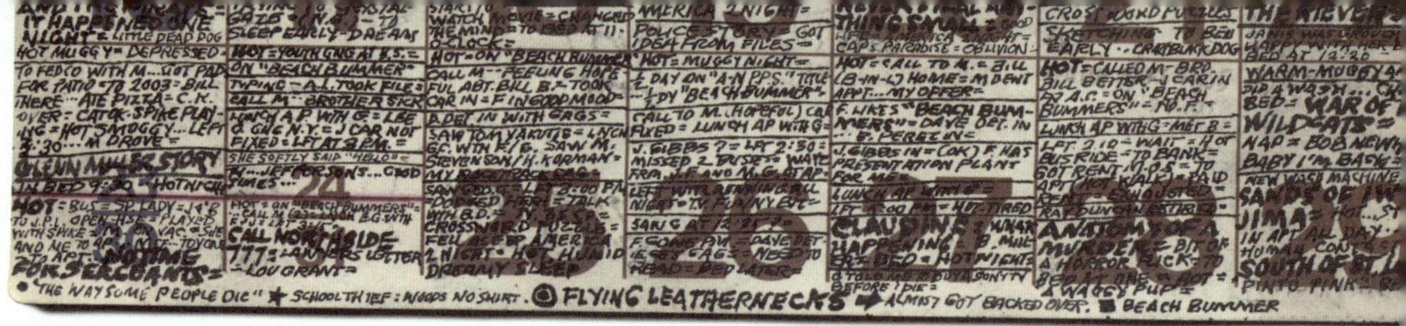

Like the open road? We offer attractive rates for recreational vehicle loans.

ALMANAC FOR JULY 1979

ALL TIMES … ARE PACIFIC STANDARD TIME

… One Hour for Daylight Saving Time When in Effect

SUNRISE, SUNSET, MOONRISE

TIDE TABLES

CONVERSION TABLE

12-HOUR DAY

24-HOUR DAY

MOON'S PHASES

First Quarter 2nd

Last Quarter 16th

New Moon 23rd

First Quarter 31st

Wednesday, July 4 Independence Day

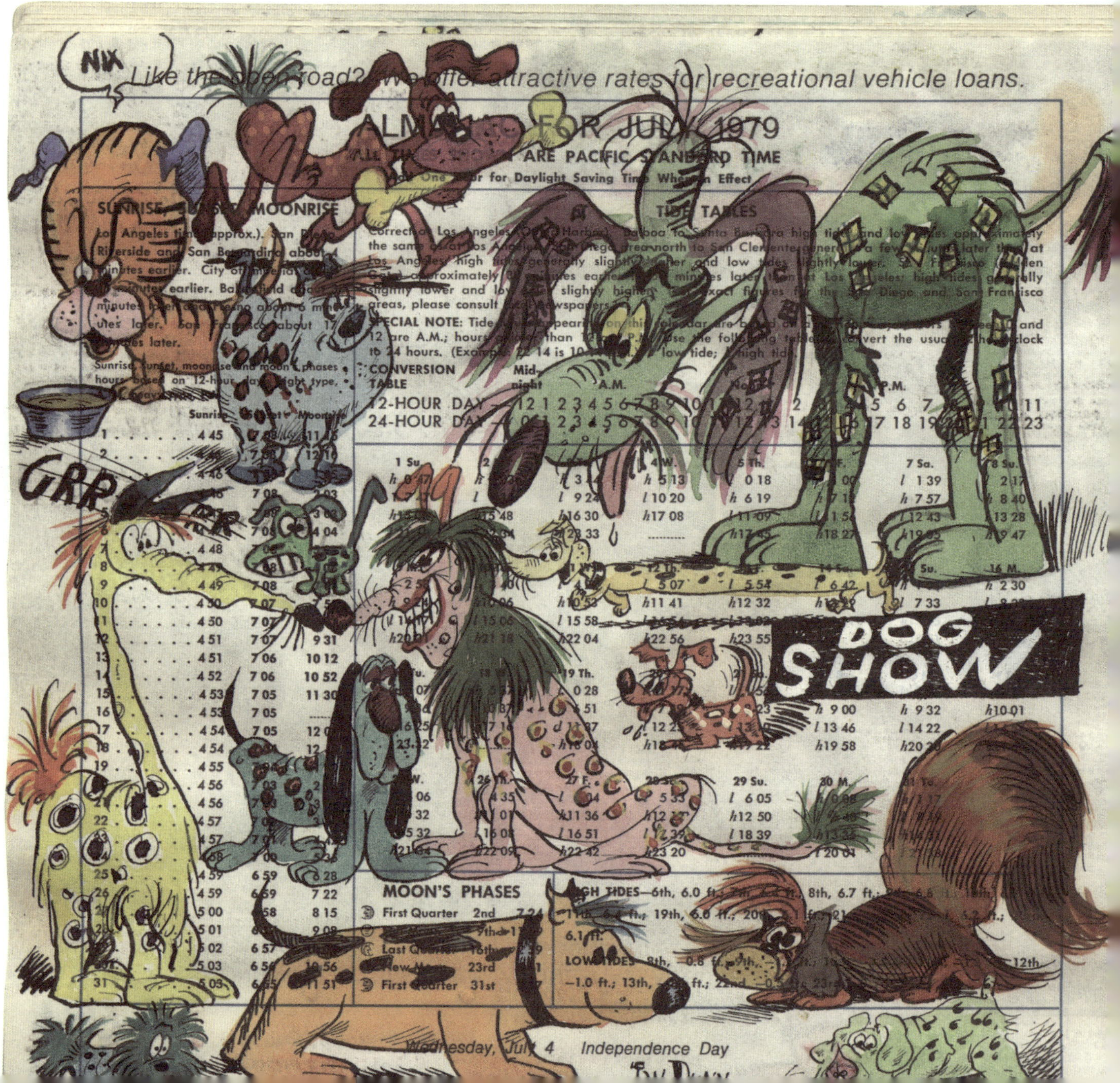

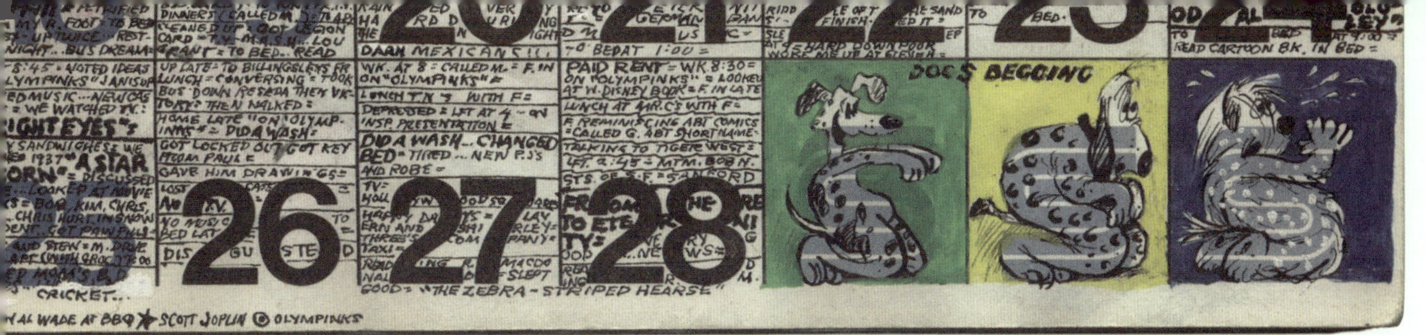

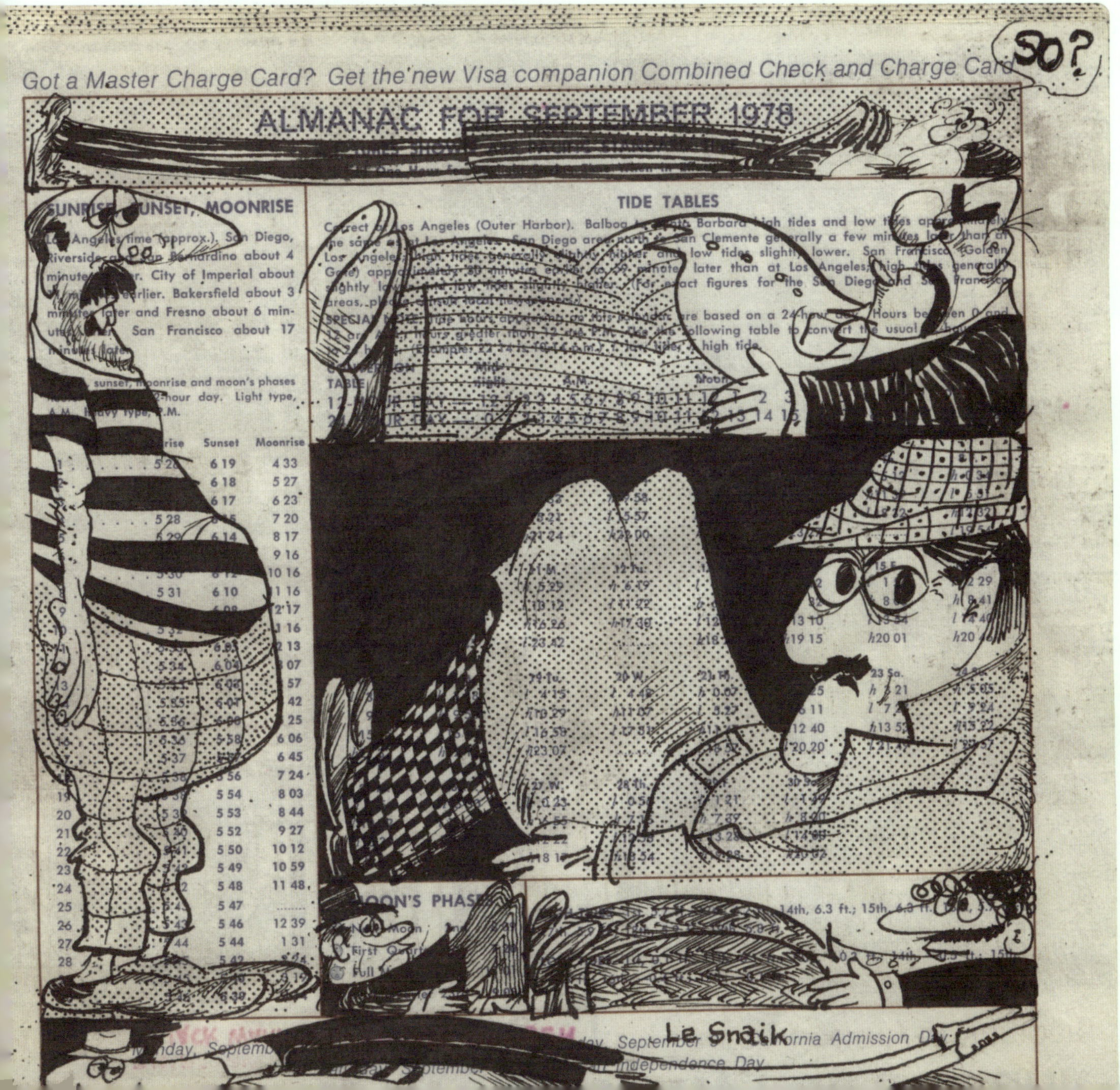

Got a Master Charge Card? Get the new Visa companion Combined Check and Charge Card

SO?

ALMANAC FOR SEPTEMBER 1978

SUNRISE, SUNSET, MOONRISE

Los Angeles time (approx.). San Diego, Riverside, San Bernardino about 4 minutes earlier. City of Imperial about … earlier. Bakersfield about 3 minutes later and Fresno about 6 minutes later. San Francisco about 17 minutes later.

… sunset, moonrise and moon's phases … 24-hour day. Light type, A.M. Heavy type, P.M.

	Sunrise	Sunset	Moonrise
1	5 2[illegible]	6 19	4 33
20	5 3[illegible]	5 53	8 44
21	[illegible]	5 52	9 27
22	[illegible]	5 50	10 12
23	[illegible]	5 49	10 59
24	[illegible]	5 48	11 48
25	[illegible]	5 47	
26	[illegible]	5 46	12 39
27	5 44	5 44	1 31
28	[illegible]	5 42	[illegible]

TIDE TABLES

Correct for Los Angeles (Outer Harbor). Balboa to Santa Barbara high tides and low tides approximately the same as at Los Angeles. San Diego area north to San Clemente generally a few minutes later than at Los Angeles; high tides generally slightly higher and low tides slightly lower. San Francisco (Golden Gate) approximately … minutes … later than at Los Angeles; high tides generally slightly lower and low tides slightly higher. (For exact figures for the San Diego and San Francisco areas, please consult local tide tables.)

SPECIAL NOTE: … are based on a 24-hour day. Hours between 0 and 12 are … following table to convert the usual … high tide.

MOON'S PHASES

New Moon …

First Quarter …

Full Moon …

14th, 6.3 ft.; 15th, 6.3 ft.

Le Snaik

Monday, September … California Admission Day

… September … Independence Day

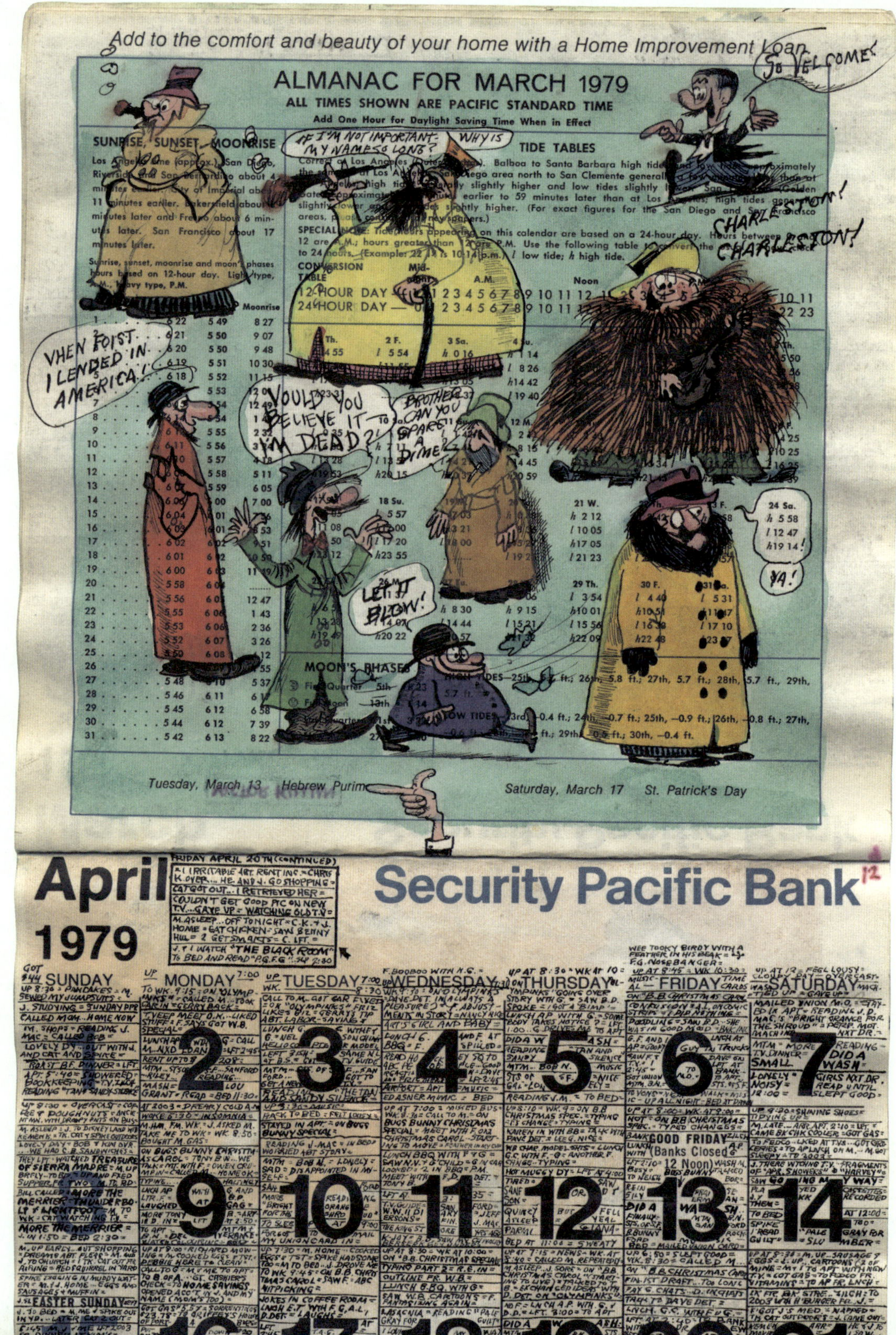
Add to the comfort and beauty of your home with a Home Improvement Loan
ALMANAC FOR MARCH 1979
ALL TIMES SHOWN ARE PACIFIC STANDARD TIME
Add One Hour for Daylight Saving Time When in Effect
SUNRISE, SUNSET, MOONRISE
TIDE TABLES
SO VELCOME!
IF I'M NOT IMPORTANT, WHY IS MY NAME SO LONG?
CHARLESTON! CHARLESTON!
VHEN FOIST I LENDED IN AMERICA!
VOULD YOU BELIEVE IT— I'M DEAD?!
BROTHER CAN YOU SPARE A DIME?
LET IT BLOW!
YA!
MOON'S PHASES
Tuesday, March 13 Hebrew Purim
Saturday, March 17 St. Patrick's Day
April 1979
Security Pacific Bank
SUNDAY MONDAY TUESDAY WEDNESDAY THURSDAY FRIDAY SATURDAY
GOOD FRIDAY (Banks Closed 12 Noon)
EASTER SUNDAY

11	12	13	14
BUNNY CHRISTMAS AL = MEET WITH F. ON STMAS CAROL – START D MOVE = FEATHER IN MY CUP H BBQ WITH F & G = N.Y. + G' CHILD = G IN CAR ED = 2 IN BBQ = P.M. WITH F. D. DET. B. 35 = UIDE = SAN FORD = JEFF II DI ARY FIN. J. MAC. NS = NG ST ORE YRS AGO Y = B.D. SAW MY CHIVALRY	T.S CHANGES = TYPING KAREN IN WTH BB = TALK WITH DAVE DET. = LEE G. NICE = WB CHAR. MODEL SHTS = LUNCH G.C. WITH F. – G = ANOTHER F. CHNGE.. TYPING = HOT MUGGY DY = LFT AT 4:00 TIRED = SAW SANF OR SON = QUINCY BUT FELL ASLEEP = YEAL PARMI GIANA = BED AT 11:00 = SWEATY	SPEC. = TYPED CHANGES = BANK **GOOD FRIDAY** ZILCH LUNCH **(Banks Closed** A.P. WITH **12 Noon)** G LFT 2:10 = WASH M. BUSY = TALKED TO NEIGH BUGS BUNNY BOR = REIN SILY SE DID A WA SH.. FINALLY.. STS. OF S.F. B.N. FORD MTM SAN B.BUNNY ROCK- FORD BED = MAILED UNION CARD =	M. LACE.. – ARR. APT. 2:10 = CAME BK CHK COOLER = TO FEDCO .. LKED AT T.V.S .. SERIES = TO AP LUNCH ON M SLEEPY = TO 2003 = J. THERE WTCHING T.V. "FRA OF "APR. SHOWERS" & "HA SAW GO ING M Y PLA YED J.Y. KK THEM = TO BED SPIKE I READ "PALE GUILT" = SLU

18	19	20	21
8:30 = WK AT 10:00 = B.B. CHRISTMAS SPECIAL D PART 2 = R.E. IN = LINE FR. W.B. = CH B.BQ. WITH G = W.B. CARTOONS = F. ASIZING AGAIN = NIA = READING "PALE FOR GUILT" MY WAY HON NCA RD	UP AT 7:15 = NEWS – WK. AT 8:40 = CALLED M. REPEATEDLY = M. ASLEEP.. J. SORE = ON "B.B. CHRISTMAS CAROL" (STARTING TO LIVE) = TALKED TO T. B. – EXCHANGED IDEAS WITH D. DET. ON "OLYMPINKS" = NO F. = LNCH A.P. WITH G. + D.D. = LFT. 3:00 = TO APT DID A W ASH = MTM B.N. SANF OF SF ROGER NUT LAUGHS A LUNC READING "PALE GRAY FOR GUILT" – J.D.M.	UP 6:50 = SLEPT GOOD = WK. 8:30 = CALLED M... ON "BB CHRISTMAS CAROL" FIN. 1ST DRAFT... TOO LONG PAY G. CHATS... D. IN CHATS TALK TO DAVE DET. = LNCH. G.C. WITH F & G. = LFT. AT 2:40 = TO BANK RENTING M. CAME GRIF T.V. M. FR. FRIED CHICKEN	UP AT 8:30 = M. UP... SAUS EGGS = J. UP... CARTOONS MINE = M + I TO APT W T.V. = GOT GAS = TO FEDCO VITAMINS = TO AP FR. L 1K FR. BK. STRE. – ZILC 2003 WITH H'BURGER FR F GOT J'S MED. = NAPP TH CAT OUTDOORS = J. CA MOVIE #1.98 MATCH GA M. UP = J. HME AT TILL 2:00 =

25	26	27	28
9:00 = WK AT 10:00 = B.B. CHRISTMAS CAR. 2ND DRAFT = INC UP SIDEWALKS = GUYS NG FLOWERS = D WITH G... MET 2 GUYS 2:45 = TOOK Y B. FEED = GOT SUPER-GLUE = OP ON CURB PLANE WI YOU GO HOME AGAIN" =	UP AT 9:30 = STAYED IN APT. ON "BUGS CHRISTMAS CAROL" DID A WASH!! CLEANED T.T. = DOWNTOWN... GOT A HAIRCUT.. TO VONS = TO APT. CHANGED BED = GOT NEW JOHN D. MACDONALD BK = READING M.T.M. ZILCH = B.N. ZILCH = SANFORD = (RECORDING) = SLEPT GOOD	UP AT 9:30 = FELT STRANGE = BALKING AT LIFE = TO WK. AT 11:15 = F. IN PALM SPS. = F. RUNNING SCARED = WB N.Y. AXED T.B.'S SHORT = BOWED OUT – TO BANK (C.F.) AT 12:15 = GOT RENT M.O. + A SMILE FRM W. = GOT COINS + CASH = TO VONS = TO APT = READING "T.E.C.S" = SAW B.N. SON = THE COPPER ROCKFORD TO BED AT 11	UP AT 9:00 = (CARTOONS BUS TO 2003 – 11:45 = J. WKE M. UP (BK. TO BD.) = BATHED SPK... HOSED PATIO UP = WE GO TO B.S. – T TO 2003... J. WASHING CA M. GAVE ME JAP BK = T.V. – MTM – #1.98 BEAUT M. ASLEEP SHOWER

NE – U P

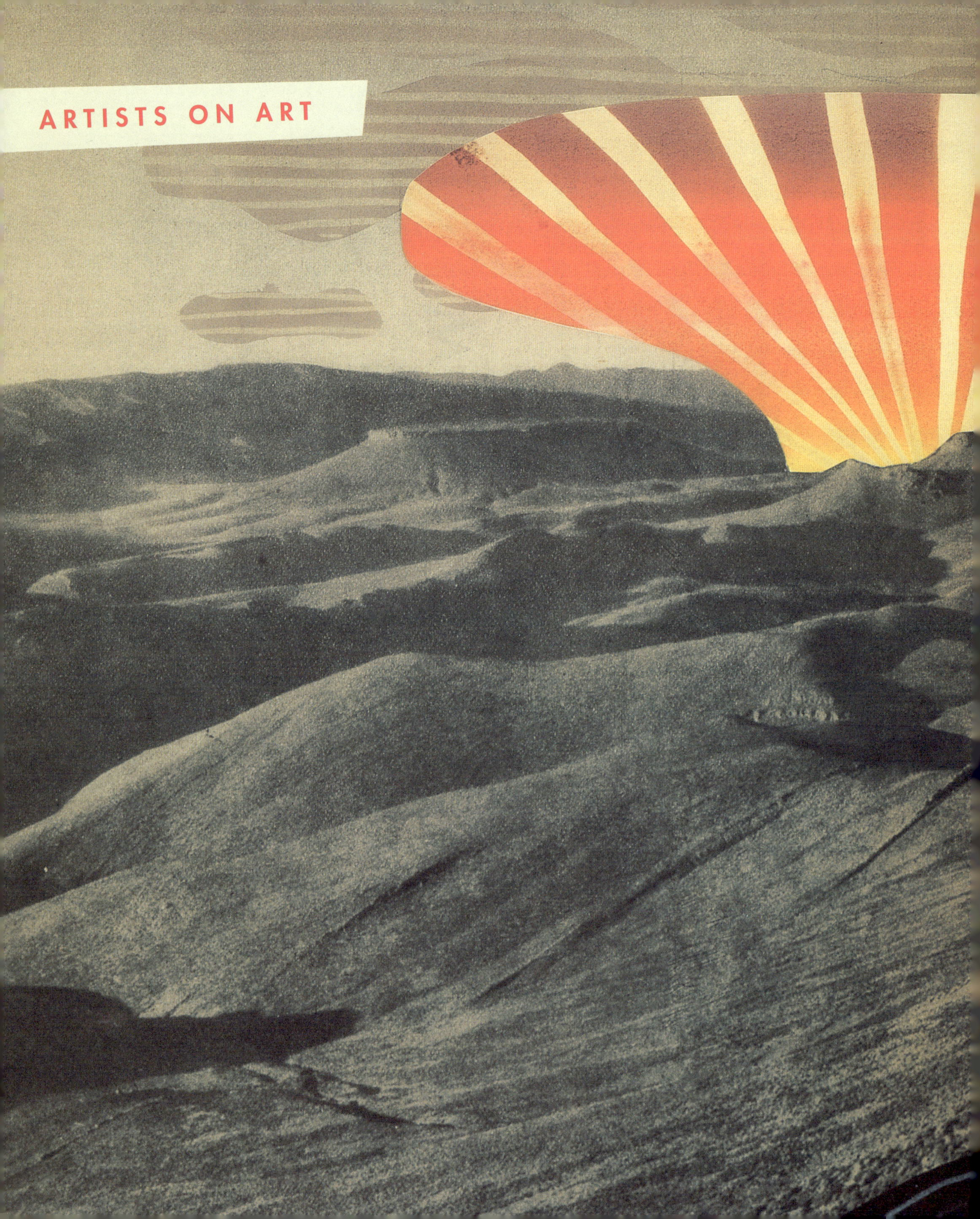
ARTISTS ON ART

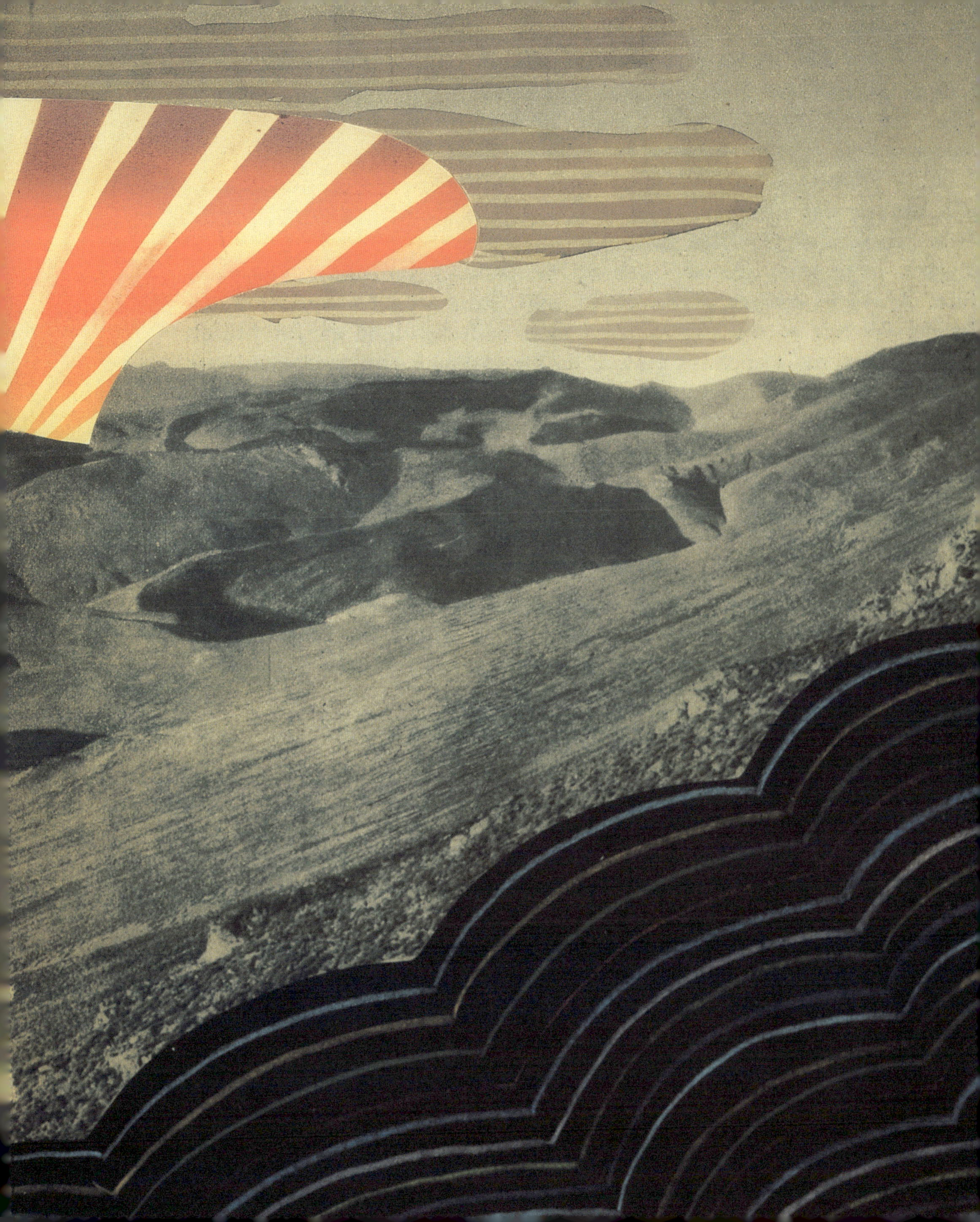

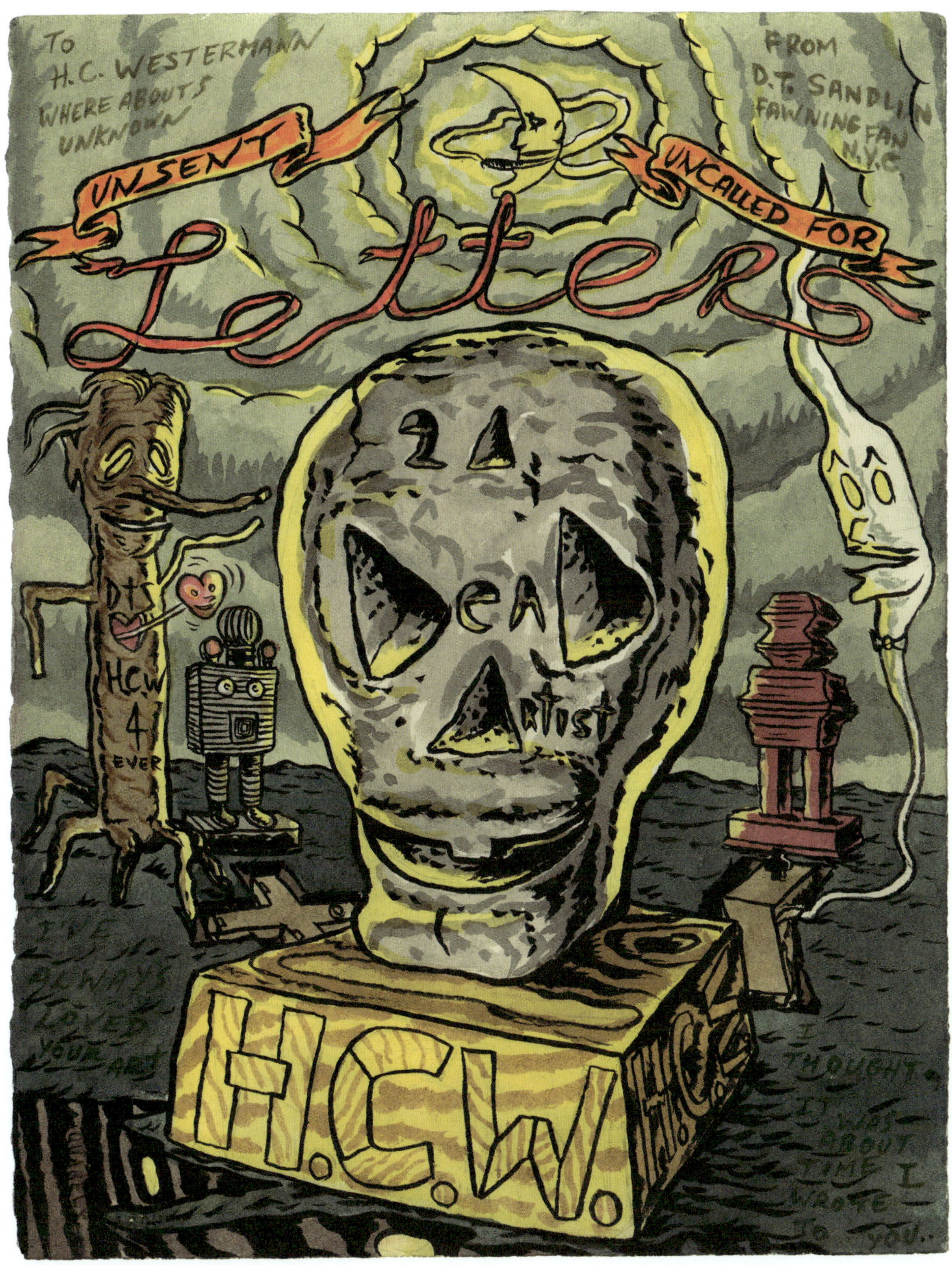
TO
H.C. WESTERMANN
WHERE ABOUTS
UNKNOWN
FROM
D.T. SANDLIN
FAWNING FAN
N.Y.C.
UNSENT
UNCALLED FOR
Letters
2 A
DeaD
Artist
D.T.
H.C.W
4
EVER
I'VE
ALWAYS
LOVED
YOUR ART
H.C.W.
H.C.
I
THOUGHT
IT WAS
ABOUT
TIME I
WROTE
TO YOU..

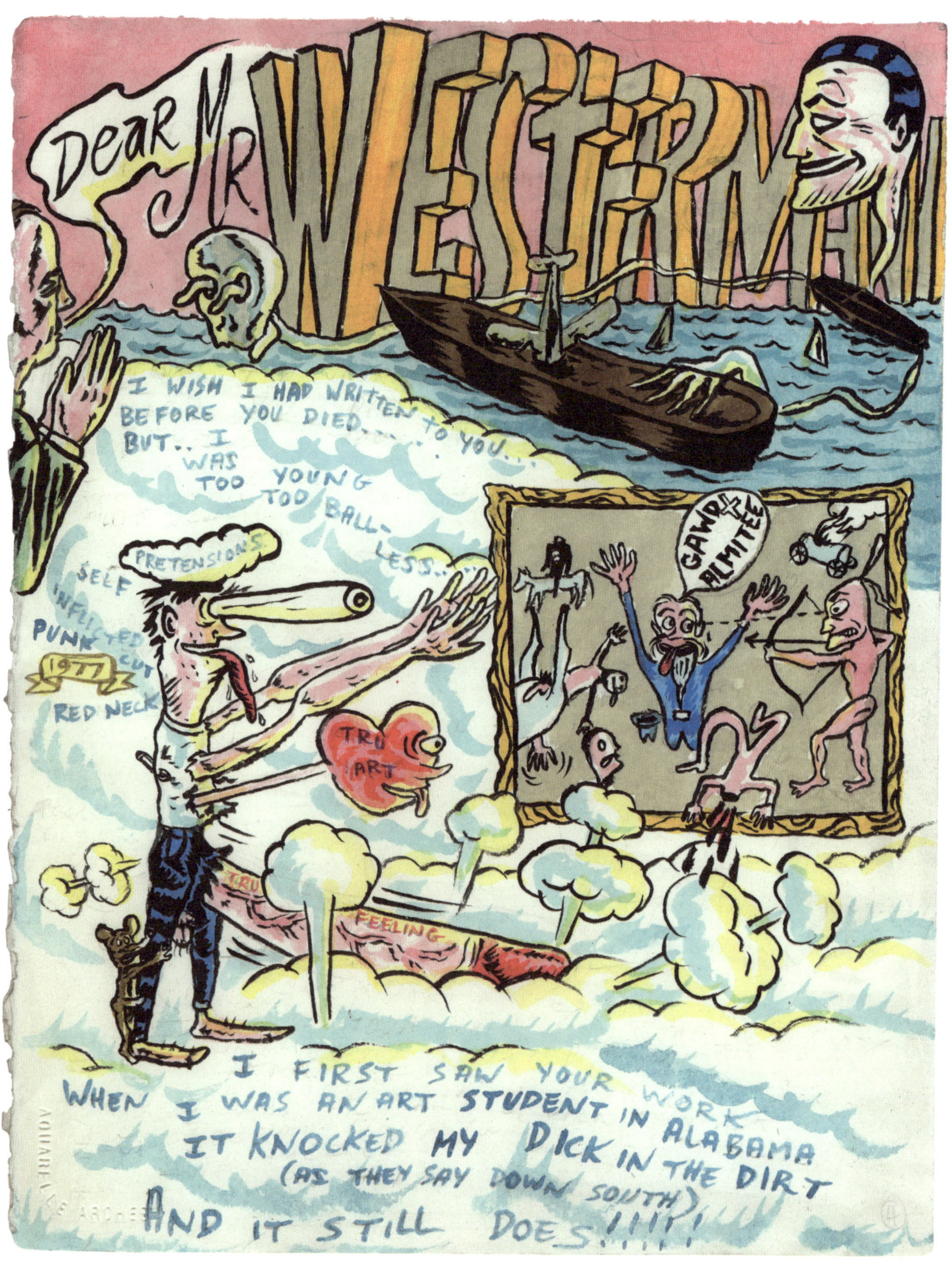

Dear Mr Westermann
I wish I had written to you...
before you died...
but.. I was too young
too ball-less...
PRETENSIONS
SELF INFLICTED PUNK CUT
1977
RED NECK
TRU ART
TRU FEELING
GAWR ALMITEE
I FIRST SAW YOUR WORK
WHEN I WAS AN ART STUDENT IN ALABAMA
IT KNOCKED MY DICK IN THE DIRT
(AS THEY SAY DOWN SOUTH)
AND IT STILL DOES!!!!!

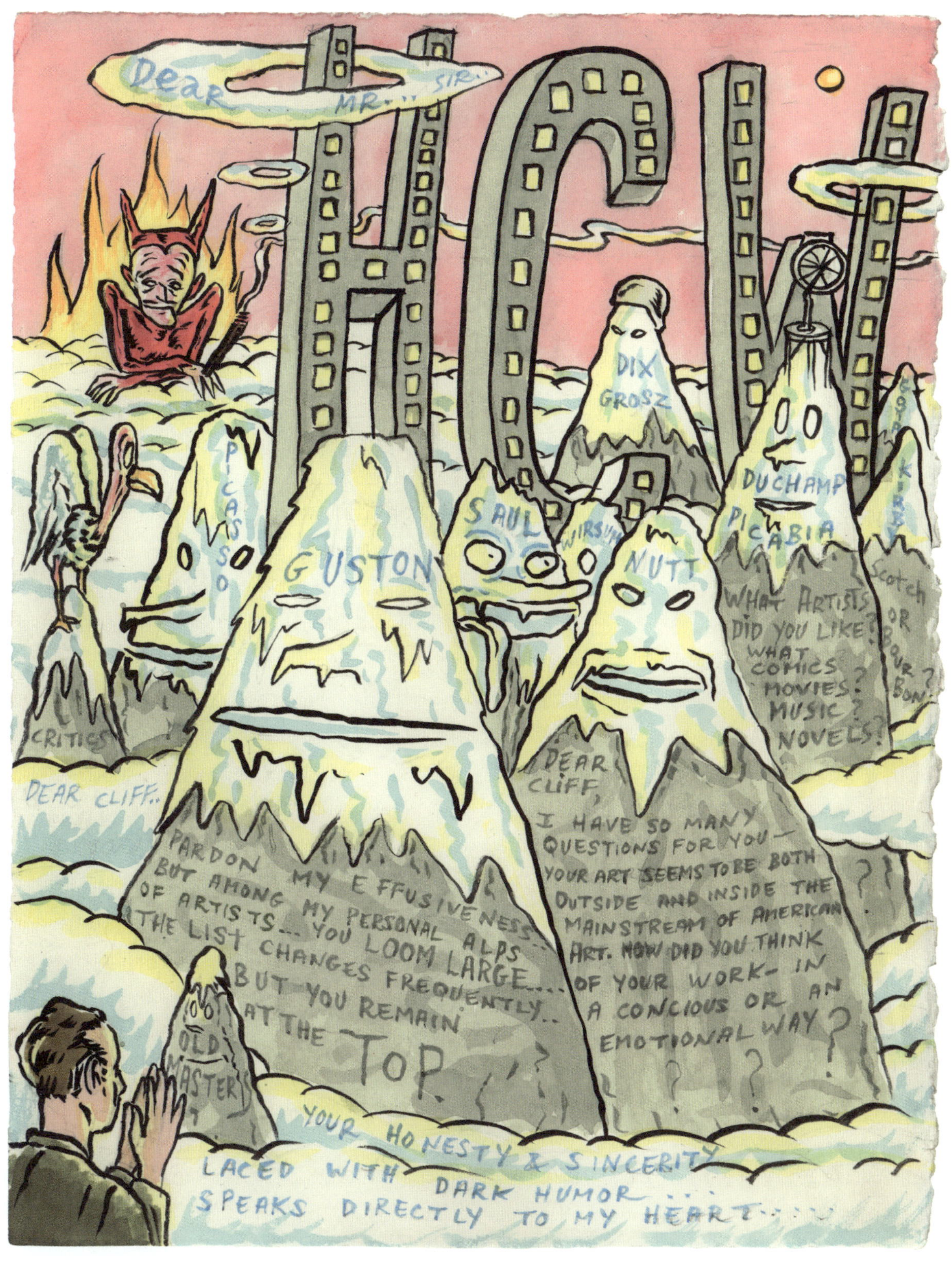

Dear MR... SIR...
HCW
PICASSO
GUSTON
SAUL
WIRSUM
NUTT
DIX
GROSZ
DUCHAMP
PICABIA
KIRBY
CRITICS
OLD MASTERS
WHAT ARTISTS DID YOU LIKE? WHAT COMICS MOVIES? MUSIC? NOVELS?
Scotch OR BOURBON?
DEAR CLIFF..
PARDON MY EFFUSIVENESS.. BUT AMONG MY PERSONAL ALPS OF ARTISTS... YOU LOOM LARGE.... THE LIST CHANGES FREQUENTLY.. BUT YOU REMAIN AT THE TOP.
DEAR CLIFF,
I HAVE SO MANY QUESTIONS FOR YOU— YOUR ART SEEMS TO BE BOTH OUTSIDE AND INSIDE THE MAINSTREAM OF AMERICAN ART. HOW DID YOU THINK OF YOUR WORK- IN A CONCIOUS OR AN EMOTIONAL WAY?
YOUR HONESTY & SINCERITY LACED WITH DARK HUMOR.... SPEAKS DIRECTLY TO MY HEART....

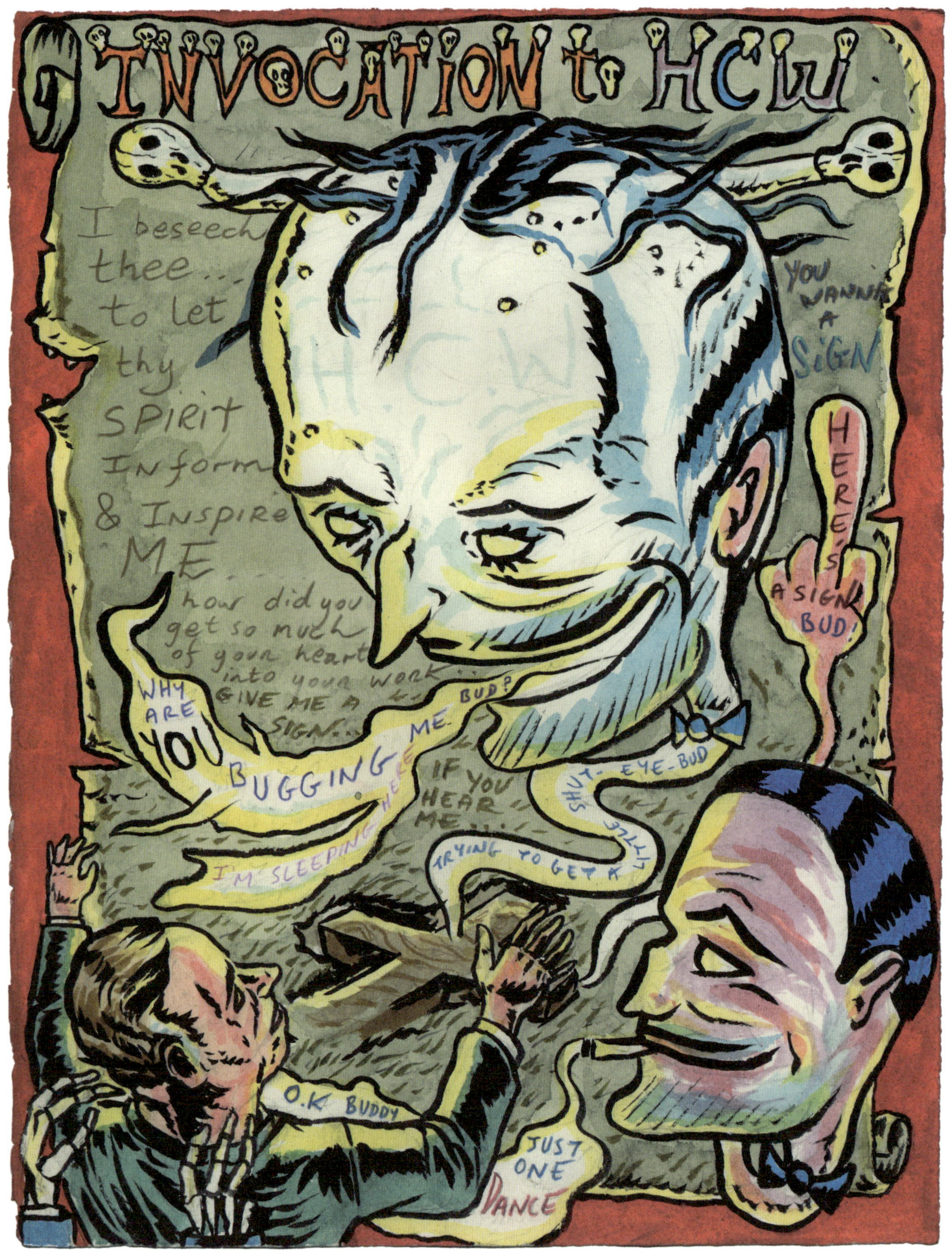
INVOCATION to HCW
I beseech thee... to let thy SPIRIT Inform & INSPIRE ME...
how did you get so much of your heart into your work...
GIVE ME A SIGN...
YOU WANNA A SIGN
HERE'S A SIGN BUD!
WHY ARE YOU BUGGING ME BUD?
IF YOU HEAR ME...
I'M SLEEPING HERE
TRYING TO GET A LITTLE SHUT-EYE-BUD
O.K BUDDY
JUST ONE DANCE

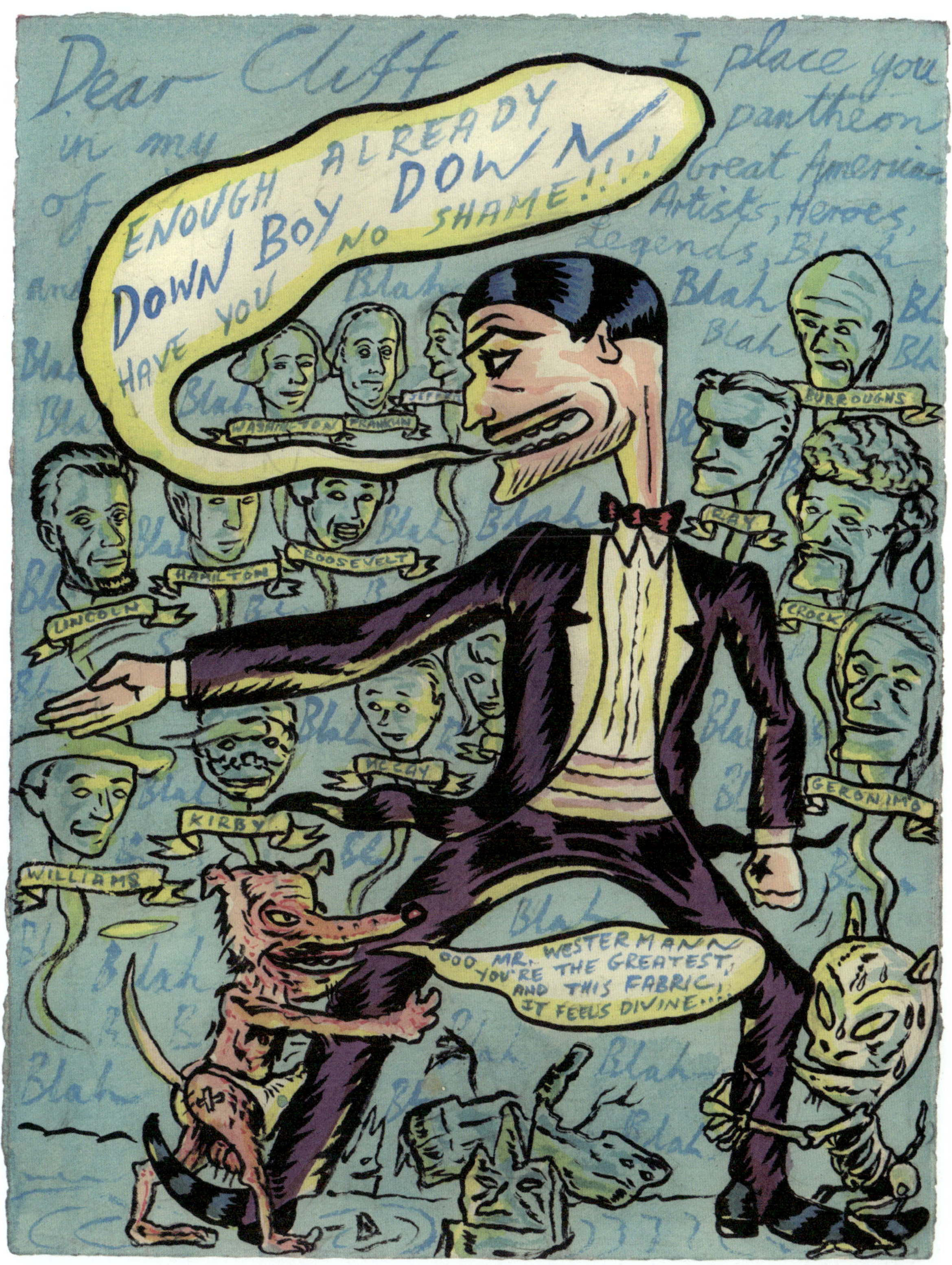
Dear Cliff I place you in my pantheon of Great American Artists, Heroes, Legends, Blah
Blah
Blah
ENOUGH ALREADY
DOWN BOY DOWN!!!!
HAVE YOU NO SHAME!!!!
WASHINGTON
FRANKLIN
BURROUGHS
LINCOLN
HAMILTON
ROOSEVELT
RAY
CROCK
McCAY
KIRBY
GERONIMO
WILLIAMS
OOO MR. WESTERMANN YOU'RE THE GREATEST, AND THIS FABRIC, IT FEELS DIVINE...

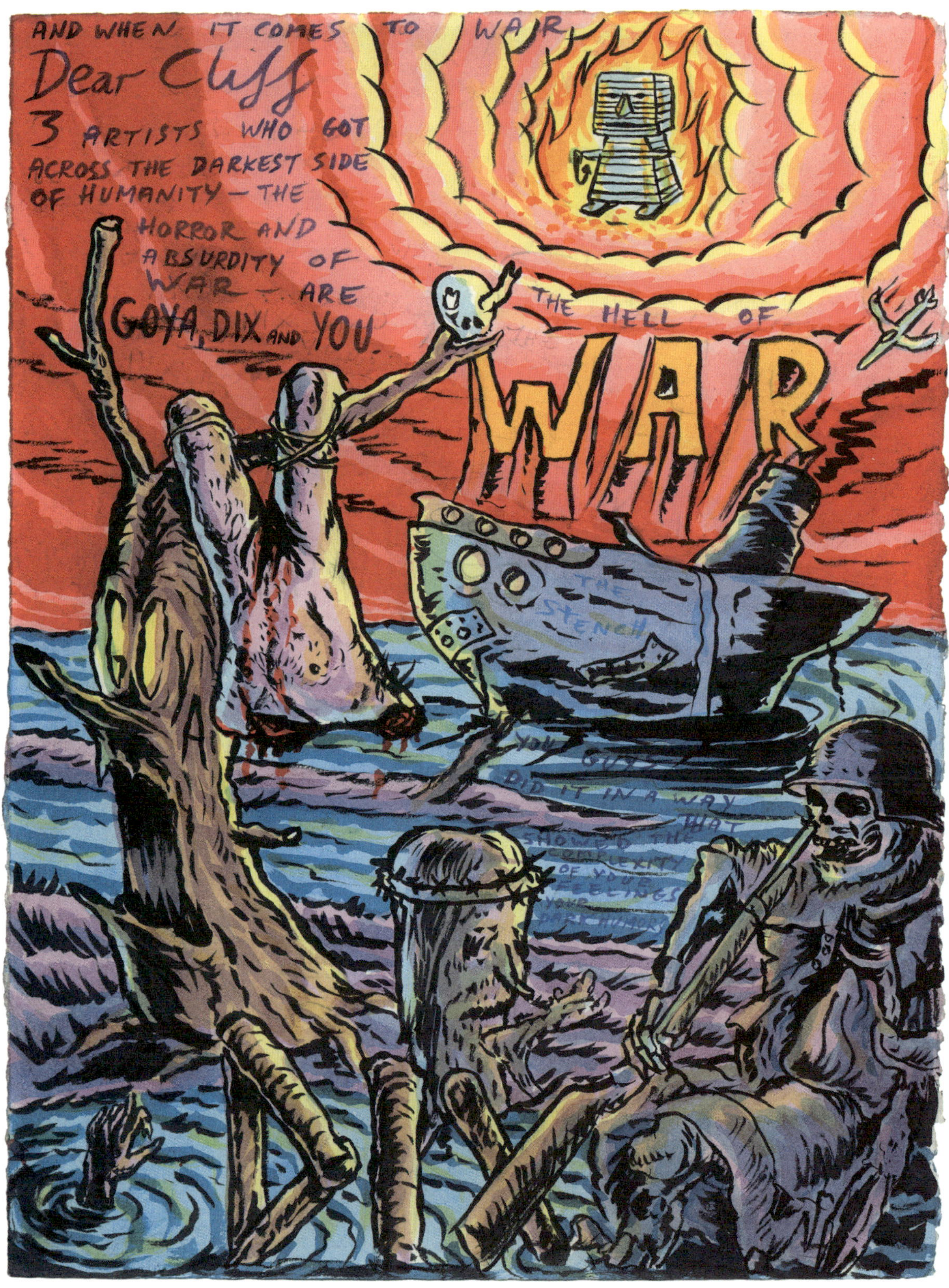

Dear Cliff
3 ARTISTS WHO GOT ACROSS THE DARKEST SIDE OF HUMANITY — THE HORROR AND ABSURDITY OF WAR — ARE GOYA, DIX AND YOU.
AND WHEN IT COMES TO WAR
THE HELL OF
WAR
THE STENCH
YOU GUYS DID IT IN A WAY THAT SHOWED THE COMPLEXITY OF YOUR FEELINGS

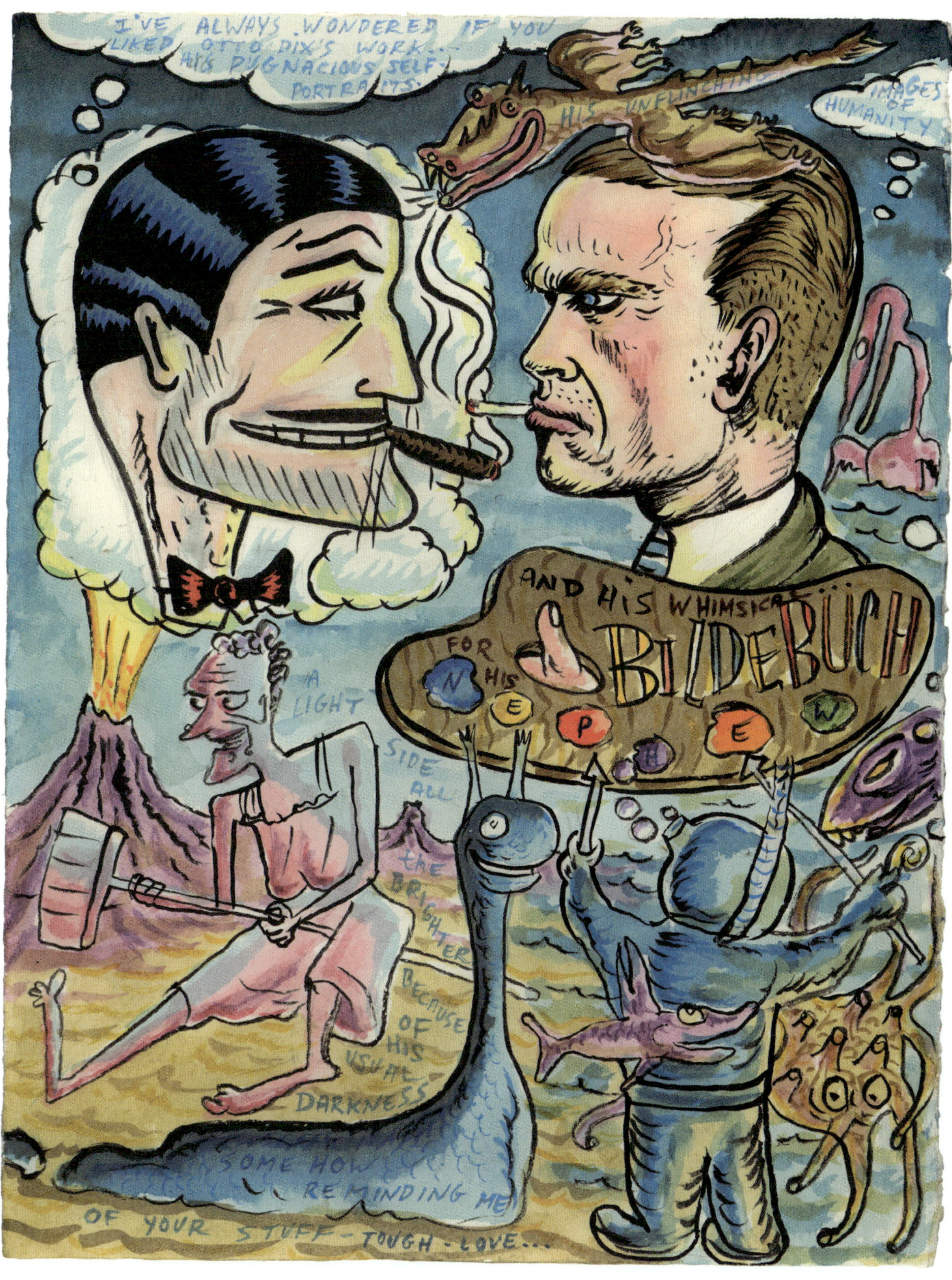

I'VE ALWAYS WONDERED IF YOU LIKED OTTO DIX'S WORK... HIS PUGNACIOUS SELF-PORTRAITS
HIS UNFLINCHING
IMAGES OF HUMANITY
AND HIS WHIMSICA
BILDEBUCH
FOR HIS
N E P H E W
A LIGHT SIDE ALL the BRIGHTER BECAUSE OF HIS USUAL DARKNESS
SOME HOW REMINDING ME
OF YOUR STUFF - TOUGH - LOVE...

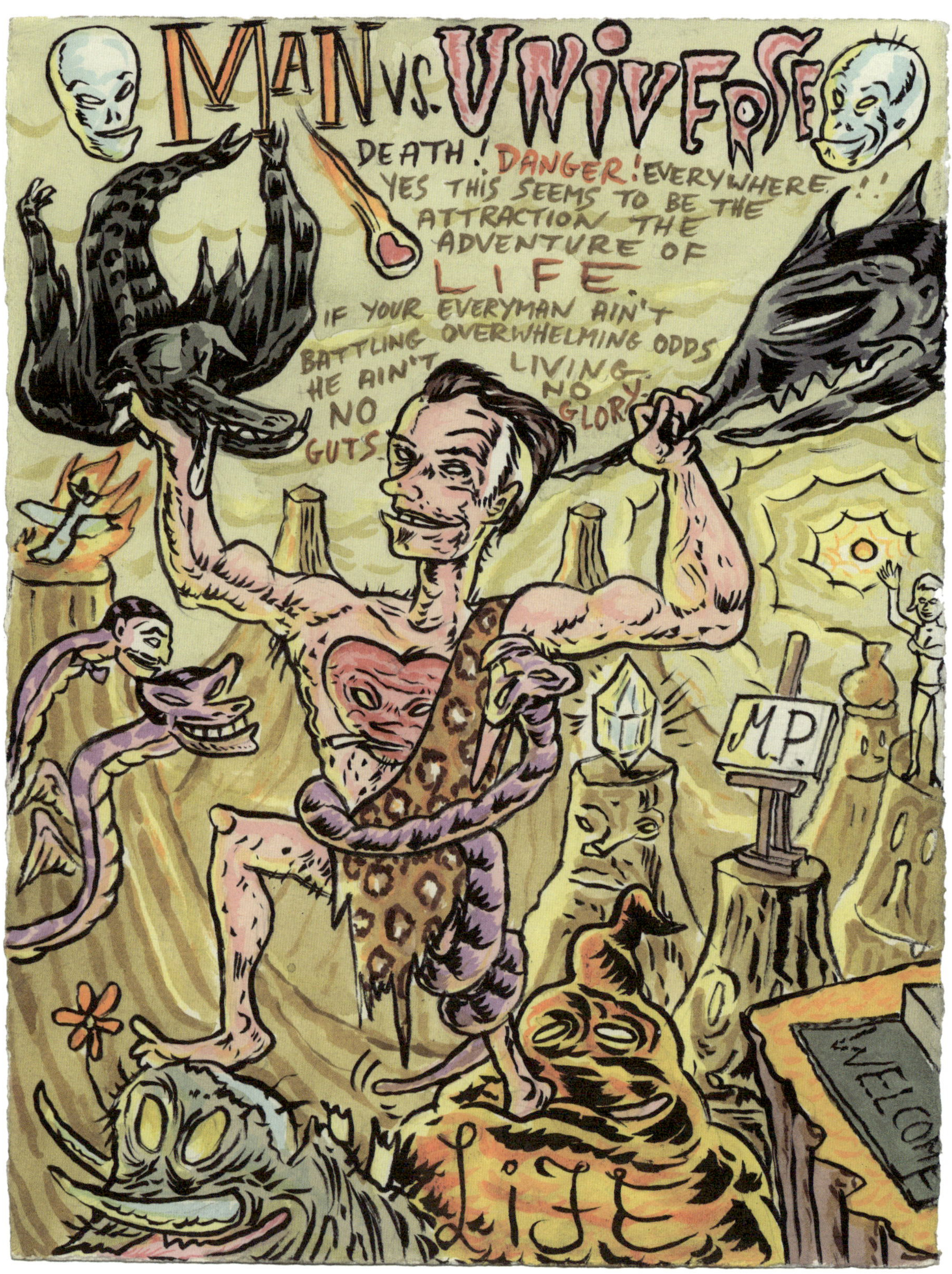
MAN VS. UNIVERSE
DEATH! DANGER! EVERYWHERE!!
YES THIS SEEMS TO BE THE
ATTRACTION THE
ADVENTURE OF
LIFE.
IF YOUR EVERYMAN AIN'T
BATTLING OVERWHELMING ODDS
HE AIN'T LIVING.
NO GUTS
NO GLORY
M.P.
WELCOME
LIFE

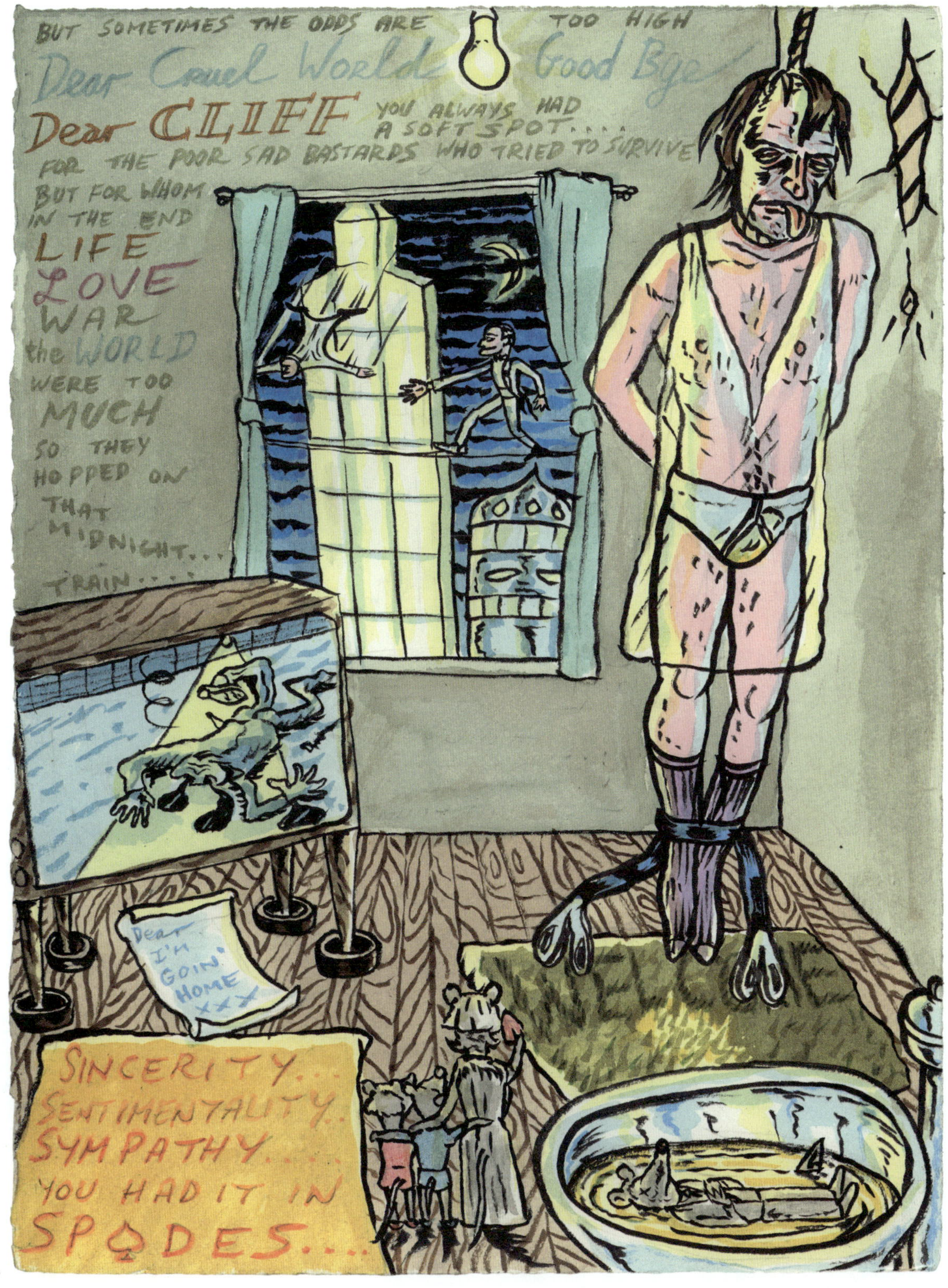
BUT SOMETIMES THE ODDS ARE TOO HIGH
Dear Cruel World Good Bye
Dear CLIFF YOU ALWAYS HAD A SOFT SPOT....
FOR THE POOR SAD BASTARDS WHO TRIED TO SURVIVE
BUT FOR WHOM IN THE END
LIFE
LOVE
WAR
the WORLD
WERE TOO
MUCH
SO THEY HOPPED ON THAT MIDNIGHT... TRAIN....
Dear I'M GOIN' HOME XXX
SINCERITY...
SENTIMENTALITY...
SYMPATHY.....
YOU HAD IT IN
SPADES....

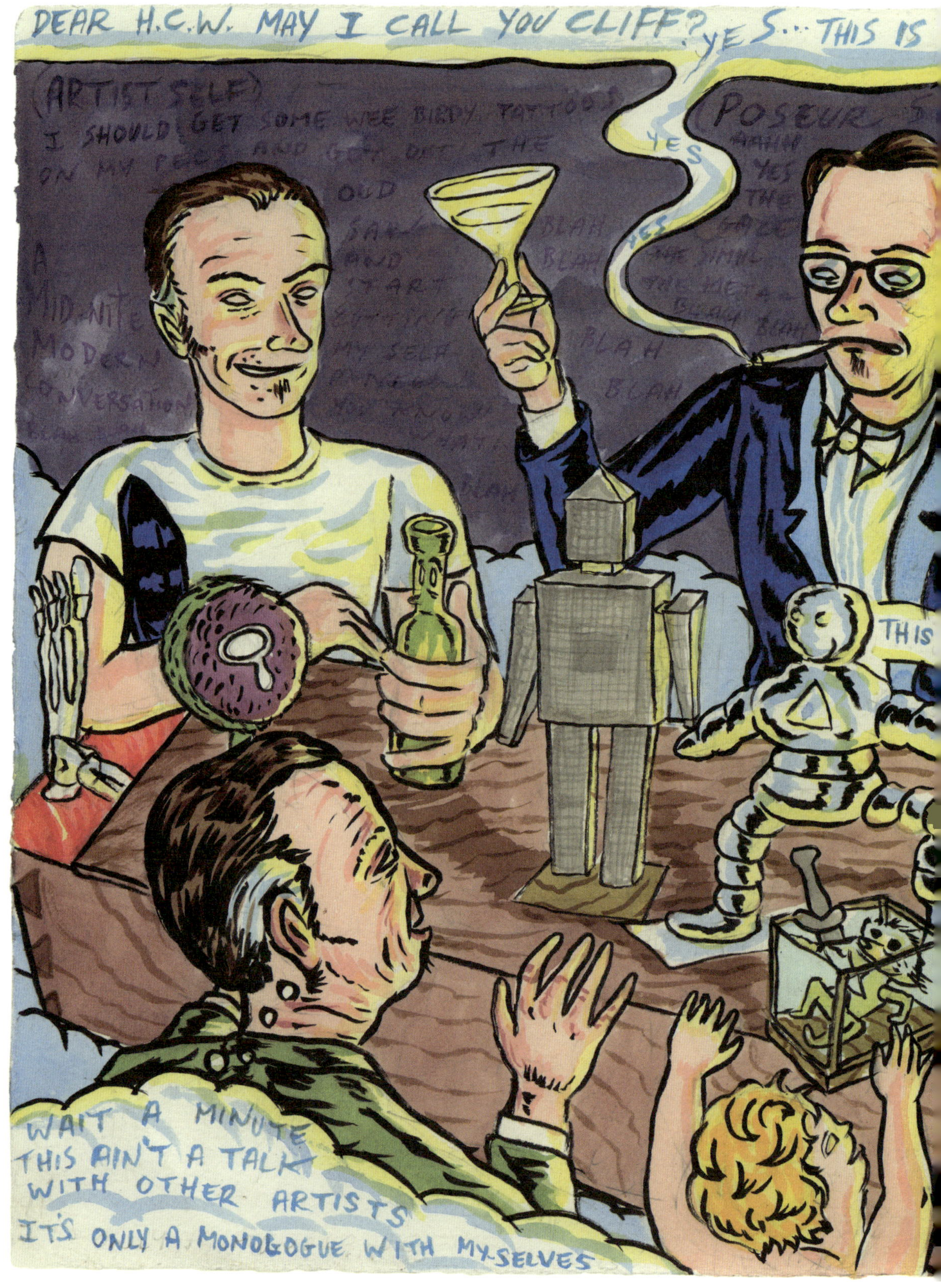
DEAR H.C.W. MAY I CALL YOU CLIFF? YES... THIS IS
(ARTIST SELF)
I SHOULD GET SOME WEE BIRDY TATTOOS
A MIDNITE MODERN CONVERSATION
POSEUR
BLAH
BLAH
BLAH
BLAH
THIS
WAIT A MINUTE
THIS AIN'T A TALK
WITH OTHER ARTISTS
IT'S ONLY A MONOLOGUE WITH MY-SELVES

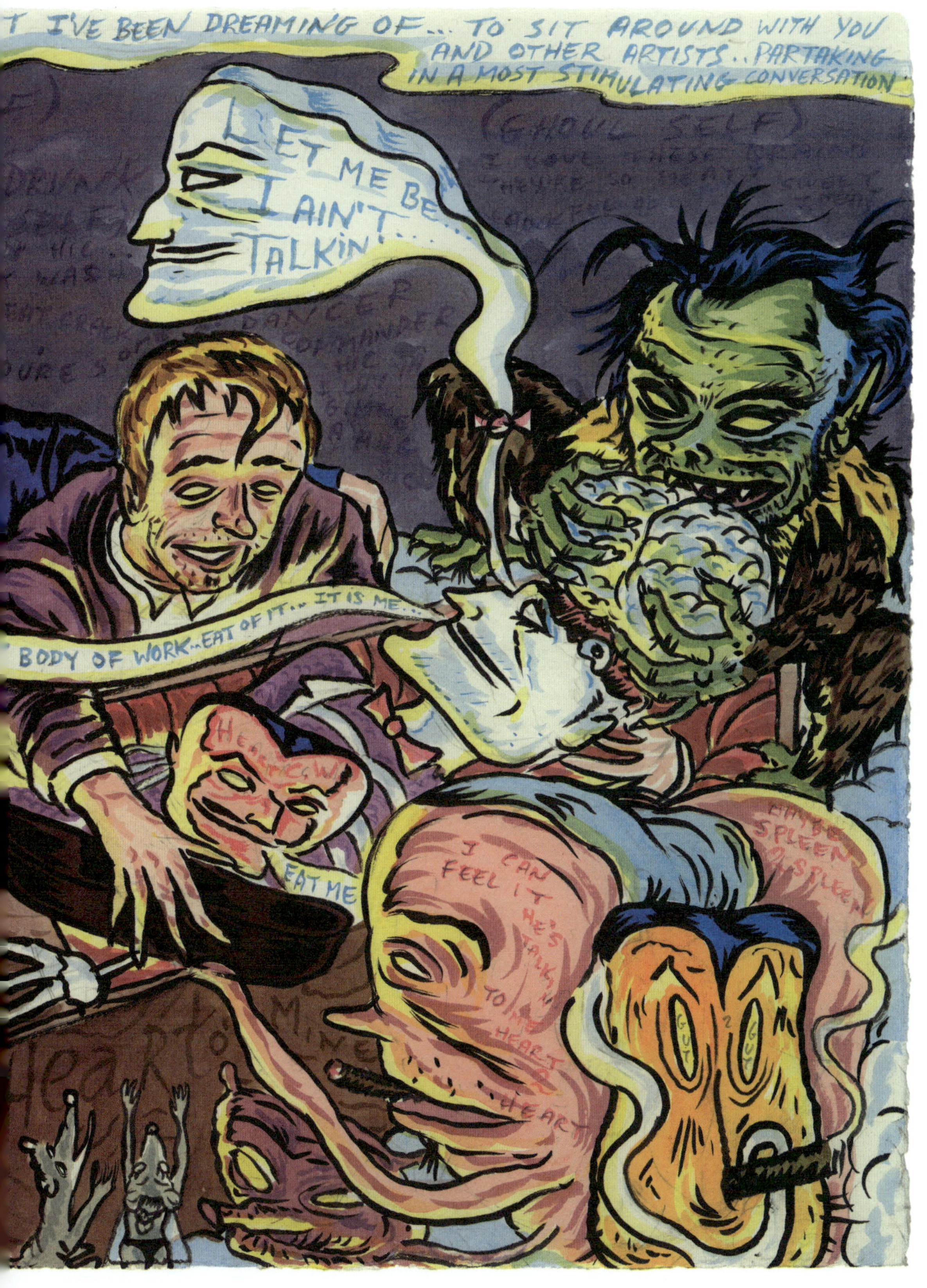
T I'VE BEEN DREAMING OF... TO SIT AROUND WITH YOU AND OTHER ARTISTS.. PARTAKING IN A MOST STIMULATING CONVERSATION"
LET ME BE... I AIN'T... TALKIN'
(GHOUL SELF)
BODY OF WORK.. EAT OF IT.. IT IS ME...
EAT ME
I CAN FEEL IT HE'S TALKIN TO ME HEART HEART
SPLEEN SPLEEN
GUT GUT

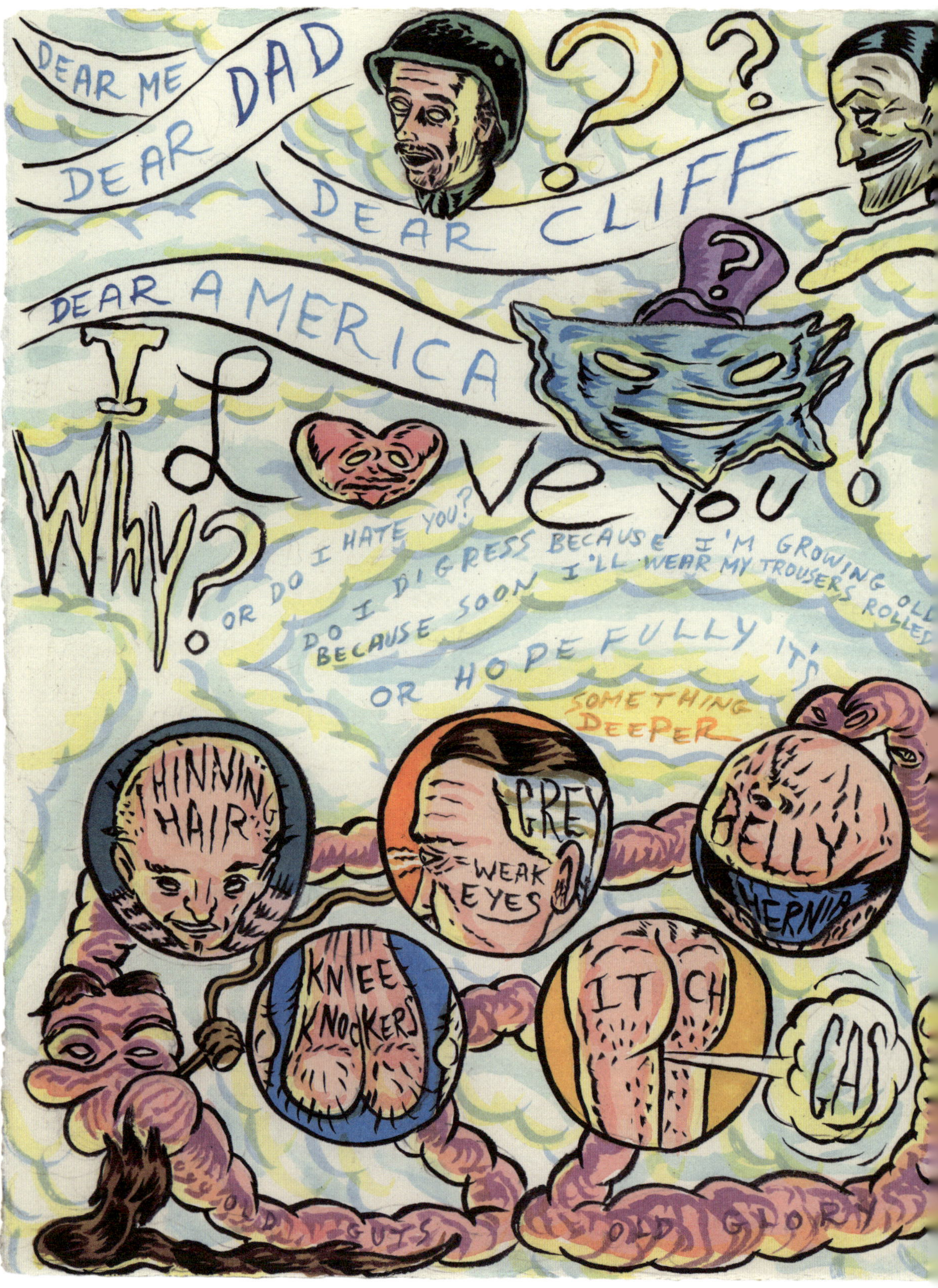
DEAR ME
DEAR DAD
DEAR CLIFF
DEAR AMERICA
I LOVE YOU
WHY? OR DO I HATE YOU?
DO I DIGRESS BECAUSE I'M GROWING OLD
BECAUSE SOON I'LL WEAR MY TROUSERS ROLLED
OR HOPEFULLY IT'S
OR
SOMETHING DEEPER
THINNING HAIR
GREY
WEAK EYES
BELLY!
HERNIA
KNEE KNOCKERS
ITCH
GAS
OLD GUTS
OLD GLORY

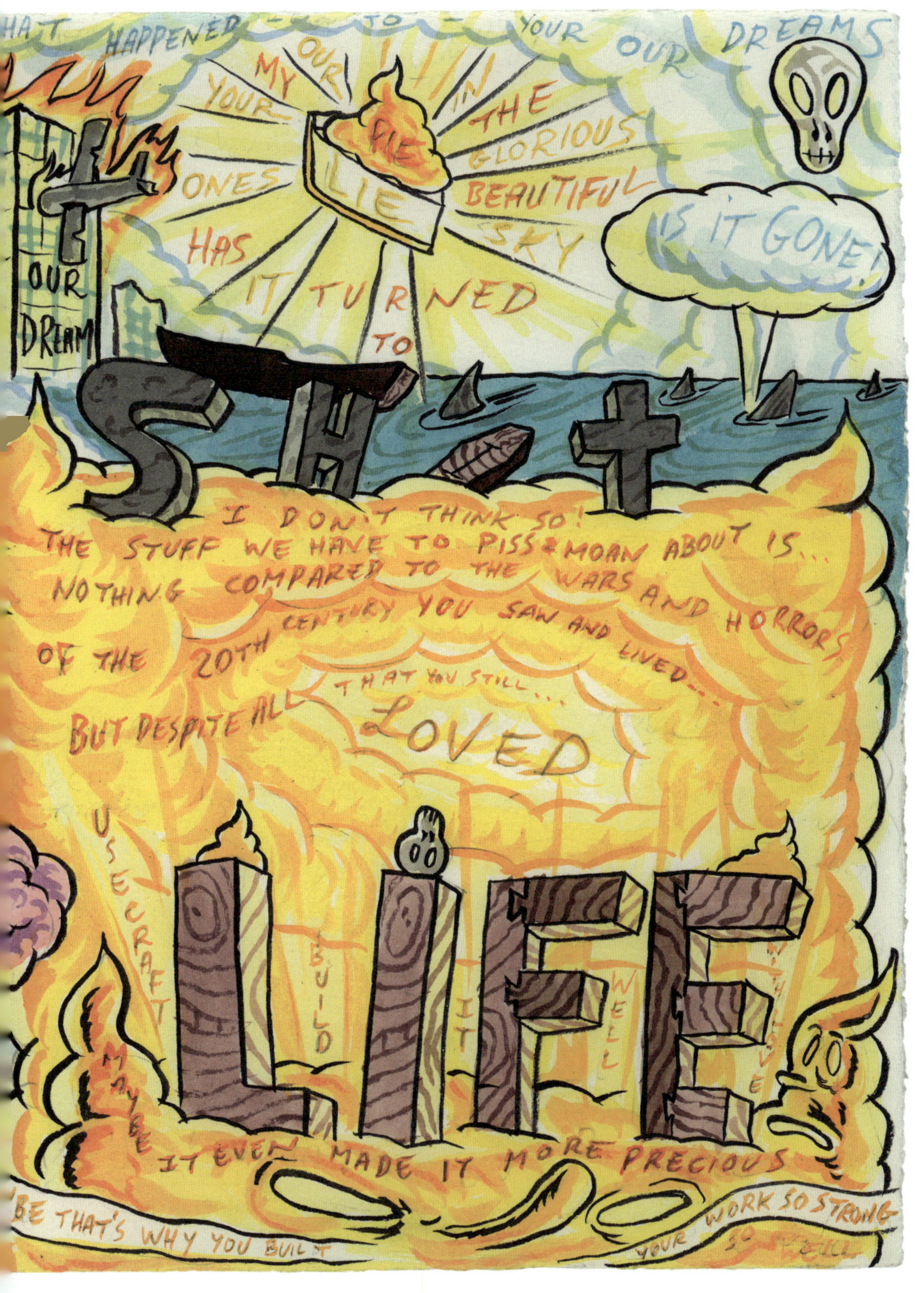

HAT HAPPENED TO YOUR OUR DREAMS
YOUR MY OUR PIE LIE IN THE GLORIOUS BEAUTIFUL SKY
ONES
HAS IT TURNED TO
OUR DREAM
IS IT GONE!
I DON'T THINK SO!
THE STUFF WE HAVE TO PISS & MOAN ABOUT IS...
NOTHING COMPARED TO THE WARS AND HORRORS
OF THE 20TH CENTURY YOU SAW AND LIVED...
BUT DESPITE ALL THAT YOU STILL...
LOVED
LIFE
USE CRAFT
BUILD IT WELL
MAYBE IT EVEN MADE IT MORE PRECIOUS
BE THAT'S WHY YOU BUILT YOUR WORK SO STRONG

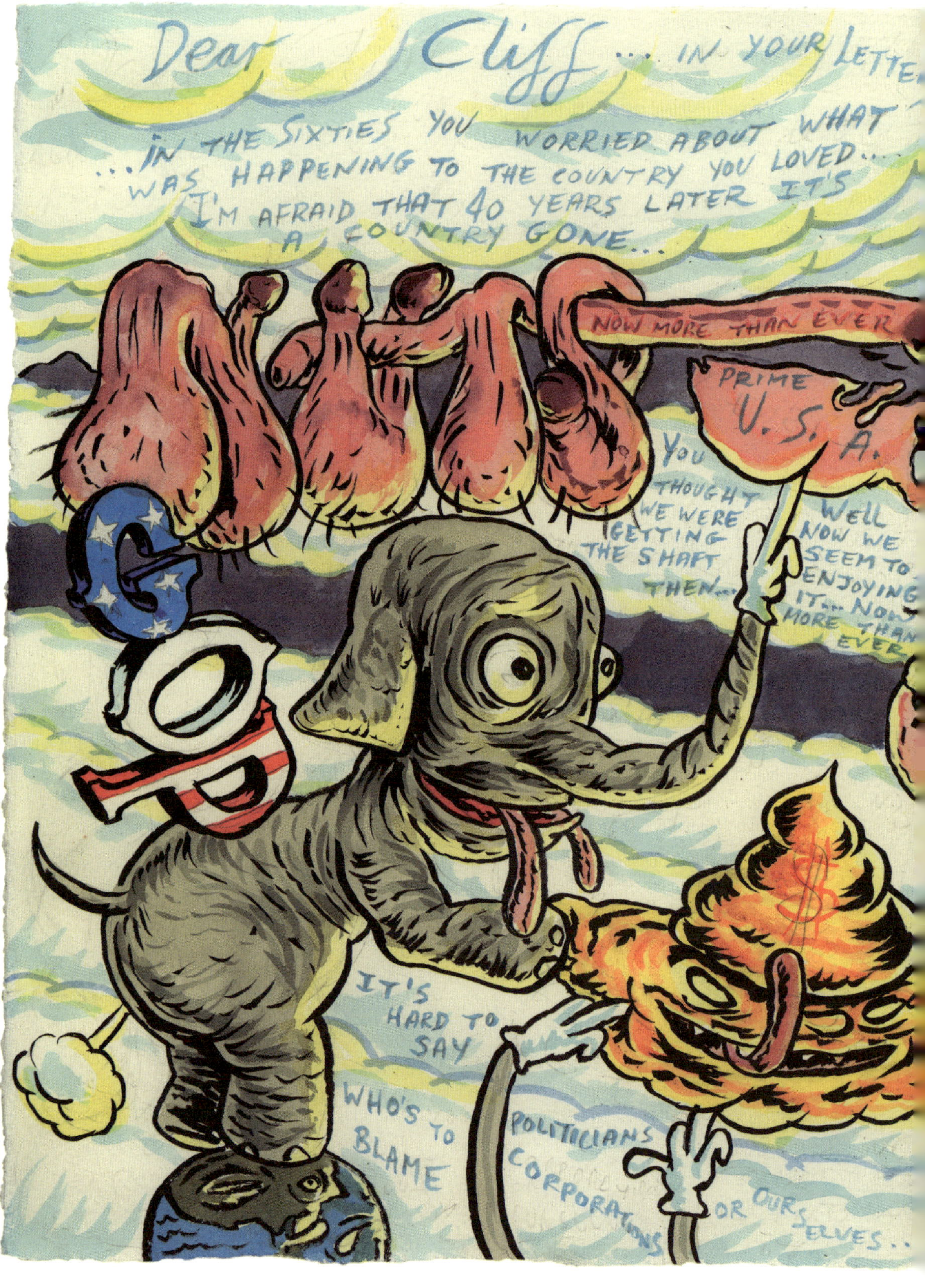
Dear Cliff ... IN YOUR LETTER
...IN THE SIXTIES YOU WORRIED ABOUT WHAT WAS HAPPENING TO THE COUNTRY YOU LOVED...
I'M AFRAID THAT 40 YEARS LATER IT'S A COUNTRY GONE...
NOW MORE THAN EVER
PRIME U.S.A.
YOU THOUGHT WE WERE GETTING THE SHAFT THEN...
WELL NOW WE SEEM TO ENJOYING IT... NOW MORE THAN EVER
GOP
IT'S HARD TO SAY
WHO'S TO BLAME
POLITICIANS
CORPORATIONS
OR OURSELVES...

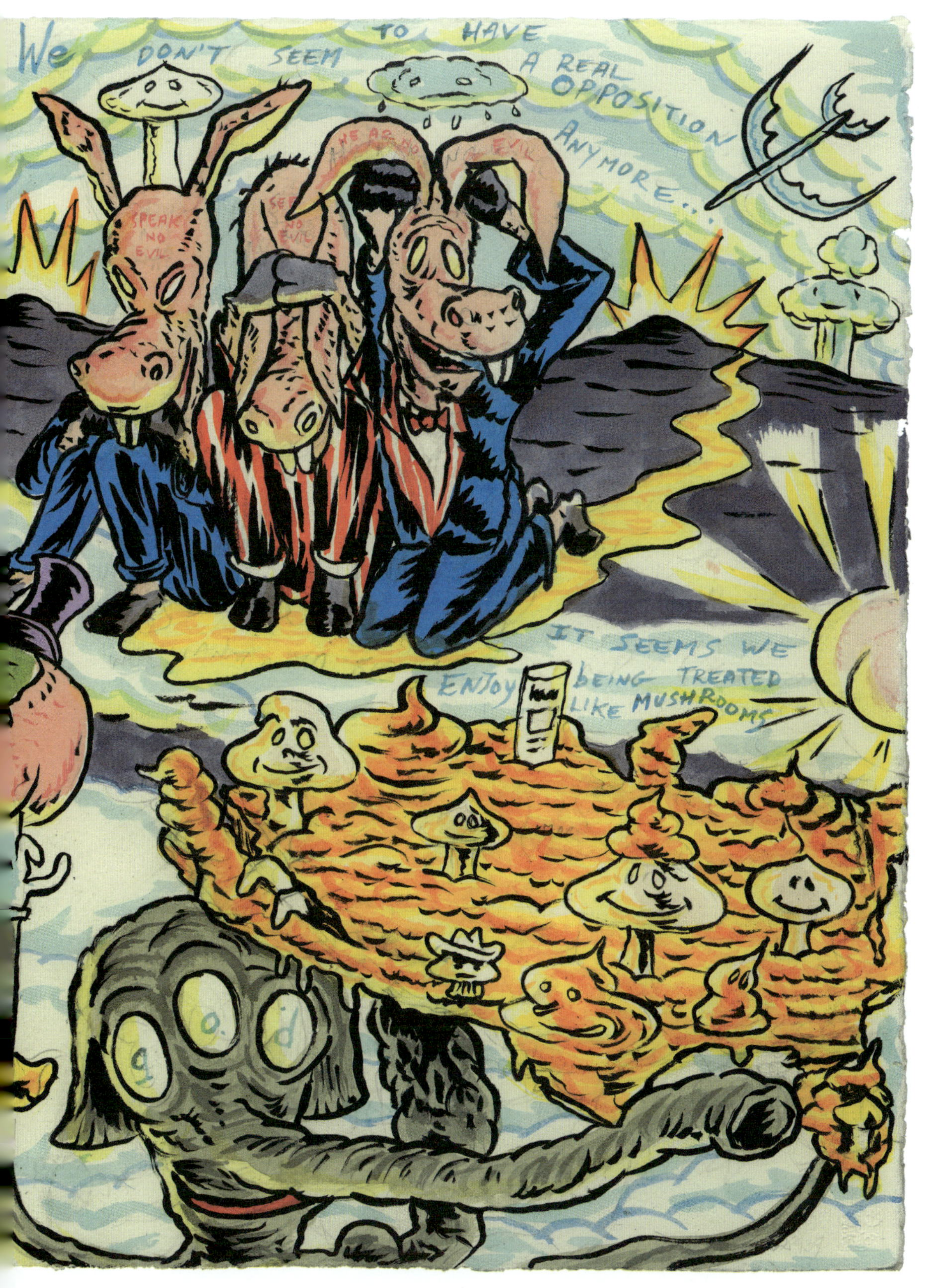

We don't seem to have a real opposition anymore....
SPEAK NO EVIL
SEE NO EVIL
It seems we enjoy being treated like mushrooms

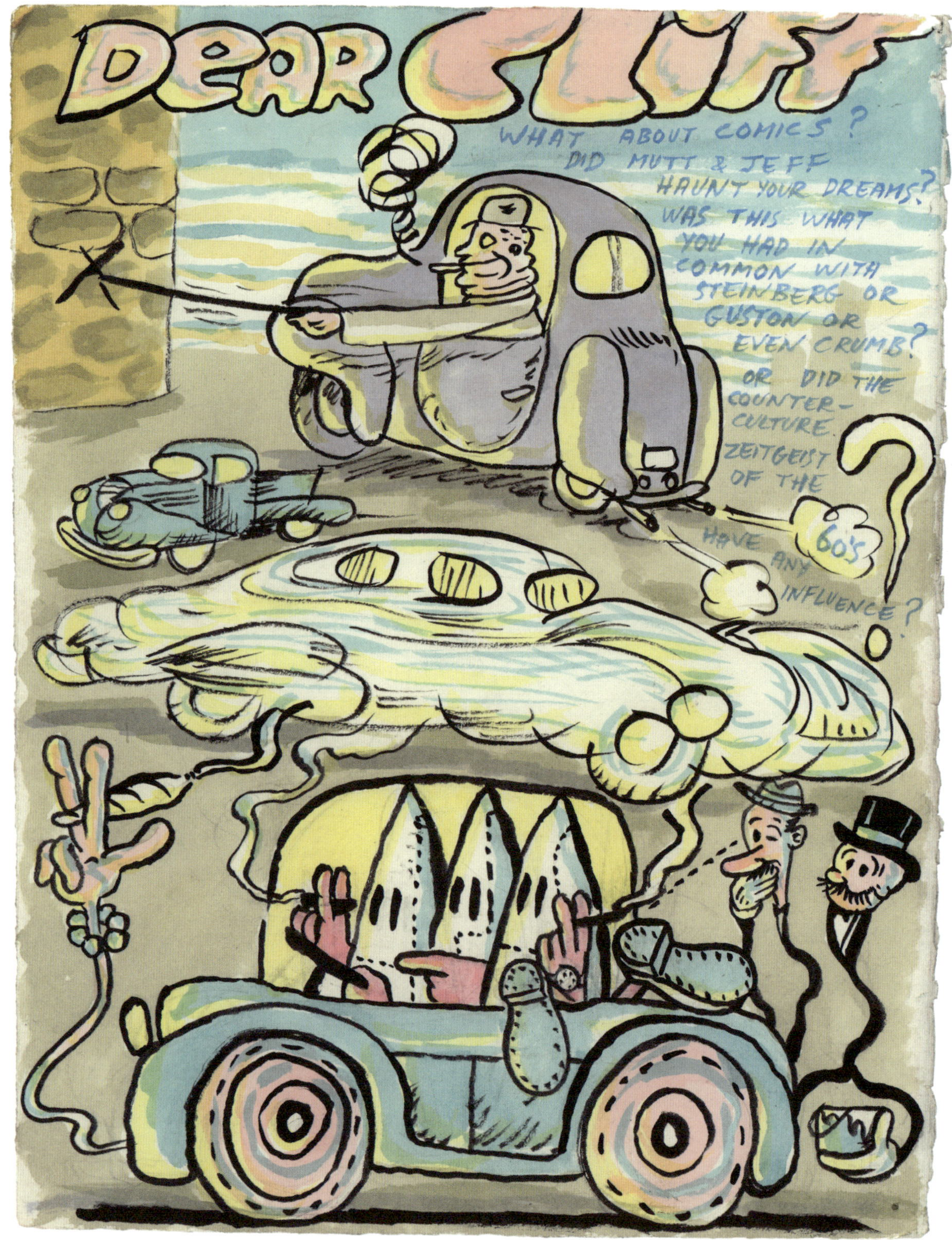
DEAR
WHAT ABOUT COMICS?
DID MUTT & JEFF
HAUNT YOUR DREAMS?
WAS THIS WHAT
YOU HAD IN
COMMON WITH
STEINBERG OR
GUSTON OR
EVEN CRUMB?
OR DID THE
COUNTER-
CULTURE
ZEITGEIST
OF THE
60's
HAVE
ANY
INFLUENCE?

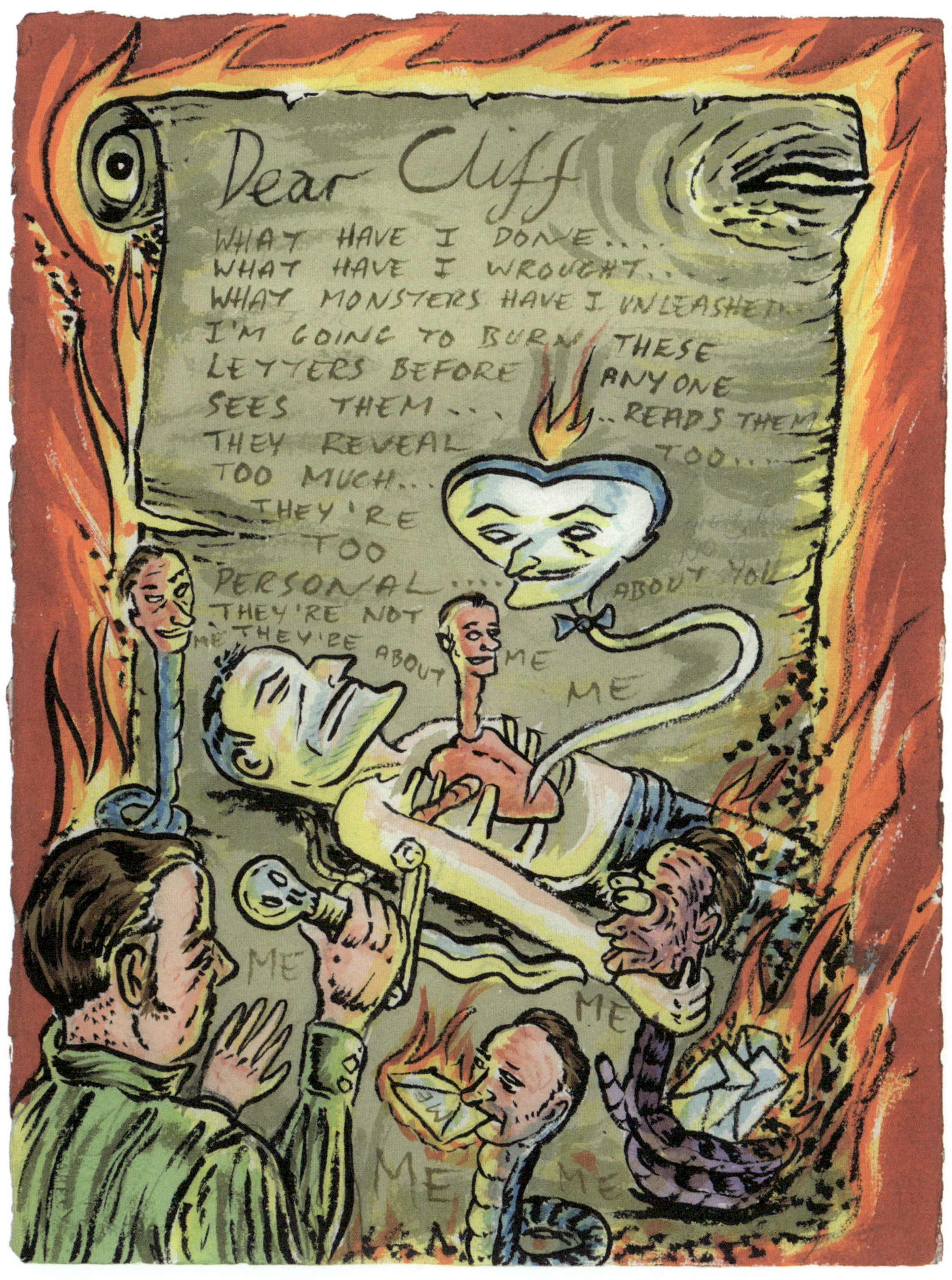
Dear Cliff
WHAT HAVE I DONE....
WHAT HAVE I WROUGHT....
WHAT MONSTERS HAVE I UNLEASHED...
I'M GOING TO BURN THESE
LETTERS BEFORE ANYONE
SEES THEM.... ..READS THEM
THEY REVEAL TOO...
TOO MUCH...
THEY'RE
TOO
PERSONAL.... ABOUT YOU
THEY'RE NOT
ME THEY'RE ABOUT ME
ME
ME
ME
ME
ME

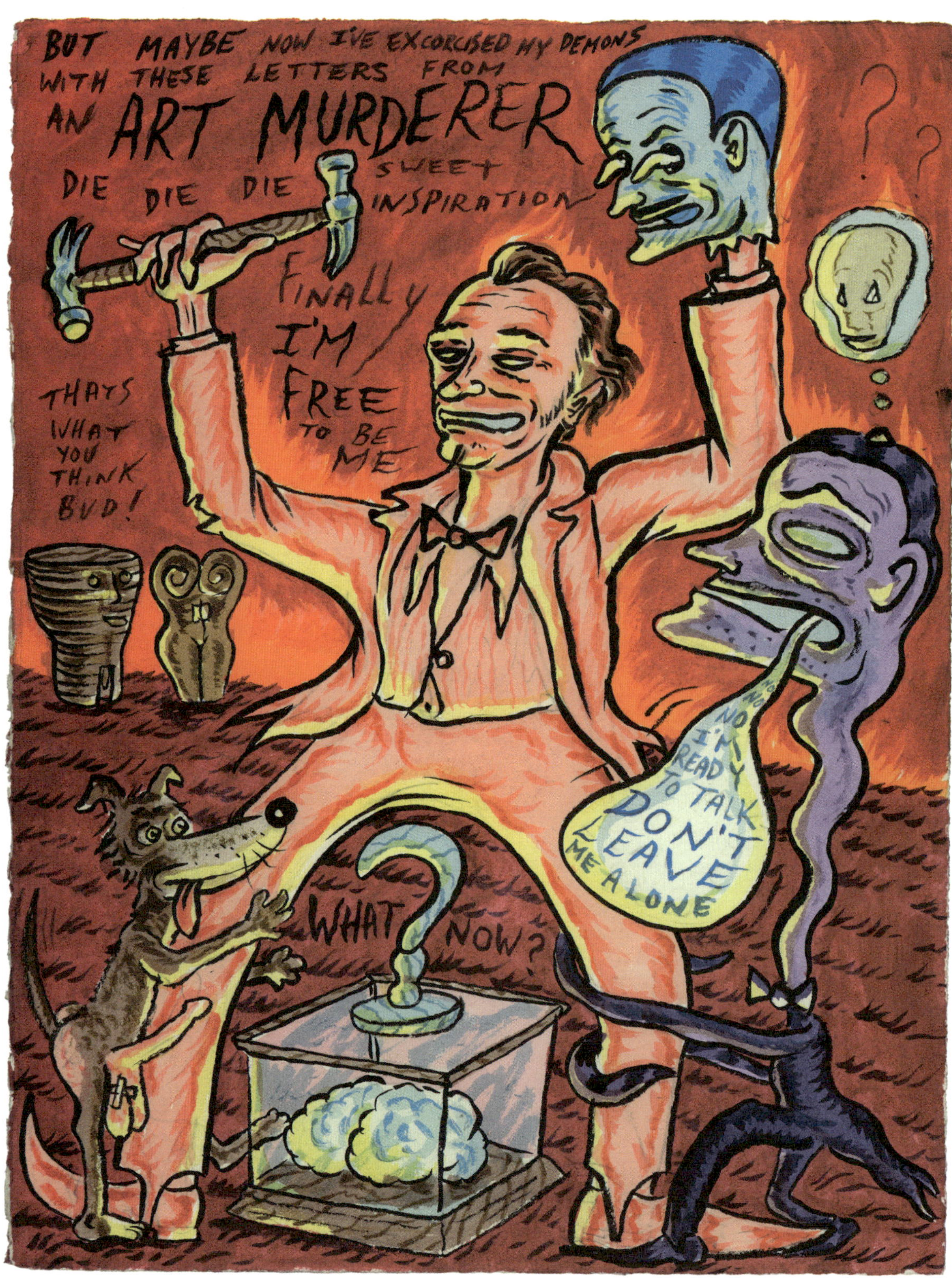
BUT MAYBE NOW I'VE EXCORCISED MY DEMONS WITH THESE LETTERS FROM AN ART MURDERER
DIE DIE DIE SWEET INSPIRATION
FINALLY I'M FREE TO BE ME
THATS WHAT YOU THINK BUD!
NO NO NO I'M READY TO TALK DON'T LEAVE ME ALONE
WHAT NOW?

H.C.W.

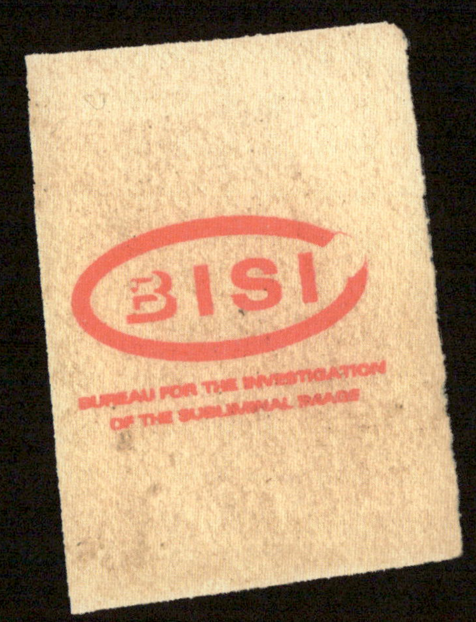

A SUBLIMINAL IMAGE is an image that is inadvertently concealed within a natural feature or manufactured object. It can be revealed only by an act of imagination on the part of the observer. Once found, its existence can be demonstrated to another: it can be solved. An imaginary solution *par excellence* (and an imagery solution as well!). Subliminal images constitute a sort of rational hallucination, and Alfred Jarry was fond of this quotation from Leibniz: "Perception is only a hallucination that is true." (***Days and Nights***)

Such a definition implies various exclusions. Deliberately manufactured visual puzzles, illusions, and the familiar "duck/rabbit" tests employed by psychologists do not qualify as subliminal images. Likewise, innumerable devotees of belief systems (religious enthusiasts, conspiracy theorists) are capable of—indeed they often cannot avoid—perceiving evidence of their monomanias in the most unlikely corners of external reality (the arrangement of pips inside vegetables, the products of mass advertising). Too often, unfortunately, these images are only perceptible to fellow zealots, which disqualifies them as objects for our investigation.

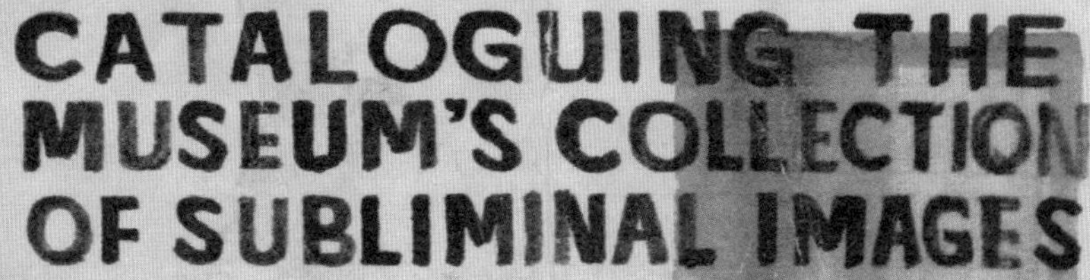

1

STAGE 1 : AN INTRODUCTION
TO THE METHODOLOGY AND
PROCEEDURES OF THE B·I·S·I

BUREAU FOR THE INVESTIGATION OF THE SUBLIMINAL IMAGE :

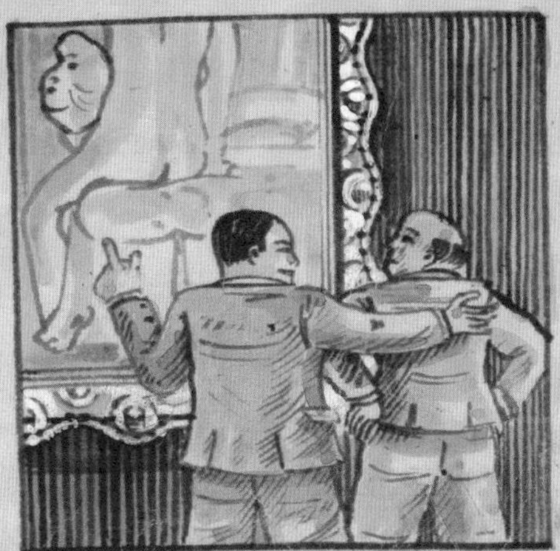

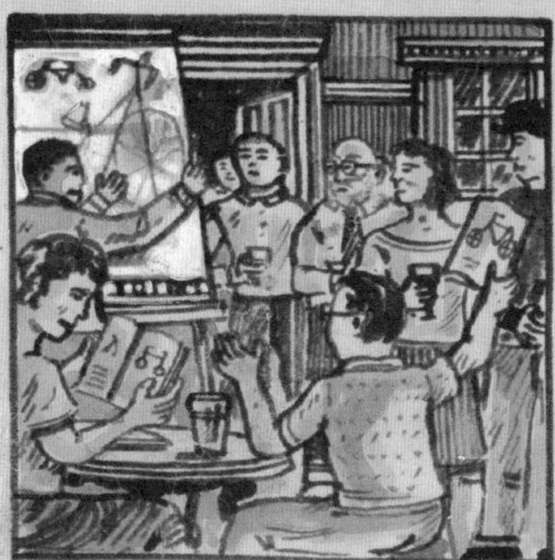

Stage 1. Public cognition of the subliminal. Museum visitors are entreated to find unseen images hidden within the fabric of famous works in the National Gallery collection. The project as a whole is outlined in the present publication.

Stage 2. Sorting subliminal images. Common categories of subliminal image are identified and isolated by the BISI (e.g. bicycles in Turner, skulls in paintings of St. Francis &c.) Refined searches are conducted to locate further overlooked subliminals.

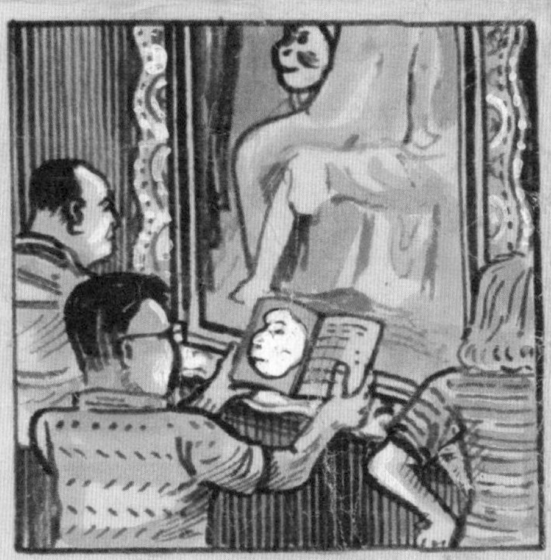

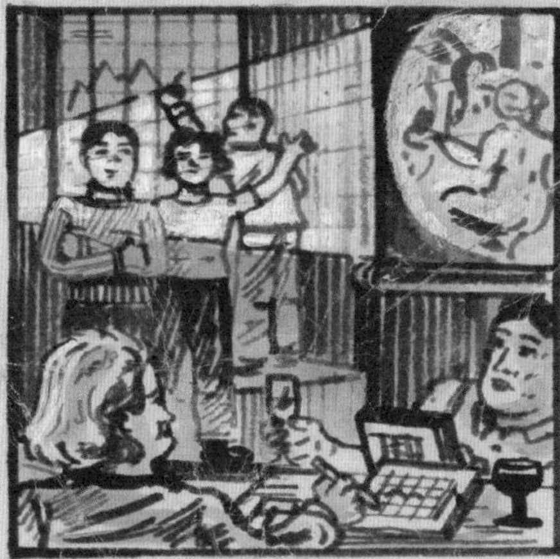

Stage 3. Validating subliminals. Handbills noting the form and location of various subliminals are employed by members of the LIP and the public to gauge the validity of the images previously discovered.

Stage 4. Collation of material. Information gathered in stage 3 is applied to a number of charts, exercises and tests. The presence of a number of subliminals is recorded and the validity of various of them is quantified.

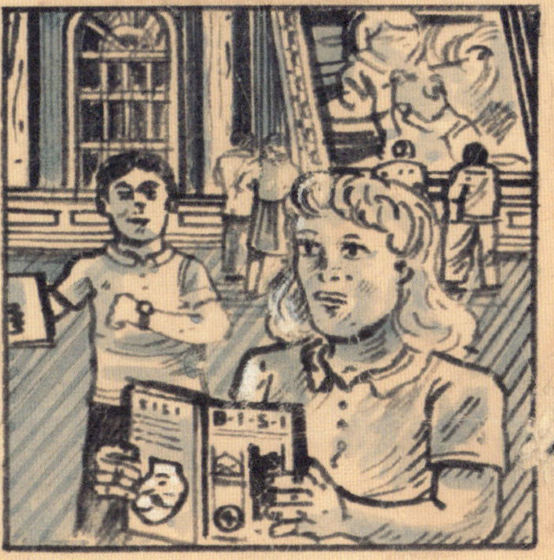

Stage 5. Initial pamphlet for public is published. The presence of refined subliminals is tested on museum visitors with various pamphlets.

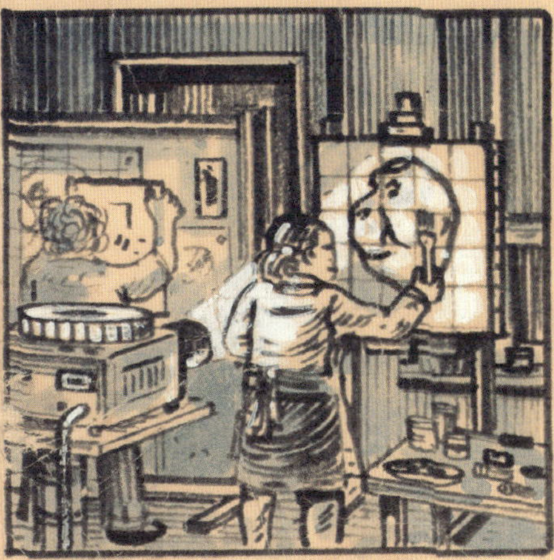

Stage 6. Graphic processing of subliminals. Skilled painters are employed to document subliminals *in situ*.

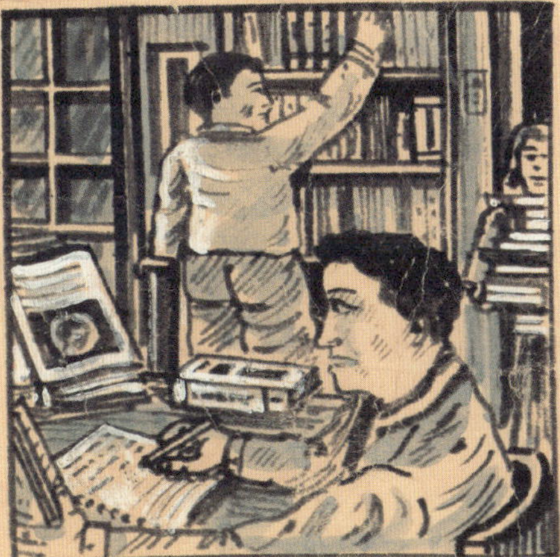

Stage 7. Construction of notional art histories. Convincing explanations of specific subliminals are researched and written up by the BISI's department of interpretation.

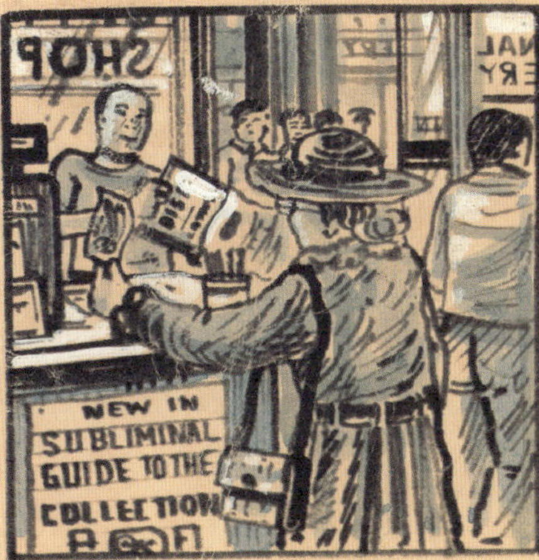

Stage 8. Publication of catalogue. A comprehensive catalogue of the museum's collection of subliminal images is offered to visitors.

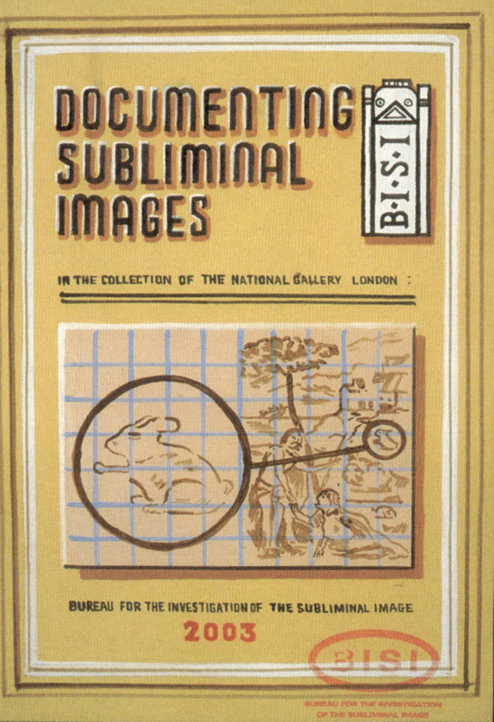
DOCUMENTING
SUBLIMINAL
IMAGES
B·I·S·I
IN THE COLLECTION OF THE NATIONAL GALLERY LONDON
BUREAU FOR THE INVESTIGATION OF THE SUBLIMINAL IMAGE
2003
BISI

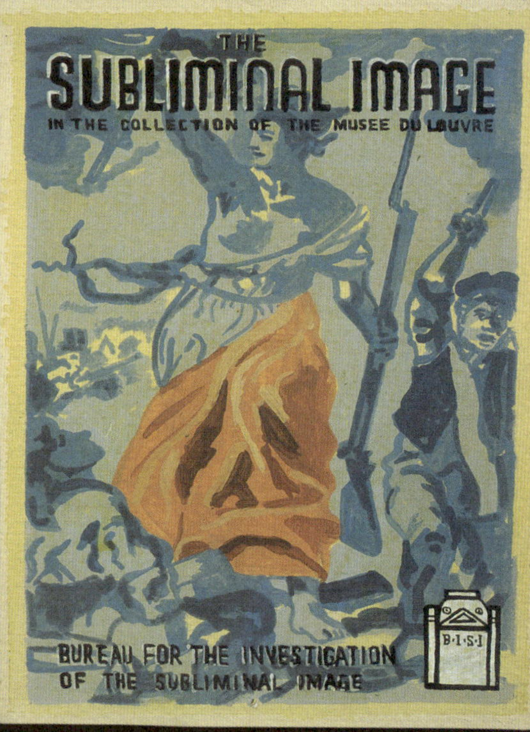
THE
SUBLIMINAL IMAGE
IN THE COLLECTION OF THE MUSEE DU LOUVRE
BUREAU FOR THE INVESTIGATION
OF THE SUBLIMINAL IMAGE
B·I·S·I

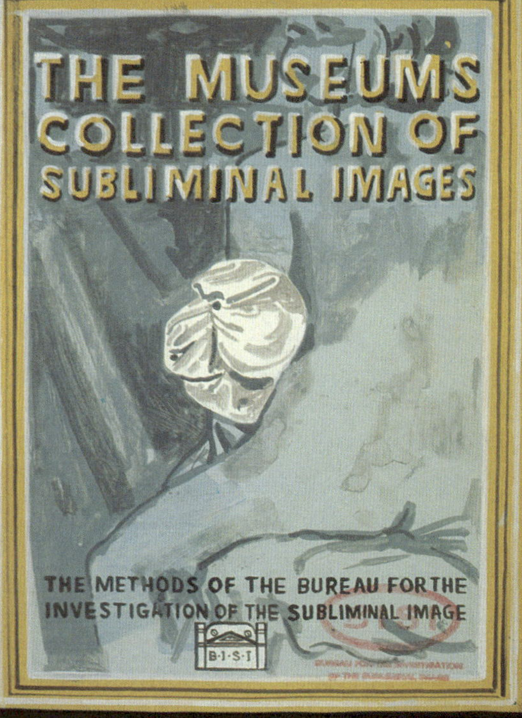
THE MUSEUMS
COLLECTION OF
SUBLIMINAL IMAGES
THE METHODS OF THE BUREAU FOR THE
INVESTIGATION OF THE SUBLIMINAL IMAGE
B·I·S·I

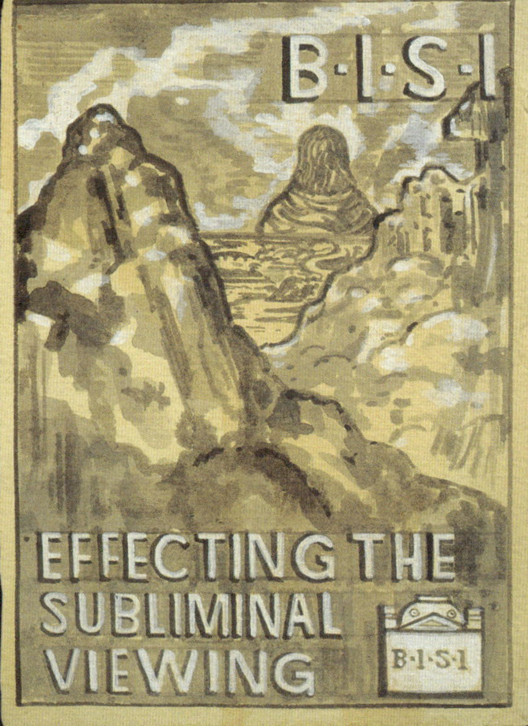
B·I·S·I
EFFECTING THE
SUBLIMINAL
VIEWING
B·I·S·I

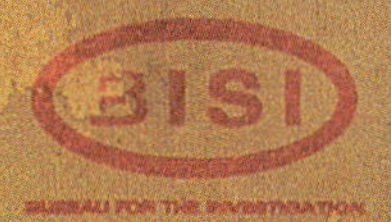

APPAREILE
SUBLIMINAL

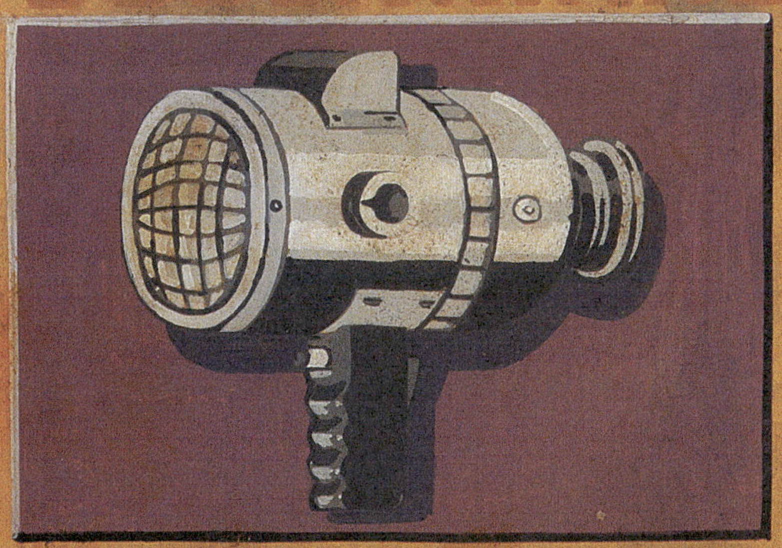

BUREAU POUR L'INVESTIGATION DE L'IMAGE SUBLIMINAL, PARIS

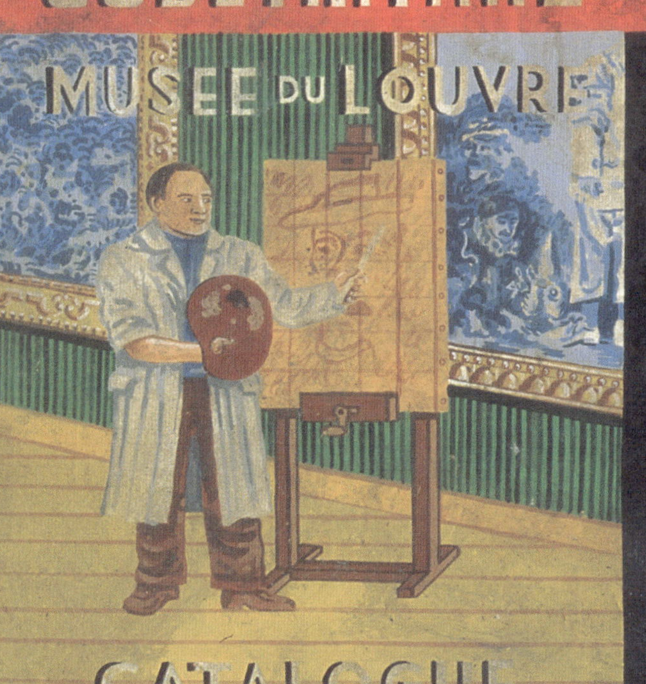
B·I·S·I
500 IMAGES ET PAROLES
SUBLIMINAL
MUSEE DU LOUVRE
CATALOGUE

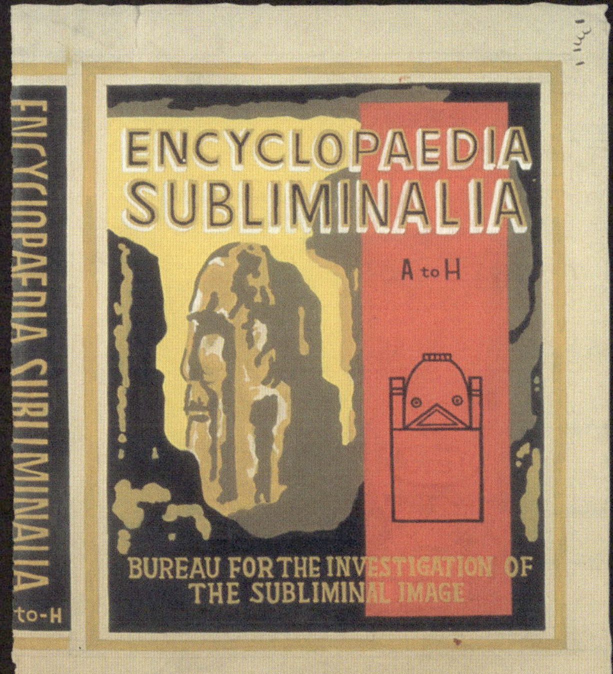

CATALOGUE

MUSEE DU LOUVRE

BISI

BUREAU FOR THE INVESTIGATION OF THE SUBLIMINAL IMAGE

BUREAU POUR L'INVESTIGATION DE L'IMAGE SUBLIMINAL

CATALOGUE : MUSEE DU LOUVRE : COLLECTION DES IMAGES SUBLIMINAL

SUBLIMINALIA

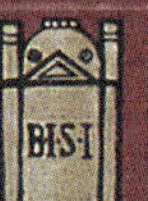

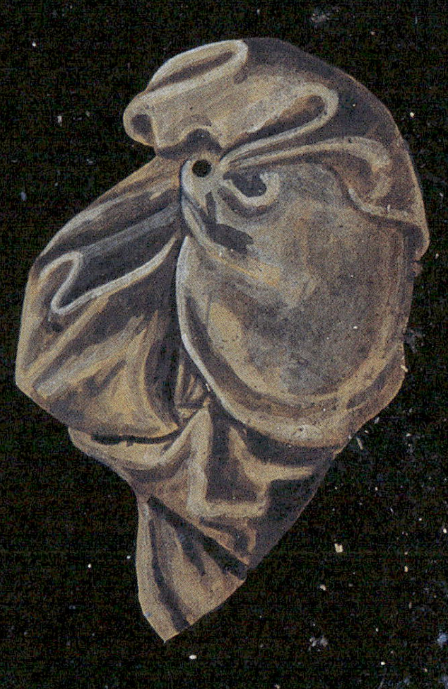

BUREAU FOR THE INVESTIGATION OF THE

SUBLIMINAL IMAGE

A PORTFOLIO OF 214 IMAGES WITH ACCOMPANYING NOTES & HISTORIES AS LOCATED, DOCUMENTED & RESEARCHED BY THE B·I·S·I IN THE PAINTING COLLECTION OF THE MUSÉE DU LOUVRE, PARIS, FRANCE. 1967.

"He [Piero] stopped to examine a wall where sick persons had used to spit, imagining that he saw there combats of horses and the most fantastic cities and extraordinary landscapes ever beheld."

—Vasari on Piero di Cosimo (from *The Lives of the Artists*)

The Bureau for the Investigation of the Subliminal Image will be publishing an illustrated *catalogue raisonné* of the National Gallery, London's collection of Subliminal Images in 2006.

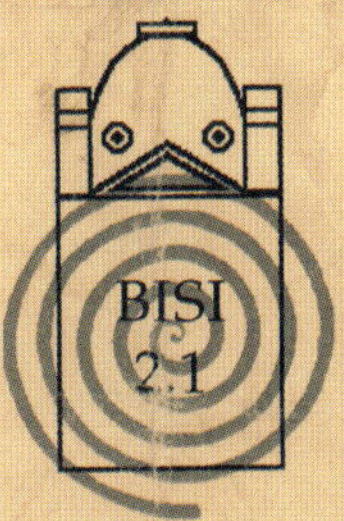

The Bureau can be contacted through The London Institute of Pataphysics.

When Dick Tracy creator Chester Gould retired from his daily chore in 1977, *The Chicago Tribune* held a Draw Dick Tracy contest. Sometime after the deadline for entry passed, Karl Wirsum took a crack at it. The results, along with a new title page, are reproduced here.

How to DRAW!

DICK TRACY

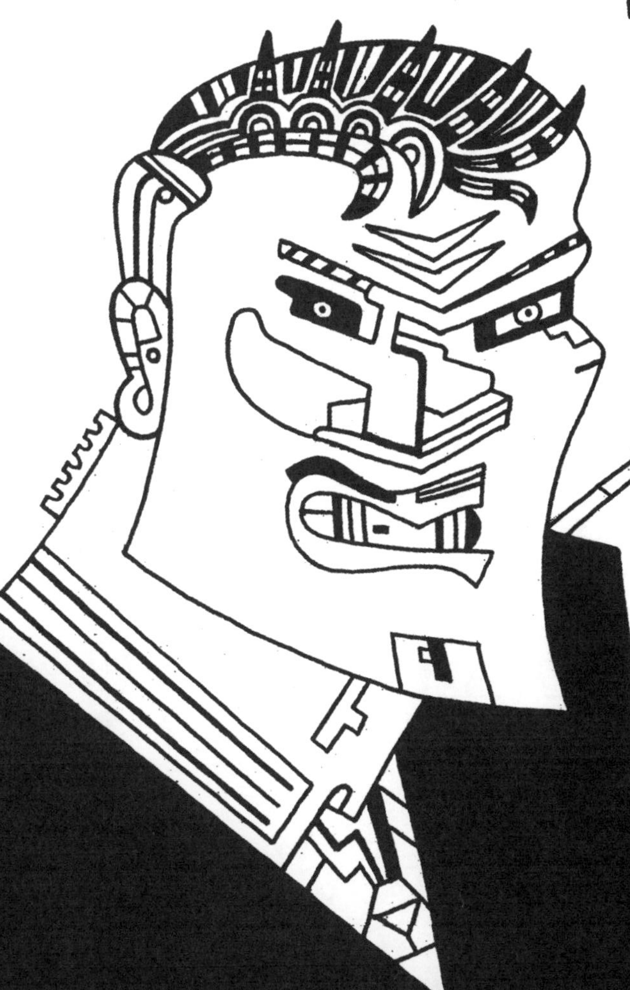

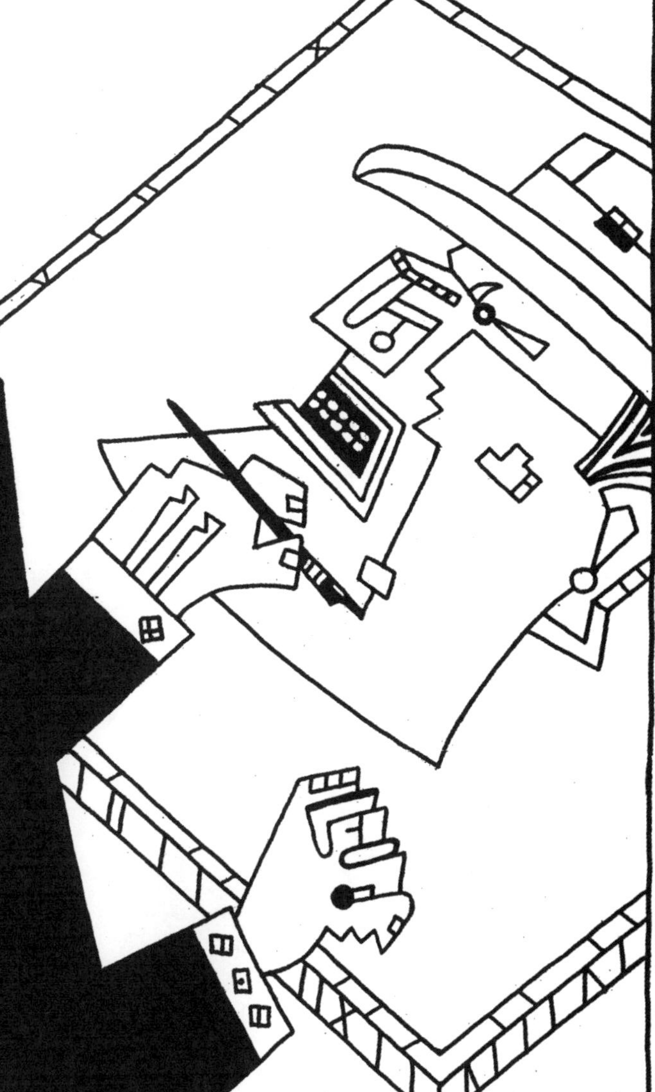

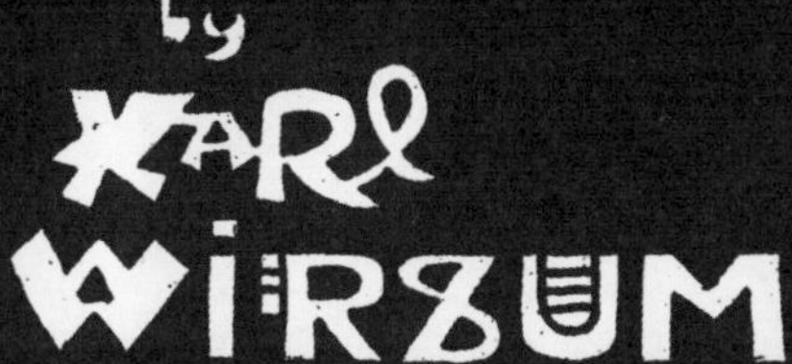

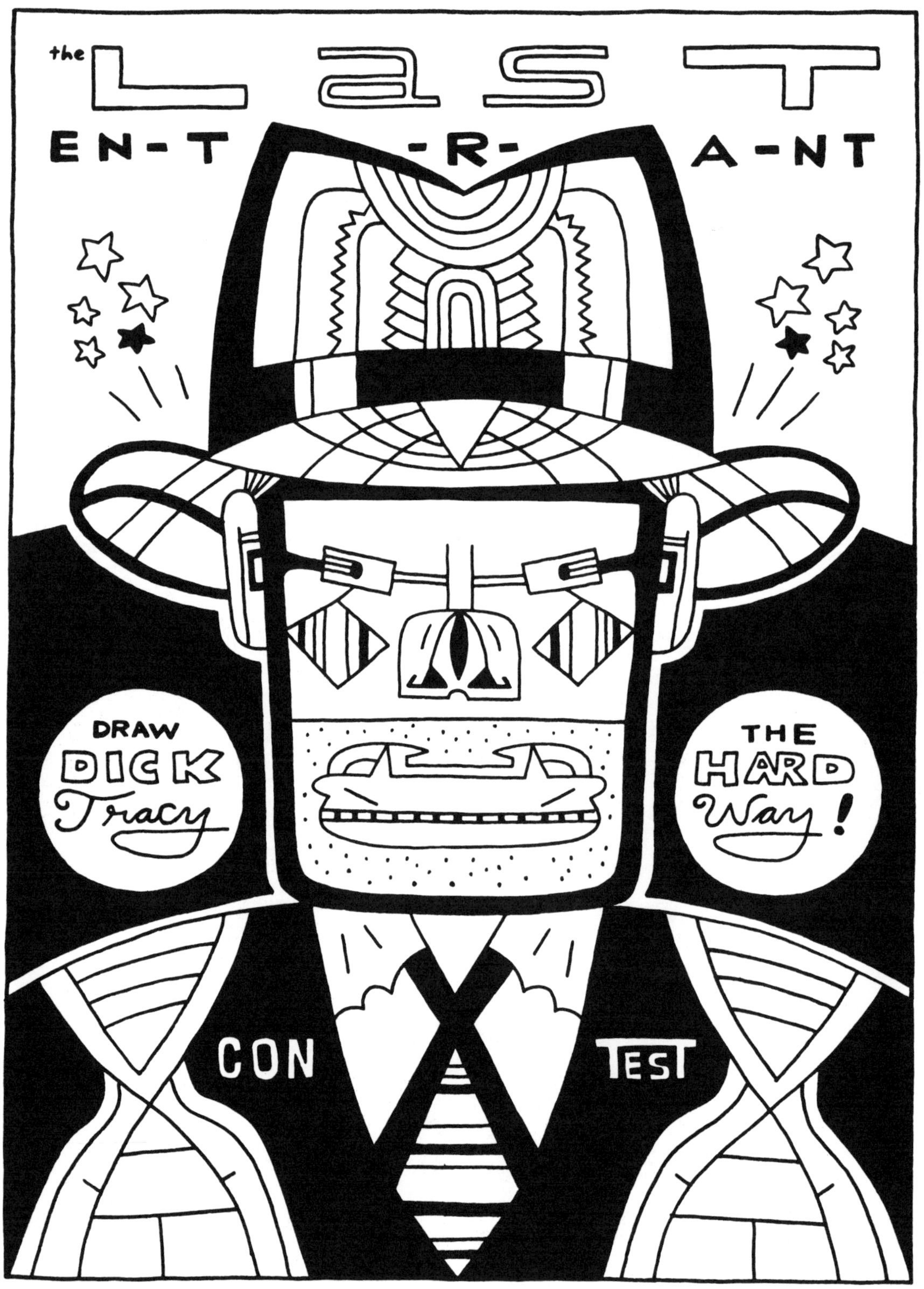
the LAST
EN-T -R- A-NT
DRAW DICK Tracy
THE HARD Way!
CON TEST

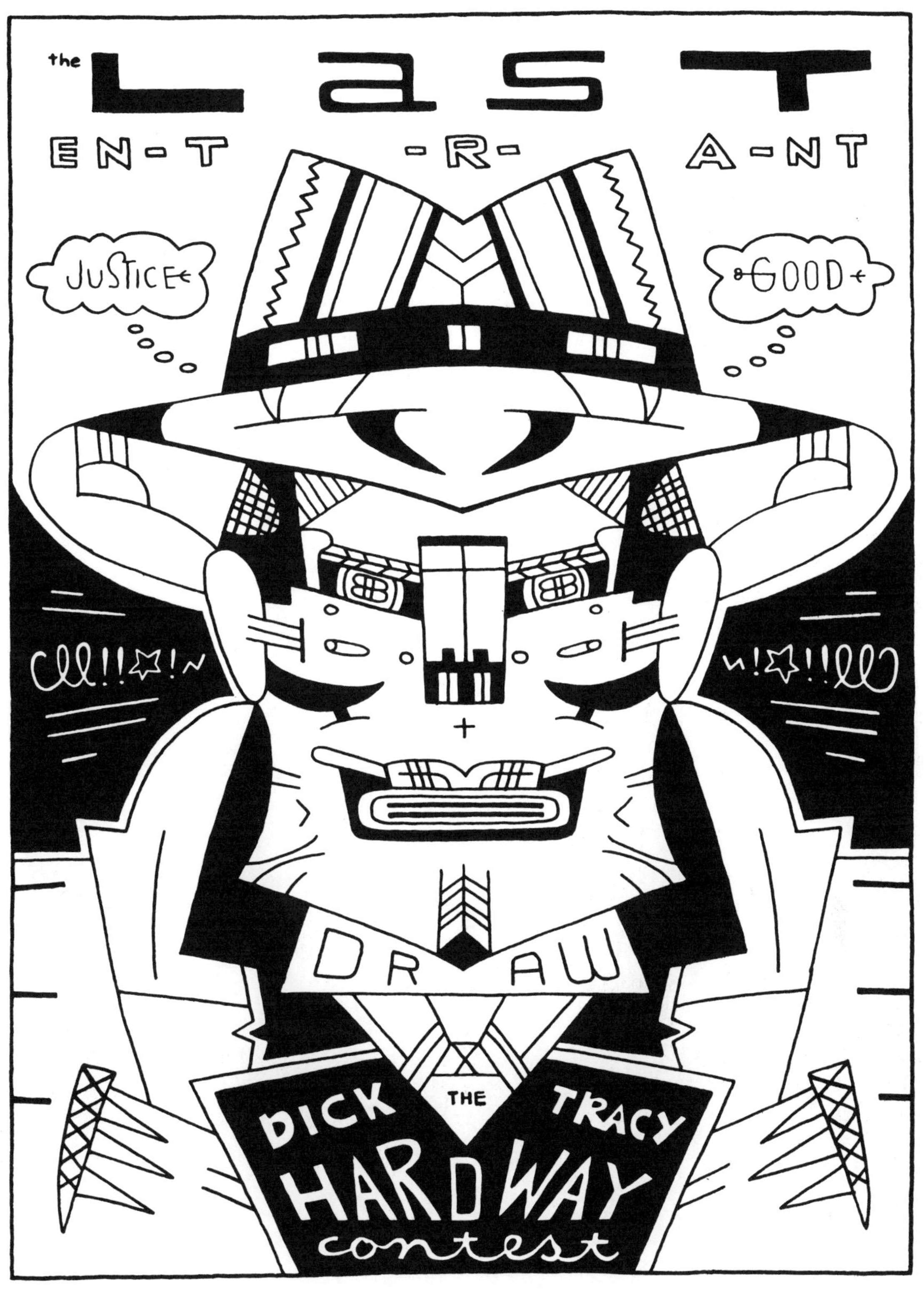
the LAST
EN-T -R- A-NT
JUSTICE
GOOD
DRAW
DICK THE TRACY
HARDWAY
contest

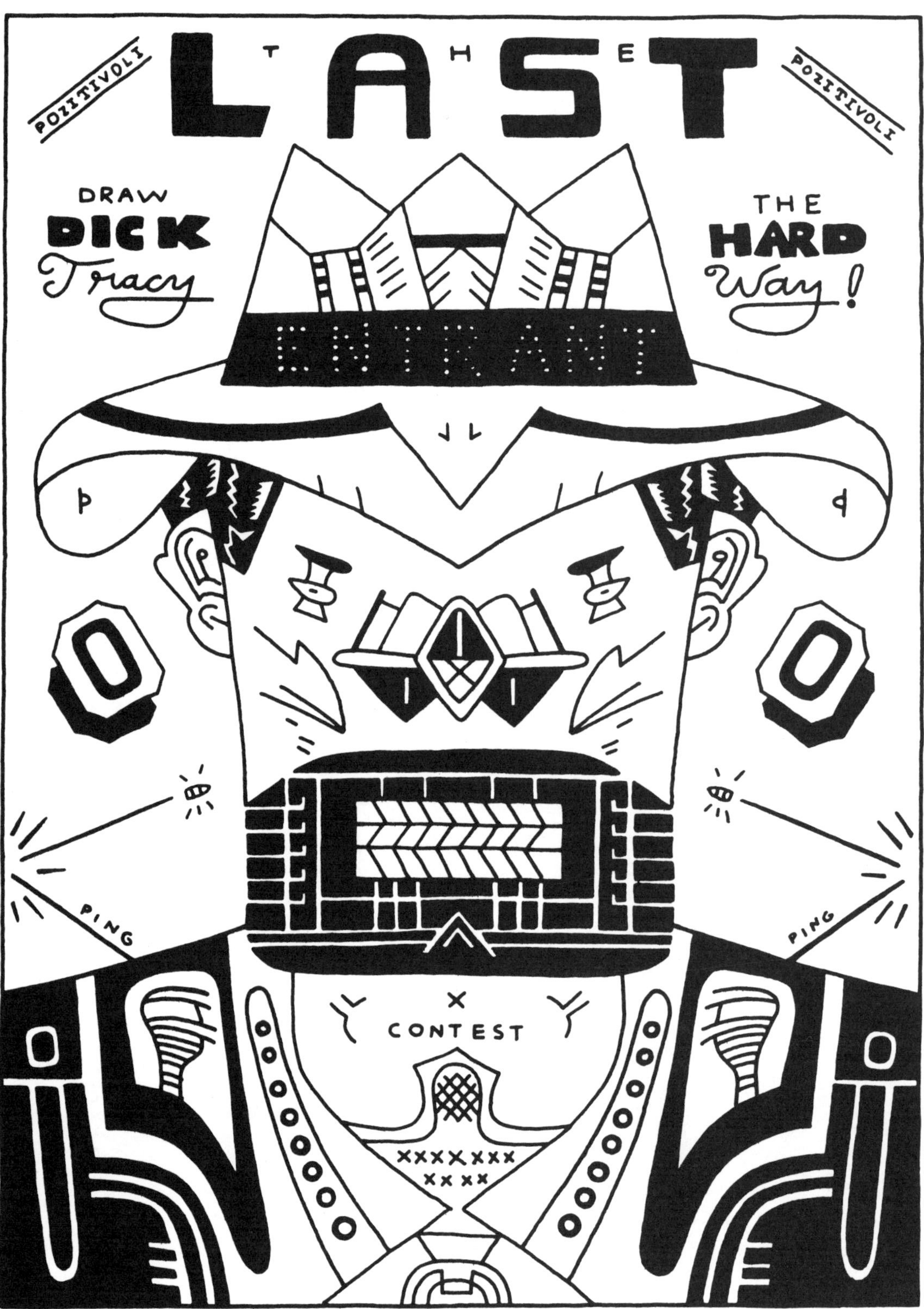

POZZITIVOLI
THE LAST
POZZITIVOLI
DRAW DICK Tracy
THE HARD Way!
ENTRANT
PING
PING
CONTEST

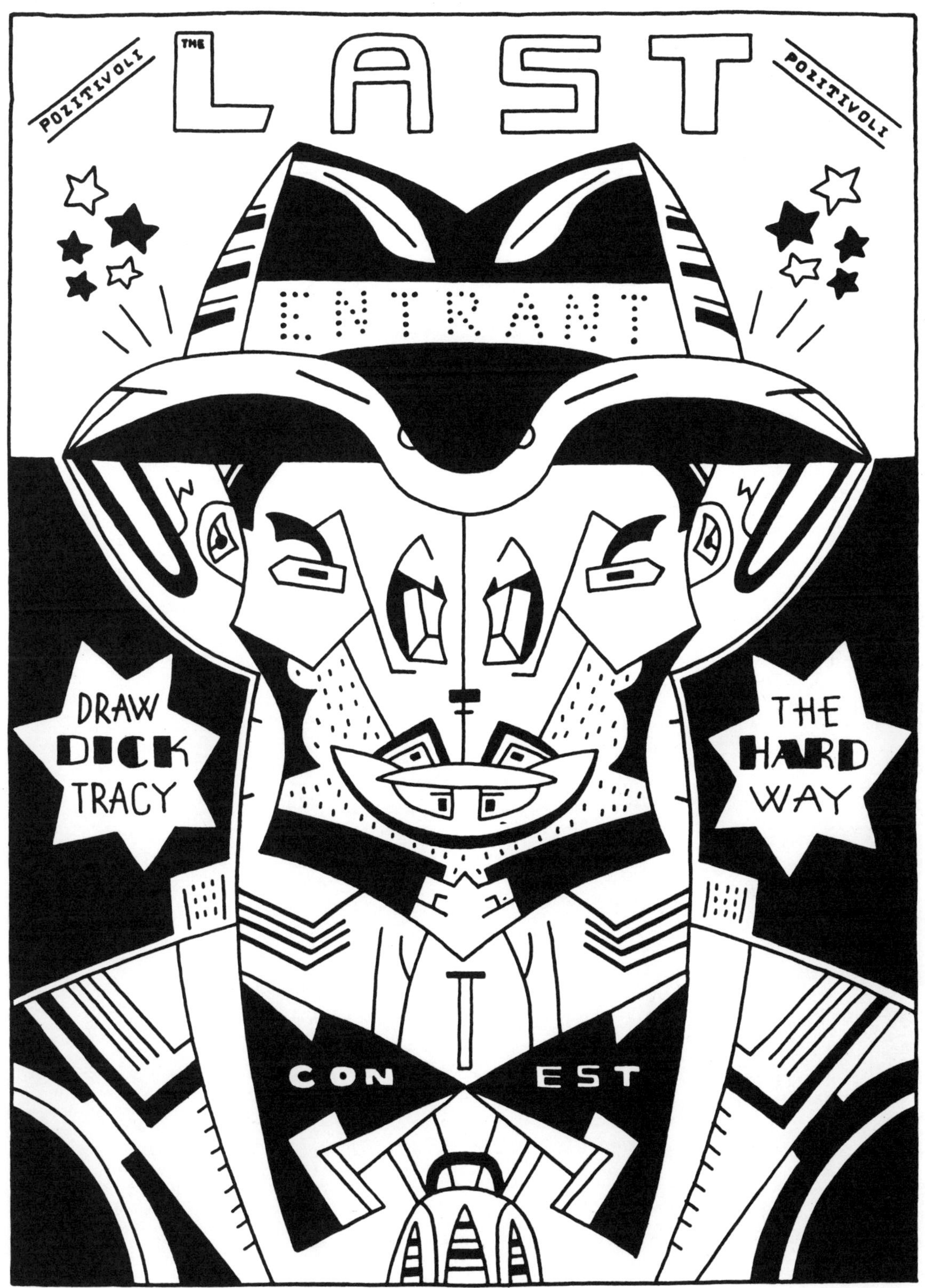
POZZITIVOLI
THE
LAST
POZZITIVOLI
ENTRANT
DRAW
DICK
TRACY
THE
HARD
WAY
CON
T
EST

PAINTINGS FOR DALI

PETER SAUL

I used Salvador Dali because he was a celebrity artist (although I had, in fact, always liked the idea of his work—because he seemed to inspire so much fear in serious Americans after World War II). It was also my perhaps crazy ambition someday to paint a picture that would have the lasting interest of the soft watch. However, when I went to see the surrealism show at the Metropolitan Museum of Art (in which I actually saw most of Dali's best pictures for the first time), I realized that he actually is a very major artist, and that he still inspires a great fear in the American art establishment (at least in *The New York Times*). He was the most looked-at artist in the surrealism show (at least the day I was there). There was a crowd in front of his paintings 70 years after they were painted.

As a result, although I had painted some soft-watch pictures in the '90s, I began at that point to put Dali in my pictures as a person, as a celebrity—the same way I have previously used Ronald Reagan, Martin Luther King, Jr., Andy Warhol, Angela Davis, and Muhammad Ali—as a celebrity bringing heat to my pictures that wouldn't have been there otherwise. These historical characters have dramatic interest for most people, including me. I've only used Salvador Dali in one major picture (he's peeing into the ear of President Bush) because it soon thereafter occurred to me that Warhol would be a hotter and more sophisticated celebrity. Consequently, I just completed my first Warhol picture since 1969, *The Birth of Pop*—it's modeled after Cabanel's *The Birth of Venus.*

I feel drunk on the thrills of subject matter and am eager to proceed with my next three Warhol epics—in which he gets shot by Valerie Solanis, meets Salvador Dali up in heaven for a little mild porn, and eventually gets executed in the electric chair. But those pictures have to be interspersed with *The Death of Captain Cook, Chinese Businessman,* and a few other laughable situations that I can hardly wait to get into.

IMAGES COURTESY NOLAN/ECKMAN GALLERY

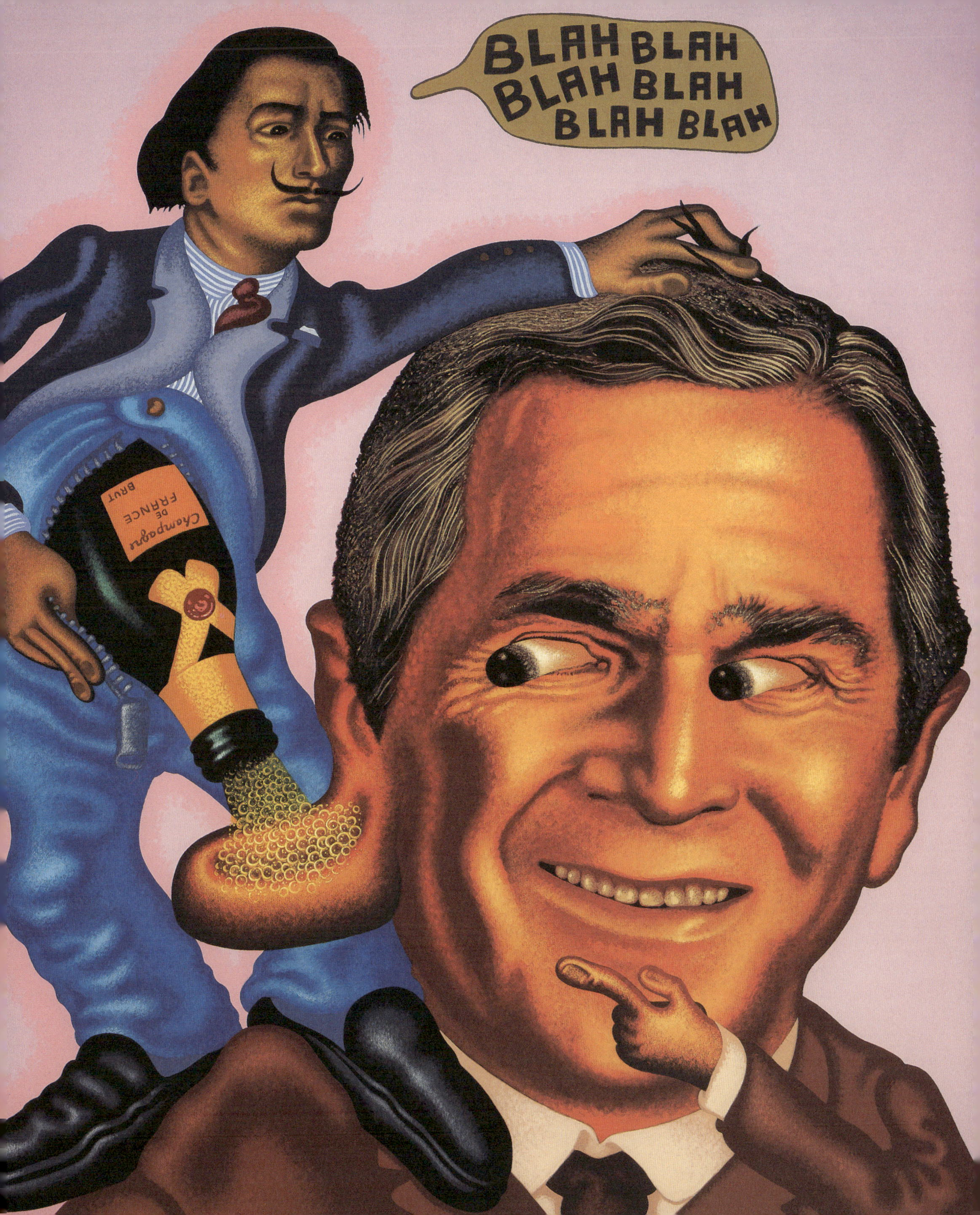
BLAH BLAH
BLAH BLAH
BLAH BLAH

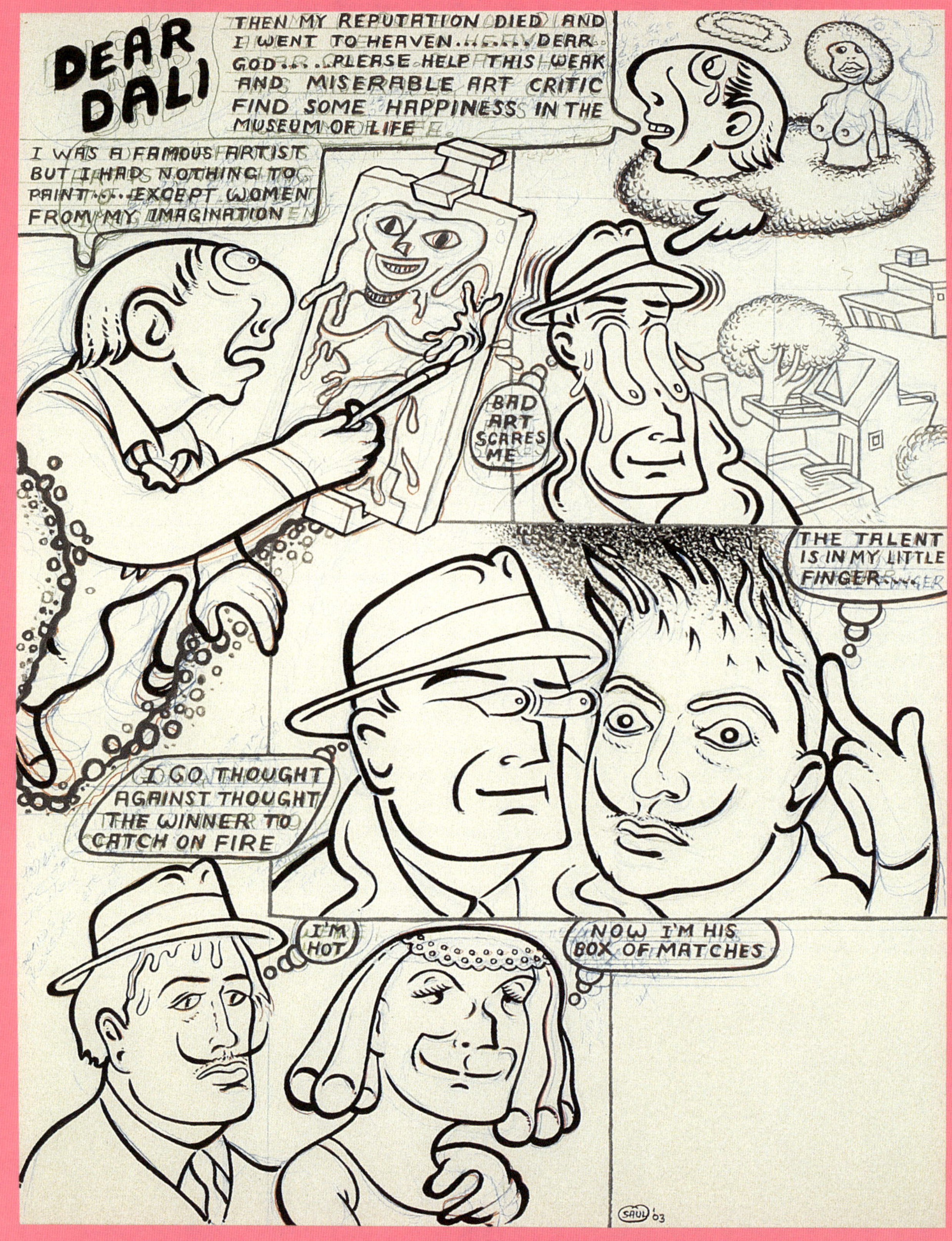
DEAR DALI
THEN MY REPUTATION DIED AND I WENT TO HEAVEN........DEAR GOD.....PLEASE HELP THIS WEAK AND MISERABLE ART CRITIC FIND SOME HAPPINESS IN THE MUSEUM OF LIFE
I WAS A FAMOUS ARTIST BUT I HAD NOTHING TO PAINT...EXCEPT WOMEN FROM MY IMAGINATION
BAD ART SCARES ME
THE TALENT IS IN MY LITTLE FINGER...
I GO THOUGHT AGAINST THOUGHT THE WINNER TO CATCH ON FIRE
I'M HOT
NOW I'M HIS BOX OF MATCHES
SAUL '03

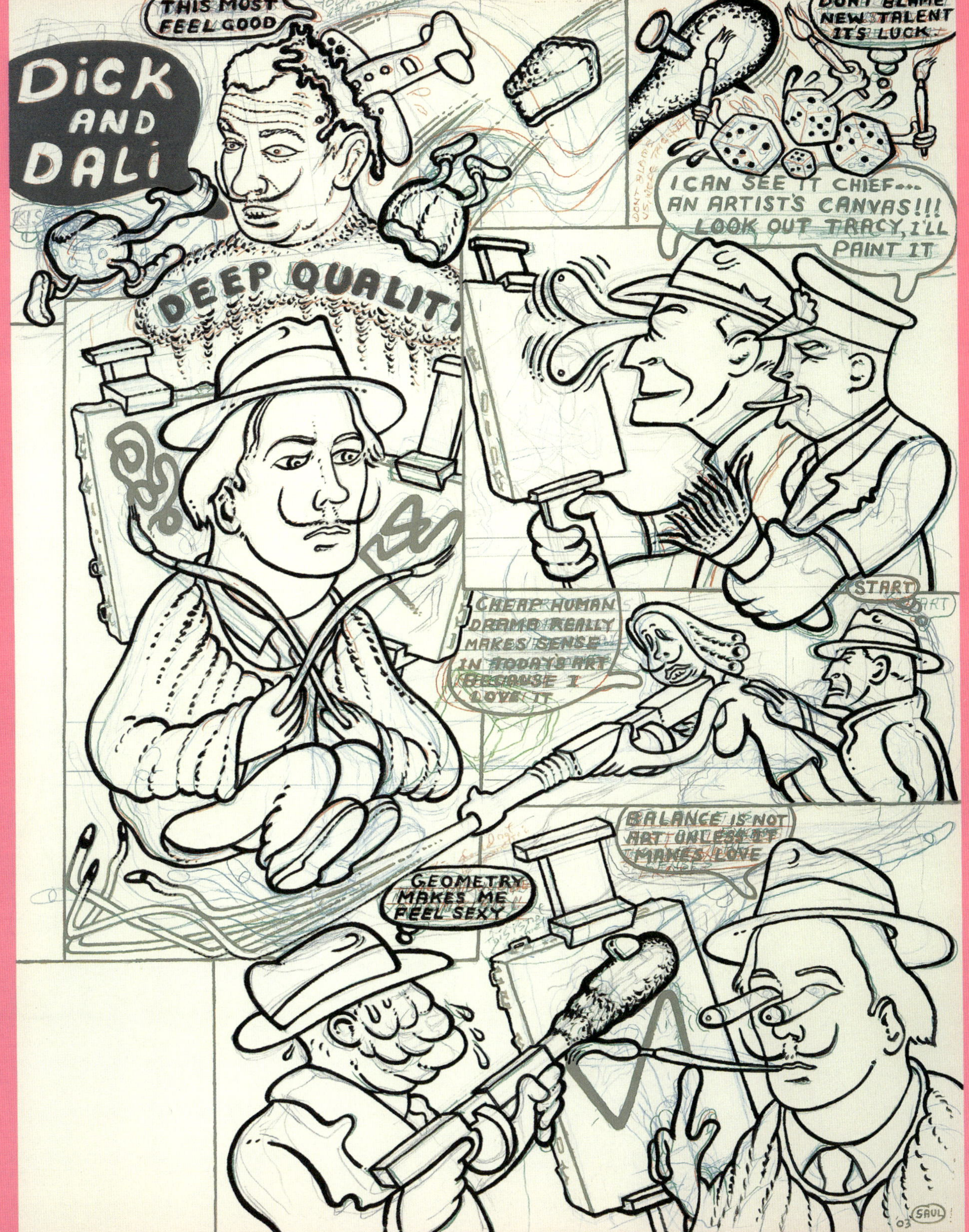
DICK AND DALI
THIS MUST FEEL GOOD
DEEP QUALITY
DON'T BLAME NEW TALENT IT'S LUCK
I CAN SEE IT CHIEF... AN ARTIST'S CANVAS!!! LOOK OUT TRACY, I'LL PAINT IT
CHEAP HUMAN DRAMA REALLY MAKES SENSE IN TODAY'S ART BECAUSE I LOVE IT
START
BALANCE IS NOT ART UNLESS IT MAKES LOVE
GEOMETRY MAKES ME FEEL SEXY
SAUL
03

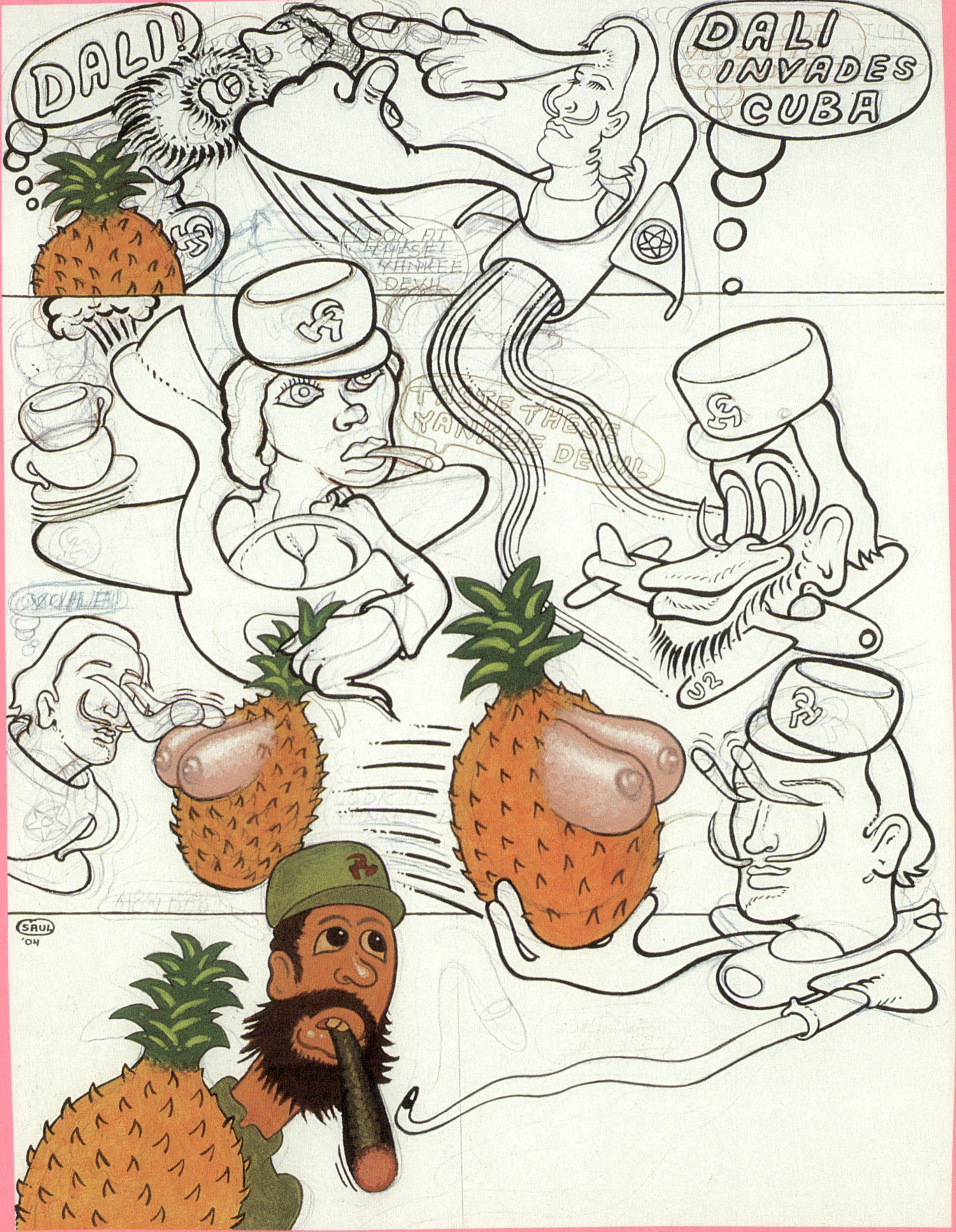
DALI!
DALI INVADES CUBA
U2
SAUL '04

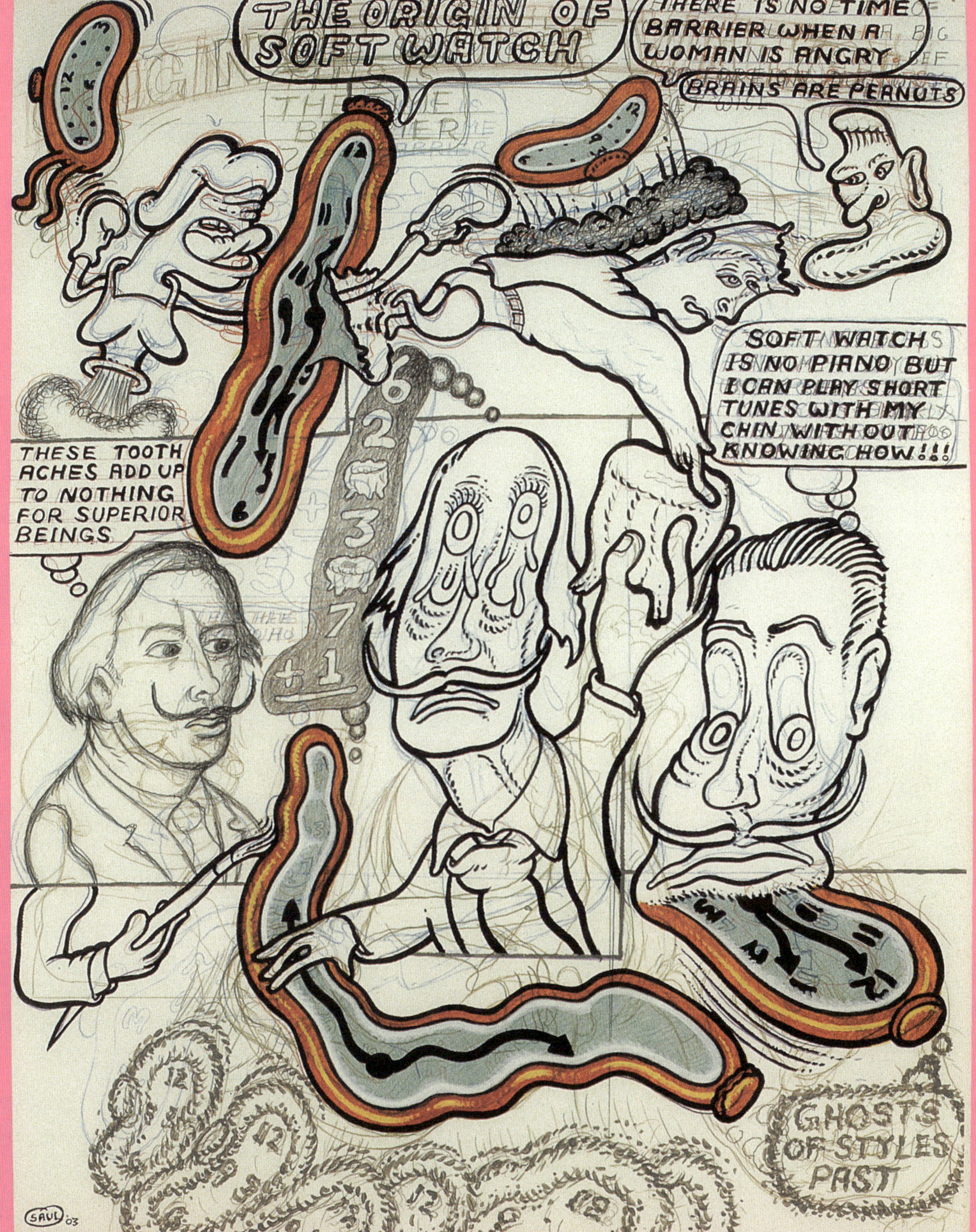
THE ORIGIN OF SOFT WATCH
THERE IS NO TIME BARRIER WHEN A WOMAN IS ANGRY
BRAINS ARE PEANUTS
SOFT WATCH IS NO PIANO BUT I CAN PLAY SHORT TUNES WITH MY CHIN WITHOUT KNOWING HOW!!!
THESE TOOTH ACHES ADD UP TO NOTHING FOR SUPERIOR BEINGS
GHOSTS OF STYLES PAST
SAUL 03

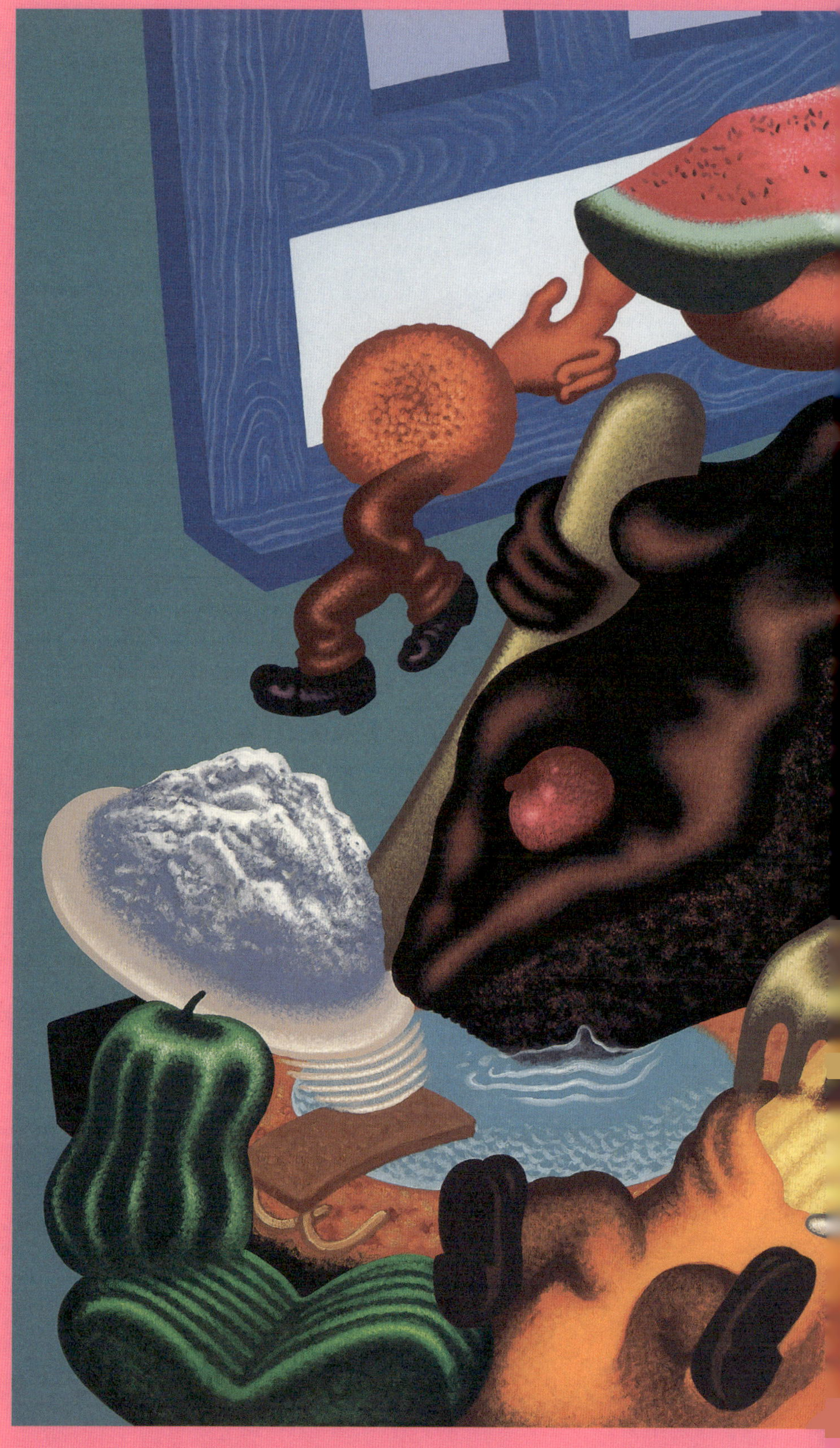

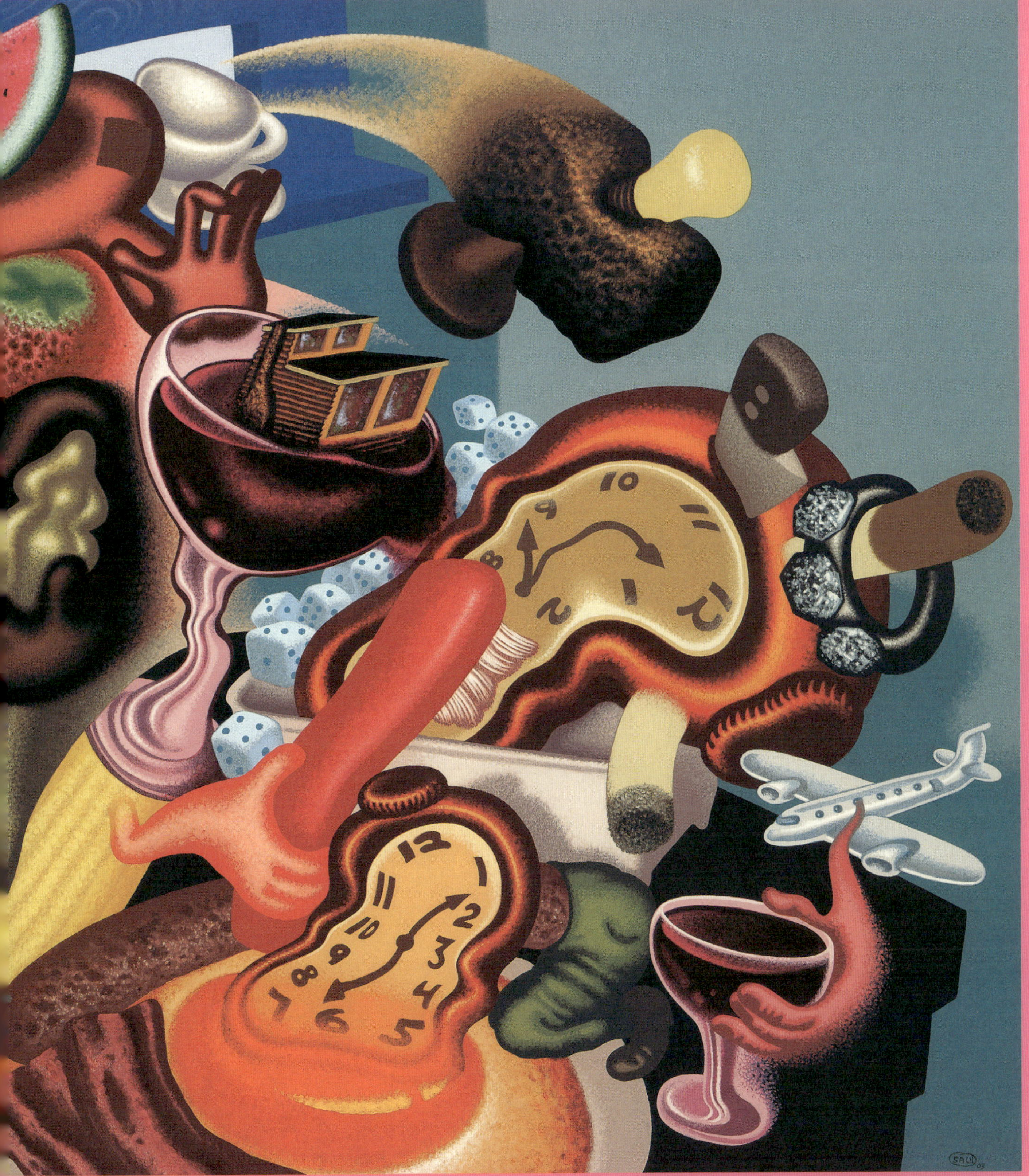

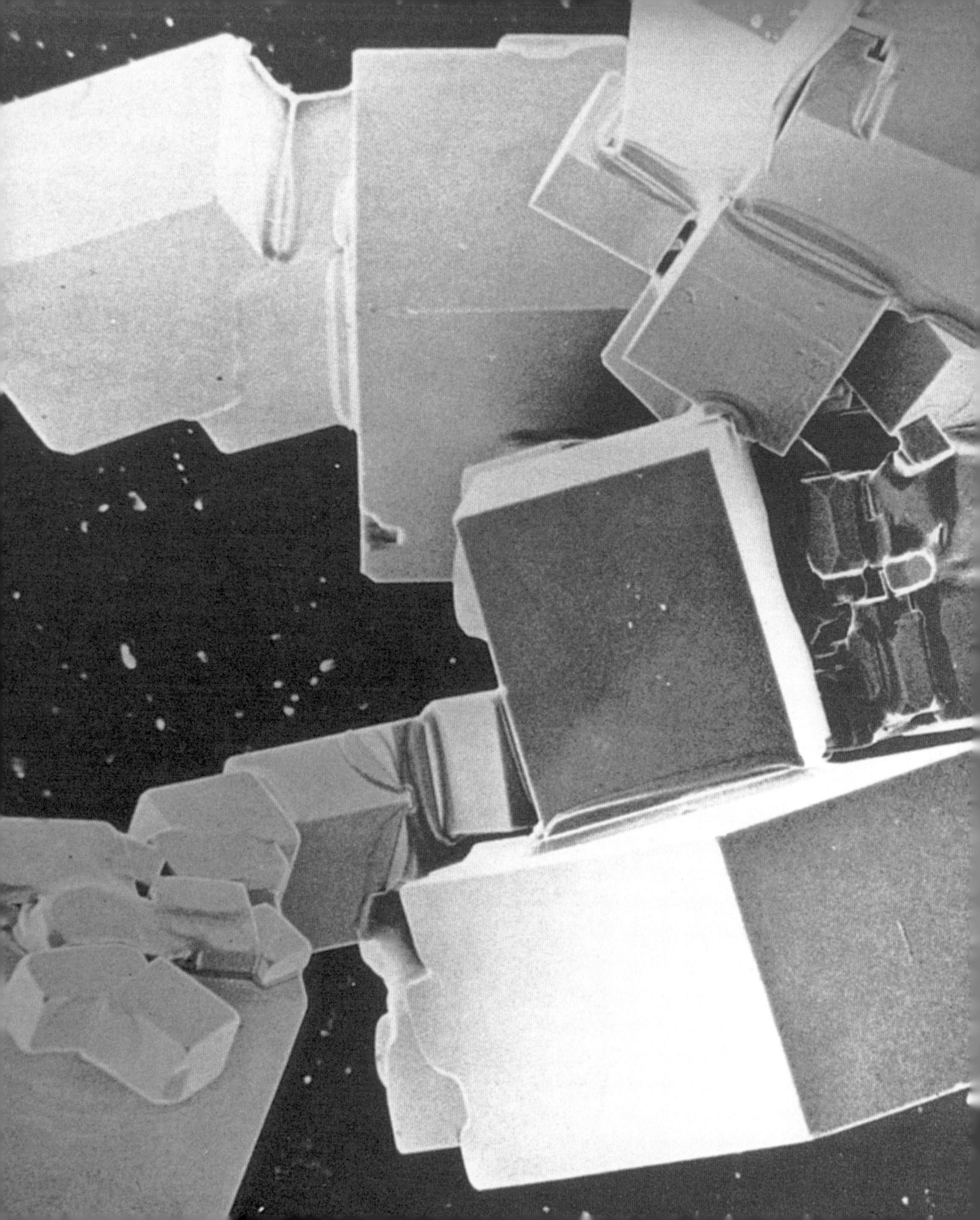

THE

ENIGMA

OF

MARIE TAGLIONI

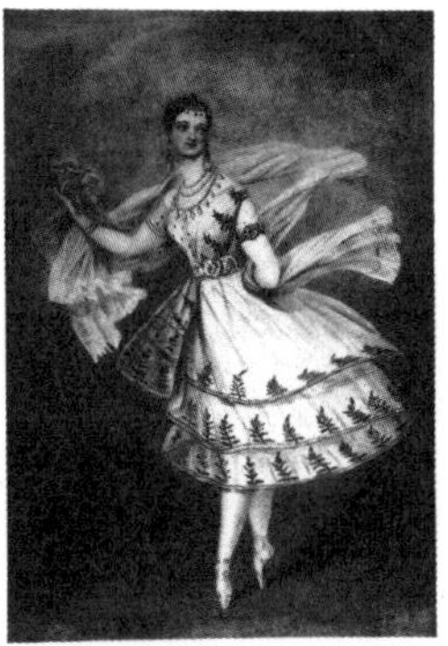

1982–1984

PAUL ETIENNE LINCOLN

"She floats like a spirit in a transparent mist of white muslin with which she loves to surround herself, and she resembles a contented soul scarcely bending the petals of celestial flowers, with the tips of her rosy feet."
THÉOPHILE GAUTIER, 1837

ABOVE: A. E. CHALON'S LITHOGRAPH OF MARIE TAGLIONI PERFORMING *La Bayadère* IN 1831
FRONTISPIECE: SODIUM CHLORIDE (SALT) TABLET TAKEN FROM HIGHWAYMAN AT 100,000X MAGNIFICATION

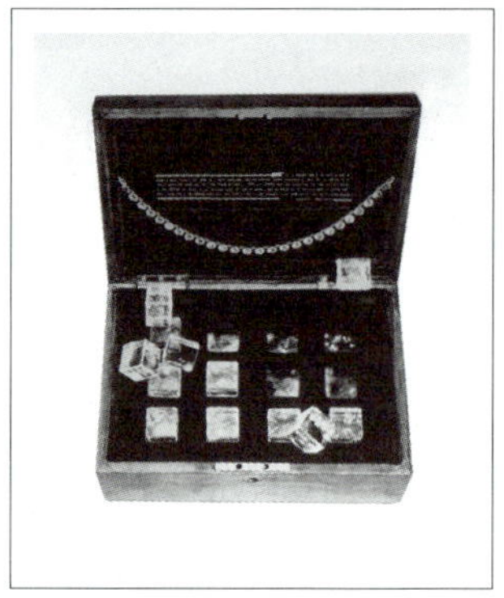

Joseph Cornell, *Taglioni's Jewel Casket*, 1940
Construction, 4¾ × 11⅞ × 8¼ inches
Museum of Modern Art, New York
Gift of James Thrall Soby

The Enigma of Marie Taglioni is an installation inspired by a text describing an experience that the famous Italian ballerina Marie Taglioni[1] had involving a highwayman outside St. Petersburg in 1835, and a legend of Taglioni's instruments for evoking that encounter. The text was found in a work constructed by the late Joseph Cornell, that great practitioner of ethereal memories: *Taglioni's Jewel Casket* (1940), now in the collection of the Museum of Modern Art, New York, is a small, dark wooden box measuring 4¾ × 11⅞ × 8¼ inches. A hinged lid opens to reveal an interior lined with brown velvet; in the base lie a dozen squares of dime-store glass fashioned to look like ice cubes.

1 Marie Taglioni (born April 23, 1804, Stockholm; died April 24, 1884, Marseille) was the first famous ballerina of the Romantic ballet era. She trained with her dancer/choreographer father, Filippo Taglioni (1777–1871), and made her debut in Vienna in 1822. In her father's ballet *La Sylphide*, introduced at the Paris Opera in 1832, she became one of the first to dance *en pointe*. It has been established that in 1832 Taglioni danced the full length of *La Sylphide en pointe*. There were almost certainly dancers before her who rose onto the tips of their toes, but it was Taglioni who pioneered and developed the technique, thus revolutionizing ballet. She transformed toe dancing, then something of a stunt, into a means of artistic expression—a dramatic as well as technical feat. Taglioni created a delicate new style, marked by floating leaps and balanced poses such as the arabesque that typified the early-nineteenth-century Romantic style. Her diaphanous white skirts later evolved into the tutu worn by most classical ballerinas. She toured throughout Europe and, after leaving the Paris Opera in 1837, took a three-year contract in St. Petersburg at the Marinsky Imperial Ballet (now known as the Kirov Ballet). Taglioni became so popular that all kinds of things were named after her: in Russia there were Taglioni caramels, Taglioni cakes, and Taglioni hairstyles. After her last performance in St. Petersburg, in 1842, a pair of her ballet shoes (made by Jannsen of Paris) sold for 200 rubles. The shoes were then cooked, garnished, served with a special sauce, and eaten by a consortium of her adoring fans. (History does not record whether the shoes had been worn.) Taglioni retired from dancing in 1847; her only choreographic work was *Le Papillon* (*The Butterfly*), 1860, created for her student Emma Liviry. In the 1870s Taglioni lived in London, where she taught social dance to children and society ladies—including Princess May of Teck, grandmother of Queen Elizabeth II, who boasted that she had been taught to curtsy by Taglioni.

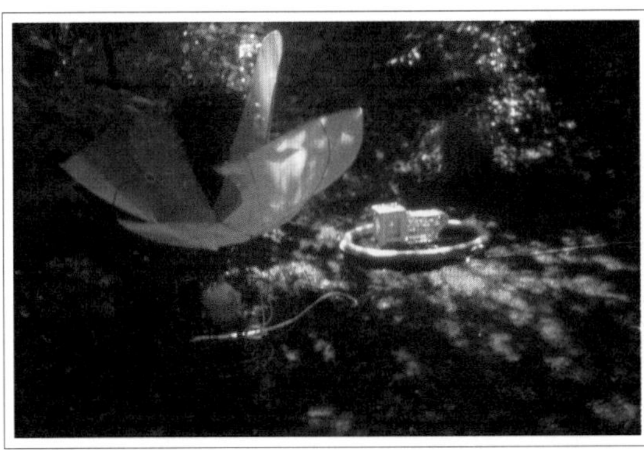

MARIE TAGLIONI AND THE RECORDING BAROGRAPH
ON THE EARLY EVENING OF APRIL 24, 1983

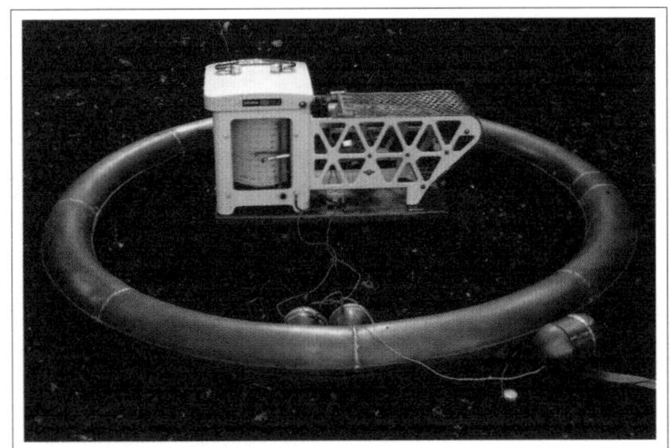

THE TEMPERATURE- AND HUMIDITY-RECORDING BAROGRAPH
SURROUNDED BY THE CIRCULAR LEAD BATTERY
WITH LIGHT-SENSOR PODS

Strung across the inside of the lid is a necklace of rhinestones. In the shallow arc formed by the necklace, recessed in the lush velour, a rectangular plate of blue glass protects a paper label bearing the following text:

> In the winter of 1835 the carriage of Marie Taglioni was halted by a Russian highwayman and that enchanting creature was commanded to dance for her audience of one upon a panther's skin spread over the snow beneath the stars. From this actuality arose the tale that to keep alive the precious memory of this adventure, Taglioni formed the habit of placing a small piece of artificial ice into a jewel casket, where, melting among the real gems, there was evoked a hint of the atmosphere of the starlit heavens above that ice-clad landscape.[2]

The Enigma of Marie Taglioni consists of five main elements: Marie Taglioni herself; the Highwayman; a circular lead battery; a barograph; and a light sensor. This cluster was installed in a shaded clearing within the wooded outcrop of Woldingham, a downland village in the southeast of England, at dusk on April 24, 1983—one year prior to the centenary of Taglioni's death.

While the mechanical and visual metaphors in *The Enigma of Marie Taglioni* are at its mnemonic core, it was atmospheric conditions that determined the initialization and operation of the installation. A barograph (a recording barometer) was used for the performance, with its graph pens touching small pieces of silver wire set at the temperature of 54°F and 51% humidity. As the cool evening drew in, casting long shadows on the softly leafed soil, the barograph recorded a temperature of 54°F; a small strip of silver wire, previously positioned to engage with the temperature-recording needle at exactly this value, received a charge from the battery. The wire in turn permitted the charge to flow to the humidity-recording needle, which, set to a value of 51%, allowed the charge to flow to the light meter, which then recorded a value that had not been previously set. As these three conditions of temperature, humidity, and light level were met, the charge then flowed directly from the battery via a lead strip to a rake mounted on the armature of the Highwayman. On receiving this charge the Highwayman became sensitized.

2 Presumably Marie Taglioni performed her role from *La Sylphide* on that fateful evening in 1835. Her formal dancing engagements in St. Petersburg began in 1837, and she opened to a full house at the St. Petersburg Bolshoi Theatre with this ballet. *La Sylphide*, created for Marie by her father, was the first great landmark in the Romantic ballet. The essence of a more romantic, even spiritual dimension was exquisitely evoked by the woodland glade of the sets and the diaphanous tulle of the costumes. The combination of *en pointe* work and ethereal allegro steps, in which Taglioni excelled, lifted the Romantic ballerina onto a pedestal.

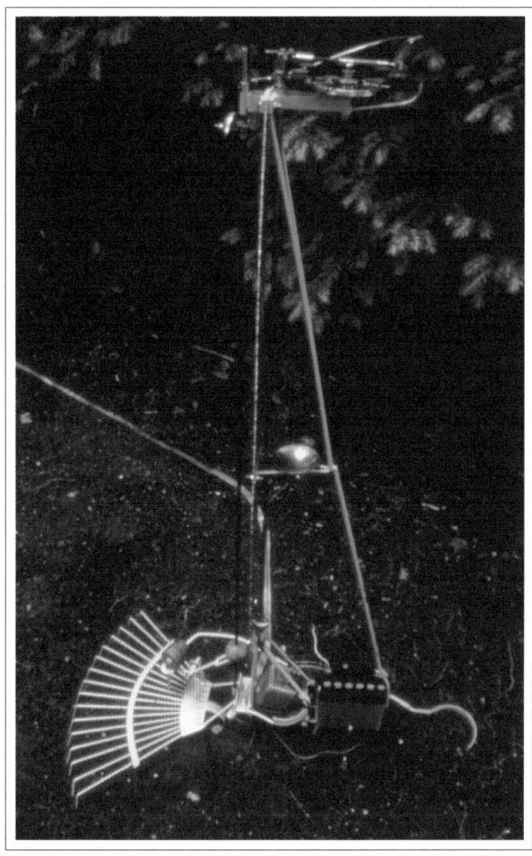

THE HIGHWAYMAN
DISPLAYING HIS MAIN COMPONENTS

The Highwayman is reminiscent of a ball-and-hammer device for measuring a man's strength—the sort found at fairground sideshows. Once sensitized, a lead weight was mechanically lifted and then dropped onto a springboard that in turn sent a ball up a steel tube at the top of which a mechanism then flicked a small tablet of salt[3] in the direction of Marie. This ritualistic offering was repeated seven times in a 30-minute performance.

3 The initial intention was to produce the seven salt tablets by crystallizing sweat released from the glands of villains. However, this rather unpleasant assignment was abandoned after research indicated that an improbably large quantity of perspiration would be required to extract even a minute quantity of salt. Moreover, the daunting task of collecting the liquid prompted the final tablets instead to be fashioned from a block of salt extracted from a Siberian mine.

THE SALT-DISPENSING MECHANISM

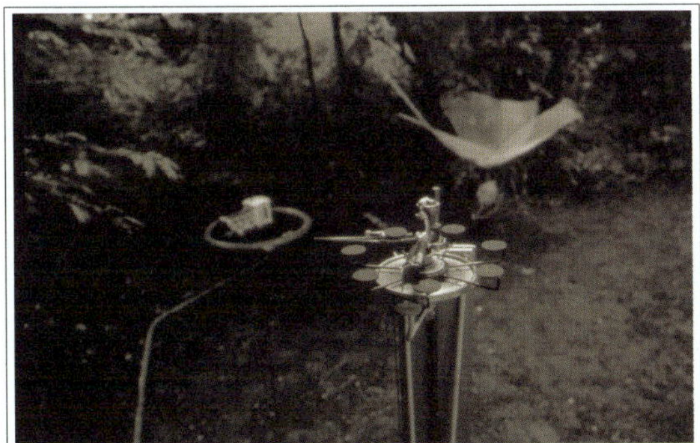

THE SALT-TABLET–DISPENSING MECHANISM SITUATED AT THE TOP OF THE HIGHWAYMAN

When the needles of the recording barograph in *The Enigma of Marie Taglioni* reached 54°F and 51% humidity on April 24, 1983, motor A on the Highwayman's armature was activated, which rotated flywheel B, thus transferring energy via drive C to SECTION 2 (see FIGS. 1–5). Flywheel B raised hammer D and then released it onto springboard E, which in turn flicked ball F up steel column G to bell H. Simultaneously, the release of hammer D allowed the ejection of the salt tablet via rod I in SECTION 2. This cycle repeated seven times.

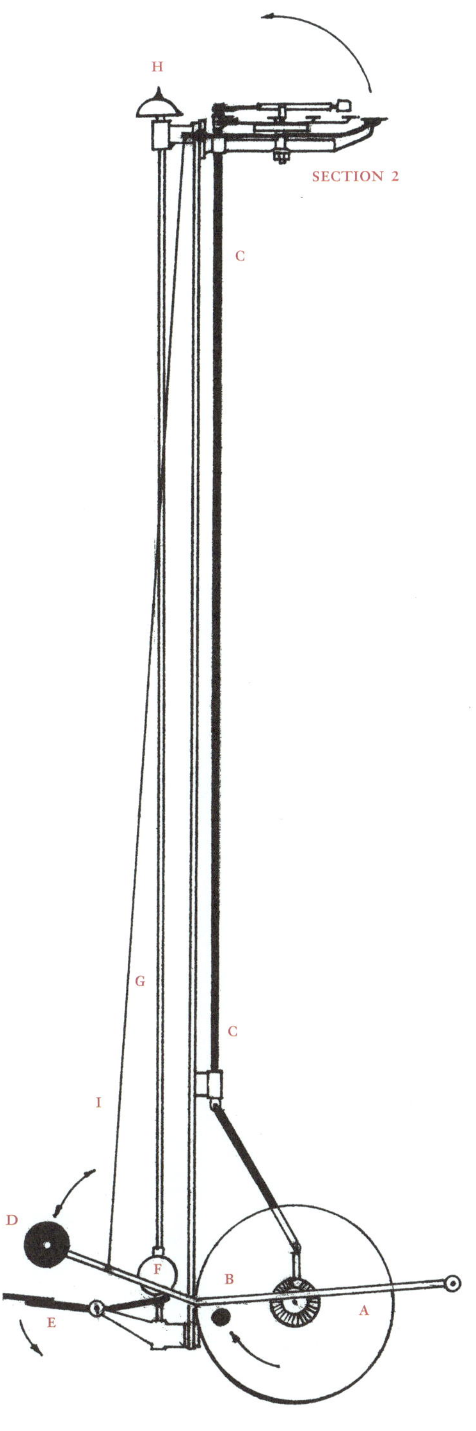

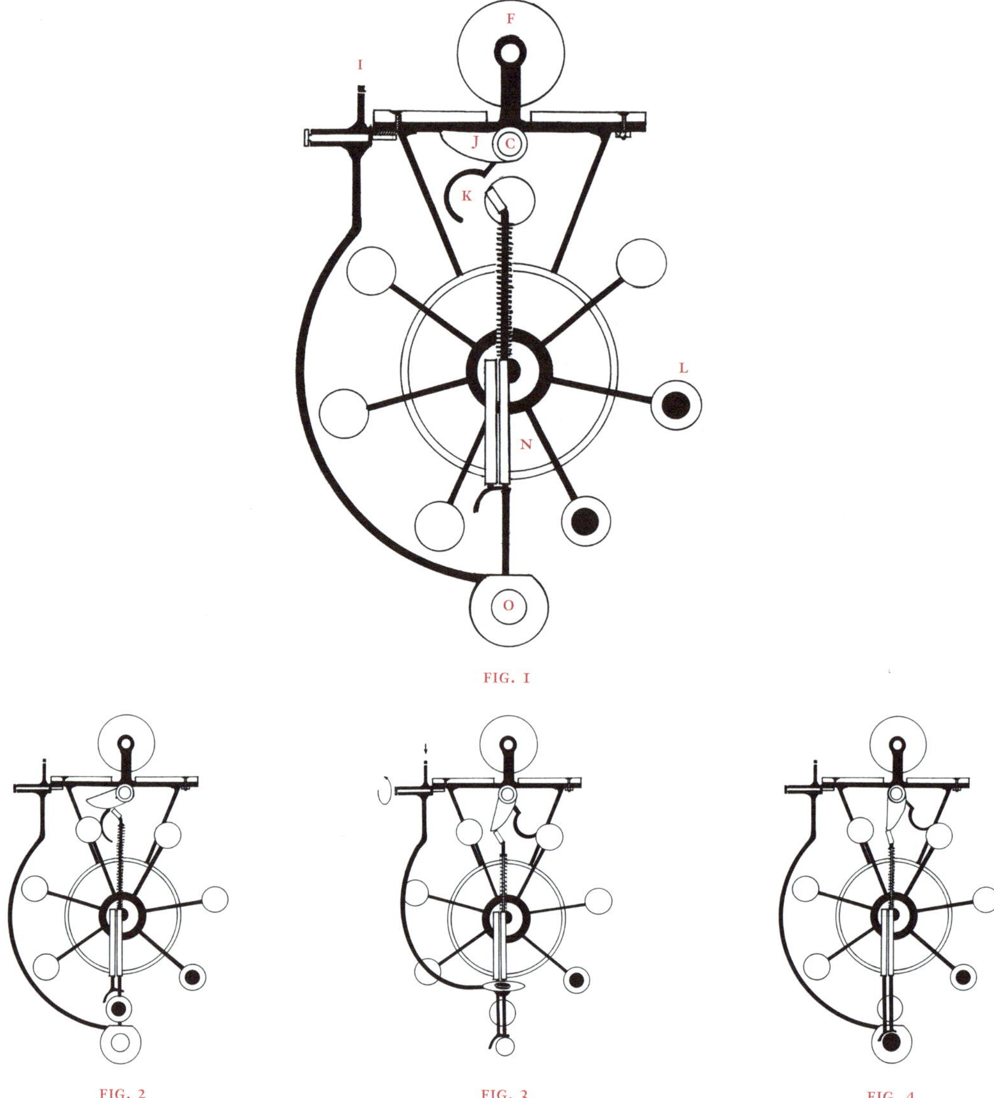

FIG. 1

FIG. 2

FIG. 3

FIG. 4

Power drawn from flywheel B in SECTION I drove cam J and hook K via drive C. Hook K advanced salt-dispensing ring L to ensure that a fresh salt tablet was in loading position. Cam J engaged with plunger N, transferring salt tablet M onto ejector trough O. Once tablet M was positioned, cam J released plunger N to its original position, and ejector rod O was activated by hammer D in SECTION I, thus completing the cycle.

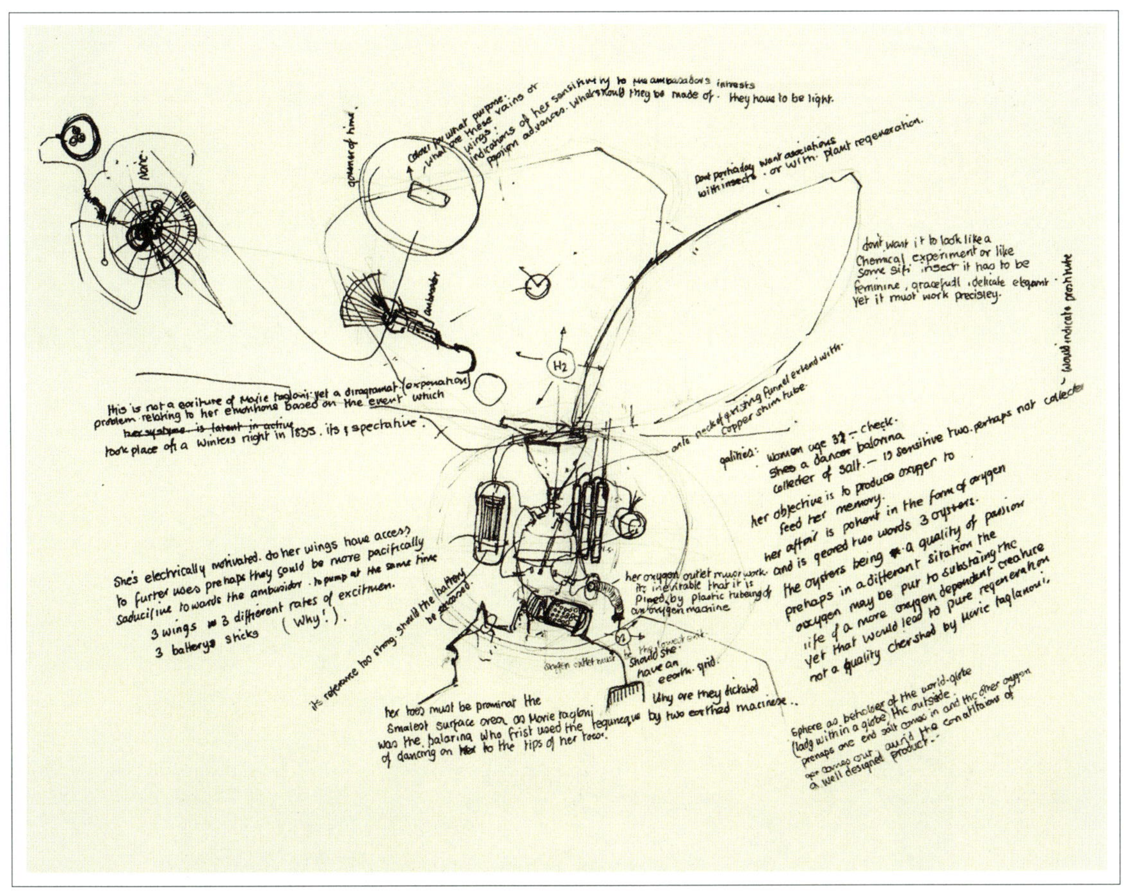

DRAWING SHOWING THE INTERNAL OPERATION OF MARIE TAGLIONI'S STOMACH

Marie had no physical connection to the barograph—her mechanisms were completely dormant until a salt tablet, ejected by the Highwayman, fell onto one of her three silk-covered vanes and descended into her paraffin-wax stomach. Marie and the Highwayman were positioned so that there was a reasonable chance that one of the salt tablets would find its way into Marie's inner pouch. Once the first tablet slid down the vanes and dissolved in the stomach's antechamber (filled with distilled water), a mechanism activated Marie's internal batteries, thus powering a small motor that orchestrated her vanes. Each of these petal-shaped vanes had a different gear ratio; the vanes moved in cycles. Some cycles had the vanes positioned to form a near-funnel, thus making her very susceptible to the ingestion of another salt tablet; other cycles left the vanes greatly extended, ensuring the salt would fall through and foul the ground.

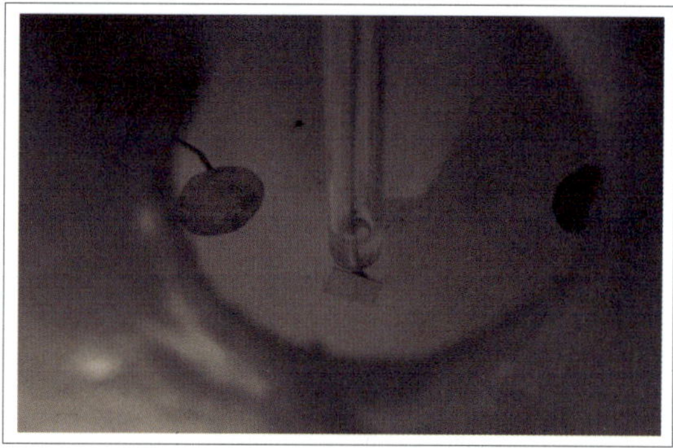

THE INTERIOR OF MARIE TAGLIONI'S STOMACH SHOWING THE GOLD AND PLATINUM ELECTRODES

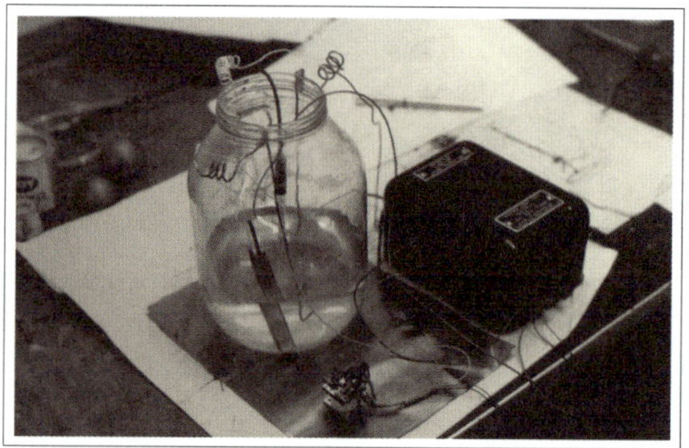

AN ELECTROLYSIS STUDY FOR MARIE TAGLIONI'S STOMACH

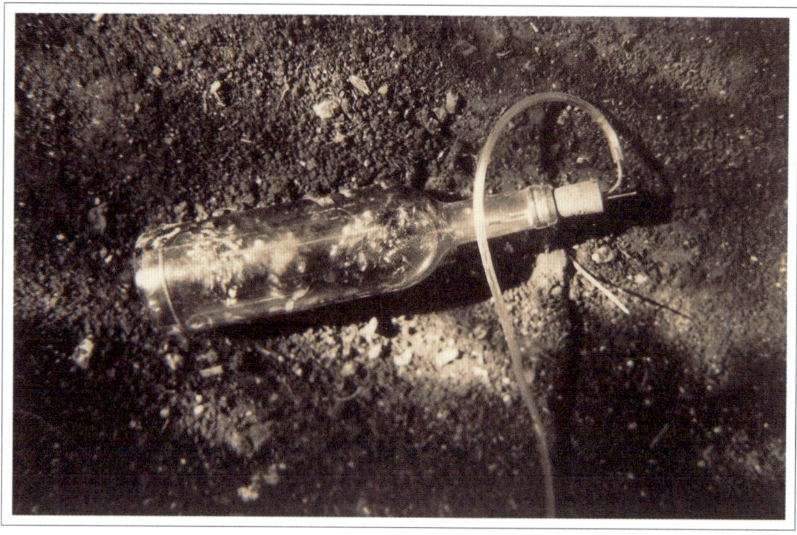

MARIE TAGLIONI'S APPENDAGE, A BOTTLE OF SCALA WINE REFILLED WITH THE THREE OYSTERS BLANKETED IN SEAWATER

As the power from Marie's batteries was energizing her motor it also flowed to two platinum- and gold-leaf electrodes within her stomach; the resulting electrolysis liberated pure oxygen (the substance by which all animal life on Earth exists) from the platinum post. As more salt entered the solution, so more oxygen was released; the oxygen was tapped from the top of the stomach and piped to a wine bottle previously filled with a wine called Scala—a reminder of that famous Milanese operatic venue. Within the wine bottle, now filled with salt water, were three live oysters. Once sensitized by the Highwayman, Marie continued to produce oxygen, pumping it to the oysters until all the energy was drained from both her batteries and those of the Highwayman.

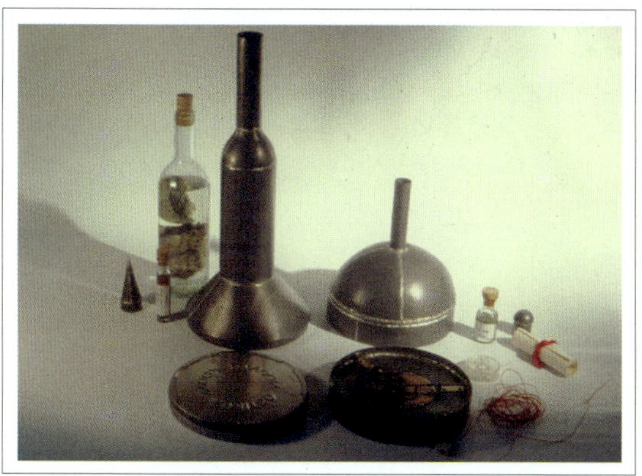

THE MEMORY CASKET UNLOCKED TO SHOW ITS CONTENTS: THE TWO MACHINES' LUBRICANTS, THE 30-MINUTE, 16-MM FILM OF THE PERFORMANCE, THE SCALA WINE BOTTLE CONTAINING THE ORIGINAL OYSTERS PRESERVED IN FORMALDEHYDE, AND THE CASKET'S LOCKING MECHANISM

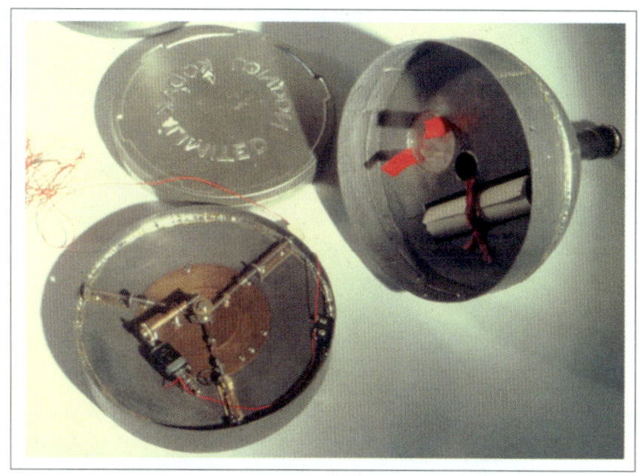

DETAIL OF THE MEMORY CASKET'S LOCKING MECHANISM, THE FILM OF THE PERFORMANCE, THE LOG OF THE OPENING OF THE CASKET, AND THE HIGHWAYMAN'S SPENT SALT TABLETS RETRIEVED FROM THE ORIGINAL PERFORMANCE

A 16-mm black-and-white film was made to document the machines' performance; the film recorded the Highwayman being disconnected from the lead battery and then the arrival of a lead casket, which was ritualistically filled with various relics and carried out of the woods. This lead casket had two ends. The ends held lubricants for both machines and denoted their genders. The end into which energy from the replenished battery entered the casket was Marie's; her lubricant consisted of Swedish watchmakers' oil and an antique scent of gypsophila and rosemary. Next to be placed in the casket were: the oysters in the Scala wine bottle, preserved in formaldehyde; an electrical lock; the film (placed in the casket after processing); the undissolved salt tablets (retrieved from the forest floor around Marie); a log of the opening of the casket; and, at the opposite pole, the lubricant of the Highwayman, made from sturgeons' oil extracted from crushed caviar and a clear alcohol of 80 proof.

When atmospheric conditions are identical to those of the original performance, the electrical lock permits the casket to be opened. The film may be viewed only during the eight to ten hours between dusk and dawn on nights that have precisely the same conditions of beauty as those experienced on April 24, 1983.[4] Marie's final act of passion—the conversion of the Highwayman's salt into pure oxygen by electrolysis of the saline in her stomach—provided a transient energy to the oysters, those richly associative ostrea, who are preserved in a wine bottle forming an encrypted message—waiting for enlightened parties of the future to decode.

4 *A Transcript to Unrequited Euphoria* was published on the occasion of the 1992 Vienna exhibition of *The Enigma of Marie Taglioni.*

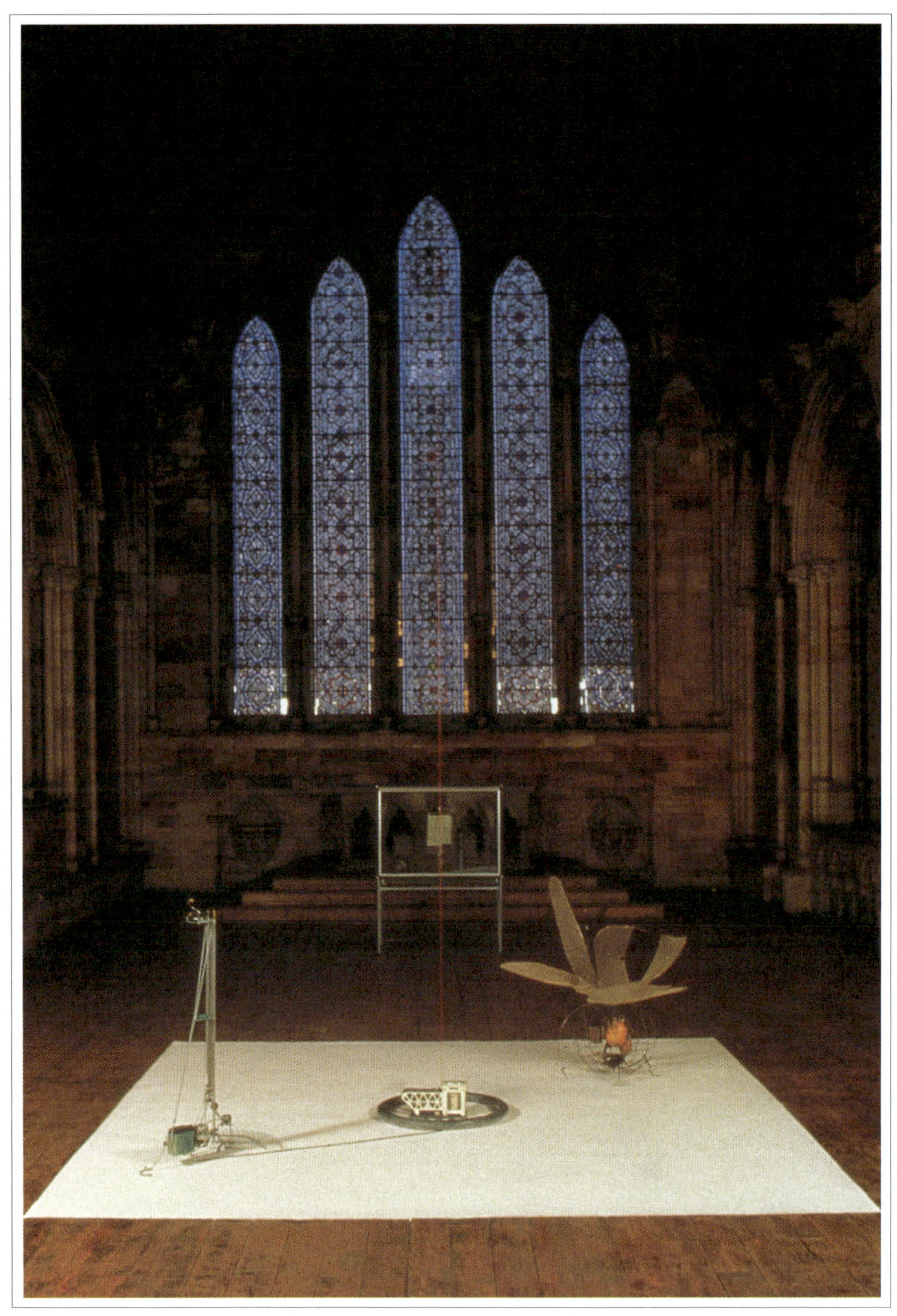

INSTALLATION VIEW OF *The Enigma of Marie Taglioni* AT ST. PAULINUS, CATTERICK, ENGLAND

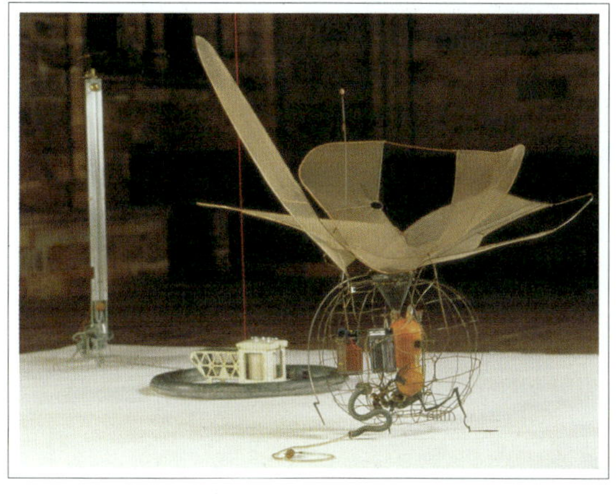

MARIE TAGLIONI ON A CARPET OF SALT
AT ST. PAULINUS, CATTERICK, ENGLAND

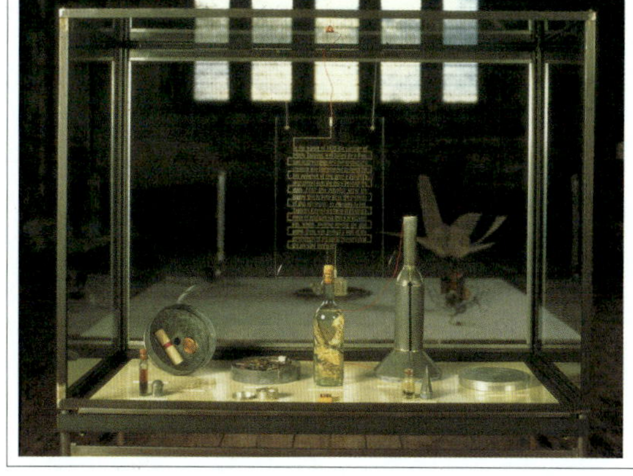

VIEW OF THE MEMORY-CASKET VITRINE
IN THE FOREGROUND OF THE ST. PAULINUS INSTALLATION

After the initial performance of *The Enigma of Marie Taglioni*, the installation has been presented three times: in Vienna in 1992; in Frankfurt in 1993; and—most recently—at St. Paulinus, in Yorkshire, England, in 1999. Each time, the five dormant elements from the original performance were presented on a plane of salt (the film may only be screened on a cloud in the sky or on a field of salt); an adjacent vitrine contained the lead casket (exceptionally opened with its treasures laid bare), together with the Cornell text (screen-printed in gilded varnish on a sheet of glass suspended in a manner resembling an electrical circuit board). A wire connected the battery, reposing on the salt plane, to the glass text. A concealed drawer at the front of the vitrine held a series of 16 line drawings detailing the inner operations of the installation's protagonists. A second, smaller vitrine held the barograph recordings for the month immediately preceding the performance, displayed with an engraving of Taglioni, and a short biography.

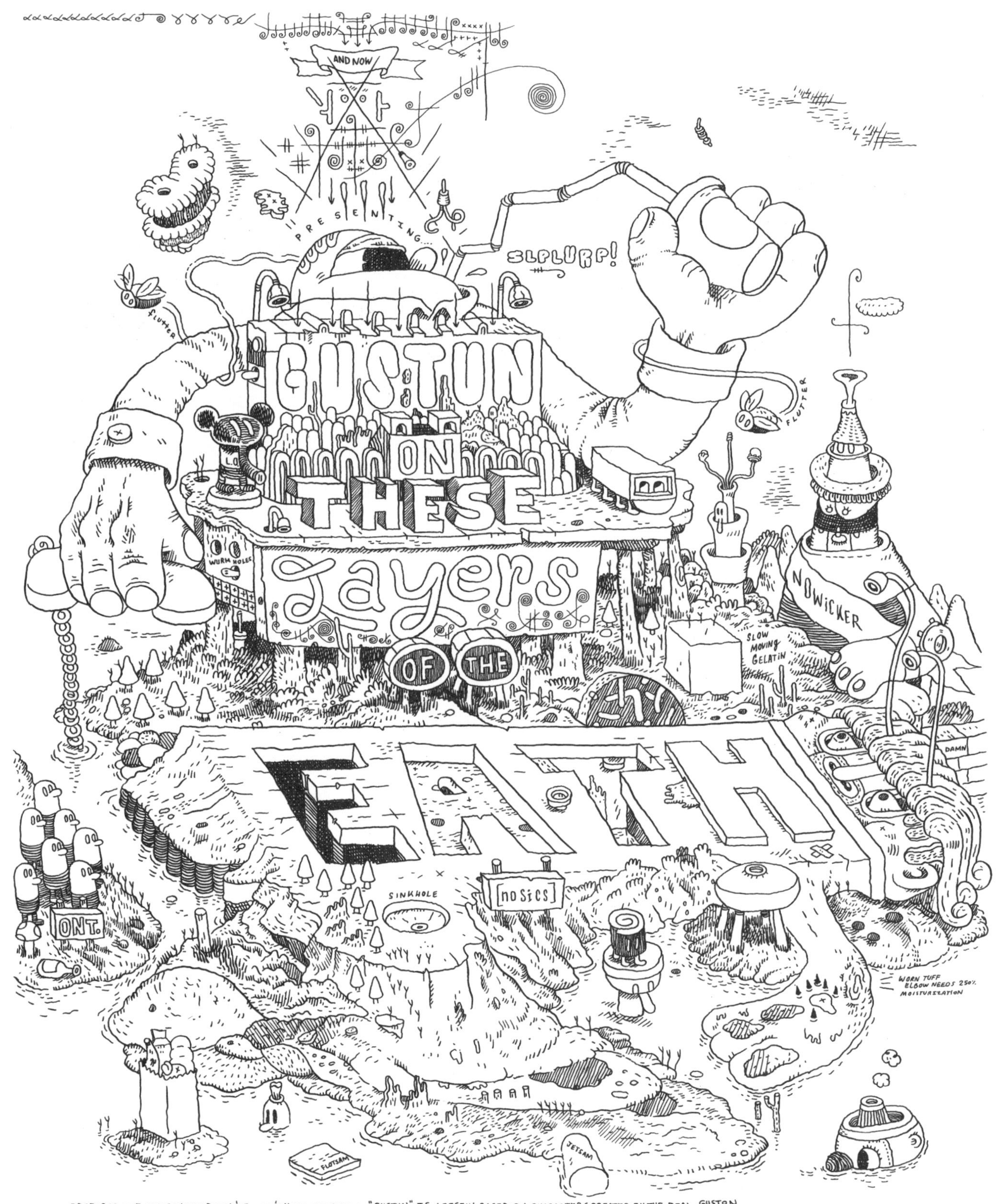

–PREPARED FOR THE GANZFELD IN '03 AND '04 BY MARC BELL. "GUSTUN" IS LOOSELY BASED ON CHARACTERS CREATED BY THE REAL GUSTON

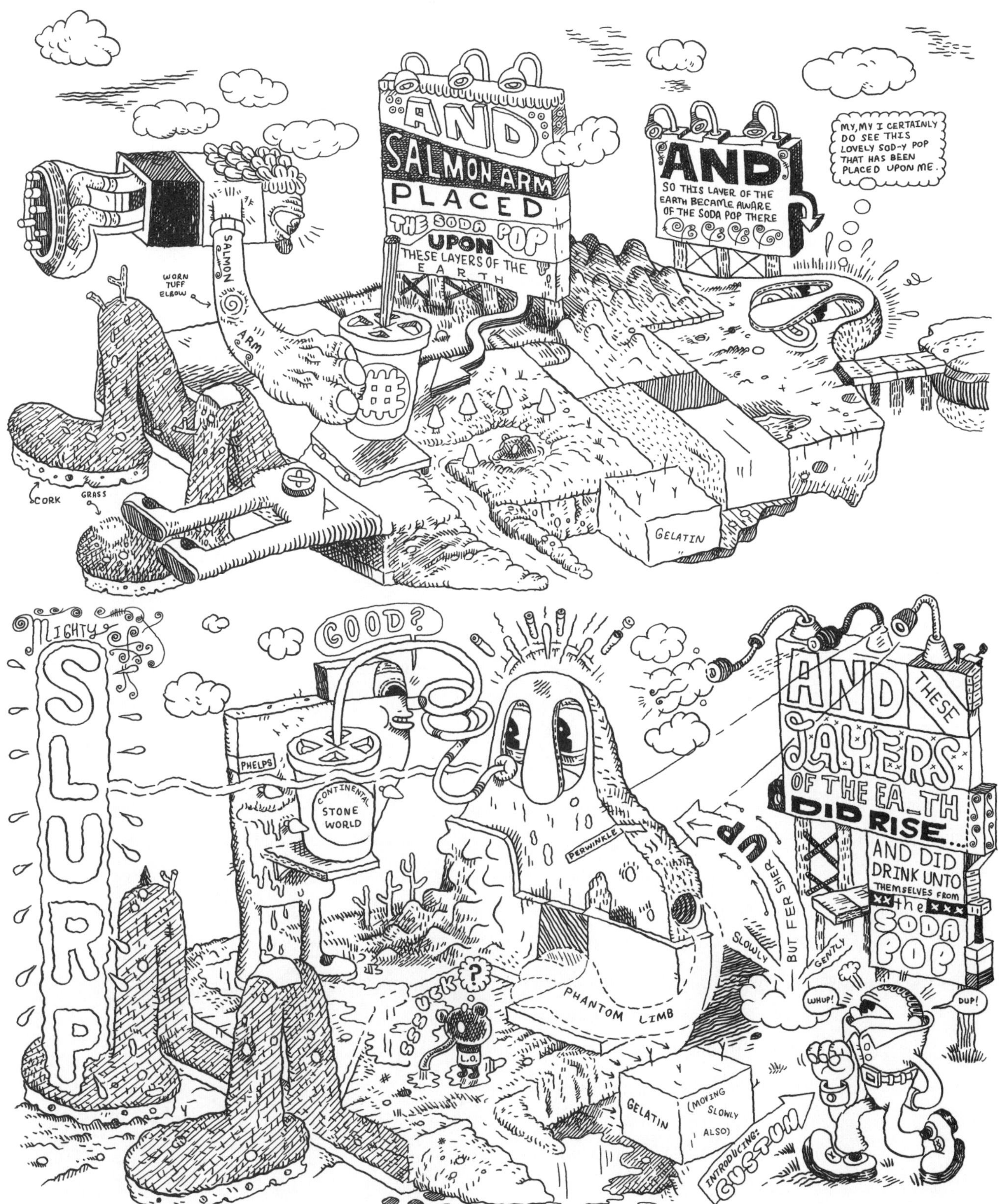
AND
SALMON ARM
PLACED
THE SODA POP
UPON
THESE LAYERS OF THE
EARTH
SALMON
ARM
WORN TUFF ELBOW
CORK
GRASS
AND
SO THIS LAYER OF THE EARTH BECAME AWARE OF THE SODA POP THERE
MY, MY I CERTAINLY DO SEE THIS LOVELY SOD-Y POP THAT HAS BEEN PLACED UPON ME.
GELATIN
MIGHTY
SLURP
GOOD?
PHELPS
CONTINENTAL STONE WORLD
PERWINKLE
PHANTOM LIMB
SSSUCK
L.O.
AND THESE
LAYERS
OF THE EA_TH
DID RISE...
AND DID DRINK UNTO THEMSELVES FROM the SODA POP
UP
SLOWLY
BUT FER SHER
GENTLY
WHUP!
DUP!
GELATIN
(MOVING SLOWLY ALSO)
INTRODUCING: GUSTUM

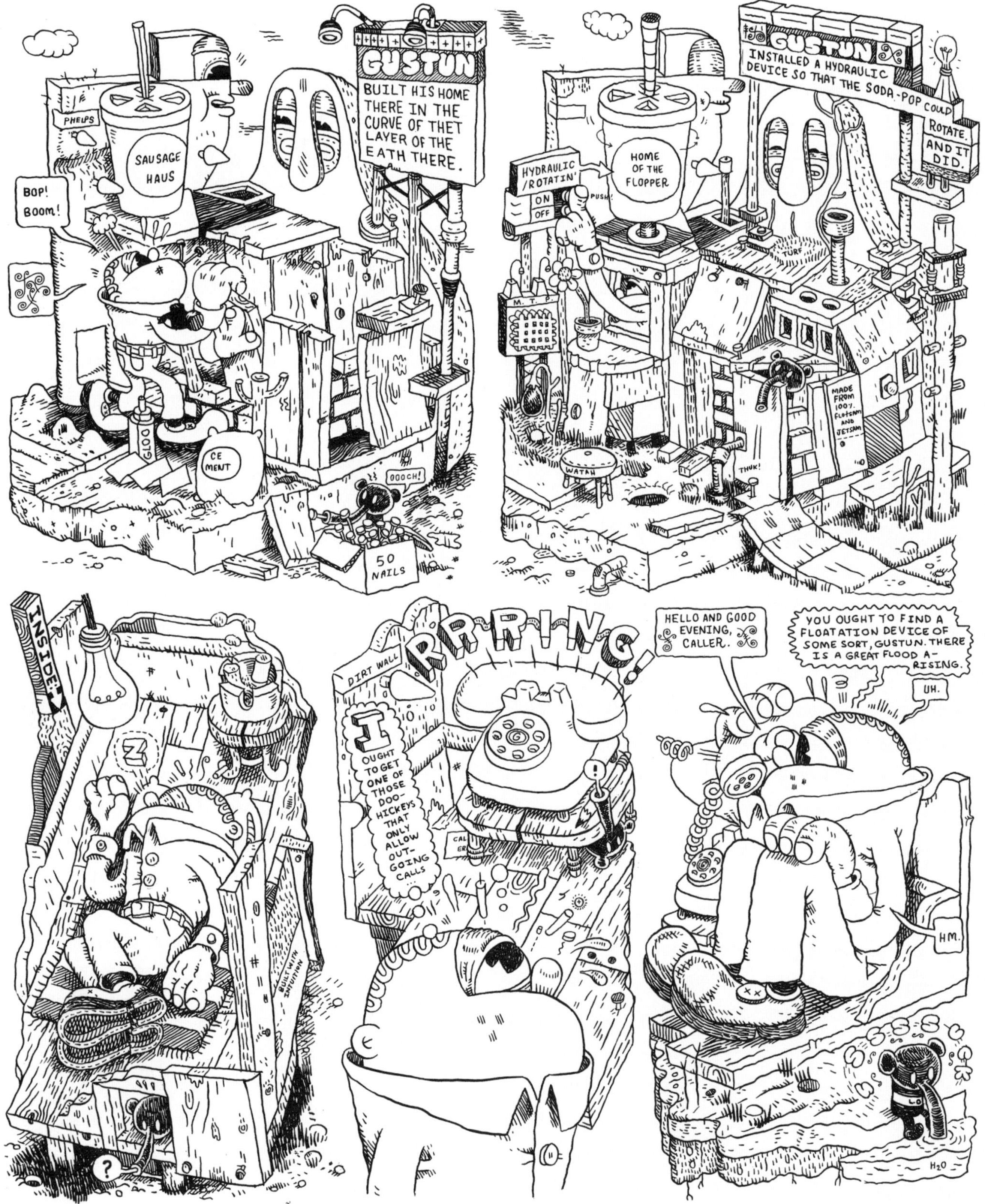
GUSTUN
BUILT HIS HOME THERE IN THE CURVE OF THET LAYER OF THE EATH THERE.
PHELPS
SAUSAGE HAUS
BOP! BOOM!
GLOO
CE MENT
OOOCH!
50 NAILS
GUSTUN
INSTALLED A HYDRAULIC DEVICE SO THAT THE SODA-POP COULD ROTATE. AND IT DID.
HYDRAULIC /ROTATIN'
ON
OFF
PUSH!
HOME OF THE FLOPPER
M. T. P.
TURF
MADE FROM 100% FLOTSAM AND JETSAM
WATAH
THUK!
INSIDE
Z
BUILT WITH INTUITION
?
DIRT WALL
RRRING!
I OUGHT TO GET ONE OF THOSE DOO-HICKEYS THAT ONLY ALLOW OUT-GOING CALLS
HELLO AND GOOD EVENING, CALLER.
YOU OUGHT TO FIND A FLOATATION DEVICE OF SOME SORT, GUSTUN. THERE IS A GREAT FLOOD A-RISING.
UH.
HM.
H2O

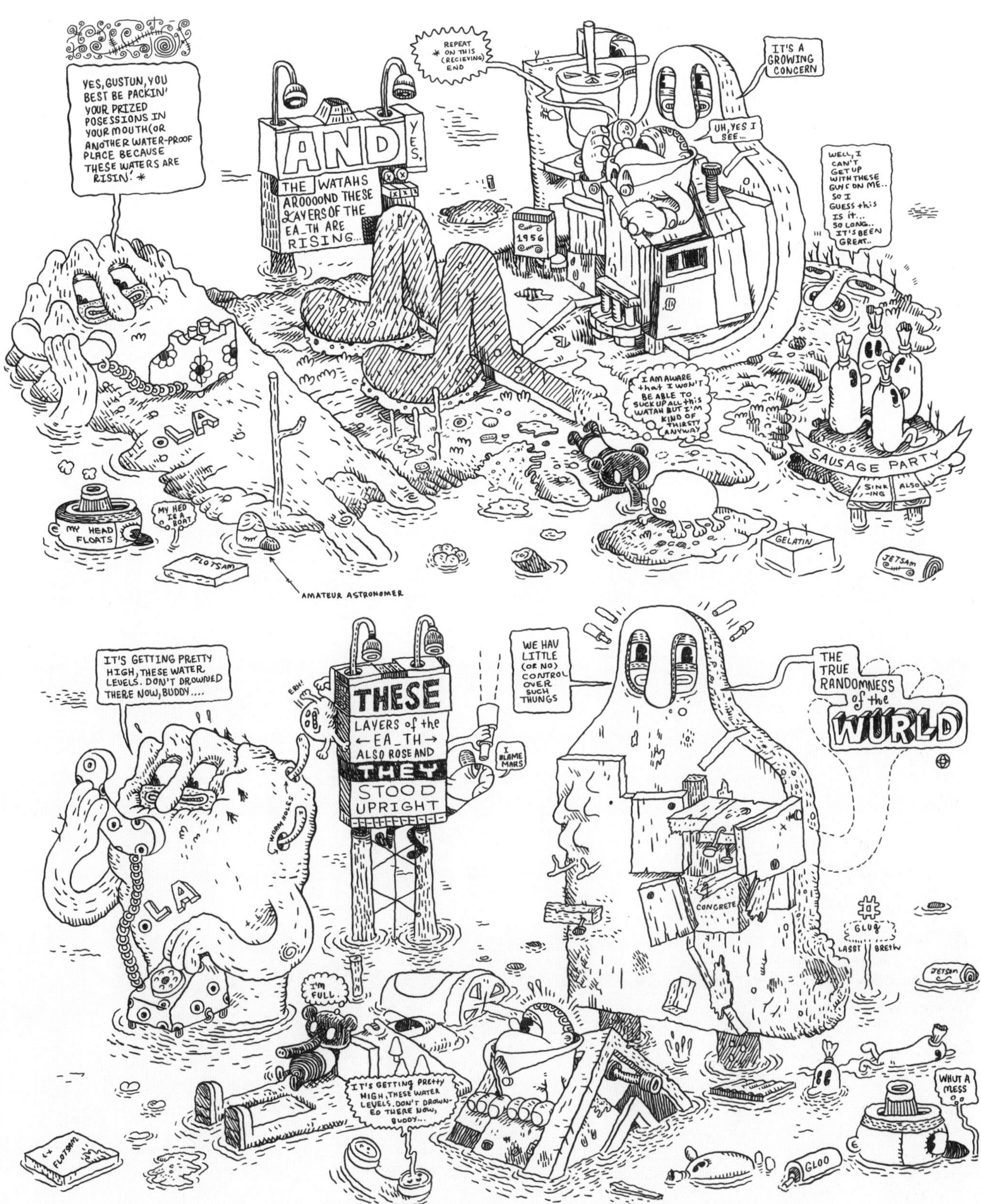
YES, GUSTUN, YOU BEST BE PACKIN' YOUR PRIZED POSESSIONS IN YOUR MOUTH (OR ANOTHER WATER-PROOF PLACE BECAUSE THESE WATERS ARE RISIN'. *
AND
YES,
THE WATAHS AROOOOND THESE LAYERS OF THE EA_TH ARE RISING...
* REPEAT ON THIS (RECIEVING) END
IT'S A GROWING CONCERN
UH, YES I SEE...
1956
WELL, I CAN'T GET UP WITH THESE GUYS ON ME.. SO I GUESS this IS it... SO LONG.. IT'S BEEN GREAT..
I AM AWARE that I WON'T BE ABLE TO SUCK UP ALL this WATAH BUT I'M KIND OF THIRSTY ANYWAY
LA
SAUSAGE PARTY
SINK -ING
ALSO
MY HEAD FLOATS
MY HED IS A BOAT
FLOTSAM
GELATIN
JETSAM
AMATEUR ASTRONOMER
IT'S GETTING PRETTY HIGH, THESE WATER LEVELS. DON'T DROWNED THERE NOW, BUDDY....
THESE
LAYERS of the ←EA_TH→ ALSO ROSE AND
THEY
STOOD UPRIGHT
I BLAME MARS
WE HAV LITTLE (OR NO) CONTROL OVER SUCH THINGS
THE TRUE RANDOMNESS of the
WURLD
WORM HOLES
LA
CONCRETE
GLUG
LASST
BRETH
JETSON
I'M FULL.
IT'S GETTING PRetty HIGH, THESE WATER LEVELS. DON'T DROWN-ED THERE NOW, BUDDY...
WHUT A MESS
FLOTSAM
GLOO

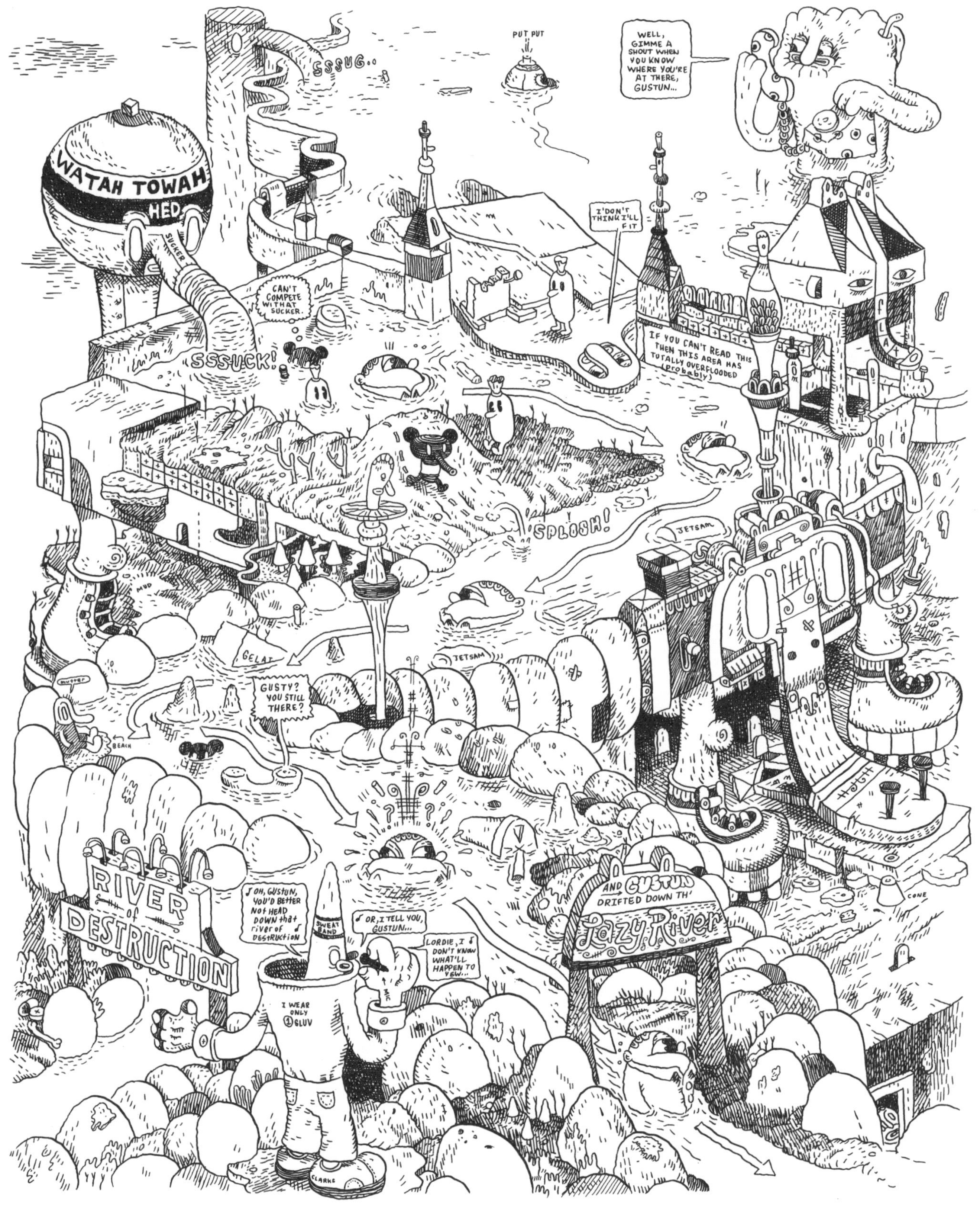
SSSUG..
PUT PUT
WELL, GIMME A SHOUT WHEN YOU KNOW WHERE YOU'RE AT THERE, GUSTUN...
WATAH TOWAH
HED
SUCKER
CAN'T COMPETE WITHAT SUCKER.
I'DON'T THINK I'LL FIT
SSSUCK!
IF YOU CAN'T READ THIS THEN THIS AREA HAS TOTALLY OVERFLOODED (probably)
SPLOSH!
JETSAM
MUD
GELAT
JETSAM
mutter
BEACH
GUSTY? YOU STILL THERE?
RIVER of DESTRUCTION
♪OH, GUSTUN, YOU'D BETTER NOT HEAD DOWN that river of DESTRUCTION♪
♪OR, I TELL YOU, GUSTUN...
LORDIE, I ♪ DON'T KNOW WHAT'LL HAPPEN TO YEW...
SWEAT BAND
MIC
I WEAR ONLY 1 GLUV
CLARKS
AND GUSTUN DRIFTED DOWN TH' Lazy River
CONE

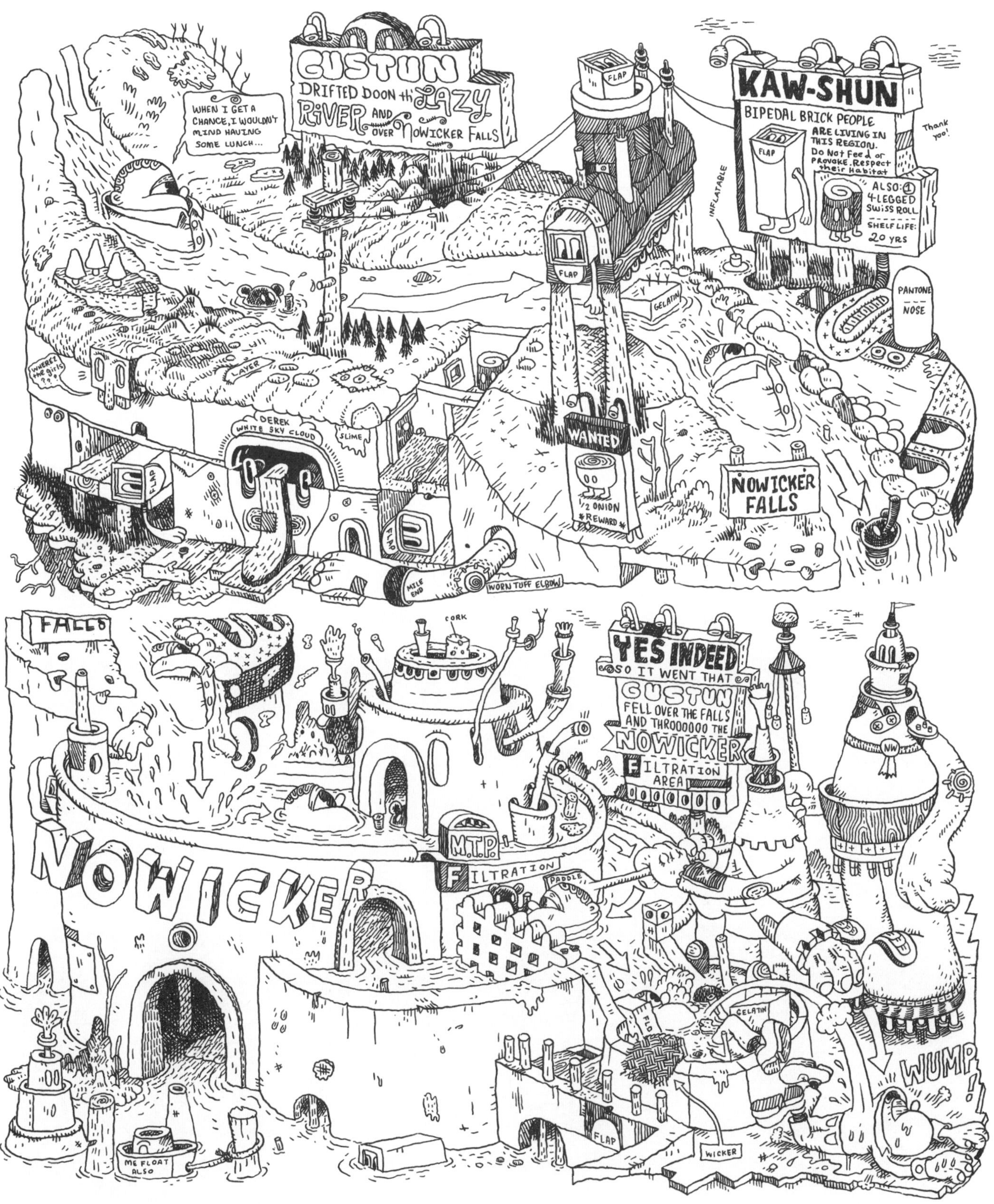

GUSTUN
DRIFTED DOON th' LAZY
RIVER AND OVER NOWICKER FALLS
WHEN I GET A CHANCE, I WOULDN'T MIND HAVING SOME LUNCH...
KAW-SHUN
BIPEDAL BRICK PEOPLE ARE LIVING IN THIS REGION. Do Not Feed or PROVOKE. Respect their Habitat
FLAP
ALSO: 1 4-LEGGED SWISS ROLL. SHELF LIFE: 20 YRS
Thank yoo!
INFLATABLE
GELATIN
PANTONE NOSE
LAYER
DEREK WHITE SKY CLOUD
SLIME
WANTED
1/2 ONION
REWARD
NOWICKER FALLS
MILE END
WORN TUFF ELBOW
FALLS
CORK
YES INDEED
SO IT WENT THAT
GUSTUN
FELL OVER THE FALLS AND THROOOOOO THE
NOWICKER
FILTRATION AREA
NOWICKER
M.T.P.
FILTRATION
PADDLE
NW
GELATIN
WUMP!
ME FLOAT ALSO
FLAP
WICKER

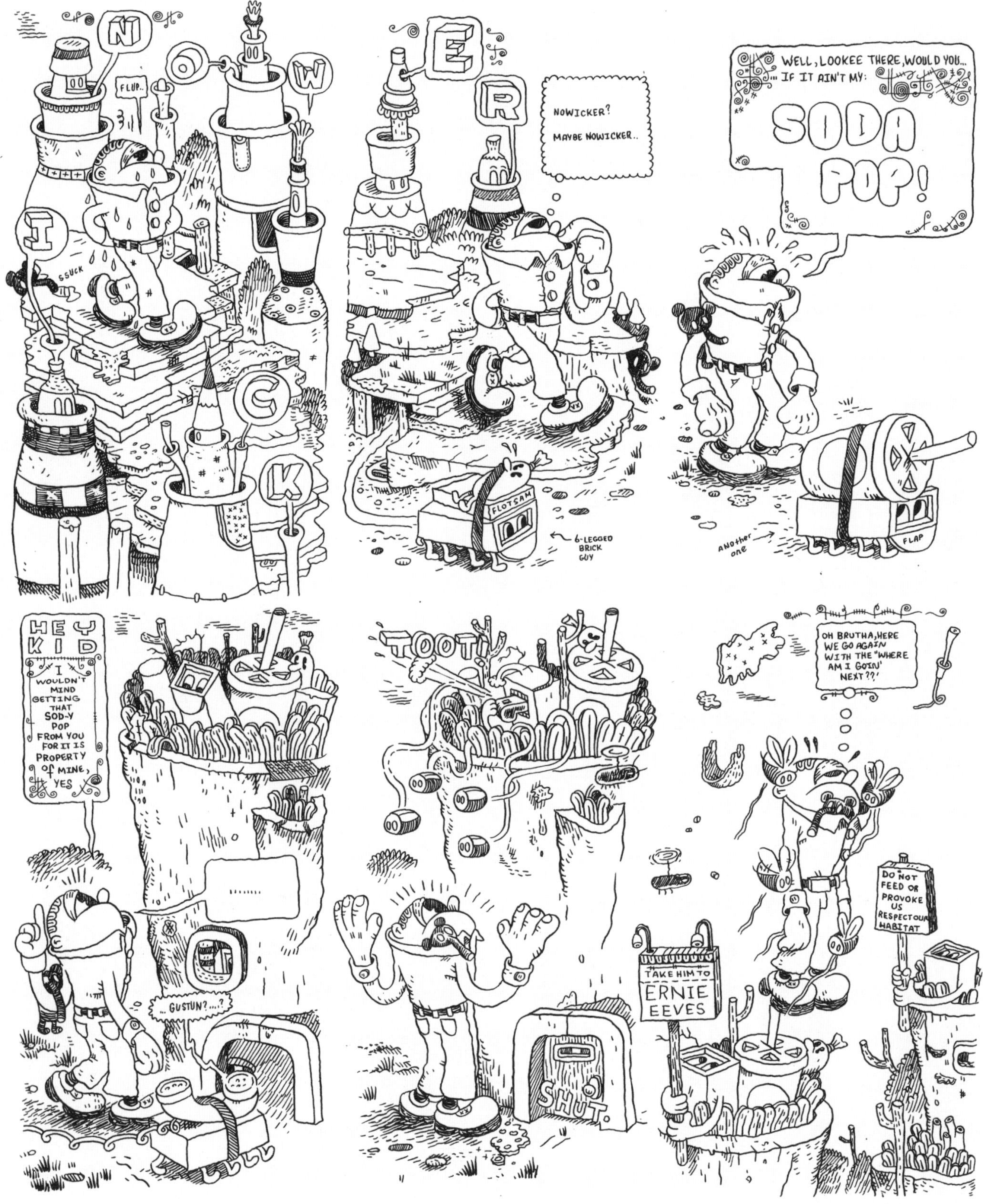
N
O
W
I
C
K
FLUP..
SSUCK
E
R
NOWICKER?
MAYBE NOWICKER..
WELL, LOOKEE THERE, WOULD YOU... IF IT AIN'T MY:
SODA POP!
FLOTSAM
6-LEGGED BRICK GUY
ANOTHER ONE
FLAP
HEY KID
I WOULDN'T MIND GETTING THAT SOD-Y POP FROM YOU FOR IT IS PROPERTY OF MINE, YES
....
...GUSTUN?...?
TOOT!
SHUT.
OH BRUTHA, HERE WE GO AGAIN WITH THE "WHERE AM I GOIN' NEXT??"
TAKE HIM TO ERNIE EEVES
DO NOT FEED OR PROVOKE US RESPECT OUR HABITAT

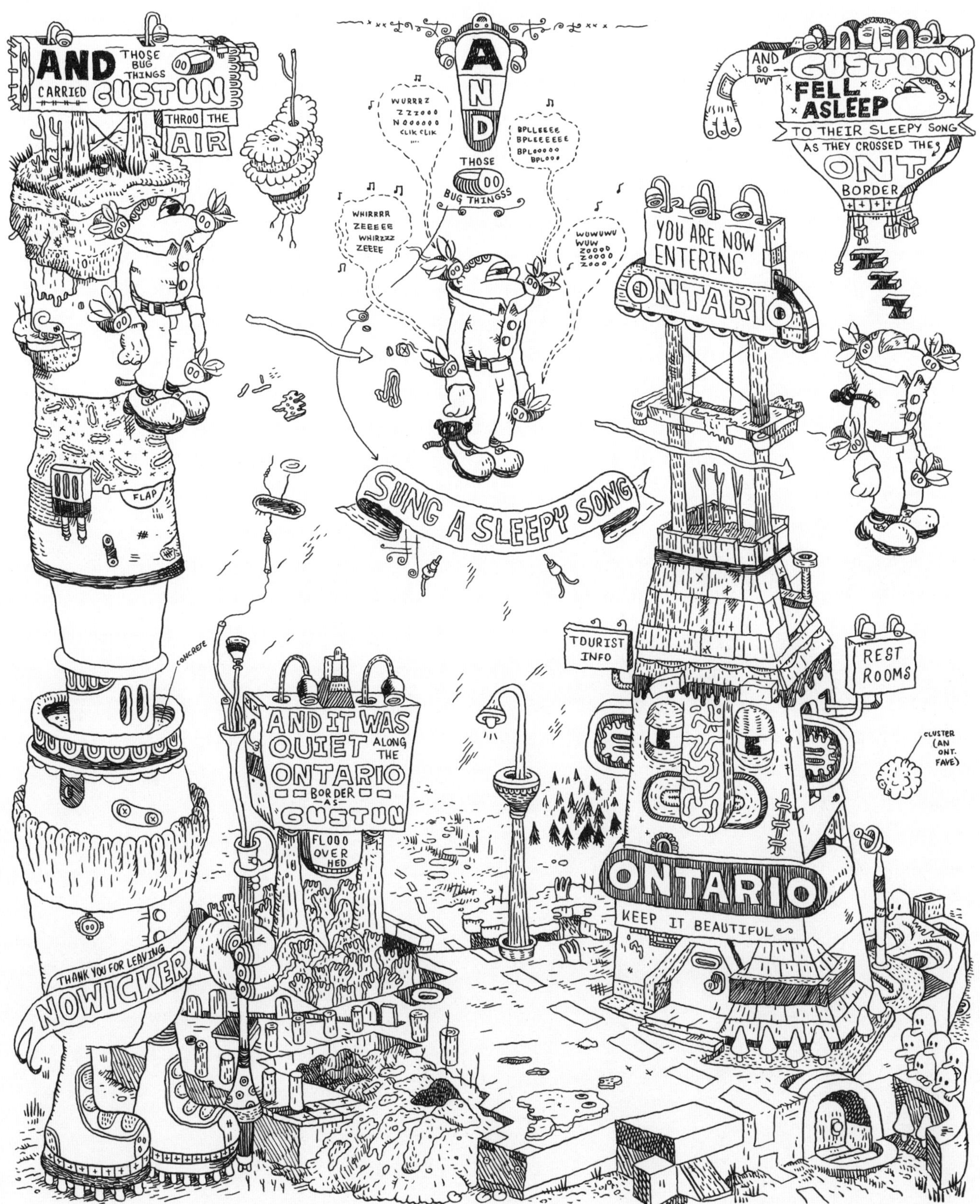
AND THOSE BUG THINGS CARRIED GUSTUN THROO THE AIR
AND
THOSE BUG THINGSS
WURRRZ ZZZOOO NOOOOOO CLIK CLIK
BPLLEEEE BPLEEEEEE BPLOOOOO BPLOOO
WHIRRRR ZEEEEE WHIRZZZ ZEEEE
WOWUWU WUW ZOOOO ZOOOO ZOOO
SUNG A SLEEPY SONG
AND SO GUSTUN FELL ASLEEP TO THEIR SLEEPY SONG AS THEY CROSSED THE ONT. BORDER
YOU ARE NOW ENTERING ONTARIO
FLAP
CONCRETE
TOURIST INFO
REST ROOMS
CLUSTER (AN ONT. FAVE)
AND IT WAS QUIET ALONG THE ONTARIO BORDER AS GUSTUN FLOOO OVER HED
ONTARIO
KEEP IT BEAUTIFUL
THANK YOU FOR LEAVING NOWICKER

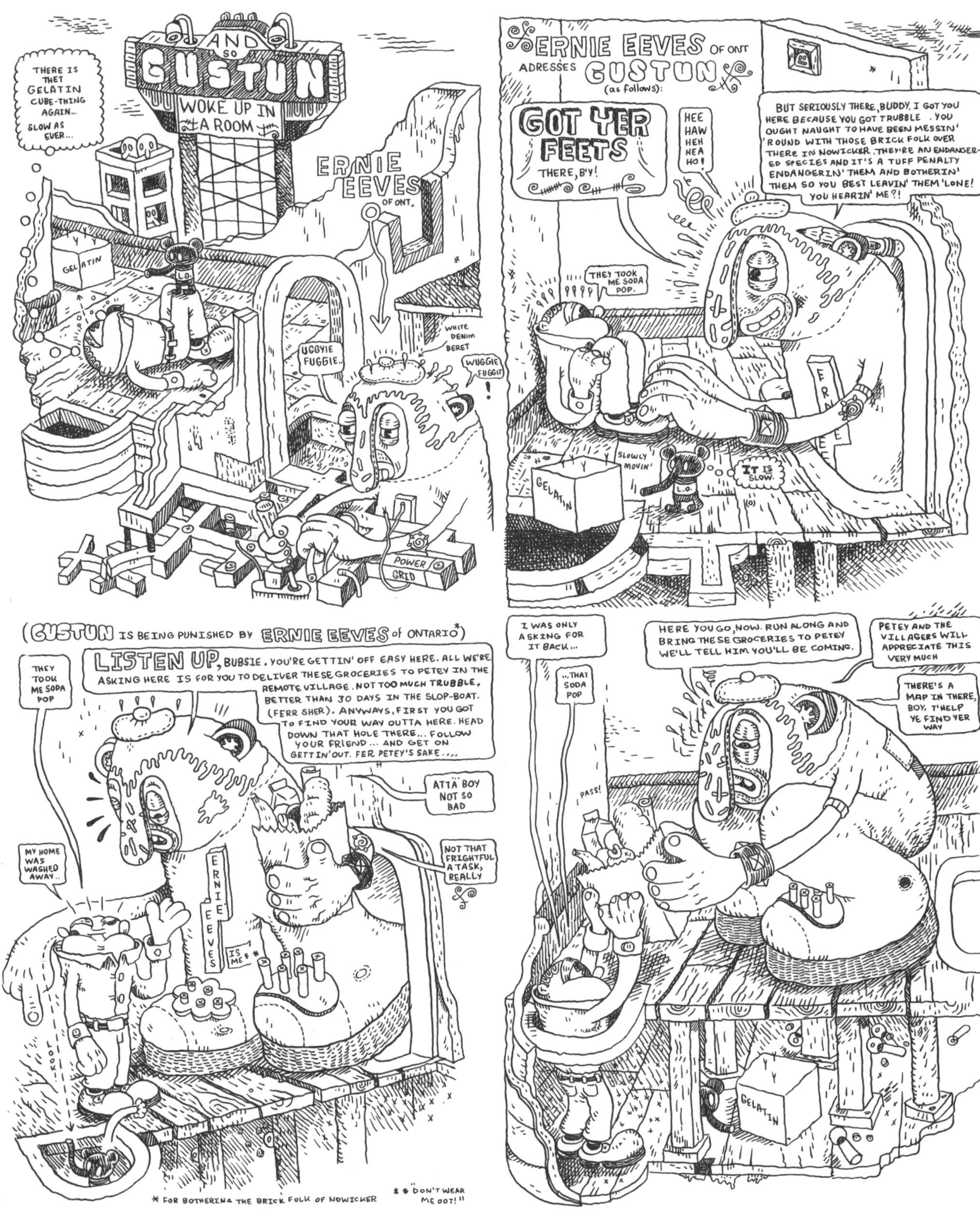

AND SO GUSTUN WOKE UP IN A ROOM
THERE IS THET GELATIN CUBE-THING AGAIN... SLOW AS EVER...
ERNIE EEVES OF ONT.
GELATIN
L.O.
UGGYIE FUGGIE..
WHITE DENIM BERET
WUGGIE FUGGIT
POWER GRID
ERNIE EEVES OF ONT ADRESSES GUSTUN (as follows):
GOT YER FEETS THERE, B'Y!
HEE HAW HEH HEA HO!
BUT SERIOUSLY THERE, BUDDY. I GOT YOU HERE BECAUSE YOU GOT TRUBBLE. YOU OUGHT NAUGHT TO HAVE BEEN MESSIN' 'ROUND WITH THOSE BRICK FOLK OVER THERE IN NOWICKER. THEY'RE AN ENDANGERED SPECIES AND IT'S A TUFF PENALTY ENDANGERIN' THEM AND BOTHERIN' THEM SO YOU BEST LEAVIN' THEM 'LONE! YOU HEARIN' ME?!
THEY TOOK ME SODA POP.
ERNIE
SLOWLY MOVIN'
IT IS SLOW.
GELATIN
L.O.
(GUSTUN IS BEING PUNISHED BY ERNIE EEVES of ONTARIO*)
THEY TOOK ME SODA POP
LISTEN UP, BUBSIE. YOU'RE GETTIN' OFF EASY HERE. ALL WE'RE ASKING HERE IS FOR YOU TO DELIVER THESE GROCERIES TO PETEY IN THE REMOTE VILLAGE. NOT TOO MUCH TRUBBLE, BETTER THAN 30 DAYS IN THE SLOP-BOAT. (FERR SHER). ANYWAYS, FIRST YOU GOT TO FIND YOUR WAY OUTTA HERE. HEAD DOWN THAT HOLE THERE... FOLLOW YOUR FRIEND... AND GET ON GETTIN' OUT. FER PETEY'S SAKE....
ATTA BOY NOT SO BAD
NOT THAT FRIGHTFUL A TASK, REALLY
MY HOME WAS WASHED AWAY..
ERNIE EEVES
IS ME**
LOOK
I WAS ONLY ASKING FOR IT BACK...
...THAT SODA POP
HERE YOU GO, NOW. RUN ALONG AND BRING THESE GROCERIES TO PETEY WE'LL TELL HIM YOU'LL BE COMING.
PETEY AND THE VILLAGERS WILL APPRECIATE THIS VERY MUCH
THERE'S A MAP IN THERE, BOY, T'HELP YE FIND YER WAY
PASS!
GELATIN
* FOR BOTHERING THE BRICK FOLK OF NOWICKER
** "DON'T WEAR ME OOT!"

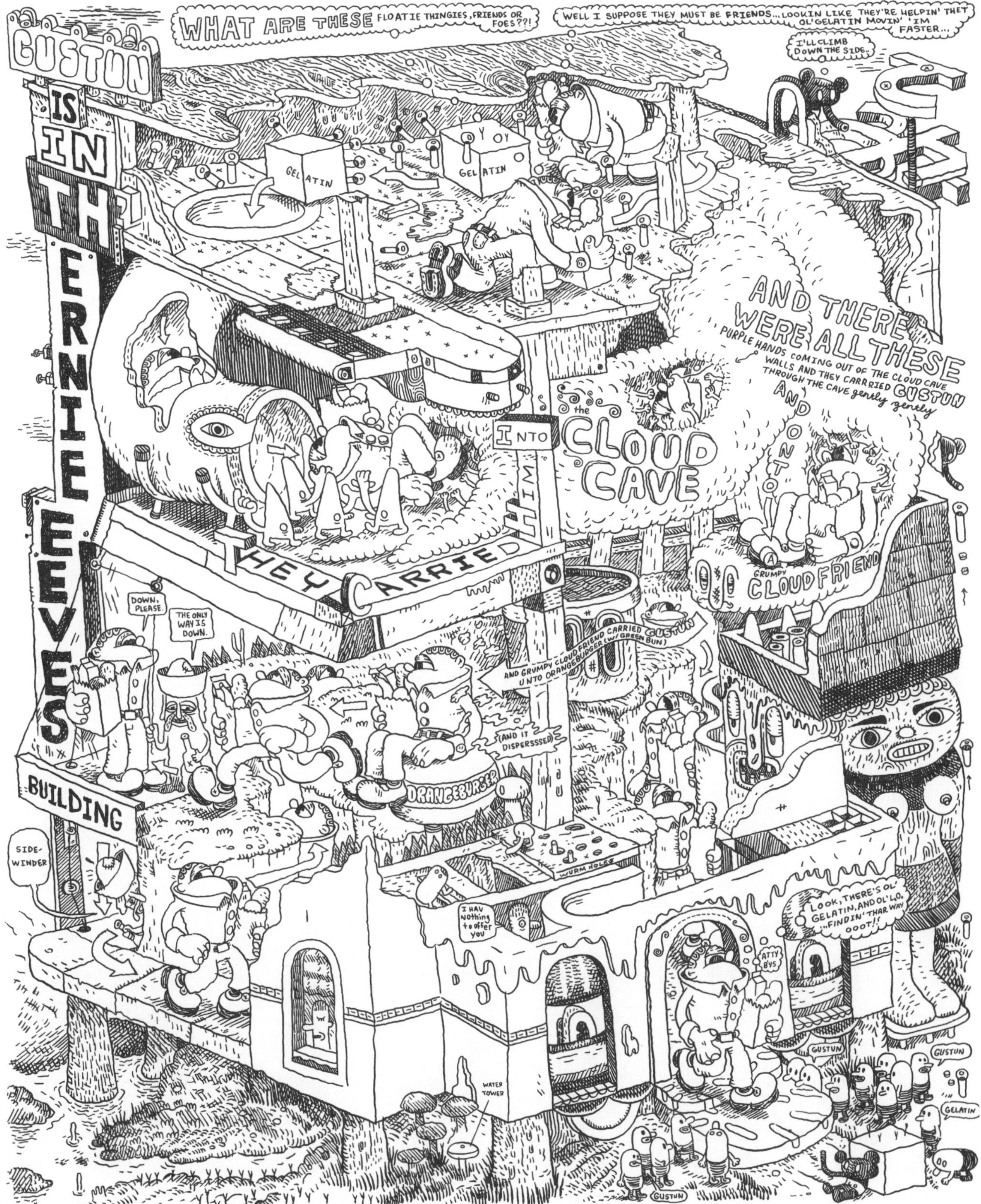
GUSTUN IS IN THE ERNIE EEVES BUILDING
WHAT ARE THESE FLOATIE THINGIES, FRIENDS OR FOES??!
WELL I SUPPOSE THEY MUST BE FRIENDS... LOOKIN LIKE THEY'RE HELPIN' THET OL' GELATIN MOVIN' 'IM FASTER...
I'LL CLIMB DOWN THE SIDE..
GELATIN
GELATIN
AND THERE WERE ALL THESE PURPLE HANDS COMING OUT OF THE CLOUD CAVE WALLS AND THEY CARRRIED GUSTUN THROUGH THE CAVE gently gently
THEY CARRIED HIM INTO the CLOUD CAVE
AND ONTO A GRUMPY CLOUDFRIEND
DOWN, PLEASE.
THE ONLY WAY IS DOWN.
AND GRUMPY CLOUDFRIEND CARRIED GUSTUN UNTO ORANGEBURGER (W/ GREEN BUN)
(AND IT DISPERSSSED)
ORANGEBURGER
WURM HOLES
SIDE-WINDER
I HAV Nothing to offer you
LOOK, THERE'S OL' GELATIN, AND OL' L.O. ...FINDIN' THAR WAY OOOT!!
ATTY BYS
WATER TOWER
GUSTUN
GUSTUN
GELATIN
GUSTUN

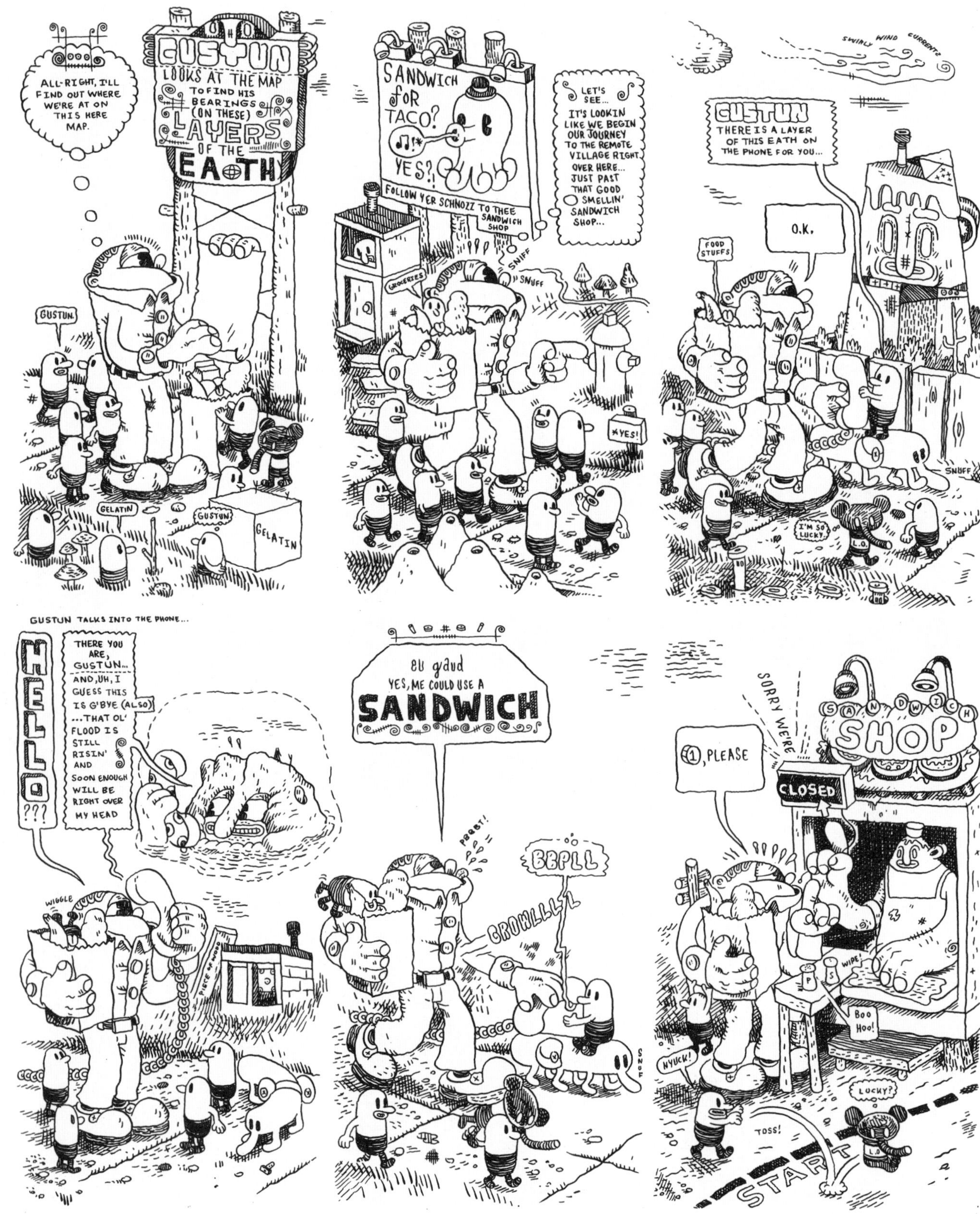
GUSTUN LOOKS AT THE MAP TO FIND HIS BEARINGS (ON THESE) LAYERS OF THE EA⊕TH
ALL-RIGHT, I'LL FIND OUT WHERE WE'RE AT ON THIS HERE MAP.
GUSTUN.
GELATIN
GUSTUN
GELATIN
SANDWICH for TACO? YES?
FOLLOW YER SCHNOZZ TO THEE SANDWICH SHOP
LET'S SEE... IT'S LOOKIN LIKE WE BEGIN OUR JOURNEY TO THE REMOTE VILLAGE RIGHT OVER HERE... JUST PAST THAT GOOD SMELLIN' SANDWICH SHOP...
SNIFF
SNUFF
GROCERIES
YES!
SWIRLY WIND CURRENTS
GUSTUN THERE IS A LAYER OF THIS EATH ON THE PHONE FOR YOU...
O.K.
FOOD STUFFS
SNUFF
I'M SO LUCKY.
GUSTUN TALKS INTO THE PHONE...
HELLO ???
THERE YOU ARE, GUSTUN... AND, UH, I GUESS THIS IS G'BYE (ALSO) ...THAT OL' FLOOD IS STILL RISIN' AND SOON ENOUGH WILL BE RIGHT OVER MY HEAD
WIGGLE
PIECE OF WOOD
eu gaud
YES, ME COULD USE A SANDWICH
BBPLL
GROWLLLL
SORRY WE'RE CLOSED
SANDWICH SHOP
①, PLEASE
WIPE!
Boo Hoo!
NYUCK!
LUCKY?
TOSS!
START

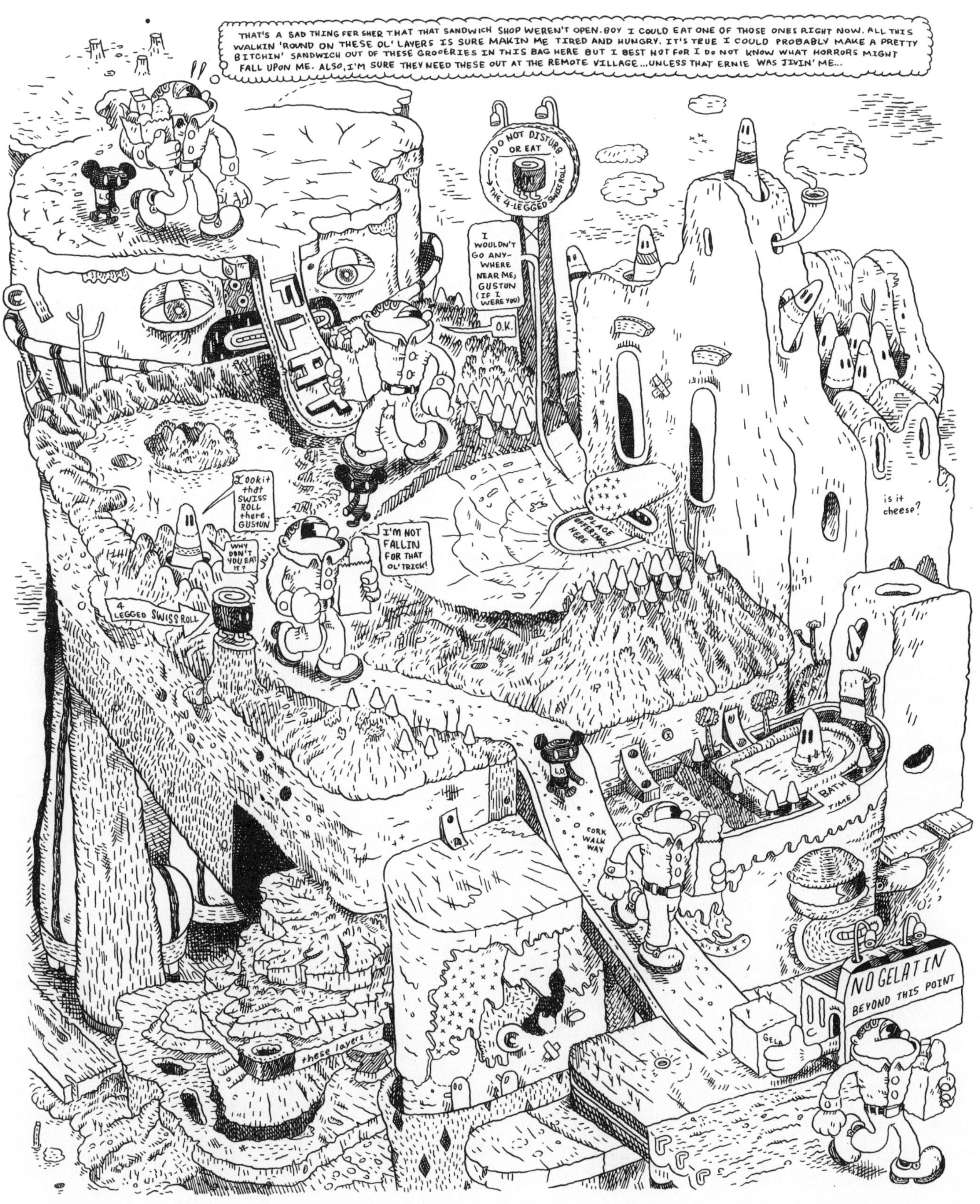
THAT'S A SAD THING FER SHER THAT THAT SANDWICH SHOP WEREN'T OPEN. BOY I COULD EAT ONE OF THOSE ONES RIGHT NOW. ALL THIS WALKIN 'ROUND ON THESE OL' LAYERS IS SURE MAKIN ME TIRED AND HUNGRY. IT'S TRUE I COULD PROBABLY MAKE A PRETTY BITCHIN' SANDWICH OUT OF THESE GROCERIES IN THIS BAG HERE BUT I BEST NOT FOR I DO NOT KNOW WHAT HORRORS MIGHT FALL UPON ME. ALSO, I'M SURE THEY NEED THESE OUT AT THE REMOTE VILLAGE...UNLESS THAT ERNIE WAS JIVIN' ME...
DO NOT DISTURB OR EAT
THE 4-LEGGED SWISS ROLL
I WOULDN'T GO ANYWHERE NEAR ME, GUSTUN (IF I WERE YOU)
O.K.
FLAT
PLACE OFFERINGS HERE
is it cheese?
Lookit that SWISS ROLL there, GUSTUN
WHY DON'T YOU EAT IT?
I'M NOT FALLIN FOR THAT OL' TRICK!
4 LEGGED SWISS ROLL
BATH TIME
CORK WALK WAY
NO GELATIN BEYOND THIS POINT
GELA
these layers

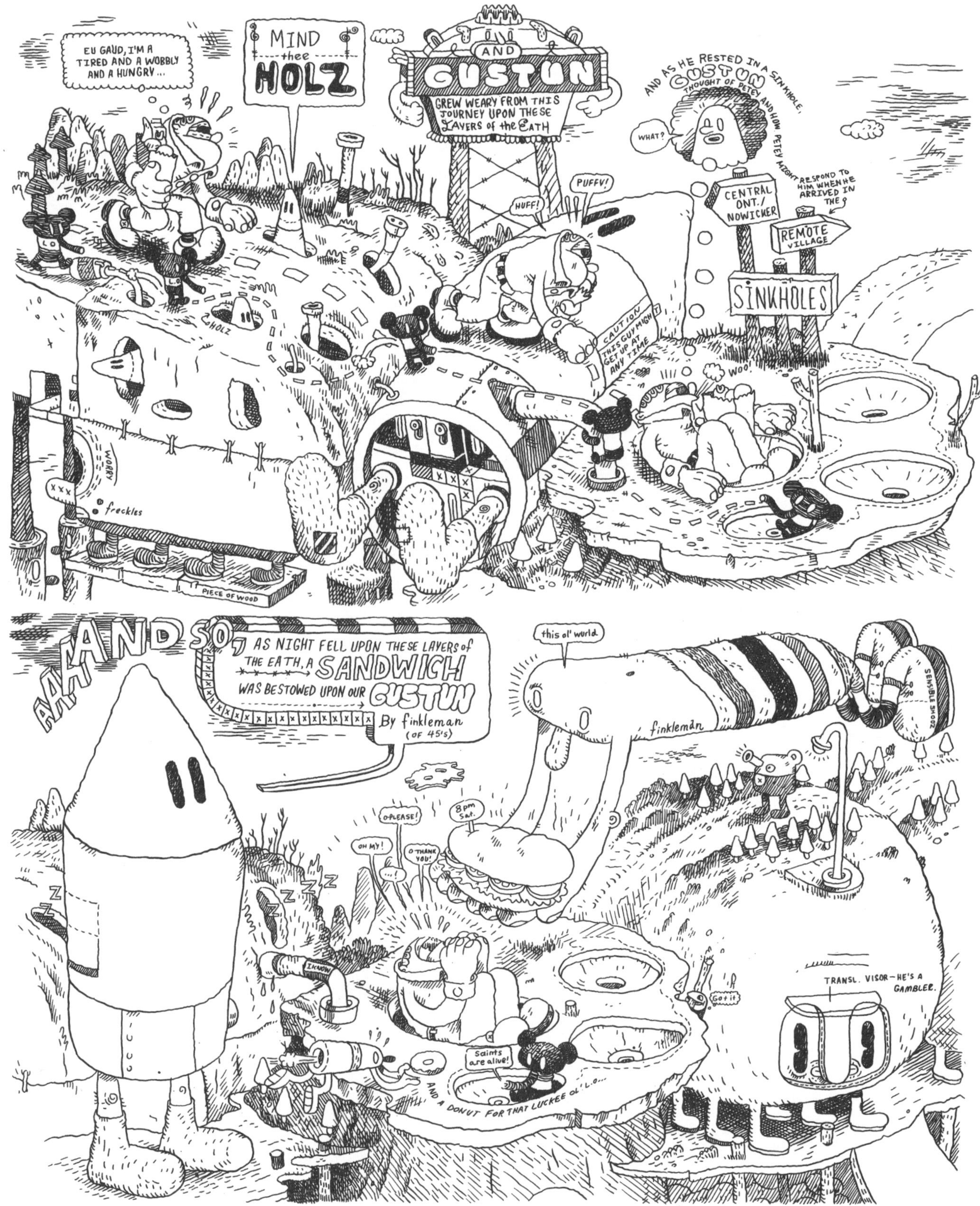

EU GAUD, I'M A TIRED AND A WOBBLY AND A HUNGRY...
MIND thee HOLZ
AND GUSTUN GREW WEARY FROM THIS JOURNEY UPON THESE LAYERS of the EATH
AND AS HE RESTED IN A SINKHOLE, GUSTUN THOUGHT OF PETEY AND HOW PETEY MIGHT RESPOND TO HIM WHEN HE ARRIVED IN THE
WHAT?
HUFF!
PUFFU!
CENTRAL ONT./ NOWICKER
REMOTE VILLAGE
SINKHOLES
HOLZ
CAUTION THIS GUY MIGHT GET UP AT ANY TIME
WOO!
WORRY
freckles
PIECE OF WOOD
AAAHH AND SO, AS NIGHT FELL UPON THESE LAYERS of THE EATH, A SANDWICH WAS BESTOWED UPON OUR GUSTUN
By finkleman (OF 45's)
this ol' world
finkleman
SENSIBLE SHOOZ
O-PLEASE!
8pm Sat.
OH MY!
O THANK YOU!
Z Z Z
TRANSL. VISOR—HE'S A GAMBLER.
Got it
Saints are alive!
AND A DONUT FOR THAT LUCKEE OL' L.O....

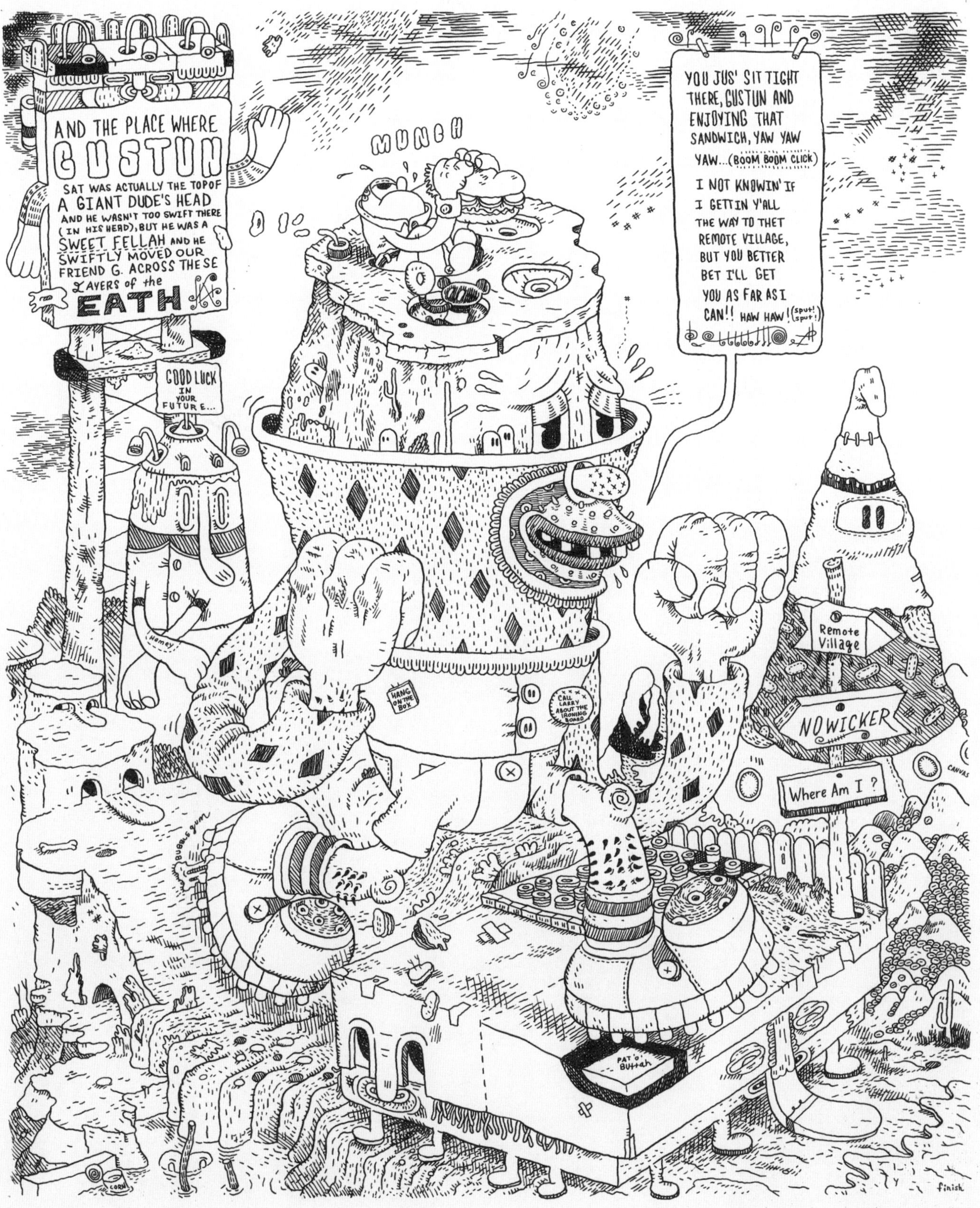
AND THE PLACE WHERE GUSTUN SAT WAS ACTUALLY THE TOPOF A GIANT DUDE'S HEAD AND HE WASN'T TOO SWIFT THERE (IN HIS HEAD), BUT HE WAS A SWEET FELLAH AND HE SWIFTLY MOVED OUR FRIEND G. ACROSS THESE LAYERS of the EATH
MUNCH
YOU JUS' SIT TIGHT THERE, GUSTUN AND ENJOYING THAT SANDWICH, YAW YAW YAW... (BOOM BOOM CLICK)
I NOT KNOWIN' IF I GETTIN Y'ALL THE WAY TO THET REMOTE VILLAGE, BUT YOU BETTER BET I'LL GET YOU AS FAR AS I CAN!! HAW HAW! (sput! sput!)
GOOD LUCK IN YOUR FUTURE...
Homey
HANG ON THE BOX
CALL LARRY ABOUT THE IRONING BOARD
Remote Village
NOWICKER
Where Am I ?
CANVAS
BUBBLE gum
PAT 'O' Buttah
CORN
finish

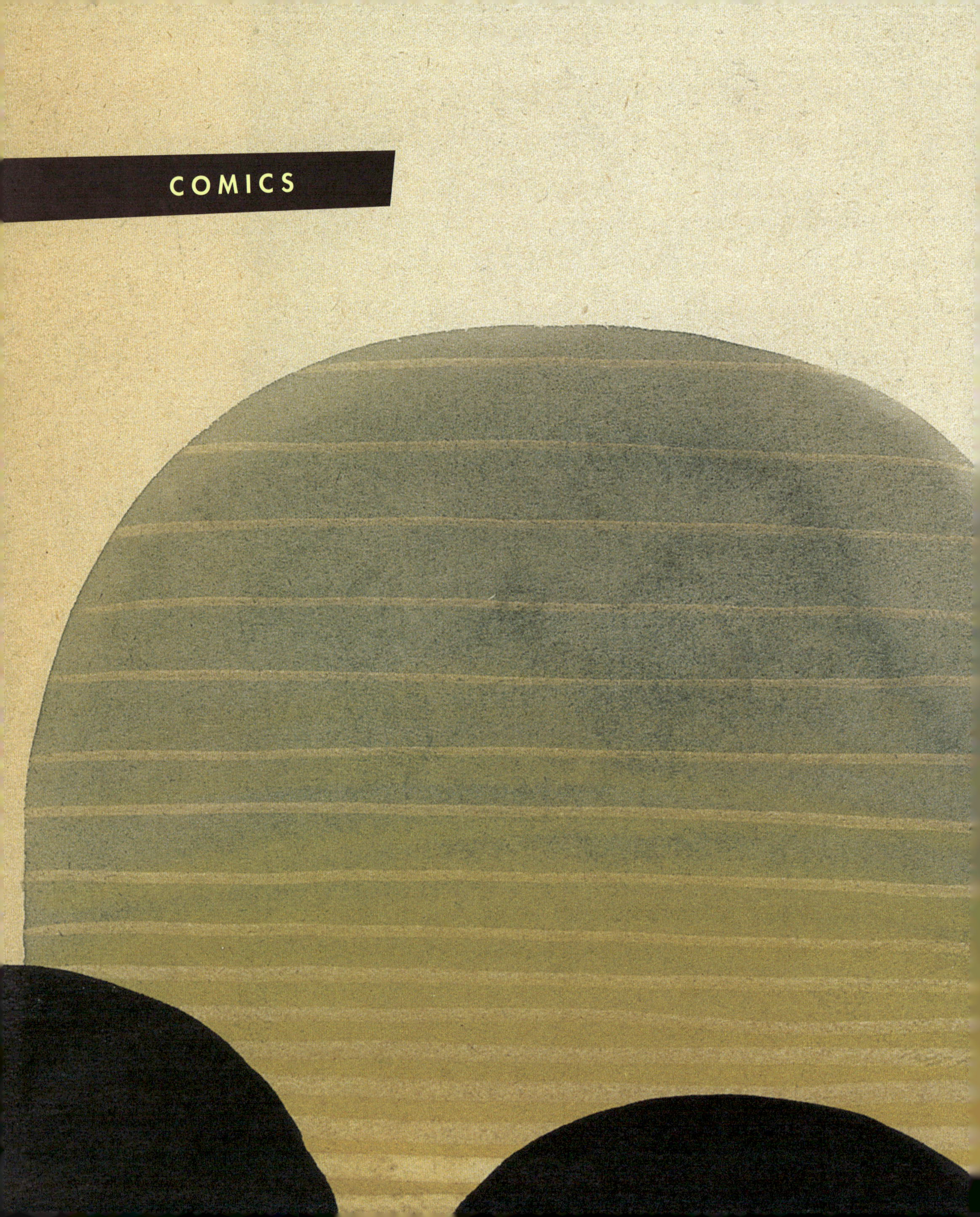

COMICS

YAZZA

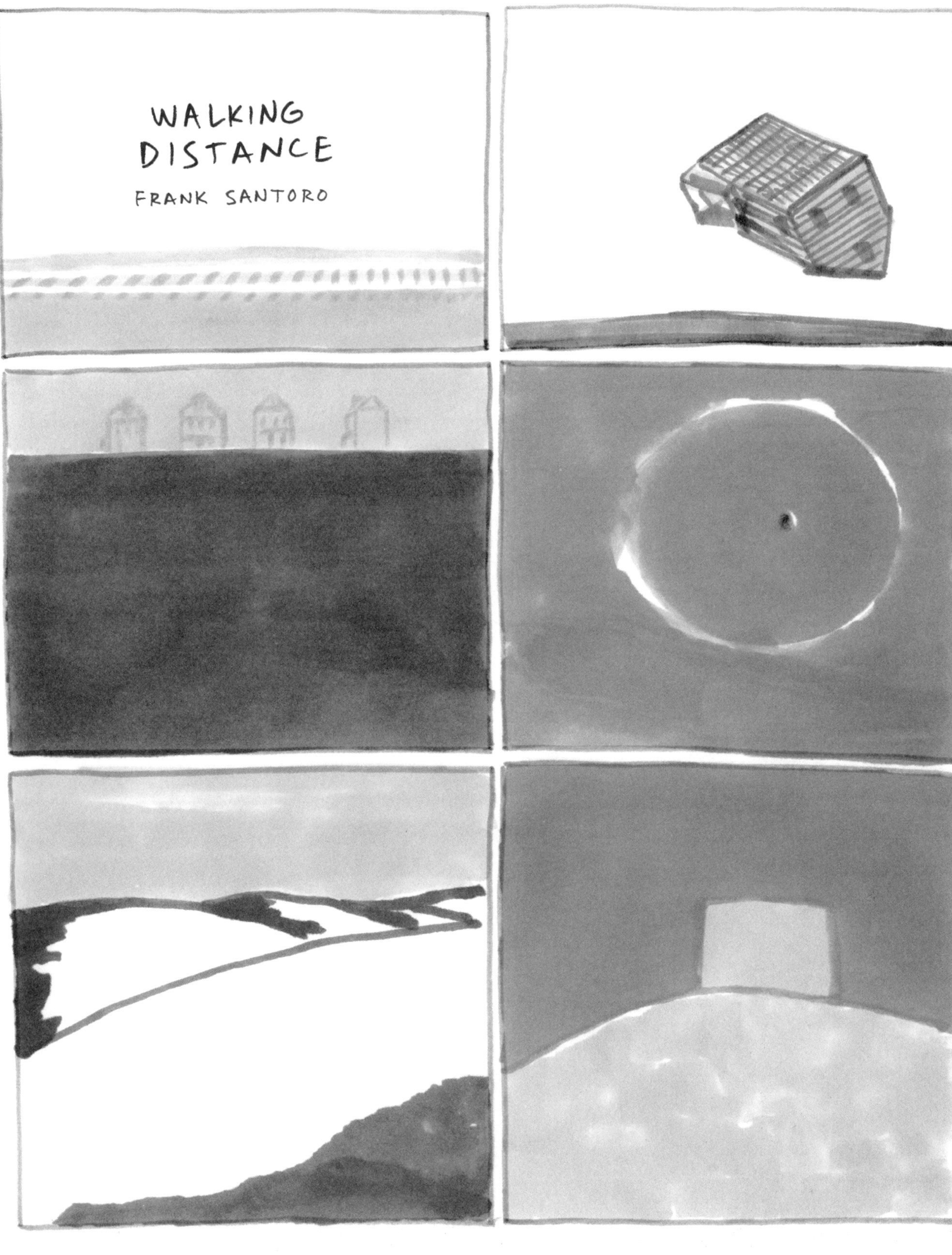
WALKING
DISTANCE
FRANK SANTORO

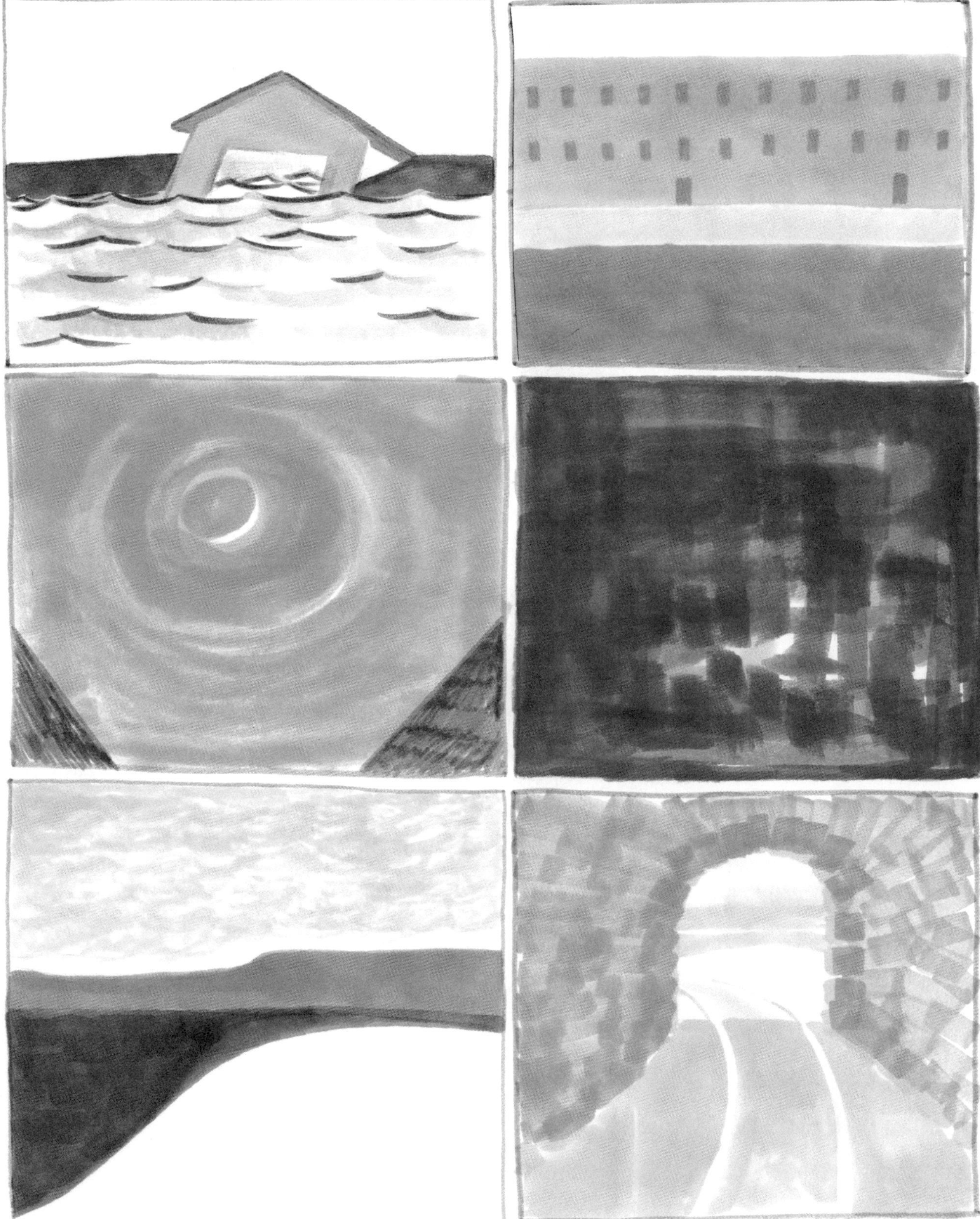

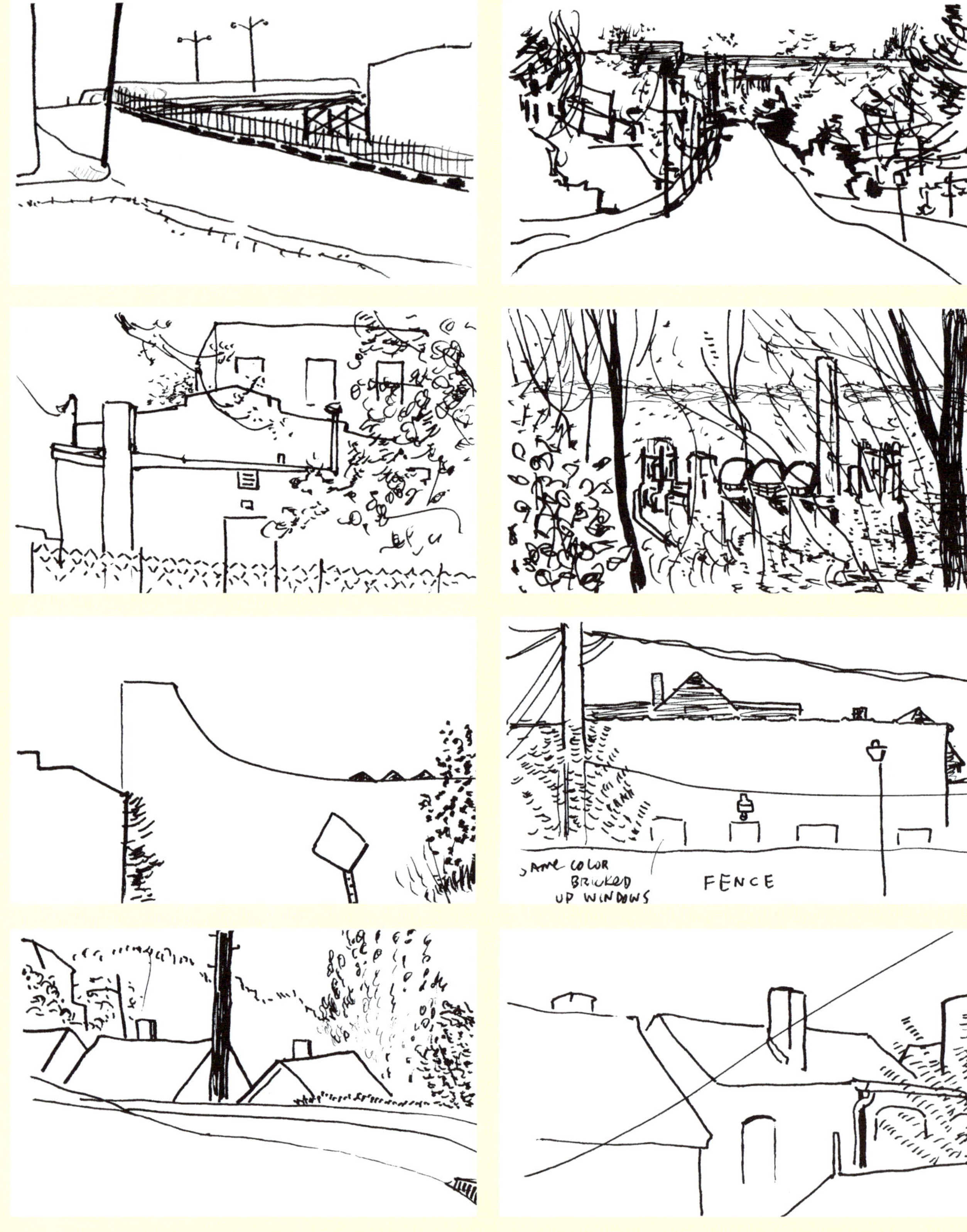
SAME COLOR
BRICKED
UP WINDOWS
FENCE

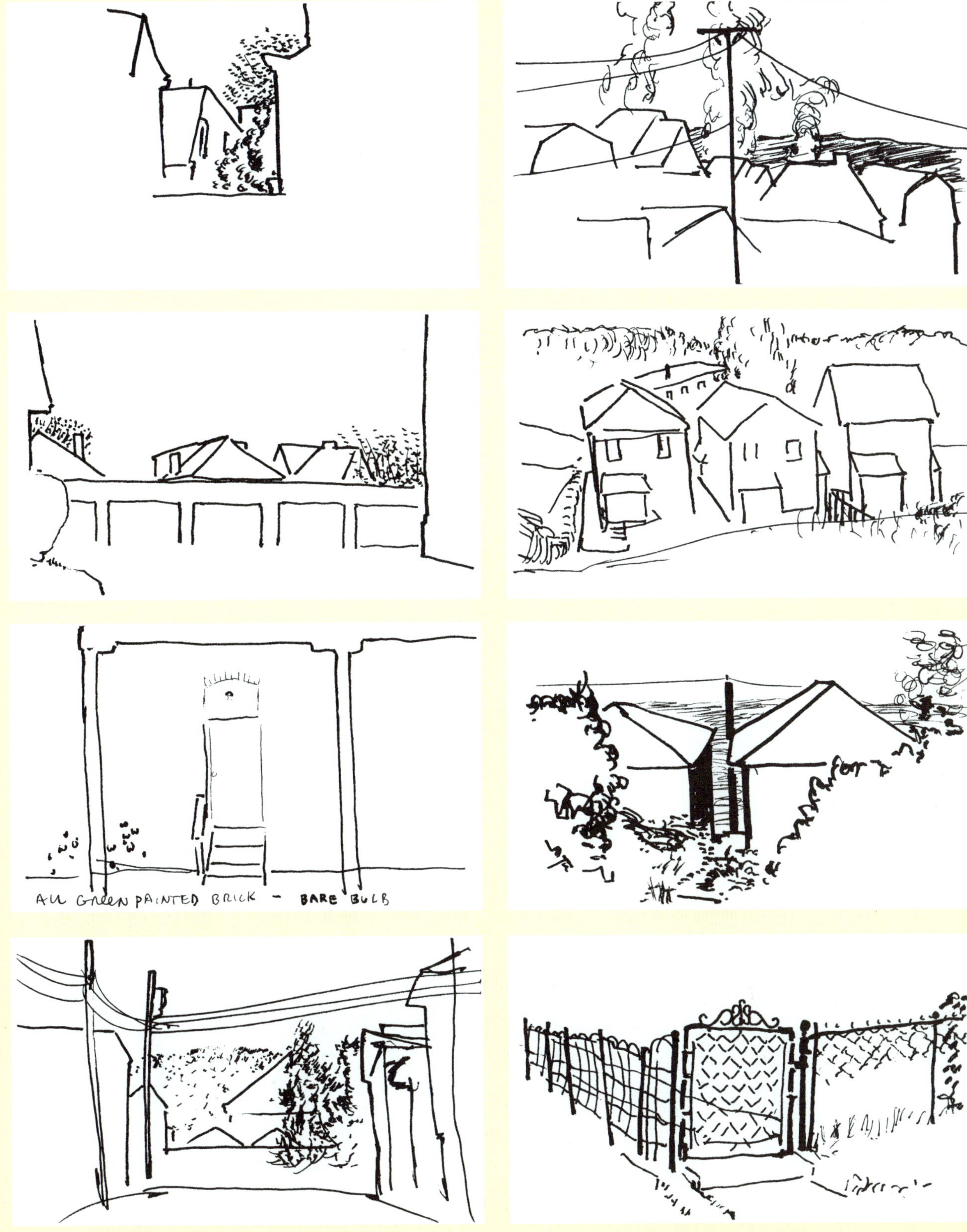
ALL GREEN PAINTED BRICK - BARE BULB

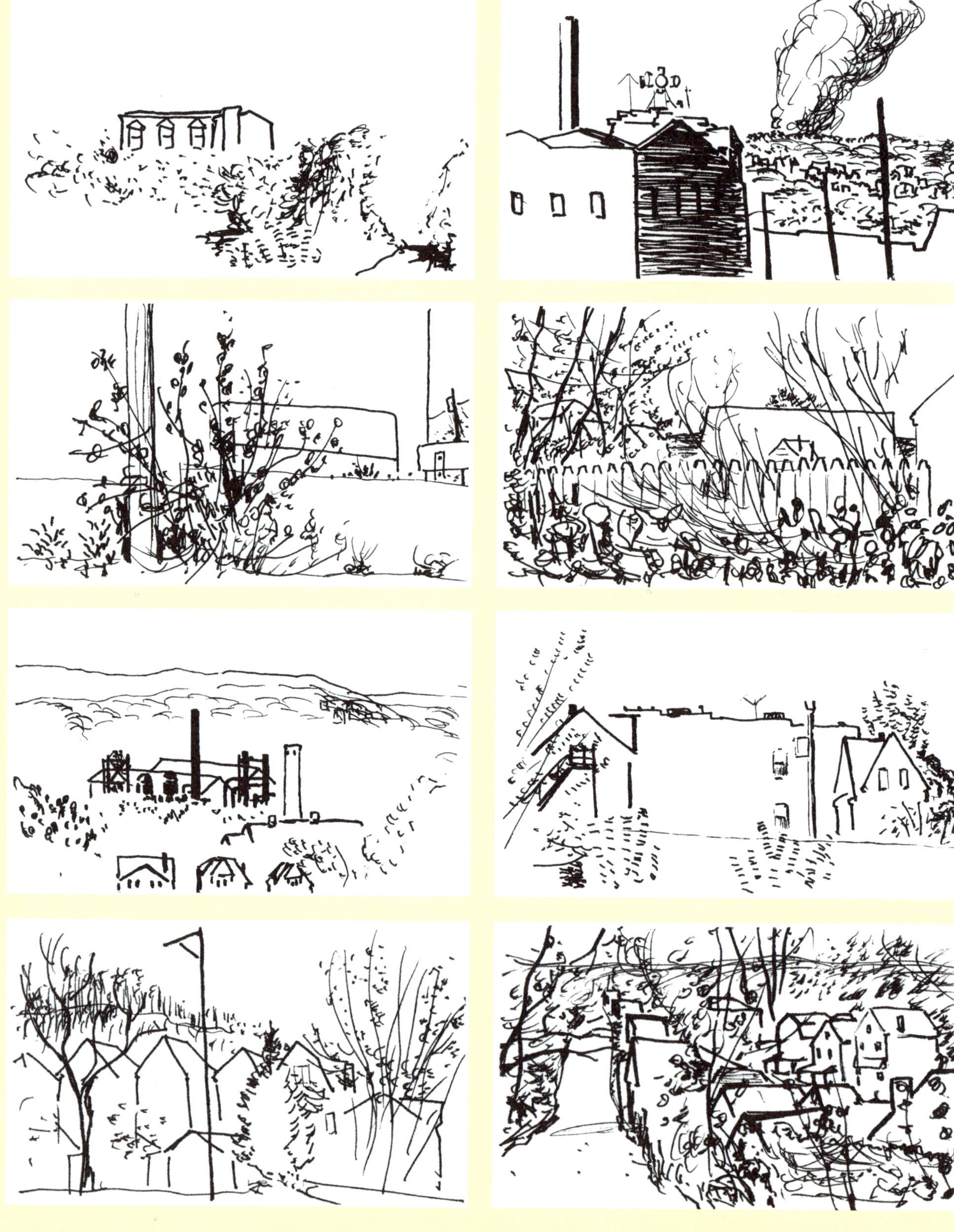

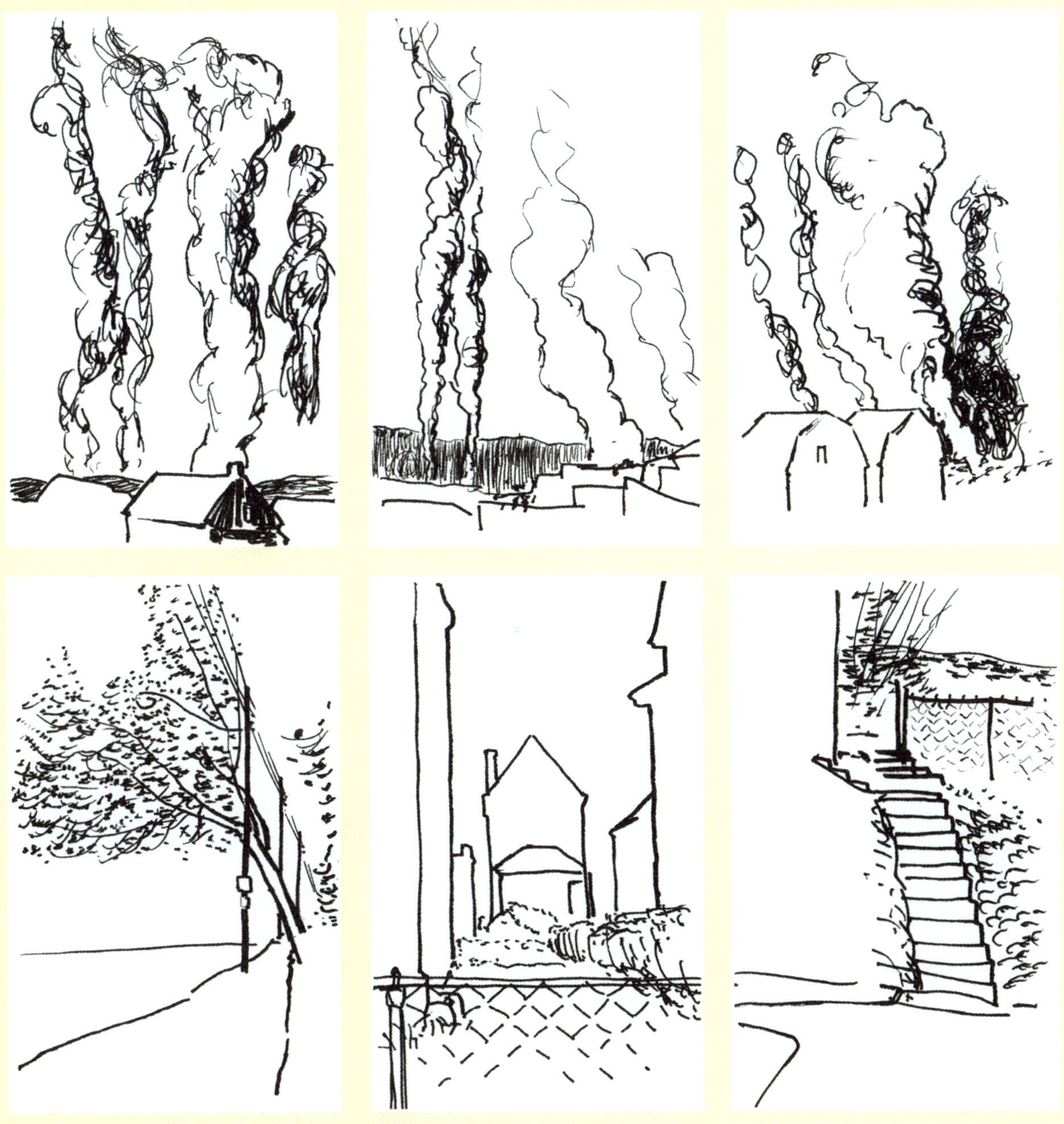

I TOOK THE TRAIN TO VISIT MOM. EARLY MAY, PITTSBURGH, PA.
ROUND THE BEND INTO BRADDOCK THE MILLS ARE STILL CLOUD FACTORIES.
WAS THAT REALLY SOMEONE CALLING MY NAME FROM A PASSING CAR?

BEQUEATH

MY MOM SAID SHE'S BEQUEATHING THE HOUSE TO ME.
I SAID IS THAT A WORD?
LOOK I'M TRYING TO TALK TO YOU ABOUT THE HOUSE.

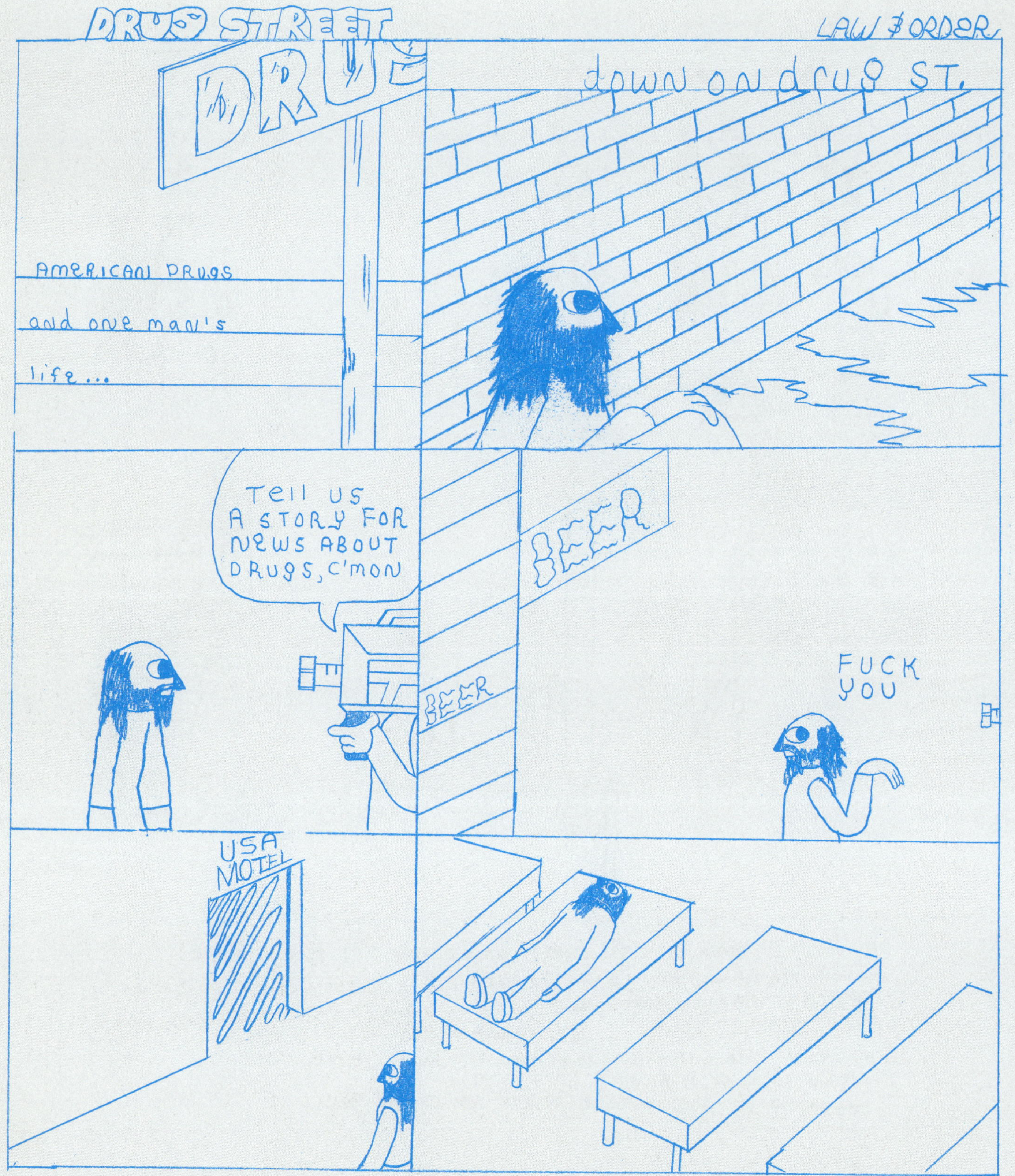
DRUG STREET
LAW $ ORDER
DRUG
down on drug ST.
AMERICAN DRUGS
and one man's
life...
Tell us
A STORY FOR
NEWS ABOUT
DRUGS, C'MON
BEER
BEER
FUCK
YOU
USA
MOTEL

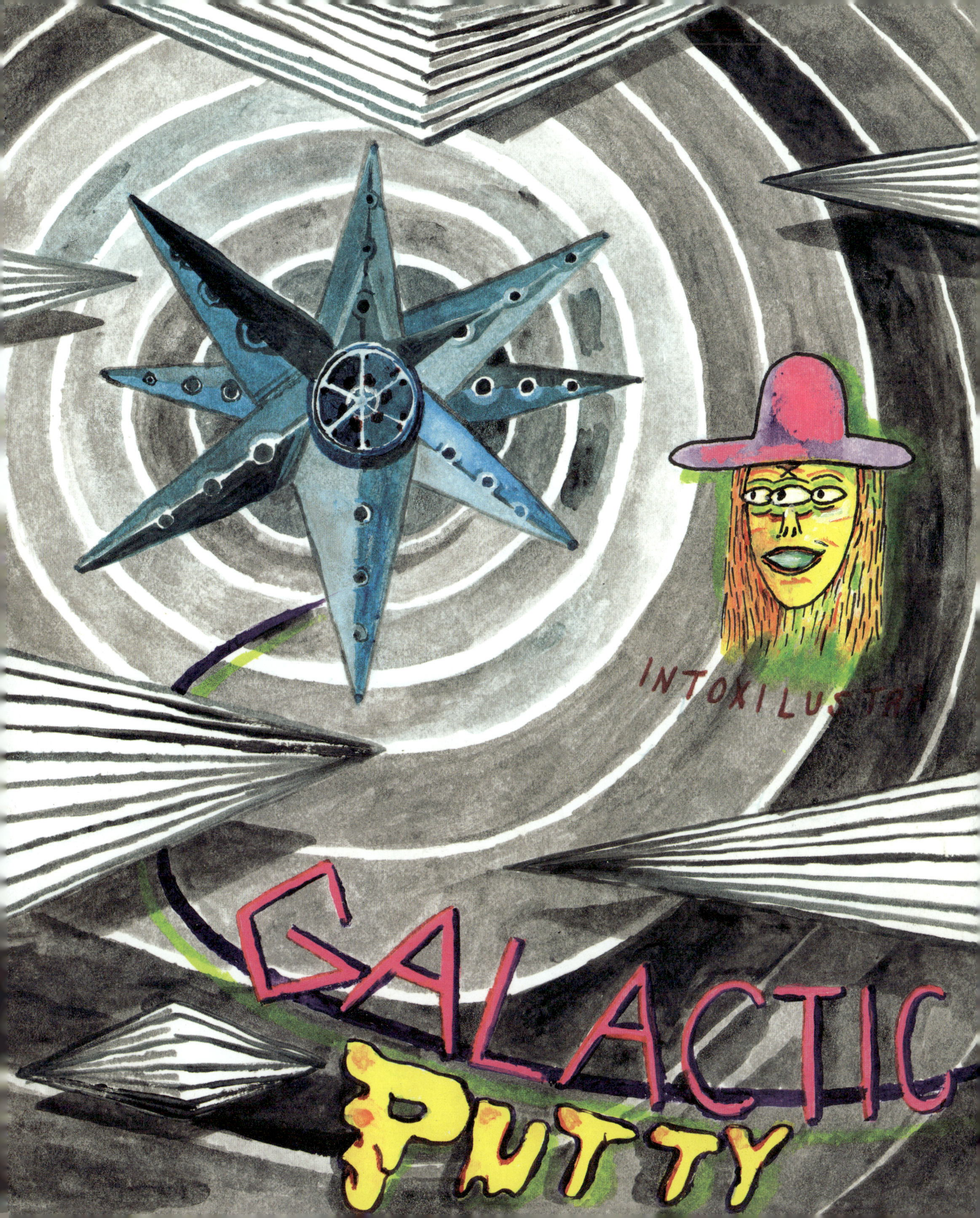
INTOXILUSTRA
GALACTIC
PUTTY

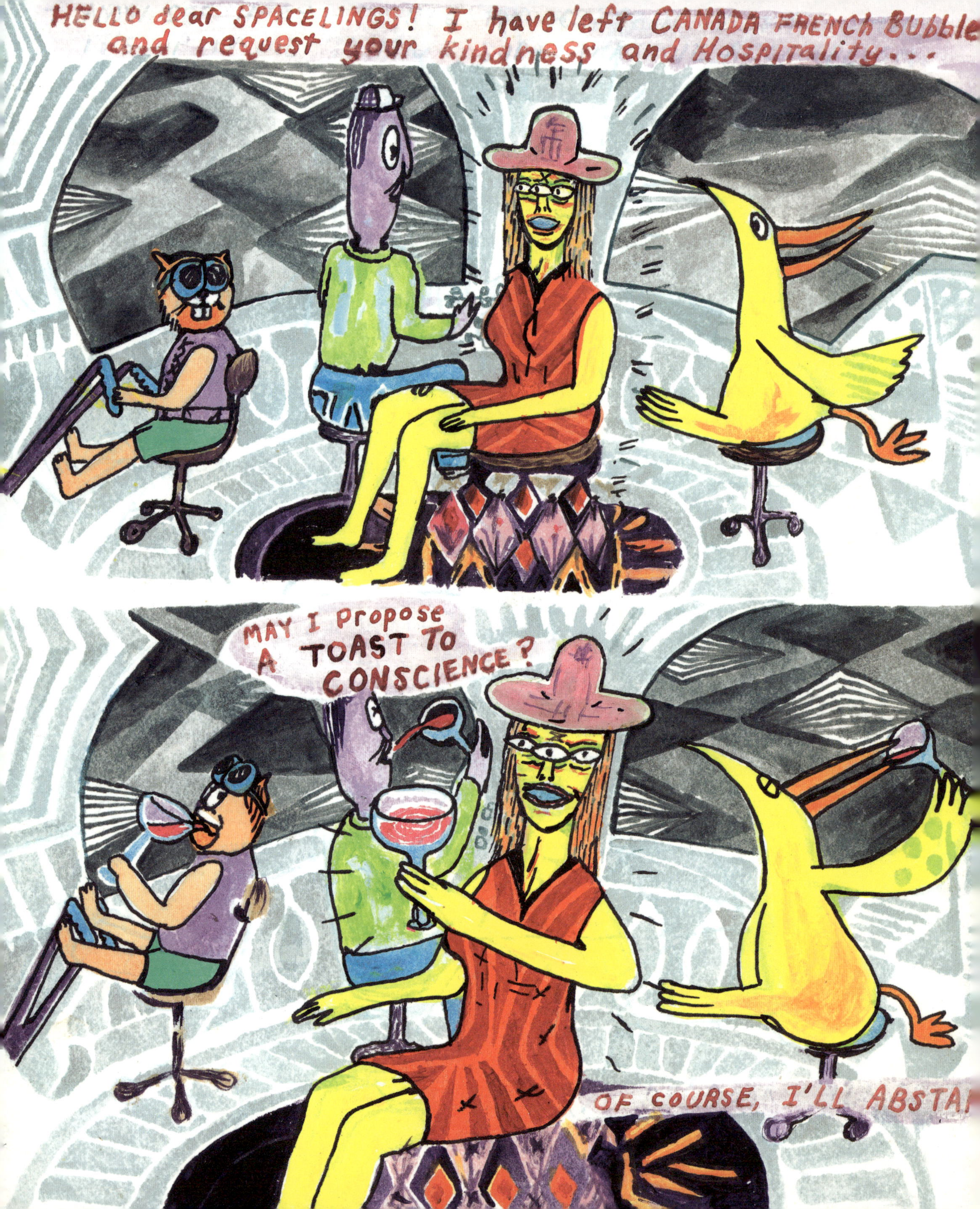
HELLO dear SPACELINGS! I have left CANADA FRENCH Bubble and request your kindness and Hospitality...
MAY I propose A TOAST TO CONSCIENCE?
OF COURSE, I'LL ABSTA

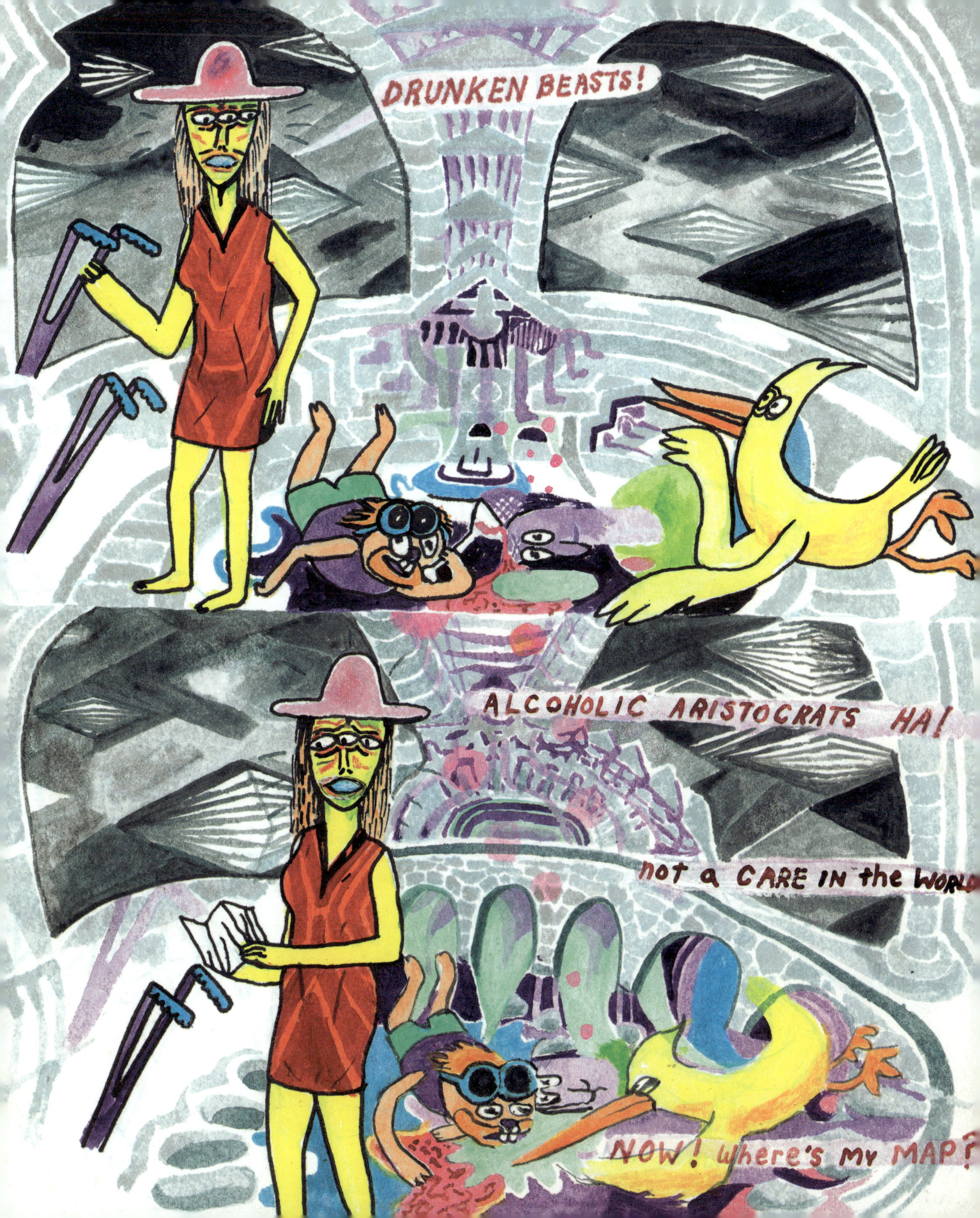
DRUNKEN BEASTS!
ALCOHOLIC ARISTOCRATS HA!
not a CARE IN the WORLD
NOW! where's MY MAP?

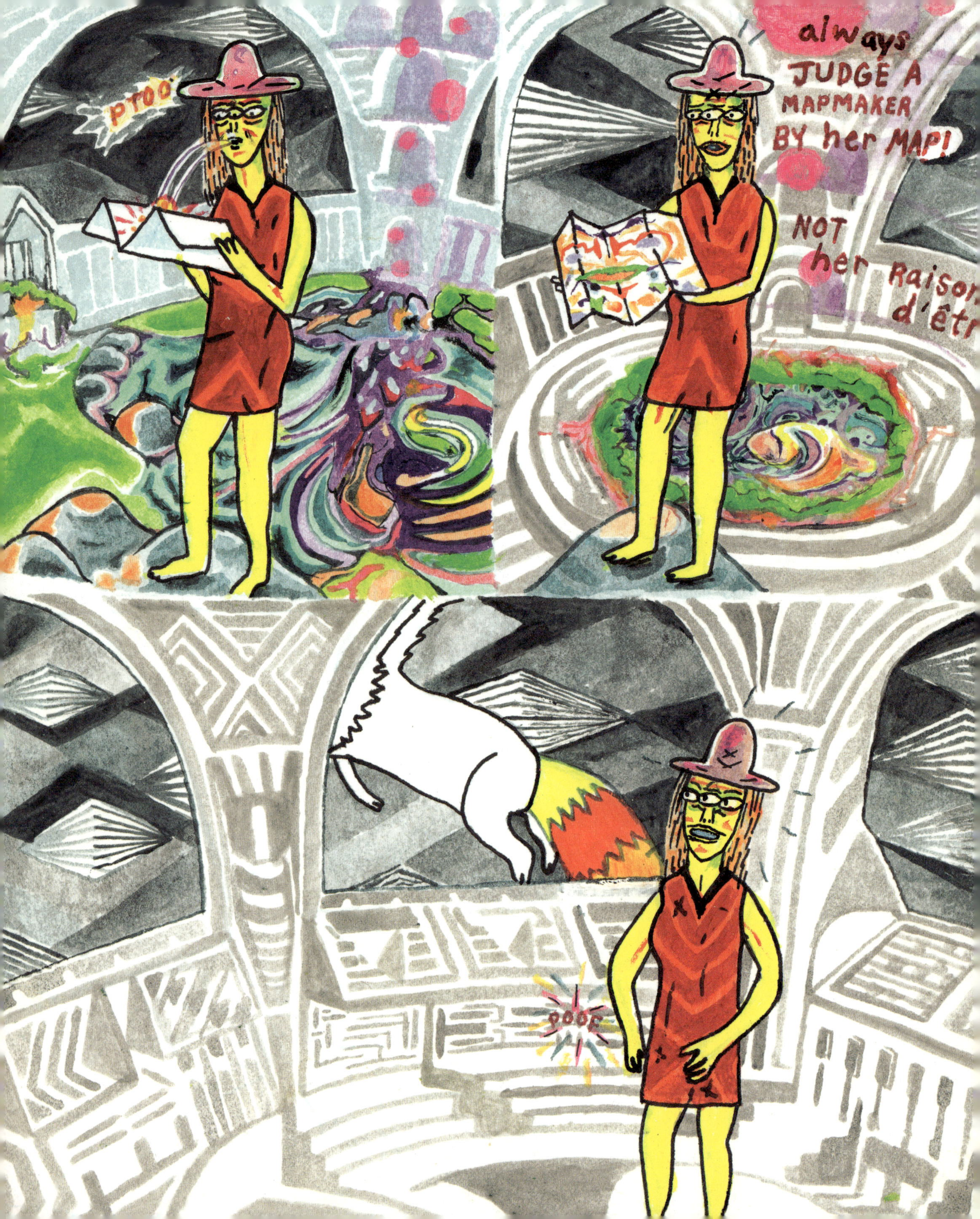
PTOO
always JUDGE A MAPMAKER BY her MAP!
NOT her Raiso
d'êtr
POOF

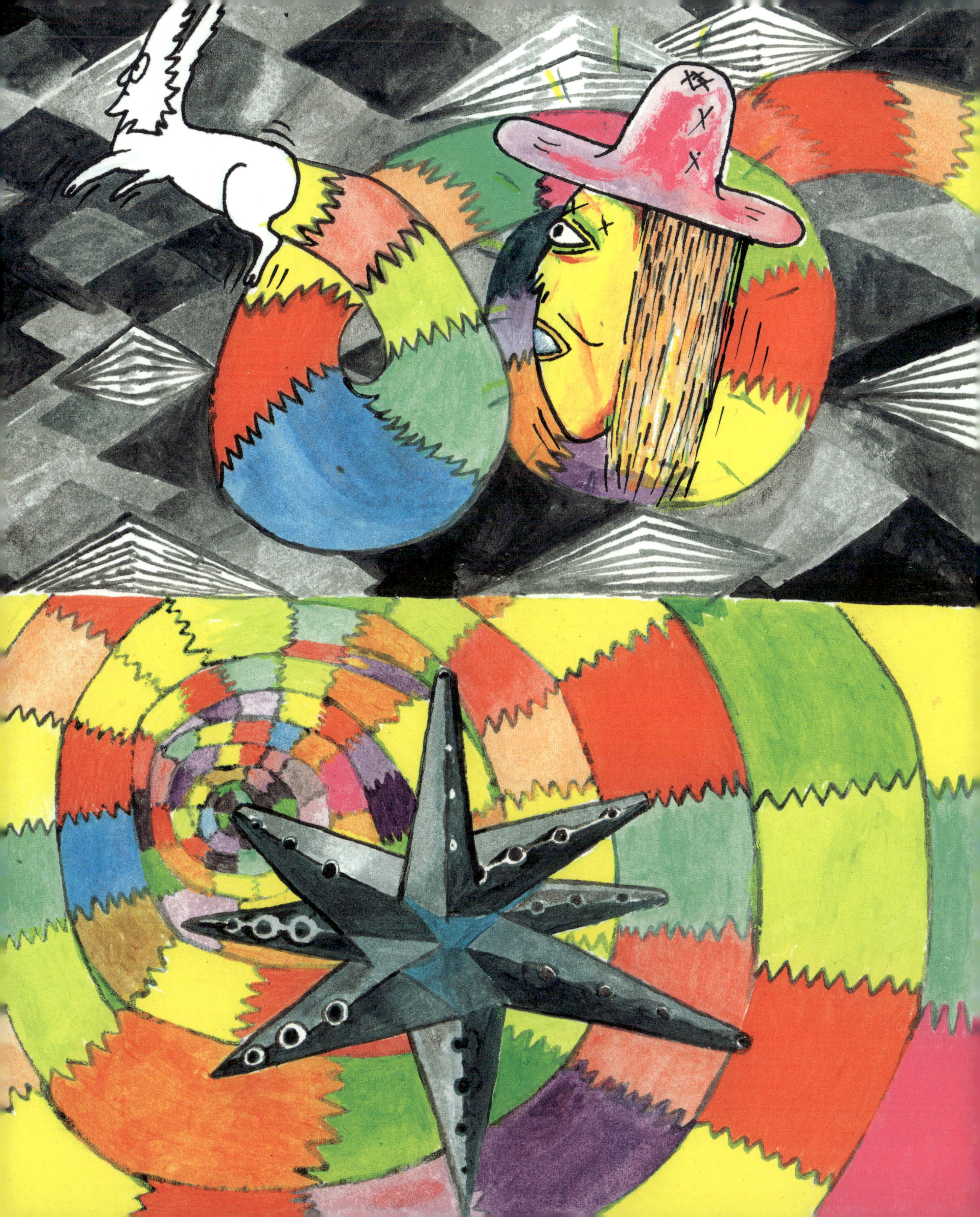

Shigeru Sugiura (1908–2000) was born in Tokyo and spent his teen years enjoying movies, and especially the silent films of Hollywood—like James Cruze's *The Covered Wagon*, John Ford's *The Iron Horse*, *The Perils of Pauline* starring Pearl White, and Laurel and Hardy comedies. Although he initially wanted to be an oil painter, in 1932 Sugiura became apprenticed to Suiho Tagawa, the creator of the *manga* series *Norakuro*, which was then the most popular *manga* in Japan. Soon thereafter, Sugiura began to draw gag comics for children's magazines, but it took him over a decade to develop his signature style. In the 1950s, his *manga* were serialized in boys' monthly magazines and published in original *manga* books; *The Last of the Mohicans* and *Monkey King Goes West* were humorous *manga* loosely based on American and Chinese classics, while *Sarutobi, the Ninja Boy* and *Mister Robot* reflected Sugiura's yearning for *terrae incognitae* and the world of fantasy. His constant incorporation of food in his *manga*—and especially the favorite foods of Japanese children—is a marked characteristic. He has even named characters after such dishes as *oden*, *katsudon*, and potato croquet.

In the 1980s, his work moved into far wilder and more surreal territory; time and space intertwined and tangled as strange creatures paraded through his frames. His work was published in a variety of magazines, and spawned a cult following. In 1985, he drew a five-page original *manga* called *Jiraiya, the Ninja Boy* for *RAW* #7. In the mid-'90s his five-volume collected work, *Shigeru Sugiura's Manga Selection*, was published in Japan. In April, 2002, The World of Shigeru Sugiura exhibition opened at the Mitaka City Gallery of Art in Tokyo. On display were 30 pages of Sugiura's scrapbook, filled with clippings from American comic books of the late 1940s and '50s, along with hundreds of his original drawings and books. Through it all, Sugiura has remained a kid at heart, and his *manga* invite us to a playground where characters move around as if play-acting Ninjas or Cowboys and Indians—in a world of his own design.

Shigeru Sugiura

by Kosei Ono

Ganmodoki, originally published in the book *Funny World of Shigeru Sugiura* (1983), marks the beginning of Sugiura's new phase. All his great loves are in play here: Hollywood films, "Anastasia," the oil paintings of Maurice Utrillo, and—of course—food.

In keeping with Japanese tradition,
Ganmodoki reads from right to left.
To accomodate for this circumstance,
Ganmodoki begins on page 247.
Turn ahead 22 pages and
continue reading
in reverse.

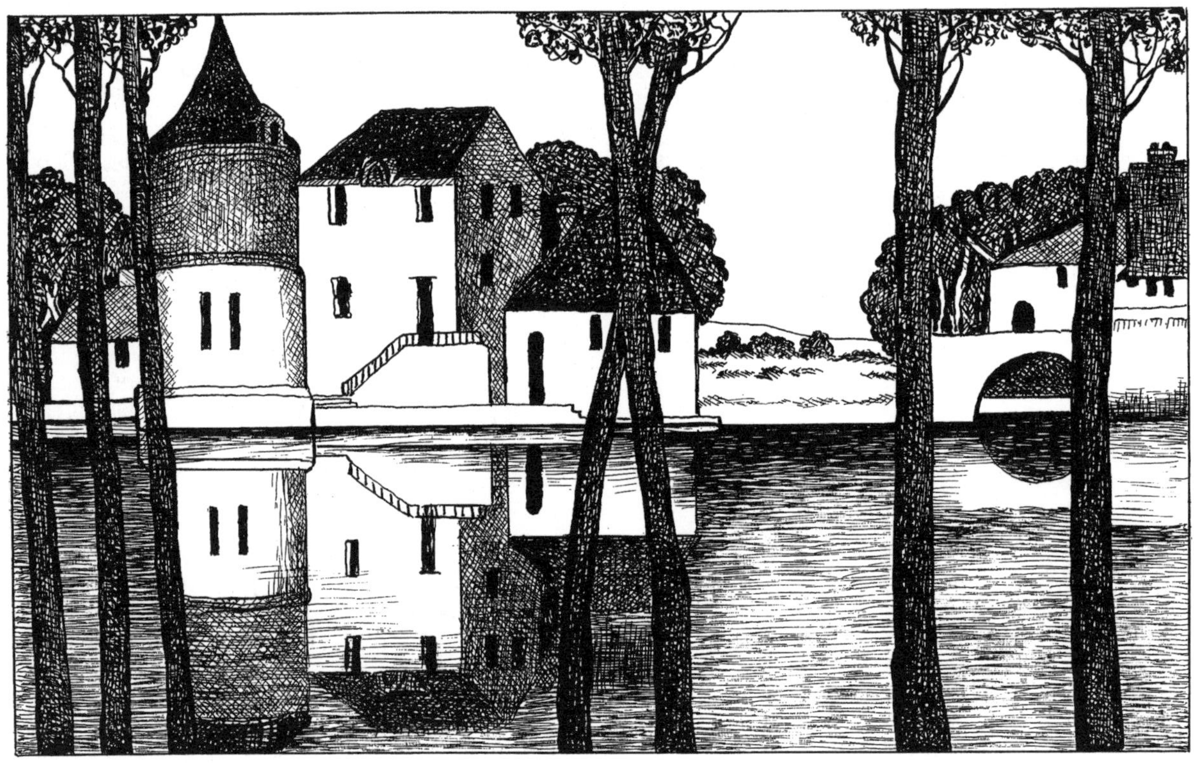

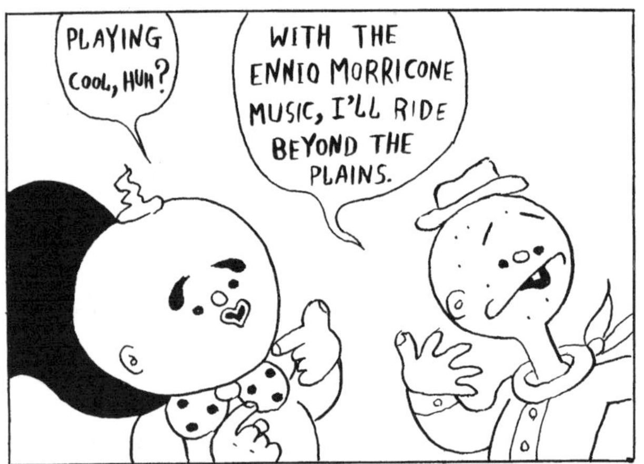

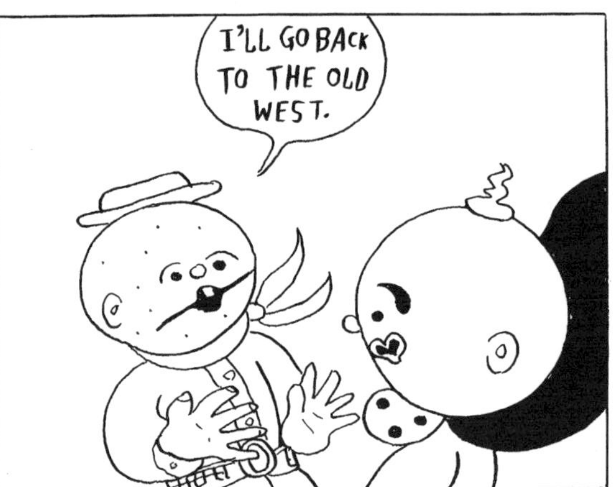

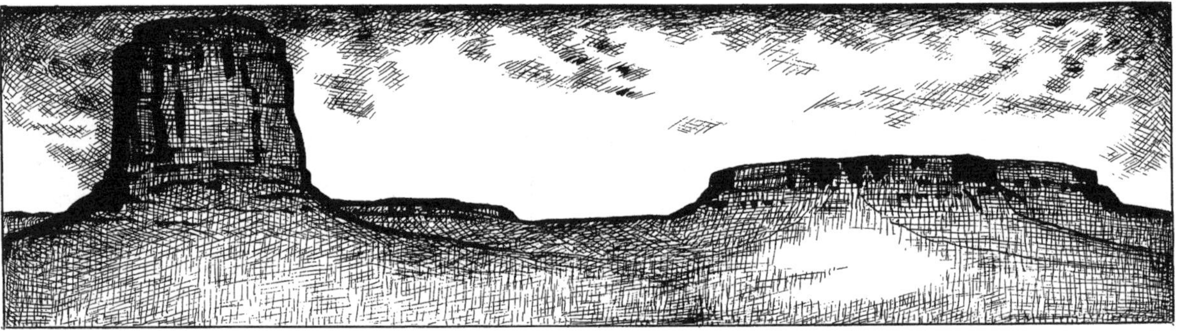

THE END

© SUGIURA TSUTOMU 2004

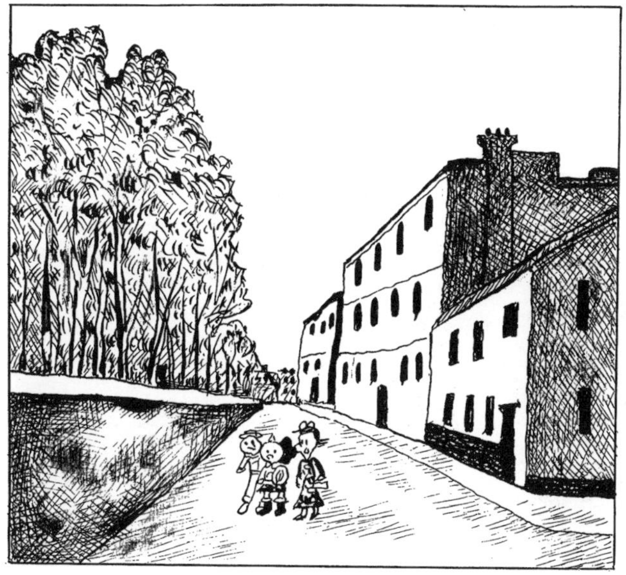

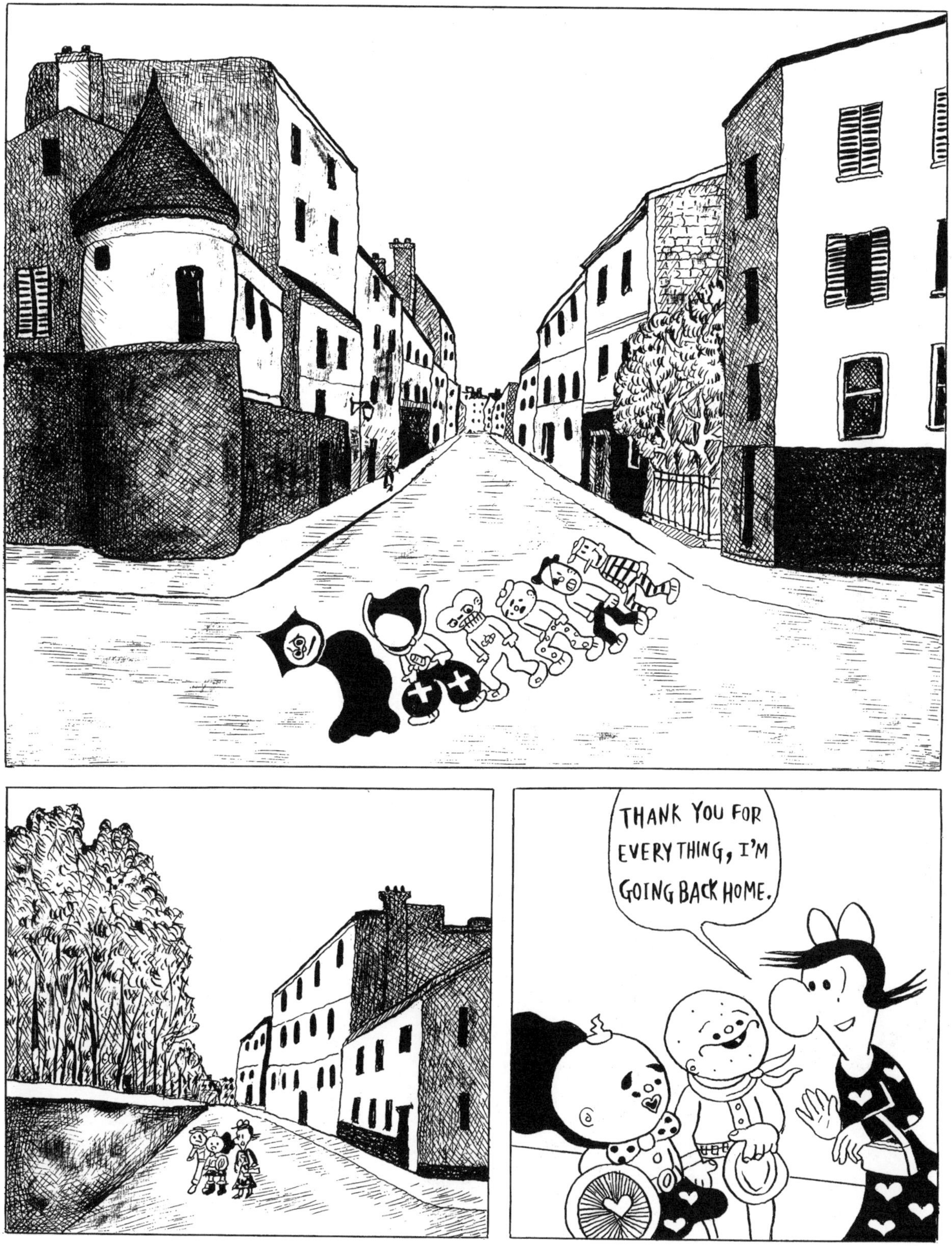

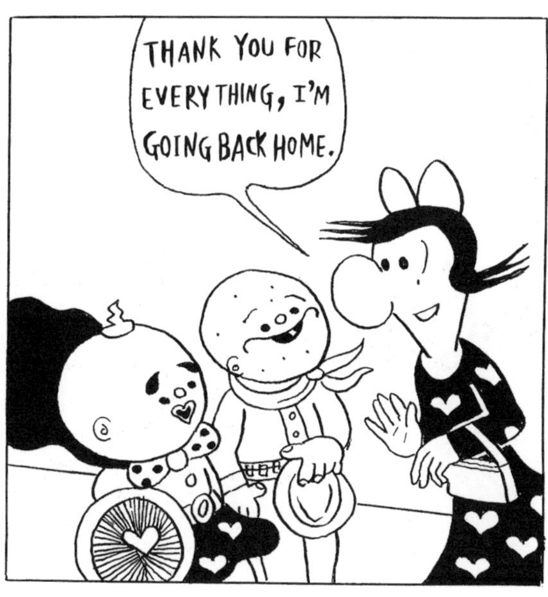
THANK YOU FOR EVERYTHING, I'M GOING BACK HOME.

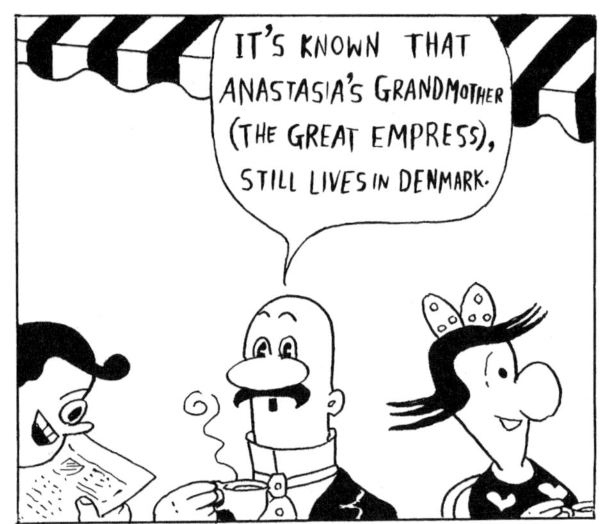
IT'S KNOWN THAT ANASTASIA'S GRANDMOTHER (THE GREAT EMPRESS), STILL LIVES IN DENMARK.

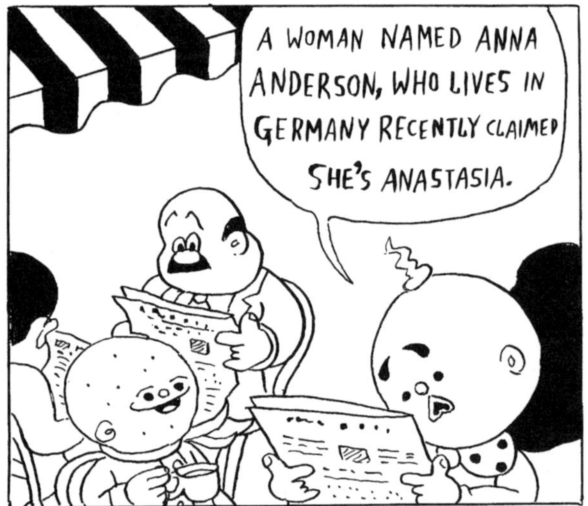
A WOMAN NAMED ANNA ANDERSON, WHO LIVES IN GERMANY RECENTLY CLAIMED SHE'S ANASTASIA.

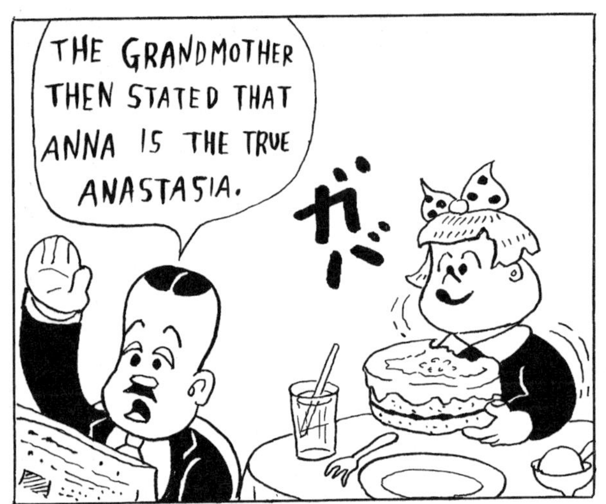
THE GRANDMOTHER THEN STATED THAT ANNA IS THE TRUE ANASTASIA.
ガバ

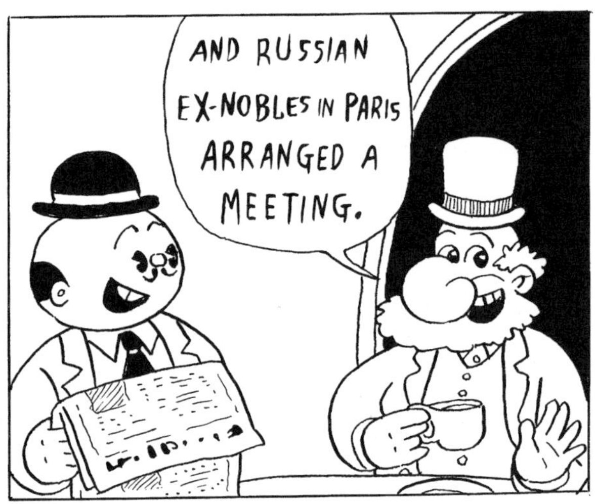
AND RUSSIAN EX-NOBLES IN PARIS ARRANGED A MEETING.

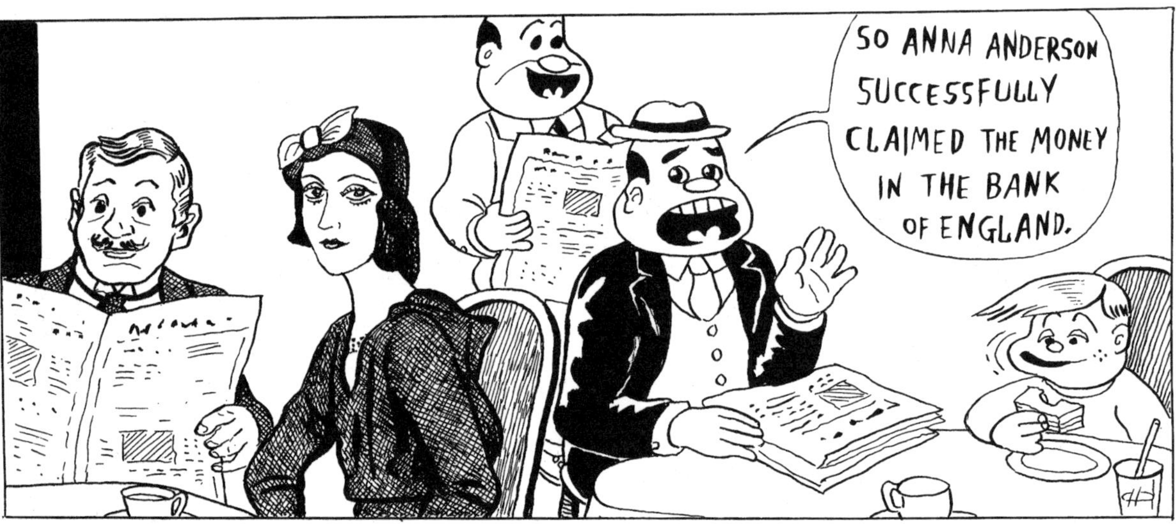
SO ANNA ANDERSON SUCCESSFULLY CLAIMED THE MONEY IN THE BANK OF ENGLAND.

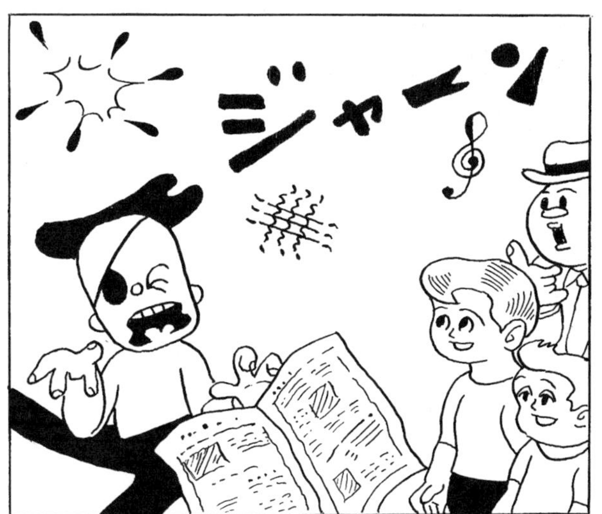
ジャーン

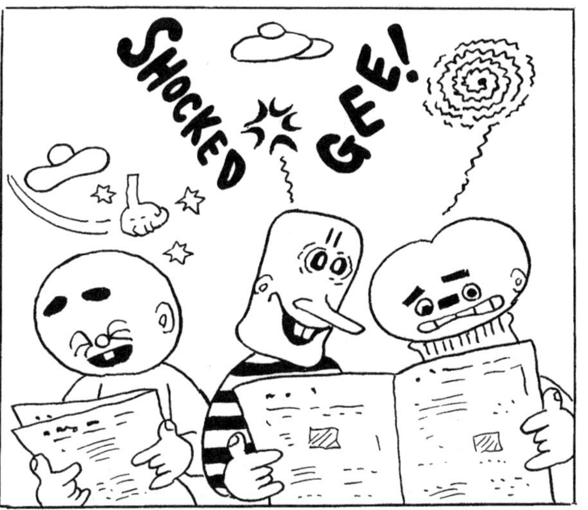
SHOCKED
GEE!

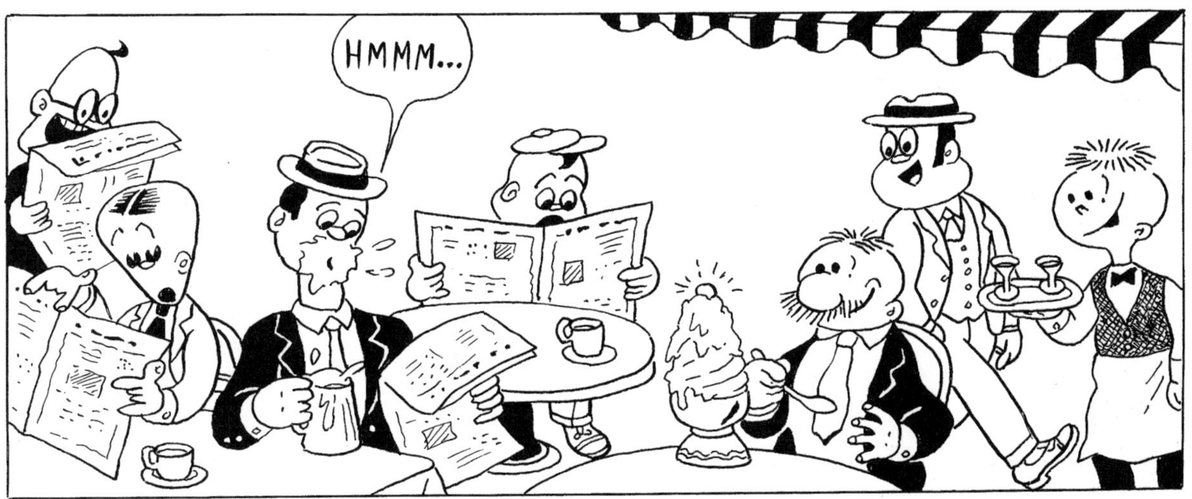
HMMM...

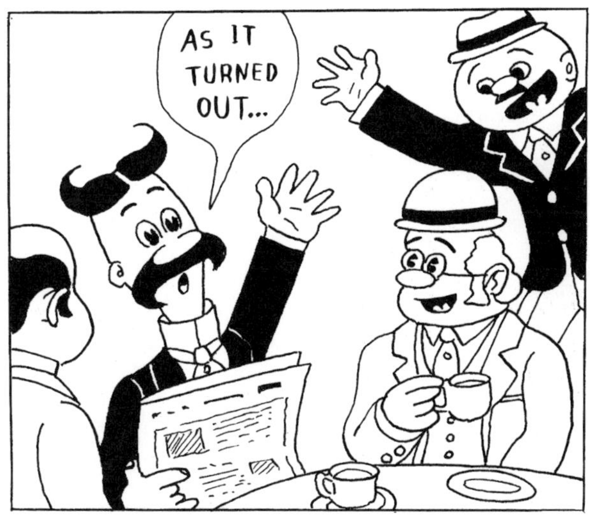
AS IT TURNED OUT...

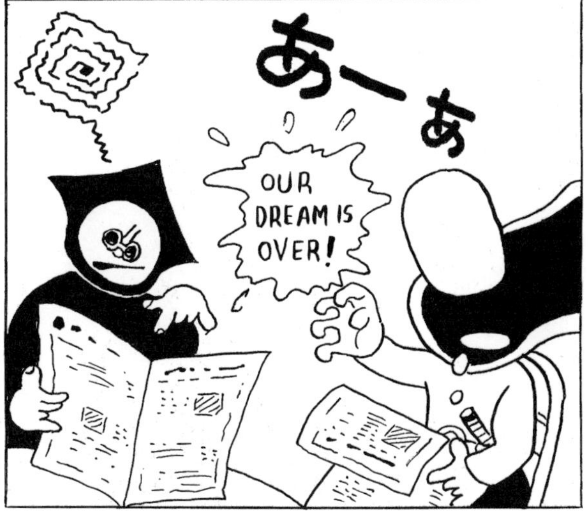
あーあ
OUR DREAM IS OVER!

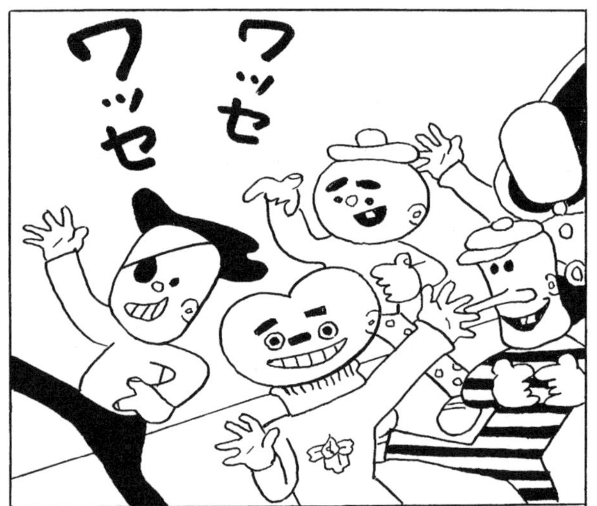

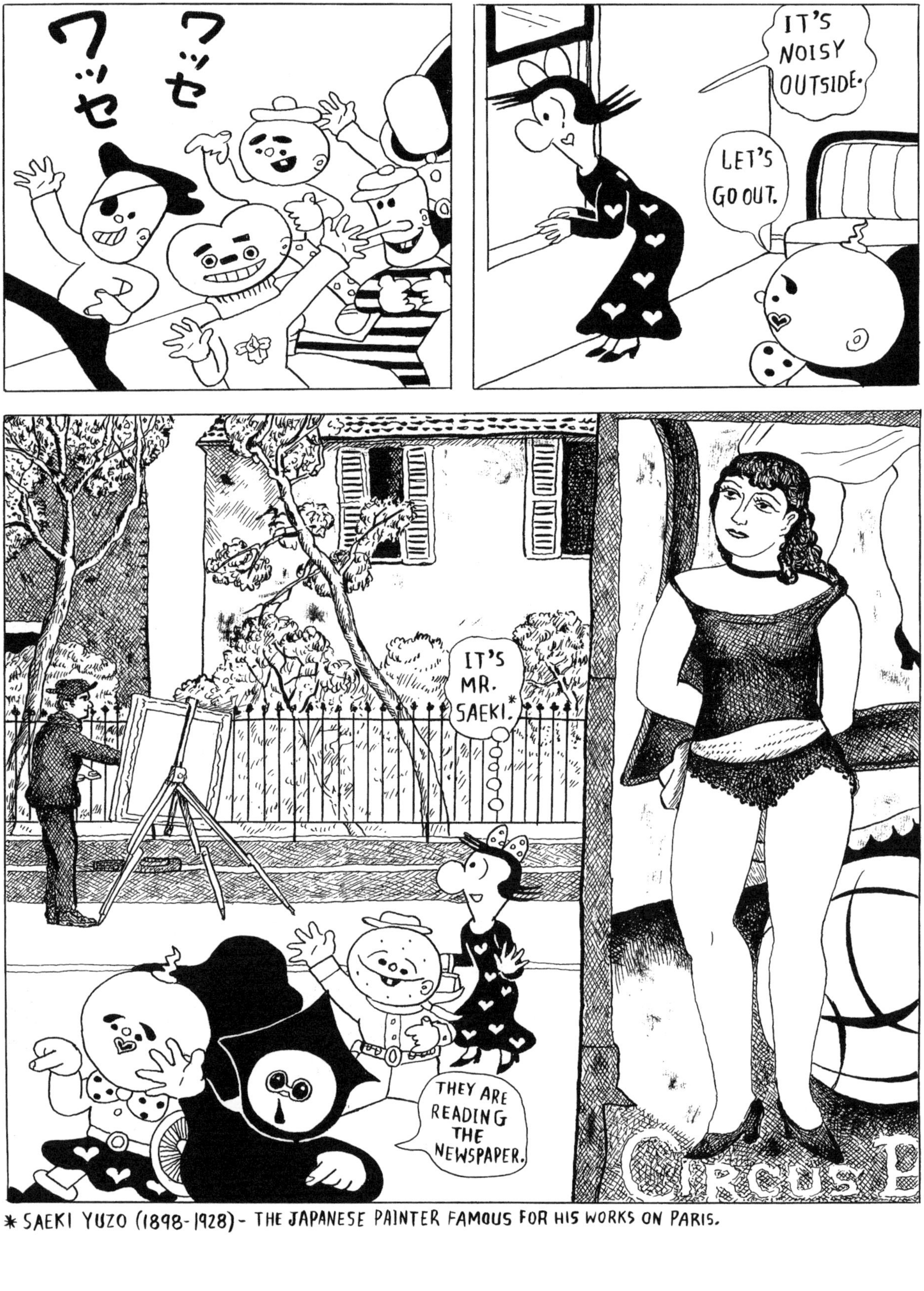

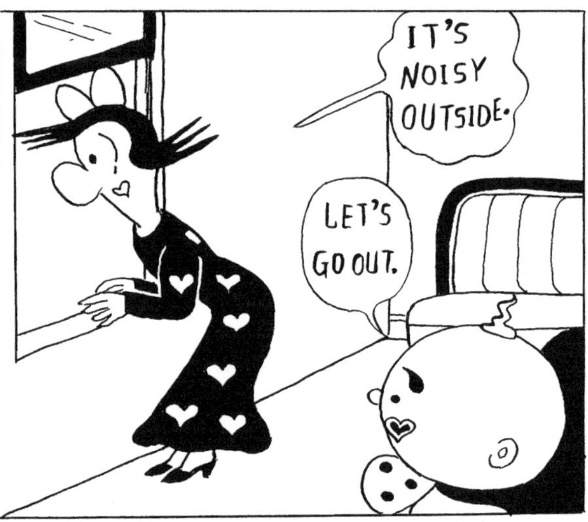

* SAEKI YUZO (1898-1928) - THE JAPANESE PAINTER FAMOUS FOR HIS WORKS ON PARIS.

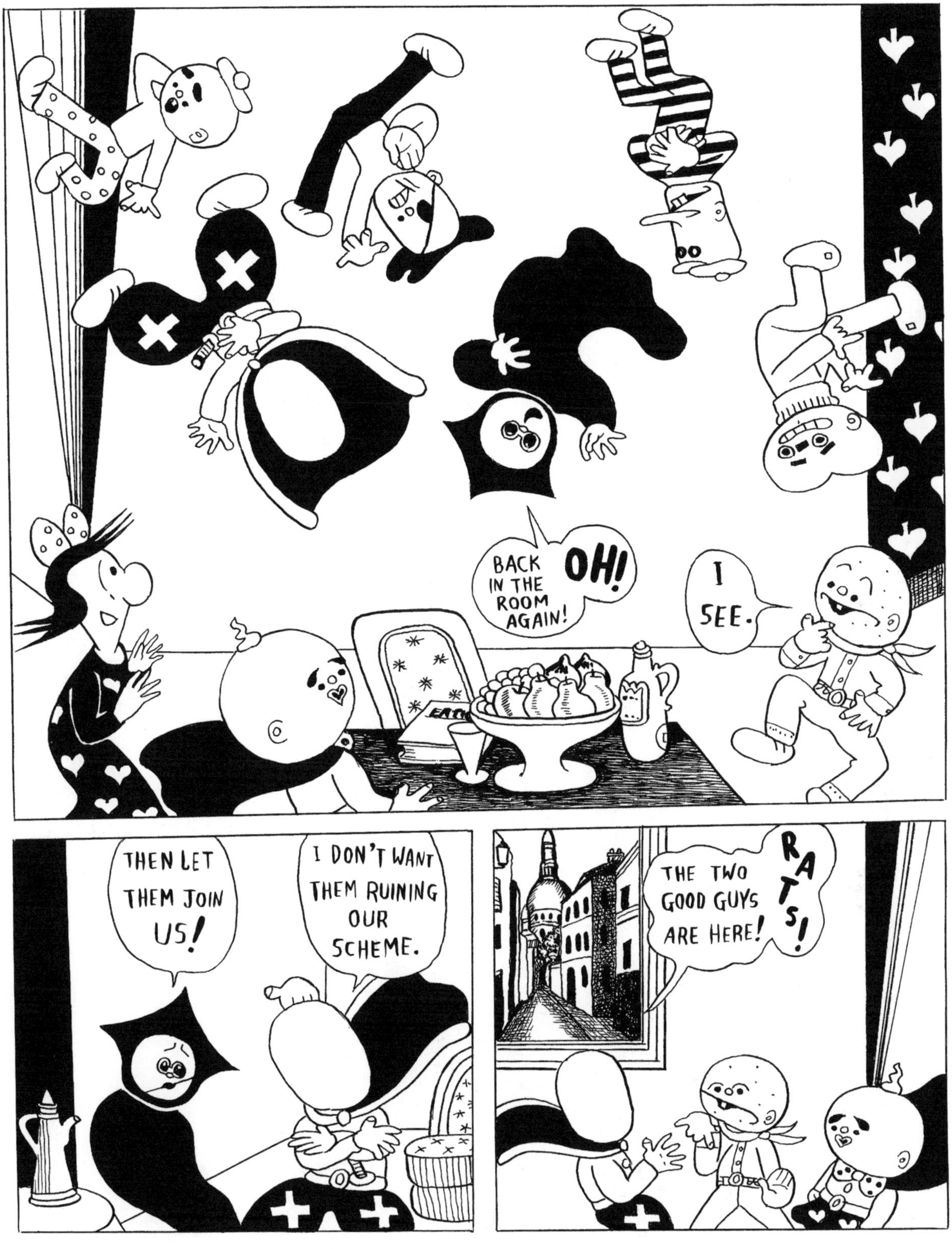

BACK IN THE ROOM AGAIN!
OH!
I SEE.

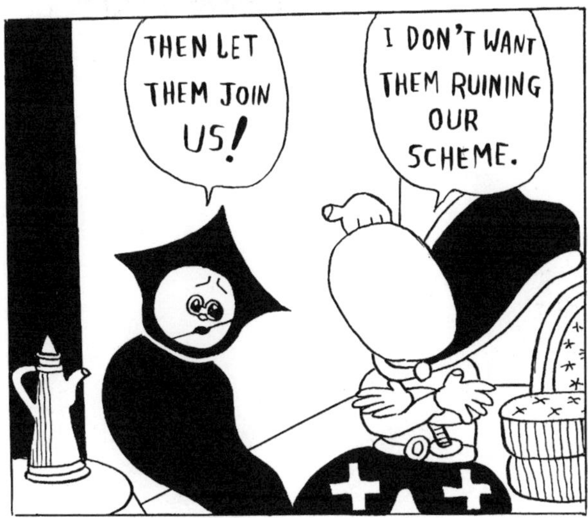
THEN LET THEM JOIN US!
I DON'T WANT THEM RUINING OUR SCHEME.

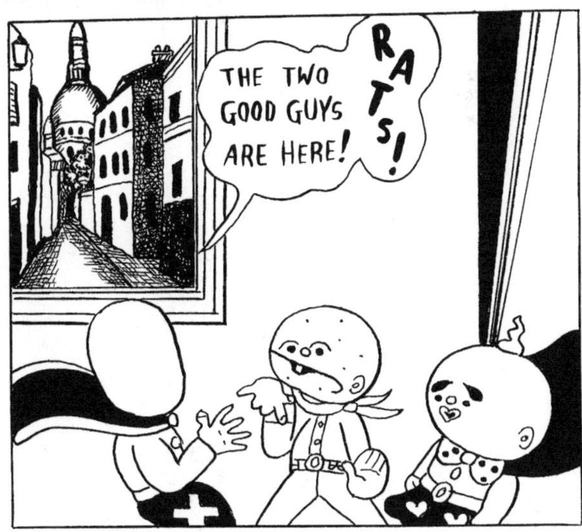
THE TWO GOOD GUYS ARE HERE!
RATS!

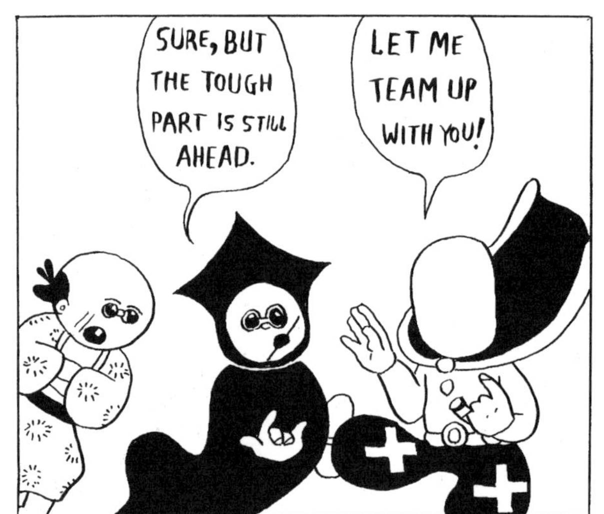
SURE, BUT THE TOUGH PART IS STILL AHEAD.
LET ME TEAM UP WITH YOU!

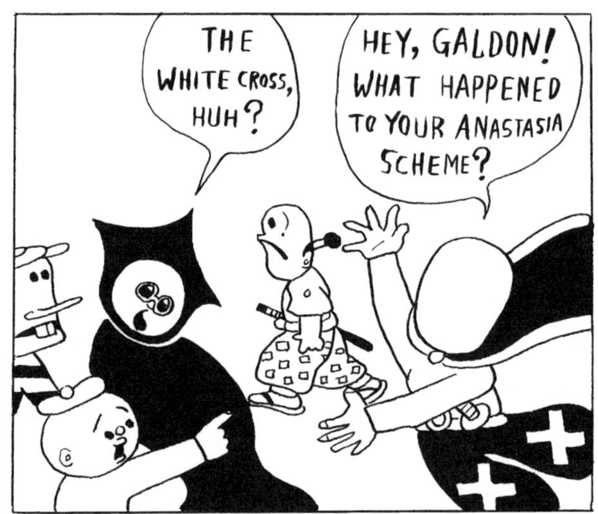
HEY, GALDON! WHAT HAPPENED TO YOUR ANASTASIA SCHEME?
THE WHITE CROSS, HUH?

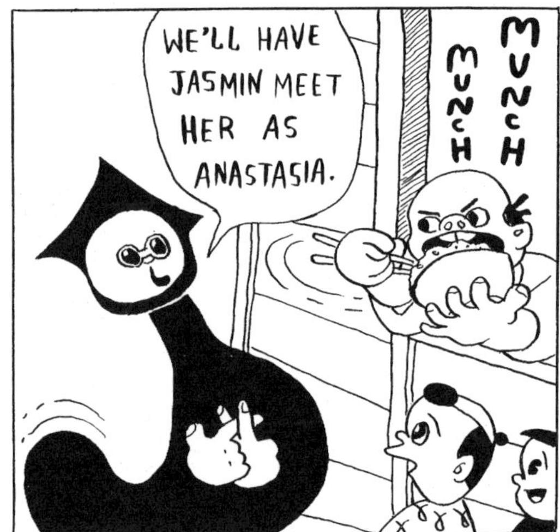
WE'LL HAVE JASMIN MEET HER AS ANASTASIA.
MUNCH
MUNCH

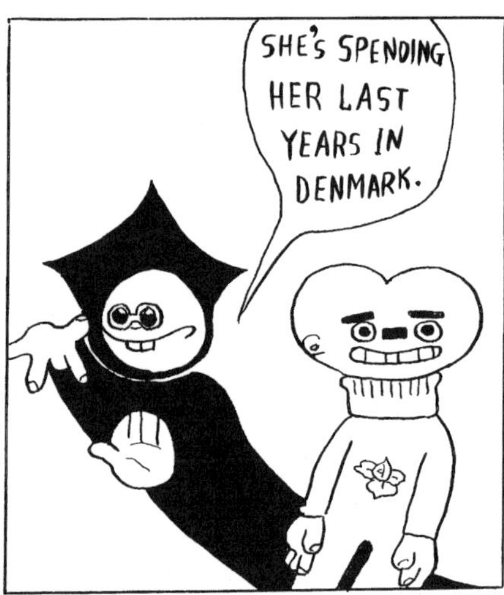
SHE'S SPENDING HER LAST YEARS IN DENMARK.

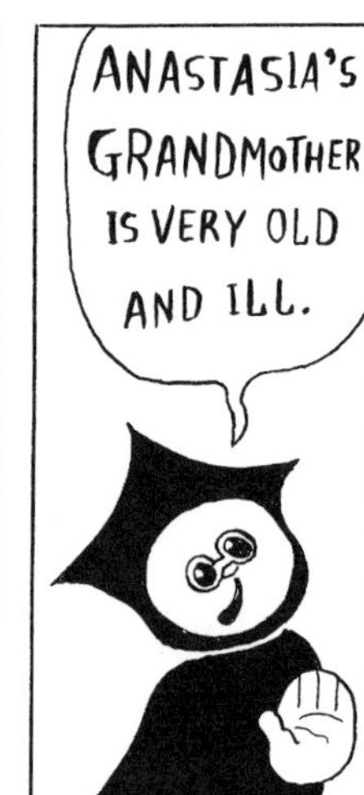
ANASTASIA'S GRANDMOTHER IS VERY OLD AND ILL.

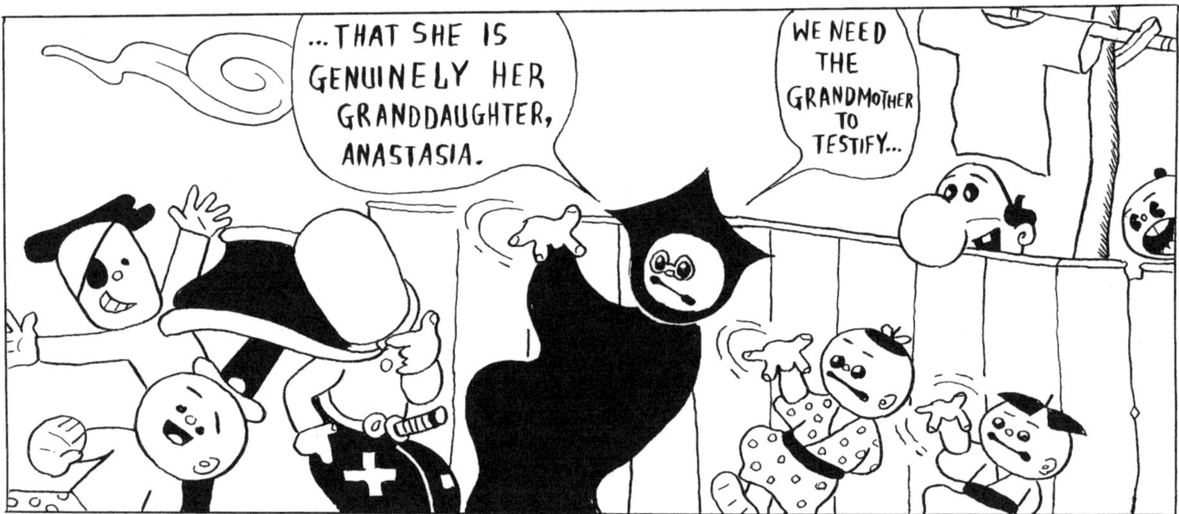
WE NEED THE GRANDMOTHER TO TESTIFY...
...THAT SHE IS GENUINELY HER GRANDDAUGHTER, ANASTASIA.

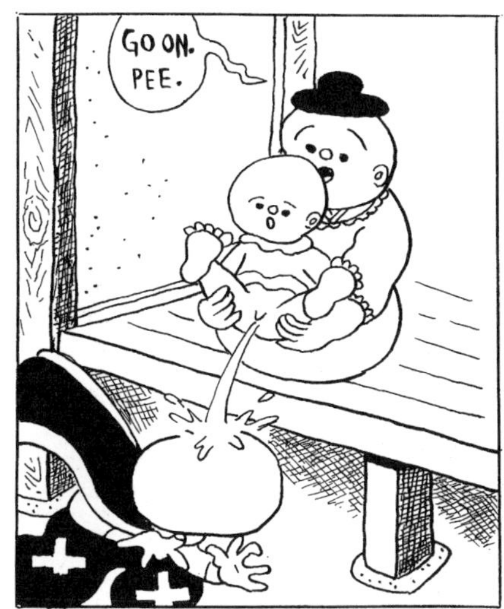
GO ON.
PEE.
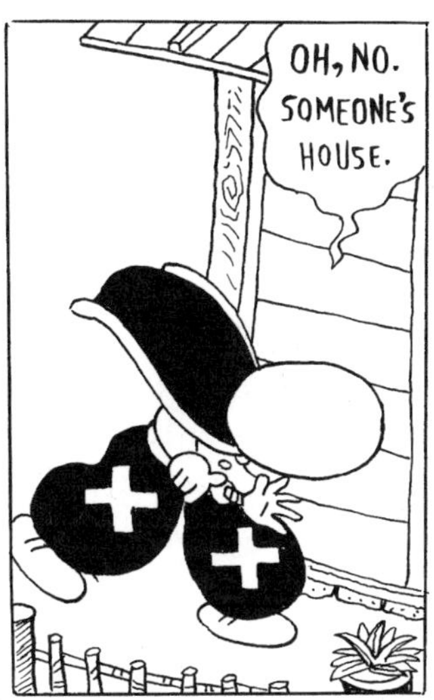
OH, NO.
SOMEONE'S
HOUSE.
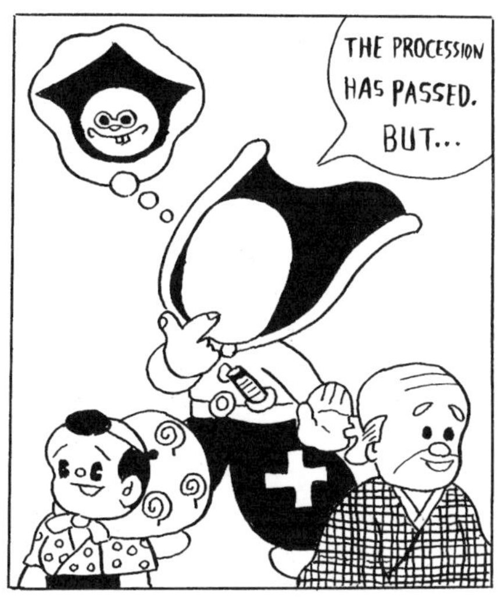
THE PROCESSION
HAS PASSED.
BUT...
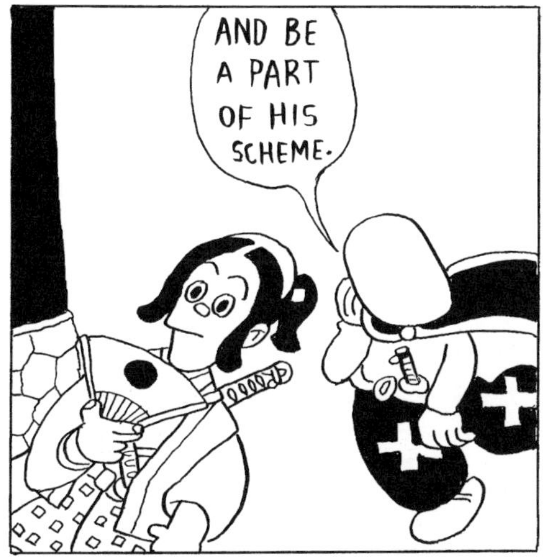
AND BE
A PART
OF HIS
SCHEME.
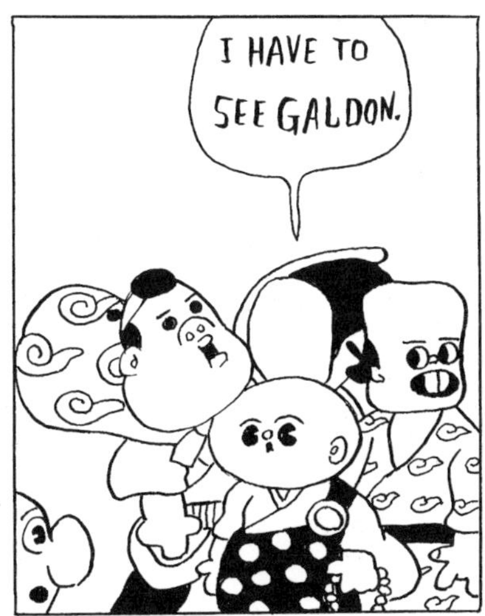
I HAVE TO
SEE GALDON.
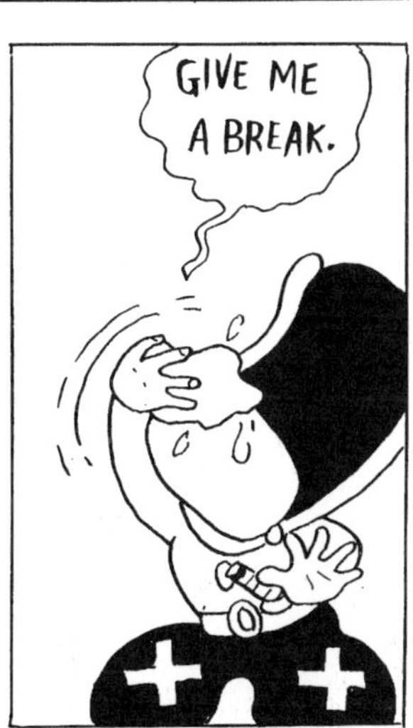
GIVE ME
A BREAK.
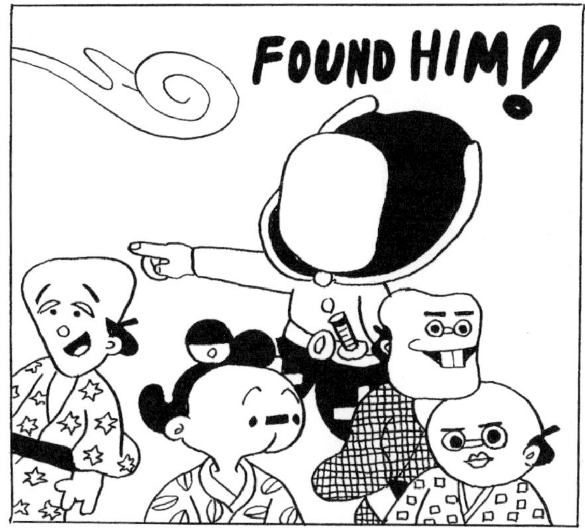
FOUND HIM!
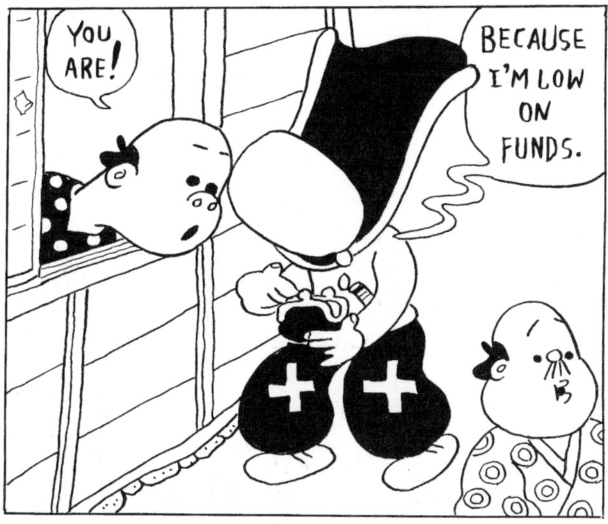
YOU
ARE!
BECAUSE
I'M LOW
ON
FUNDS.

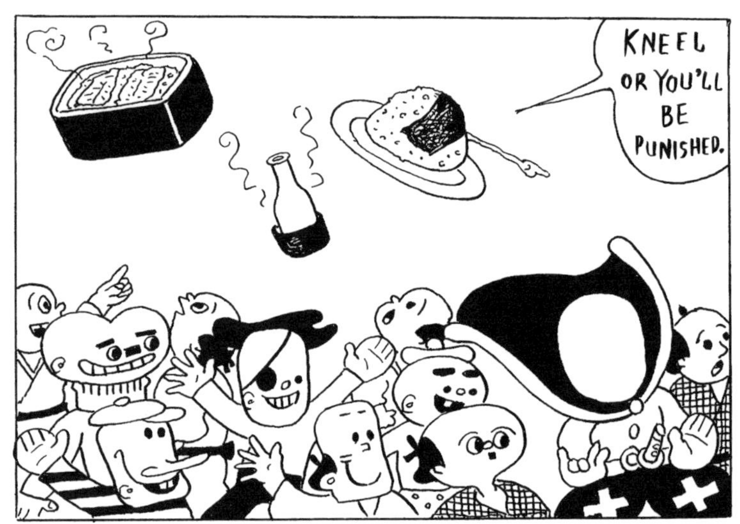
KNEEL OR YOU'LL BE PUNISHED.

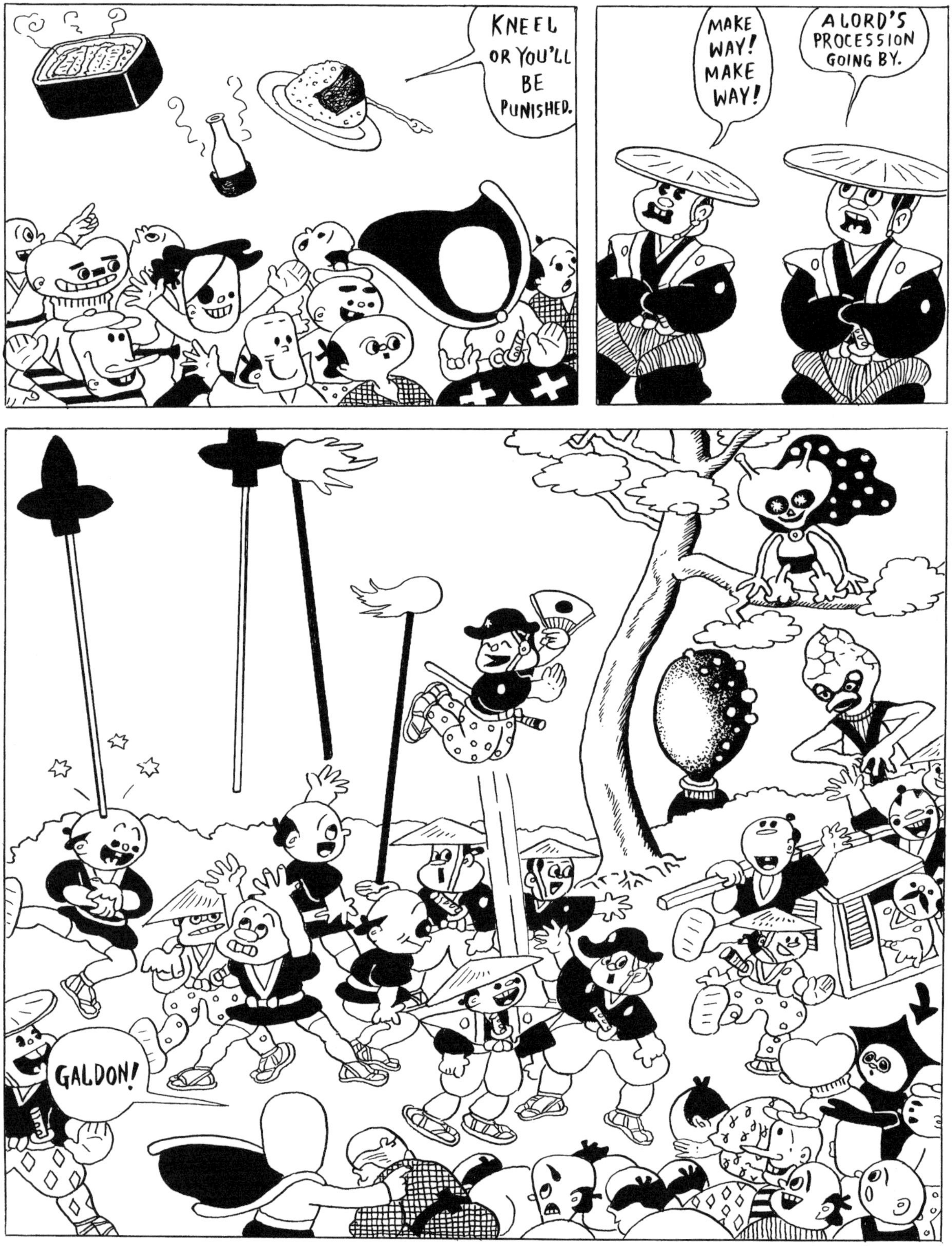

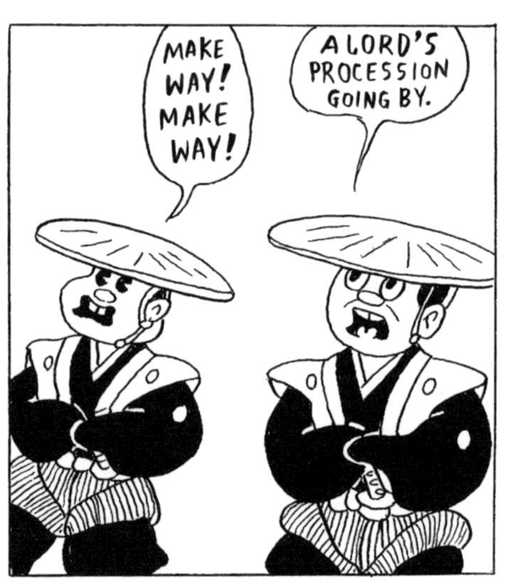
MAKE WAY! MAKE WAY!
A LORD'S PROCESSION GOING BY.

GALDON!

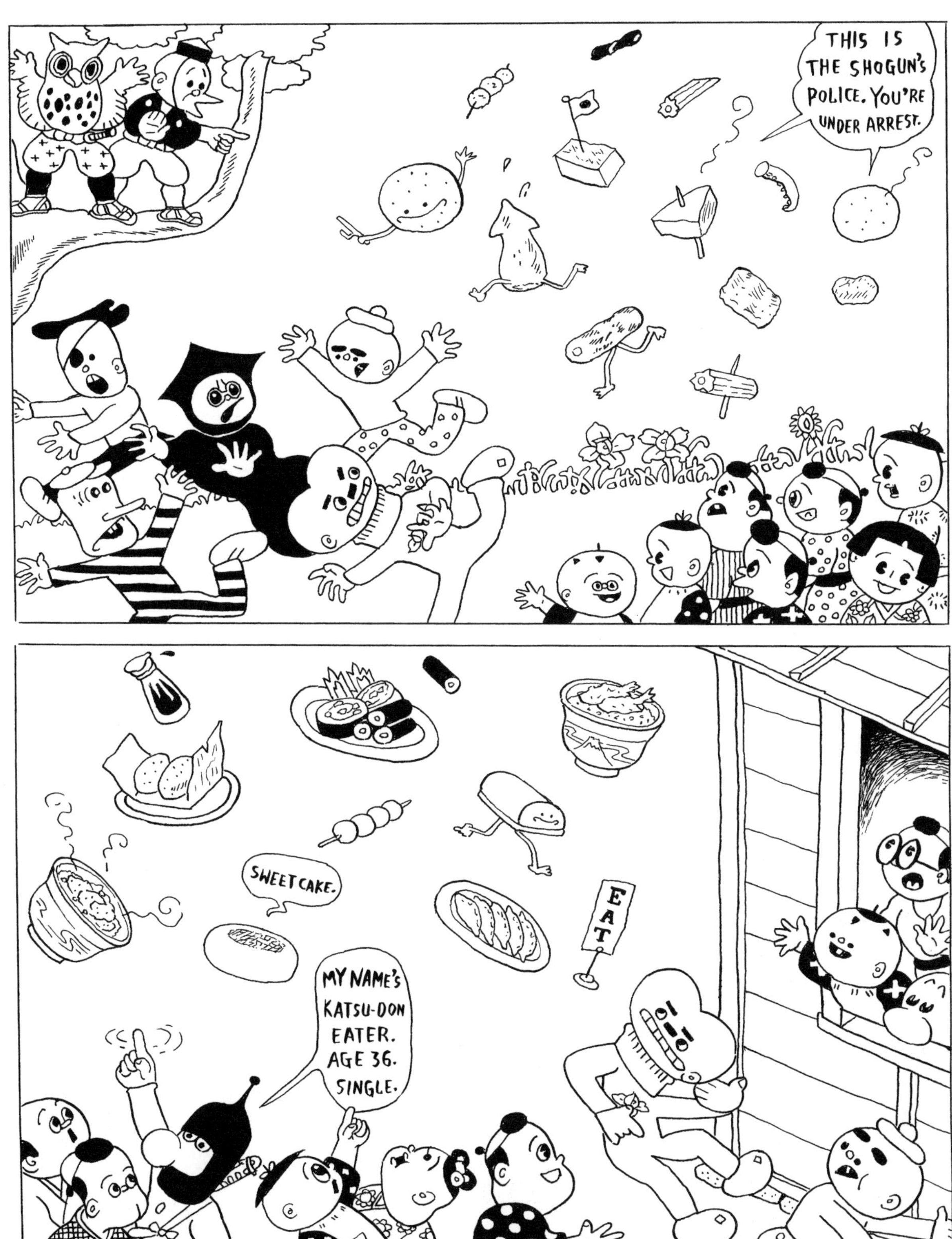
THIS IS THE SHOGUN'S POLICE. YOU'RE UNDER ARREST.
SWEET CAKE.
EAT
MY NAME'S KATSU-DON EATER. AGE 36. SINGLE.

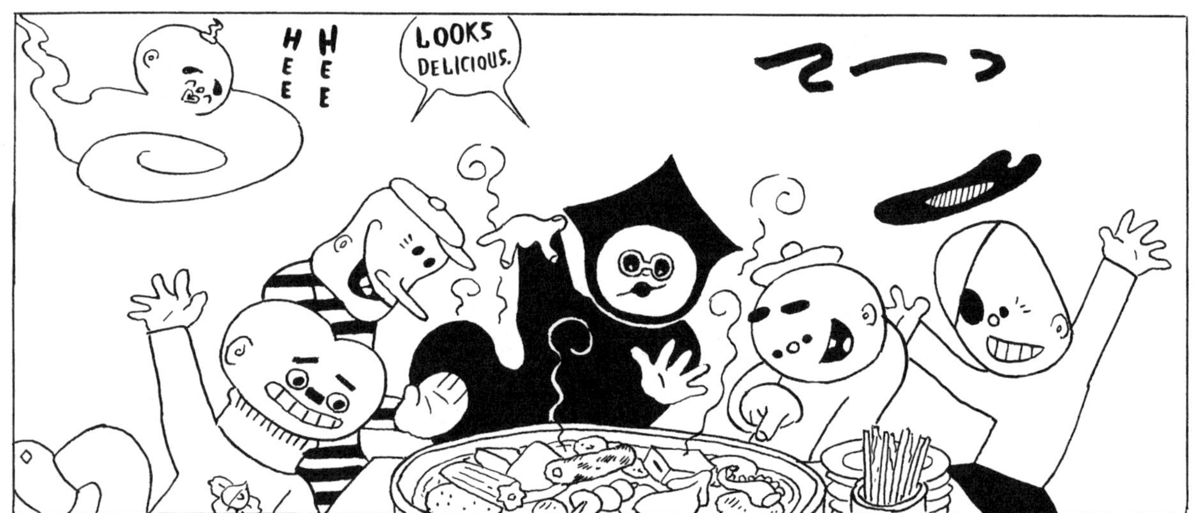
HEE HEE
LOOKS DELICIOUS.

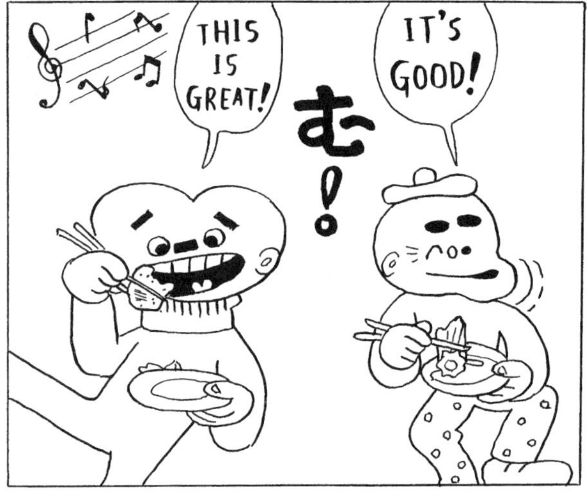
THIS IS GREAT!
IT'S GOOD!
む!

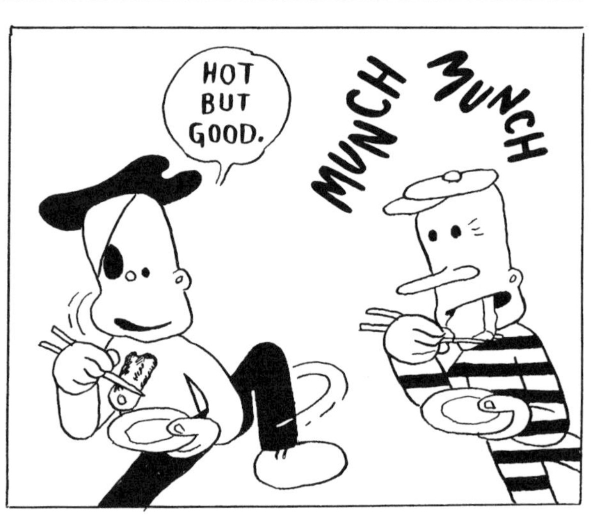
HOT BUT GOOD.
MUNCH MUNCH

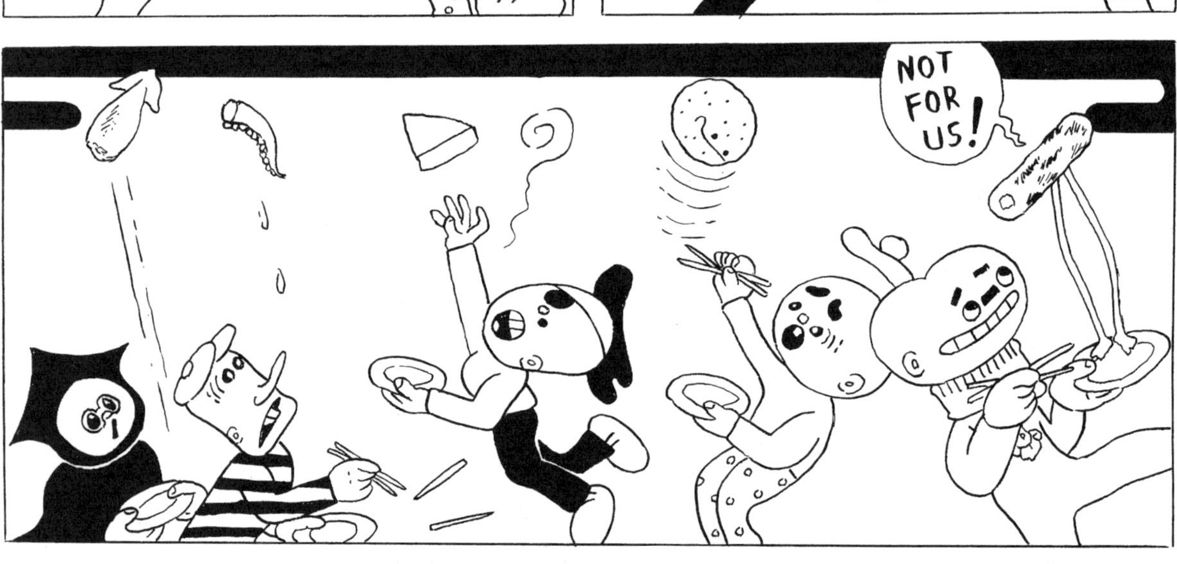
NOT FOR US!

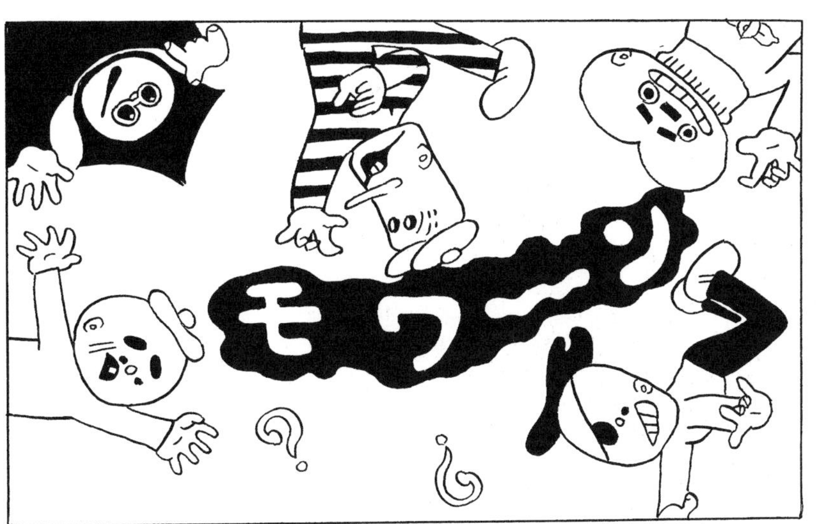

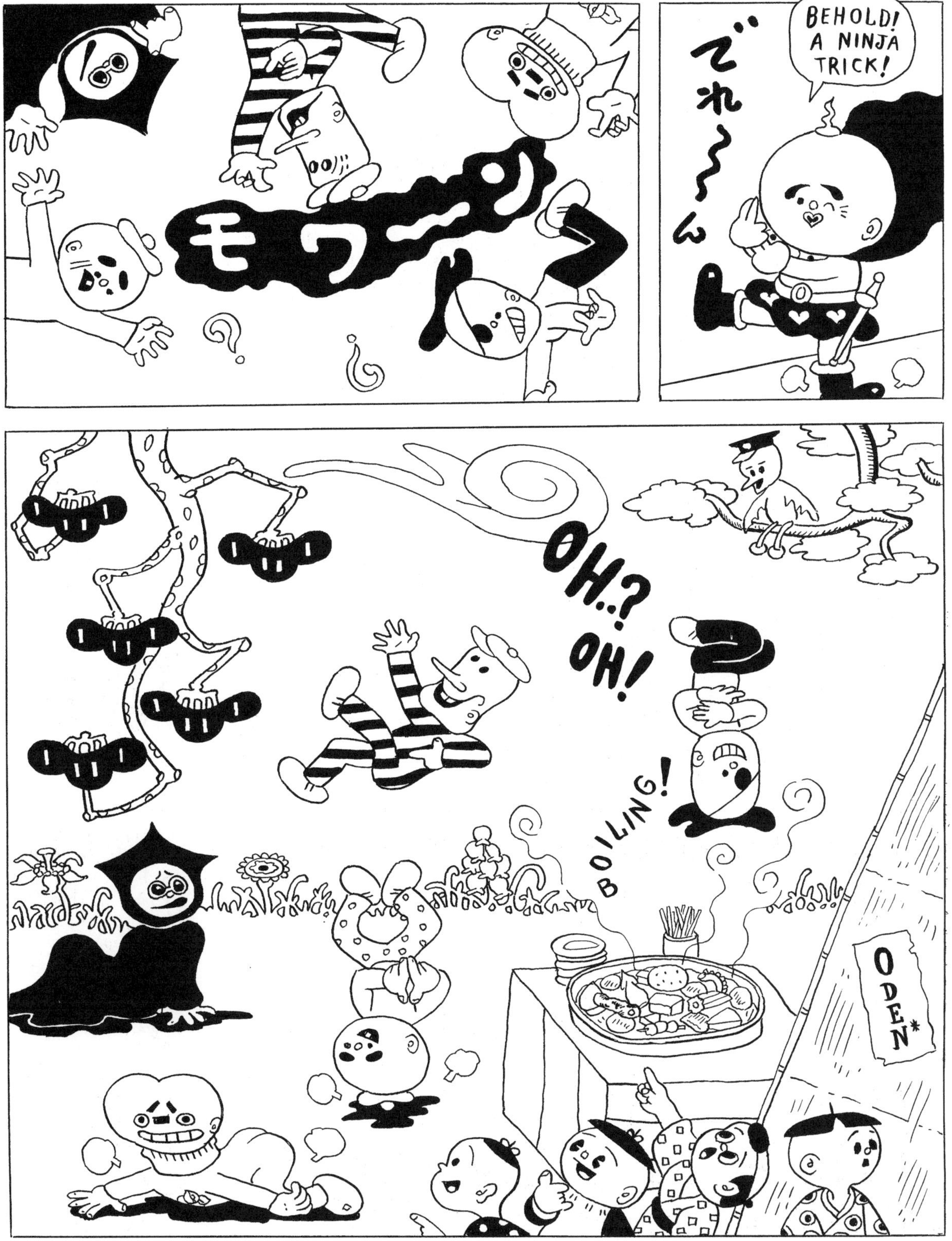

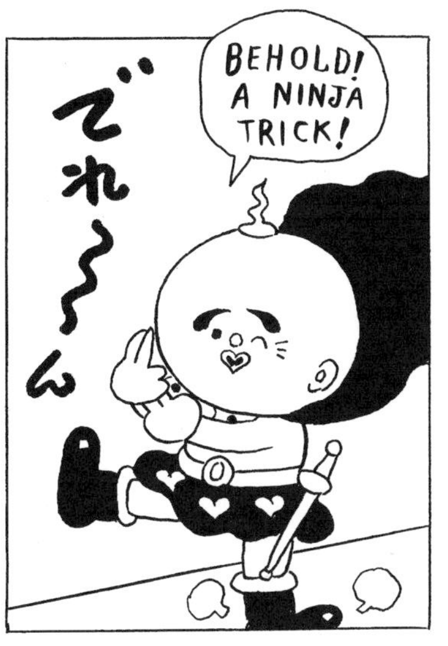

OH..? OH!

BOILING!

ODEN*

* ODEN: A POPULAR JAPANESE DISH- FISH DUMPLINGS, VEGETABLES, AND OTHERS INCLUDING GANMODOKI STEWED AND SERVED HOT.

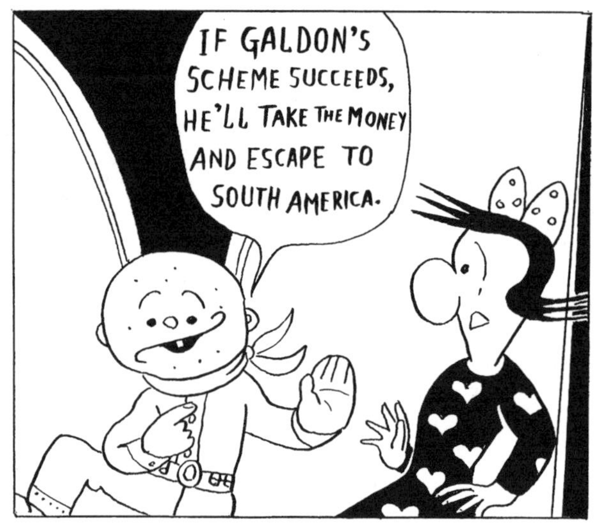
IF GALDON'S SCHEME SUCCEEDS, HE'LL TAKE THE MONEY AND ESCAPE TO SOUTH AMERICA.

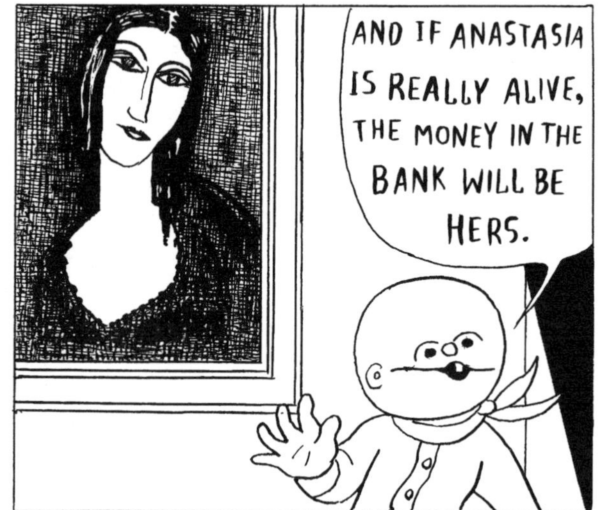
AND IF ANASTASIA IS REALLY ALIVE, THE MONEY IN THE BANK WILL BE HERS.

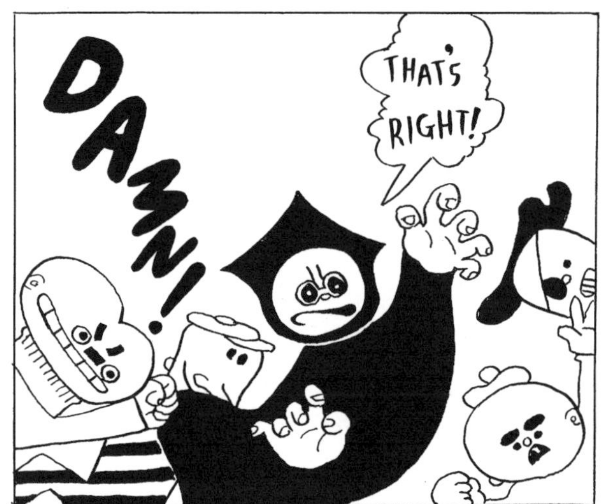
DAMN!
THAT'S RIGHT!

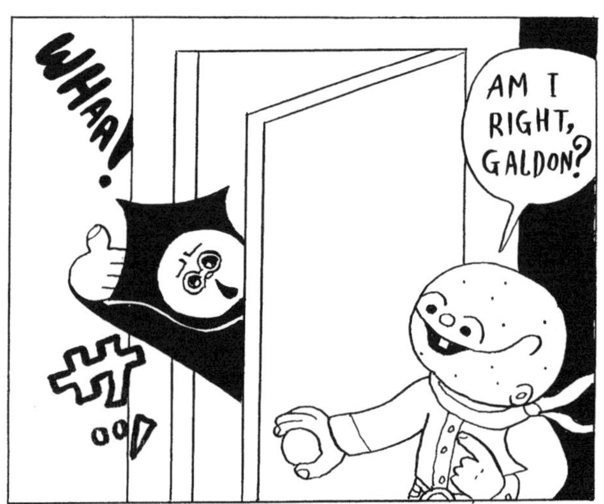
WHAA!
AM I RIGHT, GALDON?

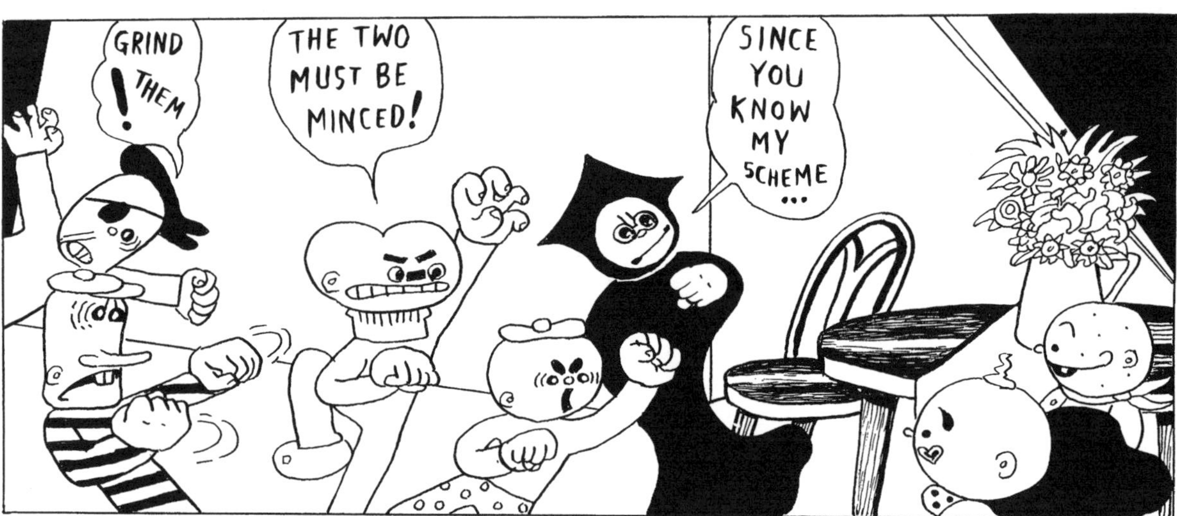
GRIND THEM!
THE TWO MUST BE MINCED!
SINCE YOU KNOW MY SCHEME...

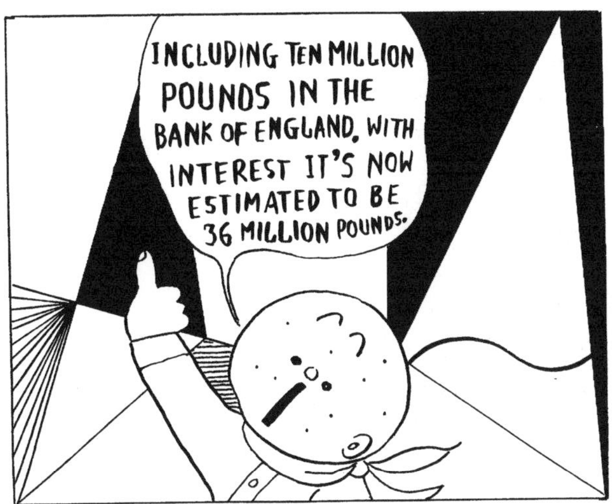

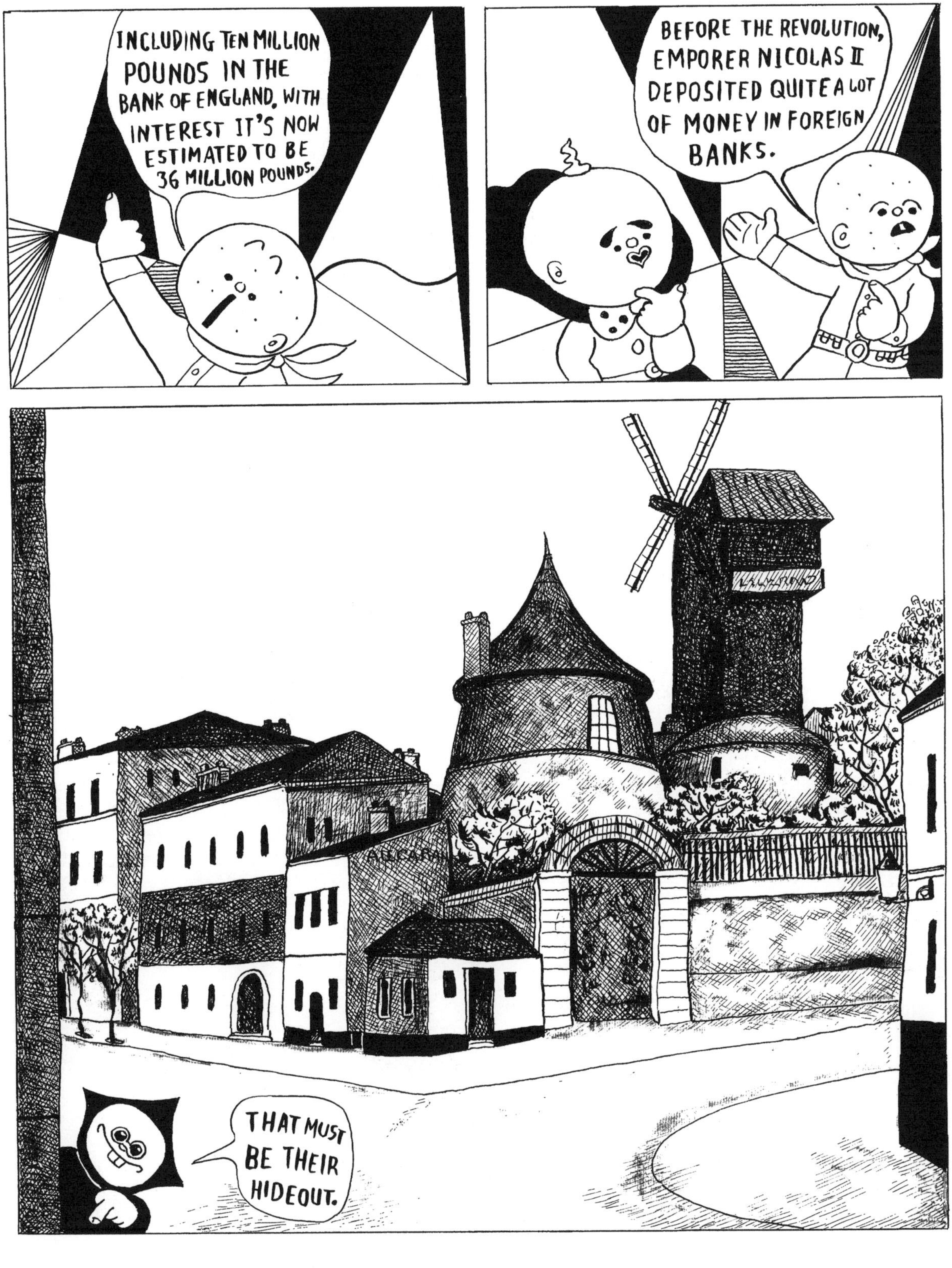

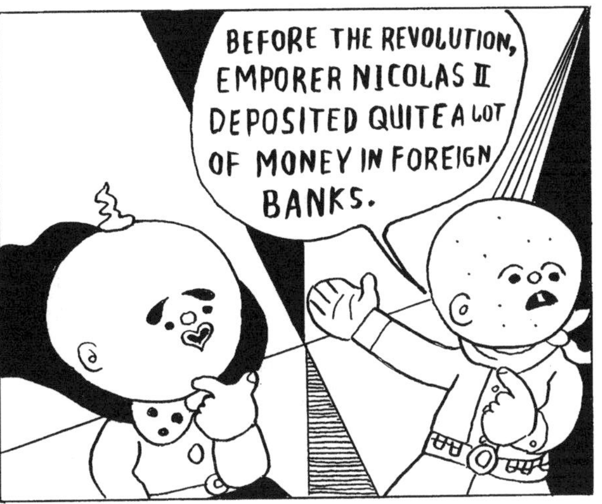

THAT MUST BE THEIR HIDEOUT.

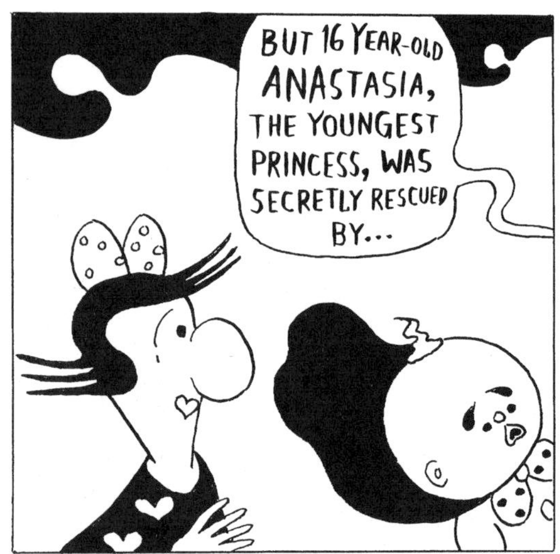
BUT 16 YEAR-OLD ANASTASIA, THE YOUNGEST PRINCESS, WAS SECRETLY RESCUED BY...

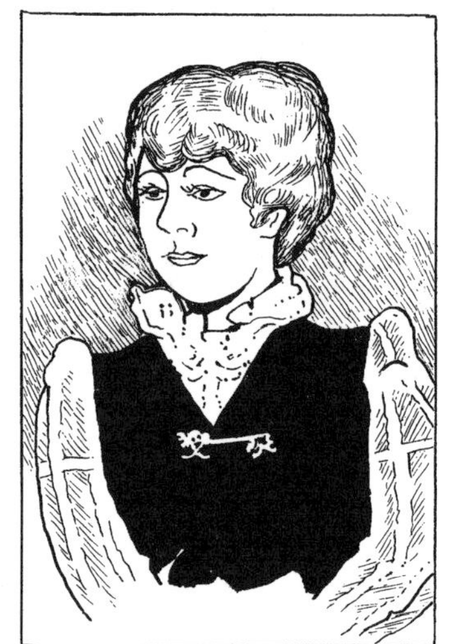

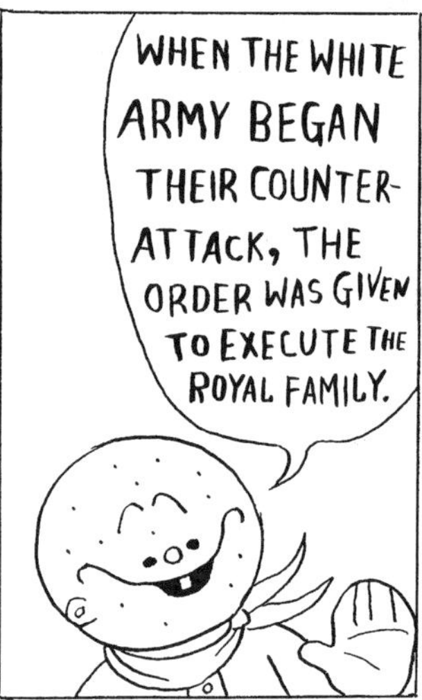
WHEN THE WHITE ARMY BEGAN THEIR COUNTER-ATTACK, THE ORDER WAS GIVEN TO EXECUTE THE ROYAL FAMILY.

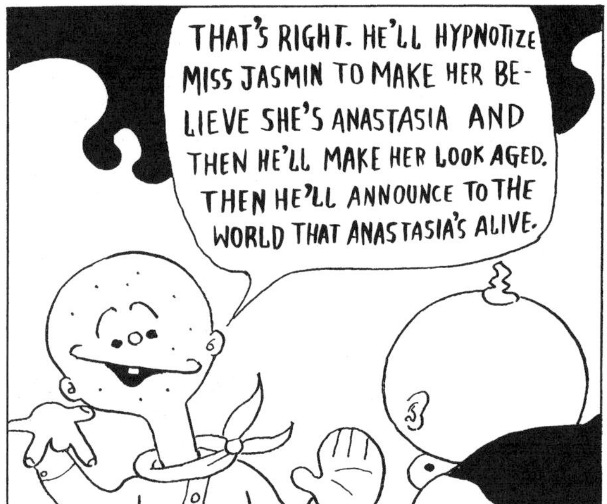
THAT'S RIGHT. HE'LL HYPNOTIZE MISS JASMIN TO MAKE HER BE-LIEVE SHE'S ANASTASIA AND THEN HE'LL MAKE HER LOOK AGED. THEN HE'LL ANNOUNCE TO THE WORLD THAT ANASTASIA'S ALIVE.

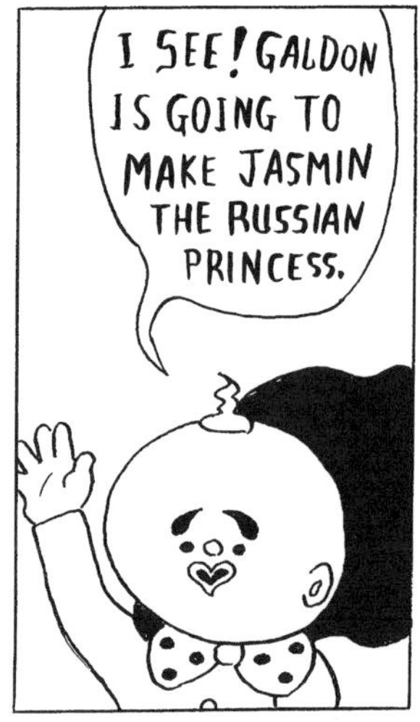
I SEE! GALDON IS GOING TO MAKE JASMIN THE RUSSIAN PRINCESS.

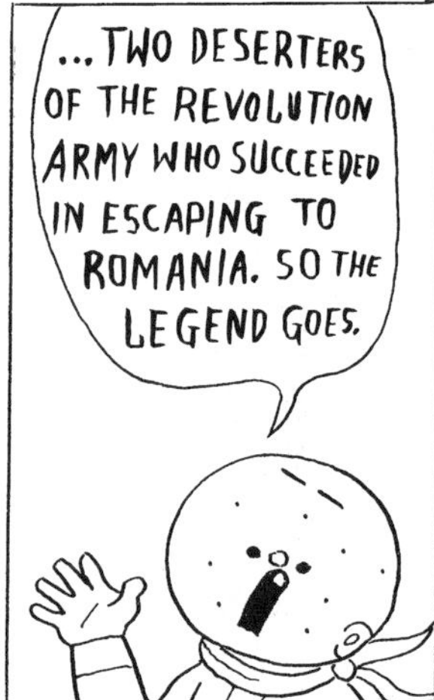
...TWO DESERTERS OF THE REVOLUTION ARMY WHO SUCCEEDED IN ESCAPING TO ROMANIA. SO THE LEGEND GOES.

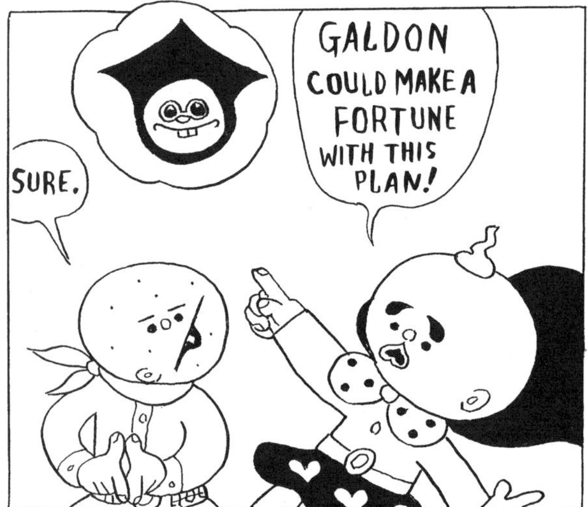
SURE.
GALDON COULD MAKE A FORTUNE WITH THIS PLAN!

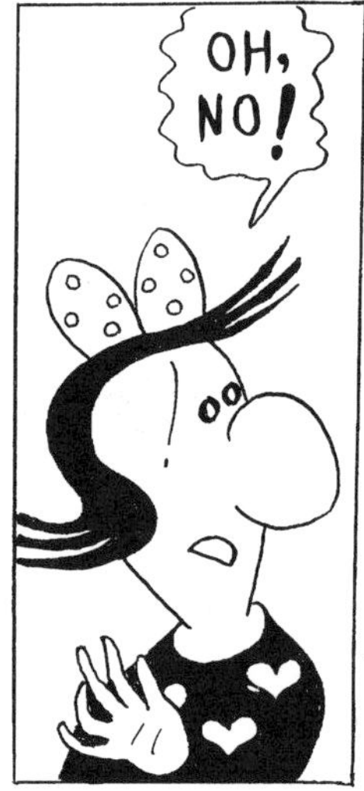
OH, NO!

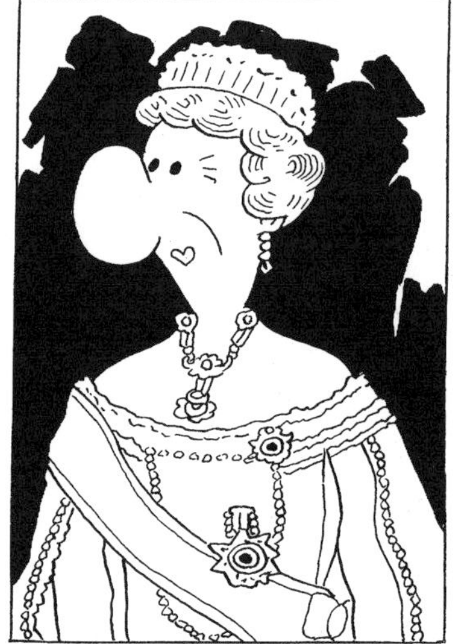

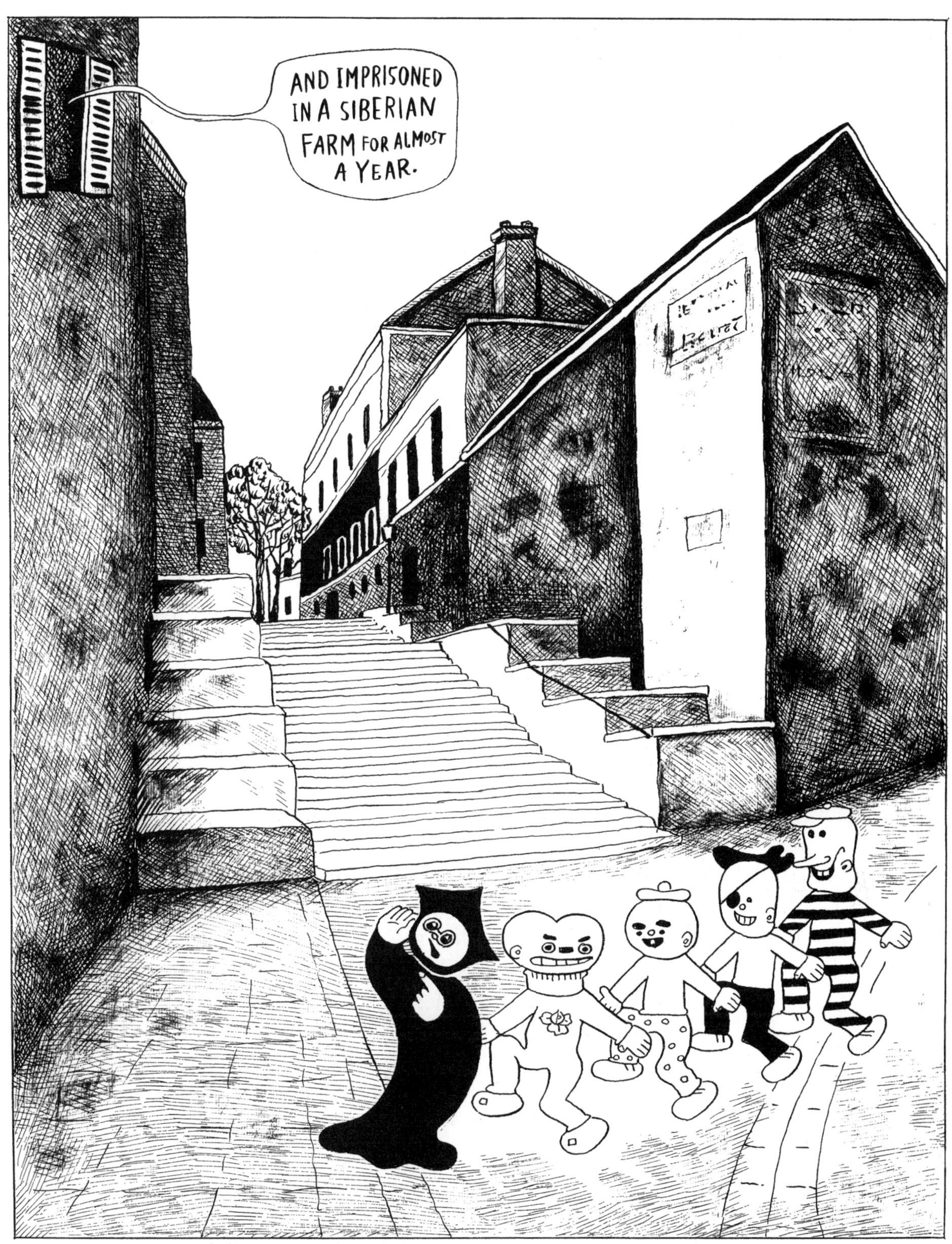
AND IMPRISONED IN A SIBERIAN FARM FOR ALMOST A YEAR.

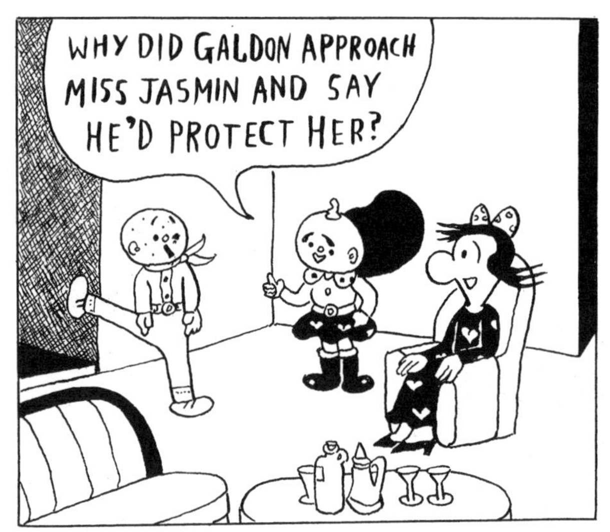
WHY DID GALDON APPROACH MISS JASMIN AND SAY HE'D PROTECT HER?

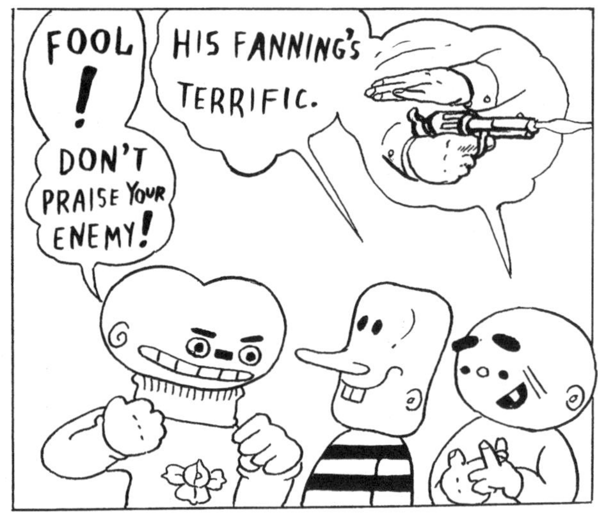
HIS FANNING'S TERRIFIC.
FOOL! DON'T PRAISE YOUR ENEMY!

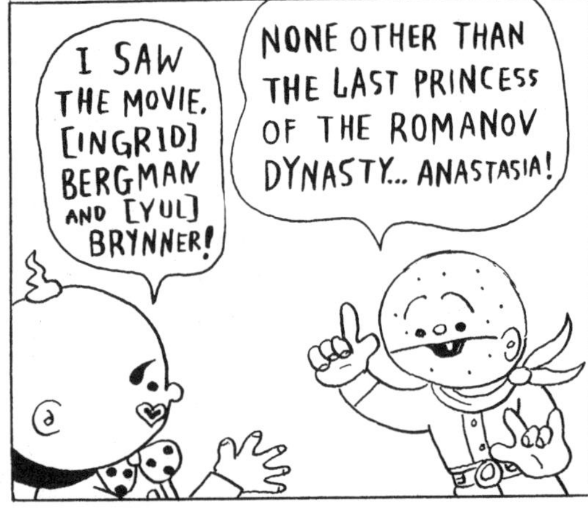
NONE OTHER THAN THE LAST PRINCESS OF THE ROMANOV DYNASTY... ANASTASIA!
I SAW THE MOVIE. [INGRID] BERGMAN AND [YUL] BRYNNER!

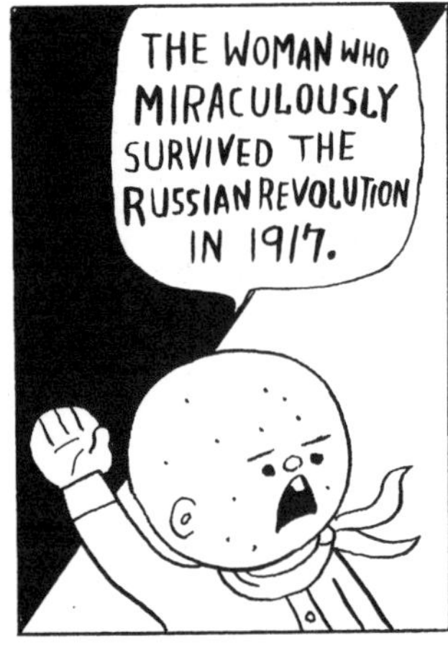
THE WOMAN WHO MIRACULOUSLY SURVIVED THE RUSSIAN REVOLUTION IN 1917.

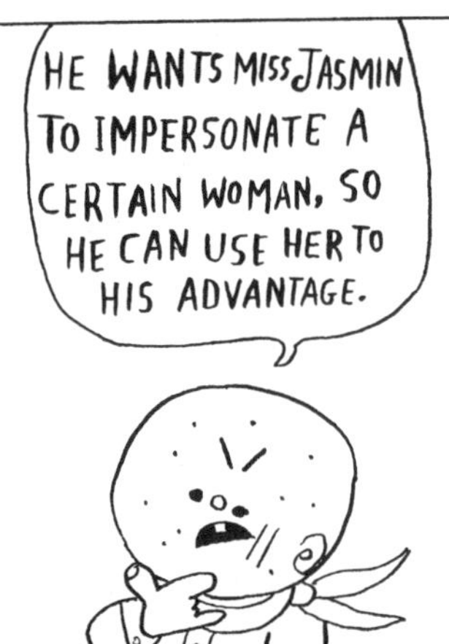
HE WANTS MISS JASMIN TO IMPERSONATE A CERTAIN WOMAN, SO HE CAN USE HER TO HIS ADVANTAGE.

ANASTASIA

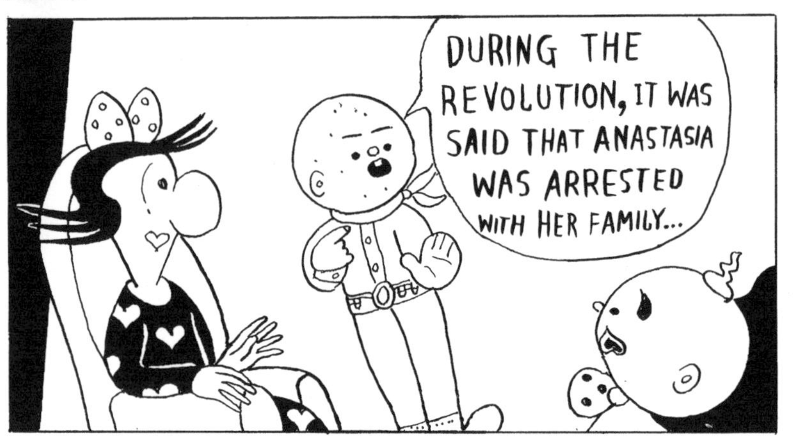
DURING THE REVOLUTION, IT WAS SAID THAT ANASTASIA WAS ARRESTED WITH HER FAMILY...

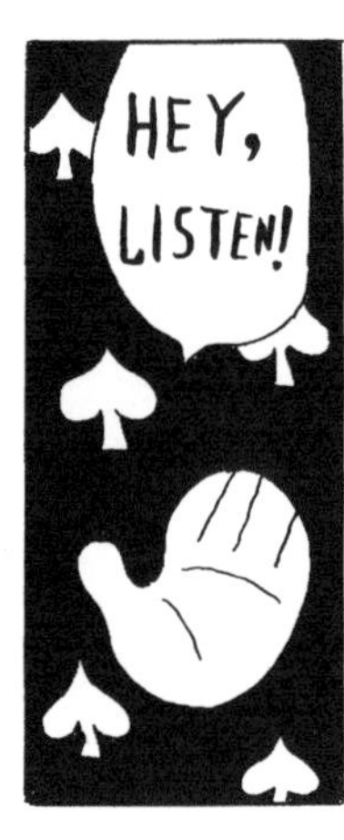
HEY, LISTEN!

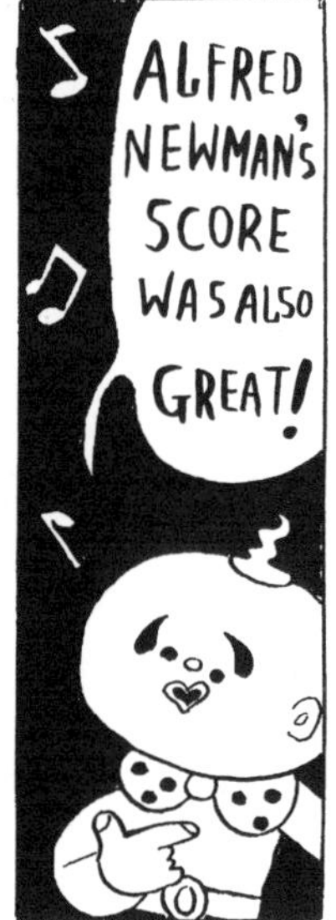
ALFRED NEWMAN'S SCORE WAS ALSO GREAT!

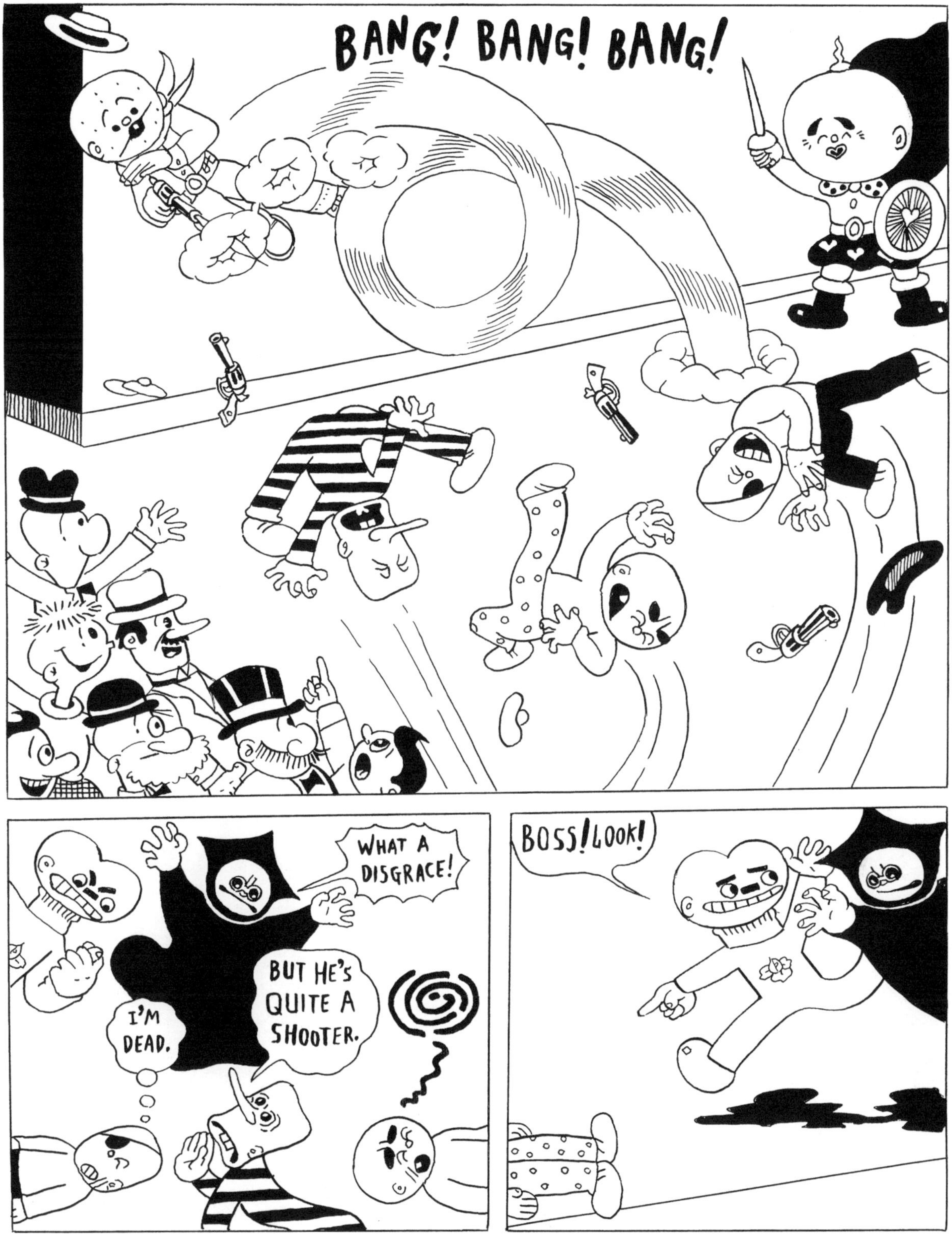

BANG! BANG! BANG!

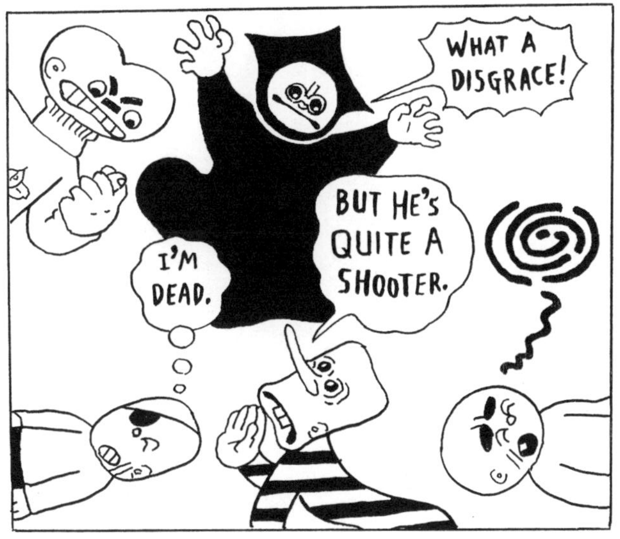

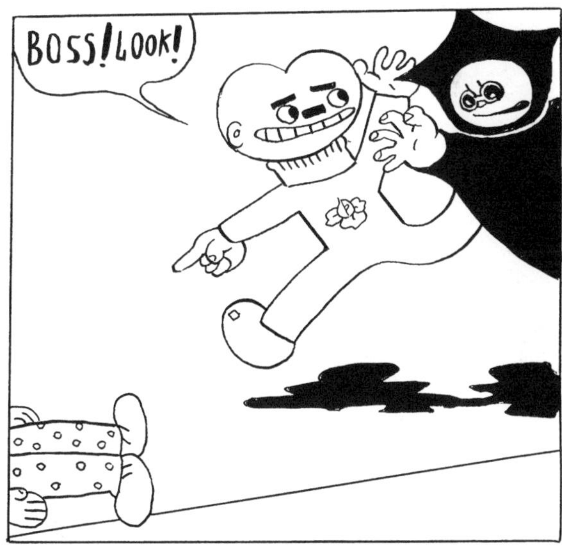

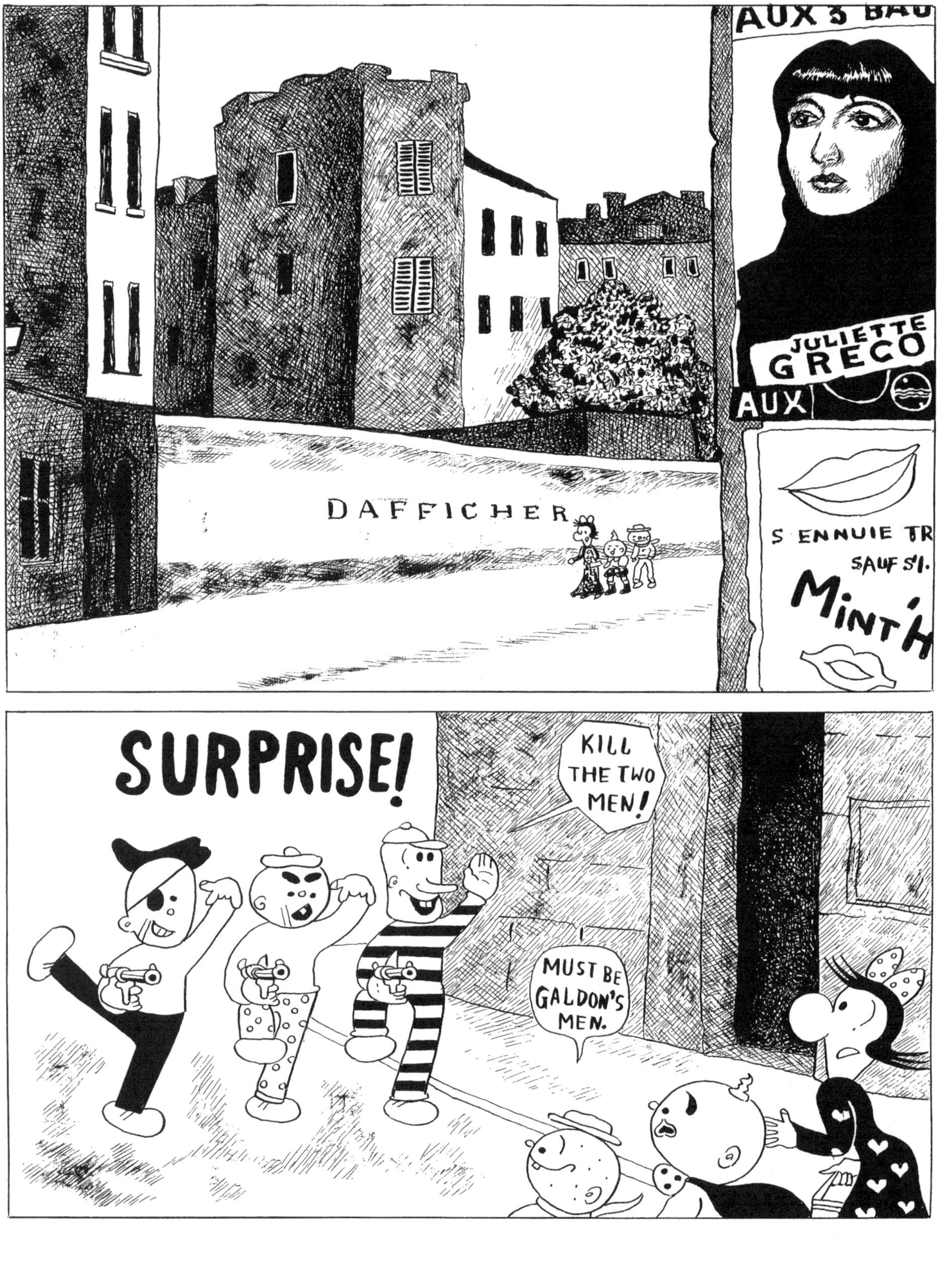

AUX 3 BAU
JULIETTE GRECO
AUX
DAFFICHER
S ENNUIE TR
SAUF S'I.
MINT'H

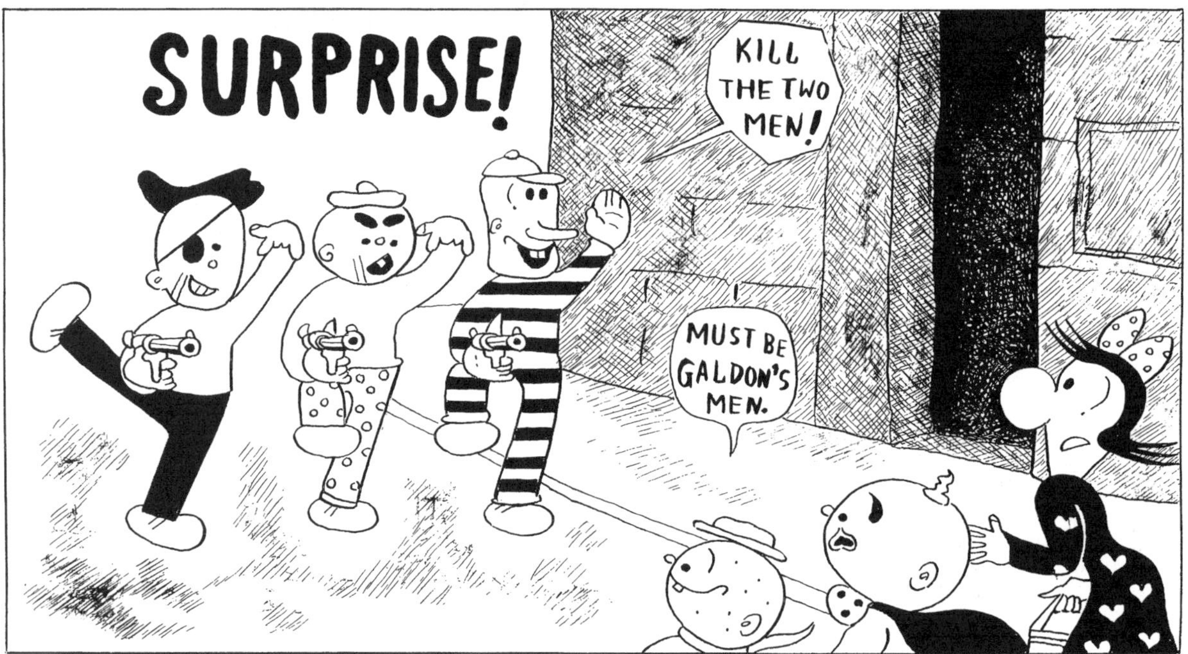
SURPRISE!
KILL THE TWO MEN!
MUST BE GALDON'S MEN.

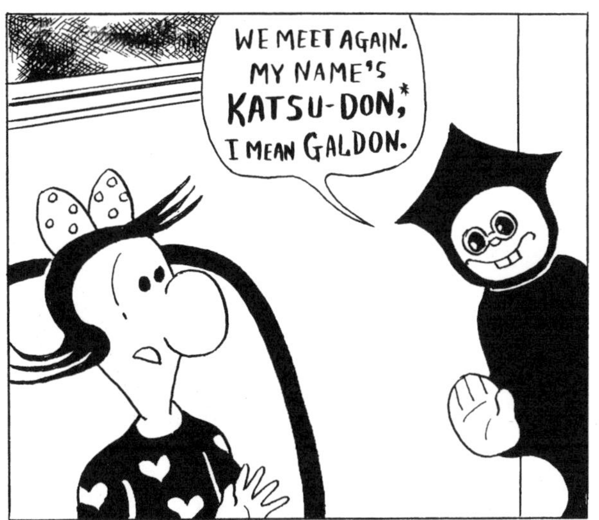

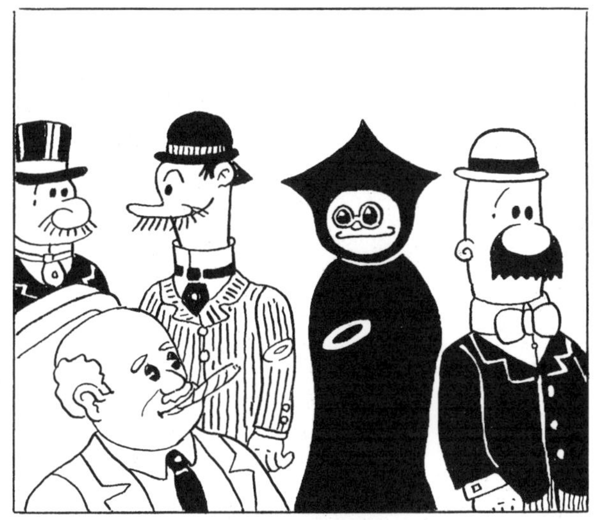

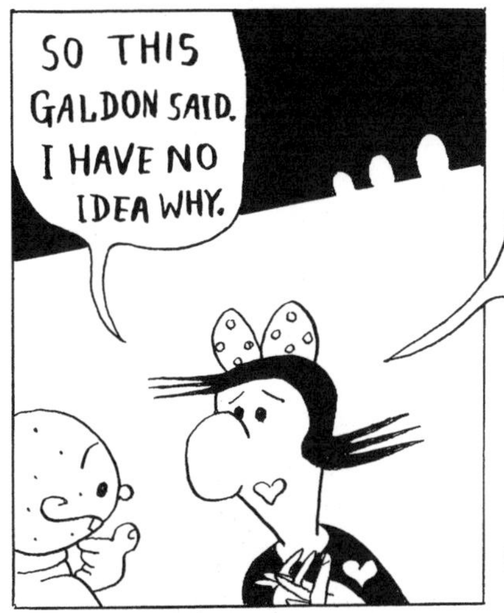

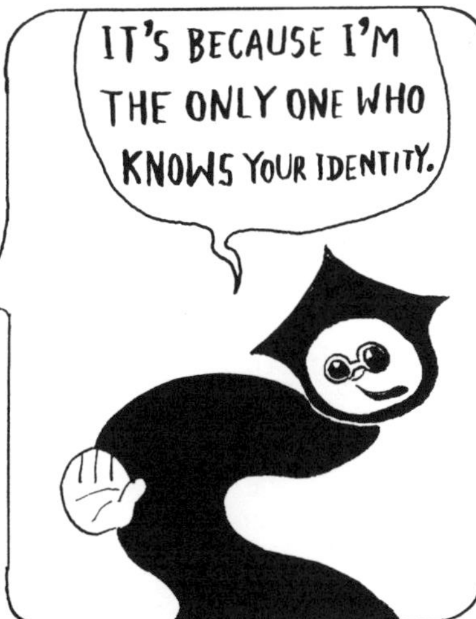

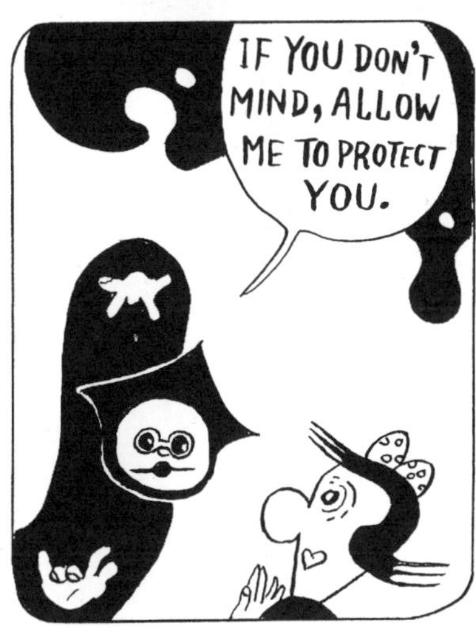

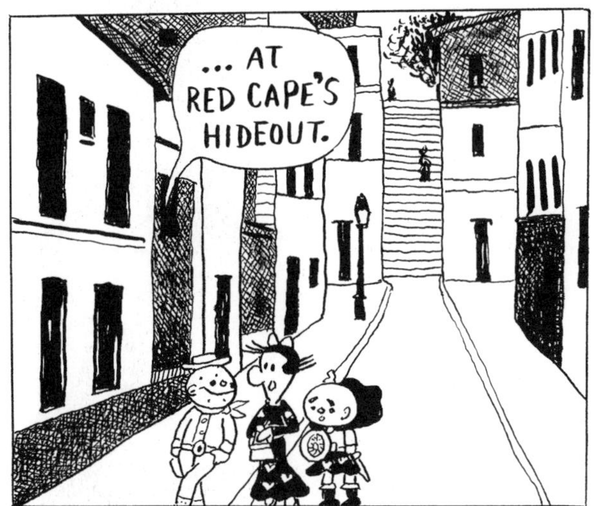

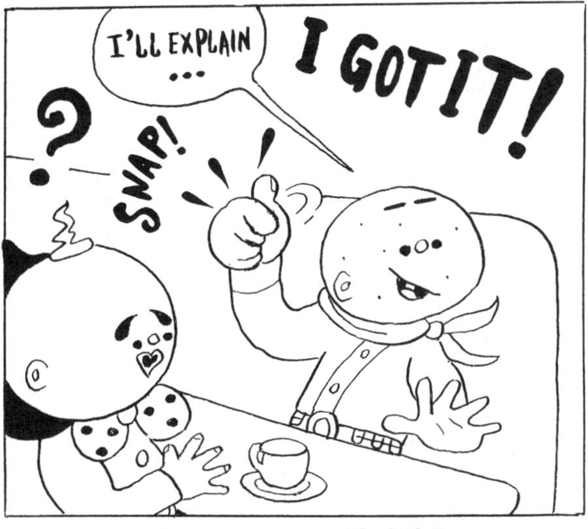

* KATSU-DON: A POPULAR JAPANESE RICE BOWL TOPPED WITH PORK CUTLETS, EGGS, AND ONIONS.

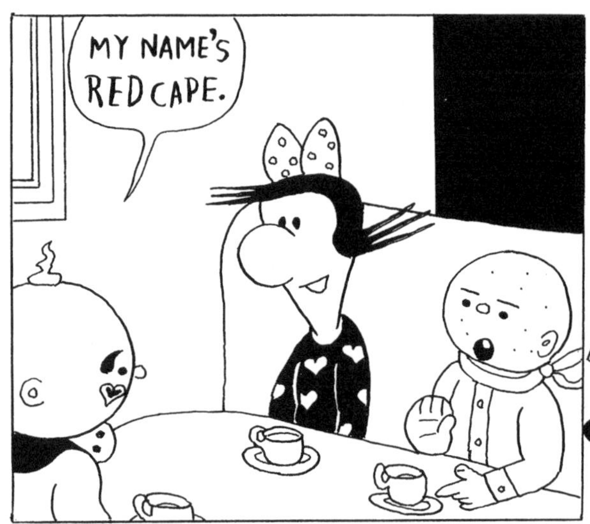

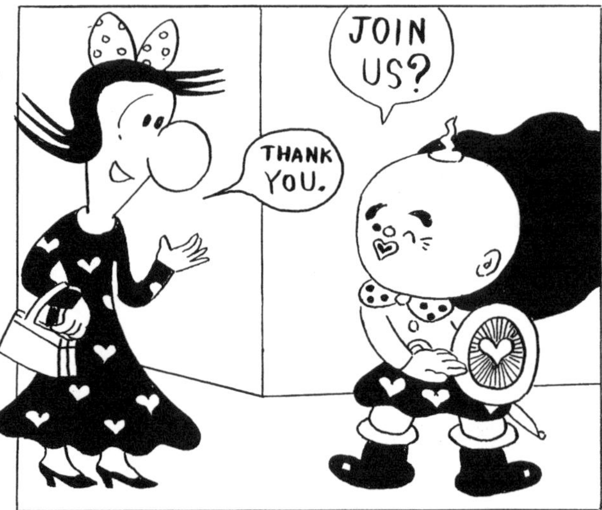

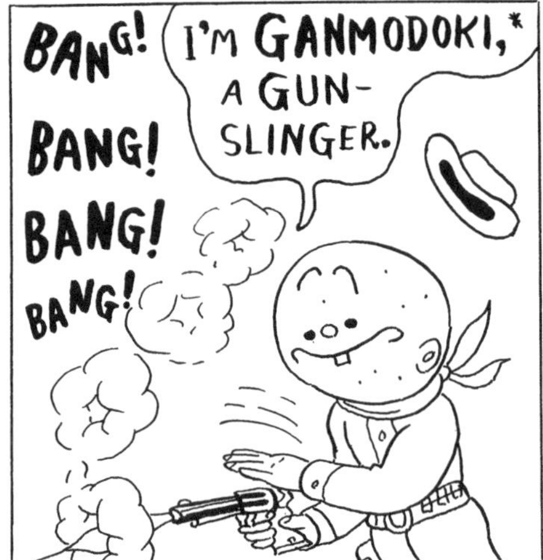

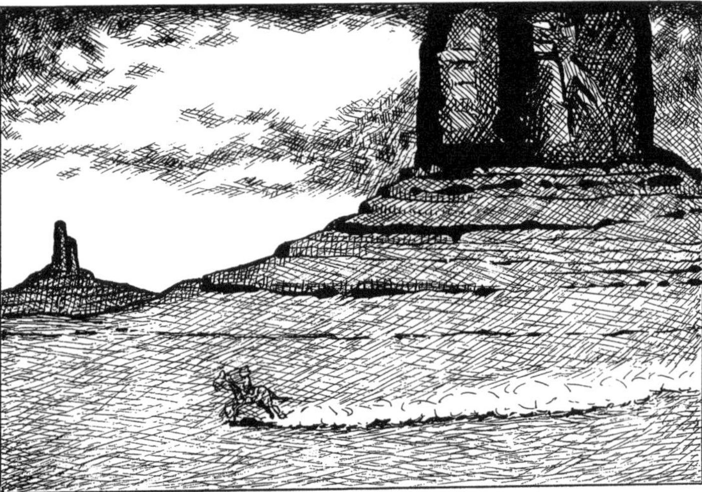

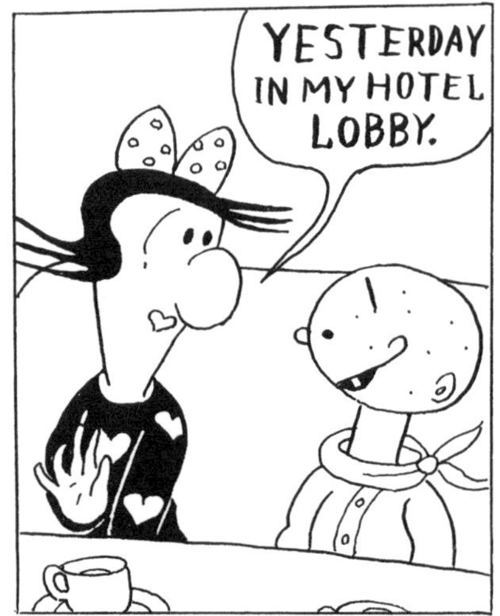

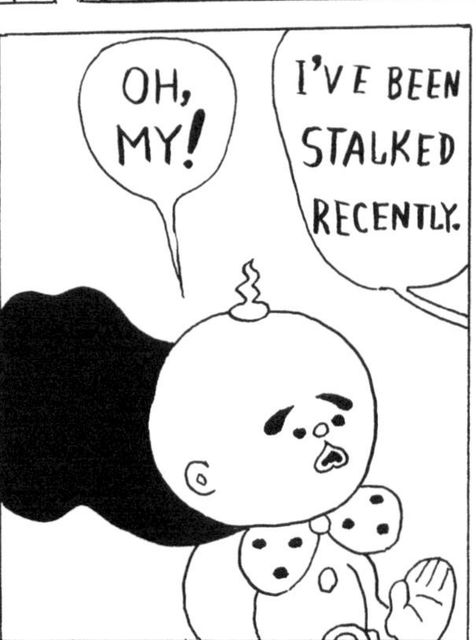

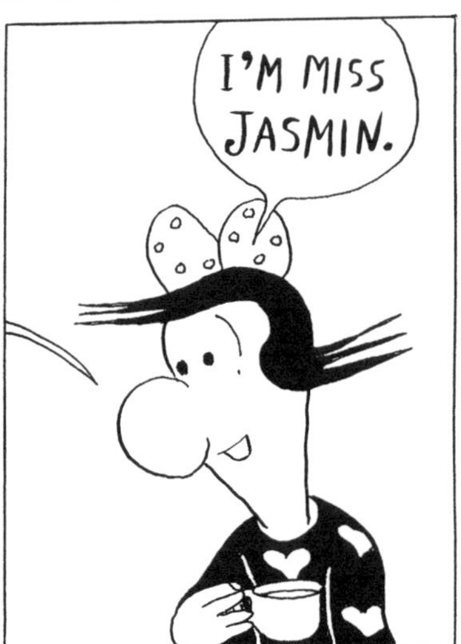

*GANMODOKI- A POPULAR JAPANESE FRIED BEAN CURD CAKE WITH VEGETABLES AND OTHER INGREDIENTS IN IT.

GANMODOKI

BY SUGIURA SHIGERU

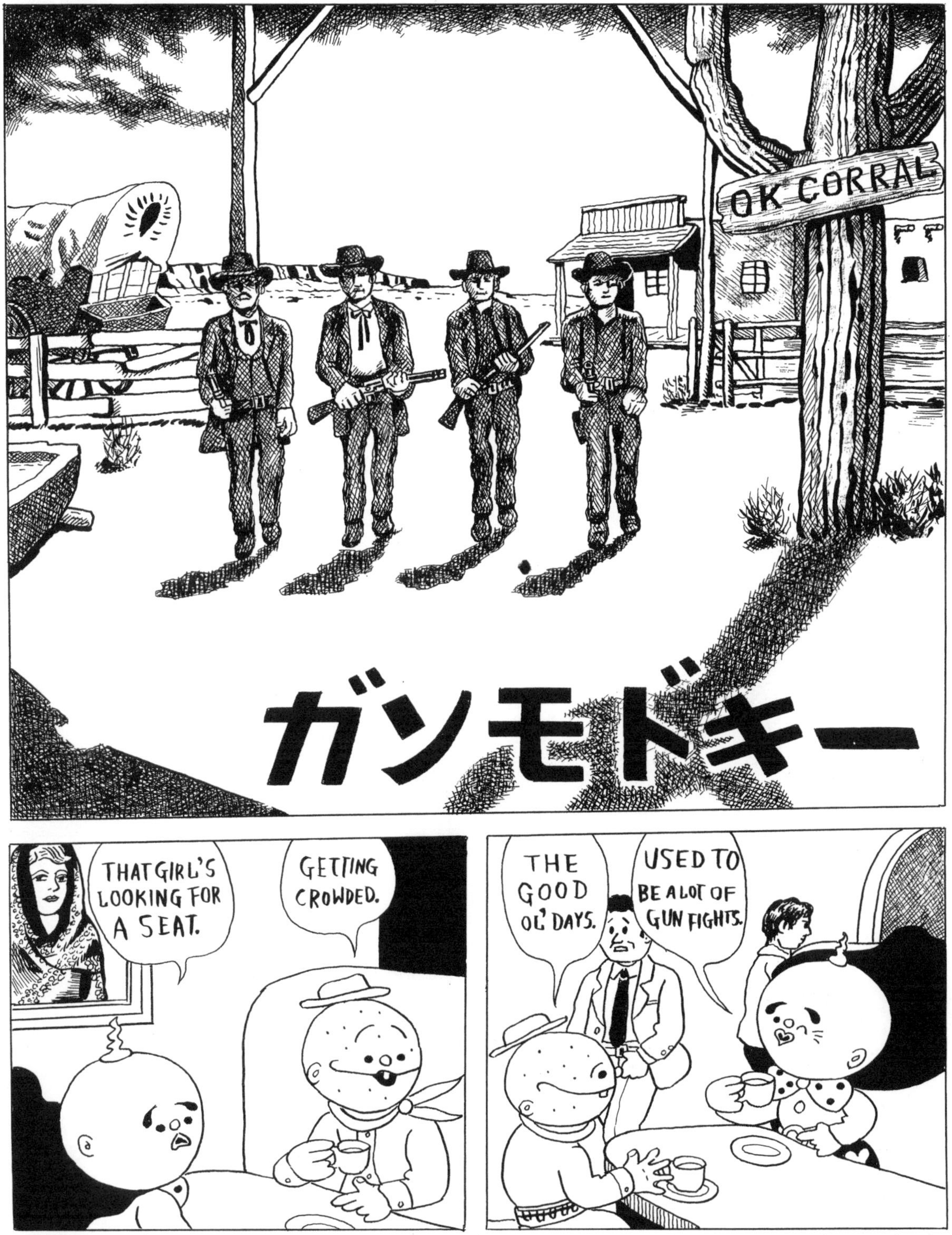

OK CORRAL

ガンモドキー

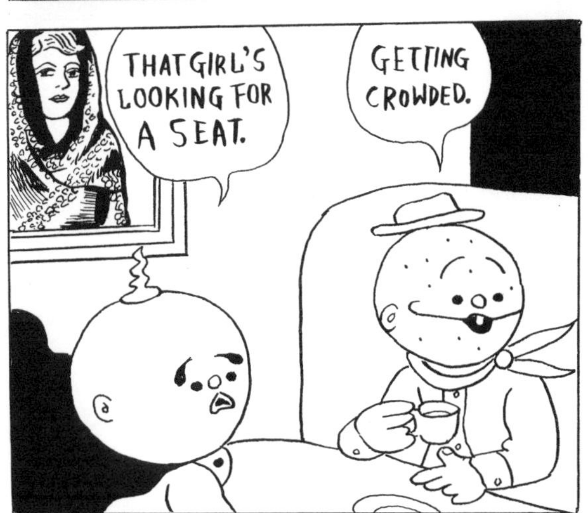

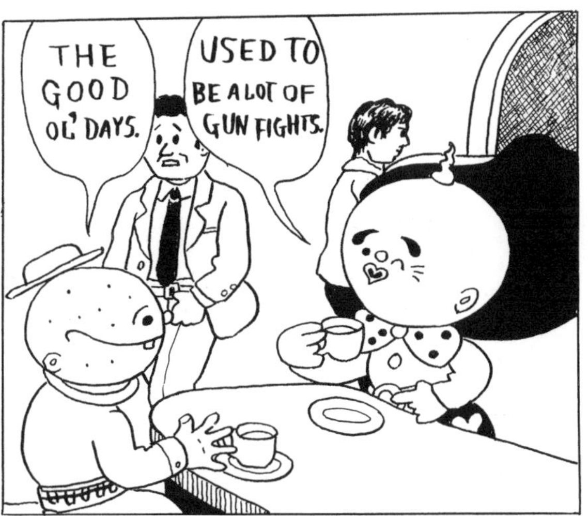

ENGLISH TRANSLATION FROM THE JAPANESE BY ONO KOSEI. LETTERING BY DAVID HEATLEY.

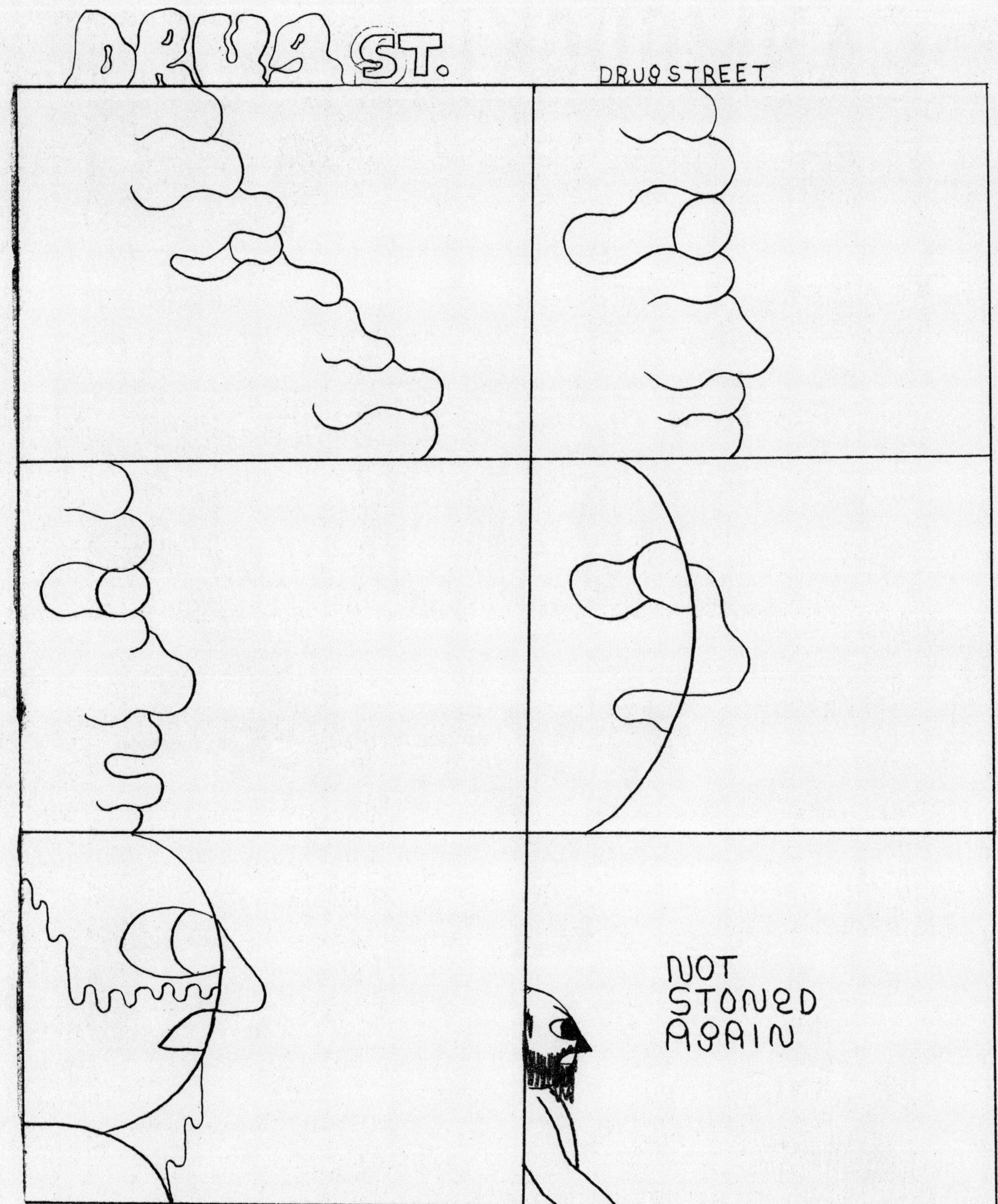
DRUG ST.
DRUG STREET
NOT
STONED
AGAIN

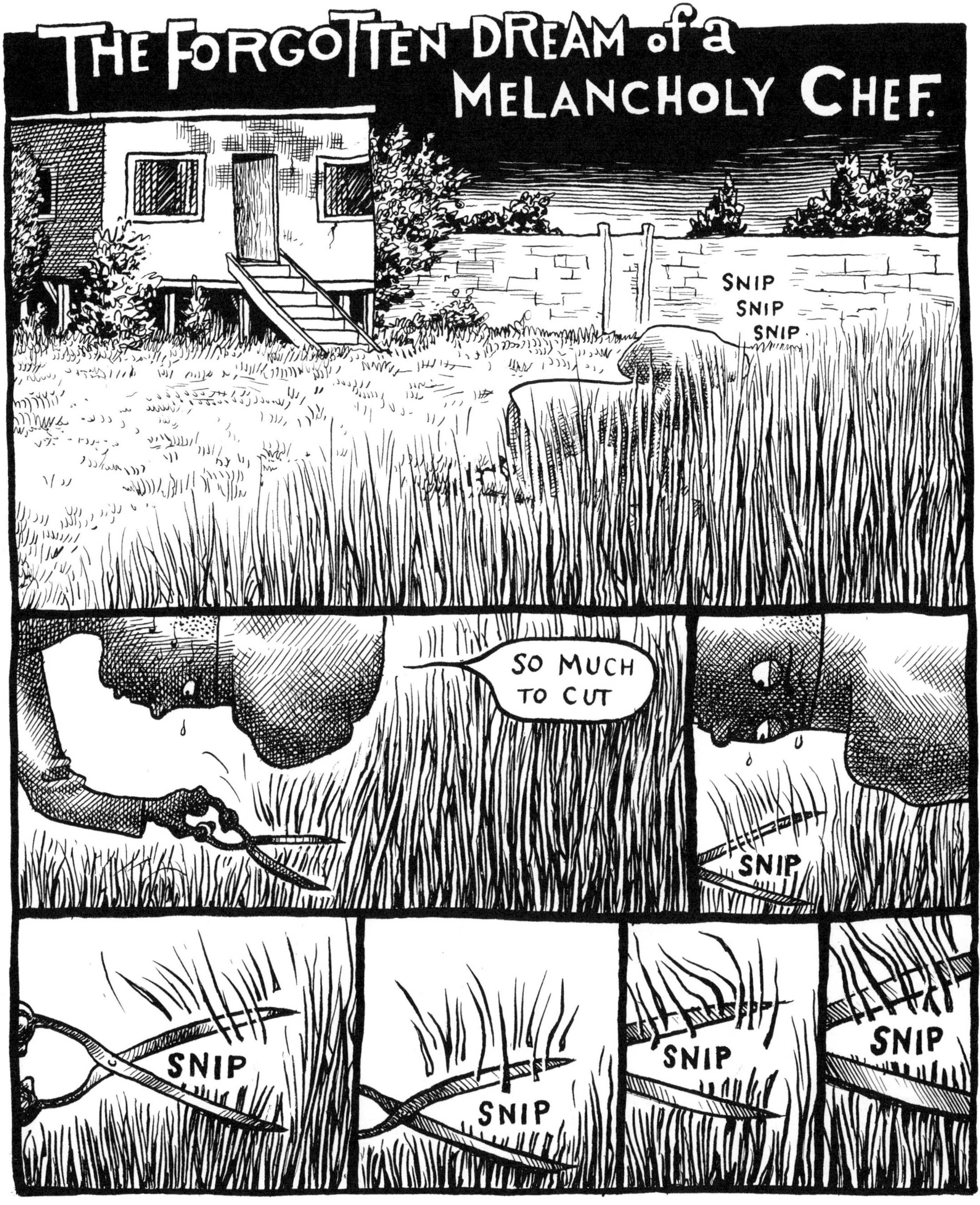
THE FORGOTTEN DREAM of a MELANCHOLY CHEF.
SNIP
SNIP
SNIP
SO MUCH TO CUT
SNIP
SNIP
SNIP
SNIP
SNIP

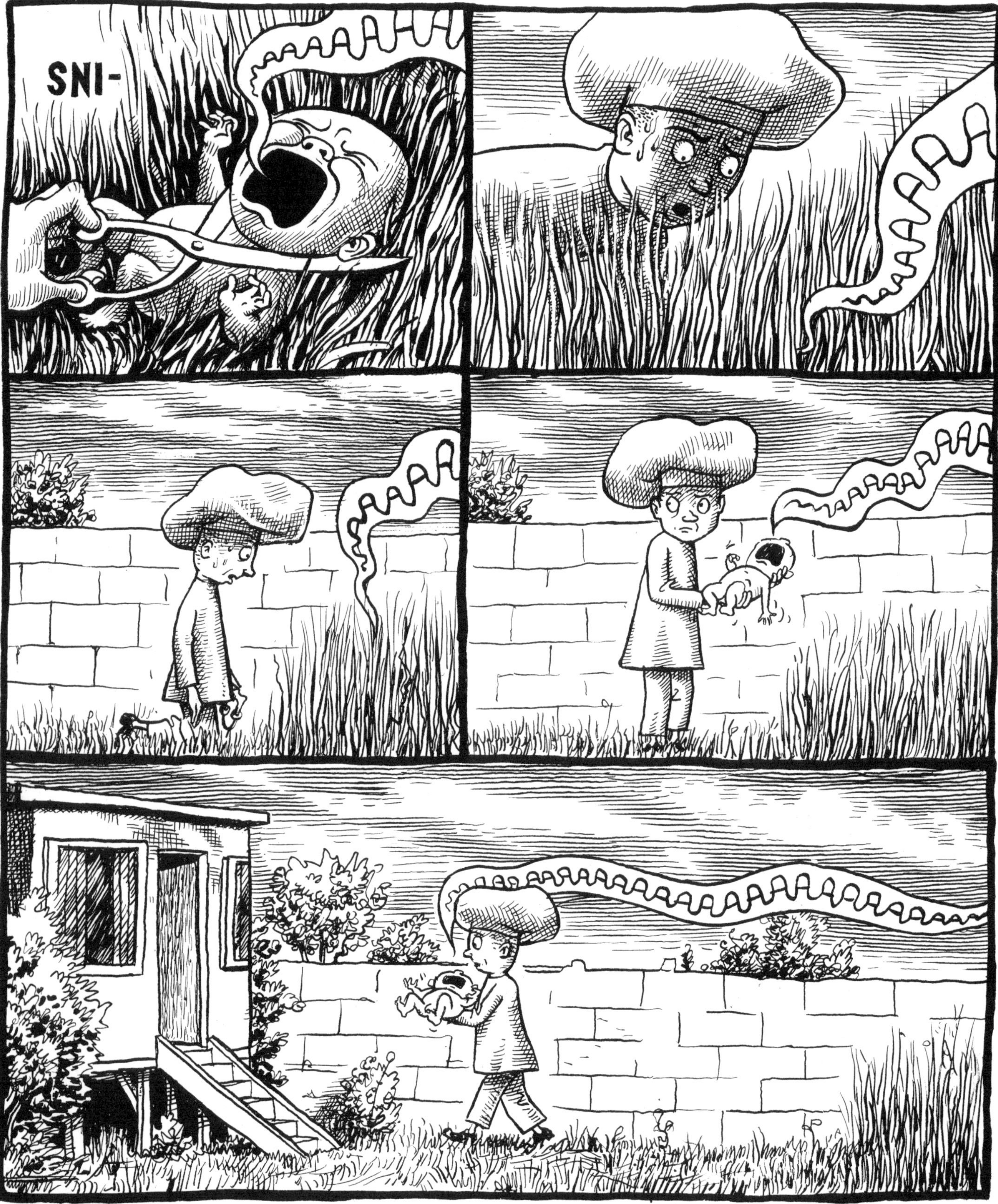
SNI-
AAAAAAHH
AAAAAAAA
AAAAAA
AAAAAAAAAAA
AAAAAAAAAAAAAAAAAAAAAAAAAAA

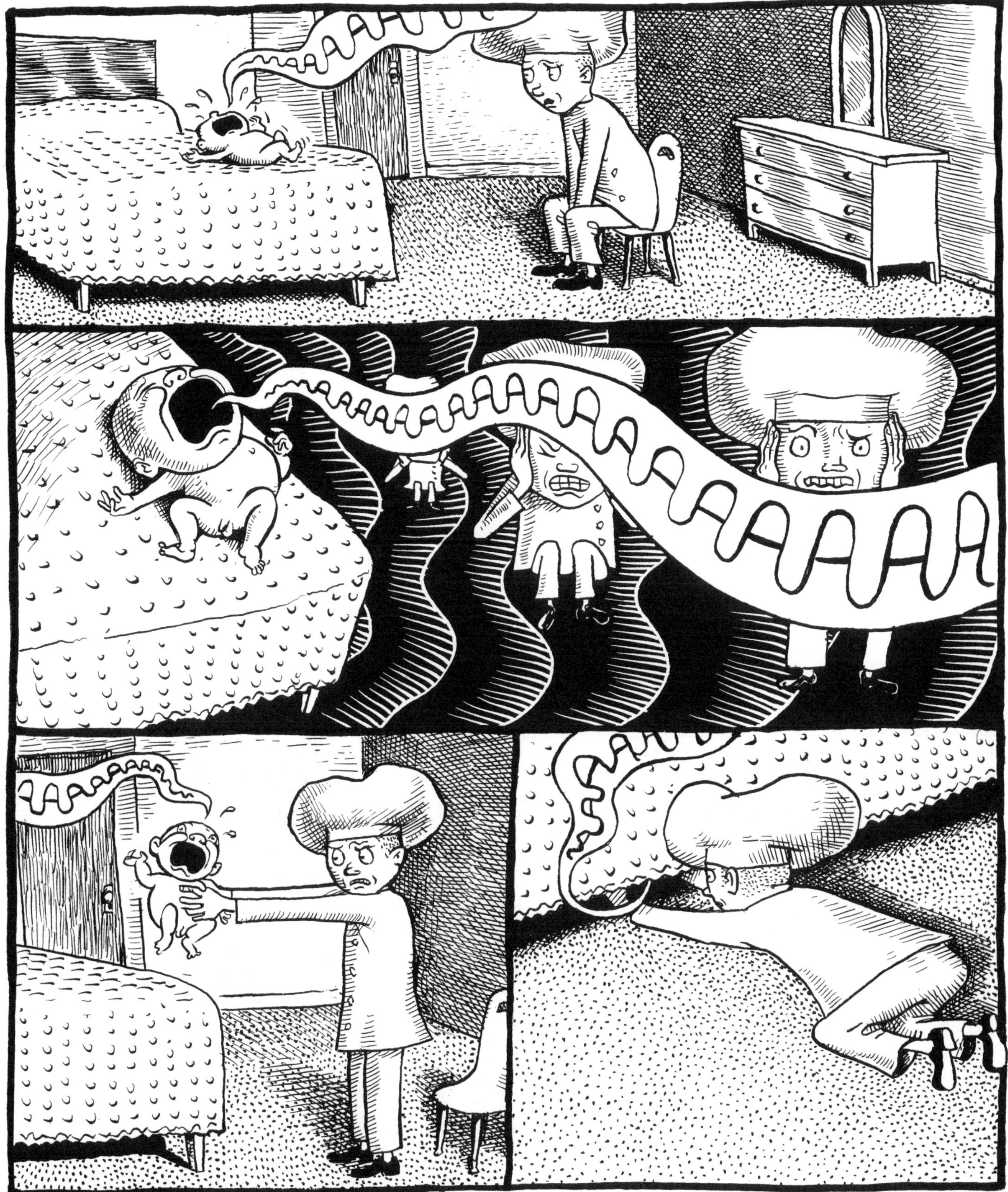

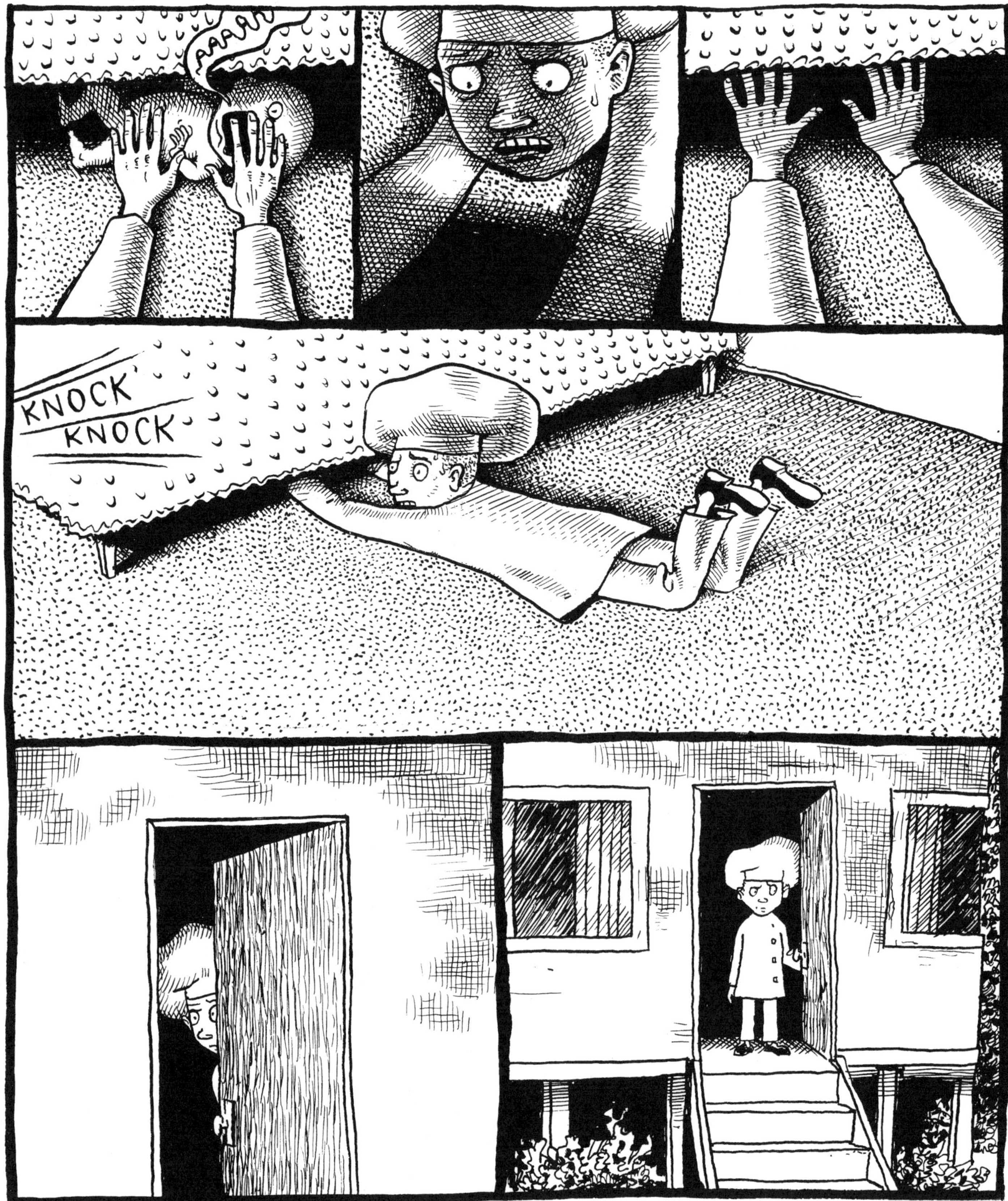
AAARR
KNOCK
KNOCK

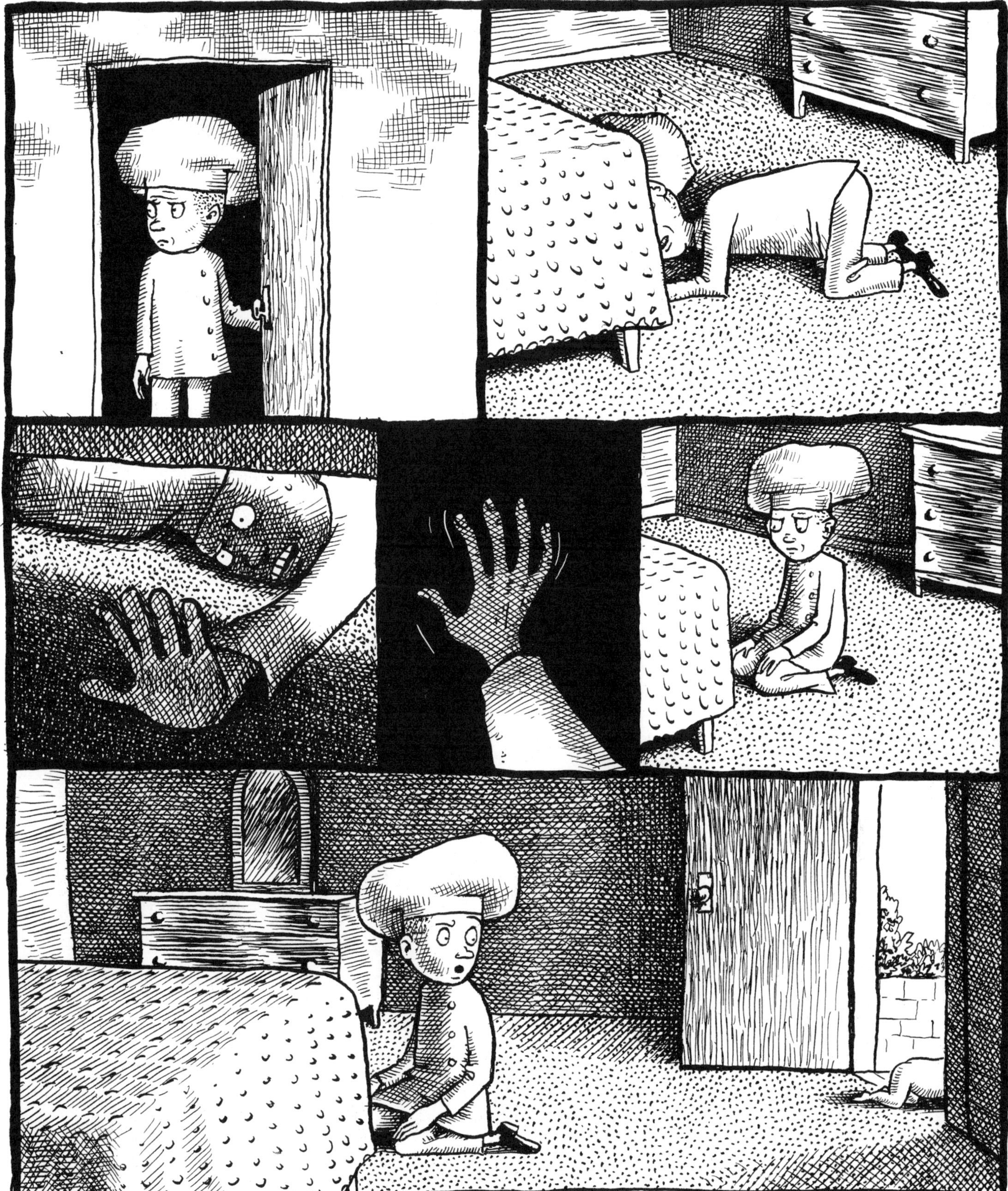

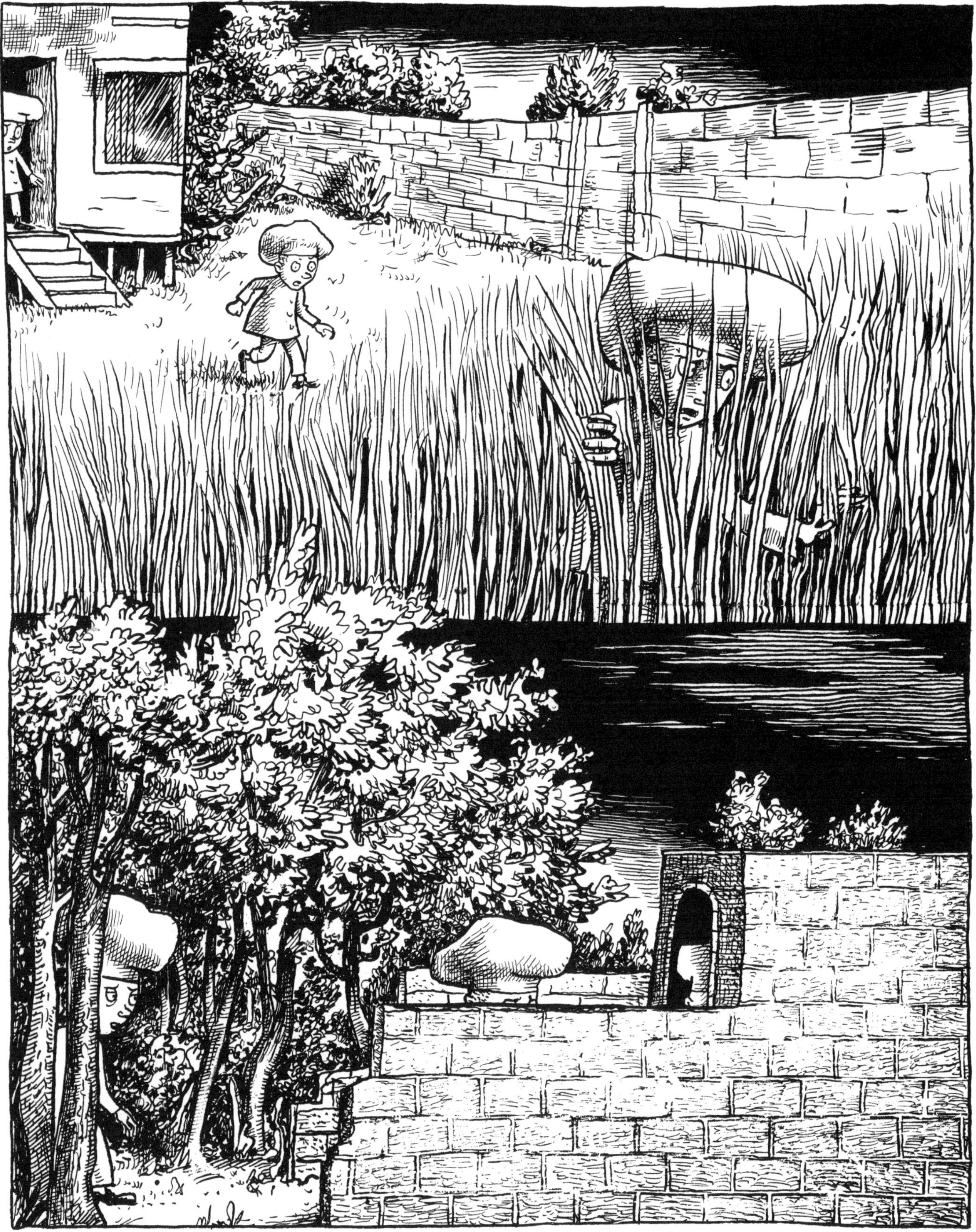

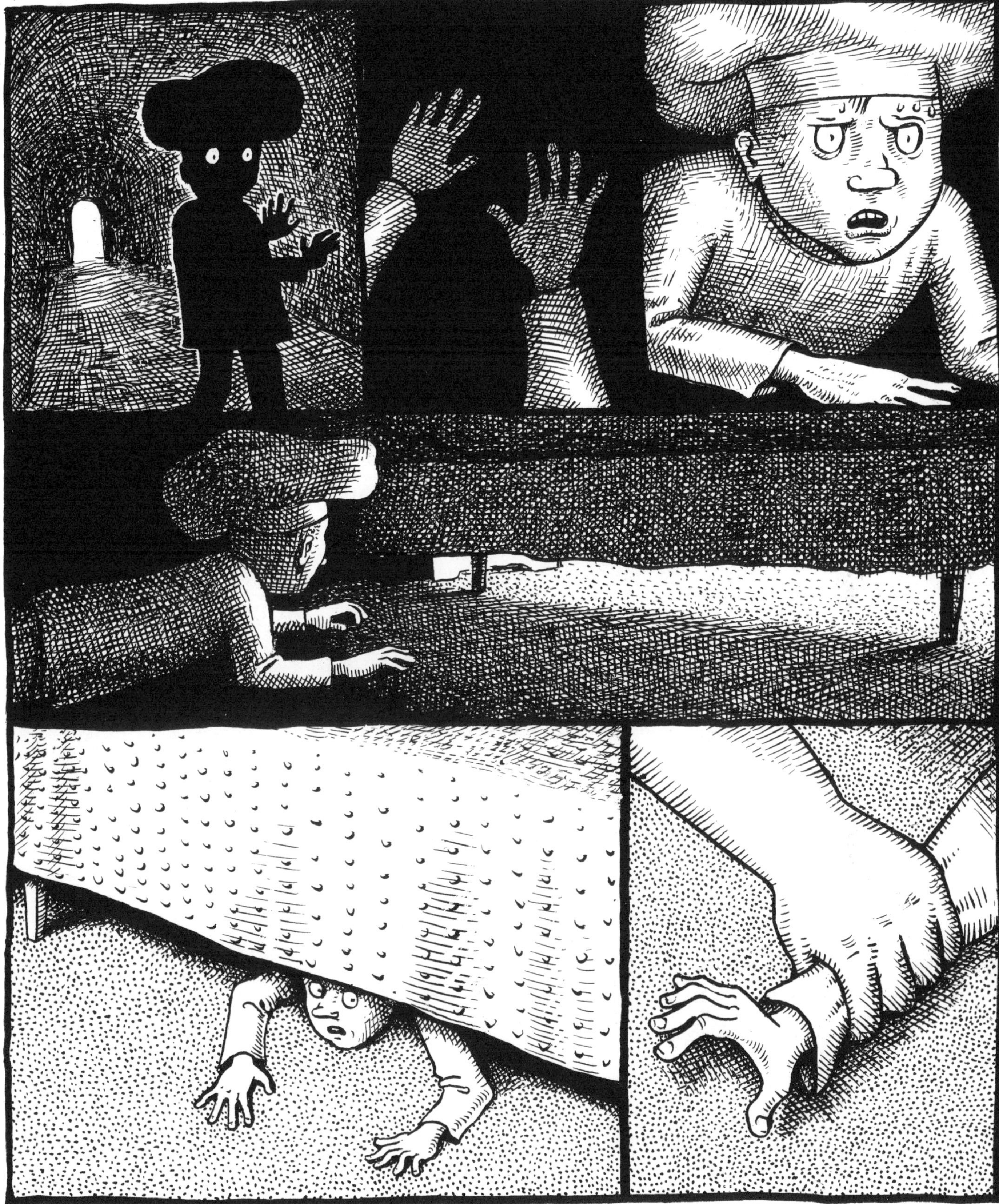

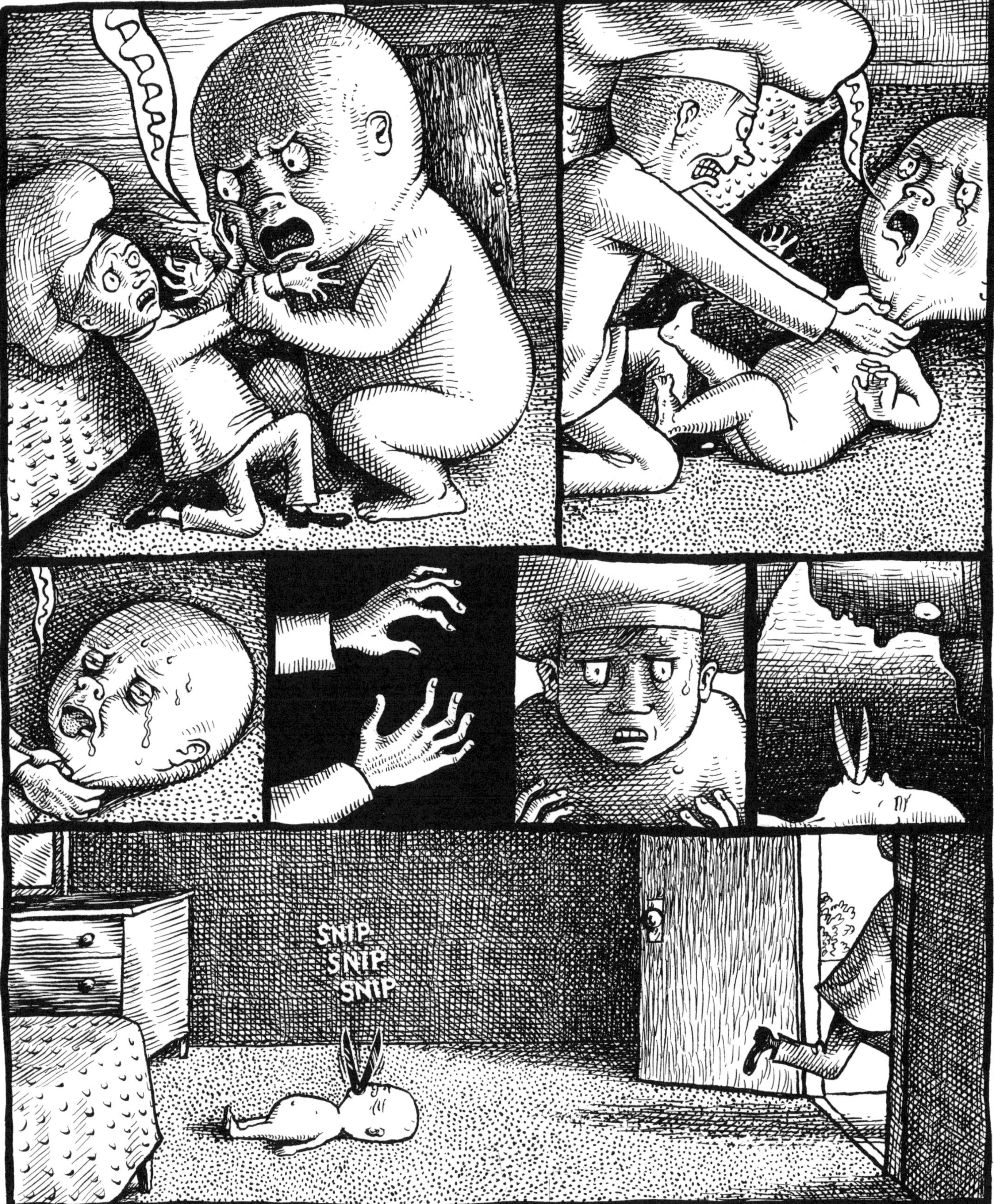
SNIP
SNIP
SNIP

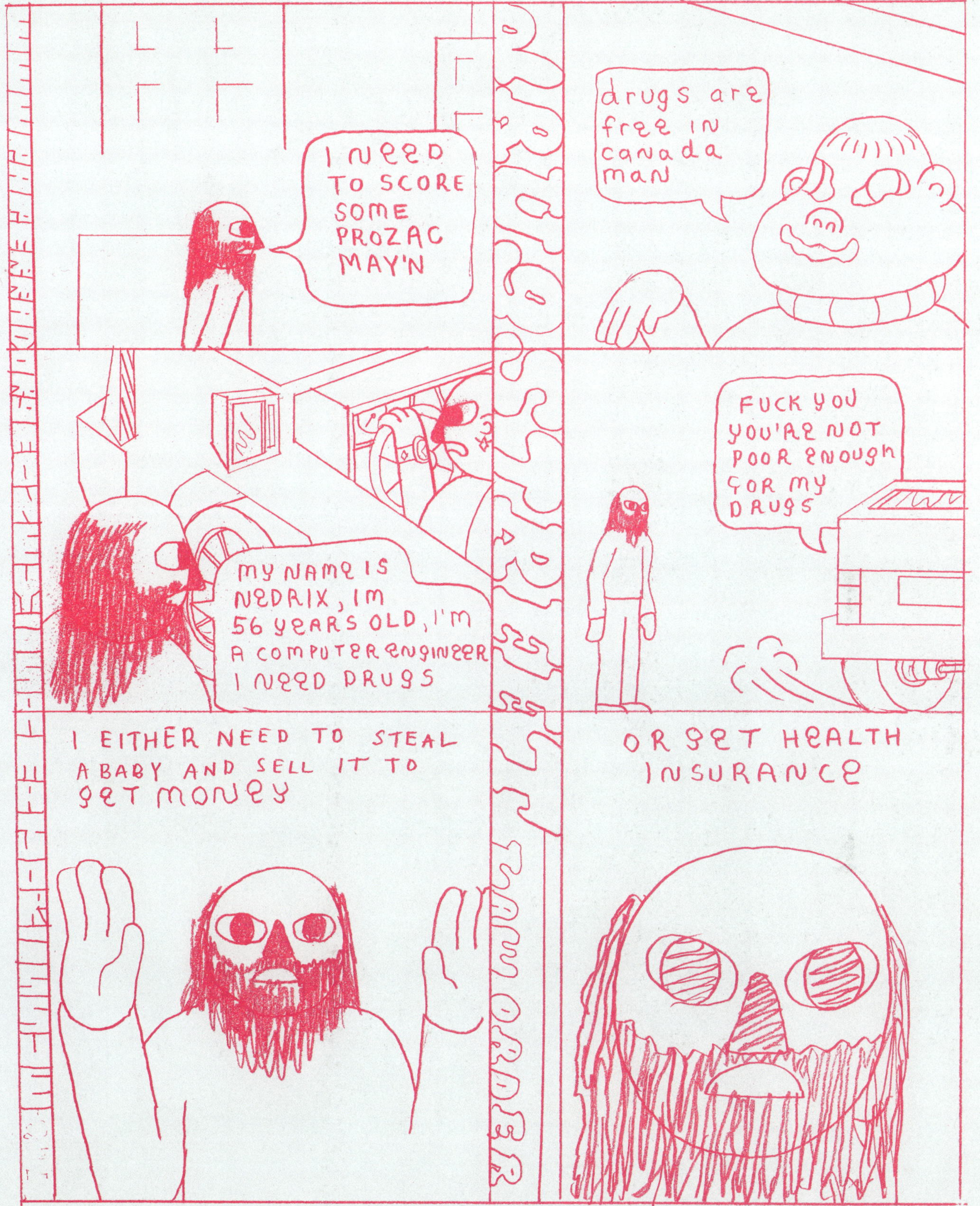
ARTURO STARRETT
I NEED TO SCORE SOME PROZAC MAY'N
drugs are free in canada man
MY NAME IS NEDRIX, IM 56 YEARS OLD, I'M A COMPUTER ENGINEER I NEED DRUGS
FUCK YOU YOU'RE NOT POOR ENOUGH FOR MY DRUGS
I EITHER NEED TO STEAL A BABY AND SELL IT TO GET MONEY
OR GET HEALTH INSURANCE
LAW ORDER

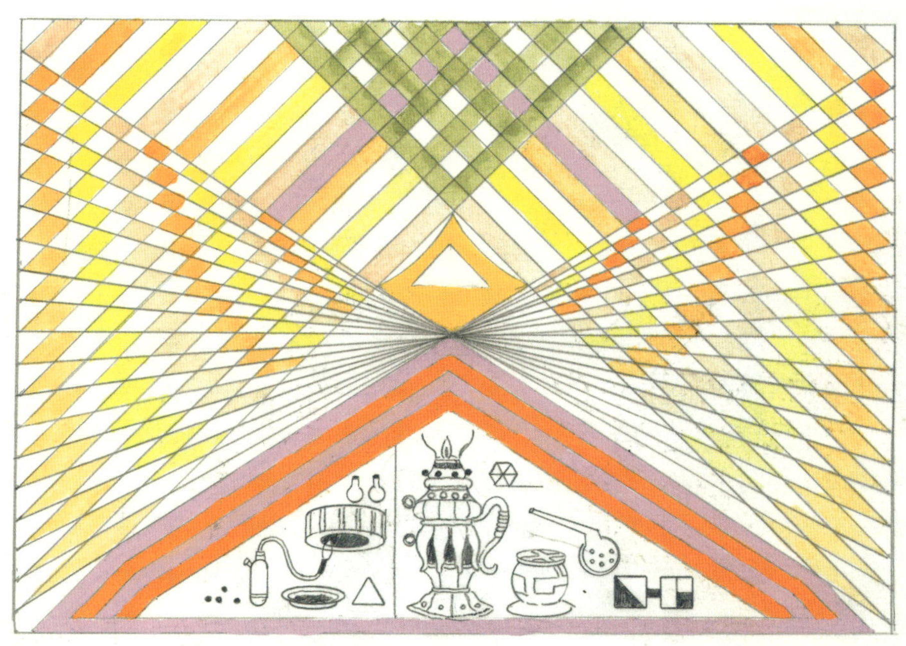

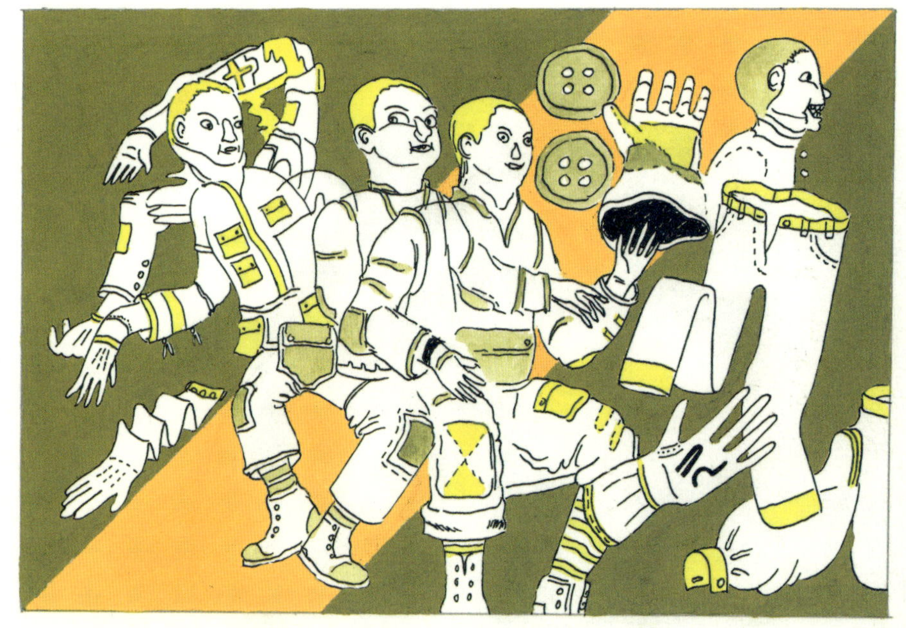

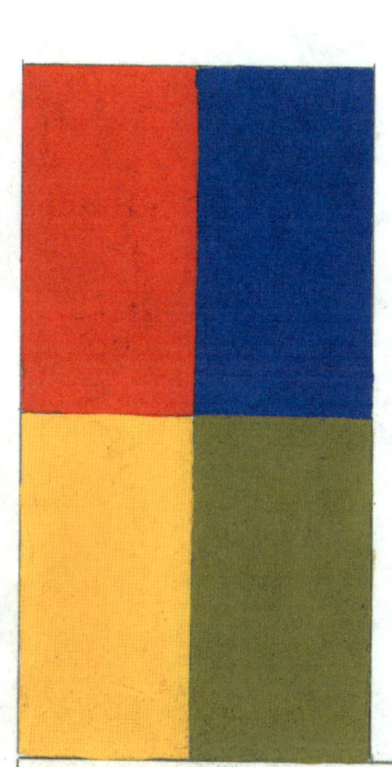

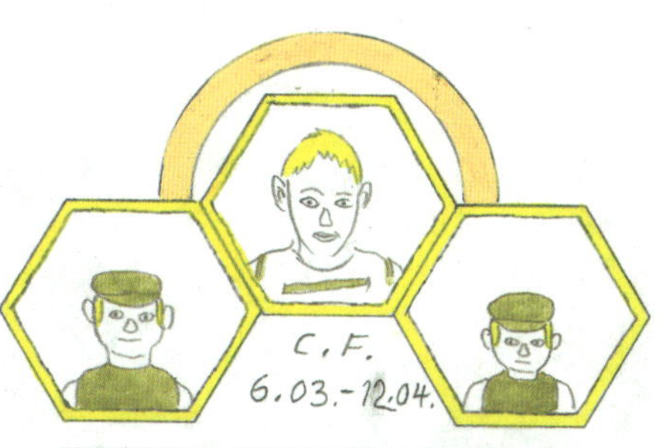

BLOND ATCHEN & THE BUMBLE BOYS
:INCLUDING WEAPONS
"IN THE SECOND'S LAIR"

DEDICATED TO JOHN GILMORE
MAIL TO: PAPER RADIO
BOX 913 PROVIDENCE R I
02901 NO NEW HOLOCAUST

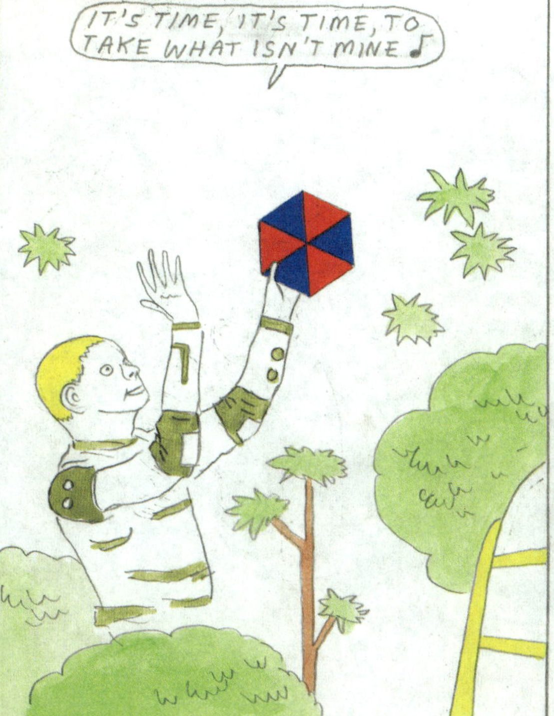

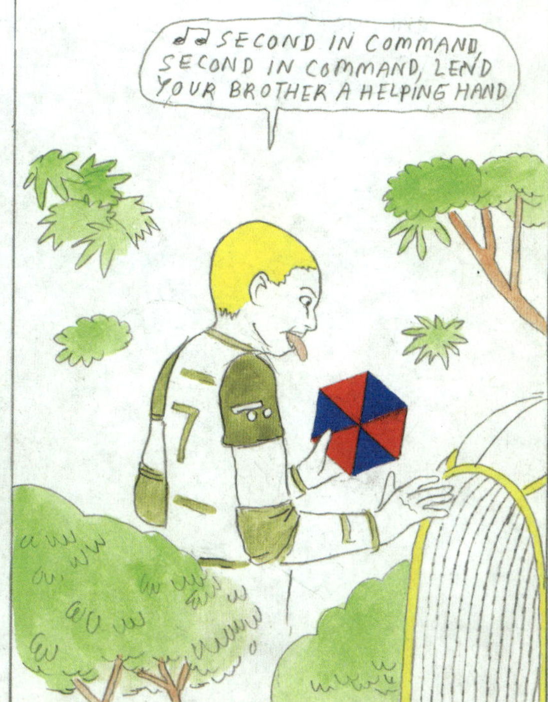

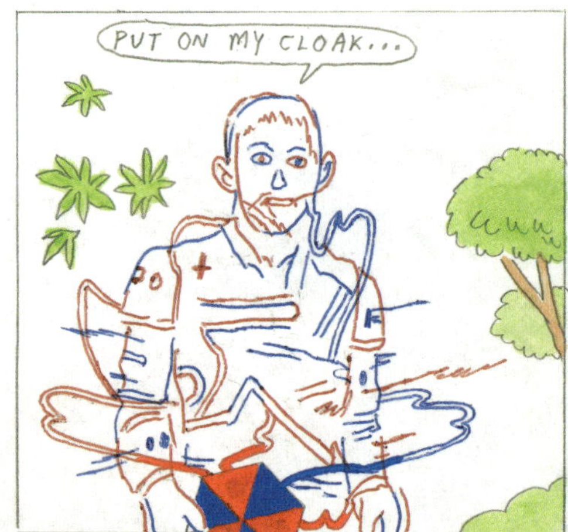
PUT ON MY CLOAK...

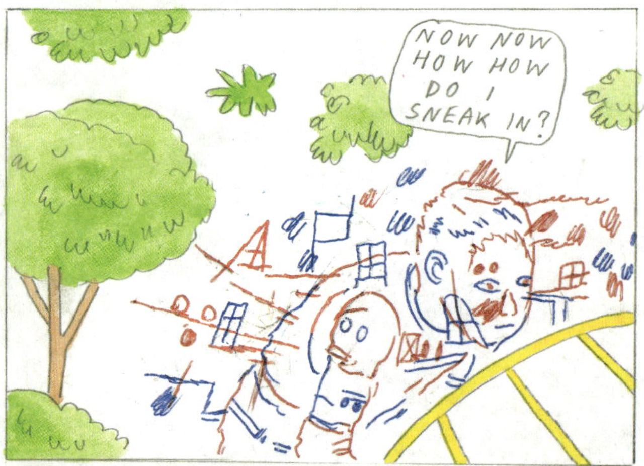
NOW NOW HOW HOW DO I SNEAK IN?

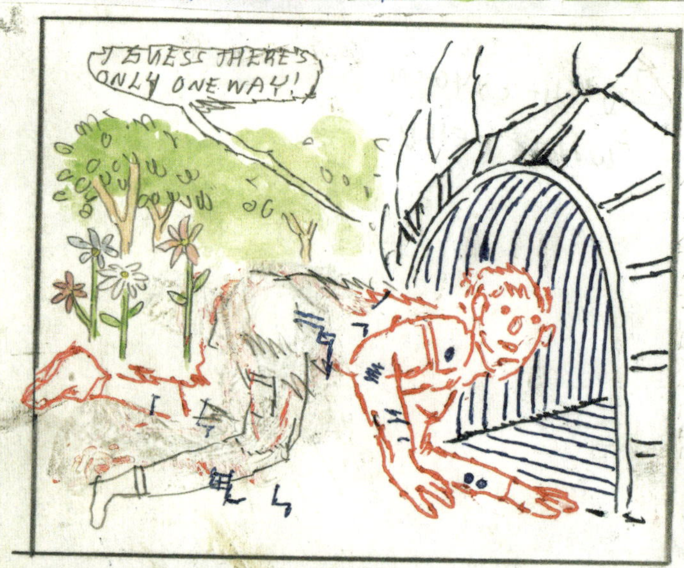
I GUESS THERE'S ONLY ONE WAY!

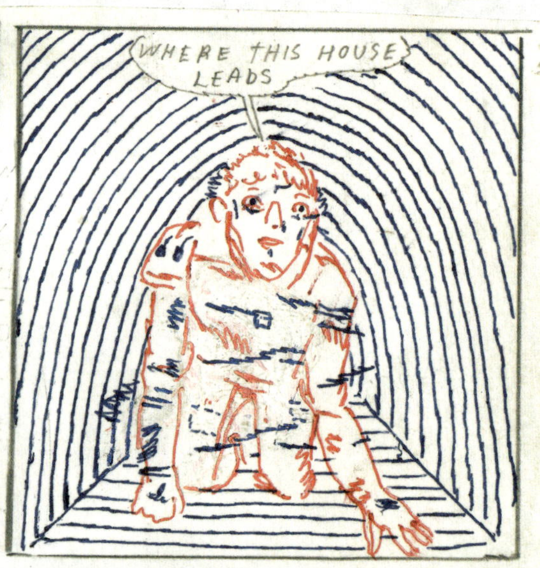
WHERE THIS HOUSE LEADS

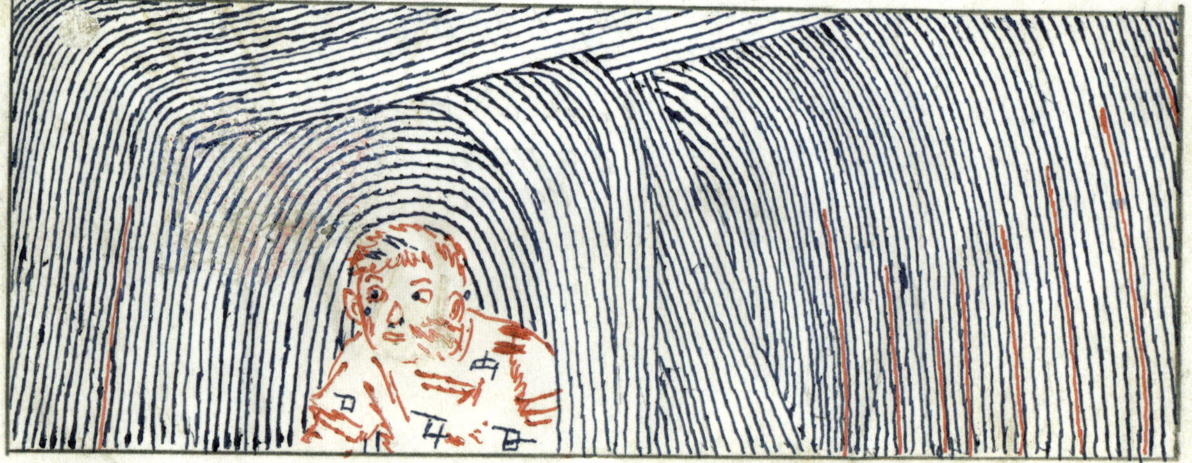

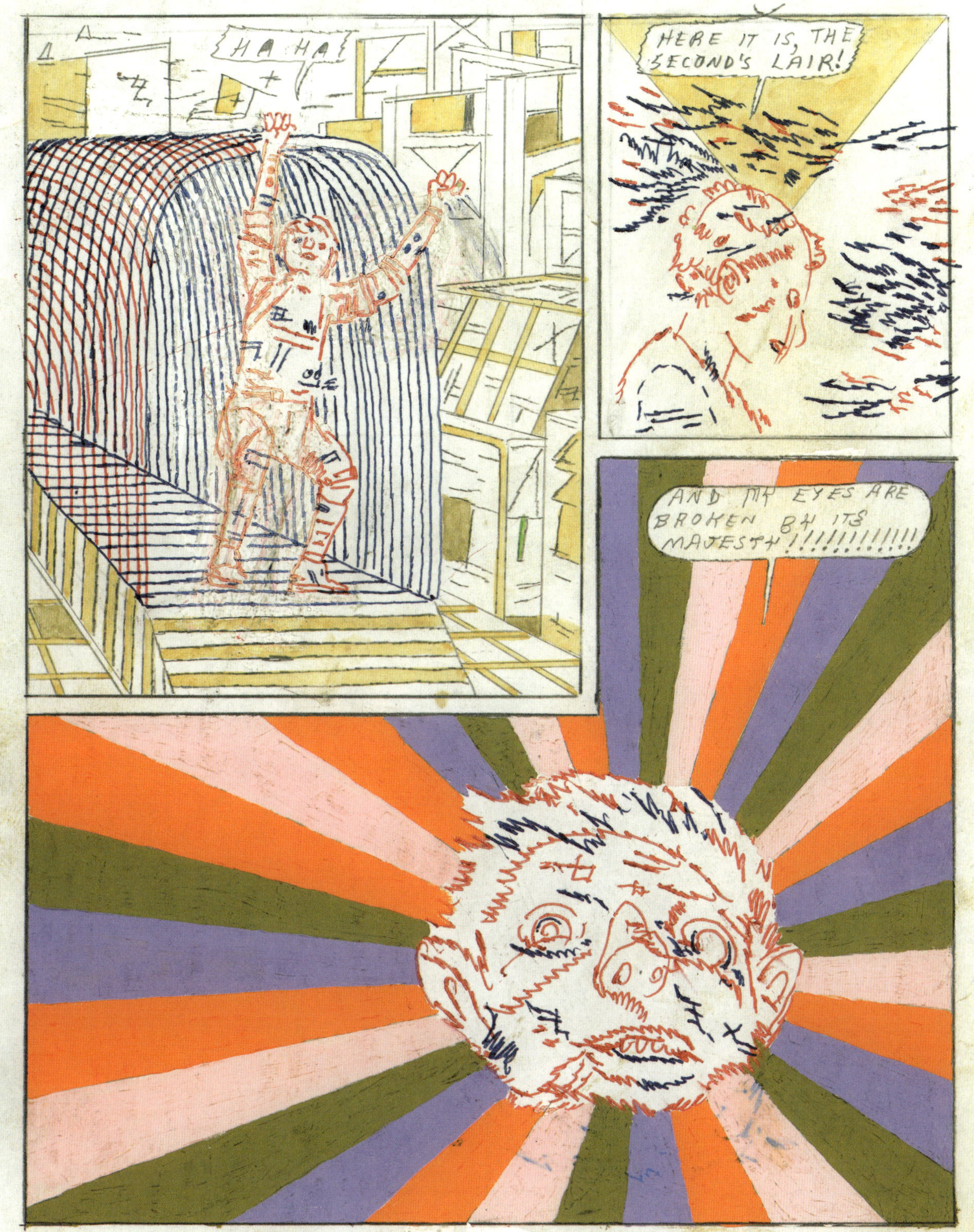
HA HA
HERE IT IS, THE SECOND'S LAIR!
AND MY EYES ARE BROKEN BY ITS MAJESTY!!!!!!!!!!!

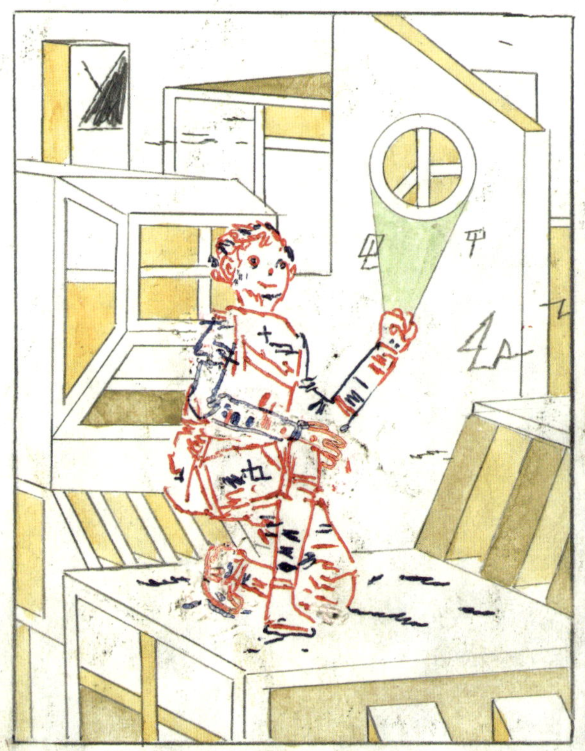

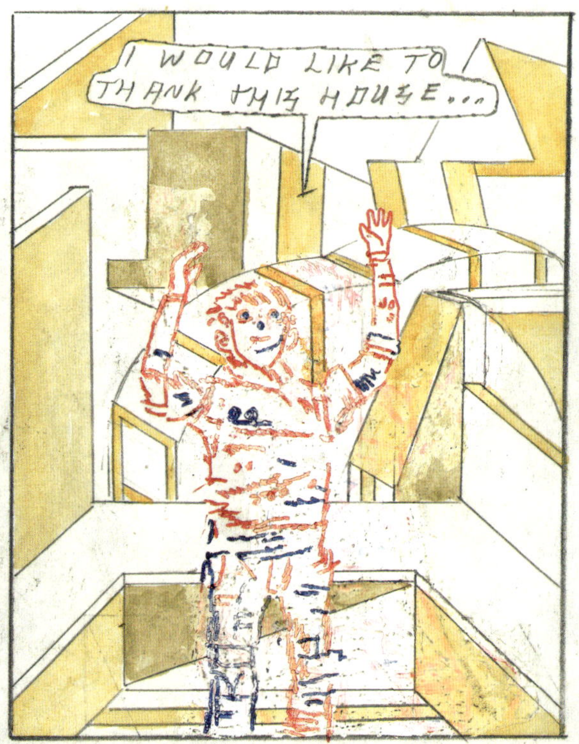
I WOULD LIKE TO THANK THIS HOUSE...

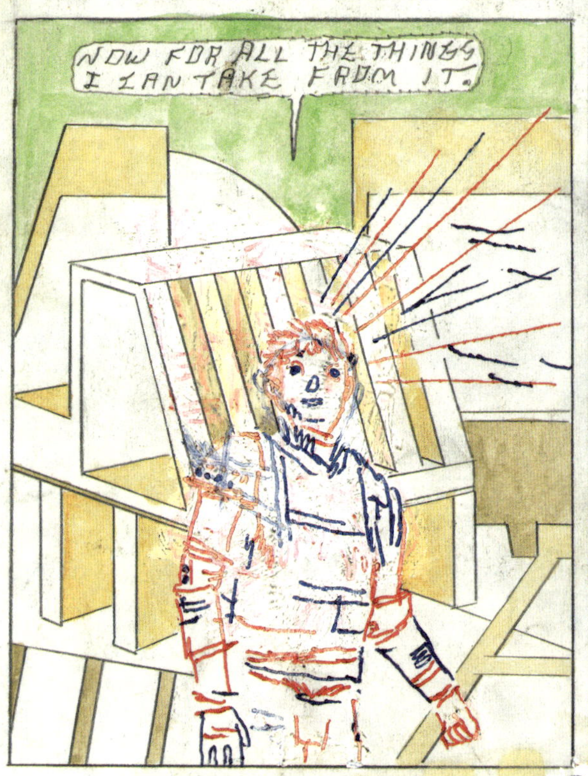
NOW FOR ALL THE THINGS I CAN TAKE FROM IT.

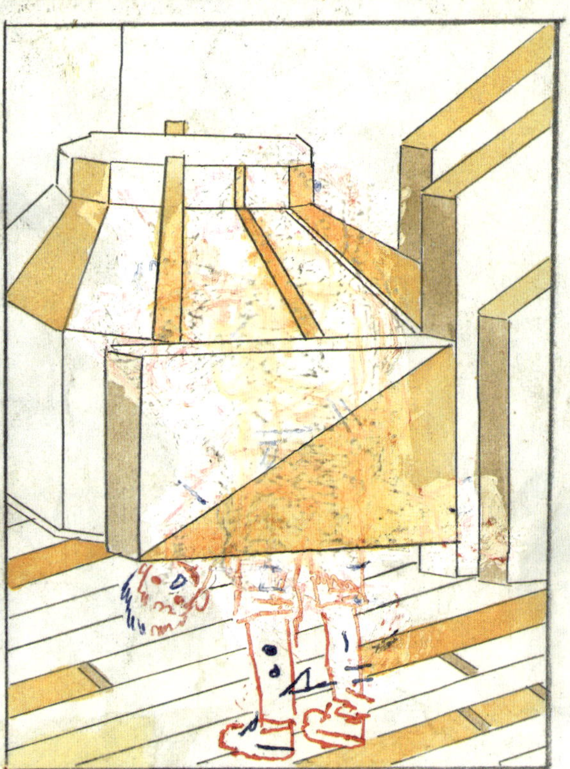

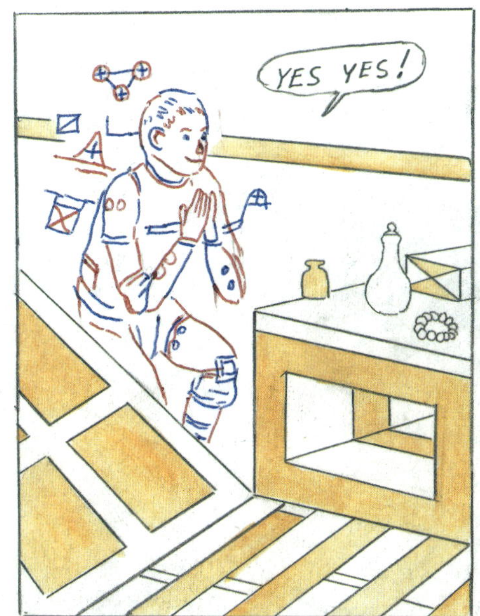
YES YES!

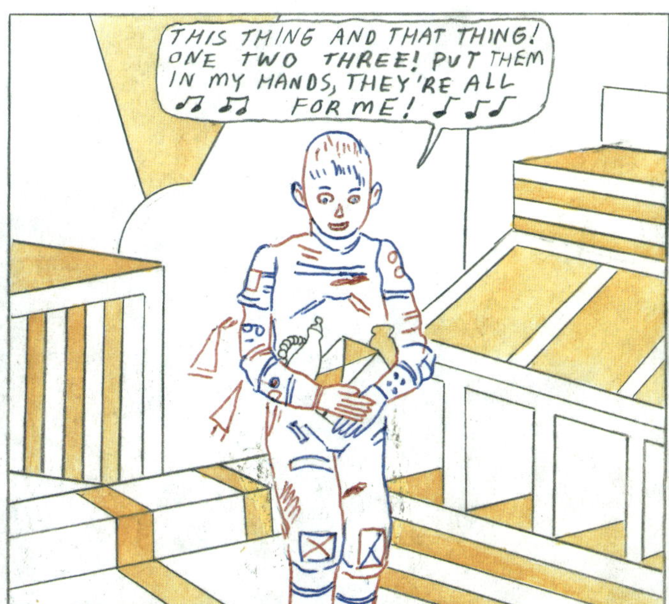
THIS THING AND THAT THING! ONE TWO THREE! PUT THEM IN MY HANDS, THEY'RE ALL FOR ME!

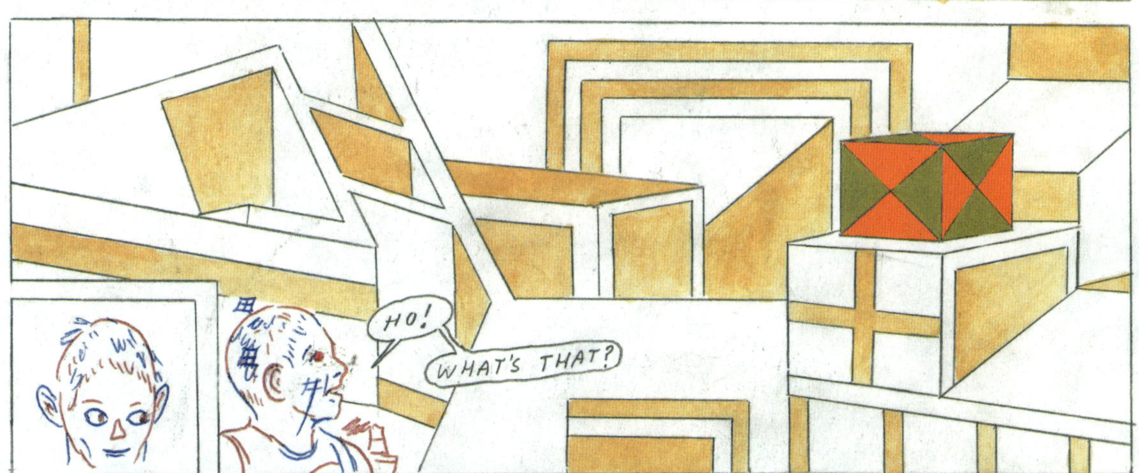
HO!
WHAT'S THAT?

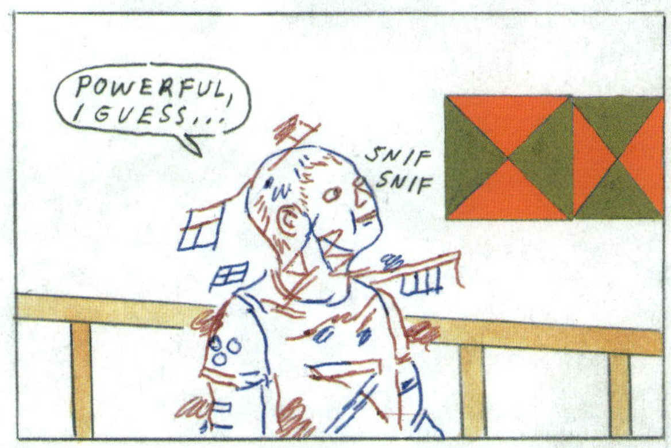
POWERFUL, I GUESS...
SNIF SNIF

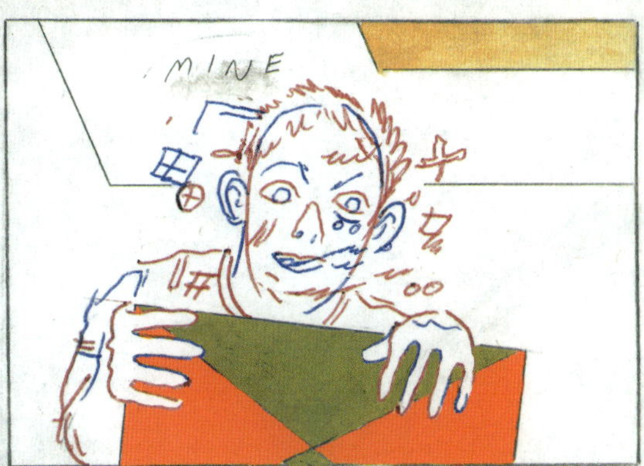
MINE

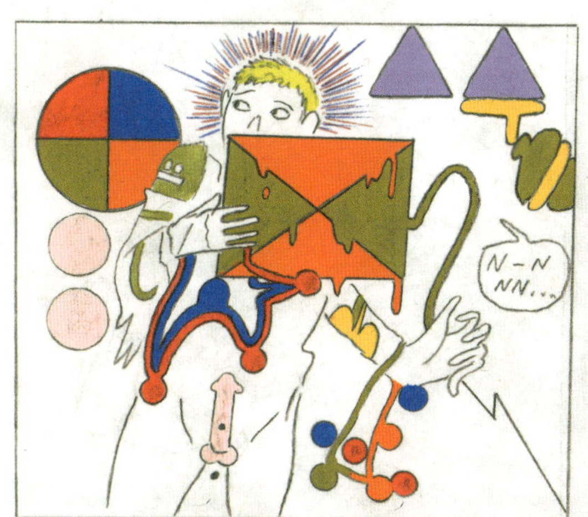
N-N
NN...

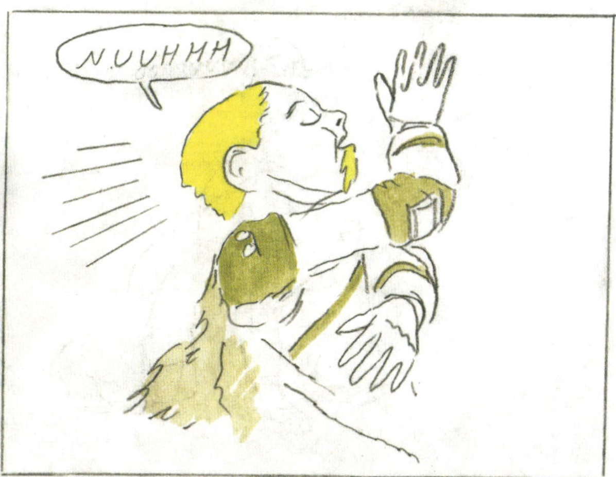
NUUHHH

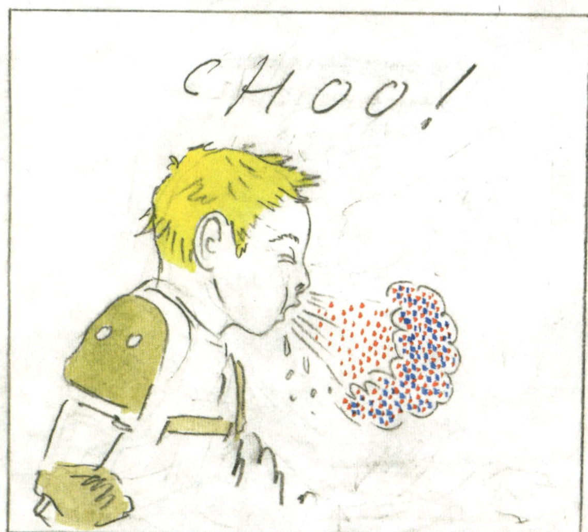
CHOO!

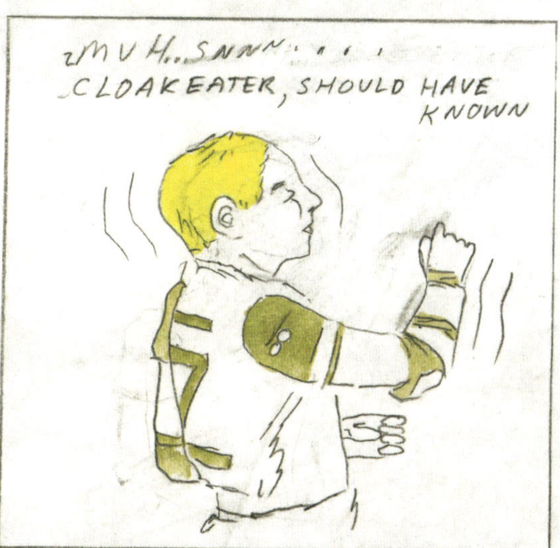
MUH...SNNN....
CLOAKEATER, SHOULD HAVE KNOWN

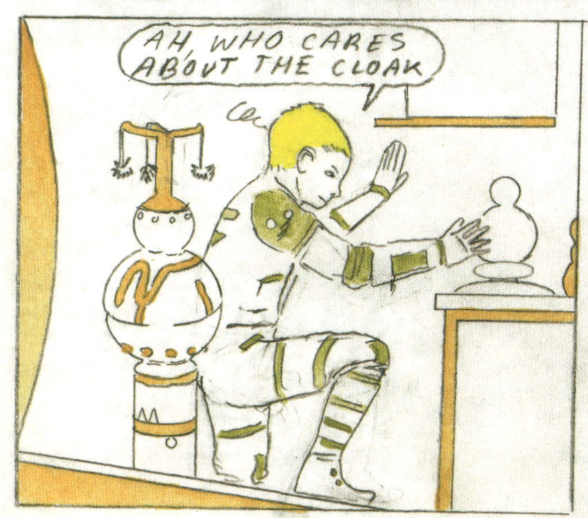
AH, WHO CARES ABOUT THE CLOAK

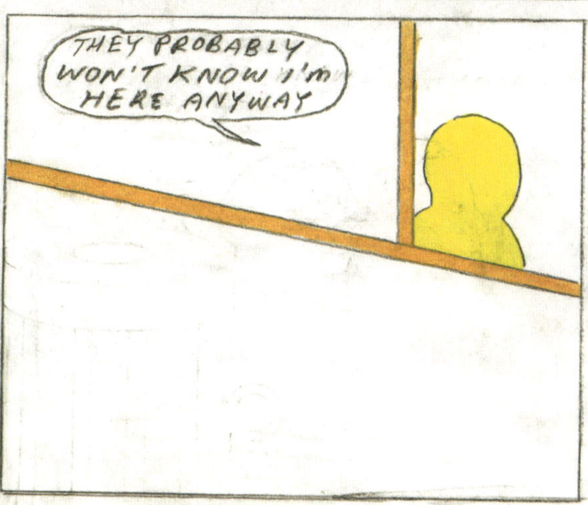
THEY PROBABLY WON'T KNOW I'M HERE ANYWAY

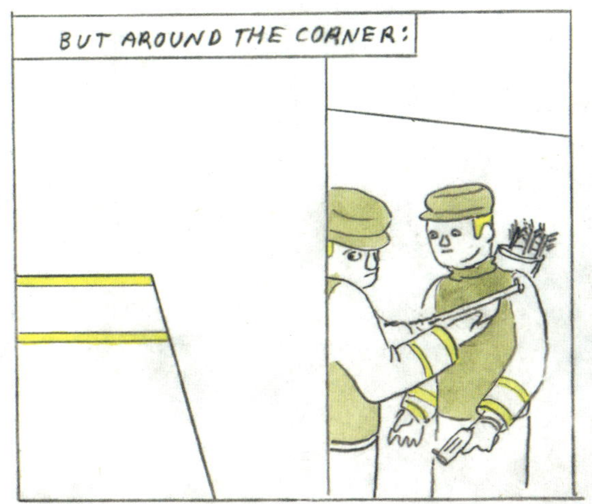
BUT AROUND THE CORNER:

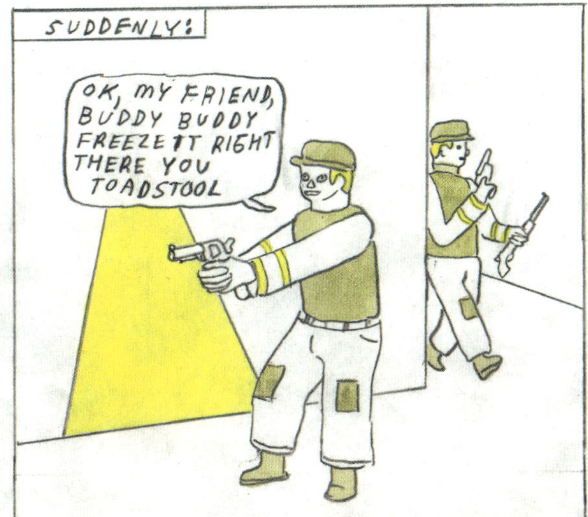
SUDDENLY:
OK, MY FRIEND, BUDDY BUDDY FREEZE IT RIGHT THERE YOU TOADSTOOL

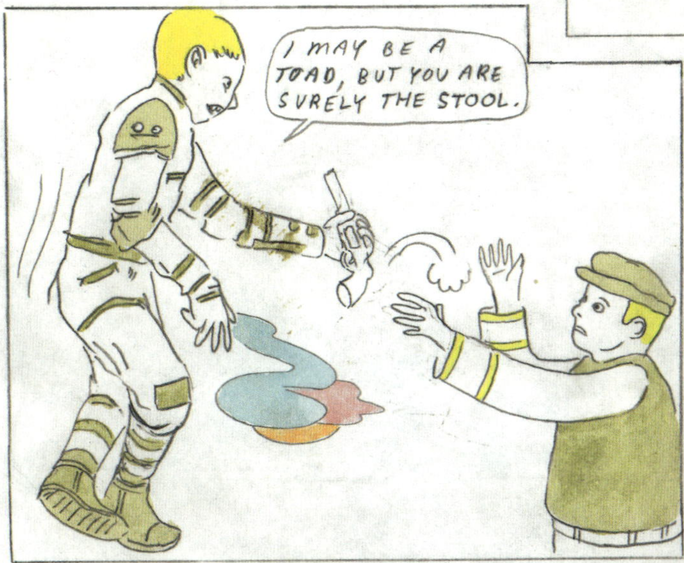
I MAY BE A TOAD, BUT YOU ARE SURELY THE STOOL.

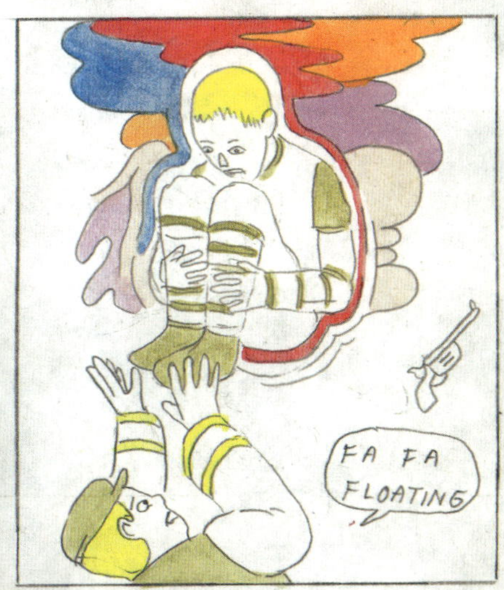
FA FA FLOATING

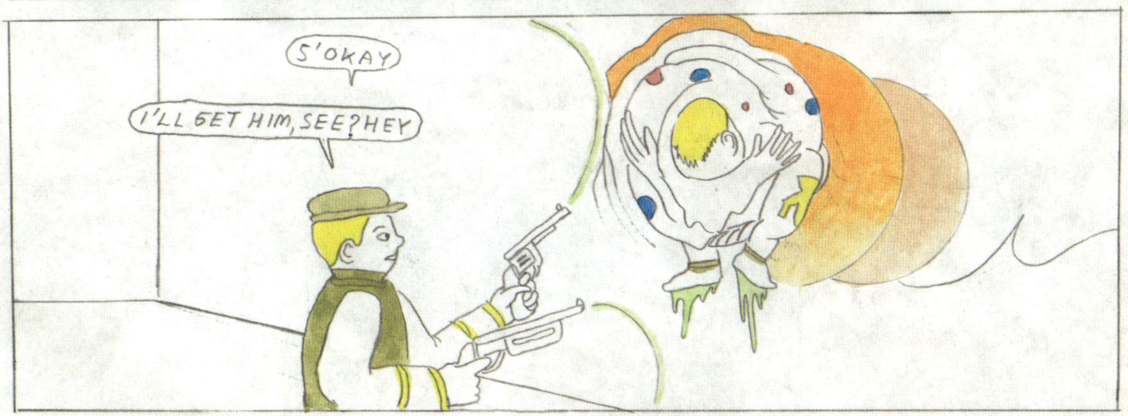
S'OKAY
I'LL GET HIM, SEE? HEY

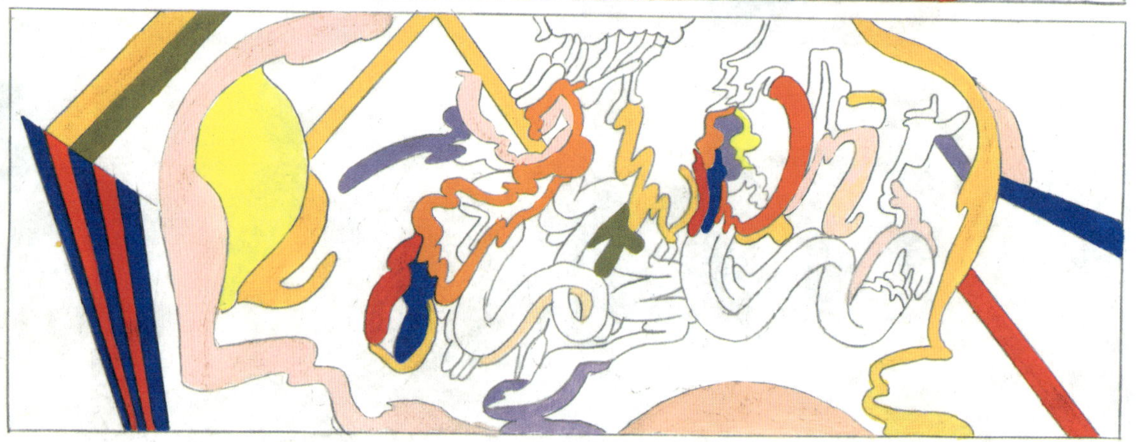

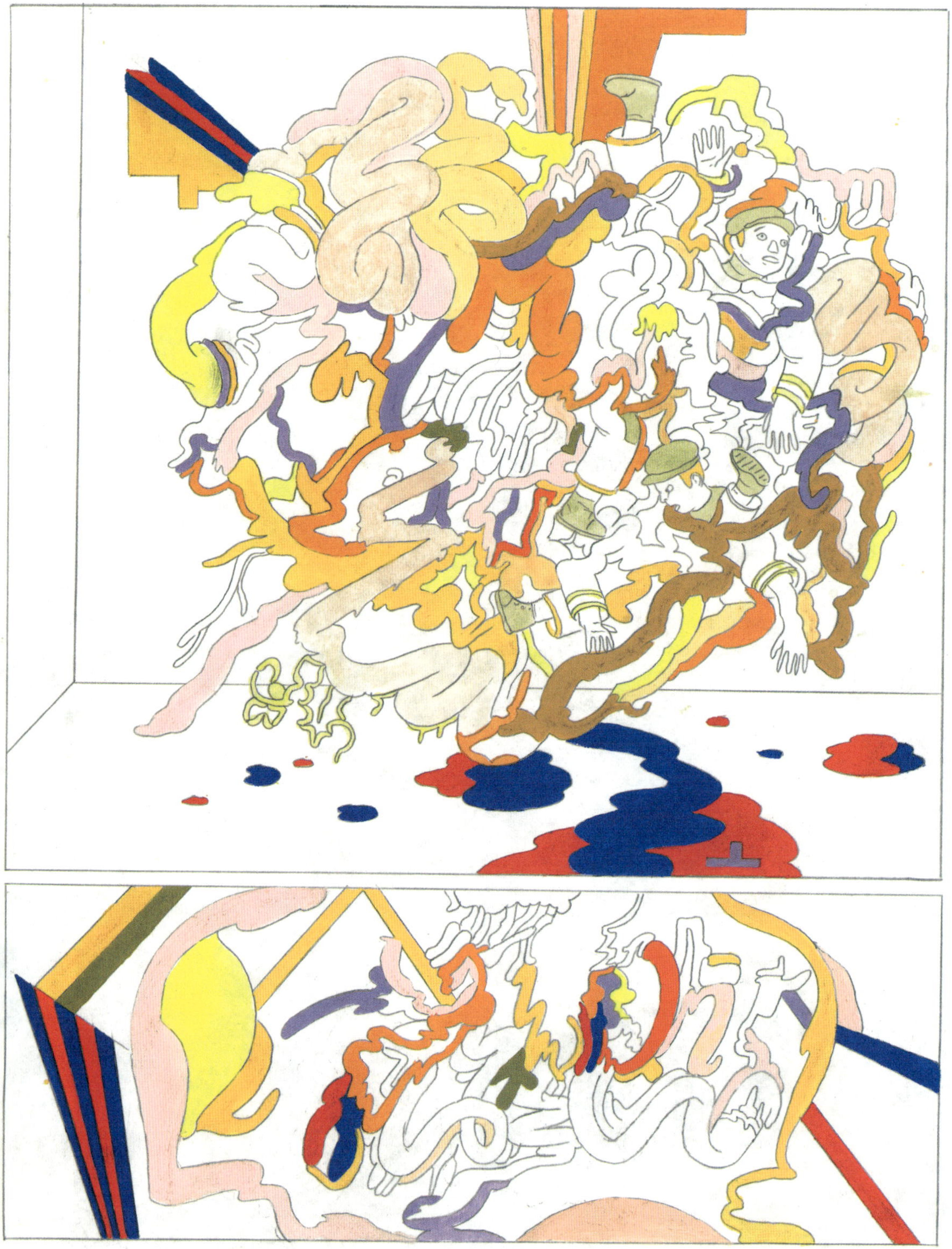

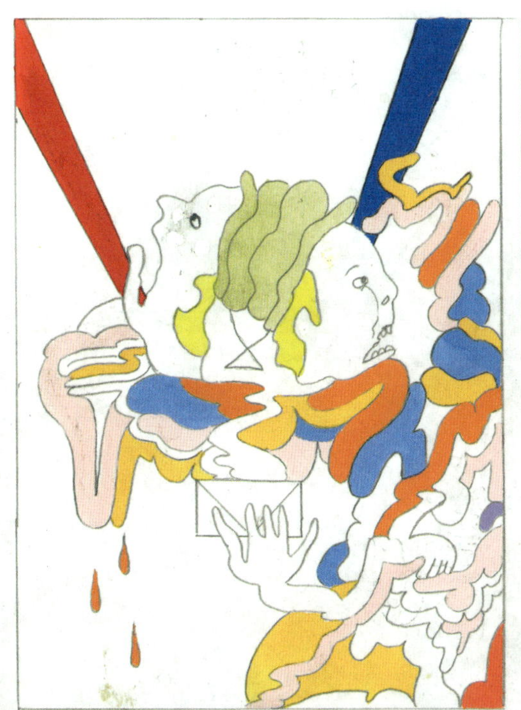

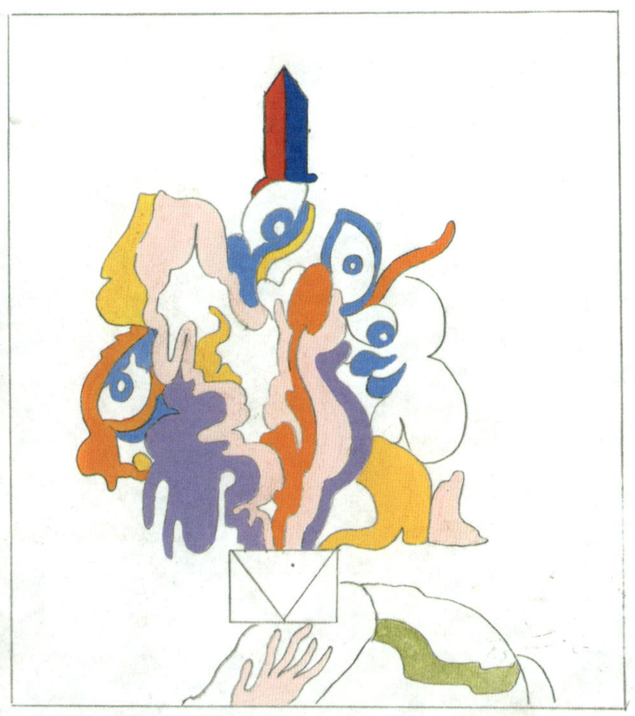

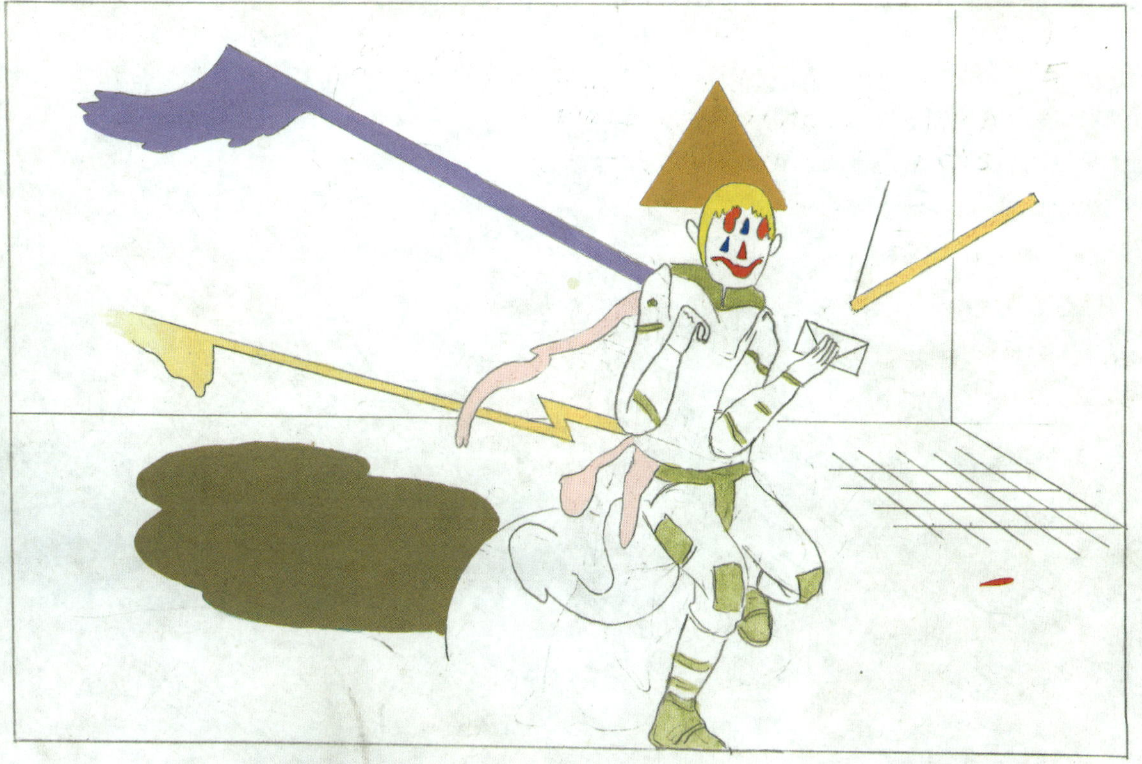

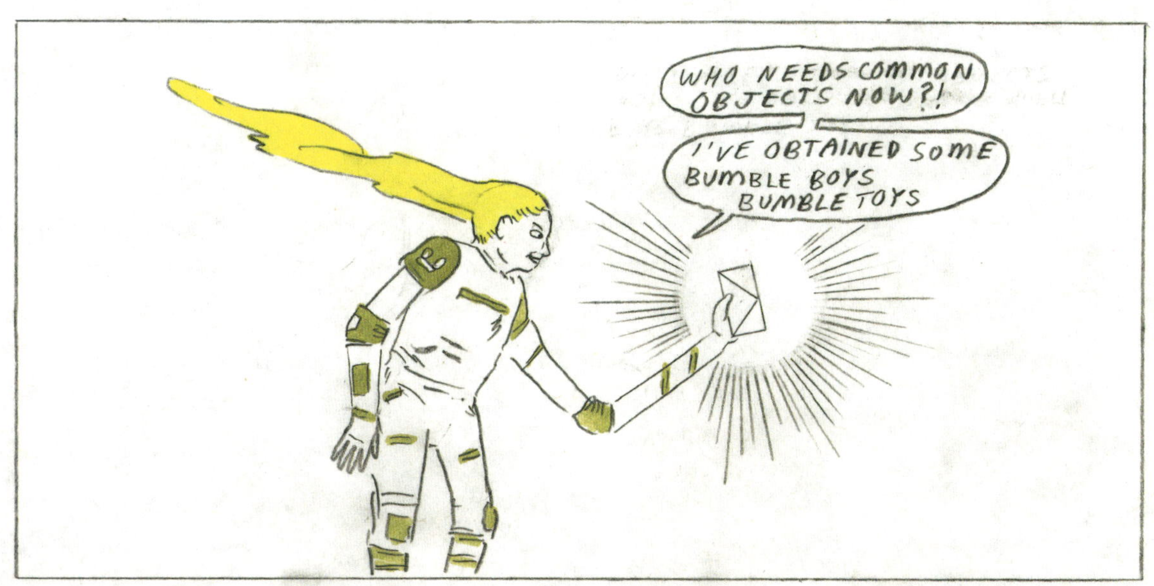
WHO NEEDS COMMON OBJECTS NOW?!
I'VE OBTAINED SOME BUMBLE BOYS BUMBLE TOYS

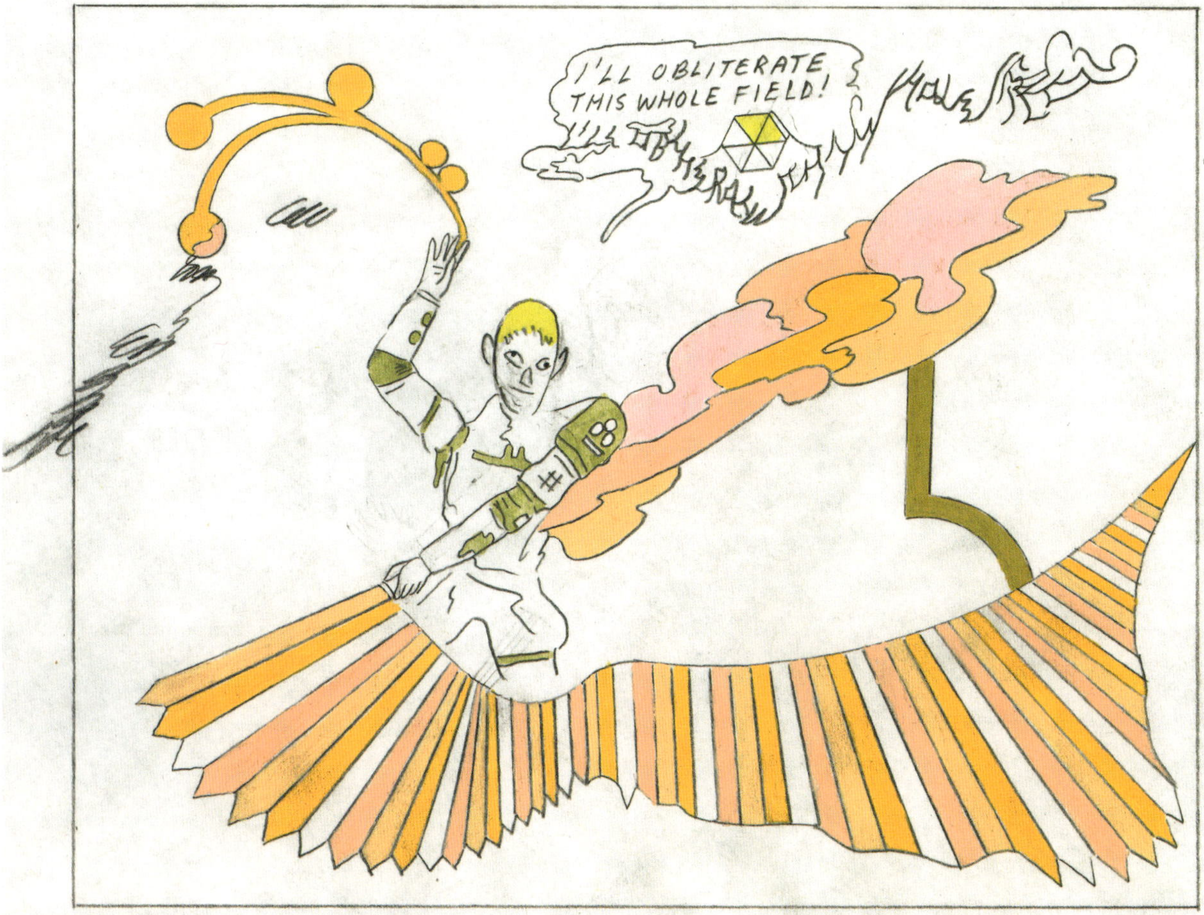

I'LL OBLITERATE THIS WHOLE FIELD!

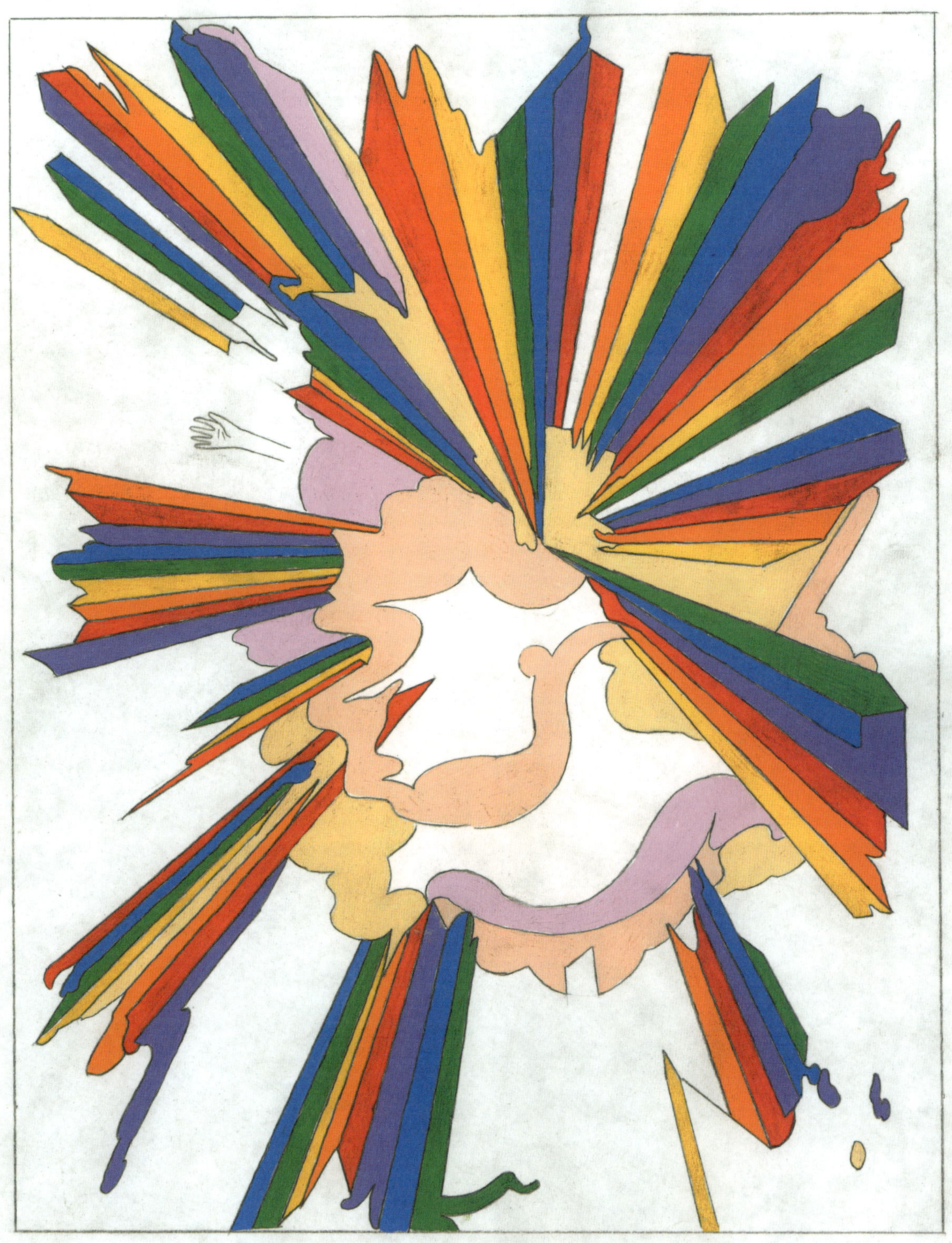

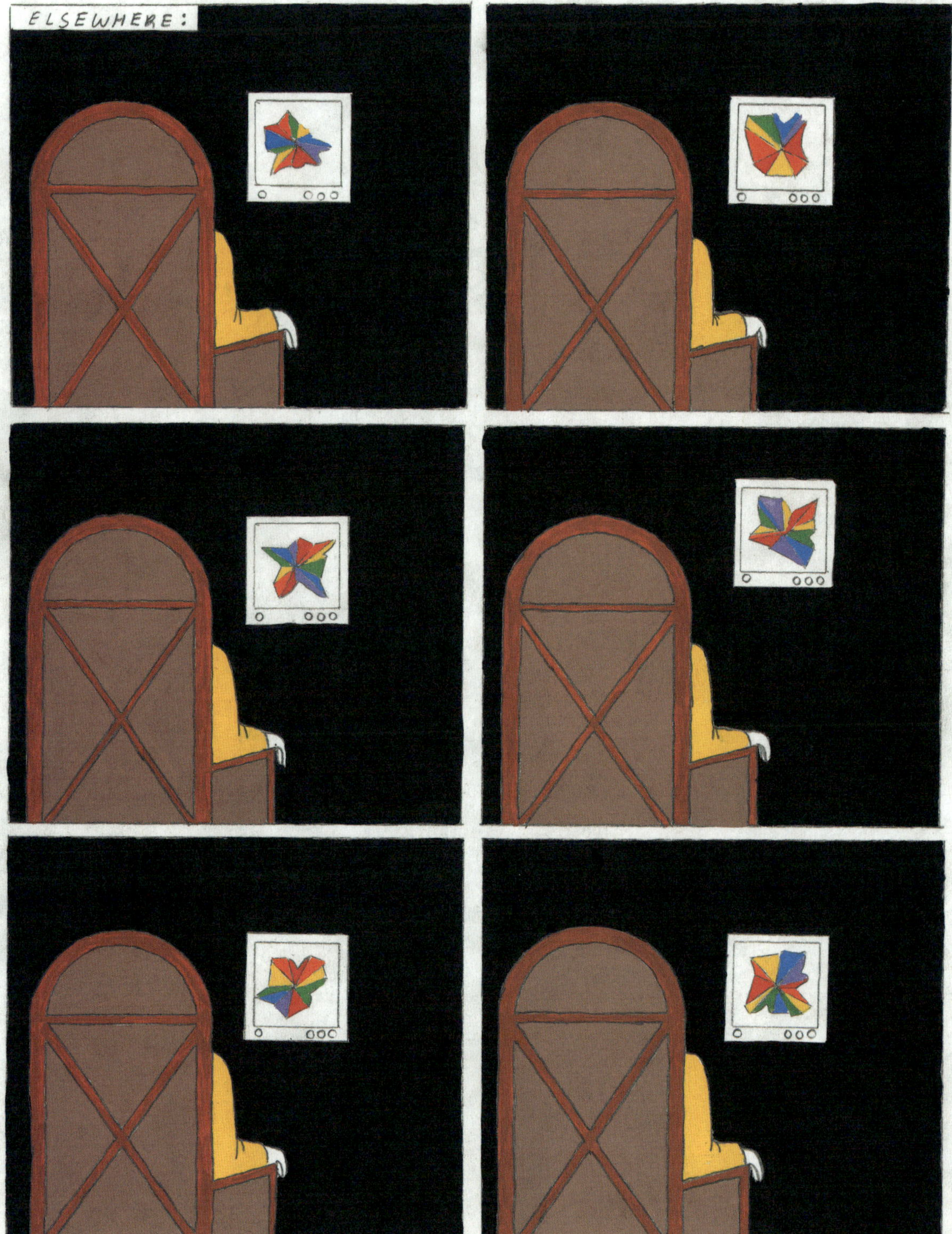
ELSEWHERE:

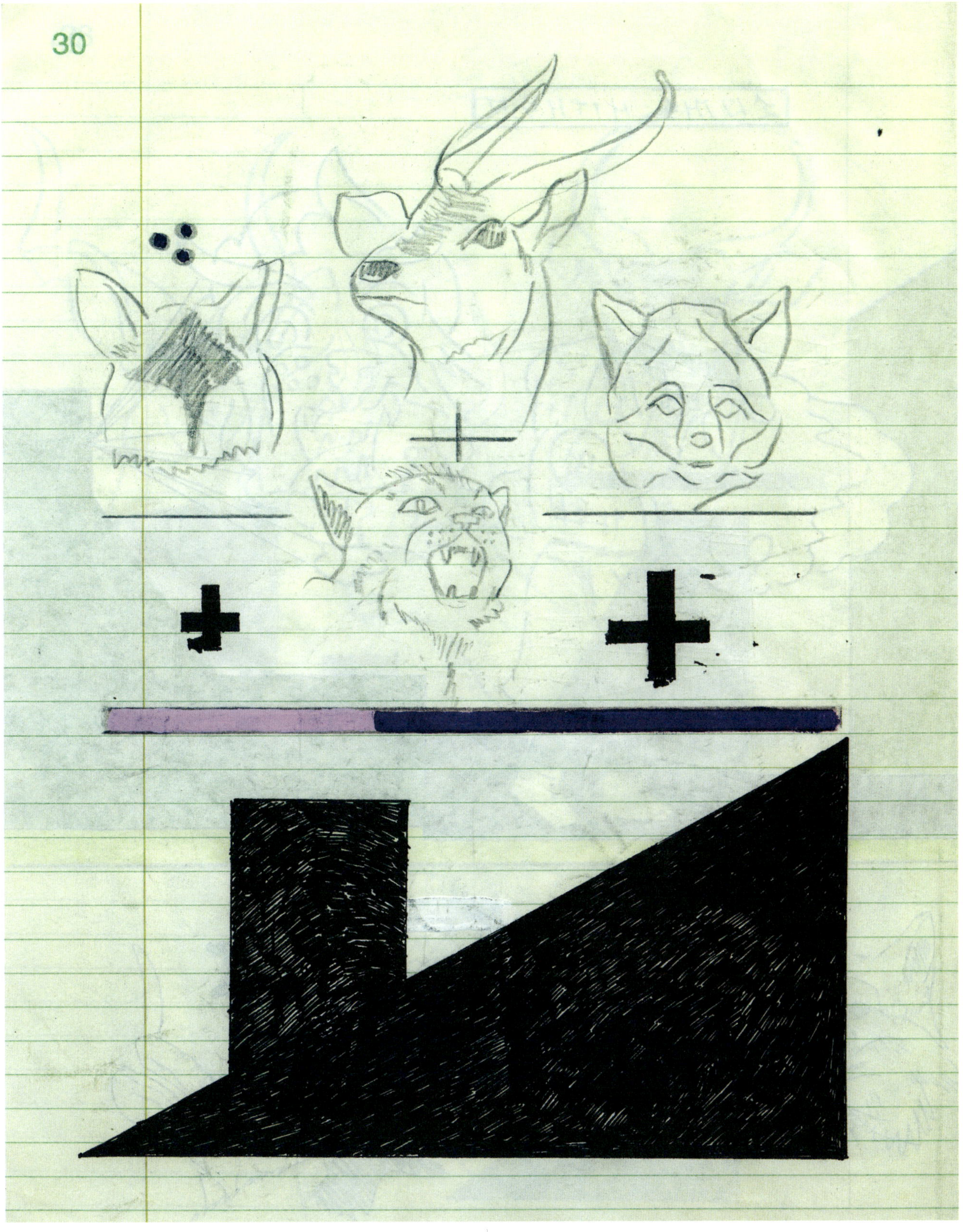
30

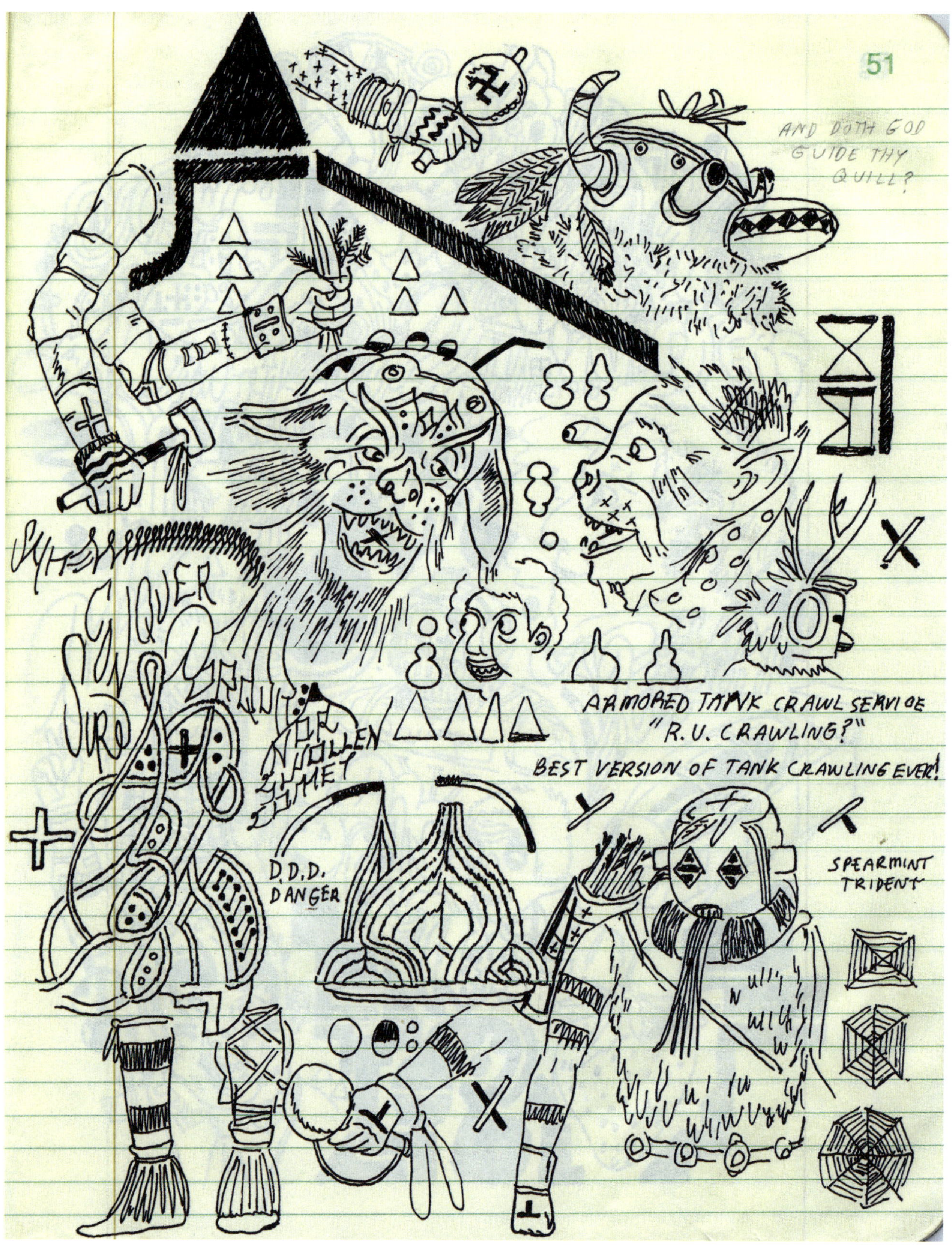
51
AND DOTH GOD
GUIDE THY
QUILL?
ARMORED TANK CRAWL SERVICE
"R.U. CRAWLING?"
BEST VERSION OF TANK CRAWLING EVER!
D.D.D.
DANGER
SPEARMINT
TRIDENT

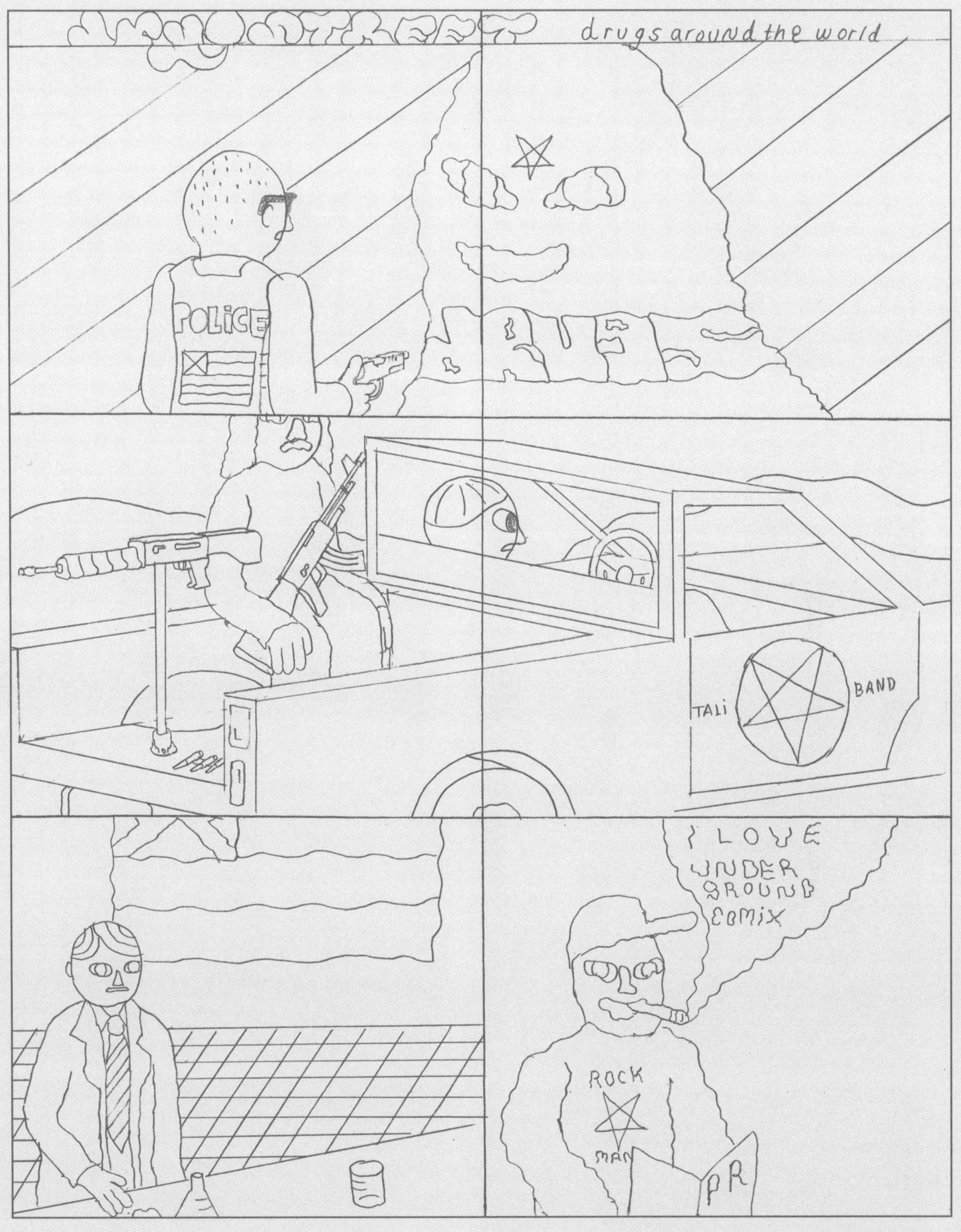
drugs around the world
POLICE
TALI
BAND
I LOVE
UNDER
GROUND
COMIX
ROCK
MAN
PR

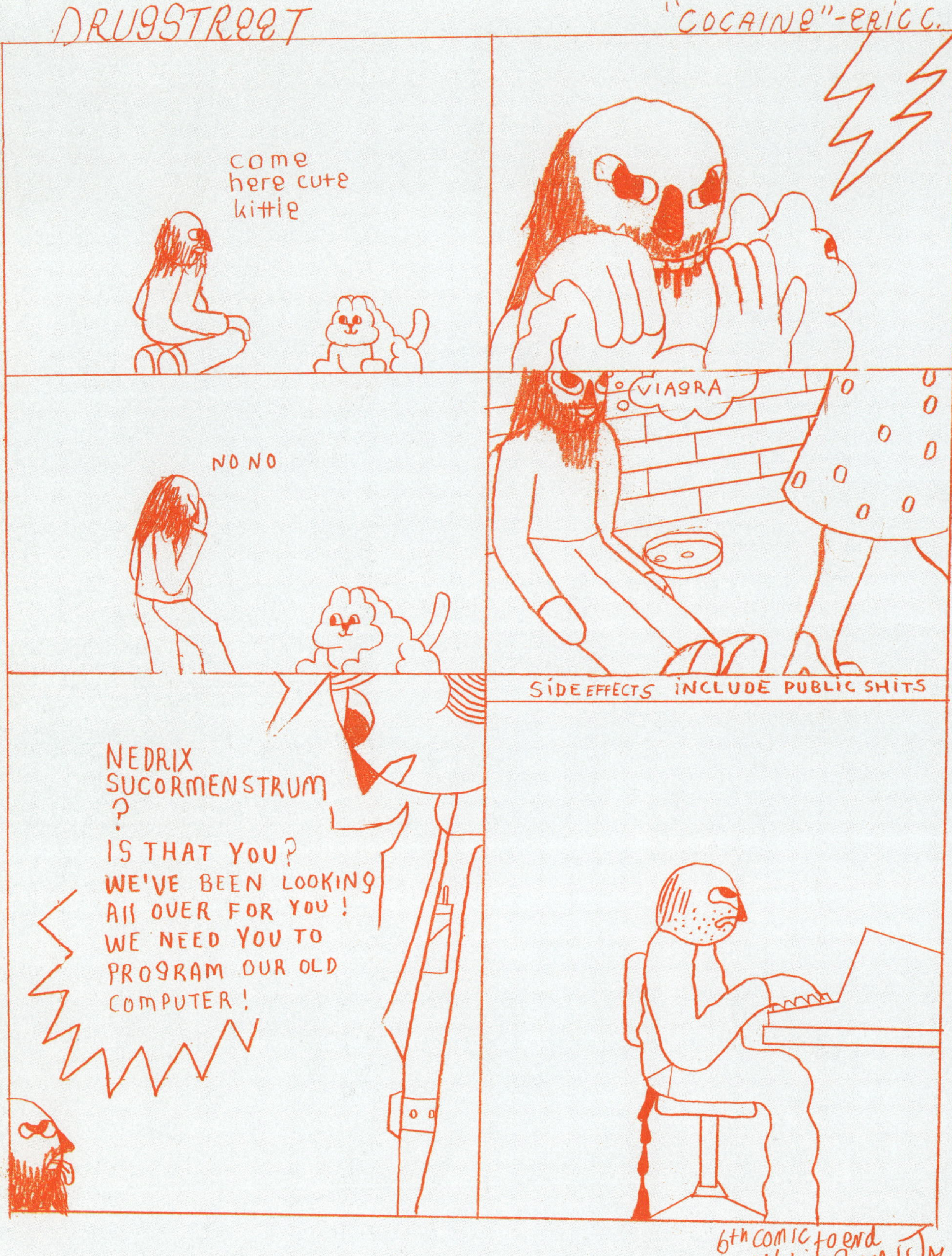
DRUGSTREET
"COCAINE" - ERIC C.
come here cute kittie
NO NO
VIAGRA
SIDE EFFECTS INCLUDE PUBLIC SHITS
NEDRIX SUCORMENSTRUM ? IS THAT YOU? WE'VE BEEN LOOKING All OVER FOR YOU! WE NEED YOU TO PROGRAM OUR OLD COMPUTER!
6th comic to end w/shit
Ben J.

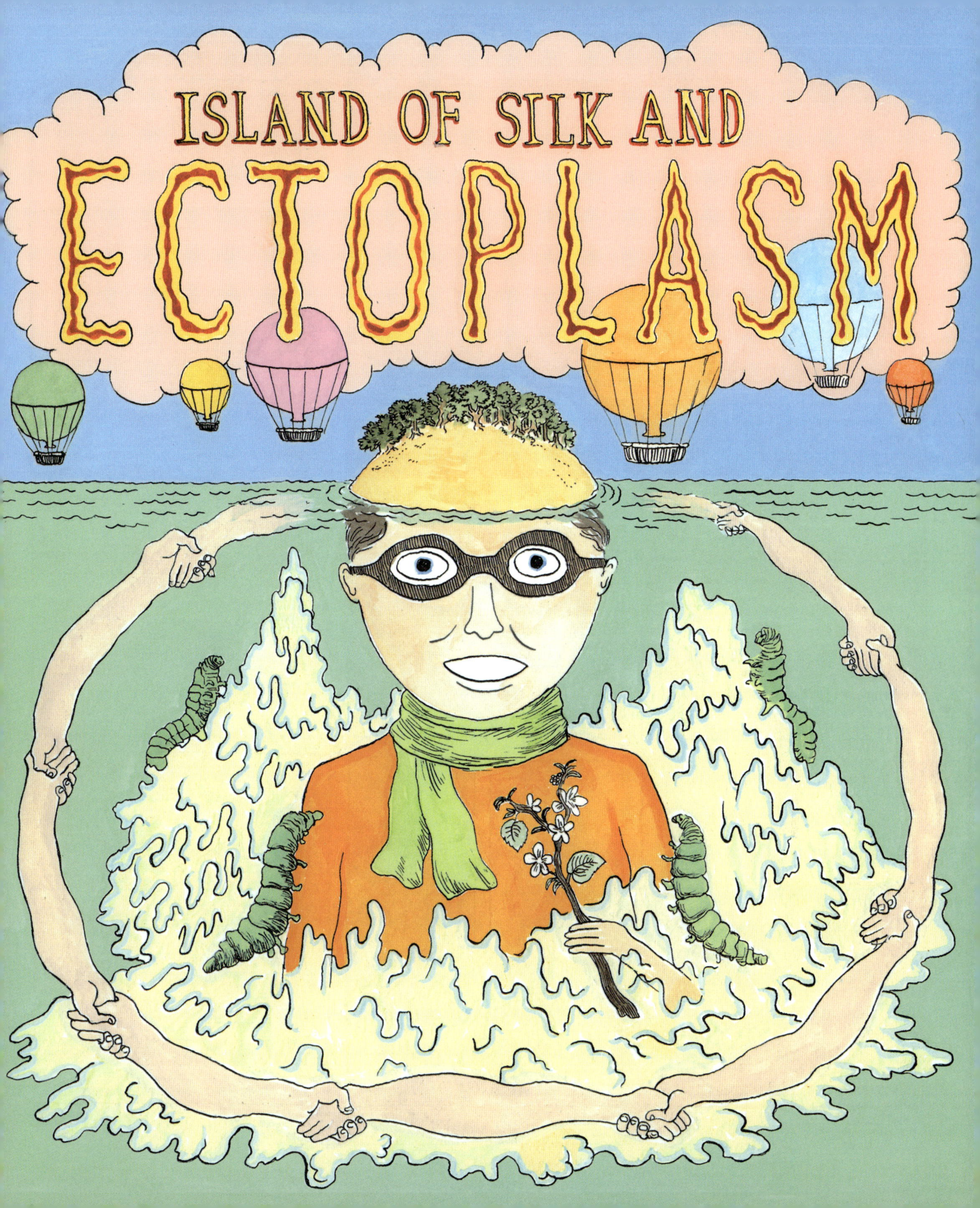
ISLAND OF SILK AND
ECTOPLASM

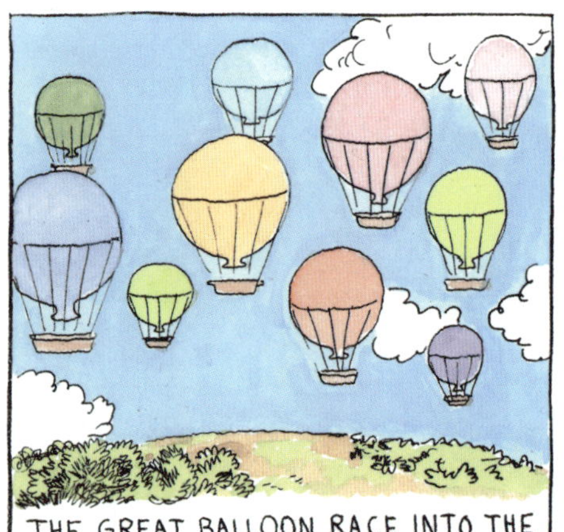
THE GREAT BALLOON RACE INTO THE BEYOND OCCURS EVERY 20 YEARS ABOVE THE ISLAND OF GUFFRE BLOMS.

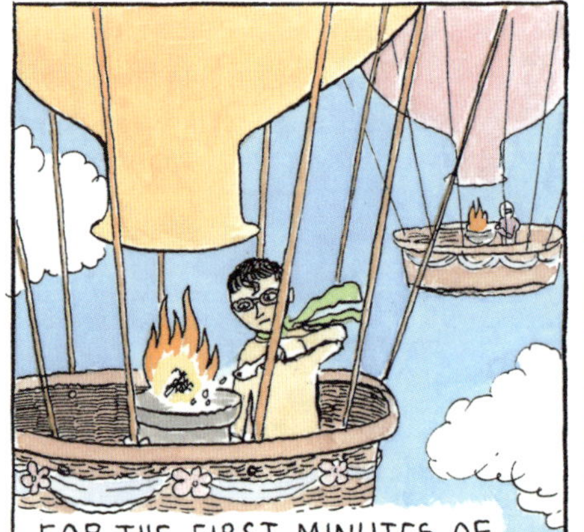
FOR THE FIRST MINUTES OF THE RACE, THE AERONAUTS BURN THEIR FUEL SUPPLY.

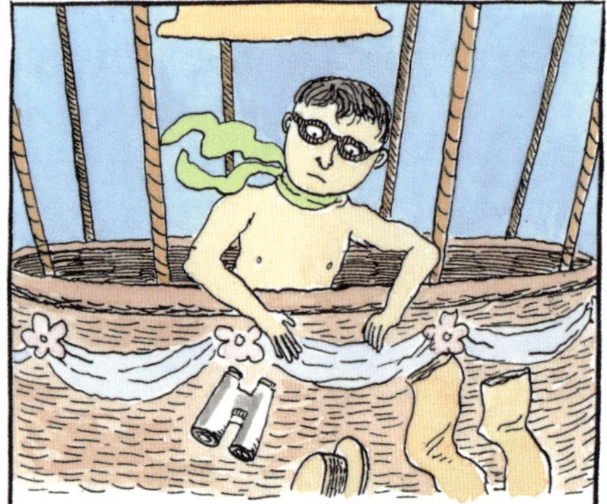
WHEN THE FUEL IS EXHAUSTED, THEY GAIN GREATER SPEED BY JETTISONING CLOTHES AND SUPPLIES.

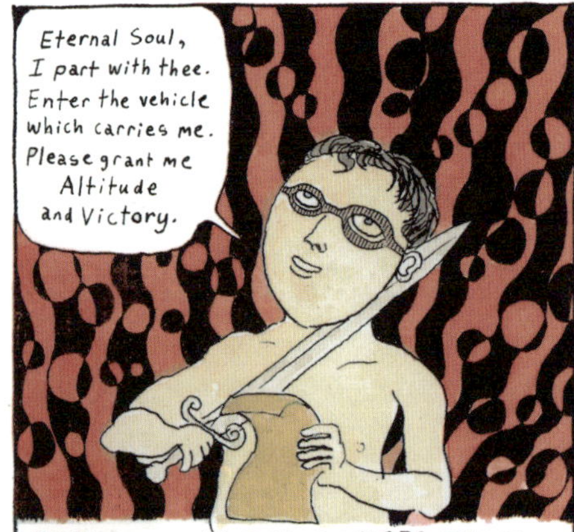
Eternal Soul, I part with thee. Enter the vehicle which carries me. Please grant me Altitude and Victory.
FINALLY, THE BALLOONISTS TAKE THEIR OWN LIVES WHILE SPEAKING ALOUD THE WORDS OF A SACRED TEXT.

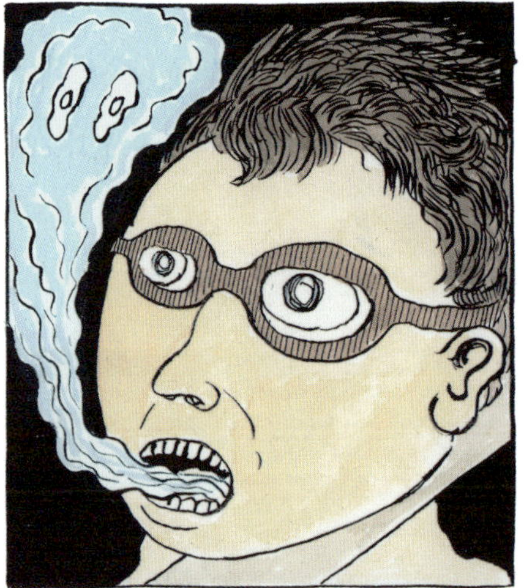

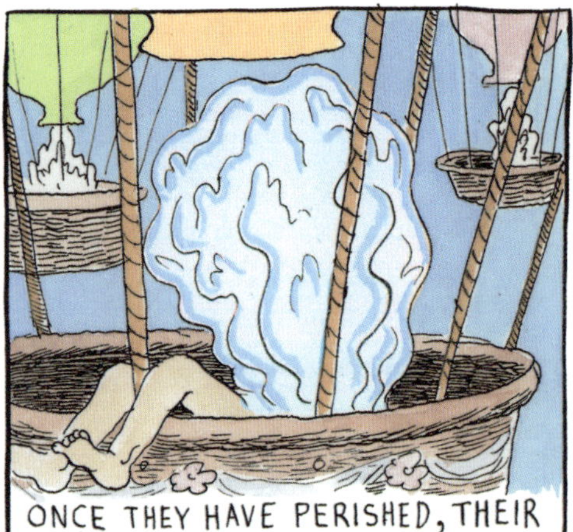
ONCE THEY HAVE PERISHED, THEIR SOULS DEPART THEIR EARTHLY STORAGE CONTAINERS.

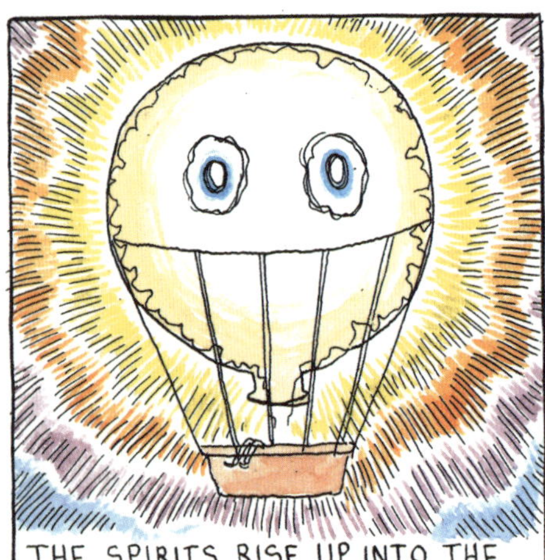
THE SPIRITS RISE UP INTO THE BALLOONS, SWELLING TO FILL THE SILK AND COATING IT WITH ECTOPLASM.

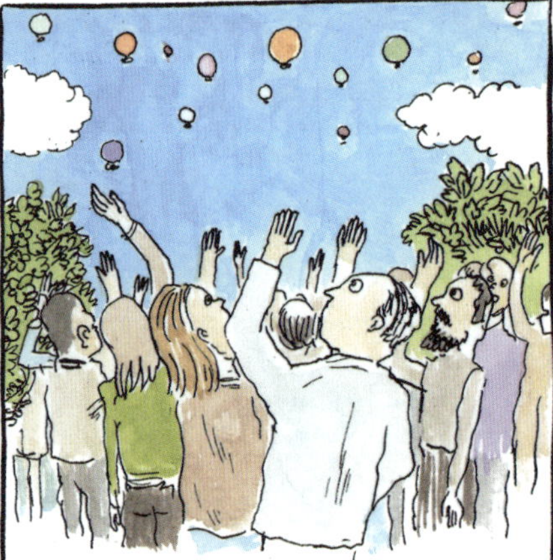
THE COMPETITORS SLOWLY DRIFT APART AS THEY MAKE THEIR WAY INTO THE AFTERLIFE

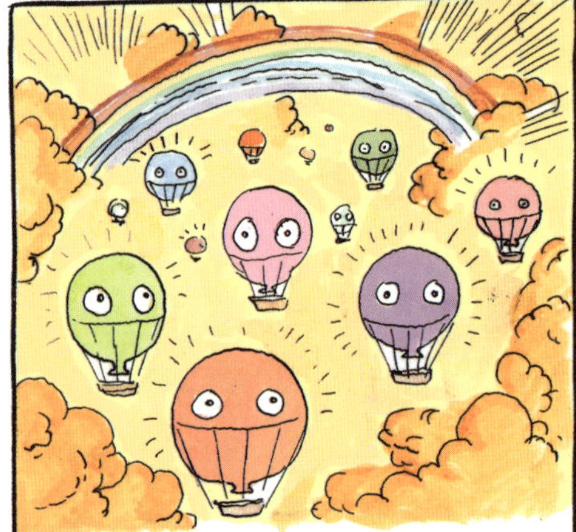
THEY HAVE ALL ATTAINED THE MOST EXALTED HEIGHTS. WHAT REWARD IS IN STORE FOR THE SOUL THAT MADE THE FASTEST ASCENT?

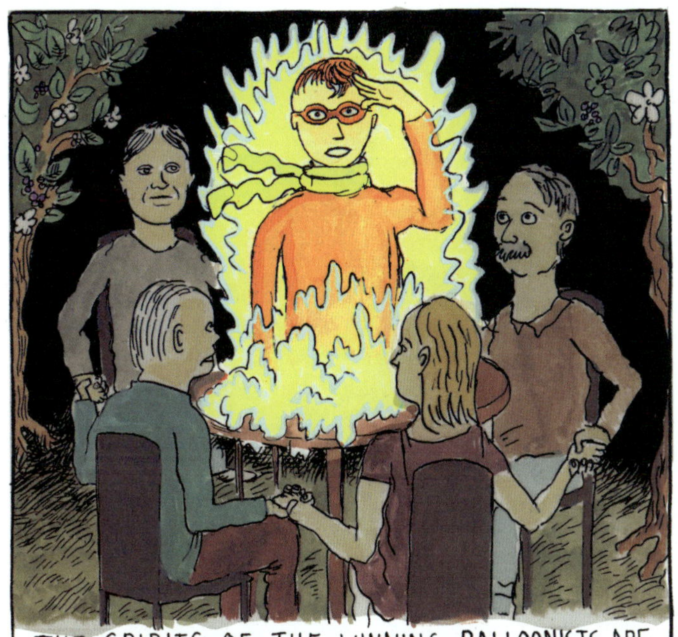
THE SPIRITS OF THE WINNING BALLOONISTS ARE SUBSEQUENTLY EMPLOYED BY THE FORESTRY DEPARTMENT IN AN IMPORTANT ROLE, WHERE SPEED IS KEY.

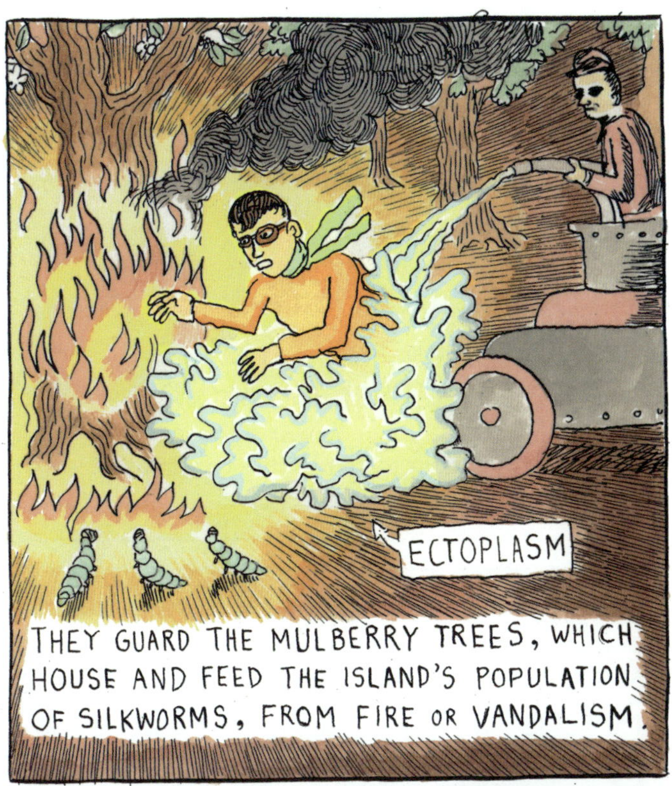
ECTOPLASM
THEY GUARD THE MULBERRY TREES, WHICH HOUSE AND FEED THE ISLAND'S POPULATION OF SILKWORMS, FROM FIRE OR VANDALISM.

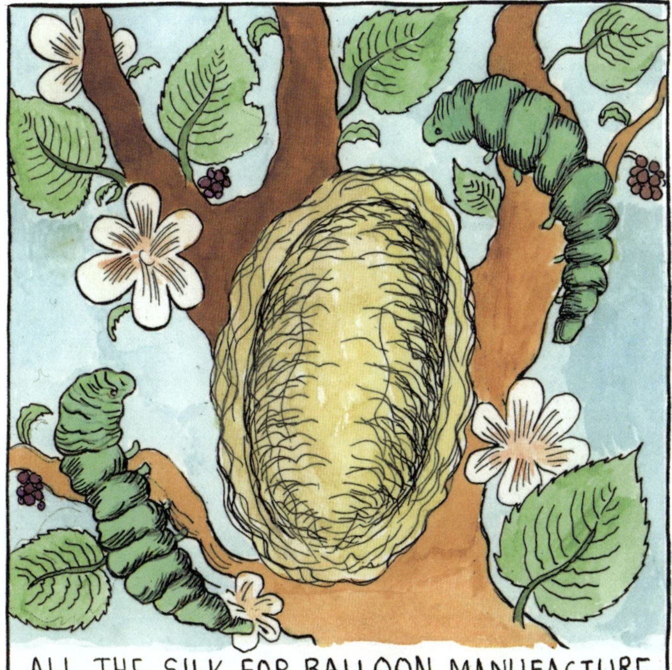
ALL THE SILK FOR BALLOON MANUFACTURE, AS WELL AS FOR THE ISLANDERS' CLOTHING, IS UNPEELED FROM THESE INSECT'S COCCOONS.

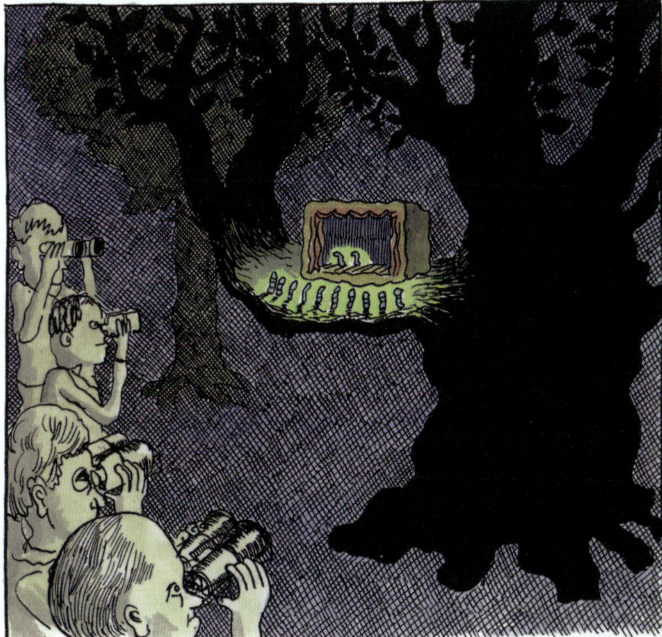
EACH YEAR THE SILKWORMS ENACT A PLAY ABOUT THEIR OWN SPIRITUAL BELIEFS, WATCHED INTENTLY THROUGH BINOCULARS BY THE ISLANDERS.

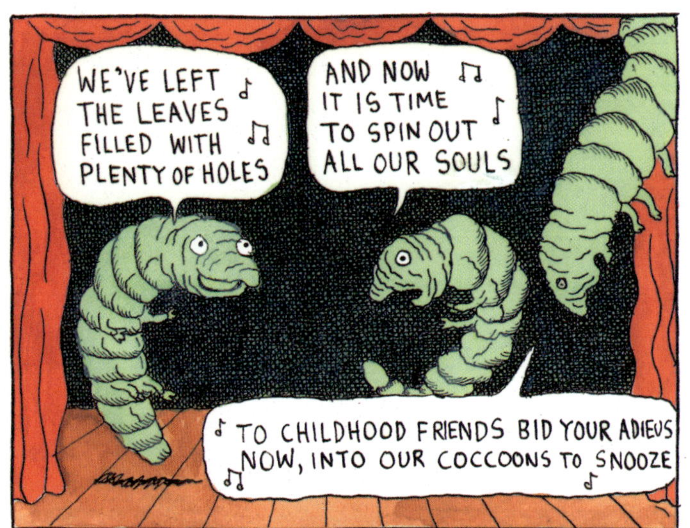
WE'VE LEFT THE LEAVES FILLED WITH PLENTY OF HOLES
AND NOW IT IS TIME TO SPIN OUT ALL OUR SOULS
TO CHILDHOOD FRIENDS BID YOUR ADIEUS NOW, INTO OUR COCCOONS TO SNOOZE

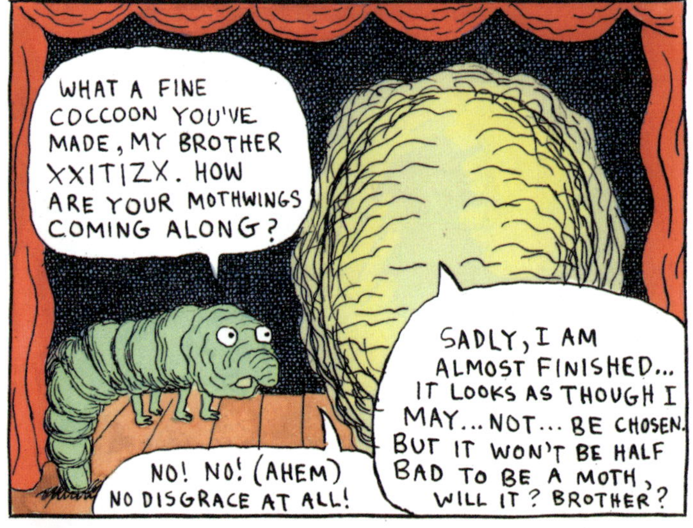
WHAT A FINE COCCOON YOU'VE MADE, MY BROTHER XXITIZX. HOW ARE YOUR MOTHWINGS COMING ALONG?
SADLY, I AM ALMOST FINISHED... IT LOOKS AS THOUGH I MAY... NOT... BE CHOSEN. BUT IT WON'T BE HALF BAD TO BE A MOTH, WILL IT? BROTHER?
NO! NO! (AHEM) NO DISGRACE AT ALL!

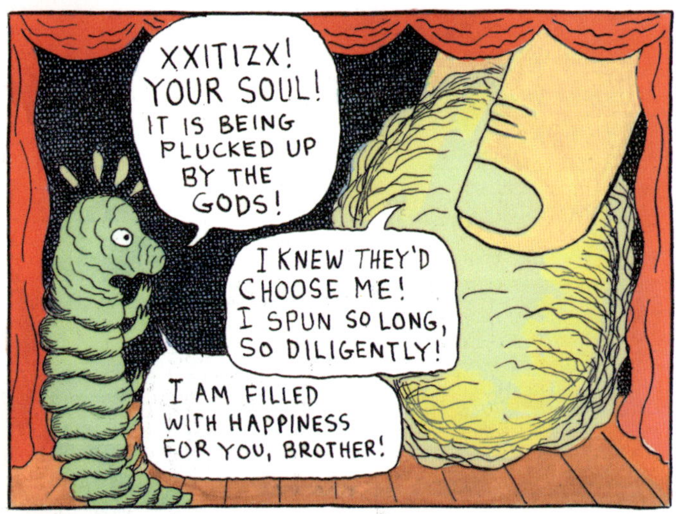
XXITIZX! YOUR SOUL! IT IS BEING PLUCKED UP BY THE GODS!
I KNEW THEY'D CHOOSE ME! I SPUN SO LONG, SO DILIGENTLY!
I AM FILLED WITH HAPPINESS FOR YOU, BROTHER!

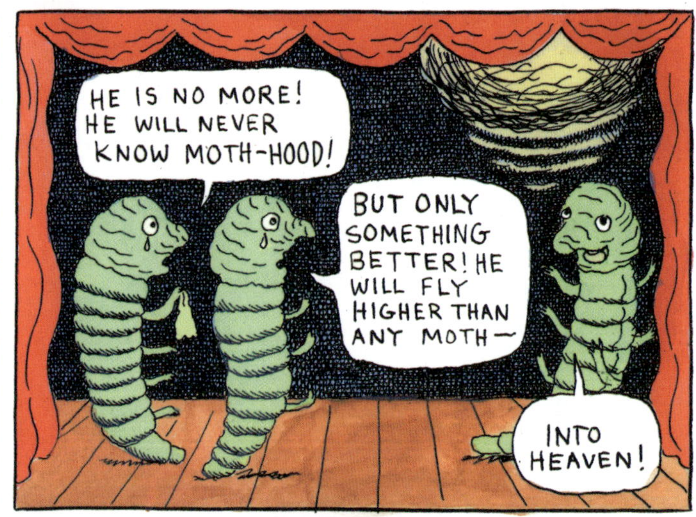
HE IS NO MORE! HE WILL NEVER KNOW MOTH-HOOD!
BUT ONLY SOMETHING BETTER! HE WILL FLY HIGHER THAN ANY MOTH—
INTO HEAVEN!

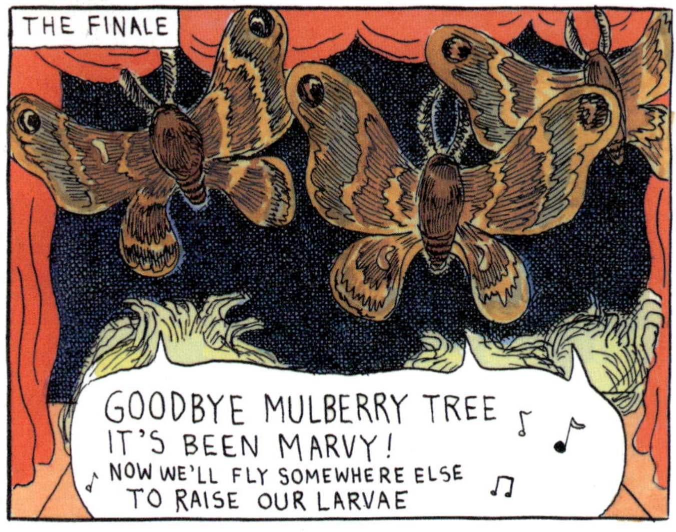
THE FINALE
GOODBYE MULBERRY TREE IT'S BEEN MARVY! NOW WE'LL FLY SOMEWHERE ELSE TO RAISE OUR LARVAE

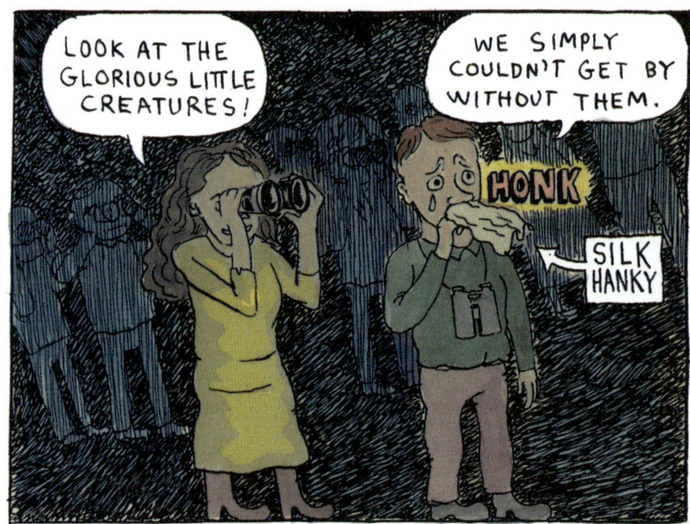
LOOK AT THE GLORIOUS LITTLE CREATURES!
WE SIMPLY COULDN'T GET BY WITHOUT THEM.
HONK
SILK HANKY

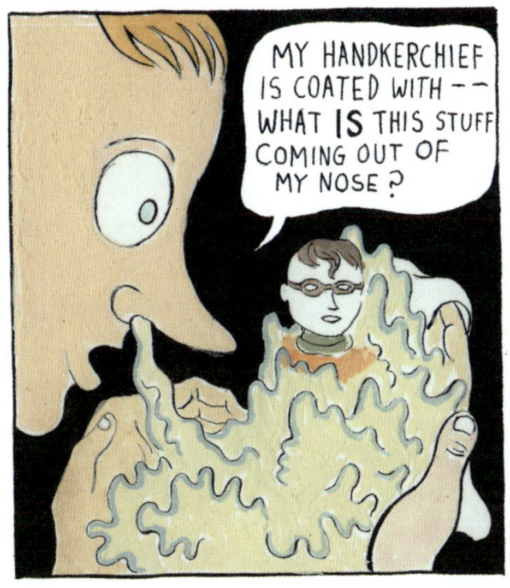
MY HANDKERCHIEF IS COATED WITH -- WHAT IS THIS STUFF COMING OUT OF MY NOSE?

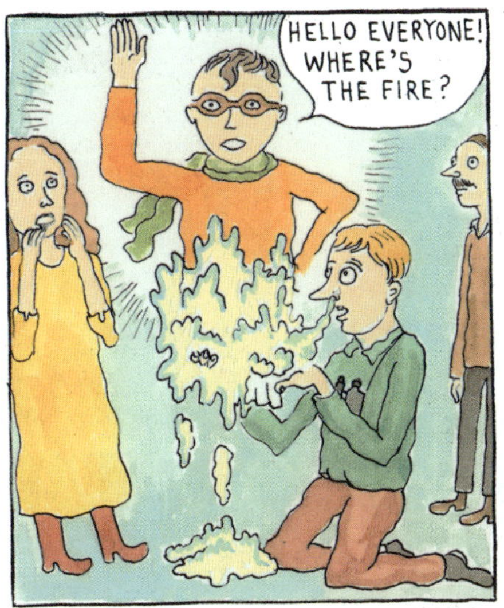
HELLO EVERYONE! WHERE'S THE FIRE?

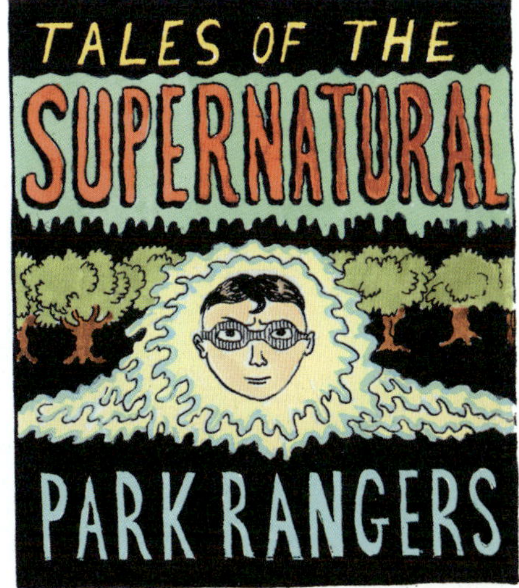
TALES OF THE
SUPERNATURAL
PARK RANGERS

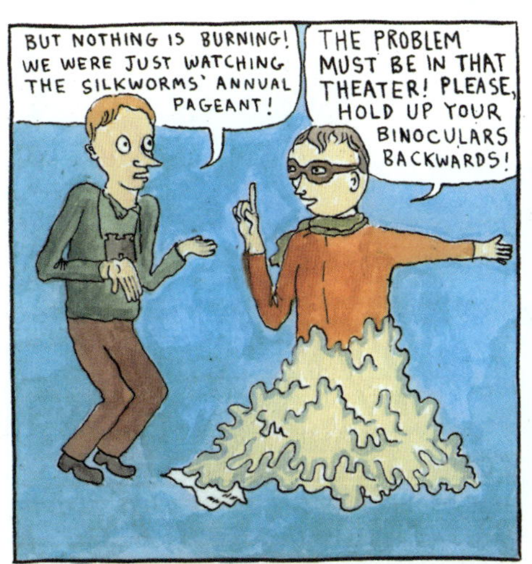
BUT NOTHING IS BURNING! WE WERE JUST WATCHING THE SILKWORMS' ANNUAL PAGEANT!
THE PROBLEM MUST BE IN THAT THEATER! PLEASE, HOLD UP YOUR BINOCULARS BACKWARDS!

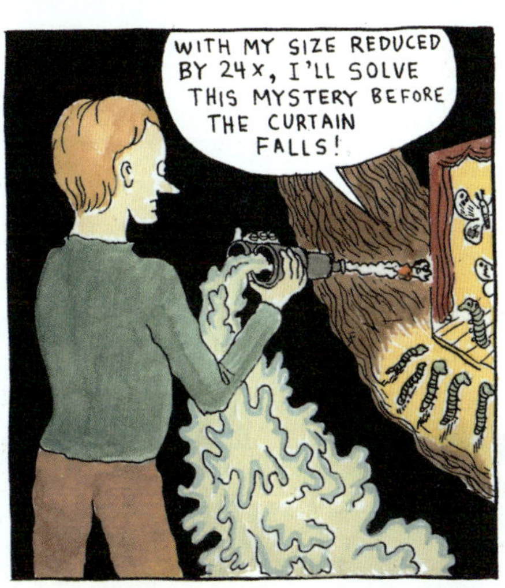
WITH MY SIZE REDUCED BY 24x, I'LL SOLVE THIS MYSTERY BEFORE THE CURTAIN FALLS!

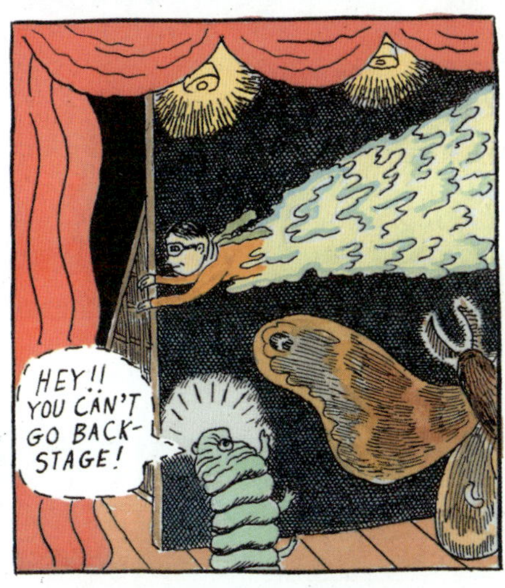
HEY!! YOU CAN'T GO BACK-STAGE!

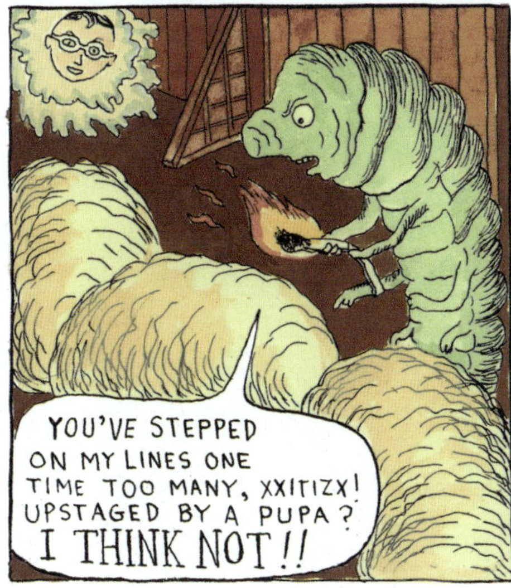
YOU'VE STEPPED ON MY LINES ONE TIME TOO MANY, XXITIZX! UPSTAGED BY A PUPA? I THINK NOT!!

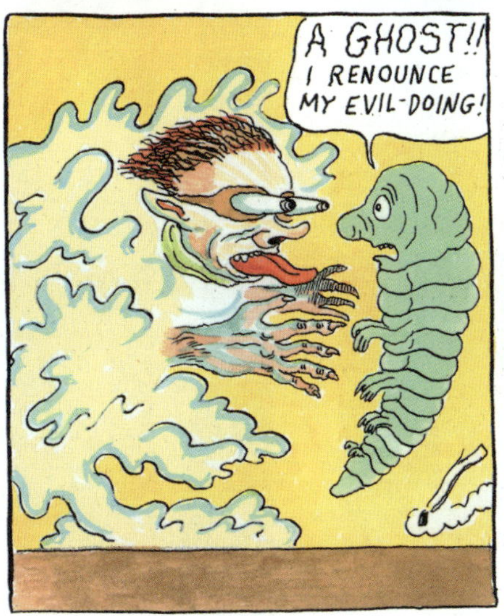
A GHOST!! I RENOUNCE MY EVIL-DOING!

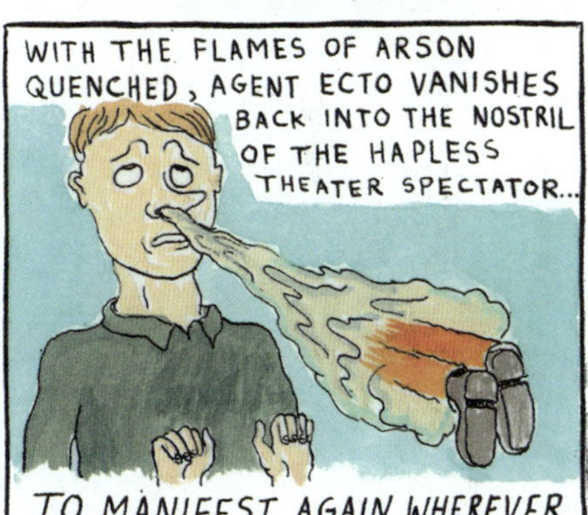
WITH THE FLAMES OF ARSON QUENCHED, AGENT ECTO VANISHES BACK INTO THE NOSTRIL OF THE HAPLESS THEATER SPECTATOR...
TO MANIFEST AGAIN WHEREVER A LEAF OF A MULBERRY TREE IS THREATENED! JOIN US FOR MORE BUBBLING ECTOPLASM AND MORE TALES OF THE SUPERNATURAL PARK RANGERS!

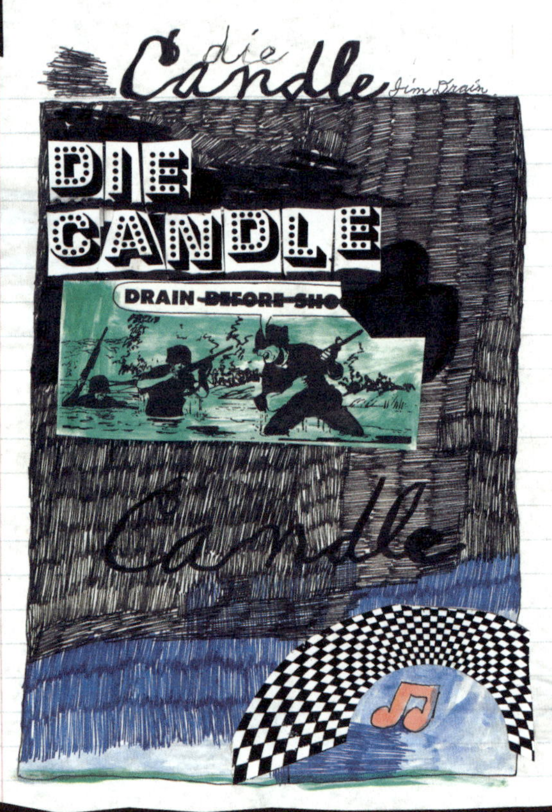
die Candle
Jim Drain
DIE CANDLE
DRAIN
Candle

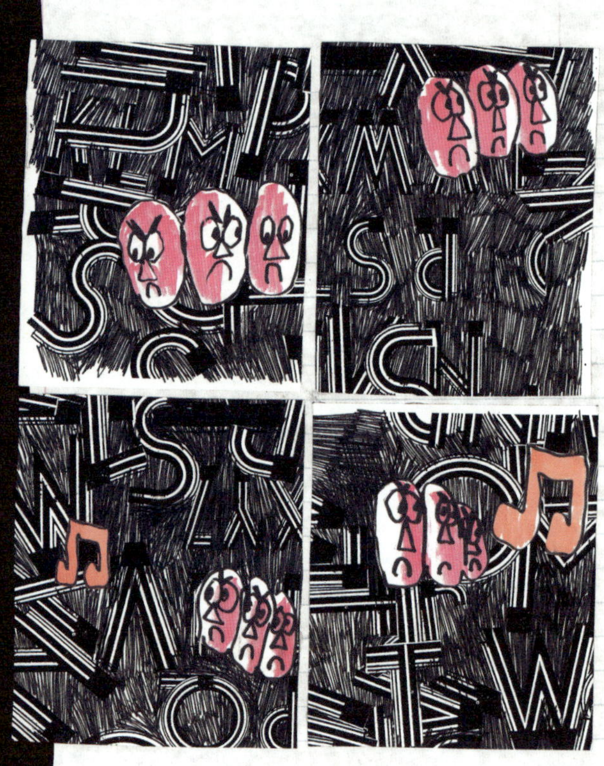

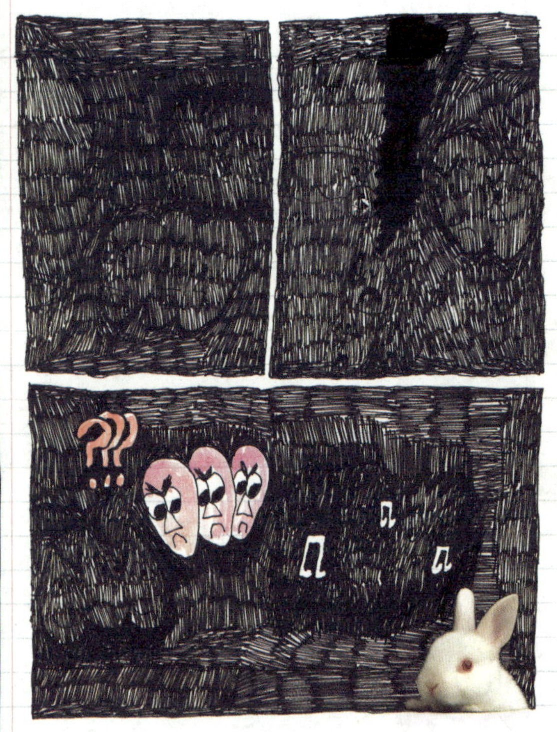

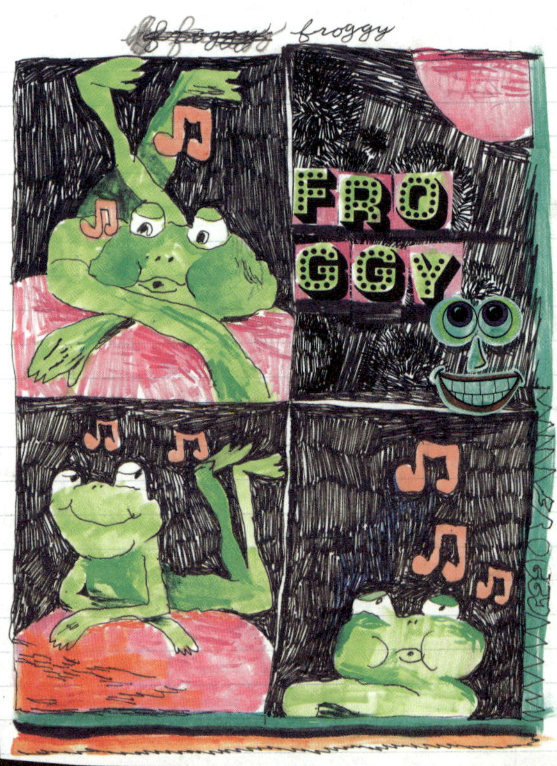
froggy
FRO GGY

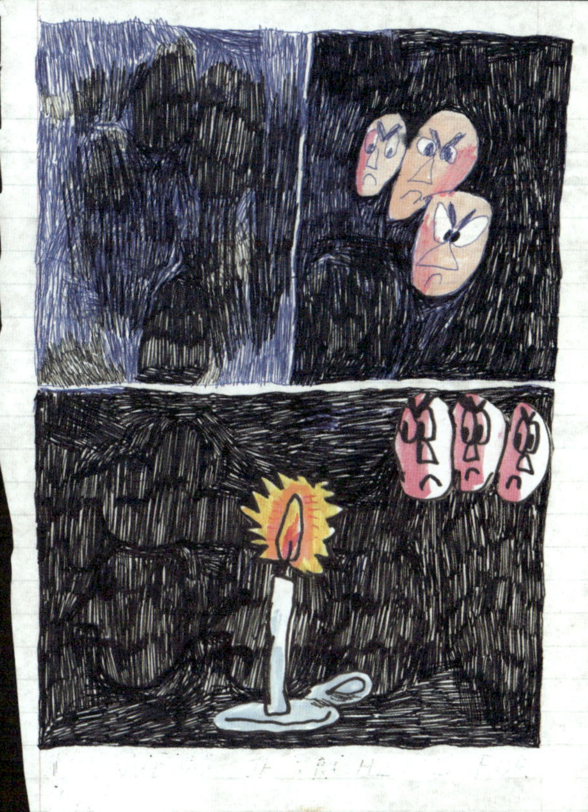

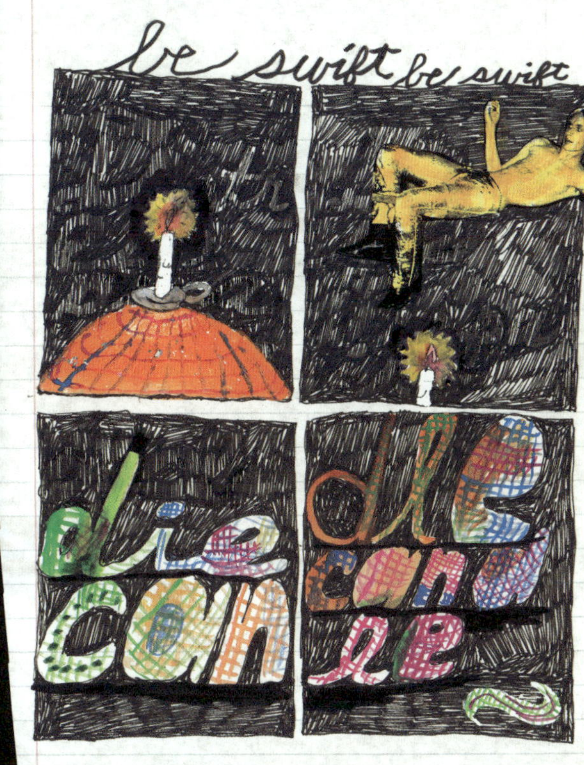
be swift be swift
die
can
die
cand
le

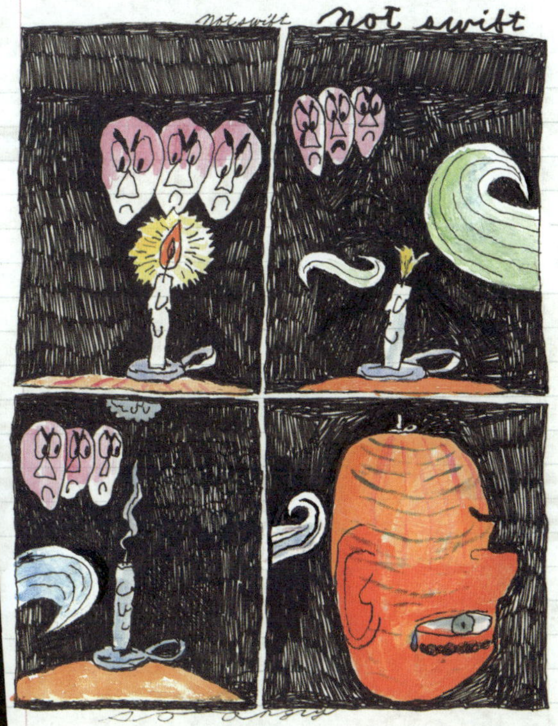
not swift
not swift

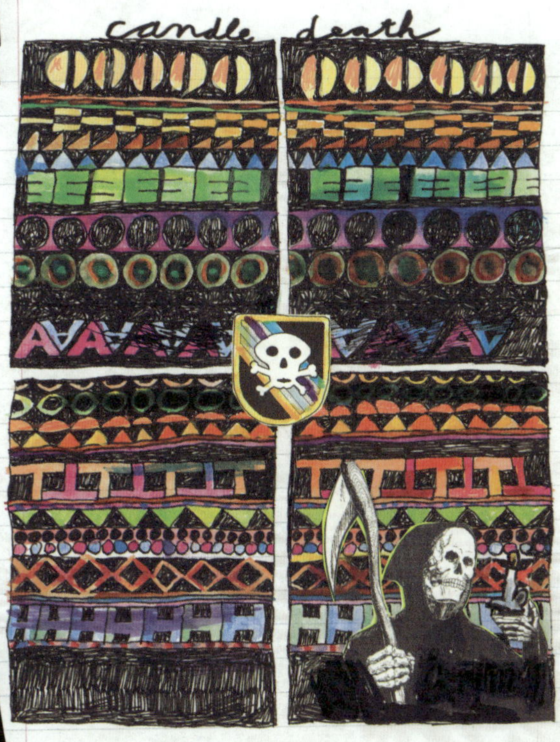
candle death

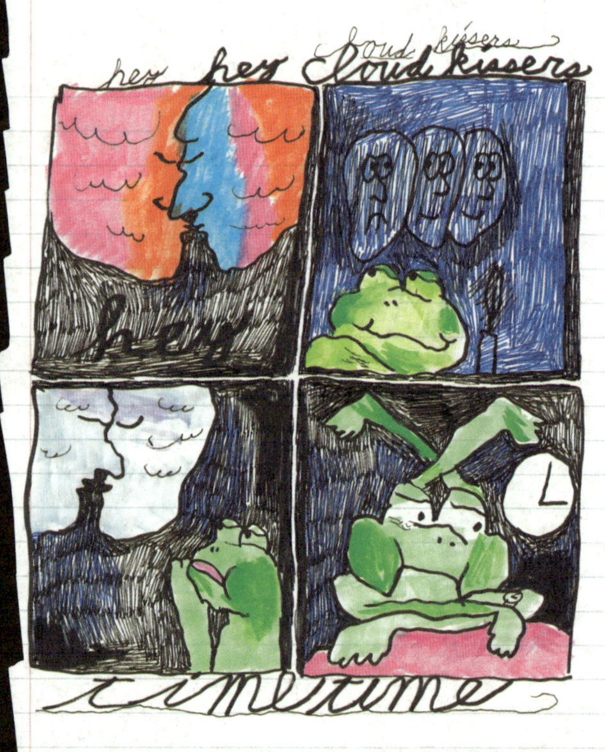
cloud kissers
hey hey cloud kissers
hey
timetime

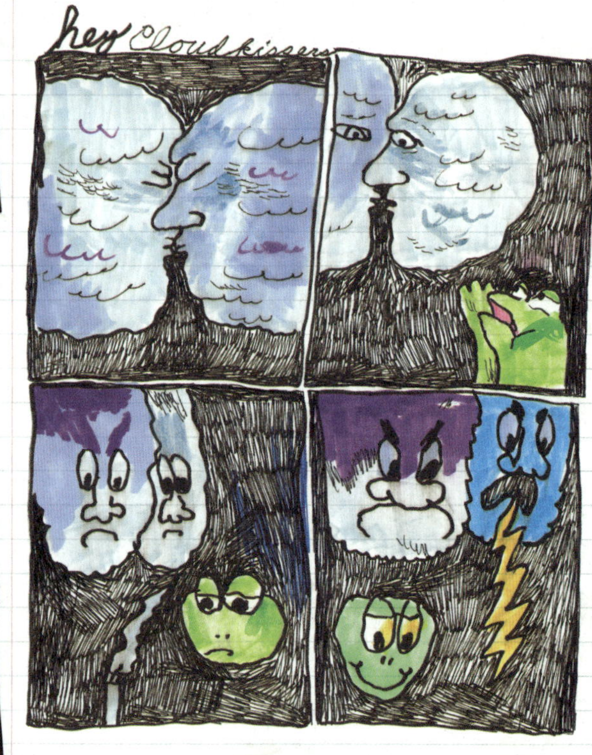
hey cloud kissers

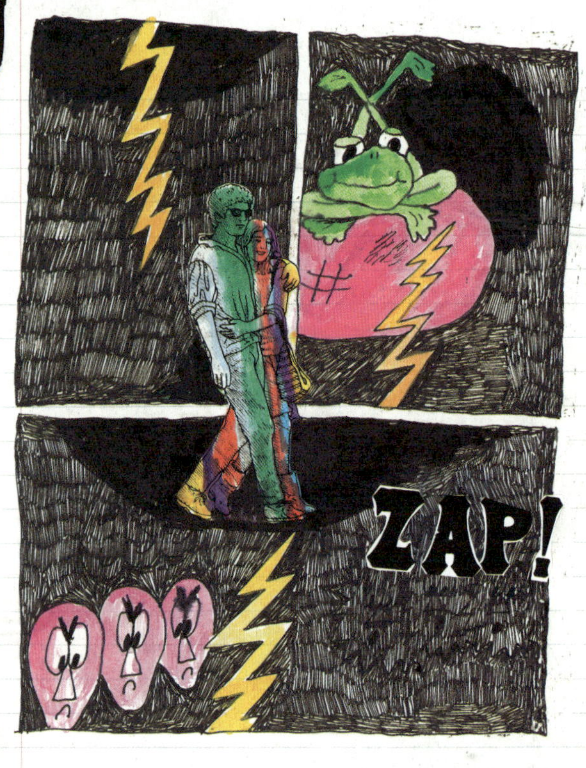
ZAP!

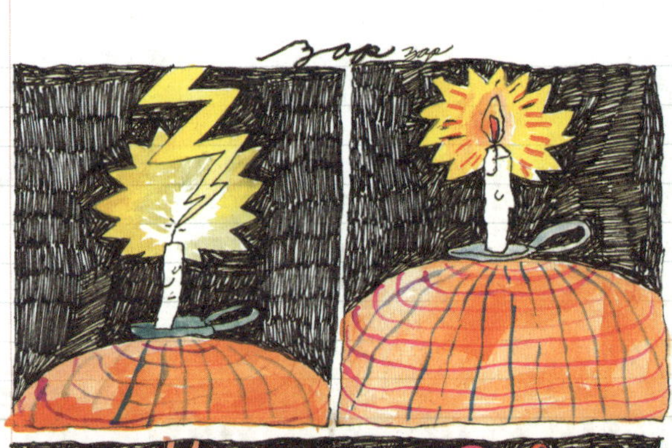
zap zap

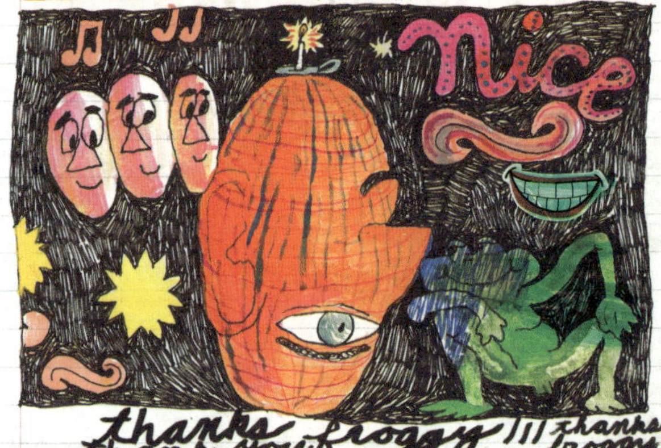
nice
thanks froggy!!!
thank you
... thanks, froggy!

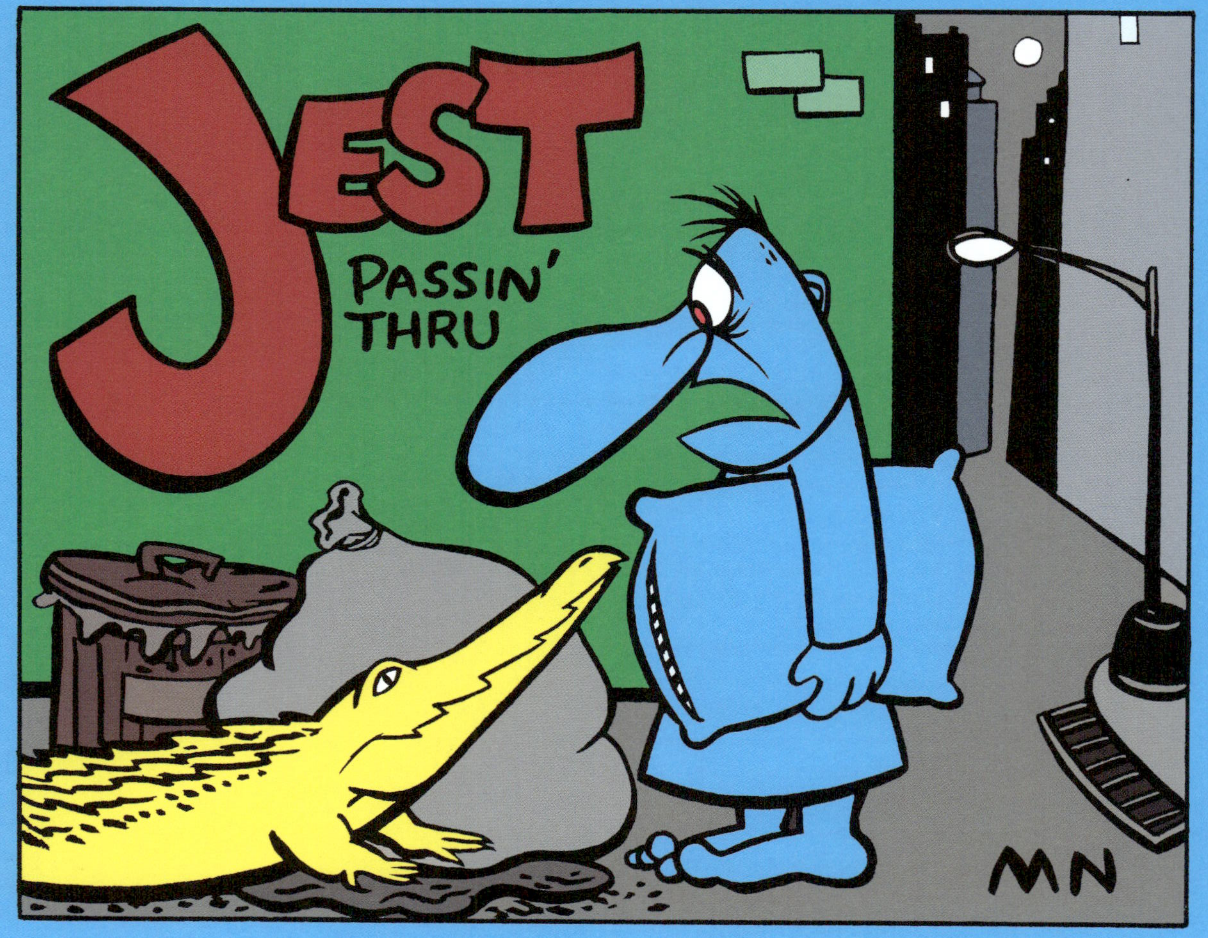

“Next to my family, nothing matters more to me than the theater. Of course my family is more important. I do have to say that, and would say it even if it weren't so very true. But—in this case—yes, it is true: my family first, the theater second. But a close second, the theater is, actually. My family—God bless 'em! But the theater is the theater.

And the theater is what sustains me. And what sustains me sustains my family in turn. And so, of course, I do—and must—love what sustains my family and myself. So I do actually love the theater foremost, although my family matters more and I always would say that, regardless. And my family, too, loves the theater, of course. We all love its vitality. Nothing is more vital, actually. Except for maybe New York. The theater and New York and my family—the Big Three in terms of vital personal importance. I mean, New York—c'mon, right?! The city, the kind of people that you get here, *The New Yorker,* the whole mindset of it being New York. You won't get that in L.A.—not like you do here! I mean, I guess you can get *The New Yorker* there, but it wouldn't be the same as getting it here, in New York. Not in terms of vitality. And the theater—the theater, of course, IS New York. That's a fact. The theater is NOT L.A. or Chicago or Florida or Vancouver. New York is NOT Mexico or Maryland or France or upstate. Right? I mean, technically it may be New York, but upstate is NOT *New York*—the theater/New York.

My family is most important to me. And New York is most vital. No—in a way the theater is actually more vital too, personally, but the theater IS New York, so New York is technically more vital than the theater because it's bigger (including upstate, although more impersonal in that case). I do consider the theater my craft. I consider the theater my craft, New York my home, and my family most important. So, if I were asked to choose, I'd choose my craft first. Of course, I'd have to choose it first—in order to sustain my home and family. That's not to say it matters most. So, although the theater is of secondary importance, it's technically my first choice—if I were asked to choose—since my family matters more, as I mentioned. And, in turn, my craft—the theater—is informed and sustained by the importance of my family and the vitality of New York, my home.

Now, my goal is, in turn, to impart back to New York the vitality of New York through my craft, the theater. I want a theater that matters. I want a theater with doors open to humanity. I want a vital theater that's not afraid to be creative and that is within reach of any New York family—like mine. Not to say my family is just any New York family. They are actually most important (to me, that is, not to anybody else, necessarily—except in terms of how they impact me and how I, in turn, impact the rest of humanity through my craft, the theater). Creativity is essential to humanity, and, in terms of creativity, I feel that I'm merely a conduit for something bigger. And that bigger thing is energy. And energy is creativity. Of course, the real creativity is New York, and I, as a mere conduit for that creativity, via my goal—informing New York, through my craft, the theater—endeavor to re-inform New York, and its families, of its own essential and vital humanity.

And perhaps something more. Because, beyond that goal, I have a dream. My dream is to expand the theater beyond my goals. Maybe it's silly. But a dream is a dream, right? I want to dare to take my vision of theater and push beyond those boundaries (although my goal is a theater with no boundaries per se). I want a theater that of its own volition expands itself exponentially beyond all boundaries—beyond family, craft, humanity, creativity, vitality, importance. Even beyond New York. I envision a living theater that can flourish in an L.A. or a Chicago or a Florida or a Vancouver. Or a Mexico or a Maryland or a France. Or even upstate. I envision a theater that is self-sustaining and self-informed—an autonomous theater that answers and matters to itself, first and foremost, even more than anything and anyone else. Even more than my family or how much my family matters to me, which is foremost. Even more than I do to me!

But, then again, maybe not. Because if I, as an individual, were not here to dare to dream of that theater-beyond-my-goal (and the theater yet beyond even that dream), then how would it even be possible to exist to override my own unimportant importance? So I take on this lonely burden. Perhaps this would be a good place to bring up art."

©2003 Mark Newgarden

CONTRIBUTORS

For Ganzfeld/PictureBox books and editions by Marc Bell, Jim Drain, Paper Rad, Frank Santoro, and Matthew Thurber, as well as back issues of *The Ganzfeld*, visit theganzfeld.com.

AMID AMIDI is the editor in chief of *Animation Blast* magazine.

MARC BELL draws comics and makes "fine aht." His latest comic book is *Worn Tuff Elbow* (published by Fantagraphics). Drawn & Quarterly published *The Stacks,* a collection of work featured in his exhibition of the same name at the Adam Baumgold Gallery (adambaumgoldgallery.com).

PETER BLEGVAD is the author of the comic strip collection *The Book of Leviathan* (Overlook Press) and a volume of writings and drawings called *Headcheese* (Atlas).

OLIVER BROUDY is a senior editor at *The Paris Review*.

TOM BURCKHARDT is a painter who lives in New York City with his wife, Kathy Butterly, and kids, Keno and Ava. He has exhibited at the Tibor de Nagy Gallery and, most recently, Caren Golden Fine Art.

C.F. is a Providence, Rhode Island–based artist. Write to him at: P.O. Box 923, Providence, RI 02701.

JOHN COHEN is songwriter and photographer. His most recent book of photographs is *Young Dylan*.

GREG COOK is a reporter and cartoonist living in beautiful Gloucester, Massachusetts, where he dreamed up his comic book *Catch As Catch Can* and is currently hard at work on more such weighty projects.

ADAM DANT is a London-based artist whose work appears in numerous publications, such as *The Independent* on Sundays. He has been a commissioned artist for the Tate Modern, and his drawings, installations, and other artworks are in the collections of the Museum of London, the Museum of Contemporary Art, Lyon, and the Museum of Modern Art, New York.

JULIE DOUCET is a used-to-be cartoonist and now a printer. Her latest book, *Lady Pep,* was published by Drawn & Quarterly.

JIM DRAIN lives in Providence, Rhode Island, and just bought a new space heater this afternoon. His old space heater broke. (It did not really break, but was dusty and he tried to fix it by blowing compressed air into it. A lot of dust came out, but to keep it short, it still did not work.) At the bottom of Jim's heart is an agate that sits underneath a heavily flowing waterfall.

JOHN GLASSIE was born in Washington, D.C., and now lives in New York. His writing has appeared in numerous publications, including *The New York Times Magazine, The Believer,* Salon.com, *Wired,* and *The Madison Review.* A book of his photographs, *Bicycles Locked to Poles,* was recently published by McSweeney's.

LEIF GOLDBERG was born in Maryland in 1975. He is currently living in Providence, Rhode Island, raising chickens and scratching on old printing plates.

TOM GUNNING is a professor of cinema and media studies at the University of Chicago. His most recent book is *The Films of Fritz Lang: Allegories of Vision and Modernity* (British Film Institute).

ALEX HANIMANN is an artist living in St. Gallen, Switzerland. He teaches at the University of Art and Design Zurich. His most recent book is *Horsepark*.

PAUL ETIENNE LINCOLN shows his artwork worldwide. His most recent publication is *The Purification of Fagus Sylvatica Var Pendula.* He is represented by Alexander and Bonin.

JONATHON LIPPINCOTT is a designer at Farrar, Straus and Giroux.

MARK NEWGARDEN is a Brooklyn-based cartoonist. He is the co-author of *Cheap Laffs: The Art of the Novelty Item. We All Die Alone,* a collection of his comics, will be released in 2005.

KOSEI ONO is the foremost translator of American comics into Japanese, having handled such works as *Little Nemo in Slumberland,* Robert Crumb's *Fritz the Cat,* and Marvel's *Spider-Man.* He is also the author of a biography of Osamu Tezuka and a history of Chinese animated films.

GARY PANTER's most recent book is *Satiro-Plastic,* a facsimile of one of his sketchbooks, published by Drawn & Quarterly. His other titles include *Jimbo in Purgatory* and *Cola Madness.* Visit him online at garypanter.com.

PHIL PATTON writes for *Esquire, The New York Times, GQ,* and many other publications.

OWEN PHILLIPS is the illustration editor of *The New Yorker* magazine, where he has also written reviews on art, photography, and restaurants. He lives in Brooklyn with his wife and three kids.

PAPER RAD is an art team based in western Massachusetts. Their new book, *Paper Rad, B.J., and da Dogs,* was published by PictureBox. Visit them online at paperrad.org.

JONATHAN ROSEN's relentlessly joyous art has been disseminated to the masses on a molecular level for over a million years. To gaze at his book *The Birth of Machine Consciousness* and various animated chemistry experiments visit www.jrosen.org.

DAVID SANDLIN's prints, paintings, and comics have been exhibited around the world and have appeared in publications including *RAW, The New York Times,* and *Rolling Stone.* His most recent book is *The Avengelist,* available at pictureboxinc.com.

FRANK SANTORO is a New York–based painter and the author of *Storeyville,* among other publications. By day, he is assistant to the painter Francesco Clemente.

PETER SAUL lives in upstate New York. He is represented by Nolan/Eckman Gallery.

HARRY SMITH was one of the preeminent musicologists and experimental filmmakers of the twentieth century. He compiled *The American Anthology of Folk Music.*

TED STEARN draws a comic book (published by Fantagraphics) called *Fuzz and Pluck,* which follows the adventures of a plucked chicken and a teddy bear. He lives in Los Angeles, working as a storyboard artist for animated cartoons.

MATTHEW THURBER grew up on Lummi Island, Washington, and now lives in Red Hook, Brooklyn. His comics have appeared in *Blood Orange, Paper Rodeo,* and in self-published books.

KARL WIRSUM's early work can be seen in *The Ganzfeld 3.* He lives and works in Chicago and is represented by the Jean Albano Gallery.

This text of this book was composed primarily in Bookman, Folio, and Futura; secondary typefaces include: Akzidenz Grotesk; Caecilia; Clarendon; Cooper; Fleece; Eclat; Helvetica Rounded; Janson; and Pioneer.

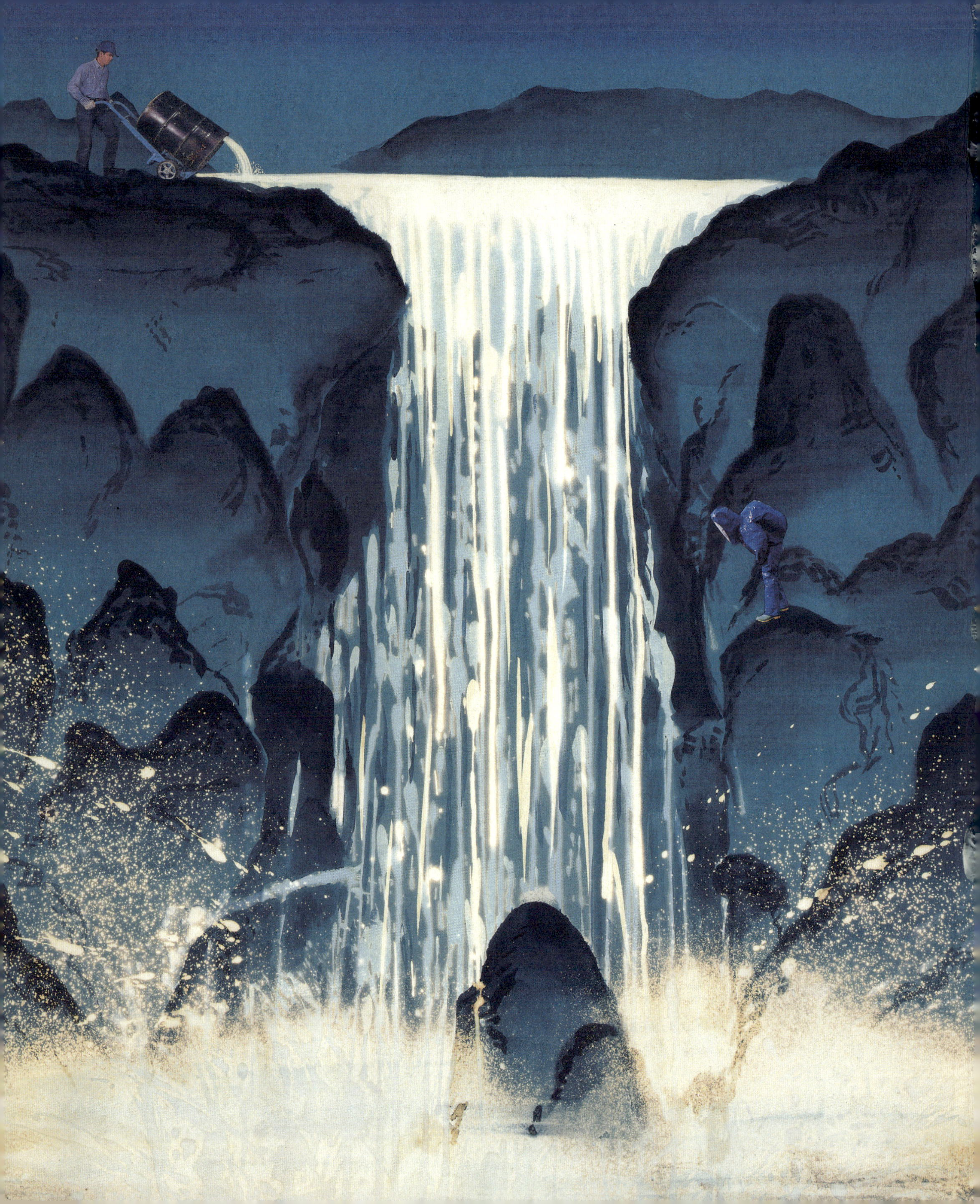